Contents at a Glance

KT-419-753

Contents

Foreword

First names are fun. It is hard to pass up reading about such facets of our own name as its origin, meaning, usage in different countries, popularity at present and in the past, variations in spelling, spin-offs, diminutives, and the important people who share the name as well as the notorious ones (hopefully not too many of the latter). Aside from the calories involved, reading about names is no different from eating popcorn—it is difficult to stop without dipping into the book for the same information about our parents, spouse, siblings, friends, and others.

An ironic feature of our name is that it says more about our parents and the period when we were born than it does about us. We had nothing to do with the choice; it was our parents (influenced by a variety of factors) who made a decision that the vast majority of us accept for the rest of our life. Parents often struggle over the choice they make. It is particularly easy for parents to torture themselves if they try to figure out what image their child's name will have and—in turn—how others will respond to the name. Yes, names do differ in their imagery. (If you have any doubts about this, compare the names of performers who have changed their names, and consider how the shift in image fits in with the performer's niche.) Seeking to make a good choice and avoid a disastrous one, many turn to books such as this one to get ideas and inspiration.

The fascination we have with names has an unfortunate consequence: it is easy to overlook special features of names that allow us to understand how our culture changes, to say nothing of the mechanisms that generate fashion and tastes. In a world in which our tastes in foods, cars, clothing, beverages, movies, music, and the like are affected by manufacturers, retailers, and industries that use high-powered advertising, subtle selling techniques, consumer research, and subliminal devices to affect the choice, names are refreshingly free of these efforts—there are no commercial efforts to influence the choices made by parents. An infant's name matters not at all to diaper manufacturers— I leave it to your imagination what does matter to them. A second important feature is that names are free: you may or may not be able to afford a fancy car or an expensive home or take a cruise (unless we include rowboat rentals), but naming choices are not restricted by income. (Yet the classes differ in their tastes even though there is no economic restriction on their choices.) Fashions occur not only in such matters as clothing and names and music; fashions and tastes are also observed in scientific topics, school curriculums, political campaigns. corporate administration, views of the role of government, tax policies and priorities, and even our manners and choice of words. The study of names helps us discover not only the pure mechanisms of fashion and taste, but also about our society and how our culture has changed through the centuries.

Here are a few illustrations of these broader considerations. In many nations, names first became a matter of fashion and taste only in the latter part of the nineteenth century. Previously, choices were much less a matter of *liking* or *disliking* a name, but rather meeting obligations (naming a child after grandparents or other relatives, and following traditional practices). And whereas parents now worry if the name they choose will be *too* popular, at one point it was common for the five most popular names for each sex to be given to 50 percent or more of the infants born in a given year. Distinctiveness was once not a virtue. Although fashions in names may seem idiosyncratic and haphazard, often they follow orderly processes. Tastes are affected by parental education, other features of social class, race, ethnic origin, immigration status, region, and the like. On the other hand, just to whet your appetite, sociologists now know of a variety of special mechanisms that operate to change tastes in names without necessarily reflecting any social processes or having any special meaning. In effect, popular explanations of cultural changes are often way off the mark—seeking meaning when there is none.

Stanley Lieberson
Abbott Lawrence Lowell Professor of Sociology
Harvard University
Author, *A Matter of Taste: How Names, Fashions, and Culture Change* (Yale University Press, 2000)

Introduction

Choosing a baby name is hard work! It's also a lot of fun, but unless you decided long ago what to name your children and your spouse or partner agreed, you may want some support, in the form of a book with tens of thousands of exciting possibilities. And you're in luck, because you're holding such a book. We're here to help you find the name that fits your little one like a glove.

However, before you even start scanning the many names here, you may want to take a step back and discuss exactly what kind of name you're going for. Do you want a cool and edgy name, or a more traditional and preppy moniker? Perhaps artsy is more your style, or were you thinking you'd like a name befitting a future jock? If you can decide up front the kind of name you want, you'll probably have an easier time narrowing your list to a manageable number of alternatives.

One approach is to choose a name from one of your families—perhaps a parent, grandparent, or favorite aunt or uncle. Some families have standing traditions of naming children after certain relatives, which you may want to investigate. Or consider using a surname—a last name—as a first for your baby. It can be a great way to keep a family name alive.

As you start to create a list of "possibles"—names that may work—it's always a good idea to check on the names' original meanings. Although the importance of meanings isn't as prominent today as it was years ago, considering a name's meaning may help you whittle down your list. You'd hate to saddle your child with a name that means "loser" or suggests he or she has a problem right from the get-go.

In addition to looking into the meanings of names, sounding them out is also smart. How does each name sound in conjunction with your last name or with the middle name you plan to use? Is it alliterative, with both names beginning with the same vowel or consonant sound? Or is it hard to pronounce? Or worse, does it create a phrase with its own meaning, such as "Jean Poole" or "Ivy Leaf"?

Although many of us want names that are distinctive, there's a fine line between "distinctive" and "disaster." Come elementary school, your child may become the butt of some very painful jokes if you select a name that suggests an unflattering nickname.

And if you have your heart set on a particular name that just isn't working as a first name, there's always the middle name, which has become more and more common since the 1950s.

But the most important factor of all is whether you like it. Beyond how it sounds, what it means, how cool or uncool it is, how many other kids have the same name, whether it will irritate your relatives, or if it breaks with a long-standing family tradition, you and your significant other need to feel good about it. You need to love it. We hope this book helps you find a name that fits your baby to a T.

How This Book Is Organized

This book is presented in two parts:

In **Part 1, "Ideas and Inspiration: The Lists,"** you'll find nearly 120 lists to help you brainstorm possible names. You can narrow your choices by the type of list presented, such as science-oriented or biblical, for instance, or read through them all for more alternatives.

Part 2, "Giant Alphabetical List of Names, Origins, and Meanings," is both a cross-reference tool for the lists in Part 1 and a resource for researching the origins, meanings, and spelling variations for names of interest—more than 30,000 of them!

Naming Rights

Check these boxes for do's and don'ts when choosing a name for your baby.

What's in a Name

These boxes provide history and little-known facts about a particular name.

Special Thanks to the Technical Reviewer

The Complete Idiot's Guide to 30,000 Baby Names was reviewed by an expert who double-checked the accuracy of what you'll learn here, to help us ensure that this book gives you everything you need to know about choosing a name for your baby. Special thanks are extended to Linda Saracino.

Acknowledgments

As you'll see once you start flipping through the pages filled with thousands of names, this book took a lot of hard work to compile and research. The authors are indebted to a number of researchers who assisted us in our efforts, including Sherrie Asbie, Marj Crum, Jackie Perrin, Lisa Steier, and LaToya Taylor. Virginia Bendall-Griffin, in particular, was a lifesaver.

We also appreciate the guidance and wisdom of our editor, Mike Sanders, and our agent, Marilyn Allen, as well as the production team, who were faced with a particularly challenging project.

Thank you all.

Marcia also wants to thank her husband, Charlie, who pitched in at various stages of the project to be sure we included more than the 30,000 names promised.

Robbi wants to thank her family, who helped keep her sane during the completion of the project. She especially wants to thank her daughter, Alexa, who spent many hours counting names.

Trademarks

All terms mentioned in this book that are known to be or are suspected of being trademarks or service marks have been appropriately capitalized. Alpha Books and Penguin Group (USA) Inc. cannot attest to the accuracy of this information. Use of a term in this book should not be regarded as affecting the validity of any trademark or service mark.

Part 1

Ideas and Inspiration: The Lists

You're going to have a baby! Congratulations. Now what will you call him or her? To jump-start the process of finding the perfect name for your baby—or babies—we've filled Part 1 with nearly 120 lists of names organized by category. Wondering what some of the cool celebrities' baby names are? We've got them. Think you might like to draw from your cultural heritage? We've got lists of Irish names, African American names, Chinese names, Hawaiian names, and more to inspire you. If you're a history buff, you'll like our lists of presidents, popes, first ladies, astronauts, even famous criminals. You'll also find famous Olympians, sports stars, musicians, and religious figures listed in Part 1.

Fame and the Name Game

Your child is, in many ways, a reflection of you—your hopes and dreams, your likes and dislikes, your personality, your quirks. So why not look to the names of people who have influenced your life in some way—celebrities, TV stars, musicians, even criminals—not that you want to name your kid after Jack the Ripper—when thinking about your baby's name?

The names in this chapter are celebrities, from the silver screen and TV, to music and musicians, from yesterday and today. If you're a rock 'n' roll fan, you'll find plenty of inspiration from the names of rock stars past and present in these pages. Or if country is more your speed, you'll see many familiar names listed here as a starting point for your baby name search.

Silver Screen Legends

Girl Names

Anne Bancroft
Audrey Hepburn
Barbara Stanwyck
Bette Davis
Claudette Colbert
Cloris Leachman
Debbie Reynolds
Dolores del Rio
Donna Reed
Elizabeth Taylor
Ellen Burstyn
Eva Marie Saint
Faye Dunaway
Gena Rowlands
Geraldine Page
Ginger Rogers
Grace Kelly
Greer Garson
Hedy Lamarr
Helen Hayes
Ingrid Bergman
Jane Wyman
Jessica Tandy
Jo Van Fleet
Joan Crawford
Joanne Woodward
Judi Dench
Julie Christie
June Allyson
Katharine Hepburn
Lee Grant
Loretta Young

Louise Fletcher
Martha Raye
Mary Pickford
Mercedes McCambridge
Myrna Loy
Norma Shearer
Olivia de Havilland
Patty Duke
Phyllis Diller
Rita Moreno
Sandy Dennis
Shelley Winters
Sophia Loren
Teresa Wright
Vanessa Redgrave
Vivien Leigh

Boy Names

Alan Alda
Alec Guinness
Anthony Quinn
Art Carney
Basil Rathbone
Bing Crosby
Broderick Crawford
Burl Ives
Burt Lancaster
Cary Grant
Charlton Heston
Clark Gable
David Niven
Don Ameche

Edmund Gwenn
Ernest Borgnine
Erroll Flynn
Frank Sinatra
Gary Cooper
George C. Scott
Gregory Peck
Henry Fonda
Humphrey Bogart
Jack Lemmon
James Cagney
James Stewart
John Houseman
Laurence Olivier
Lionel Barrymore
Marlon Brando
Maximilian Schell
Peter Finch
Peter Ustinov
Ray Milland
Red Buttons
Robert Duvall
Rod Steiger
Sidney Poitier
Spencer Tracy
Victor McLaglen
William Holden
Yul Brynner

Movie Stars

Girl Names

Actor	Movie	Actor	Movie
Angelina Jolie	*Mr. and Mrs. Smith*	Kate Winslet	*Titanic*
Brittany Murphy	*Just Married*	Kyra Sedgwick	*Phenomenon*
Cameron Diaz	*There's Something About Mary*	Lindsay Lohan	*Mean Girls*
		Meryl Streep	*The Hours*
Demi Moore	*Charlie's Angels*	Natalie Portman	*Star Wars Episodes I, II, III*
Drew Barrymore	*The Wedding Singer*		
Elisha Cuthbert	*House of Wax*	Nicole Kidman	*The Interpreter*
Glenn Close	*The Stepford Wives*	Reese Witherspoon	*Legally Blonde*
Halle Berry	*Monster's Ball*	Renée Zellweger	*Bridget Jones's Diary*
Helen Hunt	*As Good as It Gets*	Sandra Bullock	*Miss Congeniality*
Jennifer Connelly	*A Beautiful Mind*	Uma Thurman	*Kill Bill*
Jodi Foster	*The Silence of the Lambs*	Whoopi Goldberg	*Sister Act*
Julia Roberts	*Mona Lisa Smile*	Winona Ryder	*Girl, Interrupted*

Boy Names

Actor	Movie	Actor	Movie
Adam Sandler	*50 First Dates*	Kevin Bacon	*Footloose*
Al Pacino	*Scent of a Woman*	Kurt Russell	*Vanilla Sky*
Ben Affleck	*Daredevil*	Leonardo DiCaprio	*Titanic*
Brad Pitt	*Ocean's Twelve*	Liam Neeson	*Kinsey*
Colin Farrell	*Alexander*	Matt Damon	*Good Will Hunting*
Danny Glover	*Lethal Weapon*	Mel Gibson	*What Women Want*
Denzel Washington	*The Manchurian Candidate*	Orlando Bloom	*Kingdom of Heaven*
Don Cheadle	*Hotel Rwanda*	Pierce Brosnan	*James Bond 007: Everything or Nothing*
Ewan McGregor	*Moulin Rouge*		
George Clooney	*Ocean's Twelve*	Robert DeNiro	*Meet the Fockers*
Harrison Ford	*Indiana Jones*	Russell Crowe	*Master and Commander*
Jim Carrey	*Lemony Snicket's A Series of Unfortunate Events*	Samuel L. Jackson	*Coach Carter*
		Tobey Maguire	*Spiderman*
		Tom Cruise	*War of the Worlds*
Johnny Depp	*Pirates of the Caribbean*	Val Kilmer	*Mindhunters*

Movie Characters

Girl Names

Character	Actor	Movie
Ada Monroe	Nicole Kidman	*Cold Mountain*
Alicia Nash	Jennifer Connelly	*A Beautiful Mind*
Aurora Greenway	Shirley MacLaine	*Terms of Endearment*
Beatrix Kiddo	Uma Thurman	*Kill Bill*
Birdee Pruitt	Sandra Bullock	*Hope Floats*
Bree Davis	Helen Hunt	*Dr. T and the Women*
Charlotte Hollis	Olivia de Havilland	*Hush, Hush Sweet Charlotte*
Clarice Starling	Jodie Foster	*The Silence of the Lambs*
Clementine Kruczynski	Kate Winslet	*Eternal Sunshine of the Spotless Mind*
Dolly Pelliker	Cher	*Silkwood*
Elise Elliot	Goldie Hawn	*The First Wives Club*
Elle Wood	Reese Witherspoon	*Legally Blonde*
Erica Barry	Diane Keaton	*Something's Gotta Give*
Erin Brockovich	Julia Roberts	*Erin Brockovich*
Francesca Johnson	Meryl Streep	*The Bridges of Madison County*
Gracie Hart	Sandra Bullock	*Miss Congeniality*
Ilsa Laszlo	Ingrid Bergman	*Casablanca*
Jacy Farrow	Cybill Shepherd	*The Last Picture Show*
Jenny Cavilleri	Ali McGraw	*Love Story*
Jo March	Katharine Hepburn	*Little Women*
Kate McKay	Meg Ryan	*Kate and Leopold*
Lace Pennamin	Kyra Sedgwick	*Phenomenon*
Lee Holloway	Maggie Gyllenhaal	*Secretary*
Lilia Herriton	Helen Mirren	*Where Angels Fear to Tread*
Maggie Fitzgerald	Hilary Swank	*Million Dollar Baby*
Marge Gunderson	Frances McDormand	*Fargo*
Matty Walker	Kathleen Turner	*Body Heat*
Muriel Pritchett	Geena Davis	*The Accidental Tourist*
Penny Lane	Kate Hudson	*Almost Famous*
Regan MacNeil	Linda Blair	*The Exorcist*
Rose Dewitt Bukater	Kate Winslet	*Titanic*
Ruth Wonderly	Bebe Daniels	*The Maltese Falcon*
Samantha Stanton	Mary-Kate Olsen	*Switching Goals*
Susanna Kaysen	Winona Ryder	*Girl, Interrupted*
Tess McGill	Melanie Griffith	*Working Girl*
Velvet Brown	Elizabeth Taylor	*National Velvet*
Winnifred "Winnie" Foster	Alexis Bledel	*Tuck Everlasting*

Boy Names

Character	Actor	Movie
Allan Quatermain	Sean Connery	*The League of Extraordinary Gentlemen*
Amos Calloway	Danny DeVito	*Big Fish*
Ben Marco	Denzel Washington	*The Manchurian Candidate*
Boyd Redding	Morgan Freeman	*The Shawshank Redemption*
Butch Cassidy	Paul Newman	*Butch Cassidy and the Sundance Kid*
Catcher Block	Ewan McGregor	*Down with Love*
Charlie Mackenzie	Mike Myers	*So I Married an Axe Murderer*
Doyle Gipson	Samuel L. Jackson	*Changing Lanes*
Elliott (no last name)	Henry Thomas	*E.T. the Extra-Terrestrial*
Finnegan Bell	Ethan Hawke	*Great Expectations*
Forrest Gump	Tom Hanks	*Forrest Gump*
Frank Abagnale	Leonardo DiCaprio	*Catch Me If You Can*
Garth Algar	Dana Carvey	*Wayne's World*
Gordon Bombay	Emilio Estevez	*D3: The Mighty Ducks*
Herman Boone	Denzel Washington	*Remember the Titans*
Holden McNeil	Ben Affleck	*Chasing Amy*
Indiana Jones	Harrison Ford	*Indiana Jones*
Jack Aubrey	Russell Crowe	*Master and Commander*
Jason Bourne	Richard Chamberlain/ Matt Damon	*The Bourne Identity*
Jerry Fletcher	Mel Gibson	*Conspiracy Theory*
Joel Barish	Jim Carrey	*Eternal Sunshine of the Spotless Mind*
Julian Kaye	Richard Gere	*American Gigolo*
Karl Childers	Billy Bob Thornton	*Sling Blade*
Lloyd Dobler	John Cusack	*Say Anything*
Max Baron	James Spader	*White Palace*
Mickey O'Neill	Brad Pitt	*Snatch*
Mitch Albom	Hank Azaria	*Tuesdays with Morrie*
Norman Bates	Anthony Perkins	*Psycho*
Oskar Schindler	Liam Neeson	*Schindler's List*
Pete Monash	Topher Grace	*Win a Date with Tad Hamilton*
Ray Kinsella	Kevin Costner	*Field of Dreams*
Ren McCormack	Kevin Bacon	*Footloose*
Ricky McKinney	Jon Bon Jovi	*Pay It Forward*
Robert Clayton Dean	Will Smith	*Enemy of the State*
Roger Murtaugh	Danny Glover	*Lethal Weapon*
Ron Burgundy	Will Ferrell	*Anchorman*
Samuel Gerard	Tommy Lee Jones	*U.S. Marshals*
Shelly Kaplow	Alec Baldwin	*The Cooler*
Stu Shepard	Colin Farrell	*Phone Booth*
Sy Parrish	Robin Williams	*One Hour Photo*
Tom Booker	Robert Redford	*The Horse Whisperer*
Will Hunting	Matt Damon	*Good Will Hunting*
Willie Beaman	Jamie Foxx	*Any Given Sunday*
Wyatt (no last name)	Peter Fonda	*Easy Rider*

Child Stars

Girl Names

Actor	TV Show/Movie/ Claim to Fame	Actor	TV Show/Movie/ Claim to Fame
Alexis Fields	*Moesha*	Lisa Loring	*The Addams Family*
Anissa Jones	*Family Affair*	Mackenzie Phillips	*One Day at a Time*
Ashley Olsen	*Full House*	Mary-Kate Olsen	*Full House*
Candace Cameron	*Full House*	Melissa Sue Anderson	*Little House on the Prairie*
Dana Plato	*Diff'rent Strokes*		
Danica McKellar	*The Wonder Years*	Nicole Eggert	*Charles in Charge*
Gaby Hoffman	*This Is My Life*	Quinn Cummings	*The Goodbye Girl*
Heather Ripley	*Chitty Chitty Bang Bang*	Sally Field	*The Flying Nun*
		Sheila Hames	*The Many Loves of Dobie Gillis*
Inger Nilsson	*Pippi Longstocking*		
Jodie Sweetin	*Full House*	Sidney Greenbush	*Little House on the Prairie*
Kim Richards	*Escape to Witch Mountain*	Tatyana Ali	*The Fresh Prince of Bel-Air*
Kristy McNichol	*Little Darlings*		
Lark Voorhies	*Saved by the Bell*	Tempestt Bledsoe	*The Cosby Show*
Lindsay Greenbush	*Little House on the Prairie*	Tiffany Amber Thiessen	*Saved by the Bell*
		Valerie Bertinelli	*One Day at a Time*

Boy Names

Actor	TV Show/Movie/ Claim to Fame	Actor	TV Show/Movie/ Claim to Fame
Adam Rich	*Eight Is Enough*	Dustin Diamond	*Saved by the Bell*
Andrew Lawrence	*Brotherly Love*	Emmanuel Lewis	*Webster*
Barry Williams	*The Brady Bunch*	Fred Savage	*The Wonder Years*
Billy Mumy	*Lost in Space*	Henry Thomas	*E.T. the Extra-Terrestrial*
Butch Patrick	*The Munsters*		
Claude Jarman Jr.	*The Yearling*	Ilan Mitchell-Smith	*Weird Science*
Corey Feldman	*The Goonies*	Jaleel White	*Family Matters*
Corin Nemec	*Parker Lewis Can't Lose*	Jonathan Taylor Thomas	*Home Improvement*
Dan Frischman	*Head of the Class*	Leif Garrett	*Tiger Beat* pinup

Actor	TV Show/Movie/ Claim to Fame	Actor	TV Show/Movie/ Claim to Fame
Macauley Culkin	*Home Alone*	Sean Astin	*The Goonies*
Michael Oliver	*Problem Child*	Taran Noah Smith	*Home Improvement*
Noah Hathaway	*The NeverEnding Story*	Wil Wheaton	*Stand by Me*
Peter Billingsley	*A Christmas Story*	Zachery Ty Bryan	*Home Improvement*
Ricky Segall	*The Partridge Family*		

Celebrities' Babies
Girl Names

Child	Parent(s)	Child	Parent(s)
Apple	Gwyneth Paltrow and Chris Martin	Gabrielle	Donna Karan
Aquinnah	Tracy Pollan and Michael J. Fox	Gaia	Emma Thompson and Greg Wise
Ava	Reese Witherspoon and Ryan Phillippe	Georgia	Mick Jagger and Jerry Hall
Bella	Billy Bob Thornton and Connie Angland	Hazel	Julia Roberts
Brea	Eddie Murphy	Iris	Jude Law and Sadie Frost
Brooke	Chynna Phillips and Billy Baldwin	Isabella	Nicole Kidman and Tom Cruise
Camera	Arthur Ashe	Ivanka	Donald and Ivanna Trump
Carys	Catherine Zeta-Jones and Michael Douglas	Jasmine	Michael Jordan
Chelsea	Steven Tyler	Jordan	Bono
Clementine	Claudia Schiffer and Matthew Vaughn	Kaia	Cindy Crawford and Randy Gerber
Coco	Courtney Cox and David Arquette	Katia	Denzel Washington
Deva	Monica Bellucci and Vincent Cassel	Langley	Mariel Hemingway
		Leni	Heidi Klum and Flavio Briatore
Dree	Mariel Hemingway	Lola	Kelly Ripa and Mark Consuelos
Elinor	Katie Couric	Lourdes	Madonna
Ensa	Bill and Camille Cosby	Mackenzie	J. K. Rowling
Frances	Kate and Andy Spade	MaKena' lei	Helen Hunt
		Marina	Matt LeBlanc
		Mattea	Mira Sorvino
		Mia	Kate Winslet

Celebrities' Babies, continued

Child	Parent(s)
Natasha	Alex Rodriguez
Nico	Thandie Newton
Paloma	Emilio Estevez
Puma	Erykah Badu
Rainbow	Ving Rhames
Rowan	Brooke Shields
Rumer	Demi Moore and Bruce Willis
Sam	Charlie Sheen and Denise Richards
Schuyler	Tracy Pollan and Michael J. Fox

Child	Parent(s)
Scout	Demi Moore and Bruce Willis
Shea	John Grisham
Siobhan	Rebecca Lobo and Steve Rushin
Sosie	Kyra Sedgwick and Kevin Bacon
Tallulah	Demi Moore and Bruce Willis
Taylor	Garth Brooks
Willow	Will Smith and Jada Pinkett Smith
Zahra	Chris Rock
Zola	Eddie Murphy

Boy Names

Child	Parent(s)
Aidan	Lou Rawls
Aurelius	Elle MacPherson
Austin	Tommy Lee Jones
Banjo	Rachel Griffiths
Boston	Kurt Russell
Brawley	Nick Nolte
Brooklyn	Victoria and David Beckham
Caspar	Claudia Schiffer
Cosimo	Beck and Marissa Ribisi
Cruz	Victoria Beckham and David Beckham
Damian	Liz Hurley and Steve Bing
Dylan	Catherine Zeta-Jones and Michael Douglas
Ellery	Laura Dern
Finley	Holly Marie Combs
Freedom	Ving Rhames
Holden	Brendan Fraser
Indiana	Casey Affleck and Summer Phoenix
Jaden	Will Smith and Jada Pinkett Smith

Child	Parent(s)
Jett	Kelly Preston and John Travolta
Kit	Jodie Foster
Maddox	Angelina Jolie
Magnus	Will Ferrell
Marston	Hugh Hefner
Milo	Ricki Lake; Liv Tyler and Royston Langdon
Oliver	Bridget Fonda and Danny Elfman
Owen	Kevin Kline
Phinneaus	Julia Roberts
Pilot Inspektor	Jason Lee
Pirate	Jonathan Davis
Presley	Cindy Crawford
Rafferty	Jude Law and Sadie Frost
Rebel	Robert Rodriguez
Ripley	Thandie Newton
Rocco	Madonna and Guy Ritchie
Rocket	Robert Rodriguez

Child	Parent(s)	Child	Parent(s)
Roman	Debra Messing; Holly Robinson Peete and Rodney Peete	Trey	Will Smith
		True	Kirstie Alley and Parker Stevenson
Rudy	Jude Law and Sadie Frost	Truman	Rita Wilson and Tom Hanks
Ryder	Kate Hudson and Chris Robinson	Ty	Pam Dawber and Mark Harmon
Satchel	Spike Lee; Woody Allen	Weston	Nicolas Cage
Sawyer	Kate Capshaw and Steven Spielberg	Will	Mel Gibson
Sebastian	James Spader	Wolfgang	Eddie Van Halen and Valerie Bertinelli
Seven	Erykah Badu	Wyatt	Goldie Hawn and Kurt Russell
Speck	John Mellencamp and Elaine Irwin-Mellencamp	Yusef	Jesse Jackson
Taj Monroe	Steven Tyler	Zen	Corey Feldman

Dramatic Designations

Girl Names

Character	Actor	TV Show/Movie
Abigail Bartlett	Stockard Channing	*The West Wing*
Adrianna La Cerva	Drea de Matteo	*The Sopranos*
Allison DuBois	Patricia Arquette	*Medium*
Bridget DuBois	Maria Lark	*Medium*
Buffy Summers	Sarah Michelle Gellar	*Buffy the Vampire Slayer*
Catherine Willows	Marg Helgenberger	*CSI*
Connie McDowell	Charlotte Ross	*NYPD Blue*
Cordelia Chase	Charisma Carpenter	*Angel*
Felicity Porter	Keri Russell	*Felicity*
Gillian Gray	Jessica Tuck	*Judging Amy*
Grace Santiago	Valerie Cruz	*Nip/Tuck*
Jing-Mei (Deb) Chen	Ming-Na	*ER*
Jordan Cavanaugh	Jill Hennessy	*Crossing Jordan*
Kerry Weaver	Laura Innes	*ER*
Lauren Reed	Melissa George	*Alias*
Lilly Rush	Kathryn Morris	*Cold Case*

Dramatic Designations, continued

Character	Actor	TV Show/Movie
Marissa Cooper	Mischa Barton	*The O.C.*
Maxine Gray	Tyne Daly	*Judging Amy*
Natalie Teeger	Traylor Howard	*Monk*
Nora Lewin	Dianne Wiest	*Law and Order*
Paige Halliwell	Rose McGowan	*Charmed*
Piper Halliwell	Holly Marie Combs	*Charmed*
Prudence Halliwell	Shannen Doherty	*Charmed*
Rayanne Graff	A. J. Langer	*My So-Called Life*
Ruth Fisher	Frances Conroy	*Six Feet Under*
Samantha Taggart	Linda Cardellini	*ER*
Sara Sidle	Jorja Fox	*CSI*
Sharona Fleming	Bitty Schram	*Monk*
Sydney Bristow	Jennifer Garner	*Alias*
Veronica Mars	Kristen Bell	*Veronica Mars*
Vivian Johnson	Marianne Jean-Baptiste	*Without a Trace*
Willow Rosenberg	Alyson Hannigan	*Buffy the Vampire Slayer*

Boy Names

Character	Actor	TV Show/Movie
Adrian Monk	Tony Shaloub	*Monk*
Anthony (A.J.) Soprano	Robert Iler	*The Sopranos*
Arvin Sloan	Ron Rifkin	*Alias*
Brad Chase	Mark Valley	*Boston Legal*
Bruce Van Exel	Richard T. Jones	*Judging Amy*
Christian Troy	Julian McMahon	*Nip/Tuck*
Cole Turner	Julian McMahon	*Charmed*
Duncan Cane	Teddy Dunn	*Veronica Mars*
Eric Weiss	Greg Grunberg	*Alias*
Frederico Diaz	Freddy Rodriguez	*Six Feet Under*
Garrett Macy	Miguel Ferrer	*Crossing Jordan*
Gil Grissom	William Petersen	*CSI*
Graham Chase	Tom Irwin	*My So-Called Life*
Jack Bristow	Victor Garber	*Alias*
Jordan Catalano	Jared Leto	*My So-Called Life*
Joshua Lyman	Bradley Whitford	*The West Wing*

Kyle McCarty	Kevin Rahm	*Judging Amy*
Leland Stottlemeyer	Ted Levine	*Monk*
Logan Echolls	Jason Dohring	*Veronica Mars*
Luke Girardi	Michael Welch	*Joan of Arcadia*
Marshall Flinkman	Kevin Weisman	*Alias*
Martin Fitzgerald	Eric Close	*Without a Trace*
Ned Riley	Thomas McCarthy	*Boston Public*
Nick Vera	Jeremy Ratchford	*Cold Case*
Pacey Witter	Joshua Jackson	*Dawson's Creek*
Randall Disher	Jason Gray-Stanford	*Monk*
Russell Corwin	Ben Foster	*Six Feet Under*
Seth Cohen	Adam Brody	*The O.C.*
Vincent Gray	Dan Futterman	*Judging Amy*
Wallace Fennell	Percy Daggs III	*Veronica Mars*

Sitcom Sweethearts

Girl Names

Character	Actor	Sitcom
Amy McDougal-Barone	Monica Horan	*Everybody Loves Raymond*
Angie Palmero Lopez	Constance Marie	*George Lopez*
Blair Warner	Lisa Welchel	*The Facts of Life*
Bree Van De Kamp	Marcia Cross	*Desperate Housewives*
Carmen Consuelo Lopez	Stacey Haglund	*George Lopez*
Carrie Heffernan	Leah Remini	*The King of Queens*
Corky Sherwood	Faith Ford	*Murphy Brown*
Daphne Moon Crane	Jane Leeves	*Frasier*
Dylan Messinger	Ashley Williams	*Good Morning, Miami*
Edie Britt	Nicollette Sheridan	*Desperate Housewives*
Ethel Mertz	Vivian Vance	*I Love Lucy*
Gabrielle Solis	Eva Longoria	*Desperate Housewives*
Grace Adler	Debra Messing	*Will and Grace*
Heidi Keppert	Debbe Dunning	*Home Improvement*
Hillary Banks	Karyn Parsons	*The Fresh Prince of Bel-Air*
Jackie Burkhart	Mila Kunis	*That '70s Show*

Sitcom Sweethearts, continued

Character	Actor	Sitcom
Kitty Forman	Debra Jo Rupp	*That '70s Show*
Kyra Hart	Scarlett Pomers	*Reba*
Lindsay Bluth Fünke	Portia DeRossi	*Arrested Development*
Lorelai Gilmore	Lauren Graham	*Gilmore Girls*
Lucille Bluth	Jessica Walter	*Arrested Development*
Mallory Keaton	Justine Bateman	*Family Ties*
Marni Fliss	Jennifer Finnigan	*Committed*
Phoebe Buffay	Lisa Kudrow	*Friends*
Rachel Green	Jennifer Aniston	*Friends*
Rory Gilmore	Alexis Bledel	*Gilmore Girls*
Sophia Spirelli Petrillo-Weinstock	Estelle Getty	*The Golden Girls*
Syndey Hughley	Ashley Monique Clark	*The Hughleys*
Tess (no last name)	Tammy Lynn Michaels	*Committed*
Vanessa "Nessa" Thomkins	Camille Winbush	*The Bernie Mac Show*
Vivian Banks	Daphne Maxwell Reid	*The Fresh Prince of Bel-Air*
Willona Woods	Ja'net Dubois	*Good Times*
Yvonne Hughley	Elise Neal	*The Hughleys*

Boy Names

Character	Actor	Sitcom
Alex P. Keaton	Michael J. Fox	*Family Ties*
Bernie "Mac" McCullough	Bernie Mac	*The Bernie Mac Show*
Bowie James	Darius McCrary	*Committed*
Brock Hart	Christopher Rich	*Reba*
Carlos Solis	Ricardo Antonio Chivira	*Desperate Housewives*
Chandler Bing	Matthew Perry	*Friends*
Chris Peterson	Chris Elliott	*Get a Life*
Darryl Hughley	D. L. Hughley	*The Hughleys*
Deacon Palmer	Victor Williams	*The King of Queens*
Dewey Wilkerson	Erik Per Sullivan	*Malcolm in the Middle*
Douglas Heffernan	Kevin James	*The King of Queens*
Eric Forman	Topher Grace	*That '70s Show*
Francis Wilkerson	Christopher Masterson	*Malcolm in the Middle*

Character	Actor	Sitcom
George-Michael Bluth	Michael Cera	*Arrested Development*
Heathcliff Huxtable	Bill Cosby	*The Cosby Show*
Jack McFarland	Sean Hayes	*Will and Grace*
Jonas Grumby ("Skipper")	Alan Hale Jr.	*Gilligan's Island*
Keith Anderson	Ben Powers	*Good Times*
Logan Huntzberger	Matt Czuchry	*Gilmore Girls*
Luke Danes	Scott Patterson	*Gilmore Girls*
Malcolm Wilkerson	Frankie Muniz	*Malcolm in the Middle*
Michael Bluth	Jason Bateman	*Arrested Development*
Paul Young	Mark Moses	*Desperate Housewives*
Reese Wilkerson	Justin Berfield	*Malcolm in the Middle*
Rex Van De Kamp	Steven Culp	*Desperate Housewives*
Richard Gilmore	Edward Herrmann	*Gilmore Girls*
Robert Barone	Brad Garrett	*Everybody Loves Raymond*
Tobias Fünke	David Cross	*Arrested Development*
Tristan DuGray	Chad Michael Murray	*Gilmore Girls*
Van Montgomery	Steve Howey	*Reba*
Vic Palmero	Emiliano Diez	*George Lopez*
Zach Young	Cody Kasch	*Desperate Housewives*

Romance Heroes and Heroines

Girl Names

Heroine

Heroine	Romance
Aloysia Weber	*Marrying Mozart* by Stephanie Cowell
Althea Almott	*Picking Up the Pieces* by Barbara Gale
Ardys Trevallon	*The Queen's Fencer* by Caitlin Scott Turner
Beatrix Carmichael	*Our Husband* by Stephanie Bond
Caitlan Claiborne	*Irish Fire* by Jeanette Baker
Callie Quinn	*Callie's Convict* by Heidi Betts
Camryn O'Brien	*From Boardwalk with Love* by Nina Bangs
Dani Strauss	*The Mommy Fund* by Madeline J. Jacob
Deidre Doyle	*Silver Wedding* by Maeve Binchy
Eden Beckett	*A Man of Affairs* by Ann Barbour
Elspeth Stewart	*Ride the Fire* by Pamela Clare

Romance Heroes and Heroines, continued

Heroine	Romance
Emmaline Denford	*Something About Emmaline* by Elizabeth Boyle
Felicity Chambeau	*Her Forever Man* by Leanne Banks
Fonda Blayne	*Spotlight* by Carole Bellacera
Georgiana Escott	*One Night of Passion* by Elizabeth Boyle
Hester Poitevant	*The Bridemaker* by Rexanne Becnel
Jillian Fitzgerald	*Nell* by Jeanette Baker
Jo Beth Jensen	*The Cowboy Way* by Candace Schuler
Kaylynn Summers	*Spirit's Song* by Madeline Baker
Kirby Greenland	*I Am Not Esther* by Fleur Beale
Lacey O'Neill	*Kiss River* by Diane Chamberlain
Lauren Remington	*Born to Be Wild* by Patti Berg
Madeline Breton	*The Bride Finder* by Susan Carroll
Margrete Trewsbury	*The Maiden's Heart* by Julie Beard
Olivia FitzDurham	*Glass Houses* by Stella Cameron
Piper Devon	*Hush* by Jo Leigh
Prudence Reynolds	*Texas Star* by Elaine Barbieri
Quinn McKenzie	*Crazy for You* by Jennifer Crusie
Ripley Logan	*Private Investigations* by Tori Carrington
Sierra Lavotini	*Drag Strip* by Nancy Bartholomew
Sophia Armitage	*Irresistible* by Mary Balogh
Tempe Walsh	*Hot Stuff* by Flo Fitzpatrick
Thea Garrett	*Swear by the Moon* by Shirlee Busbee
Tru Van Dyne	*Unraveled* by C. J. Barry
Vivianna Greentree	*Lessons in Seduction* by Sara Bennett
Zoe Beckett	*A Man of Affairs* by Ann Barbour

Boy Names

Hero	Romance
Adrian Hawke	*The Bridemaker* by Susan Carroll
Aiden Flynn	*Glass Houses* by Stella Cameron
Anatole St. Leger	*The Bride Finder* by Susan Carroll
Britt Cameron	*Cameron* by Beverly Barton
Brock Logan	*Her Forever Man* by Leanne Banks
Ciaran Tamberlane	*My Forever Love* by Marsha Canham
Caldwell Star	*Texas Star* by Elaine Barbieri
Clay O'Neill	*Kiss River* by Diane Chamberlain

Hero	Romance
Desmond Doyle	*Silver Wedding* by Maeve Binchy
Devlin McCloud	*Leaping Hearts* by Jessica Bird
Donal O'Flaherty	*Nell* by Jeanette Baker
Gideon Cole	*To Love a Thief* by Julie Ann Long
Grayson St. Cyre	*Mad Jack* by Catherine Coulter
Harry Benson	*Picking Up the Pieces* by Barbara Gale
Ian Rufford	*The Companion* by Susan Squires
Jake Bannister	*Western Rose* by Lynna Banning
Lex Tanner	*The Countdown* by Ruth Wind
Max Wilde	*Born to Be Wild* by Patti Berg
Morgan Farrell	*Looking for a Hero* by Patti Berg
Neil Ellsworth	*Shadows on the Lake* by Leona Karr
Nicholas Devoncroix	*The Passion* by Donna Boyd
Oliver Montegomery	*Lessons in Seduction* by Sara Bennett
Patrick Blackburne	*Swear by the Moon* by Shirlee Busbee
Rayce Coburne	*Unraveled* by C. J. Barry
Roan Benedict	*Roan* by Jennifer Blake
Seth Lindow	*A Man of Affairs* by Ann Barbour
Shane Jeffrey	*Ashes of Dreams* by Ruth Ryan Langan
Stuart Chesterton	*Kiss the Bride* by Patricia Cabot
Tobin de Clare	*Wicked* by Jill Barnett
Trace Winslow	*Hush* by Jo Leigh
Tucker Johnston	*Inventing Savannah* by Susan Shapiro Barash/Joanne Lara
Vic Drummond	*Do You Believe?* by Ann Lawrence
Wade Mason	*Callie's Convict* by Heidi Betts

Soap Opera Hunks and Hussies
Girl Names

Hussy	Soap Opera	Hussy	Soap Opera
Ambrosia Moore	*The Bold and the Beautiful*	Calliope Jones	*Days of Our Lives*
		Cricket Blair	*The Young and the Restless*
Belle Black	*Days of Our Lives*		
Billie Reed	*Days of Our Lives*	Dahlia Ventura	*As the World Turns*

Soap Opera Hunks and Hussies, continued

Hussy	Soap Opera	Hussy	Soap Opera
Drucilla Winters	*The Young and the Restless*	Marlena Black	*Days of Our Lives*
Eden August	*Guiding Light*	Nikki Munson	*As the World Turns*
Felicia Jones Scorpio	*General Hospital*	Olivia Winters	*The Young and the Restless*
Frannie Hughes	*As the World Turns*	Opal Cortlandt	*All My Children*
Hope Brady	*Days of Our Lives*	Pilar Santos	*Passions*
Jennifer Devereaux	*Days of Our Lives*	Rosanna Cabot	*As the World Turns*
Katie Pereti Coleman	*As the World Turns*	Sage Snyder	*As the World Turns*
Kendall Hart	*All My Children*	Sheridan Crane Lopez-Fitzgerald	*Passions*
Lahoma Vale Lucas	*Another World*		
Lien Hughes	*As the World Turns*	Skye Chandler	*All My Children*
Marah Lewis	*Guiding Light*	Tara Martin	*All My Children*

Boy Names

Hunk	Soap Opera	Hunk	Soap Opera
Abe Carver	*Days of Our Lives*	Lucas Roberts	*Days of Our Lives*
Blade Bladeson	*The Young and the Restless*	Marcus Taggert	*General Hospital*
Brock Reynolds	*The Young and the Restless*	Mateo Santos	*All My Children*
Burke Donovan	*As the World Turns*	Neil Winters	*The Young and the Restless*
Damon Porter	*The Young and the Restless*	Niko Kelly	*All My Children*
Deacon Sharpe	*The Bold and the Beautiful*	Pierce Riley	*All My Children*
Dillon Quartermaine	*General Hospital*	Ridge Forrester	*The Bold and the Beautiful*
Emilio Ramirez	*Days of Our Lives*		
Evan Webster	*Another World*	Royce Keller	*As the World Turns*
Frisco Jones	*General Hospital*	Snapper Foster	*The Young and the Restless*
Harlan Barrett	*General Hospital*	Sven Petersen	*Another World*
Holden Snyder	*As the World Turns*	Tad Martin	*All My Children*
Jagger Cates	*General Hospital*	Trey Kenyon	*All My Children*
Jory Andros	*Guiding Light*	Wade Larson	*As the World Turns*
Judge Grange	*Another World*	Walker Daniels	*As the World Turns*
Keemo Volien Abbott	*The Young and the Restless*	Zander Smith	*General Hospital*

TV Talk-Show Hosts
Girl Names

Host	Show
Asha Blake	*Later Today*
Barbara Walters	*The View*
Cybill Shepherd	*Men Are from Mars, Women Are from Venus*
Ellen DeGeneres	*The Ellen Show*
Iyanla Vanzant	*Iyanla*
Joan Rivers	*Still Talking*
Jodi Applegate	*Later Today*
Joy Browne	*Dr. Joy Browne Show*
Katie Couric	*Today Show*
Kelly Ripa	*Regis and Kelly*
Leeza Gibbons	*Leeza*
Meredith Vieira	*The View*
Oprah Winfrey	*The Oprah Winfrey Show*
Queen Latifah	*Queen Latifah in the House*
Ricki Lake	*Ricki Lake*
Rosie O'Donnell	*The Rosie O'Donnell Show*
Ruth Westheimer (Dr.)	*Dr. Ruth*
Sam Phillips	*Men Are from Mars, Women Are from Venus*
Sarah Ferguson, Duchess of York	*Larry King Live*
Star Jones Reynolds	*The View*
Tyra Banks	*Tyra*
Vickie Gabereau	*Vickie Gabereau Live*

Boy Names

Host	Show
Adam Carolla	*The Man Show*
Andy Richter	*Late Night*
Arsenio Hall	*Arsenio*
Bill Maher	*Politically Incorrect*
Carson Daly	*Last Call*
Chris Rock	*The Chris Rock Show*
Craig Ferguson	*The Late, Late Show*
Ernie Kovacs	*The Tonight Show*
Garry Shandling	*The Larry Sanders Show*
Geraldo Rivera	*Rivera Live*
Howard Stern	*The Howard Stern Show*
Jay Leno	*The Tonight Show*
Jesse Ventura	*Jesse Ventura Show*
Jimmy Kimmel	*The Man Show*
Joey Bishop	*The Joey Bishop Show*
Keenen Wayans	*Vibe*
Mario Lopez	*The Other Half*
Matt Lauer	*Today Show*
Montel Williams	*The Montel Williams Show*
Morton Downey Jr.	*Morton Downey Jr. Show*
Regis Philbin	*Regis and Kelly*
Richard Simmons	*Dreammaker*
Rondell Sheridan	*Men Are from Mars, Women Are from Venus*
RuPaul	*The RuPaul Show*

TV Talk Show Hosts, continued

Host	Show	Host	Show
Rush Limbaugh	*The Rush Limbaugh Show*	Tom Green	*The Tom Green Show*
Sinbad	*Vibe*	Wayne Brady	*The Wayne Brady Show*
Tavis Smiley	*The Tavis Smiley Show*		

Newscasters/Journalists

Girl Names

Newscaster	Network/Show	Newscaster	Network/Show
Alexis Glick	CNBC	Gerri Willis	CNN
Alisha Davis	CNN	Greta Van Susteren	FOX
Anita Vogel	FOX	Heidi Collins	CNN
Ashleigh Banfield	NBC	Jamie Colby	FOX
Alisyn Camerota	FOX	Jessica Yellin	MSNBC
Alex Witt	MSNBC	Josie Burke	CNN
Barbara Walters	ABC	Juliet Huddy	FOX
Bertha Coombs	CNBC	Kara Henderson	CNN
Bianca Solorzano	MSNBC	Kelly Arena	CNN
Brigitte Quinn	FOX	Kiran Chetry	FOX
Campbell Brown	MSNBC	Kitty Pilgrim	CNN
Claudia Cowan	FOX	Kristine Johnson	CNN
Christiane Amanpour	CNN	Leslie Laroche	CNBC
Claudia DiFolco	MSNBC	Linda Stouffer	CNN
Connie Chung	NBC	Lis Wiehl	FOX
Contessa Brewer	MSNBC	Lisa Ling	*Ultimate Explorer,* National Geographic
Dagen McDowell	FOX		
Dari Alexander	FOX	Maria Bartiromo	MSNBC/CBC
Dawna Friesen	NBC	Maya Kulycky	CNBC
Daryn Kagan	MSNBC	Megyn Kendall	FOX
Elizabeth Cohen	CNN	Milissa Rehberger	NBC
Erica Hill	CNN	Mercedes Colwin	MSNBC
Flavia Colgan	MSNBC	Molly Henneberg	FOX
Fredricka Whitfield	CNN		

Newscaster	Network/Show	Newscaster	Network/Show
Nanette Hansen	MSN	Sibila Vargas	CNN
Natalie Allen	NBC	Soledad O'Brien	CNN
Norah Odonnell	NBC	Sumi Das	MSNBC
Page Hopkins	FOX	Tracye Hutchins	CNN
Rebecca Gomez	FOX	Uma Pemmaraju	FOX
Rosey Edeh	MSNBC	Veronica De La Cruz	CNN
Rudi Bakhtiar	CNN	Whitney Casey	CNN
Sachi Koto	CNN	Willow Bay	NBC
Shanon Cook	CNN		

Boy Names

Newscaster	Network/Show	Newscaster	Network/Show
Aaron Brown	CNN	James Rosen	FOX
Adam Housley	FOX	Jason Carroll	CNN
Anderson Cooper	CNN	Jerry Nachman	MSNBC
Bill O'Reilly	FOX	Jesse Ventura	MPR News
Bob Simon	CBS	Joe Kernen	CNBC
Brad Goode	CNBC	John Gibson	FOX
Brian Kilmeade	FOX	Julian Phillips	FOX
Brit Hume	FOX	Keith Olbermann	MSNBC
Carl Quintanilla	MSNBC	Kendis Gibson	CNN
Charlie Rose	CBS	Kevin Sites	NBC
Chip Reid	NBC	Kris Osborn	CNN
Chris Matthews	MSNBC	Larry King	CNN
Dan Abrams	MSNBC	Leon Harris	FOX
Dan Rather	CBS	Lester Holt	MSNBC
David Faber	MSNBC	Lou Dobbs	CNN
Dennis Miller	CNBC	Matt Lauer	MSNBC
Ed Bradley	CBS	Maurice DuBois	MSNBC
Geraldo Rivera	FOX	Miguel Marquez	CNN
Greg Palkot	FOX	Mike Galanos	CNN
Harris Whitbeck	CNN	Miles O'Brien	CNN
Jack Cafferty	CNN	Morley Safer	ABC

Newscasters/Journalists, continued

Newscaster	Network/Show	Newscaster	Network/Show
Neil Cavuto	FOX	Shepard Smith	FOX
Nic Robertson	CNN	Steve Doocy	FOX
Peter Jennings	ABC	Stone Phillips	NBC
Randy Meier	MSNBC	Thomas Roberts	CNN
Reney Miguel	CNN	Tom Brokaw	NBC
Richard Engel	MSNBC	Tony Snow	FOX
Rick Sanchez	MSNBC	Trace Gallagher	FOX
Rob Marciano	CNN	Tucker Carlson	PBS
Sam Shane	MSNBC	Walter Cronkite	CBS
Sanjay Gupta	CNN	William La Jeunesse	FOX
Sean McLaughlin	MSNBC	Wolf Blitzer	CNN

Celebrity Chefs

Girl Names

Alexandra Ewald	Diane Forley	Maryann Esposito	Rachael Ray
Alice Waters	Helene Darroze	Melissa Kelly	Roxanne Klein
Amy Scherber	Jody Adams	Mina Newman	Sara Moulton
Anita Lo	Julia Child	Mindy Segal	Sarah Stegner
Ann Nurse	Katy Sparks	Ming Tsai	Sue Torres
Anne Rosenzweig	Lidia Bastianich	Mollie Katzen	Susan Feniger
Barbara Kafka	Madeleine Kamman	Monique Barbeau	Susan O'Rourke
Barbara Lynch	Marion Cunningham	Nathalie Dupree	Zarela Martines
Biba Caggiano	Martha Stewart	Nigella Lawson	Zov Karamardian
Caprial Pence	Mary Bergin	Odette Fada	
Carrie Nahabedian	Mary Sue Milliken	Patricia Yeo	

Boy Names

Alain Ducasse
Allen Susser
Alton Brown
Anthony Bourdain
Antoine Careme
Bobby Flay
Charlie Palmer
Charlie Trotter
Daniel Boulud
David Burke
David Ruggerio

Emeril Lagasse
Fritz Maytag
Gordon Ramsay
Graham Kerr
Jacques Pepin
James Beard
Jamie Oliver
Jean-Georges Vongerichten
Jeff Smith
Jody Denton

José Andrés
Marcel Desaulniers
Marcus Samuelsson
Mario Batali
Michael Ginor
Michael Lomonaco
Michael McCarty
Morgan Larsson
Nobu Matsuhisa
Norman Van Aken
Paul Prudhomme

Reed Hearon
Rick Bayless
Roberto Donna
Rocco DiSpirito
Sanford D'Amato
Steve Johnson
Thomas Keller
Todd English
Todd Gray
Wolfgang Puck

Famous Criminals

Girl Names

Aileen Wuornos
Andrea Yates
Amy Fisher
Anne Bonny
Bambi Bembeneck
Belle Starr
Beverly Allitt
Bonnie Parker
Carolyn Warmus

Charlotte de Berry
Claudine Longet
Darlie Router
Diane Downs
Dorothea Puente
Frances Creighton
Genene Jones
Grace O'Malley
Jean Harris

Judith Anne Neelley
Karla Faye Tucker
Kate "Ma" Barker
Kathleen Folbigg
Leslie Nelson
Lizzie Borden
Lynette "Squeaky" Fromme
Madelaine Smith
Marie Antoinette

Martha Beck
Mary Kay Letourneau
Nannie Doss
Patty Hearst
Rae Carruth
Ruth Snyder
Sue Basso
Velma Barfield
Winnie Ruth Judd

Boy Names

Al Capone
Albert Anastasia
Andrew Gigante
Arnold Rothstein
Benjamin Siegel
Burt Alvord
Caryl Chessman

Charles Arthur "Pretty Boy" Floyd
Christopher Marlowe
Clyde Barrow
Cole Younger
Cullen Baker
Frank Costello

David Berkowitz
Dion O'Banion
Edmund Kemper
Edward Gein
Eric Robert Rudolph
Francisco Pancho Villa
Floyd Hamilton

Gary Gilmore
George "Machine Gun" Kelly
Harry Longabaugh, a.k.a. "The Sundance Kid"
Harvey Logan, a.k.a. "Kid Curry"

Famous Criminals, continued

Henry Plummer

Hugh Anderson

Ira Einhorn

Jack the Ripper

Jake Bird

James "Wild Bill" Hickok

Jefferson Randolph Smith, a.k.a. "Soapy Smith"

Jeffrey Dahmer

Jesse James

Jim Jones

Joe Ball

John Gotti

John Wayne Gacy

Jose Chavez

Juan Corona

Lee Harvey Oswald

Lester Gillis, a.k.a. "Baby Face Nelson"

Logan Belt

Lucky Luciano

Luke Short

Meyer Lansky

Micajah Harp

Mike McCluskie

Paul Bernardo

Pedro Lopez

Polk Wells

Reggie Kray

Robert Clay Anderson

Ronnie Kray

Roy Gardner

Ted Bundy

Terry Nichols

Salvatore Zappola

Sam Sheppard

Steve Long

Thayne Archibald

Timothy McVeigh

Tony Accardo

Vincent "Chin" Gigante

Vito Genovese

Wesley Elkins

Wiley Harp

William Bonney a.k.a. "Billy the Kid"

Zip Wyatt

Rock Kings and Queens
Girl Names

Alanis Morissette

Ani DiFranco

Annie Lennox, Eurythmics

Aretha Franklin

Belinda Carlisle, Go-Gos

Billie Holiday

Brenda Lee

Carly Simon

Carole King

Cass Elliot, The Mamas and the Papas

Chrissie Hynde, Pretenders

Cindy Wilson, B-52s

Cleotha Staples, The Staple Singers

Deborah Harry, Blondie

Diana Ross, The Supremes

Donna Godchaux, Grateful Dead

Dusty Springfield

Etta James

Gladys Knight, Gladys Knight and the Pips

Grace Slick, Jefferson Airplane

Janis Joplin

Joan Armatrading

Joni Mitchell

Linda Ronstadt

Martha Reeves, Martha and the Vandellas

Maureen Tucker, Velvet Underground

Michelle Phillips, The Mamas and the Papas

Natalie Merchant, 10,000 Maniacs

Pat Benatar

Patti LaBelle, LaBelle

Sade

Sam Phillips

Stevie Nicks, Fleetwood Mac

Susanna Hoffs, The Bangles

Tina Turner

Tina Weymouth, Talking Heads

Boy Names

Ace Frehley, Kiss
Alice Cooper
Axl Rose, Guns 'n' Roses
Billy Idol
Bo Diddley
Bob Dylan
Bob Marley
Bono, U2
Bruce Springsteen
Buck Roeser, Blue Oyster Cult
Buddy Holly
Carlos Santana, Santana
Cesar Rosas, Los Lobos
Chuck Berry
David Bowie
Dewey Martin, Buffalo Springfield
Don Henley, The Eagles
Eddie Vedder, Pearl Jam

Elton John
Elvis Costello
Elvis Presley
Eric Clapton
Frank Zappa
Freddie Mercury, Queen
Gene Simmons, Kiss
George Harrison, The Beatles
Hilton Valentine, The Animals
Isaac Hayes
James Brown
Jerry Garcia, Grateful Dead
Jim Morrison, The Doors
Jimi Hendrix
John Lennon, The Beatles
Jon Bon Jovi, Bon Jovi
Mick Jagger, Rolling Stones
Neil Young, Crosby, Stills, Nash and Young

Otis Redding
Paul McCartney, The Beatles
Pete Townshend, The Who
Phil Rudd, AC/DC
Phillard Williams, Earth, Wind and Fire
Ray Charles
Ric Ocasek, The Cars
Ringo Starr, The Beatles
Robert Plant, Led Zeppelin
Rod Stewart
Roger Daltrey, The Who
Simon Gallup, The Cure
Steven Tyler, Aerosmith
Sting, The Police
Syd Barrett, Pink Floyd
Tom Petty, Tom Petty and the Heartbreakers
Van Morrison
Woody Guthrie

Country Stars
Girl Names

Alison Krauss
Amber Dotson
Anne Murray
Barbara Mandrell
Becky Hobbs
Bonnie Raitt
Brenda Lee
Carlene Carter
Caryl Mack Parker
Chalee Tennison
Claudia Church

Connie Smith
Crystal Gayle
Danni Leigh
Dolly Parton
Dottie West
Emmylou Harris
Faith Hill
Gretchen Wilson
Jamie O'Neal
Jennifer Day
Jessi Alexander

Jo Dee Messina
Julie Harris
Kasey Chambers
Kathy Mattea
Kippi Brannon
Kylie Harris
Lari White
LeAnn Rimes
Lee Ann Womack
Loretta Lynn
Lynn Anderson

Martina McBride
Mary Chapin Carpenter
Mindy McCready
Miranda Lambert
Noah Kelley
Patsy Cline
Patsy Montana
Patty Loveless
Reba McEntire
Rebecca Lynn Howard

Country Singers, continued

Rheanne Rivers	Shelly Fairchild	Tammy Wynette	Trisha Yearwood
Sara Evans	Sherrié Austin	Tanya Tucker	Wynonna Judd
Shania Twain	Suzanne Alexander	Tara Lyn Hart	

Boy Names

Aaron Lines	Dierks Bentley	Johnny Cash	Ronnie Dun
Alan Jackson	Don Williams	Keith Anderson	Ronnie Milsap
Bill Anderson	Dusty Drake	Keith Whitely	Roy Acuff
Billy Dean	Dwight Yoakam	Keni Thomas	Royal Wade Kimes
Billy Ray Cyrus	Earl Thomas Conley	Kenny Chesney	Sammy Kershaw
Blaine Larsen	Eddie Rabbitt	Kenny Rogers	Shane Minor
Blake Shelton	Eddy Arnold	Kix Brooks	Tim McGraw
Brad Paisley	Ernest Tubb	Larry Gatlin	Toby Keith
Buck Owens	Garth Brooks	Leroy Van Dyke	Trace Adkins
Charley Pride	Gary Allan	Marty Robbins	Trini Triggs
Charlie Daniels	Gene Autry	Mel Tillis	Ty Herndon
Charlie Rich	Gene Watson	Merle Haggard	Vern Gosdin
Chet Atkins	George Jones	Mickey Gilley	Vince Gill
Clint Black	George Strait	Paul Overstreet	Waylon Jennings
Conway Twitty	Glen Campbell	Randy Travis	Willie Nelson
Damon Gray	Hank Snow	Rhett Akins	
Davis Daniel	Hank Williams	Ricky Scaggs	
Deryl Dodd	Jerry Jeff Walker	Roger Miller	

Gospel Singers

Girl Names

Albertina Walker	Blind Mamie Forehand	Doris Akers	Fanny Crosby
Amy Grant	Cassietta George	Dorothy Norwood	Frances Preston
Anna Carter	Cece Winans	Dottie Rambo	Gloria Gaither
Annie Herring	Clara Ward	Ethel Waters	Inez Andrews
Bertha Lee	Clarice Baxter	Eva Mae LeFevre	Jan Buckner
Bessie Johnson	Cleotha Staples	Evie Tornquist	Janis Lewis Phillips

Jerri Morrison
Lena "Mom" Speer
Lonnie MnIntorsh
Mahalia Jackson
Mary Ann Gaither

Mary Nelson
Maude LeFevre
Mavis Staples
Miggie Lewis
Nelly Griesen

Polly Lewis
Reba Rambo
Rose Carter
Sallie Martin
Sandi Patty

Sherrill Nielsen
Shirley Ceasar
Vestal Goodman
Wendy Bagwell

Boy Names

Adger Pace
Al Green
Albert Brumley
Alphus LeFevre
Andrae Crouch
Andrew Ishee
Anthony Burger
Armond Morales
Asa Brooks Everett
Austin Coleman
Ben Speer
Bentley Ackley
Billy Graham
Blind Willie Davis
Bo Weavil Jackson
Bob Hartman
Bobby Butler
Booker White
Brock Speer
Bryan Hutson
Buck Rambo
Buddy Liles
Bukka White
Charley Patton
Clarence Fountain
Cleavant Derricks
Cliff Barrows

Connor Hall
D. P. "Dad" Carter
Danny Gaither
Dennis Crumpton
Denver Crumpler
Derrell Stewart
Don Breland
Doyle Blackwood
Eddie Head
Edward Clayborn
Edwin Hawkins
Elvis Presley
Frank Palmes
G. T. "Dad" Speer
Gary McSpadden
George Scott
Glen Payne
Greg Hough
Haldor Lillenas
Herman Harper
Hobart Evans
Homer Rodeheaver
Hovie Lister
Ira Stanphill
J.D. Sumner
Jake Hess
James Cleveland

Jarrell McCracken
Jaybird Coleman
Jerry Martin
Jimmy Carter
Joe Taggart
Joey Williams
John DeGroff Petra
Keith Green
Kirk Franklin
Kurt Kaiser
Larry Norman
Lee Roy Abernathy
Les Beasley
Lewis Phillips
"Little" Roy Lewis
Lloyd Orrell
Lon "Deacon"
  Freeman
Lou Hildreth
Lowell Mason
Mark Ellerbee
Marvin Norcross
Matthew Ward
Mosie Lister
Noel Fox
Oliver Cooper
Oren Parris

Otis Jones
P.P. Bliss
Parker Jonathan
Pat Boone
Perry Morgan
Powell Hassell
Ralph Carmichael
Ray Dean Reese
Rex Humbard
Ricky McKinnie
Robert Summers
Roger Breeland
Ron Page
Roosevelt Graves
Smitty Gatlin
Steve Sanders
Stuart Hamblen
Tennessee Ernie Ford
Tim Lovelace
Thomas Dorsey
Tommy Fairchild
Tony Brown
Urias LeFevre
Versey Smith
Wally Fowler
William Smith
Willie Wynn

Pop Princes and Princesses

Girl Names

Aaliyah	Christina Milian	Joss Stone	Michelle Branch
Alicia Keys	Faith Evans	Kelly Clarkson	Missy Elliott
Amerie	Fantasia Barrino	Kylie	Natalie Imbruglia
Ashanti	Gwen Stefani	Lil' Kim	Natasha Bedingfield
Ashlee Simpson	Hilary Duff	Lindsay Lohan	Nina Sky
Avril Lavigne	Janet Jackson	Madonna	Nivea
Beyoncé Knowles	Jennifer Lopez	Mandy Moore	Shakira
Britney Spears	Jessica Simpson	Mariah Carey	Vanessa Carlton
Christina Aguilera	JoJo	Mary J. Blige	

Boy Names

Baby Bash	Jay-Z	Mario	Ryan Cabrera
Babyface	Jesse McCartney	Michael Jackson	Sean "P. Diddy" Combs
Eminem	John Mayer	Nick Carter	Usher
Frankie J.	Justin Timberlake	Papa Roach	Will Smith
Gavin DeGraw	Kanye West	R. Kelly	Wyclef Jean
Howie Day	Ludacris	Rob Thomas	

Names from Songs

Girl Names

Name	Artist	Song
Adia	Sarah McLachlan	*Adia*
Adrienne	The Calling	*Adrienne*
Alethea	Robin Trower	*Alethea*
Angie	The Rolling Stones	*Angie*
Arabella	The Kinks	*Wicked Arabella*
Beth	Kiss	*Beth*
Black Betty	Ram Jam	*Black Betti*
Billy Jean	Michael Jackson	*Billy Jean*
Carrie	Dr. Hook and the Medicine Show	*Carry Me Carrie*
Charlotte	The Cure	*Charlotte Sometimes*
Cynthia	Blue Rodeo	*Cynthia*

Name	Artist	Song
Darlene	Led Zepplin	*Darlene*
Diane	John Mellencamp	*Jack and Diane*
Elvira	Oak Ridge Boys	*Elvira*
Emma	Hot Chocolate	*Emma*
Felicia	Blues Traveler	*Felicia*
Francine	ZZ Top	*Francine*
Georgia	Ray Charles	*Georgia on My Mind*
Glynis	Smashing Pumpkins	*Glynis*
Guinnevere	Crosby, Stills and Nash	*Guinnevere*
Iris	Goo Goo Dolls	*Iris*
Isabel	John Denver	*Isabel*
Jamie	Van Halen	*Jamie's Crying*
Jenny	Tommy Tutone	*867-5309/Jenny*
Josephine	George Thorogood	*Ride on Josephine*
Kim	Concrete Blonde	*Songs for Kim*
Layla	Eric Clapton	*Layla*
Lily	The Who	*Pictures of Lily*
Lola	The Kinks	*Lola*
Mabel	Goldfinger	*Mabel*
Maggie May	The Beatles	*Maggie May*
Mandy	Barry Manilow	*Mandy*
Mariah	The Kingston Trio	*They Call The Wind Mariah*
Nancy	Frank Sinatra	*Nancy with the Laughing Face*
Natalie	The Killers	*Believe me Natalie*
Ophelia	The Band	*Ophelia*
Peggy Sue	Buddy Holly	*Peggy Sue*
Penny	Hanson	*Penny and Me*
Rebecca	The Bee Gees	*Rebecca*
Rhiannon	Fleetwood Mac	*Rhiannon*
Rhonda	The Beach Boys	*Help Me Rhonda*
Rosalinda	Billy Joel	*Rosalinda's Eyes*
Rosanna	Toto	*Rosanna*
Roxanne	The Police	*Roxanne*
Sara	Fleetwood Mac	*Sara*
Sheila	Ready for the World	*Oh, Sheila*
Sherry	The Four Seasons	*Sherry*
Virginia	Tori Amos	*Virginia*
Wendy	The Beach Boys	*Wendy*

Boy Names

Name	Artist	Song
Achilles	Led Zeppelin	*Achilles Last Stand*
Adam	Aerosmith	*Adam's Apple*
Al	Paul Simon	*You Can Call Me Al*
Andy	The Killers	*Andy You're a Star*
Billy	Bo Donaldson and the Heywoods	*Billy Don't Be a Hero*
Boris	The Who	*Boris the Spider*
Brian	Barenaked Ladies	*Brian Wilson*
Casey	Grateful Dead	*Casey Jones*
Charlie	The Coasters	*Charlie Brown*
Daniel	Elton John	*Daniel*
Dave	The Roches	*Uncle Dave*
Earl	Dixie Chicks	*Goodbye Earl*
Eddie	The Teen Queens	*Eddie My Love*
Edmund	Gordon Lightfoot	*The Wreck of the Edmund Fitzgerald*
Frankie	Connie Francis	*Frankie*
Henry	Lowest of the Low	*Henry Needs a New Pair of Shoes*
Jack	John Mellencamp	*Jack and Diane*
Jeremy	Pearl Jam	*Jeremy*
Jesse	Carly Simon	*Jesse*
Joe	Frank Zappa	*Joe's Garage*
Johnny	Bruce Springsteen	*Johnny Bye Bye*
Kenneth	R.E.M.	*What's the Frequency Kenneth?*
Leroy	Jim Croce	*Bad, Bad Leroy Brown*
Louie	The Kingsmen	*Louie, Louie*
Mickey	Tony Basil	*Mickey*
Nathan	The Supremes	*Nathan Jones*
Neil	Carole King	*Oh, Neil*
Noah	Harry Belafonte	*Noah*
Norman	Sue Thompson	*Norman*
Oliver	Elvis Costello	*Oliver's Army*
Oskar	Our Lady Peace	*Hello Oskar*
Peter	XTC	*Ballad of Peter Pumpkinhead*
Quinn	Bob Dylan	*Mighty Quinn*
Ray	Aimee Mann	*Ray*
Sam	Olivia Newton-John	*Sam*
Shane	Liz Phair	*Shane*
Simon	Lifehouse	*Simon*
Steve	Sheryl Crow	*Steve McQueen*
Sue	Johnny Cash	*A Boy Named Sue*
Wayne	Chantal Kreviazuk	*Wayne*
Willie Joe	The Mystery Trio	*Willie Joe*

Noteworthy Names

When choosing a name for your baby, you might decide to imbue him or her with a powerful superhero name such as those featured in this chapter's list of superheroes' secret identities. Or maybe you feel like going silly with one of the names featured in the cartoon-character name lists.

In this chapter, you'll also find lists of actors' and actresses' "before and after" names. If you're looking for an alliterative or initialed moniker, you'll find those in this chapter as well.

In addition, you'll find some nicknames you can bestow upon your newborn and classic names that have been around for decades. And to help avoid any naming no-no's, we also include a list of names to avoid.

Cartoon Characters

Girl Names

Character	Cartoon
Angelica Pickles	*Rugrats*
Aurora (no last name)	*Sleeping Beauty*
Belle (no last name)	*Beauty and the Beast*
Bianca (no last name)	*The Rescuers*
Clementine (no last name)	*Caillou*
Daisy Duck	*Donald Duck*
Daphne Blake	*Scooby-Doo*
Daria	*Beavis and Butthead*
Dora (no last name)	*Dora the Explorer*
Dory (no last name)	*Finding Nemo*
Esmeralda (no last name)	*Hunchback of Notre Dame*
Jasmine (no last name)	*Aladdin*
Josie McCoy	*Josie and the Pussycats*
Kim Possible	*Kim Possible*

Character	Cartoon
Lilo (no last name)	*Lilo and Stitch*
Lois Griffin	*Family Guy*
Luanne Platter	*King of the Hill*
Marge Simpson	*The Simpsons*
Marianne Thornberry	*The Wild Thornberrys*
Megan Griffin	*Family Guy*
Melody Valentine	*Josie and the Pussycats*
Nala (no last name)	*The Lion King*
Nora (no last name)	*Pete's Dragon*
Pearl (no last name)	*Finding Nemo*
Pocahontas (no last name)	*Pocahontas*
Trixie (no last name)	*Speed Racer*
Veronica Lodge	*Archie*

Boy Names

Character	Cartoon
Aladdin (no last name)	*Aladdin*
Albert (no last name)	*Fat Albert*
Arthur (no last name)	*Sword in the Stone*
Bart Simpson	*The Simpsons*
Bernard (no last name)	*The Rescuers*
Casper (no last name)	*Casper the Friendly Ghost*
Dennis Mitchell	*Dennis the Menace*
Dexter (no last name)	*Dexter's Laboratory*
Diego (no last name)	*Dora the Explorer*
Dudley Do-Right	*Rocky and Bullwinkle*
Dylan "Dil" Pickles	*Rugrats*
Elmer Fudd	*Looney Tunes*
Elroy Jetson	*The Jetsons*

Character	Cartoon
Fred Flintstone	*The Flintstones*
Gaston (no last name)	*Beauty and the Beast*
Hank Hill	*King of the Hill*
Linus Van Pelt	*Peanuts*
Marlin (no last name)	*Finding Nemo*
Mickey Mouse	*Mickey Mouse*
Nemo (no last name)	*Finding Nemo*
Nigel Thornberry	*The Wild Thornberrys*
Rocket J. Squirrel	*Rocky and Bullwinkle*
Simba (no last name)	*The Lion King*
Theodore (no last name)	*Alvin and the Chipmunks*
Timmy Turner	*The Fairly OddParents*

Secret Identities of Superheroes

Girl Names

Superhero	Secret Identity	Superhero	Secret Identity
Batgirl	Barbara Gordon	Oracle	Barbara Gordon
Bionic Woman	Jaimie Summers	Queen of Swords	Maria Teresa Alvarado
Black Scorpion	Darcy Walker	Supergirl	Linda Danvers
Cat Woman	Selina Kyle	Witchblade	Sara Pezzini
The Girl from U.N.C.L.E.	April Dancer	Wonder Girl	Drusilla Prince
		Wonder Woman	Yeoman Diana Prince

Boy Names

Superhero	Secret Identity	Superhero	Secret Identity
Batman	Bruce Wayne	Mr. Fantastic	Reed Richards
Captain America	Steve Rogers	Mr. Terrific	Stanley Beamish
Captain Marvel	Billy Batson	Penguin	Oswald Chesterfield Cobblepot
Captain Midnight	Captain Jim "Red" Albright	Phantom	Kit Walker Jr.
Captain Nice	Carter Nash	Riddler	Edward "E" Nigma
The Crow	Eric Draven	Robin, Boy Wonder	Dick Grayson
The Flash	Barry Allen	Robin Hood	Sir Robin of Loxley
Gemini Man	Sam Casey	The Saint	Simon Templar
Green Hornet	Britt Reid	Scarlet Pimpernel	Sir Percy Blakeney
Incredible Hulk	Dr. David Bruce Banner	Six Million Dollar Man	Col. Steve Austin
Invisible Man	Daniel Westin	Spiderman	Peter Parker
Iron Man	Tony Stark	Submariner	Lord Namor
Jetman	Oscar North	Superman	Clark Kent
Jon Sable	Nicholas Flemming	Tarzan	John Clayton III, Lord Greystoke
Lone Ranger	John Reid	Ultra Man	Andrew Clements
Man from Atlantis	Mark Harris	Zorro	Don Diego de la Vega
The Mighty Thor	Dr. Don Blake		

Before They Were Famous—Name Changers

Girl Names

Celebrity Name	Original Name	Celebrity Name	Original Name
Alicia Keys	Alicia Cook	Kelly Preston	Kelly Smith
Anna Nicole Smith	Vickie Lynn Hogan	Lauren Bacall	Betty Joan Perske
Carmen Electra	Tara Patrick	Leelee Sobieski	Liliane Sobieski
Cher	Cherilyn La Piere	Macy Gray	Natalie McIntyre
Courtney Love	Michelle Harrison	Marilyn Monroe	Norma Jean Mortensen
Demi Moore	Demetria Guynes	Michelle Phillips	Holly Gilliam
Elle MacPherson	Eleanor Gow	Pink	Alicia Moore
Faith Hill	Audrey Faith Perry	Portia de Rossi	Amanda Rogers
Goldie Hawn	Goldie Jean Studlendegehawn	Queen Latifah	Dana Owens
		Shania Twain	Eileen Regina Edwards
Jodie Foster	Alicia Christian Foster	Tina Turner	Annie Mae Bullock
Julianne Moore	Julie Anne Smith	Winona Ryder	Winona Horowitz
Kate Capshaw	Kathleen Sue Nail		

Boy Names

Celebrity Name	Original Name	Celebrity Name	Original Name
Alan Alda	Alphonse D'Abruzzo	Moby	Richard Melville Hall
Bernie Mac	Bernard Jeffery McCullough	Muhammed Ali	Cassius Clay
		Nicolas Cage	Nicholas Kim Coppola
Bill Clinton	William Jefferson Blythe IV	Rodney Dangerfield	Jacob Cohen
		Snoop Dogg	Calvin Broadus
Bono	Paul Hewson	Spike Lee	Shelton Jackson Lee
Brad Pitt	William Bradley Pitt	Sting	Gordon Matthew Sumner
Chad Lowe	Charles Lowe		
Christian Slater	Christian Michael Hawkins	Sylvester Stallone	Michael Stallone
Coolio	Artis Ivey Jr.	Taye Diggs	Scott Diggs
Elton John	Reginald Kenneth Dwight	Tim McGraw	Samuel Timothy Smith
		Tom Cruise	Thomas Cruise Mapother IV
Eminem	Marshall Mathers III		
Jay Leno	James Leno	Vin Diesel	Mark Vincent
Jon Bon Jovi	Jon Bongiovi	Warren Beatty	Henry Warren Beaty
Kareen Abdul-Jabbar	Ferdinand Lewis Alcindor Jr.	Woody Allen	Allen Stewart Konigsberg

Alliterative Names

Girl Names

Name	Claim to Fame	Name	Claim to Fame
Barbara Bush	First lady	Janet Jackson	Singer
Brigitte Bardot	Actress	Katie Couric	*Today Show* host
Brooke Burns	Actress	Kim Cattrall	Actress
Courteney Cox	Actress	Laura Linney	Actress
Cybill Shepherd	Actress	Lucy Liu	Actress
Dana Delany	Actress	Martina McBride	Country singer
Dominique Dawes	Gymnast	Michael Michele	Actress
Dorothy Dandridge	Actress	Parker Posey	Actress
Faith Ford	Actress	Rachel Ray	Chef
Farrah Fawcett	Actress	Rene Russo	Actress
Greta Garbo	Actress	Susan Sarandon	Actress
Holly Hunter	Actress	Tina Turner	Singer

Boy Names

Name	Claim to Fame	Name	Claim to Fame
Arthur Ashe	Tennis pro	Lyle Lovett	Singer
Barry Bonds	Baseball pro	Mark McGuire	Baseball pro
Benjamin Bratt	Actor	Matthew McConaughey	Actor
Bjorn Borg	Tennis pro	Mike Myers	Actor
Calvin Coolidge	U.S. president	Nick Nolte	Actor
Chevy Chase	Actor	Ozzy Osbourne	Rock 'n' roller
Clark Kent	Superman	Pablo Picasso	Artist
David Duchovny	Actor	Paul Prudhomme	Chef
Ernie Els	Golf pro	Sammy Sosa	Baseball pro
Gilbert Gottfried	Actor	Sylvester "Sly" Stallone	Actor
Hubert Humphrey	U.S. vice president	Ted Turner	Entrepreneur/ CNN founder
James Joyce	Author	Travis Tritt	Country musician
Jesse Jackson	Clergyman	Walt Whitman	Poet
Kirk Cameron	Actor	Zig Ziglar	Business consultant
Lennox Lewis	Boxer		

Double Names

Girl Names

Carrie-Ann Moss

Catherine Mary Stewart

Eva Marie Saint

Hallie Kate Eisenberg

Joey Lauren Adams

Julia Louis-Dreyfus

Mary-Kate Olsen

Mary-Louise Parker

Penelope Ann Miller

Rachel Leigh Cook

Sarah Jessica Parker

Summer Joy Phoenix

Tammy Faye Baker

Tiffany Amber Theissen

Boy Names

Anthony Michael Hall

Billy Bob Thornton

Brian Austin Green

David James Elliot

Edward James Olmos

Haley Joel Osment

Jan-Michael Vincent

Jason James Richter

Jean-Claude Van Damme

Jonathan Taylor Thomas

Michael Thomas Dunn

Neil Patrick Harris

Richard Dean Anderson

Scott William Winters

Sean Patrick Flanery

Tommy Lee Jones

Initial Names

Girl Names

Name	Claim to Fame
C. C. Bloom	*Beaches* character
C. J. Cregg	*The West Wing* character
J. B. Fletcher	*Murder She Wrote* character
K. D. Lang	Singer
P. J. Soles	Actress

Boy Names

Name	Claim to Fame
D. B. Sweeney	Actor
F. Lee Bailey	Attorney
I. M. Pei	Architect
J. C. Chasez	*NSYNC singer
LL Cool J	Rapper
P. T. Barnum	Showman

Unusual Names

Girl Names

Apple Martin

Blue Angel Evans

Chastity Bono

Daisy Boo Oliver

Diva Zappa

Fifi Trixibelle Geldof

Heavenly Hirani Tigerlilly
  Hutchence

Ima Hogg

Ione Sky

Justice Mellencamp

Liberty Kasem

Moon Unit Zappa

Nell Marmalade Eliot

Rumer Willis

Soleil Moon Frye

Starlite Berenson

Peaches Honeyblossom
  Geldof

Pia Zadora

Pixie Geldof

Sistine Stallone

Boy Names

Audio Science Sossamon

Banjo Griffiths

Denim Kole Braxton Lewis

Dweezil Zappa

Edsel Ford

ESPN ("Espen") Malachi McCall

Fuddy Wayans

Hud Mellencamp

Ib Melchior

Mumtaz Wonder

Pirate Inspector Davis

Rock Brynner

Rolan Bolan

Speck Mellencamp

Tara Gabriel Galaxy
  Gramophone Getty

Taro Hart

Topo McGuire

Zowie Bowie

Gothic/Vampire Names

Girl Names

Bela	Claudia	Karayan	Nicki
Bianca	Estelle	Lucine	Pandora
Bronwen	Gabrielle	Madeleine	Wynn
Celeste			

Boy Names

Akasha	Asphar	Eamen	Rashid
Aleron	Athan	Enkil	Raven
Amadeo	Avicus	Flavius	Rune
Amarande	Blaine	Kern	Santiago
Ambrose	Carden	Lestat	Tainn
Andros	Damian	Louis	Tariq
Arjun	Danton	Merrick	Vega
Armand			

Classic Names

Girl Names

Ann Russell	Elsa Lanchester	Kim Novak	Tabitha Whitney
Bette Davis	Estelle Getty	Maggie Riley	Vanessa Redgrave
Carrie Abrams	Ethel Waters	Patricia Neal	Zsa Zsa Gabor
Deborah Kerr	Jane Marple	Ruth Hale	
Donna Reed	Juliet Mills	Sarah Whitney	

Boy Names

Andrew Turck	Gene Hackman	John Baker	Quincy Whitney
Anthony Flynn	George Blair	Joseph Johnson	Robert Smith
David Wideman	Ira Prosser	Levi Stainton	Ronald Ferguson
Donald Sutherland	Isaac Newton	Orrin Reed	Russell Squier
Edmund Trebus	James Joyce	Paul Newman	Sean Connery
Elliott Andrus	Joel Stebbins	Phillip Crane	William Price
Garrett Kinney			

Winners, Winners, and More Winners

Every parent wants his or her little girl or boy to be successful. We dream of our baby making it big. Maybe she'll be the next Julia Roberts or he the next Tom Hanks. If we're lucky, maybe she'll be as talented as Michelle Kwan or as successful as Tiger Woods. Whatever your passion—whether it's a hobby, a sport, a form of entertainment, or an indulgence—you're sure to find it here, followed by a long list of winners in that area.

You'll find great thinkers, such as Pulitzer prize and Nobel Prize winners, as well as names of performers, including Oscar winners, Tony Award winners, Emmy winners, and Grammy winners. Among sports greats, you'll spot everyone from golfers to football players, tennis aces, ice-skating champs, Olympic medalists, NASCAR racers, gymnasts, and hockey players, in addition to basketball and baseball heavy-hitters.

Pulitzer Prize Winners

Girl Names

Winner	Category	Winner	Category
Amy Lowell	Poetry	Leonora Speyer	Poetry
Annalynn Swan	Biography	Linda Greenhouse	Beat reporting
Carol Guzy	Photography	Lisa Pollak	Feature writing
Carolyn Cole	Photography	Liz Balmaseda	Commentary
Cheryl Diaz Meyer	Photography	Louise Gluck	Poetry
Connie Schultz	Commentary	Margo Jefferson	Criticism
Cornelia Grumman	Editorial writing	Marilynne Robinson	Fiction
Deanne Fitzmaurice	Photography	Martha Rial	Photography
Diana Sugg	Beat reporting	Maureen Dowd	Commentary
Doris Kearns Goodwin	History	Melinda Wagner	Music
Dorothy Rabinowitz	Commentary	Michiko Kakutani	Criticism
Edith Wharton	Novel	Paula Vogel	Drama
Edna St. Vincent Millay	Poetry	Samantha Power	General nonfiction
Eileen McNamara	Commentary	Sara Teasdale	Poetry
Gail Caldwell	Criticism	Sari Horwitz	Investigative reporting
Gretchen Morgenson	Beat reporting		
Isabel Wilkerson	Feature writing	Sonia Nazario	Feature writing
Joan Hedrick	Biography	Stacy Schiff	Biography
Julia Keller	Feature writing	Stephanie Welsh	Photography
Katharine Graham	Biography	Margaret Widdemer	Poetry
Kim Murphy	International reporting	Tina Rosenberg	General nonfiction
		Willa Cather	Novel
Laura E. Richards	Biography	Zona Gale	Drama

Boy Names

Winner	Category	Winner	Category
Aaron Jay Kernis	Music	Jared Diamond	General nonfiction
Albert Beveridge	Biography	Jesse Lynch Williams	Drama
Alex Raksin	Editorial writing	Joel Pett	Editorial cartooning
Alva Johnston	Reporting	Justin Smith	History
Angelo Henderson	Feature writing	Kevin Helliker	Explanatory reporting
Barry Bearak	International reporting	Kirke Simpson	Reporting
Bernard Stein	Editorial writing	Leon Dash	Explanatory journalism
Booth Tarkington	Novel	Leonard Pitts Jr.	Commentary
Burton Hendrick	History	Lloyd Schwartz	Criticism
Byron Acohido	Beat reporting	Louis Seibold	Reporting
Carl Sandburg	Poetry	Magner White	Reporting
Chuck Philips	Beat reporting	Matt Davies	Editorial cartooning
Clarence Williams	Photography	Morton Gould	Music
Clifford Levy	Investigative reporting	Nelson Harding	Editorial cartooning
Colbert King	Commentary	Nigel Jaquiss	Investigative reporting
Daniel Golden	Beat reporting	Nilo Cruz	Drama
Dele Olojede	International reporting	Owen Davis	Drama
Edwin Arlington Robinson	Poetry	Philip Roth	Fiction
Emory Holloway	Biography	Robert Frost	Poetry
Eugene O'Neill	Drama	Rollin Kirby	Editorial cartooning
Frank O'Brien	Editorial writing	Samuel Flagg Bemis	History
Franz Wright	Poetry	Sidney Howard	Drama
Gareth Cook	Explanatory reporting	Sinclair Lewis	Novel
Gunther Schuller	Music	Steven Stucky	Music
Harold Littledale	Reporting	Walt Handelsman	Editorial cartooning
Hamlin Garland	Biography	William Cabell Bruce	Biography
Horton Foote	Drama	Wynton Marsalis	Music
Ian Johnson	International reporting		

Nobel Prize Winners

Girl Names

Prize Winner	Category	Prize Winner	Category
Alva Myrdal	Peace	Mairead Corrigan	Peace
Barbara McClintock	Medicine	Marie Curie	Physics, Chemistry
Bertha von Suttner	Peace		
Betty Williams	Peace	Nadine Gordimer	Literature
Christiane Nusslein-Volhard	Medicine	Nelly Sachs	Literature
Daw Aung Suu Kyi	Peace	Pearl Buck	Literature
Elfriede Jelinek	Literature	Rigoberta Menchu	Peace
Emily Balch	Peace	Rosalyn Sussman Yalow	Medicine
Gabriela Mistral	Literature	Selma Lagerof	Literature
Gertrude Elion	Medicine	Shirin Ebadi	Peace
Gerty Radnitz Cori	Biochemistry	Sigrid Undset	Literature
Grazia Deledda	Literature	Mother Teresa	Peace
Irene Curie	Chemistry	Toni Morrison	Literature
Jody Williams	Peace	Wangari Maathai	Peace
Linda Buck	Medicine	Wislawa Szymborska	Literature

Boy Names

Prize Winner	Category	Prize Winner	Category
Aaron Ciechanover	Chemistry	Koichi Tanaka	Chemistry
Alexei Abrikosov	Physics	Kurt Wuthrich	Chemistry
Arvid Carlsson	Medicine	Leland Hartwell	Medicine
Avram Hershko	Chemistry	Masatoshi Koshiba	Physics
Clive Granger	Economics	Peter Agre	Chemistry
Daniel Kahneman	Economics	Riccardo Giacconi	Physics
David Gross	Physics	Richard Axel	Medicine
Edward Prescott	Economics	Roderick MacKinnon	Chemistry
Finn Kydland	Economics	Ryogi Noyori	Chemistry
Frank Wilczek	Physics	Sydney Brenner	Medicine
Gao Xingjian	Medicine	Tim Hunt	Medicine
Imre Kertész	Medicine	Vernon Smith	Economics
Irwin Rose	Chemistry	Vitaly Ginzburg	Physics
Joseph Stiglitz	Economics	Wolfgang Ketterle	Physics
Kofi Annan	Peace	Zhores Alferov	Physics

Oscar Winners*
Girl Names

Winner	Character	Movie
Angelina Jolie	Lisa Rowe	*Girl, Interrupted*
Barbra Streisand	Fanny Brice	*Funny Girl*
Cate Blanchett	Katharine Hepburn	*The Aviator*
Catherine Zeta-Jones	Velma Kelly	*Chicago*
Charlize Theron	Aileen Wuornos	*Monster*
Dianne Wiest	Holly	*Hannah and Her Sisters*
Emma Thompson	Margaret Schlegel	*Howards End*
Estelle Parsons	Blanche Barrow	*Bonnie and Clyde*
Faye Dunaway	Diana Christensen	*Network*
Geena Davis	Muriel	*The Accidental Tourist*
Gwyneth Paltrow	Viola De Lesseps	*Shakespeare in Love*
Halle Berry	Leticia Musgrove	*Monster's Ball*
Hilary Swank	Brandon Teena/Teena Brandon Maggie Fitzgerald	*Boys Don't Cry* *Million Dollar Baby*
Holly Hunter	Ada McGrath	*The Piano*
Jessica Lange	Carly Marshall, Julie Nichols	*Blue Sky, Tootsie*
Jodie Foster	Clarice Starling, Sarah Tobias	*The Silence of the Lambs, The Accused*
Julia Roberts	Erin Brockovich	*Erin Brockovich*
Katharine Hepburn	Ethel Thayer	*On Golden Pond*
Kim Basinger	Lynn Bracken	*L.A. Confidential*
Lee Grant	Felicia Carr	*Shampoo*
Marisa Tomei	Mona Lisa Vito	*My Cousin Vinny*
Marlee Matlin	Sarah Norman	*Children of a Lesser God*
Mercedes Ruehl	Anne (no last name)	*The Fisher King*
Mira Sorvino	Linda Ash	*Mighty Aphrodite*
Nicole Kidman	Virginia Woolf	*The Hours*
Olympia Dukakis	Rose Castorini	*Moonstruck*
Renée Zellweger	Ruby Thewes	*Cold Mountain*
Shirley MacLaine	Aurora Greenway	*Terms of Endearment*
Sissy Spacek	Loretta Lynn	*Coal Miner's Daughter*
Susan Sarandon	Sister Helen Prejean	*Dead Man Walking*
Tatum O'Neal	Addie Loggins	*Paper Moon*
Vanessa Redgrave	Julia (no last name)	*Julia*

*Information from 1964 through 2004.

Boy Names

Winner	Character	Movie
Adrien Brody	Wladyslaw Szpilman	*The Pianist*
Al Pacino	Lt. Col. Frank Slade	*Scent of a Woman*
Anthony Hopkins	Dr. Hannibal Lecter	*The Silence of the Lambs*
Ben Kingsley	Mahatma Gandhi	*Ghandi*
Benicio Del Toro	Javier Rodriguez	*Traffic*
Christopher Walken	Nick (no last name)	*The Deer Hunter*
Cuba Gooding Jr.	Rod Tidwell	*Jerry Maguire*
Daniel Day-Lewis	Christy Brown	*My Left Foot*
Denzel Washington	Alonzo	*Training Day*
Dustin Hoffman	Raymond Babbitt	*Rain Man*
	Ted Kramer	*Kramer vs. Kramer*
Gene Hackman	Jimmy "Popeye" Doyle	*The French Connection*
	Little Bill Daggett	*Unforgiven*
Gig Young	Rocky	*They Shoot Horses, Don't They?*
Haing S. Ngor	Dith Pran	*The Killing Fields*
Jamie Foxx	Ray Charles	*Ray*
Jeremy Irons	Claus Von Bulow	*Reversal of Fortune*
Jon Voight	Luke Martin	*Coming Home*
Kevin Spacey	Lester Burnham	*American Beauty*
Louis Gossett Jr.	Sgt. Emil Foley	*An Officer and a Gentleman*
Marlon Brando	Don Vito Corleone	*The Godfather*
Michael Caine	Elliot (no last name)	*Hannah and Her Sisters*
Morgan Freeman	Eddie Scrap-Iron Dupris	*Million Dollar Baby*
Nicolas Cage	Ben Sanderson	*Leaving Las Vegas*
Rex Harrison	Professor Henry Higgins	*My Fair Lady*
Richard Dreyfuss	Elliot Garfield	*The Goodbye Girl*
Roberto Benigni	Guido Orefice	*Life Is Beautiful*
Robin Williams	Sean McGuire	*Good Will Hunting*
Russell Crowe	Maximus Decimus Meridius	*Gladiator*
Sean Penn	Jimmy Markum	*Mystic River*
Tim Robbins	Dave Boyle	*Mystic River*
Tom Hanks	Andrew Beckett	*Philadelphia*
	Forrest Gump	*Forrest Gump*
William Hurt	Luis Molina	*Kiss of the Spider Woman*

Tony Winners

Girl Names

Winner	Category	Play
Anita Waxman	Revival, play	*The Real Thing*
Audra McDonald	Actress, play	*Master Class*
Bebe Neuwirth	Actress, musical	*Chicago*
Bernadette Peters	Actress, musical	*Annie Get Your Gun*
Cady Huffman	Actress, musical	*The Producers*
Charlene Marshall	Play, revival	*Long Day's Journey into Night*
Cherry Jones	Actress, play	*Doubt*
Florence Klotz	Costume designer	*Show Boat*
Frances Edelstein	Tony Honors for Excellence in Theater	
Gillian Gregory	Choreographer	*Me and My Girl*
Idina Menzel	Actress, musical	*Wicked*
Harriet Harris	Actress, musical	*Thoroughly Modern Millie*
Heather Headley	Actress, musical	*Aida*
Kara Medoff	Play, revival	*Long Day's Journey into Night*
Kristin Chenoweth	Actress, musical	*You're a Good Man, Charlie Brown*
Lillias White	Actress, musical	*The Life*
Lindsay Duncan	Actress, play	*Private Lives*
Margo Lion	Producer, musical	*Hairspray*
Marissa Jaret Winokur	Actress, musical	*Hairspray*
Natasha Katz	Lighting designer	*Aida*
Phylicia Rashad	Actress, play	*A Raisin in the Sun*
Robyn Goodman	Producer, musical	*Avenue Q*
Sutton Foster	Actress, musical	*Thoroughly Modern Millie*
Twyla Tharp	Choreographer	*Movin' Out*
Uta Hagen	Actress, drama	*Who's Afraid of Virginia Woolf*
Viola Davis	Actress, play	*King Hedley II*
Yasmina Reza	Writer, play	*Art*
Zoe Caldwell	Actress, play	*Master Class*

Boy Names

Winner	Category	Play
Alfred Uhry	Book, musical	*Parade*
André Bishop	Producer, musical	*Contact*
Bernard Gersten	Producer, revival	*Our Town*
Billy Joel	Orchestrations	*Movin' Out*
Boyd Gaines	Actor, musical	*Contact*
Christopher Plummer	Actor, play	*Barrymore*
Darren Bagert	Producer, revival	*Long Day's Journey into Night*
Dick Latessa	Actor, musical	*Hairspray*
Douglas Besterman	Orchestration	*Fosse*
Ellis Rabb	Director, play	*The Royal Family*
Elton John	Original musical score	*Aida*
Frank Langella	Actor, play	*Fortune's Fool*
Garth Fagan	Choreographer	*The Lion King*
Hugh Jackman	Actor, musical	*The Boy from Oz*
Jefferson Mays	Actor, play	*I Am My Own Wife*
Jules Fisher	Lighting designer	*Bring in 'da Noise/Bring in 'da Funk*
Ken Billington	Lighting designer	*Chicago*
Lloyd Richards	Director, play	*Fences*
Maury Yeston	Original musical score	*Titanic*
Nathan Lane	Actor, musical	*The Producers*
Nigel Levings	Lighting designer	*La Bohème*
Owen Teale	Actor, play	*A Doll's House*
Rick Steiner	Producer, musical	*Hairspray*
Ruben Santiago-Hudson	Actor, play	*Seven Guitars*
Shuler Hensley	Actor, musical	*Oklahoma!*
Stuart Malina	Orchestrations	*Movin' Out*
Tharon Musser	Lighting designer	*Dreamgirls*
Trevor Nunn	Director, musical	*Les Misérables*
Wilson Jermaine Heredia	Actor, musical	*Rent*

Emmy Winners

Girl Names

Winner	Category	Show
Aisha Wagle	Coordinating producer	*A Baby Story*
Audrey Jones	Producer	*The View*
Candice Bergen	Actress	*Murphy Brown*
Casey Childs	Director	*All My Children*
Cynthia Nixon	Actress	*Sex and the City*
Dana Goodman	Producer	*The View*
Erin Irwin	Producer	*The Wayne Brady Show*
Frances Reid	Actress	*Days of Our Lives*
Gena Rowlands	Actress	*Hysterical Blindness*
Haleigh Safran	Producer	*The View*
Isabel Sanford	Actress	*The Jeffersons*
Jakki Taylor	Coordinating producer	*The View*
Kirstie Alley	Actress	*Cheers; David's Mother*
Krysia Plonka	Supervising producer	*The Wayne Brady Show*
Lindsay Wagner	Actress	*The Bionic Woman*
Liz Naylor	Producer	*A Baby Story*
Lorri Leighton	Producer	*A Baby Story*
Maria Notaras	Producer	*The Wayne Brady Show*
Mary-Louise Parker	Actress	*Angels in America*
Nan Schwieger	Producer	*Reading Rainbow*
Nicole Silver	Producer	*Reading Rainbow*
Rachel Ames	Actress	*General Hospital*
Roseanne Arnold	Actress	*Roseanne*
Sarah Jessica Parker	Actress	*Sex and the City*
Shelly Moore	Writer	*General Hospital*
Sudie Anning	Producer	*Reading Rainbow*
Tamara Grady	Stage manager	*All My Children*
Twila Liggett	Director	*Reading Rainbow*
Tyne Daly	Actress	*Judging Amy*
Vanessa Marcil	Actress	*General Hospital*
Vivian Gundaker	Producer	*As the World Turns*

Boy Names

Winner	Category	Show
Albert Finney	Actor	*The Gathering Storm*
Beau Bridges	Actor	*The Second Civil War*
Bill Geddie	Executive producer	*The View*
Bradley Whitford	Actor	*The West Wing*
Burt Reynolds	Actor	*Evening Shade*
Carroll O'Connor	Actor	*All in the Family; In the Heat of the Night*
Craig T. Nelson	Actor	*Coach*
Don Hastings	Actor	*As the World Turns*
Ed Wiseman	Producer	*Reading Rainbow*
Freddy Rodriguez	Supporting actor	*Six Feet Under*
Garin Wolf	Writer	*General Hospital*
Glenn Davish	Producer	*The View*
Hal Holbrook	Actor	*Sandburg's Lincoln*
Jerry Pilato	Associate director	*All My Children*
Jordi Vilasuso	Actor	*Guiding Light*
Josh Gilbert	Producer	*The Wayne Brady Show*
Judd Hirsch	Actor	*Taxi*
Kelsey Bay	Coordinating producer	*As the World Turns*
Lee Farber	Producer	*The Wayne Brady Show*
Levar Burton	Executive producer	*Reading Rainbow*
Maurice Benard	Actor	*General Hospital*
Michael Loman	Executive producer	*Sesame Street*
Neil Cohen	Executive producer	*A Baby Story*
Orly Wiseman	Producer	*Reading Rainbow*
Rocky Schmidt	Senior producer	*Jeopardy!*
Rusty Swope	Stage manager	*All My Children*
Shane Farley	Producer	*The Wayne Brady Show*
Shia Labeouf	Actor	*Even Stevens*
Sid Caesar	Actor	*Caesar's Hour*
Telly Savalas	Actor	*Kojak*
Wayne Brady	Actor	*Whose Line Is It Anyway?*

Grammy Winners
Girl Names

Musician	Category	Musician	Category
Alannah Myles	Rock	K. D. Lang	Traditional pop
Amy Grant	Gospel	Kathy Mattea	Country
Ani DiFranco	Packaging	Lauryn Hill	R&B
Anita Baker	R&B	Lena Horne	Jazz
Anne Sofie von Otter	Classical	Macy Gray	Pop
Barbra Streisand	Pop	Madonna	Pop
Bette Midler	Pop	Mary Youngblood	Folk
Brandy	R&B	Melissa Etheridge	Rock
CeCe Winans	Gospel	Missy Elliott	Rap
Cecilia Bartoli	Classical	Monica	R&B
Celia Cruz	Latin	Mya	Pop
Celine Dion	Pop	Naomi Judd	Country
Chaka Khan	R&B	Natalie Cole	Jazz
Cher	Pop	Nelly Furtado	Pop
Cissy Houston	Gospel	Norah Jones	Pop
Cyndi Lauper	Pop	Pam Tillis	Country
Debby Boone	Gospel	Paula Cole	Rock
Dee Dee Bridgewater	Jazz	Patti Page	Traditional pop
Dianne Reeves	Jazz	Pink	Rock
Dionne Warwick	Pop	Queen Latifah	Rap
Donna Summer	Pop	Renée Fleming	Classical
Enya	New Age	Sarah McLachlan	Pop
Faith Hill	Country	Shawn Colvin	Folk
Fiona Apple	Rock	Sheena Easton	Pop
Gloria Estefan	Latin	Shelby Lynne	Country
Irene Cara	Pop	Sheryl Crow	Rock
Janet Jackson	Pop	Shirley Horn	Jazz
Joan Sebastian	Latin	Susan Graham	Classical
Jody Watley	Pop	Thelma Houston	R&B
Juice Newton	Country	Toni Braxton	R&B
June Carter Cash	Country	Tracy Chapman	Rock
		Whitney Houston	R&B

Boy Names

Musician	Category	Musician	Category
Aaron Neville	Country	LL Cool J	Rap
Al Jarreau	R&B	Lenny Kravitz	Rock
André Previn	Classical	Lionel Richie	Pop
Art Neville	Rock	Lou Rawls	R&B
Barry White	R&B	Luis Miguel	Latin
Beck	Rock	Luther Vandross	R&B
Billy Joel	Rock	Lyle Lovett	Country
Bobby Brown	R&B	Marvin Gaye	R&B
Bruce Hornsby	Pop	McCoy Tyner	Jazz
Burt Bacharach	Composing	Michael Bolton	Pop
Chick Corea	Jazz	Miles Davis	Jazz
Christopher Cross	Arranging	Murray Perahia	Classical
Coolio	Rap	Nat "King" Cole	Pop
Dave Matthews	Rock	Nelly	Rap
David Russell	Classical	Ozzy Osbourne	Rock
Dominick Argento	Classical	Pat Metheny	New Age
Donald Fagen	Pop	Paul Simon	Pop
Elvis Costello	Pop	Peabo Bryson	Pop
Emanuel Ax	Classical	Pete Seeger	Folk
Enrique Iglesias	Latin	Peter Gabriel	Music video
George Winston	New Age	Phil Collins	Composing
Grover Mitchell	Jazz	Quincy Jones	Jazz
Harry Connick Jr.	Jazz	R. Kelly	R&B
Herbie Hancock	Jazz	Randy Brecker	Jazz
Jack White	Rock	Ricky Skaggs	Country
James Taylor	Pop	Robert Palmer	Rock
Jeff Beck	Rock	Rubén Blades	Latin
Jimmy Page	Rock	Seal	Pop
Jimmy Sturr	Polka	Sergio Mendes	World
Joe Jackson	Pop	Stevie Wonder	R&B
John Fogerty	Rock	Tito Puente	Latin
Jon Secada	Latin	Tony Bennett	Traditional pop
José Feliciano	Latin	Travis Tritt	Country
Joshua Bell	Classical	Warren Zevon	Folk
Julio Iglesias	Latin	Waylon Jennings	Country
Kenny Loggins	Pop	Willie Nelson	Country
Kurt Cobain	Alternative	Wynton Marsalis	Jazz
		Yo-Yo Ma	Classical

Olympic Medalists
Girl Names

Winner	Sport	Winner	Sport
Amanda Beard	Swimming	Janica Kostelic	Alpine skiing
Angel Martino	Swimming	Katarina Witt	Figure skating
Bente Skari	Cross-country skiing	Katja Seizinger	Alpine skiing
Carly Patterson	Gymnastics	Kristi Yamaguchi	Figure skating
Claudia Boyarskikh	Cross-country skiing	Mariel Zagunis	Fencing
		Marion Jones	Track and field
Daniela Ceccarelli	Alpine skiing	Mary Lou Retton	Gymnastics
Dara Torres	Swimming	Merlene Ottey	Track and field
Diann Roffe-Steinrotter	Alpine skiing	Nadia Comaneci	Gymnastics
Ecaterina Szabo	Gymnastics	Nikki Stone	Freestyle skiing
Ethelda Bleibtrey	Swimming	Oksana Baiul	Figure skating
Florence Griffith-Joyner	Track and field	Picabo Street	Alpine skiing
Galina Kulakova	Cross-country skiing	Shannon Miller	Gymnastics
		Tara Lipinski	Figure skating
Gwen Torrence	Track and field	Valerie Brisco-Hooks	Track and field
Jackie Joyner-Kersee	Track and field	Wilma Rudolph	Track and field

Boy Names

Winner	Sport	Winner	Sport
Alberto Tomba	Alpine skiing	Jean-Claude Killy	Alpine skiing
Alexei Yagudin	Figure skating	Jesse Owens	Track and field
Brian Boitano	Figure skating	Lasse Kjus	Alpine skiing
Carl Lewis	Track and field	Lenny Krayzelburg	Swimming
Casey FitzRandolph	Speed skating	Matt Biondi	Swimming
Derek Parra	Speed skating	Matti Nykanen	Ski jumping
Dick Button	Figure skating	Maurice Greene	Track and field
Eric Heiden	Speed skating	Michael Johnson	Track and field
Fritz Strobl	Alpine skiing	Neil Walker	Swimming
Gary Hall Jr.	Swimming	Oscar De La Hoya	Boxing
Georg Hackl	Luge	Pernell Whitaker	Boxing
Ilia Kulik	Figure skating	Scott Hamilton	Figure skating
Irving Jaffee	Speed skating	Tommy Moe	Alpine skiing
Jason Lezak	Swimming	Viktor Petrenko	Figure skating

Heisman Trophy Winners

Girl Names

Not applicable.

Boy Names

Winner	School	Winner	School
Andre Ware	University of Houston	Howard Cassady	Ohio State University
Angelo Bertelli	University of Notre Dame	Jason White	University of Oklahoma
		Jay Berwanger	University of Chicago
Bo Jackson	Auburn University	Jim Plunkett	Stanford University
Bruce Smith	University of Minnesota	Joe Bellino	Navy
Carson Palmer	University of Southern California	John Huarte	University of Notre Dame
Charles White	University of Southern California	Johnny Rodgers	University of Nebraska
		Larry Kelley	Yale University
Chris Weinke	Florida State University	Leon Hart	University of Notre Dame
Clint Frank	Yale University		
Danny Wuerffel	University of Florida	Les Horvath	Ohio State University
Davey O'Brien	Texas Christian University	Marcus Allen	University of Southern California
Desmond Howard	University of Michigan	Mike Garrett	University of Southern California
Doak Walker	Southern Methodist University	Nile Kinnick	University of Iowa
Earl Campbell	University of Texas	Peter Dawkins	Army
Eric Crouch	University of Nebraska	Rashaan Salaam	University of Colorado
Ernie Davis	Syracuse University	Ricky Williams	University of Texas
Felix Blanchard	Army	Roger Staubach	Navy
Frank Sinkwich	University of Georgia	Steve Spurrier	University of Florida
Gary Beban	University of California-Los Angeles	Terry Baker	Oregon State University
George Rogers	University of South Carolina	Tim Brown	University of Notre Dame
Gino Torretta	University of Miami	Ty Detmer	Brigham Young University
Glenn Davis	Army	Vic Janowicz	Ohio State University
Herschel Walker	University of Georgia	Vinny Testaverde	University of Miami

Series MVPs

Girl Names

MVP	Sport	MVP	Sport
Ashley Earley	Basketball	Milena Tomova	Basketball
Crystal Kelly	Basketball	Ofa Wright	Basketball
Dee-Dee Wheeler	Basketball	Reka Cserny	Basketball
Elisha Turek	Basketball	Rolanda Monroe	Basketball
Eva Cunningham	Basketball	Sancho Lyttle	Basketball
Jazz Covington	Basketball	Shay Doron	Basketball
Jillian Robbins	Basketball	Sugiery Monsac	Basketball
Khara Smith	Basketball	Tan White	Basketball
Kiera Hardy	Basketball	Tanisha Wright	Basketball
Leilani Mitchell	Basketball	Tori Talbert	Basketball
Meg Bulger	Basketball		

Boy Names

MVP	Sport	MVP	Sport
Bart Starr	Football	Marcus Allen	Football
Bucky Dent	Baseball	Mariano Rivera	Baseball
Charles Barkley	Basketball	Moses Malone	Basketball
Darrell Porter	Baseball	Orel Hershiser	Baseball
Desmond Howard	Football	Oscar Robertson	Basketball
Dexter Jackson	Football	Pedro Guerrero	Baseball
Emmitt Smith	Football	Phil Simms	Football
Franco Harris	Football	Randy White	Football
Gene Tenace	Baseball	Reggie Jackson	Baseball
Hakeem Olajuwon	Basketball	Roberto Clemente	Baseball
Harvey Martin	Football	Roger Staubach	Football
Jake Scott	Football	Rollie Fingers	Baseball
Jose Rijo	Baseball	Sandy Koufax	Baseball
Julius Erving	Basketball	Scott Brosius	Baseball
Kareem Abdul-Jabbar	Basketball	Shaquille O'Neal	Basketball
Karl Malone	Basketball	Terrell Davis	Football
Kurt Warner	Football	Troy Aikman	Football
Lew Burdette	Baseball	Whitey Ford	Baseball
Livan Hernandez	Baseball	Willis Reed	Basketball
Lynn Swann	Football	Wilt Chamberlain	Basketball

NBA/NCAA All-Stars

Girl Names

All-Star	Team
Alison Bales	Duke University Blue Devils
Amber Flynn	Bowling Green State University Falcons
Anna Chappell	University of Arizona Wildcats
Brie Madden	Kansas State University Wildcats
Brittney Keil	College of the Holy Cross Crusaders
Caprice Smith	DePaul University Blue Demons
Casmir Patterson	DePaul University Blue Demons
Cavanaugh Hagen	Canisius College Golden Griffins
Chelsea Whitaker	Baylor University Bears
Corinne Turner	George Washington University Colonials
Danielle Adefeso	University of Arizona Wildcats
Daphne Andre	University of Houston Lady Cougars
Denita Plain	Coppin State College Lady Eagles
Ebony Franklin	Alcorn State Lady Braves
Erica Taylor	Louisiana Tech University Lady Techsters
Jaci McCormack	Illinois State University Redbirds
Janese Hardrick	University of Georgia Lady Bulldogs
Joy Hollingsworth	University Arizona Wildcats
Karly Chesko	Canisius College Golden Griffins
Kenisha Daniels	Alcorn State University Lady Braves
Kia Alexander	Alcorn State University Lady Braves

All-Star	Team
Lashawn Johnson	Illinois State University Redbirds
Leisel Harry	Coppin State College Lady Eagles
Margaret DeCiman	Louisiana Tech Lady Techsters
Monique Currie	Duke University Blue Devils
Natasha Dennis	Alcorn State University Lady Braves
Nia Capuano	Canisius College Golden Griffins
Nina Simokes	University of Louisville Cardinals
Patrika Barlow	University of Louisville Cardinals
Quianna Chaney	Louisiana State University Lady Tigers
Rachael Carney	DePaul University Blue Demons
Sakima Smith	Bowling Green State University Falcons
Sarah Placek	College of the Holy Cross Crusaders
Sherill Baker	University of Georgia Lady Bulldogs
Sophia White	Baylor University Bears
Sylvia Fowles	Louisiana State University Lady Tigers
Talia Sutton	Coppin State College Lady Eagles
Tanika Price	University of Hartford Hawks
Tosha Christmas	Louisiana Tech Lady Techsters
Wanisha Smith	Duke University Blue Devils
Whitney Taylor	Bowling Green University Falcons

Boy Names

All-Star	Team	All-Star	Team
Alonzo Mourning	Miami Heat	Larry Bird	Boston Celtics
Amare Stoudemire	Phoenix Suns	LeBron James	Cleveland Cavaliers
Antoine Walker	Boston Celtics	Magic Johnson	Los Angeles Lakers
Baron Davis	Golden State Warriors	Michael Jordan	Chicago Bulls
Bryon Russell	Denver Nuggets	Moses Malone	Portland Trail Blazers
Brad Miller	Sacramento Kings	Otis Thorpe	New Orleans Hornets
Carlos Boozer	Utah Jazz	Pau Gasol	Memphis Grizzlies
Carmelo Anthony	Denver Nuggets	Peja Stojakovic	Sacramento Kings
Chauncey Billups	Detroit Pistons	Radoslav Nesterovic	San Antonio Spurs
Clyde Drexler	Portland Trail Blazers	Reggie Miller	Indiana Pacers
Dale Davis	Indiana Pacers	Ricky Davis	Boston Celtics
Darryl Dawkins	Detroit Pistons	Robert Parish	Chicago Bulls
Derek Fisher	Golden State Warriors	Sam Perkins	Indiana Pacers
Dikembe Mutombo	Houston Rockets	Scottie Pippen	Chicago Bulls
Dirk Nowitzki	Dallas Mavericks	Shaquille O'Neal	Miami Heat
Dolph Schayes	New York Knicks	Shareef Abdur-Rahim	Portland Trail Blazers
Eddy Curry	Chicago Bulls	Stephon Marbury	New York Knicks
Emanuel Ginobili	San Antonio Spurs	Terry Porter	San Antonio Spurs
Gilbert Arenas	Washington Wizards	Toni Kukoc	Milwaukee Bucks
Hakeem Olajuwon	Toronto Raptors	Tracy McGrady	Houston Rockets
Hersey Hawkins	New Orleans Hornets	Tree Rollins	Indiana Pacers
Isiah Thomas	Detroit Pistons	Tyson Chandler	Chicago Bulls
Jerome Kersey	San Antonio Spurs	Vern Mikkelsen	Minneapolis Lakers
Jo Jo White	Boston Celtics	Vince Carter	New Jersey Nets
Julius Erving	Philadelphia 76ers	Vlade Divac	Los Angeles Lakers
Kareem Abdul-Jabbar	Los Angeles Lakers	Wes Unseld	Baltimore Bullets
Karl Malone	Los Angeles Lakers	Willis Reed	New York Knicks
Kenyon Martin	Denver Nuggets	Yao Ming	Houston Rockets
Kiki Vandeweghe	Denver Nuggets	Zydrunas Ilgauskas	Cleveland Cavaliers
Kobe Bryant	Los Angeles Lakers		

Hockey Hunks and Babes

Girl Names

Hockey Babe	Team	Hockey Babe	Team
Annika Ahlen	Sweden	Jeanine Sobek	Team USA
Bettina Evers	Germany	Kristina Bergstrand	Sweden
Cammie Granato	Team USA	Lina Huo	China
Danielle Goyette	Team Canada	Manon Rheume	Team Canada
Emma Bowles	Great Britain	Nina Gall	Germany
Fiona Smith	Team Canada	Robyn Ann Armour	Australia
Gretchen Ulion	Team USA	Sabine Schumacher	Switzerland
Isabelle Minier	Team Canada	Yuka Oda	Japan

Boy Names

Hockey Hunk	Team	Hockey Hunk	Team
Aaron Ward	Carolina Hurricanes	Kip Brennan	Los Angeles Kings
Andreas Lilja	Florida Panthers	Lance Ward	Anaheim Mighty Ducks
Ari Ahonen	New Jersey Devils		
Brett Lysak	Carolina Hurricanes	Marek Zidlicky	Nashville Predators
Brooks Laich	Washington Capitals	Mattias Weinhandl	New York Islanders
Bryce Lampman	New York Rangers	Mikko Luoma	Edmonton Oilers
Chad Wiseman	New York Rangers	Neil Little	Philadelphia Flyers
Christian Backman	St. Louis Blues	Nikita Alexeev	Tampa Bay Lightning
Claude Lapointe	Philadelphia Flyers	Nolan Baumgartner	Vancouver Canucks
Daymond Langkow	Phoenix Coyotes	Pascal Leclaire	Columbus Blue Jackets
Drake Berehowsky	Toronto Maple Leafs		
Duvie Westcott	Columbus Blue Jackets	Quintin Laing	Chicago Blackhawks
		Ramzi Abid	Pittsburg Penguins
Emmanuel Legace	Detroit Red Wings	Ryan Barnes	Detroit Red Wings
Francis Lessard	Atlanta Thrashers	Sebastien Aubin	Pittsburg Penguins
Guillaume Lefebvre	Pittsburg Penguins	Stu Barnes	Dallas Stars
Henrik Zetterberg	Detroit Red Wings	Trevor Letowski	Columbus Blue Jackets
Ian Laperriere	Los Angeles Kings		
Jere Lehtinen	Dallas Stars	Vincent Lecavalier	Tampa Bay Lightning
Jesse Wallin	Detriot Red Wings	Wes Waltz	Minnesota Wild
Jozef Balej	Montreal Canadiens	Zac Bierk	Phoenix Coyotes
Kevyn Adams	Boston Bruins		

Gymnast Guys and Gals

Girl Names

Gymnast	Country	Gymnast	Country
Aurelia Dobre	Romania	Nadia Comaneci	Romania
Brandy Johnson	USA	Nelli Kim	Soviet Union
Catalina Ponor	Romania	Oksana Omeliantchik	Soviet Union
Chellsie Memmel	USA	Olga Bicherova	Soviet Union
Dominique Dawes	USA	Pearl Perkins	USA
Ecaterina Szabo	Romania	Rachel Tidd	USA
Elise Ray	USA	Shannon Miller	USA
Hollie Vise	USA	Svetlana Boginskaia	Soviet Union
Jaycie Phelps	USA	Tatiana Gutsu	Soviet Union
Julianne McNamara	USA	Terin Humphrey	USA
Kerri Strug	USA	Vera Caslavska	Czechoslovakia
Kim Zmeskal	USA	Yang Bo	China
Lilia Podkopayeva	Ukraine	Yelena Mukhina	Soviet Union
Marcia Frederick	USA	Zhu Zheng	China
Mohini Bhardwaj	USA		

Boy Names

Gymnast	Country	Gymnast	Country
Alexander Artemev	USA	Kip Simons	USA
Bart Conner	USA	Kurt Thomas	USA
Blaine Wilson	USA	Lance Ringnald	USA
Boris Shakhlin	Soviet Union	Leon Stukelj	Slovenia
Brett McClure	USA	Marshall Avener	USA
Chainey Umphrey	USA	Mihai Bagiu	USA
Conrad Voorsanger	USA	Mitch Gaylord	USA
Ed Hennig	USA	Morgan Hamm	USA
Frank Cumiskey	USA	Nikolay Andrianov	Soviet Union
Georges Miez	Switzerland	Paul Hamm	USA
Guard Young	USA	Raj Bhavsar	USA
Jair Lynch	USA	Rusty Mitchell	USA
Jarrod Hanks	USA	Scott Keswick	USA
Josh Stein	USA	Trent Dimas	USA
Kerry Huston	USA	Vitaly Scherbo	Soviet Union

NASCAR Names

Girl Names

Ann Bunselmeyer
Christine Beckers
Ethel Mobley
Fifi Scott

Goldie Parsons
Janet Guthrie
Lella Lombardi
Louise Smith

Marian Pagan
Patty Moise
Robin McCall

Sara Christian
Shawna Robinson
Stacy Compton

Boy Names

Allan Grice
Alton Jones
Andy Belmont
Austin Cameron
Baxter Price
Blair Aiken
Bobby Allison
Boris Said
Brandon Ash
Brent Elliott
Brett Bodine
Buck Baker
Buddy Arrington
Cale Yarborough
Carl Adams
Chad Blount
Charlie Rudolph
Chet Fillip
Chuck Wahl
Clark Dwyer
Clay Young
Casey Atwood
Christian Fittipaldi
Dale Earnhardt Jr.
Darrell Waltrip
Davey Allison
Derrike Cope
Dick Whalen

Doc Faustina
Donnie Allison
Doug Wheeler
Earl Ross
Edward Cooper
Eldon Dotson
Elliott Forbes-
 Robinson
Ernie Cline
Fonty Flock
Frank Warren
Gary Baker
George Wiltshire
Gil Roth
Glen Francis
Gordon Johncock
Graham Taylor
Grant Adcox
Harry Goularte
Henley Gray
Hermie Sadler
Howard Rose
Hut Stricklin
Ivan Baldwin
Jack Donohue
Jason Hedlesky
Jeremy Mayfield
Jerry Nadeau

Jimmy Walker
Joey Arrington
John Alexander
Keith Davis
Kenny Wallace
Kerry Earnhardt
Kevin Harvick
Kirk Bryant
Klaus Graf
Kurt Busch
Kyle Petty
Lake Speed
Laurent Rioux
Lee Raymond
Loy Allen
Marty Robbins
Marv Acton
Matt Kenseth
Maurice Randall
Mickey Gibbs
Mike Alexander
Morgan Shepard
Neil Bonnett
Nelson Oswald
Norm Palmer
Oma Kimbrough
Pancho Carter
Paul Dean Holt

Phil Barkdoll
Ralph Jones
Randy Renfrow
Ray Elder
Richard White
Rodney Combs
Roger McCluskey
Roland Wlodyka
Ruben Garcia
Rusty Wallace
Salt Walther
Sam Ard
Satch Worley
Scott Autrey
Shane Hall
Stanley Smith
Strout Wayne
Ted Fritz
Terry Ryan
Tom Williams
Tony Ave
Travis Kvapil
Trevor Boys
Vince
 Giamformaggio
Walter Wallace
Ward Burton
Wayne Watercutter

Spinners and Stunners—Ice Skaters
Girl Names

Andrea Ehrig

Barbara Ann Scott

Beatrix Schuba

Bonnie Blair

Carol Heiss

Catriona Le May Doan

Cecilia Colledge

Christa Luding-Rothenburger

Christina Kaiser

Claudia Pechstein

Connie Carpenter

Dagmar Lurz

Debi Thomas

Dianna Holum

Dorothy Hamill

Ekaterina Gordeeva

Elizabeth Manley

Ethel Mukelt

Eva Pawlik

Gabriele Seyfert

Gunda Niemann-Stirnemann

Ingrid Wendl

Irina Rodnina

Jacqueline du Bief

Jayne Torvill

Jeanne Ashworth

Jill Trenary

Karin Kania

Katarina Witt

Kira Ivanova

Kristi Yamaguchi

Lee-Kyung Chun

Lidiva Skoblikova

Linda Fratianne

Madge Syers

Maribel Vinson

Michelle Kwan

Nancy Kerrigan

Nicole Bobek

Oksana Baiul

Peggy Fleming

Radka Kovarikova

Regine Heitzer

Rosalynn Sumners

Sarah Hughes

Sonja Henie

Tai Babilonia

Tara Lipinski

Tenley Albright

Theresa Weld

Vivi-Anne Hulten

Yvonne Van Gennip

Boy Names

Alain Calmat

Aleksey Urmanov

Andreas Krogh

Arthur Cumming

Brian Boitano

Charles Tickner

David Jenkins

Dick Button

Elvis Stojko

Ernst Baier

Felix Kaspar

Geoffrey Hall-Say

Georges Gautschi

Gillis Grafstrom

Hans Gerschwiler

Hayes Alan Jenkins

Helmut Seibt

Ilya Kulik

James Grogan

John Curry

Josef Sabovcik

Karl Schafer

Manfred Schnelldorfer

Martin Stixrud

Montgomery Wilson

Ondrej Nepela

Patrick Pera

Paul Wylie

Philippe Candeloro

Rene Novotny

Richard Johannson

Robert Van Zeebroeck

Robin Cousins

Ronnie Robertson

Scott Hamilton

Sergey Chetveroukhin

Tim Wood

Toller Cranston

Ulrich Salchow

Viktor Petrenko

Vladimir Kovalev

Willy Bockl

Wolfgang Schwarz

Grand Slammers–Tennis Players

Girl Names

Abigail Spears
Alicia Molik
Amelie Mauresmo
Amy Frazier
Anastasia Myskina
Anna Kournikova
Anke Huber
Arantxa Sanchez Vicario
Billie Jean King
Chris Evert
Conchita Martinez
Elena Bovina

Elena Dementieva
Elena Likhovtseva
Evonne Goolagong Cawley
Gabriela Sabatini
Hana Mandlikova
Helena Sukova
Iva Majoli
Jana Novotna
Jelena Jankovic
Jennifer Capriati
Jill Craybas
Justine Henin-

Hardenne
Kim Clijsters
Lindsay Davenport
Maria Sharapova
Marissa Irvin
Martina Hingis
Martina Navratilova
Mary Pierce
Mary Jo Fernandez
Monica Seles
Nadia Petrova
Natasha Zvereva

Nathalie Dechy
Pam Shriver
Patty Schnyder
Serena Williams
Steffi Graf
Svetlana Kuznetsova
Tatiana Golovin
Tracy Austin
Venus Williams
Vera Zvonareva
Virginia Wade

Boy Names

Adriano Panatta
Andre Agassi
Andy Roddick
Arthur Ashe
Bjorn Borg
Bobby Riggs
Boris Becker
Carlos Moya
David Nalbandian
Dominik Hrbaty
Gaston Gaudio
Goran Ivanisevic
Guillermo Canas
Guillermo Coria

Guillermo Vilas
Gustavo Kuerten
Ilie Nastase
Ivan Lendl
Ivan Ljubicic
Jan Kodes
Jim Courier
Jimmy Connors
Joachim Johansson
Johan Kriek
John McEnroe
John Newcombe
Lleyton Hewitt

Manuel Orantes
Marat Safin
Mario Ancic
Mats Wilander
Michael Chang
Michael Stich
Nikolay Davydenko
Pat Cash
Patrick Rafter
Pete Sampras
Petr Korda
Radek Stepanek
Rafael Nadal

Richard Krajicek
Rod Laver
Roger Federer
Sergi Bruguera
Stan Smith
Stefan Edberg
Thomas Johansson
Thomas Muster
Tim Henmen
Tommy Robredo
Vitas Gerulaitis
Yannick Noah
Yevgeny Kafelnikov

Golf Pros

Girl Names

Annika Sorenstam	Emilee Klein	Karrie Webb	Natalie Gulbis
Beth Bauer	Gloria Park	Kim Saiki	Nicole Perrot
Beth Daniel	Grace Park	Kristi Albers	Pat Hurst
Birdie Kim	Heather Bowie	Laura Davies	Paula Creamer
Brandie Burton	Hee-Won Han	Laura Diaz	Rachel Hetherington
Candie Kung	Helen Alfredsson	Leta Lindley	Reilley Rankin
Carin Koch	Janice Moodie	Liselotte Neumann	Rosie Jones
Catriona Matthew	Jennifer Rosales	Lorena Ochoa	Se Ri Pak
Christina Kim	Jeong Jang	Lorie Kane	Shi Hyun Ahn
Cristie Kerr	Jill McGill	Maria Hjorth	Silvia Cavalleri
Danielle Ammaccapane	Jimin Kang	Meg Mallon	Stacy Prammanasudh
Dawn Coe-Jones	Joo Mi Kim	Mi Hyun Kim	Tina Barrett
Deb Richard	Juli Inkster	Michele Redman	Wendy Ward
Dorothy Delasin	Karen Stupples	Moira Dunn	Young Kim
	Karine Icher		

Boy Names

Adam Scott	Fred Couples	K. J. Choi	Scott Verplank
Angel Cabrera	Fred Funk	Kenny Perry	Sergio Garcia
Arnold Palmer	Graeme McDowell	Kirk Triplett	Shaun Micheel
Bart Bryant	Greg Norman	Lee Westwood	Shigeki Maruyama
Bernhard Langer	Hal Sutton	Luke Donald	Stephen Ames
Bob Tway	Hank Kuehne	Mark Hensby	Stewart Cink
Bobby Jones	Harrison Frazar	Miguel Jimenez	Stuart Appleby
Brett Quigley	Ian Poulter	Mike Weir	Tag Ridings
Carl Pettersson	Jack Nicklaus	Nick O'Hern	Thomas Bjorn
Chad Campbell	Jaxon Brigman	Padraig Harrington	Tiger Woods
Chris DiMarco	Jay Haas	Paul Casey	Tim Clark
Colin Montgomerie	Jeff Maggert	Per-Ulrik Johansson	Titch Moore
Corey Pavin	Jesper Parnevik	Peter Lonard	Todd Hamilton
Craig Parry	Jim Furyk	Phil Mickelson	Tom Lehman
Darren Clarke	Joey Sindelar	Pierre Fulke	Trevor Immelman
David Toms	John Daly	Retief Goosen	Vaughn Taylor
Davis Love III	Jonathan Kaye	Robert Allenby	Vijay Singh
Duffy Waldorf	José Maria Olazabal	Rod Pampling	Zach Johnson
Ernie Els	Justin Leonard	Rory Sabbatini	

Money Monikers

If you fancy your son or daughter as a future corporate leader, take a look at some of the names of today's CEOs of the Fortune 1000 for naming ideas. You'll spot the names of all the women currently heading U.S. corporations, as well as a mix of men holding the same top spot.

Or scan the names of some of the world's best-known entrepreneurs. Important historical figures such as Andrew Carnegie and John D. Rockefeller are here, too, as are some of today's hot-shot entrepreneurs, such as Jeff Bezos and Liz Lange.

For even more fun, peek at some of the brand names some parents have given their kids. From liqueur to cars to shoes, you'll see quite a variety to choose from. Or you may be inspired to use one of your own favorite brands.

CEOs

Girl Names

CEO	Company
Andrea Jung	Avon
Anne Mulcahy	Xerox
Brenda Barnes	Sara Lee
Dona Davis Young	Phoenix Technologies
Dorrit Bern	Charming Shoppes
Eileen Scott	Pathmark Stores
Janet Robinson	*The New York Times*
Kathleen Ligocki	Tower Automotive
Margaret Whitman	eBay
Marion Sandler	Golden West Financial Corp.

CEO	Company
Mary Forté	Zale Corporation
Mary Agnes Wilderotter	Citizens Communications
Mary Sammons	Rite Aid
Patricia Gallup	PC Connection
Patricia Russo	Lucent Technologies
Paula Rosput	AGL Resources
S. Marce Fuller	Mirant
Stephanie Streeter	Banta
Susan Ivey	Reynolds American

Boy Names

CEO	Company
Alan Lafley	Procter and Gamble
Aldo Zucaro	Old Republic International
Bernard Girod	Harman International Industries
Blake Nordstrom	Nordstrom
Bradbury Anderson	Best Buy
Burton Tansky	Neiman Marcus
Charles Prince	Citigroup
Clarence Otis	Darden Restaurants
Dane Miller	Biomet
David Edmondson	Radio Shack
Derek Hathaway	Harsco Corporation
Edmond English	TJX Companies, Inc.
Edward Rust Jr.	State Farm Insurance Companies
Elden Smith	Fleetwood Enterprises
Eli Harari	SanDisk
G. Richard Wagoner Jr.	General Motors
H. Lee Scott	Wal-Mart Stores
Harris DeLoach Jr.	Sonoco Products
Hector Ortino	Ferro

CEO	Company
Henry Paulson Jr.	Goldman Sachs Group
Ian McCarthy	Beezer Homes USA
Jay Fishman	St. Paul Travelers Cos.
Jeffrey Immelt	General Electric
Jim Donald	Starbucks Corporation
Joel Johnson	Hormel Foods
Jose Maria Alapont	Federal-Mogul
Kelly Conlin	Primedia
Kenneth Chenault	American Express
Lamar Norsworthy	Holly Corporation
Lee Raymond	Exxon Mobil
Marijn Dekkers	Thermo Electron
Mark Hurd	Hewlett-Packard
Michael Eskew	United Parcel Service
Morry Weiss	American Greetings
Myron Ullman	J.C. Penney
Nolan Archibald	Black and Decker
Owsley Brown II	Brown-Forman
Patrick Stokes	Anheuser-Busch
Rajiv Gupta	Rohm and Haas
Ralph Hake	Maytag

CEO	Company	CEO	Company
Reuben Mark	Colgate-Palmolive	Theodore Solso	Cummins
Richard Parsons	Time Warner	Walden O'Dell	Diebold
Richmond McKinnish	Carlisle	Wallace Barr	Caesars Entertainment
Robert Iger	Disney		
Samuel Palmisano	IBM	Warren Buffett	Berkshire Hathaway
Seymour Sternberg	New York Life Insurance	Wendell Weeks	Corning
		Wesley von Schack	Energy East
Sherrill Hudson	TECO Energy	William Perez	Nike
Stanley O'Neal	Merrill Lynch		

Entrepreneurs

Girl Names

Entrepreneur	Company/ Industry	Entrepreneur	Company/ Industry
Anita Roddick	The Body Shop	Lillian Vernon	Lillian Vernon
Betsey Johnson	Betsey Johnson	Liz Lange	Liz Lange Maternity
Coco Chanel	Chanel	Martha Stewart	Martha Stewart Living Omnimedia
Donna Karan	Donna Karan Corp.		
Jenny Craig	Jenny Craig International	Mary Kay Ash	Mary Kay Cosmetics
		Oprah Winfrey	Harpo, Inc.
Josie Natori	Natori Lingerie	Vera Wang	Vera Wang
Kimora Lee Simmons	Baby Phat		

Boy Names

Entrepreneur	Company/ Industry	Entrepreneur	Company/ Industry
Andrew Carnegie	Steel industry	Paul Allen	Microsoft
Donald Burr	People Express	Pierre Omidyar	eBay
George Lucas	Lucasfilm Ltd.	Ray Kroc	McDonald's
Howard Schultz	Starbucks	Sam Walton	Wal-Mart
Jeff Bezos	Amazon.com	Sean "P. Diddy" Combs	Sean Jean
Jerry Yang	Yahoo!	Steve Jobs	Apple Computer
Leon Leonwood "L.L." Bean	L.L. Bean	Sumner Redstone	Viacom
		Ted Turner	Turner Broadcasting
Michael Dell	Dell Computer	Walt Disney	The Walt Disney Co.

Brands

Girl Names

Name	Product	Name	Product
Alize	Fruity wine	Evian	Water
Armani	Fashion designer	Fanta	Soft drink
Breck	Shampoo	Halston	Fashion designer
Cambria	Car	Infiniti	Car
Camry	Car	L'Oréal	Cosmetics
Catera	Car	Lexus	Luxury car
Celica	Car	Melitta	Coffee filter
Chanel	Fashion designer	Mercedes	Luxury car
Chloe	Perfume	Meridian	Phone products
Clinique	Cosmetics	Nautica	Clothing
Cristal	Champagne	Nivea	Skin cream
Dakota	Dodge truck	Porsche	Sports car
Dannon	Yogurt	Shasta	Soda
Delta	Airline	Skyy	Vodka
Dior	Fashion designer	Tiffany	Jeweler
Eternity	Perfume		

Boy Names

Name	Product	Name	Product
Acura	Car	Guinness	Beer
Armani	Fashion designer	Harley	Motorcycle
Avis	Car rental	Hennessy	Liqueur
Baxter	Health care	Hyatt	Hotel
Canon	Camera	Ikea	Furniture
Cartier	Jeweler	Jaguar	Luxury car
Corvette	Car	Jameson	Whiskey
Courvoisier	Liqueur	Killian	Beer
Delmonte	Fruits and vegetables	Ronrico	Rum
Denim	Cologne	Skyy	Vodka
Disney	Corporation	Stetson	Cologne
Elgin	Watch	Timberland	Shoes
Ford	Car		

Political Names

You might relate to a famous leader from the past, be it a president, world leader, or an activist. If you're thinking of honoring someone political by naming your child after him or her, this is the chapter to check out.

The lists in this chapter open up a world of possibilities for baby names, from president and first lady names to the names of their children. Names of peacemakers and patriots are also featured in this historical, politically active chapter.

World Leaders, Past and Present

Girl Names

Leader	Title	Country
Adrienne Clarkson	Governor-General	Canada
Benzir Bhutto	Prime Minister	Pakistan
Gloria Macapagal-Arroyo	President	Philippines
Golda Meir	Prime Minister	Israel
Gro Harlem Brundtland	Prime Minister	Norway
Helen Clark	Prime Minister	New Zealand
Indira Gandhi	Prime Minister	India
Ivy Dumont	Governor-General	The Bahamas
Margaret Thatcher	Prime Minister	United Kingdom
Mary Eugenia Charles	Prime Minister	Dominica
Mary McAleese	President	Ireland
Mary Robinson	President	Ireland
Pearlette Louisy	Governor General	Saint Lucia
Tarja Halonen	President	Finland
Vigdis Finnbogadottir	President	Iceland
Violeta Barrios de Chamorro	President	Nicaragua

Boy Names

Leader	Title	Country
Abel Pacheco	President	Costa Rica
Adolf Hitler	Chancellor	Germany
Alfredo Palacio	President	Ecuador
Ariel Sharon	Prime Minister	Israel
Charlemagne (no last name)	Emperor	Europe
Colville Young	Governor-General	Belize
Festus Mogae	President	Botswana
Hamid Karzai	President	Afghanistan
Heinz Fischer	President	Austria
Horst Koehler	President	Germany
Hugo Chavez	President	Venezuela

Leader	Title	Country
Jacques Chirac	President	France
Jintao Hu	President	China
Junichiro Koizumi	Prime Minister	Japan
Karolos Papoulias	President	Greece
Leonel Fernandez	President	Dominican Republic
Macky Sall	Prime Minister	Senegal
Manmohan Singh	Prime Minister	India
Martin Torrijos	President	Panama
Michael Jeffery	Governor-General	Australia
Nestor Kirchner	President	Argentina
Omar Karami	Prime Minister	Lebanon
Patrick Manning	Prime Minister	Trinidad and Tobago
Paul Biya	President	Cameroon
Ricardo Lagos	President	Chile
Samuel Schmid	President	Switzerland
Silvio Berlusconi	Prime Minister	Italy
Soe Win	Prime Minister	Burma
Thabo Mbeki	President	South Africa
Tony Blair	Prime Minister	United Kingdom
Vaclav Klaus	President	Czech Republic
Vicente Fox	President	Mexico
Viktor Yushchenko	President	Ukraine
Vladimir Putin	President	Russia
Winston Churchill	Prime Minister	United Kingdom

Royalty

Girl Names

Royalty	Title	Country
Alexandra	Princess	England
Alexandra Feodorovna	Empress	Russia
Anastasia Romanov	Grand Duchess	Russia
Anne	Queen	England
Beatrice Elizabeth Mary	Princess of York	England
Beatrix (no last name)	Queen	The Netherlands
Birgitte Eva van Deurs	Duchess of Gloucester	England
Anne Elizabeth Alice Louise	The Princess Royal of England	England
Camilla Rosemary Shand	Duchess of Cornwall	England
Catherine of Aragon	Queen	England
Diana Frances Spencer	Princess of Wales	England
Elizabeth I	Queen	England
Eugenie Victoria Helena	Princess of York	England
Henrietta Maria	Queen	England
Jane Grey	Queen	England
Margaret of Anjou	Queen	England
Margrethe II (no last name)	Queen	Denmark
Maria-Feodorovna	Empress	Russia
Marie-Christine von Reibnitz	Princess	England
Mary	Queen	England
Matilda	Queen	England
Olga Nicholaevna Romanova	Grand Duchess	Russia
Sarah Ferguson	Duchess of York	England
Sophia August Frederika	Empress Catherine II ("Catherine the Great")	Russia
Sophie Rhys-Jones	Countess of Wessex	England
Tatiana Romanov	Grand Duchess	Russia

Boy Names

Royalty	Title	Country
Aleksey Romanov	Tsar	Russia
Alexander	Emperor	Russia
Alfred the Great	King	England
Angus Ogilvy	Earl of Airlie	England
Athelstan	King	England
Augustus Henry Fitzroy	Duke of Grafton	England
Canute the Dane	King	England
Charles Philip Arthur George	Prince of Wales	England
Edred	King	England
Edward Anthony Richard Lewis	Earl of Wessex	England
Ethelbert	King of Kent	England
Ethelwolf	King	England
Edwin	King of Northumbria	England
Frederick "Lord North"	Earl of Guildford	England
George Augustus	King	England
Godwin	Earl of Kent	England
Hardicanute	King	England and Denmark
Henry Charles Albert Davis	Prince of Wales	England
Ina	King of the West Saxons	England
Malcolm III	King	Scotland
Offa	King of Mercia	England
Oswald	King of Northumbria	England
Penda	King of Mercia	England
Piers Gaveston	Earl of Cornwall	England
Richard Alexander Walter George	Duke of Gloucester	England
Simon de Montfort	4th Count Earl of Liecester	England
William Arthur Philip Louis	Prince	England

U.S. Presidents

Girl Names

Not applicable.

Boy Names

Abraham Lincoln

Andrew Jackson

Andrew Johnson

Benjamin Harrison

Calvin Coolidge

Chester Arthur

Dwight Eisenhower

Franklin Pierce

Franklin Roosevelt

George Herbert Walker Bush

George Walker Bush

George Washington

Gerald Ford

Grover Cleveland

Harry S. Truman

Herbert Hoover

Hiram Ulysses S. Grant

James Buchanan

James Garfield

James Madison

James Monroe

James Polk

Jimmy Carter

John Adams

John Fitzgerald Kennedy

John Quincy Adams

John Tyler

Lyndon Baines Johnson

Martin van Buren

Millard Fillmore

Richard Nixon

Ronald Reagan

Rutherford Birchard Hayes

Theodore Roosevelt

Thomas Jefferson

Warren Harding

William Jefferson Clinton

William Henry Harrison

William Howard Taft

William McKinley

Woodrow Wilson

Zachary Taylor

First Ladies

Girl Names

Abigail Powers Fillmore

Abigail Smith Adams

Anna Eleanor Roosevelt

Anna Tuthill Symmes Harrison

Barbara Pierce Bush

Caroline Lavinia Scott Harrison

Claudia "Lady Bird" Taylor Johnson

Dolley Payne Todd Madison

Edith Bolling Galt Wilson

Edith Kermit Carow Roosevelt

Eleanor Rosalynn Smith Carter

Eliza McCardle Johnson

Elizabeth "Bess" Virginia Wallace Truman

Elizabeth "Betty" Bloomer Warren Ford

Elizabeth "Eliza" Kortright Monroe

Ellen Lewis Herndon Arthur

Florence Kling DeWolf Harding

Frances Folsom Cleveland

Grace Anna Goodhew Coolidge

Hannah Hoes Van Buren

Helen Herron Taft

Hillary Rodham Clinton

Ida Saxton McKinley

Jane Means Appleton Pierce

Jacqueline Lee Bouvier Kennedy

Julia Dent Grant

Julia Gardiner Tyler

Laura Welch Bush

Lou Henry Hoover

Louisa Catherine Johnson Adams

Lucretia Rudolph Garfield

Lucy Ware Webb Hayes

Margaret Mackall Smith Taylor

Martha Dandridge Custis Washington

Martha Wayles Skelton Jefferson

Mary "Mamie" Geneva Doud Eisenhower

Mary Todd Lincoln

Nancy Davis Reagan

Rachel Donelson Robards Jackson

Sarah Childress Polk

Thelma Patricia "Pat" Catherine Ryan Nixon

Boy Names
Not applicable.

Presidents' Kids

Girl Names

First Kid	Father
Abigail "Nabby" Adams Smith	John Adams
Alice Lee Roosevelt Longworth	Theodore Roosevelt
Amy Carter Wentzel	James Carter Jr.
Anna Tuthill Harrison Taylor	William Henry Harrison
Anne Margaret Mackall Taylor Wood	Zachary Taylor
Barbara Pierce Bush	George W. Bush
Caroline Kennedy Schlossberg	John F. Kennedy
Chelsea Victoria Clinton	William Clinton
Dorothy "Doro" Bush Koch	George Herbert Walker Bush
Eleanor "Nellie" Randolph Wilson McAdoo	Woodrow Wilson
Eliza Arabella "Trot" Garfield	James A. Garfield
Elizabeth "Lizzie" Tyler Waller	John Tyler
Ellen Wrenshall "Nellie" Grant Sartoris Jones	Ulysses S. Grant
Esther Cleveland Bosanquet	Grover Cleveland
Ethel Carow Roosevelt Derby	Theodore Roosevelt
Fanny Hayes Smith	Rutherford B. Hayes

Presidents' Kids, continued

First Kid	Father
Helen Herron Taft Manning	William Howard Taft
Ida McKinley	William McKinley
Jane Randolph Jefferson	Thomas Jefferson
Jenna Welch Bush	George W. Bush
Jessie Woodrow Wilson Sayre	Woodrow Wilson
Julia Tyler Spencer	John Tyler
Julie Nixon Eisenhower	Richard M. Nixon
Katherine "Katie" McKinley	William McKinley
Letitia (Letty) Tyler Semple	John Tyler
Louisa Catherine Adams	John Quincy Adams
Luci Baines Johnson Turpin	Lyndon Baines Johnson
Lucy Elizabeth I	Thomas Jefferson
Lynda Bird Johnson Robb	Lyndon Baines Johnson
Maria Hester Monroe Gouverneur	James Monroe
Margaret Woodrow Wilson	Woodrow Wilson
Martha "Patsy" Parke Custis	George Washington
Maureen Reagan Revell	Ronald Reagan
Mary Abigail "Abby" Fillmore	Millard Fillmore
Octavia Pannel Taylor	Zachary Taylor
Patricia "Patti Davis" Ann Reagan	Ronald Reagan
Pauline Robinson "Robin" Bush	George Herbert Walker Bush
Pearl Tyler Ellis	John Tyler
Ruth Cleveland	Grover Cleveland
Sarah Knox Taylor Davis	Zachary Taylor
Susan Ford Vance Bales	Gerald Ford
Susanna Adams	John Adams
Tricia Nixon Cox	Richard M. Nixon

Boy Names

First Kid	Father
Abraham van Buren	Martin van Buren
Abram Garfield	James A. Garfield
Allan Henry Hoover	Herbert Clark Hoover

First Kid	Father
Andrew Jackson Jr.	Andrew Jackson
Archibald "Archie" Bulloch Roosevelt	Theodore Roosevelt
Benjamin Pierce	Franklin Pierce
Birchard Austin Hayes	Rutherford B. Hayes
Calvin Coolidge Jr.	Calvin Coolidge
Carter Bassett Harrison	William Henry Harrison
Charles Adams	John Adams
David Gardiner "Gardie" Tyler	John Tyler
Donnell Jeffrey "Jeff" Carter	James Carter Jr.
Doud Dwight "Ikky" Eisenhower	Dwight D. Eisenhower
Edward Baker "Eddie" Lincoln	Abraham Lincoln
Elliott Roosevelt	Franklin Delano Roosevelt
Eugene Marshall "Pete" DeWolfe	Warren G. Harding
Francis Grover Cleveland	Grover Cleveland
Frank Robert Pierce	Franklin Pierce
Franklin Roosevelt	Franklin Delano Roosevelt
Fredrick Dent Grant	Ulysses S. Grant
George Washington Adams	John Quincy Adams
Harry Augustus "Hal" Garfield	James A. Garfield
Herbert Hoover Jr.	Herbert Clark Hoover
Irvin McDowell Garfield	James A. Garfield
James Earl "Chip" Carter III	James Carter Jr.
James Rudolf Garfield	James A. Garfield
Jesse Root Grant	Ulysses S. Grant
John Alexander "Alex" Tyler	John Tyler
Kermit Roosevelt	Theodore Roosevelt
Lachlan Tyler	John Tyler
Lyon Gardiner Tyler	John Tyler
Manning Force Hayes	Rutherford B. Hayes
Marion Cleveland Dell Amen	Grover Cleveland
Marshall Polk	James K. Polk
Martin Van Buren Jr.	Martin Van Buren
Marvin Pierce Bush	George H. W. Bush
Michael Gerald Ford	Gerald Ford
Millard Powers Fillmore	Millard Fillmore

Presidents' Kids, continued

Neil Mallon Bush	George H. W. Bush
Oscar Folsom Cleveland	Grover Cleveland
Patrick Bouvier Kennedy	John F. Kennedy
Quentin Roosevelt	Theodore Roosevelt
Richard Folsom "Dick" Cleveland	Grover Cleveland
Robert Alphonso Taft	William Howard Taft
Ronald Prescott Reagan	Ronald Reagan
Russell Benjamin Harrison	Benjamin Harrison
Rutherford Platt Hayes	Rutherford B. Hayes
Smith Thompson van Buren	Martin van Buren
Steven Meigs Ford	Gerald Ford
Tazewell Tyler	John Tyler
Theodore "Ted" Roosevelt Jr.	Theodore Roosevelt
Thomas Boylston Adams	John Adams
Ulysses Simpson "Buck" Grant Jr.	Ulysses S. Grant
William Henry Harrison Jr.	William Henry Harrison
William Lewis Arthur Chester	Alan Arthur

Patriots/Military Leaders

Girl Names

Abigail Adams
Anna Comnena
Betsy Ross
Deborah Sampson
Martha Washington
Mercy Otis-Warren
Phillis Wheatley

Boy Names

Ben Franklin
Colin Powell
George Washington
H. Norman Schwarzkopf
John Adams
Nelson Mandela
Patrick Henry
Stonewall Jackson
Thomas Jefferson

Warriors

Girl Names

Eleanor of Castile

Emma, Countess of Norfolk

Hippolyte

Marguerite de Provence

Thyra, Queen of Denmark

Xianthippe

Boy Names

Atilla the Hun

Vernon Baker

William Carney

Peacemakers

Girl Names

Peacemaker	Area/Country of Work	Peacemaker	Area/Country of Work
Alva Myrdal	Sweden	Jody Williams	Int'l Campaign to Ban Landmines
Aung San Suu Kyi	Burma		
Bertha von Suttner	Austria	Kathy Kelly	United States
Betty Williams	United Kingdom	Mairead Corrigan	Northern Ireland
Emily Balch	United States	Mother Teresa	India
Helen Caldicott	Australia	Rigoberta Menchu Tum	Guatemala
Jane Addams	United States	Shirin Ebadi	Iran
Jane Hamilton-Merritt (Dr.)	United States	Wangari Maathai	Kenya

Boy Names

Peacemaker	Area/Country of Work	Peacemaker	Area/Country of Work
Abuna Elias Chacour	Israel	Craig Kielburger	United States
Adolfo Perez Esquivel	Argentina	Dag Hammarskjold	Sweden
Albert Lutuli	South Africa	David Trimble	Northern Ireland
Alfonso Garcia Robles	Mexico	Desmond Tutu	South Africa
Andrei Sakharov	USSR	Elie Wiesel	United States
Aristide Briand	France	Elihu Root	United States
Carlos Filipe Belo (Archbishop)	East Timor	Elisaku Sato	Japan
		Gerson Perez	Colombia
Cordell Hull	United States	Henry Kissinger	United States

Peacemakers, continued

Peacemaker	Area/Country of Work	Peacemaker	Area/Country of Work
Jimmy Carter	United States	Mohamed Anwar al-Sadat	Egypt
Jose Ramos Horta	East Timor	Nelson Mandela	South Africa
Joseph Rotblat	Canada	Norman Borlaug	United States
Kim Dae-jung	South Korea	Oscar Arias Sanchez	Costa Rica
Kofi Annan	United Nations	Ralph Bunche	United States
Lars Olaf Soderblom	Sweden	Rene Cassin	France
Lech Walesa	Poland	Sean MacBride	Ireland
Leon Jouhaux	France	Shimon Peres	Israel
Linus Pauling	United States	Tenzin Gyatso (Dalai Lama)	Tibet
Mahatma Ghandi	India		
Martin Luther King	United States	Tobias Asser	The Netherlands
Menachem Begin	Israel	Willy Brandt	Germany
Michael Scharf	United States	Yasser Arafat	Palestine
Mikhail Gorbachev	Russia	Yitzhak Rabin	Israel

Black History/Civil Rights Leaders

Girl Names

Bessie Coleman	Eliza Bryant	Mary McLeod Bethune
Biddy Mason	Ella Fitzgerald	Maya Angelou
Billie Holiday	Fannie Lou Hamer	Rita Dove
Cathay Williams	Harriet Tubman	Rosa Parks
Charlotte Forten Grimke	Ida Wells Barnett	Sally Hemings
Diana Fletcher	Josephine Baker	Sojourner Truth
Dorothy Dandridge	Mahalia Jackson	Susan McKinney
Edmonia Lewis	Marian Anderson	Zelma Watson George

Boy Names

Asa Philip Randolph	George Washington Carver	Matthew Henson
Benjamin Banneker	Jesse Owens	Nat King Cole
Carter Woodson	Jim Beckwourth	Paul Laurence Dunbar
Charles Drew	Jim Crow	Percy Lavon Julian
Duke Ellington	Langston Hughes	Ralph Bunche
Eldridge Cleaver	Louis Armstrong	Salem Poor
Ernest Just	Louis Farrakhan	Scott Joplin
Erroll Garner	Malcolm X	Thelonious Monk
Eubie Blake	Marcus Garvey	Whitney Moore Young
Frederick Douglass	Martin Luther King Jr.	William Edward Burghardt (W.E.B.) DuBois

Activists

Girl Names

Name	Cause
Heather Mills	Anti-Land mines
Jane Akre	Milk safety
Julia Bonds	Anti-Mountaintop removal mining
Kaisha Atakhanova	Nuclear waste reform
Melissa Poe	Clean environment
Stephanie Roth	Anti-gold mining in Romania

Boy Names

Name	Cause
Adam Werbach	Conservationist
Corneiele Ewango	Environmental protection
Dailan Pugh	Environmental
Isidro Baldenegro Lopez	Forestry reform activist
John Corkill	Environmental
Jose Andres Cortez (Father)	Environmental
Peter Rawlinson	Forests
Robert Hunter	Eco-crusader
Steve Wilson	Milk safety

Scientific Suggestions

If science is your thing, or you'd like your little one to be inspired by the subject, we've compiled several lists to generate some ideas. We've got Nobel Prize winners as well as world-renowned scientists, celebrated inventors, and scientists who shoot for the stars—astronauts and pilots, that is.

Whether you hope your baby will make a mark on history or you'd like to honor someone in the scientific community who already has, the lists in this chapter are sure to provide some suggestions.

Scientists

Girl Names

Name	Science	Time Period
Anna Atkins	Botany	1799–1871
Augusta Lovelace	Inventor of early computer	1815–1852
Caroline Herschel	Discovered comet	1750–1848
Celia Borromeo	Natural philosopher	Middle Ages
Clemence Royer	Encyclopedist	1830–?
Cornelia Clapp	Zoology	1849–1934
Dorotea Bucca	Physician	Middle Ages
Eliza Pinckney	Agriculture	1723–1766
Emilie de Breteuil	Physicist	1706–1749
Florence Nightingale	Nurse statistician	1820–1910
Georgia Rooks	Physician	20th century
Grace Hopper	Mathematician	1906–1992
Henrietta Leavitt	Astronomer	1868–1921
Hertha Ayrton	Physicist	1854–1923
Ida Tacke	Physicist	20th century
Josephine Kablick	Botanist	18th century
Kate Gleason	Engineer	1865–1933
Laura Bassi	Physicist	1711–1778
Lise Meitner	Physicist	1878–1968
Lucy Hobbs Taylor	Dentist	1833–1910
Martha Logan	Horticulturist	1702–1779
Maud Menten	Biologist	20th century
Nettie Stevens	Biologist	1861–1912
Nor Mahal	Inventor	17th century
Olive Beech	Aviation	1920–1986
Patsy Sherman	Inventor	20th century
Rosalind Franklin	Chemist	1920–1957
Sadie Delany	Home economics	1891–1999
Sethanne Howard	Astronomer	1944–
Sophia Brahe	Astronomer	1556–1643
Themista	Natural philosopher	Ancient Greece
Williamina Fleming	Astronomer	1857–1911

Boy Names

Name	Science	Time Period
Albert Einstein	Father of Modern Science	1879–1955
Alessandro Volta	Battery inventor	1745–1827
Amedeo Avogadro	Chemist	1776–1856
Blaise Pascal	Mathematician	1623–1662
Carl Sagan	Astronomer	1934–1996
Christiaan Huygens	Mathematician	1629–1695
Daniel Bernoulli	Mathematician	1700–1782
Edme Mariotte	Physicist	1620–1684
Ernest Haeckel	Biologist	1843–1919
Evangelista Torricelli	Physicist	1608–1647
Francis Crick	Molecular biologist	1916–2004
Friedrich Wohler	Chemist	1800–1882
Galileo Galilei	Astronomer	1564–1642
Giovanni Venturi	Physicist	1745–1822
Gregor Mendel	Anthropologist	1822–1884
Gustav Hertz	Physicist	1887–1975
Hannes Olof Alfven	Physicist	1908–1995
Humphry Davy	Chemist	1778–1829
Isaac Newton	Mathematician and physicist	1642–1727
Jacques Charles	Aeronaut	1746–1823
Johann Kepler	Astronomer	1571–1630
Konrad Lorenz	Ethologist	1903–1989
Leonardo da Vinci	Artist and engineer	1452–1519
Max Planck	Physicist	1858–1947
Nicolas Copernicus	Astronomer	1473–1543
Nikola Tesla	Inventor	1856–1943
Niels Bohr	Physicist	1885–1962
Pierre Curie	Radiologist	1859–1906
René Descartes	Mathematician	1596–1650
Stephen Hawking	Physicist	1942–
Thomas Edison	Inventor	1847–1931
Tycho Brahe	Astronomer	1546–1601
Wilhelm Rontgen	Physicist	1845–1923

Inventors and Discoverers

Girl Names

Inventor	Invention/Discovery
Alice Parker	Gas furnace
Ann Moore	Snugli baby carrier
Anna Keichline	Combined sink and washtub; first female architect
Barbara Askins	Film processing system
Bette Graham	Liquid Paper
Beulah Henry	Bobbinless sewing machine
Carol Wior	Slimming swimsuit
Frances Gabe	Self-cleaning house
Gertrude Elion	Leukemia-fighting drug
Grace Hopper	Computing improvements
Harriet Tracy	Safety elevator
Josephine Cochran	Dishwasher
Julie Newmar	Ultra-sheer pantyhose
Lillian Russell	Dresser trunk
Margaret Knight	Flat-bottom bags
Marion Donovan	Disposable diapers
Marjorie Joyner	Permanent hairstyling system
Martha Coston	Signal flares
Mary Dixon Kies	Weaving process
Mary Phelps Jacob	Bra
Patricia Bath	Medical improvement
Patsy Sherman	Scotchgard
Ruth Handler	Barbie doll
Sarah Boone	Ironing board improvement
Stephanie Kwolek	Kevlar
Sybilla Masters	Corn mill
Virginia Apgar	Newborn screening system

Boy Names

Inventor	Invention/Discovery
Albert Einstein	Theory of relativity
Alexander Graham Bell	Telephone
Art Fry	Post-it Notes
Benjamin Rubin	Vaccination needle
Carl Sontheimer	Cuisinart
Chester Carlson	Photocopying
Clarence Birdseye	Commercial frozen food
Earle Dickson	Band-Aids
Edwin Land	Polaroid photography
Elias Howe	Sewing machine
Galileo Galilei	Planets revolve around sun
George Washington Carver	Peanut butter; agriculture improvements
Henry Ford	Assembly line auto production
Sir Isaac Newton	Telescope; the three laws of physics
Jerome Lemelson	Bar code readers; cassette players
Johannes Gutenberg	Moveable type
Jonas Salk	Polio vaccine
Levi Strauss	Blue jeans
Louis Pasteur	Discovered germs; pasteurization process
Martin Cooper	Modern cell phone
Ole Evinrude	Outboard motor
Percy Spencer	Microwave oven
Pierre Lorillard	Tuxedo
Ralph Samuelson	Waterskiing
Samuel Morse	Telegraph
Schulyer Wheeler	Electric fan
Thomas Edison	Phonograph
Tim Berners-Lee	World Wide Web
Walt Disney	Feature-length animated films
Whitcomb Judson	Early zipper
Willis Carrier	Air conditioning

Sky-High Names—Astronauts and Aviators

Girl Names

Agnes Firth
Amelia Earhart
Amelie Beese
Anna Fisher
Bessie Coleman
Bonnie Dunbar
Catherine Coleman
Cheridah de Beauvoir Stocks
Christa McAuliffe
Claudie Haignere
E. Lilian Todd
Eileen Collins

Ellen Baker
Ellen Ochoa
Enid Hibbard
Ester Vietta
Eugenia Shakhovskaya
Florence Seidel
Helen Sharman
Helene Dutrieu
Hilda Beatrice Hewlitt
Jeanne Herveux
Julia Clark
Kalpana Chawla
Kathryn Sullivan

Laurel Clark
Leda Richberg Hornsby
Lydia V. Zvereva
Mae Jemison
Margaret Rhea Seddon
Marie Marvingt
Marie-Louise Driancourt
Marsha Ivins
Mary Cleave
Nancy Currie
Pamela Melroy

Peggy Whitson
Roberta Bondar
Rosina Ferrario
Sally Ride
Sandra Magnus
Shannon Lucid
Susan Kilrain
Suzanne Bernard
Tamara Jernigan
Valentina Tereshkova
Willa Beatrice Brown

Boy Names

Alan Shepard
Arch Hoxsey
Armstrong Drexel
Bentfield Hucks
Bernard Harris Jr.
Beryl Williams
Bill Anders
Bruce McCandless
Buzz Aldrin
Calbraith Rodgers
Chauncy Vought
Curtis Brown
Dale Gardner
David Scott
Dirk Frimont

Donn Eisele
Duane Carey
Emile Dubonnet
Frank Borman
Franklin Chang-Diaz
Fred Haise
Guion Bluford
Gus Grissom
Hans Grade
Hubert Latham
James Irwin
Jerome Apt
Jerry Ross
Jim Lovell
Joe Walker

John Glenn
John Swigert
Jules Vedrines
Ladis Lewkowicz
Leroy Gordon Cooper
Loren Acton
Max Lillie
Michael Anderson
Neil Armstrong
Norman Thagard
Orville Wright
Osbert Edwin Williams
Otto Brodie
Owen Garriott

Patrick Baudry
Pete Conrad
Raymond Saulnier
Rene Barrier
Rexford Smith
Rick Husband
Ronald McNair
Silas Christofferson
St. Croix Johnstone
Story Musgrave
Taylor Wang
Wally Schirra
Weldon Cooke
Wilbur Wright

Pure and Natural Possibilities

For parents who want their child to be in touch with the earth, the planet, and its ultimate possibility, the lists in this chapter offer name choices from the world in which we live—from the stars and planets that hover above us to the mountains, valleys, rivers, and lakes that make up the world's geography.

If you want your child's name to embrace the minerals, jewels, and gems mined from the earth's surface, you'll find lists of those names here as well. Names for flowers, fruits, animals, and colors also abound. If you're looking for a name that speaks to your connection to the earth, you're sure to find something here.

Stars and Planets

Girl Names

Adhara	Cassiopeia	Jana	Rishima
Amaris	Celine	Luna	Shaula
Andromeda	Chandrama	Moon	Soleil
Antlia	Columba	Nokomis	Tainn
Apus	Dyan	Norma	Vega
Ara	Hina	Polaris	Venus
Badriya	Hydra	Rigel	Virgo
Bellatrix	Indu		

Boy Names

Altair	Centaurus	Leo	Procyon
Antares	Cepheus	Lupus	Regulus
Aquarius	Cetus	Mars	Sagittarius
Aquila	Charon	Mercury	Saturn
Arcturus	Circinus	Orion	Shivendu
Aries	Corvus	Pavo	Sirius
Auriga	Cygnus	Pegasus	Som
Bootes	Draco	Perseus	Sun
Caelum	Eridanus	Phoenix	Taurus
Cancer	Hadar	Pluto	Uranus
Capricornus	Hydrus	Pollux	Vikesh
Castor			

Mountains and Valleys

Girl Names

Aase	Denver	Kendall	Olympia
Alba	Elam	Kia	Orea
Ashland	Gayora	Kiona	Peri
Aspen	Gelilah	Kiri	Sierra
Cyd	Glenna	Kirima	Tarin
Dale	Glyn	Madison	Vail
Dallon	Hallam	Marcy	Whitney
Deanna	Hollace	Montana	Yama
Deena	Kalinda	Odina	Zaltana
Deiondre			

Boy Names

Aaron	Clifford	Everest	Mitchell
Adams	Crawford	Geordi	Montana
Alban	Craig	Gibbes	Montego
Arlo	Cyd	Glen	Montenegro
Banagher	Dale	Hallam	Montgomery
Bartholomew	Dallon	Hamilton	Ogden
Belden	Dalton	Heaton	Orestes
Berg	Deiondre	Holden	Percival
Blackburn	Denver	Kendall	Rainier
Braden	Dix	Knox	Roden
Brent	Doane	Lamont	Sheldon
Buckley	Elam	Lincoln	Tarin
Camden	Elbert	McKinley	Vail

Lakes and Rivers

Girl Names

Afton	Hachi	Narmada	Shannon
Arnon	Ivria	Naiyah	Tamesis
Avon	Jamuna	Nile	Tanginika
Avonmora	Jordan	Nimiani	Tapati
Belisma	Kaveri	Ohio	Tarangini
Blaine	Lake	Rhea	Teleri
Carey	Laken	Riva	Triveni
Clodagh	Lindsay	Ryo	Tyne
Darya	Mallow	Sarita	Varana
Delta	Manda	Saryu	Yamuna
Guadalupe			

Boy Names

Afram	Chilton	Kelby	Ohio
Afton	Clifford	Kelvin	Orrin
Annan	Clyde	Lachlan	Redford
Arnon	Deverell	Laken	Rio
Avon	Douglas	Mallow	River
Avonmore	Ford	Mansfield	Romney
Ballinamore	George	Marland	Ryo
Blaine	Guadalupe	Max	Severin
Caldwell	Inis	Melborn	Tarik
Cameron	Jafar	Merton	Tiberius
Carlow	Jiang	Monroe	Tyne
Cary	Johnavon	Moses	Vytharana
Chad	Jordan	Niger	Wade

Jewels, Gems, and Minerals

Girl Names

Agate	Carnelian	Hazel	Pearl
Alexandrite	Chalcedony	Heliotrope	Peridot
Allirea	Cinnabar	Iolite	Prunella
Amethyst	Citrine	Ivory	Quartz
Aquamarine	Coral	Jacinth	Rose Quartz
Auburn	Crisiant	Jade	Sapphire
Azure	Crystal	Jewel	Sienna
Basalt	Cyanite	Lilac	Spodumene
Beryl	Diamond	Madge	Tangerine
Biana	Ebony	Malachite	Tawny
Blanca	Emerald/Emeraude	Mauve	Teal
Blanche	Fawn	Moonstone Adularia	Topaz
Bloodstone	Garnet	Moss Agate	Tourmaline
Beryl	Gemma	Noire	Turquoise
Calcite	Ghita	Olivine	Violet
Cameo	Goldie	Onyx	Zoisite
Cara	Greta	Opal	

Boy Names

Almas	Flint	Jet	Sterling
Bernstein	Geode	Mica	Stone
Bruno	Gold	Obsidian	Ulexite
Bronze	Indigo	Platinum	Yahto
Copper	Jasper	Slate	Zircon
Carnelian			

Animals

Girl Names

Name	Derivation/Meaning	Name	Derivation/Meaning
Aqualina	Like an eagle	Loni	Lion
Ariella	God's lioness	Melissa	Honeybee
Arva	Eagle	Merle	Blackbird
Ava	Little bird	Merlyn	Falcon
Ayala	Deer	Mink	Weasel
Brena	Raven	Orpah	Fawn
Brenda	Small raven	Orsa	Female bear
Bunny	Rabbit	Paloma	Dove
Calandra	Lark	Penelope	Duck
Chenoa	White dove	Rachel	Ewe
Columbine	Dove	Raven	Blackbird
Danuta	Little deer	Robin	Bird
Deborah	Bee	Rosalind	From word for horse
Delphine	Dolphin	Rosamond	From word for horse
Dorcas	Gazelle	Tabitha	Doe
Fawn	Young deer	Teal	Water bird
Hinda	Female deer	Una	Lamb
Jemima	Dove	Ursula	Female bear
Jena	Little bird	Ushi	Ox
Lark	Skylark	Yona	Dove
Leandra	Lion woman	Zera	Wolf
Leona	Lioness	Zippora	Bird

Boy Names

Name	Derivation/Meaning	Name	Derivation/Meaning
Adelard	Old eagles	Hart	Red deer
Adler	Eagle	Hawk	Bird
Adolphus	Noble wolf	Hawkins	Little hawk
Andor	Thundering eagle	Herring	Small fish
Ari	Lion	Hershel	Deer
Aries	Ram	Jackal	Wild dog
Arno	Eagle-wolf	Jay	Jaybird
Barend	Firm bear	Jonah	Dove
Barrett	Bear strength	Kaleb	Dog
Berend	Bearlike	Leo	Lion
Bertram	Bright raven	Lionel	Young lion
Bram	Raven	Lowell	Young wolf
Brock	Badger	Merle	Blackbird
Bronco	Wild horse	Newt	Small salamander
Buck	Male deer	Oisin	Little deer
Castor	Beaver	Orsen	Little bear
Colin	Young animal	Osborn	Divine bear
Colt	Young horse	Raynard	Fox
Conall	Strong wolf	Reno	Reindeer
Corbett	Raven	Rodolf	Famous wolf
Dolf	Noble wolf	Roe	Small deer
Dov	Bear	Roebuck	Male deer
Drake	Dragon	Roswald	Mighty horse
Dyani	Deer	Rudi	Famous wolf
Eachan	Brown horse	Tahatan	Hawk
Eden	Bear cub	Tiger	Tiger
Falk	Falcon	Tod	Fox
Finch	Songbird	Ursel	Bear
Fox	Fox	Wolfe	Wolf
Gawain	Battle hawk	Yonas	Dove
Giles	Young goat	Zvi	Deer
Harshul	Deer		

Flowers and Trees

Girl Names

Alona	Cocoa	Ivy	Petunia
Ashley	Daisy	Jasmine	Phyllis
Ayana	Daphne	Juniper	Poppy
Azalea	Fauna	Laura	Raisa
Azhaar	Fern	Laurel	Rhoda
Blossom	Flora	Lian	Rose
Bryony	Florence	Lily	Sage
Burnet	Gardenia	Linnea	Sugar
Calendula	Ginger	Magnolia	Susan
Calla	Hana	Marigold	Varda
Camillia	Hazel	Myrtle	Viola
Carmel	Heather	Narcissus	Violet
Cerise	Holly	Nawar	Willow
Cherise	Hyacinth	Olive	Yasmeen
Cherry	Ione	Olivia	Yolanda
Cheryl	Iris	Pansy	Zinnia

Boy Names

Aiken	Elder	Hickory	Lennox
Alder	Ellery	Hollis	Lyndon
Aster	Elmore	Ivo	Oakes
Basil	Forrest	Jacek	Oliver
Berry	Garth	Kai	Oren
Birch	Glanville	Keith	Perry
Boyce	Grover	Landon	Shelly
Cedar	Hawthorne	Lee	Vernon
Cochise	Heath		

Fruits
Girl Names

Alani	Cherise	Evelina	Sabra
Anzu	Cherry	Jana	Tao
Apple	Clementine	Minaku	Xiu Mei
Cam	Elma	Mora	Zabrina
Carmen	Eustacia	Prunella	Zerdali

Boy Names

Berry	Perry
Ephraim	Ringo
Frasier	

Colors
Girl Names

Affera	Flavia	Kala	Scarlet
Afra	Garnet	Lilia	Silver
Amber	Ginger	Midori	Talutah
Azure	Hong	Nelia	Violet
Debbani	Hyacinth	Ornat	Xantha
Devaki	Jacinta	Ruby	Zukra
Ebony	Jette		

Boy Names

Adham	Donovan	Hinto	Odhran
Al-Ashab	Dwyer	Kadir	Porfio
Blake	Earc	Kieran	Rad
Bruno	Flavian	Lloyd	Roy
Cerny	Floyd	Matlal	Russell
Conroy	Gorman	Mustanen	Zeleny
Cronan	Harkin	Nila	

Artistic Appellations

Many of you likely grew up admiring an author, or perhaps you saw a painting in an art gallery and became enamored of that artist's work. This chapter offers names of famous artists, best-selling authors, and characters from literature as well as names of those immortal characters who have peopled William Shakespeare's works.

For those of you interested in science fiction and fantasy, we've also included a section of names with sci-fi/fantasy flair. For parents who have never given up their love of children's literature, you'll find a list of the boys and girls who filled the pages of your favorite books.

Named for Artists

Girl Names

Andrea Mantegna

Anna Atkins

Berenice Abbott

Berthe Morisot

Doris Ulmann

Dorothea Tanning

Elizabeth Butler

Evelyn de Morgan

Francesca della Piero

Georgia O'Keeffe

Judith Lyster

Leonora Carrington

Grandma Moses

Marie Bracquemond

Mary Cassatt

Rita Angus

Rosa Bonheur

Simone Martini

Tilly Kettle

Boy Names

Adam Elsheimer

Albrecht Altdorfer

Alexandre Cabanel

Alfred Sisley

Alonso Cano

Antonio Allegri Corregio

Auguste Rodin

Balthasar van der Ast

Benjamin West

Benvenuto Cellini

Camille Pissarro

Caspar David Friedrich

Charles Le Brun

Claude Monet

Dante Gabriel Rossetti

David Hockney

Dirck van Baburen

Domenico Ghirlandaio

Edgar Degas

Edward Hopper

Edvard Munch

El Greco

Eugene Boudin

Federico Barocci

Fra Angelico

Francis Bacon

Franz Marc

Gerard Davis

Giovanni Bellini

Gustave Caillebotte

Hendrick Avercamp

Henri Rousseau

Hieronymus Bosch

Honore Daumier

Jackson Pollock

James Tissot

Jan Vermeer

Jasper Cropsey

Jeanne-Baptiste Simeon
  Chardin

Jesse Trevino

Joan Miro

John Constable

Joseph Cornell

Joshua Shaw

Leonardo da Vinci

Lorenzo di Piero de' Medici

Luca Della Robbia

Lucian Freud

Michelangelo Buonarroti

Nehemiah Partridge

Nicholas Hilliard

Norman Rockwell

Odilon Redon

Paul Cézanne

Peter Paul Rubens

Pierre-Auguste Renoir

Pieter Bruegel

Raffaello Sanzio Raphael

Rembrandt van Rijn

Robert Campin

Ron Kitaj

Salvadore Dali

Sandro Botticelli

Stuart Davis

Theodore Chasseriau

Thomas Cole

Titian

Vincent van Gogh

Wassily Kandinsky

William Blake

Yves Tanguy

Zacharie Astruc

Favorite Children's Book/Show Characters

Girl Names

Character	Children's Book/Show	Character	Children's Book/Show
Alanna	*Alanna: The First Adventure*	Jane	*Fun with Dick and Jane*
Alice	*Alice in Wonderland*	Jenny Linsky	*Jenny and the Cat Club*
Amanda	*Amanda Pig and Her Big Brother Oliver*	Judy	*Runaway Pony*
Amelia Bedelia	*Amelia Bedelia* series	Laura Ingalls	*Little House on the Prairie*
Anastasia	*Anastasia Krupnik*	Lizzie	*Berenstain Bears*
Anne Shirley	*Anne of Green Gables*	Lucy	*The Chronicles of Narnia*
Arrietty	*The Borrowers*	Madeline	*Mad About Madeline*
Barbie	*Barbie Fairytopia*	Manyara	*Mufaro's Beautiful Daughters*
Beezus	*Beezus and Ramona*	Nan Bobbsey	*Bobbsey Twins Go to the Seashore*
Betsy	*Betsy-Tacy* books	Nancy Drew	*Nancy Drew Mysteries*
Caitlin Seeger	*Caitlin's Way*	Nina	*Runaway Pony*
Candy Quackenbush	*Abarat: Days of Magic, Nights of War*	Olivia	*Olivia*
Charlotte	*Charlotte's Web*	Sam Bangs	*Sam Bangs and Moonshine*
Clarissa	*Clarissa Explains It All*	Sophie	*When Sophie Gets Angry—Really, Really Angry*
Claudia	*From the Mixed-Up Files of Mrs. Basil E Frankweiler*	Tacy	*Betsy-Tacy* books
Dorothy	*The Wizard of Oz*	Violet Baudelaire	*Lemony Snicket's Series of Unfortunate Events*
Ella Sarah	*Ella Sarah Gets Dressed*	Wanda	*The Hundred Dresses*
Ellen	*Edgar and Ellen*	Wednesday Addams	*The Addams Family*
Eloise	*Eloise*	Willa	*Tell Me Something Before I Go to Sleep*
Emily Elizabeth	*Clifford the Big Red Dog*	Sunny Baudelaire	*Lemony Snicket's Series of Unfortunate Events*
Fern	*Charlotte's Web*		
Flossie Bobbsey	*Bobbsey Twins Go to the Seashore*		
Hermione Granger	*Harry Potter* series		

Favorite Children's Book/Show Characters, continued

Boy Names

Character	Children's Book/Show
Alec	*The Black Stallion*
Alexander Cold	*City of the Beasts*
Artemis Fowl	*Artemis Fowl*
Arthur	*Arthur*
Bo	*The Thief Lord*
Bert Bobbsey	*Bobbsey Twins Go to the Seashore*
Braid Beard	*How I Became a Pirate*
Charlie Bucket	*Charlie and the Chocolate Factory*
Christopher Robin	*Winnie the Pooh*
Clifford	*Clifford the Big Red Dog*
Crispin	*Crispin: Cross of Lead*
Damian Cray	*Eagle Strike: An Alex Rider Adventure*
Danny	*Danny and the Dinosaur*
Dennis	*Dennis the Menace*
Dexter	*Dexter's Laboratory*
David	*No, David!*
Dick	*Fun with Dick and Jane*
Eddie McDowd	*100 Deeds for Eddie McDowd*
Edgar	*Edgar and Ellen*
Freddie Fernortner	*Fearless First Grader*
Gordon	*Thomas the Tank Engine*

Character	Children's Book/Show
Harold	*Harold and the Purple Crayon*
Harry Potter	*Harry Potter* series
Jack	*Magic Tree House #14: Day of the Dragon King*
James	*James and the Giant Peach*
Jeremy Jacob	*How I Became a Pirate*
Joaquin Murieta	*Bandit's Moon*
Joe	*Time Warp Trio*
Marshall Teller	*Eerie, Indiana*
Max	*Where the Wild Things Are*
Mickey	*In the Night Kitchen*
Mike Mulligan	*Mike Mulligan and His Steam Shovel*
Milo	*The Phantom Tollbooth*
Omri	*Indian in the Cupboard*
Pete Wrigley	*The Adventures of Pete and Pete*
Prosper	*The Thief Lord*
Ron Weasley	*Harry Potter* series
Sam	*Time Warp Trio*
Stuart	*Stuart Little*
Thomas	*Thomas the Tank Engine*

Science-Fiction/Fantasy Names

Girl Names

Aari	Elani	Karana	Merla	Tayna
Alandra	Eliann	Katarra	Narra	Tendra
Allaya	Eudana	Kierra	Neema	Tierna
Anara	Fayla	Kilana	Nevala	Umali
Ariana	Fiolla	K'Rene	Nori	Vima
Arissa	Gaeriel	Latika	Onaya	Wrenn
Ayala	Gilora	Leosa	Philana	Yareena
Beata	Hela	Lisea	Qatai	Zarabeth
Brixie	Isela	Losira	Ravis	
Chalan	Jaya	Lysia	Renora	
Deila	Jesmin	Mala	Salia	
Demma	Jira	Marayna	Sayana	
Duenna	Kambrea	Marna	Shenna	

Boy Names

Adin	Boromir	Eris	Liko	Rivan
Alzen	Brin	Ezral	Lohden	Rondon
Amanin	Cindel	Faramir	Macias	Sarin
Amaros	Corin	Farran	Mavek	Sauron
Aragorn	Darod	Hogan	Mordock	Tabris
Arturis	Dathan	Inyri	Narik	Talar
Athan	Dillard	Ishan	Odan	Tarquin
Azen	Doran	Kainon	Orlando	Valen
Balin	Draylan	Kalin	Parell	Vima
Batai	Droe	Kir	Peregrin	Webb
Belar	Dwalin	Larell	Quarren	Yareth
Berik	Elrond	Lidell	Ramsey	Zolan

Literary Characters

Girl Names

Character	Book
Ántonia Shimerda	*My Ántonia*
Aureliano Buendia	*One Hundred Years of Solitude*
Celie (no last name)	*The Color Purple*
Clarissa Dalloway	*Mrs. Dalloway*
Claudine (no last name)	*Claudine at School*
Daisy Buchanan	*The Great Gatsby*
Frankie Addams	*The Member of the Wedding*
Hana	*The English Patient*
Hazel Motes	*Wise Blood*
Holly Golightly	*Breakfast at Tiffany's*
Janie Crawford	*Their Eyes Were Watching God*
Jean Brodie	*The Prime of Miss Jean Brodie*
Lily Bart	*House of Mirth*
Lolita	*Lolita*
Margaret Schlegel	*Howards End*
Mary Katherine Blackwood	*We Have Always Lived in the Castle*
Molly Bloom	*Ulysses*
Nora Charles	*The Thin Man*
Phoebe Caulfield	*The Catcher in the Rye*
Scout Finch	*To Kill a Mockingbird*
Sula Peace	*Sula*

Boy Names

Character	Book
Alden Pyle	*The Quiet American*
Alex Portnoy	*Portnoy's Complaint*
Arthur "Boo" Radley	*To Kill a Mockingbird*
Atticus Finch	*To Kill a Mockingbird*
Augustus McCrae	*Lonesome Dove*
Benjy	*The Sound and the Fury*
Bigger Thomas	*Native Son*
Binx Bolling	*The Moviegoer*
Charles Kinbote	*Pale Fire*

Character	Book
Christopher Tietjens	*Parade's End*
Clyde Griffiths	*An American Tragedy*
Dean Moriarty	*On the Road*
Eugene Henderson	*Henderson the Rain King*
Geoffrey Firmin	*Under the Volcano*
George Smiley	*Tinker, Tailor, Soldier, Spy*
Gregor Samsa	*The Metamorphosis*
Henry Chinaski	*Post Office*
Holden Caulfield	*The Catcher in the Rye*
Humbert	*Lolita*
Ignatius Reilly	*A Confederacy of Dunces*
Jake Barnes	*The Sun Also Rises*
James Bond	*Casino Royale*
Jay Gatsby	*The Great Gatsby*
Jeeves	*My Man Jeeves*
Joseph K.	*The Trial*
Lennie Small	*Of Mice and Men*
Leopold Bloom	*Ulysses*
Maurice Bendrix	*The End of the Affair*
Nathan Zuckerman	*My Life as a Man*
Neddy Merrill	*The Swimmer*
Newland Archer	*The Age of Innocence*
Nick Adams	*In Our Time*
Oskar Matzerath	*The Tin Drum*
Peter Pan	*The Little White Bird*
Philip Marlowe	*The Big Sleep*
Quentin Compson	*The Sound and the Fury*
Rabbit Angstrom	*Rabbit, Run*
Sam Spade	*The Maltese Falcon*
Santiago	*The Old Man and the Sea*
Seymour Glass	*Nine Stories*
Sebastian Flyte	*Brideshead Revisited*
Sherlock Holmes	*The Hound of the Baskervilles*
Stephen Dedalus	*A Portrait of the Artist as a Young Man*
Tarzan	*Tarzan of the Apes*
Tom Ripley	*The Talented Mr. Ripley*
Willie Stark	*All the King's Men*
Yossarian	*Catch-22*
Yuri Zhivago	*Dr. Zhivago*

Best-Selling Authors

Girl Names

Author	Work
Agatha Christie	*The Mysterious Mr. Quin*
Alice Sebold	*The Lovely Bones*
Amy Tan	*The Joy Luck Club*
Ann Rule	*Every Breath You Take*
Anna Quindlen	*A Short Guide to a Happy Life*
Anne Rice	*Interview with the Vampire*
Ayn Rand	*Atlas Shrugged*
Barbara Delinsky	*The Summer I Dared*
Beatrix Potter	*The Tale of Peter Rabbit*
Charlotte Brontë	*Jane Eyre*
Danielle Steel	*Safe Harbour*
Debbie Macomber	*Angels Everywhere*
Edith Wharton	*The House of Mirth*
Evelyn Waugh	*Scoop*
Fern Michaels	*Pretty Woman*
Flannery O'Connor	*The Complete Stories of Flannery O'Connor*
Frances Hodgson Burnett	*Little Lord Fauntleroy*
Gertrude Stein	*Three Lives and Tender Buttons*
Harper Lee	*To Kill a Mockingbird*
Harriet Beecher Stowe	*Uncle Tom's Cabin*
Heidi Murkoff	*What to Expect the First Year*
Iris Johansen	*Countdown*
J. K. Rowling	*Harry Potter* series
Jane Austen	*Pride and Prejudice*
Janet Evanovich	*Back to the Bedroom*
Jean Auel	*Clan of the Cave Bear*
Jennifer Crusie	*Charlie All Night*
Jennifer Weiner	*Good in Bed*
Joan Collins	*Misfortune's Daughters*
Jodi Picoult	*My Sister's Keeper*
Joyce Carol Oates	*We Were the Mulvaneys*

Author	Work
Karen Robards	*Superstition*
Kate Douglas Wiggin	*Rebecca of Sunnybrook Farm*
Kate White	*If Looks Could Kill*
Kitty Kelley	*The Family: The Real Story of the Bush Dynasty*
Laura Ingalls Wilder	*The Little House* series
Laurell Hamilton	*A Stroke of Midnight*
Lilian Jackson Braun	*Cat Who Talked Turkey*
Louisa May Alcott	*Little Women*
Lucy Maud Montgomery	*Anne of Green Gables*
Maeve Binchy	*Nights of Rain and Stars*
Margaret Atwood	*Handmaid's Tale*
Margaret Mitchell	*Gone with the Wind*
Margery Williams	*Velveteen Rabbit*
Marietta Holley	*Around the World with Josiah Allen's Wife*
Marilynne Robinson	*Housekeeping*
Mary Higgins Clark	*No Place Like Home*
Maya Angelou	*I Know Why the Caged Bird Sings*
Nicole Krauss	*The History of Love: A Novel*
Nora Roberts	*Black Rose*
Patricia Cornwell	*Predator*
Rebecca Wells	*Divine Secrets of the YA-YA Sisterhood*
Sandra Brown	*White Hot*
Sarah Vowell	*Assassination Vacation*
Sojourner Truth	*Book of Life*
Sue Grafton	*R Is for Ricochet*
Sue Monk Kidd	*Secret Life of Bees*
Susan Orlean	*The Orchid Thief: A True Story of Beauty and Obsession*
Suze Orman	*The Money Book for the Young, Fabulous & Broke*
Toni Morrison	*Beloved*
Virginia Woolf	*Mrs. Dalloway*
Willa Cather	*My Ántonia*
Zora Neale Hurston	*Their Eyes Were Watching God*

Boy Names

Author	Work
Alexander McCall Smith	*The No. 1 Ladies' Detective Agency*
Arthur Agatston	*The South Beach Diet Good Fats/Good Carbs Guide*
Buzz Bissinger	*Three Nights in August: Strategy, Heartbreak and Joy: Inside the Mind of a Manager*
Charles Dickens	*Great Expectations*
Clive Cussler	*Polar Shift*
Dan Brown	*The Da Vinci Code*
Dave Barry	*Big Trouble*
David Baldacci	*Split Second*
David McCullough	*1776*
Dean Koontz	*Velocity*
Deepak Chopra	*The Book of Secrets: Unlocking the Dimensions of Your Life*
Don Miguel Ruiz	*The Four Agreements* (*Toltec Wisdom* series)
Douglas Adams	*Ultimate Hitchhiker's Guide to the Galaxy*
Edgar Allan Poe	*The Murders in the Rue Morgue*
Ernest Hemingway	*The Old Man and the Sea*
F. Scott Fitzgerald	*The Great Gatsby*
Gregg Hurwitz	*Do No Harm*
Harlan Coben	*Just One Look*
Henry James	*The Portrait of a Lady*
Herman Melville	*Moby Dick*
Ian McEwan	*Saturday*
Jack London	*The Call of the Wild*
James Patterson	*The Lake House*
Jared Diamond	*Collapse: How Societies Choose to Fail or Succeed*
Jim Collins	*Built to Last: Successful Habits of Visionary Companies*
John Gray	*Men Are from Mars: Woman Are from Venus: The Classic Guide to Understanding the Opposite Sex*
John Grisham	*The Broker*
John Irving	*Until I Find You*
John Le Carre	*The Constant Gardener*
John Saul	*Perfect Nightmare*
Jon Stewart	*The Daily Show with Jon Stewart Presents America (The Book): A Citizen's Guide to Democracy Inaction*

Author	Work
Jonathan Kellerman	*Rage*
Joseph Wambaugh	*The Onion Field*
Ken Follett	*Pillars of the Earth*
Khaled Hosseini	*The Kite Runner*
Leo Tolstoy	*Anna Karenina*
Malcolm Gladwell	*Blink: The Power of Thinking Without Thinking*
Mark Twain	*The Adventures of Huckleberry Finn*
Michael Connelly	*The Closers*
Michael Crichton	*Jurassic Park*
Mitch Albom	*The Five People You Meet in Heaven*
Nathaniel Hawthorne	*The Scarlet Letter*
Nelson DeMille	*Night Fall*
Nicholas Sparks	*The Notebook*
Oscar Wilde	*The Picture of Dorian Gray*
Philip McGraw	*Family First*
Rick Warren	*The Purpose Driven Life: Why on Earth Am I Here For?*
Ridley Pearson	*Cut and Run*
Robert Fulghum	*All I Really Needed to Know I Learned in Kindergarten*
Robert Kiyosaki	*The ABC's of Real Estate Investing: What the Rich Invest in That The Poor and Middle Class Do Not!*
Robert Louis Stevenson	*Treasure Island*
Robert Ludlum	*The Bourne Identity*
Scott Turow	*Reversible Errors*
Sinclair Lewis	*Babbitt*
Spencer Johnson	*Who Moved My Cheese?*
Stephen King	*The Shining*
Steven Levitt	*Freakonomics: A Rogue Economist Explores the Hidden Side of Everything*
Tom Clancy	*The Teeth of the Tiger*
Upton Sinclair	*The Jungle*
Wally Lamb	*She's Come Undone*
Washington Irving	*Legend of Sleepy Hollow*
William Bernhardt	*Hate Crime: A Novel of Suspense*
William Shakespeare	*Hamlet*

Names from Shakespeare

Girl Names

Character	Play
Adriana	*The Comedy of Errors*
Aemilia	*The Comedy of Errors*
Alice	*Henry IV*
Andromache	*Troilus and Cressida*
Anne Page	*The Merry Wives of Windsor*
Audrey	*As You Like It*
Beatrice	*Much Ado About Nothing*
Bianca	*The Taming of the Shrew, Othello*
Calpurnia	*Julius Caesar*
Cassandra	*Troilus and Cressida*
Celia	*As You Like It*
Ceres	*The Tempest*
Charmian	*Antony and Cleopatra*
Cleopatra	*Antony and Cleopatra*
Constance	*King John*
Cordelia	*King Lear*
Cressida	*Troilus and Cressida*
Desdemona	*Othello*
Diana	*All's Well That Ends Well, Pericles*
Dionyza	*Pericles*
Dorcas	*The Winter's Tale*
Emilia	*The Winter's Tale, Othello*
Francisca	*Measure for Measure*
Gertrude	*Hamlet*
Goneril	*King Lear*
Helen	*Troilus and Cressida, Cymbeline*
Helena	*A Midsummer Night's Dream, All's Well That Ends Well*
Hermia	*A Midsummer Night's Dream*
Hermione	*The Winter's Tale*
Hero	*Much Ado About Nothing*

Character	Play
Hippolyta	*A Midsummer Night's Dream*
Imogen	*Cymbeline*
Iras	*Antony and Cleopatra*
Iris	*The Tempest*
Isabella	*Measure for Measure*
Jessica	*The Merchant of Venice*
Julia	*The Two Gentlemen of Verona*
Juliet	*Romeo and Juliet, Measure for Measure*
Juno	*The Tempest*
Katharina	*The Taming of the Shrew*
Lavinia	*Titus Andronicus*
Luce	*The Comedy of Errors*
Lucetta	*The Two Gentlemen of Verona*
Luciana	*The Comedy of Errors*
Lychorinda	*Pericles*
Margaret	*Much Ado About Nothing*
Maria	*Twelfth Night*
Mariana	*All's Well That Ends Well, Measure for Measure*
Marina	*Pericles*
Miranda	*The Tempest*
Mopsa	*The Winter's Tale*
Nerissa	*The Merchant of Venice*
Octavia	*Antony and Cleopatra*
Olivia	*Twelfth Night*
Ophelia	*Hamlet*
Patience	*Henry VIII*
Paulina	*The Winter's Tale*
Perdita	*The Winter's Tale*
Phebe	*As You Like It*
Phrynia	*Timon of Athens*

Character	Play
Portia	The Merchant of Venice, Julius Caesar
Regan	King Lear
Rosalind	As You Like It
Rosaline	Romeo and Juliet
Silvia	The Two Gentlemen of Verona
Tamora	Titus Andronicus
Thaisa	Pericles

Character	Play
Timandra	Timon of Athens
Titania	A Midsummer Night's Dream
Ursula	Much Ado About Nothing
Valeria	Coriolanus
Viola	Twelfth Night
Violenta	All's Well That Ends Well
Virgilia	Coriolanus
Volumnia	Coriolanus

Boy Names

Character	Play
Abraham	Romeo and Juliet
Adam	As You Like It
Adriano	Love's Labor's Lost
Agamemnon	Troilus and Cressida
Alonso	The Tempest
Amiens	As You Like It
Angus	Macbeth
Archidamus	The Winter's Tale
Balthazar	The Comedy of Errors
Bardolph	The Merry Wives of Windsor, Henry V
Bassanio	The Merchant of Venice
Bassett	King Henry VI
Bates	Henry V
Benedick	Much Ado About Nothing
Boyet	Love's Labor's Lost
Caius	Titus Andronicus
Camillo	The Winter's Tale
Cassio	Othello
Cato	Julius Caesar
Chiron	Titus Andronicus
Cicero	Julius Caesar
Claudio	Much Ado About Nothing, Measure for Measure
Cleon	Pericles

Character	Play
Conrade	Much Ado About Nothing
Costard	Love's Labor's Lost
Cromwell	Henry VIII
Curan	King Lear
Curtis	The Taming of the Shrew
Dion	The Winter's Tale
Donalbain	Macbeth
Dromio	The Comedy of Errors
Dumaine	Love's Labor's Lost
Duncan	Macbeth
Edgar	King Lear
Escanes	Pericles
Fabian	Twelfth Night
Falstaff (Sir John)	The Merry Wives of Windsor
Fenton	The Merry Wives of Windsor
Ferdinand	The Tempest, Love's Labor's Lost
Feste	Twelfth Night
Ford	The Merry Wives of Windsor
Francisco	Hamlet, The Tempest
Gallus	Antony and Cleopatra
Gremio	The Taming of the Shrew
Griffith	Henry VIII
Guildenstern	Hamlet

Names from Shakespeare, continued

Character	Play	Character	Play
Hamlet	*Hamlet*	Orlando	*As You Like It*
Hector	*Troilus and Cressida*	Osric	*Hamlet*
Horatio	*Hamlet*	Othello	*Othello*
Iachima	*Cymbeline*	Pandarus	*Troilus and Cressida*
Iago	*Othello*	Philo	*Antony and Cleopatra*
Jamy	*Henry V*	Pindarus	*Julius Caesar*
Julius Caesar	*Julius Caesar*	Priam	*Troilus and Cressida*
Laertes	*Hamlet*	Proteus	*The Two Gentlemen of Verona*
Launce	*The Two Gentlemen of Verona*	Quince	*A Midsummer Night's Dream*
Laurence (Friar)	*Romeo and Juliet*	Quintus	*Titus Andronicus*
Lennox	*Macbeth*	Reynaldo	*Hamlet*
Leontes	*The Winter's Tale*	Romeo	*Romeo and Juliet*
Longaville	*Love's Labor's Lost*	Ross	*Macbeth*
Lorenzo	*The Merchant of Venice*	Rugby	*The Merry Wives of Windsor*
Lucio	*Measure for Measure*	Sampson	*Romeo and Juliet*
Lysander	*A Midsummer Night's Dream*	Sebastian	*The Tempest, Twelfth Night*
Macbeth	*Macbeth*	Seyton	*Macbeth*
Macduff	*Macbeth*	Strato	*Julius Caesar*
Macmorris	*Henry V*	Theseus	*A Midsummer Night's Dream*
Marcellus	*Hamlet*	Timon	*Timon of Athens*
Mardian	*Antony and Cleopatra*	Titus	*Coriolanus, Timon of Athens*
Mark Antony	*Antony and Cleopatra*	Tranio	*The Taming of the Shrew*
Menelaus	*Troilus and Cressida*	Tybalt	*Romeo and Juliet*
Montague	*Romeo and Juliet*	Ulysses	*Troilus and Cressida*
Montano	*Othello*	Varrius	*Antony and Cleopatra*
Nathaniel	*Love's Labor's Lost*	Verges	*Much Ado About Nothing*
Nestor	*Troilus and Cressida*	William	*As You Like It*
Oberon	*A Midsummer Night's Dream*		
Octavius	*Julius Caesar*		

Names of Poets

Girl Names

Alice Cary
Anne Sexton
Barbara Guest
Carol Ann Duffy
Diane DiPrima
Dorothy Auchterlonie
Elaine Feinstein
Elizabeth Bishop
Emily Dickinson
Erica Jong

Ethel Anderson
Fanny Howe
Felicia Hemans
Fleur Adcock
Gwendolyn Bennett
Gwendolyn Brooks
Janet Frame
Joanna Baillie
Joy Harjo
June Jordan

Lisa Jarnot
Lucille Clifton
Margaret Atwood
Mary Wedderburn
  Cannon
Mathilde Blind
Maura Dooley
Maya Angelou
Michelle Cliff
Norma Cole
Pam Ayres

Penelope Fitzgerald
Phoebe Cary
Rae Armantrout
Rita Dove
Sandra Cisneros
Susanne Blamire
Sylvia Plath
Thea Astley
Tina Darragh
Wanda Coleman

Boy Names

Alexander Hume
Albert Gordon Austin
Allen Fisher
Allen Ginsberg
Anselm Berrigan
Arthur Henry Adams
Asa Benveniste
Austin Clarke
Ben Jonson
Bernard Barton
Bob Cobbing
Brian Coffey
Bruce Andrews
Carl Sandburg
Charles Causely
Constantine Cavafy

David Ball
Denis Devlin
Douglas Dunn
Ebenezer Elliot
E. E. Cummings
Edmund Blunden
Edward Dorn
Edwin Atherstone
Elijah Fenton
Ezra Pound
Geoffrey Chaucer
George Chapman
Gilbert Adair
Harold Acton
Henry Carey
Jack Clarke

Jack Kerouac
James Tate
Jesse Ball
John Ashbery
Joseph Addison
Keith Douglas
Ken Barratt
Lawrence Ferlinghetti
Leigh Hunt
Lewis Carroll
Lex Banning
Mark Akenside
Matthew Arnold
Maurice Biggs
Michael Davidson
Miles Champion

Oliver Wendell
  Holmes
Peter Bladen
Ralph Waldo Emerson
Randall Jarrell
Ray DiPalma
Richard Caddel
Robert Frost
Samuel Bishop
Simon Armitage
Stanley Kunitz
Theodore Roethke
Thomas Ashe
Trevor Joyce
Wendell Berry
William Carlos
  Williams

Composers

Girl Names

Agathe Backer Grondahl

Angela Morley

Anne Boleyn

Annette von Droste-Hülshoff

Barbara White

Beth Anderson

Bunita Marcus

Carla Bley

Caroline Sheridan Norton

Caterina Assandra

Cécile Chaminade

Cecilia Maria Barthelemon

Clara Schumann

Eleanor Hovda

Elisabeth Lutyens

Ellen Wright

Elodie Lauten

Ethel Smyth

Eve Beglarian

Fanny Mendelssohn

Frances Allitsen

Francesca Caccini

Germaine Tailleferre

Gertrude van den Bergh

Grace Williams

Helene de Montgeroult

Joan La Barbara

Johanna Mathieux Kinkel

Josephine Lang

Julia Wolfe

Kaija Saariaho

Laurie Spiegel

Lili Boulanger

Lois Vierk

Louise Talma

Maddalena Cassulana

Madeleine Dring

Maria Teresa Agnesi

Marion Bauer

Maryanne Amacher

Meredith Monk

Nadia Boulanger

Pauline Oliveros

Rebecca Clarke

Ruth Crawford-Seeger

Settimia Caccini

Shulamit Ran

Sofia Gubaidulina

Tekla Badarzewska

Thea Musgrave

Usha Khanna

Wendy Carlos

Boy Names

Aaron Copland

Alexander Scriabin

Andrew Lloyd Webber

Antonín Dvořák

Antonini Vivaldi

Archangelo Corelli

Arnold Schoenberg

Arthur Sullivan

Béla Bartók

Benjamin Britten

Carl von Weber

Charles Gounod

Christoph Gluck

Claude Debussy

Claudio Monteverdi

Dmitri Shostakovich

Dominick Argento

Edvard Grieg

Felix Mendelssohn

François Couperin

Franz Liszt

Franz Schubert

Frederic Chopin

Gabriel Fauré

Georg Telemann

George Gershwin

George Handel

Giacomo Puccini

Gian Carlo Menotti

Gioacchino Rossini

Giovanni Gabrieli

Giuseppe Verdi

Gustav Mahler

Hector Berlioz

Heinrich Schütz

Henry Purcell

Igor Stravinsky

Jean Sibelius

Jean-Baptiste Lully

Jean-Philippe Rameau

Johann Pachelbel

Johann Sebastian Bach

Johannes Brahms

John Philip Sousa

Joseph Haydn

Kurt Weill

Leonard Bernstein

Ludwig van Beethoven

Manuel de Falla

Maurice Ravel

Nicolo Paganini

Piotr Ilyitch Tchaikovsky

Ralph Vaughan Williams

Richard Wagner

Robert Schumann

Samuel Barber

Serge Prokofiev

Sergei Rachmaninoff

Wolfgang Amadeus Mozart

Opera Singers' Names

Girl Names

Adria Firestone
Alessandra Marc
Angela Brown
Anna Netrebko
Beverly Sills
Birgit Nilsson
Catherine Hayes
Cecilia Bartoli
Chon Wolson
Christine Brewer
Dagmar zum Hingst
Deborah Voigt
Denyce Graves

Dolora Zajick
Edita Gruberova
Ellen Denham
Eva Marton
Fabiana Bravo
Felicity Lott
Frederica von Stade
Hayley Westenra
Hildegard Behrens
Jane Eaglen
Janice Baird
Jennifer Larmore
Joan Sutherland

Karen Parks
Kathleen Battle
Kirsten Flagstad
Lesley Garrett
Leontyne Price
Lotte Lehmann
Luana DeVol
Lucia Aliberti
Mara Kelley
Marcella Sembrich
Maria Callas
Marilyn Horne
Mary Bella

Mirella Freni
Patricia Caicedo
Renata Tebaldi
Renée Fleming
Rosemary Wagner-
  Scott
Ruth Ann Swenson
Stella Scott
Suzanne Mentzer
Tania Melanie Marsh
Teresa Zykus-Gara
Vivica Genaux

Boy Names

Andreas Bocelli
Bryn Terfel
David Faircloth
Dennis Jesse
Dietrich Fisher-
  Dieskau
Dmitri Hvorostovsky
Enrico Caruso
Ezio Pinza
Franco Corelli
François le Roux
Fredrick Redd

Fritz Wunderlich
Gerard Edery
Giovanni Meoni
Grant Doyle
Ian Gray
James Anest
Jerry Hadley
John Davies
José Carreras
Joseph Shore
Josh Groban
Jussi Bjorling

Luciano Pavarotti
Louis Quilico
Mark Evans
Matthias Goerne
Miguel Velasquez
Nathaniel Watson
Nicolai Gedda
Nolan Van Way
Paul Carey Jones
Peter Schreier
Phillip Mentor
Placido Domingo

Richard Tucker
Robert Sims
Russell Watson
Ryan Taylor
Samuel Ramsey
Scott Russell
Stuart Neill
Thomas Hampson
Warren Leonard
William Warfield

Dancers' Names

Girl Names

Dancer	Form of Dance	Dancer	Form of Dance
Adeline Genée	Ballet	Jennifer Lopez	Hip-hop
Agnes Letestu	Ballet	Karen Kain	Ballet
Alicia Markova	Ballet	Kathrine Dunham	Jazz
Ann Miller	Tap	Lucile Grahn	Ballet
Anna Pavlova	Ballet	Margot Fonteyn	Ballet
Aurelie Dupont	Ballet	Maria Alexandrova	Ballet
Britney Spears	Hip-hop	Mathilde Kschessinska	Ballet
Christina Aguilera	Hip-hop	Melissa Hayden	Ballet
Darcey Bussell	Ballet	Missy Elliot	Hip-hop
Devora Canario	Hip-hop	Olga Preobrajenska	Ballet
Eleanor Powell	Tap	Patricia McBride	Ballet
Elisabeth Maurin	Ballet	Ruby Keeler	Tap
Fanny Cerito	Ballet	Suzanne DiNunzio	Hip-hop
Gwen Verdon	Jazz	Suzanne Farrell	Ballet
Janet Jackson	Hip-hop	Sylvie Guillem	Ballet
		Vera Ellen	Tap

Boy Names

Dancer	Form of Dance	Dancer	Form of Dance
Anton Dolin	Ballet	Jeremie Belingard	Ballet
Barry Lather	Hip-hop	Joe Frisco	Jazz
Bill Robinson "Bojangles"	Tap	John Bubbles	Tap
Bob Fosse	Jazz	Jose Manuel Carreno	Ballet
Charles Jude	Ballet	Justin Timberlake	Hip-hop
Cyril Atanassoff	Ballet	Marcelo Gomes	Ballet
Darrin Henson	Hip-hop	Michael Vester	Ballet
Emmanuel Thibault	Ballet	Mikhail Baryshnikov	Ballet
Erik Bruhn	Ballet	Nicolas Lerich	Ballet
Ethan Stiefel	Ballet	Nino Ananiashvili	Ballet
Fred Astaire	Tap	Pavel Gerdt	Ballet
Gene Kelly	Tap	Rolando Sarabia	Ballet
Gregory Hines	Tap	Rudolf Nureyev	Ballet
Gus Giordano	Jazz	Sammy Davis Jr.	Tap
Howard "Sandman" Sims	Tap	Savion Glover	Tap
Jean-Pierre Bonnefous	Ballet	Seth Stewart	Hip-hop
		Yuri Soloviev	Ballet

Naming Nationwide

It's funny: choosing a baby name is such a personal decision and yet many parents often choose the same name for their child as their neighbors, friends, and family members chose for their child. Take a look at this chapter's lists of the most popular baby names worldwide, as well as some of the frequent choices by region, state, and city in the United States.

You may also find inspiration by checking out popular names from the past, such as in our lists of top baby names by decade. Or skim the list of the top 100 names nationwide for more recent hot picks.

Top Baby Names by Country

Note: Following each country name are the top three most popular names, in descending order of popularity.

Girl Names

Africa	Aamoir, Fatima, Leetefa	**Israel**	Janna, Ariel, Ada
Australia	Emily, Jessica, Chloe	**Italy**	Maria, Anna, Giuseppina
Austria	Sarah, Anna, Juli	**Japan**	Misaki, Aoi, Nanami
Czech Republic	Tereza, Katerina, Natalie	**Kenya**	Saada, Jamila, Basha
Chile	Maria, Ana Rosa	**Mexico**	Gabriella, Cierra, Rosa
China	Bao, Min, Zan	**Netherlands**	Sanne, Lotte, Emma
Denmark	Emma, Julie, Mathilde	**Nigeria**	Fabayo, Abagbe, Chinue
England/Wales	Chloe, Emily, Megan	**Norway**	Emma, Ida, Thea
Finland	Maria, Emilia, Sofia	**Poland**	Anna, Maria, Katarzyna
France	Lea, Manon, Chloe	**Russia**	Sofia, Anna, Elena
Germany	Maria, Sophia, Katharina	**Scotland**	Chloe, Sophie, Emma
Greece	Sappho, Eugina, Calliope	**Spain**	Lucia, Maria, Paula
Iceland	Guðrún, Sigríður, Kristín	**Sweden**	Emma, Madja, Ida
Ireland	Emma, Katie, Chloe	**Vietnam**	Thu, Nhung, Kim

Boy Names

Africa	Harun, Muhhamad, Salim	**Israel**	Isaiah, Aaron, Benjamin
Australia	Joshua, Lachlan, Jack	**Italy**	Giuseppe, Giovanni, Antonio
Austria	Lukas, Florian, Tobias	**Japan**	Shun, Tukami, Shou
Chile	Jose, Juan, Luis	**Kenya**	Pandu, Cheja, Taalib
China	An, Quon, Yen	**Mexico**	Felix, Antonio, Rafael
Czech Republic	Jakub, Jan, Tomas	**Nigeria**	Abiade, Madu, Danjuma
Denmark	Mikkel, Frederick, Mathias	**Netherlands**	Sem, Daan, Thomas
England/Wales	Jack, Thomas, James	**Norway**	Mathias, Tobias, Andreas
Finland	Mikael, Juhani, Johannes	**Poland**	Piotr, Jan, Andrzej
France	Thomas, Lucas, Theo	**Russia**	Maximilian, Paul, David
Germany	Alexander, Maximilian, Paul	**Scotland**	Jack, Lewis, Cameron
Greece	Diokles, Arcadicus, Hippias	**Spain**	Alejandro, Daniel, Pablo
Iceland	Sigríður, Guðmundur, Jón	**Sweden**	William, Filip, Oscar
Ireland	Jack, Matthew, Adam	**Vietnam**	Due, Quang, Minh

Most Popular Names by U.S. Region

Girl Names

Northeast Emily, Samantha, Sarah, Jessica, Ashley, Nicole, Amanda, Elizabeth, Taylor, Kayla

Southeast Ashley, Jessica, Taylor, Emily, Brittany, Sarah, Kayla, Hannah, Samantha, Alexis

Midwest Jessica, Ashley, Emily, Samantha, Taylor, Sarah, Megan, Amanda, Rachel, Brittany

Northwest Jessica, Emily, Ashley, Samantha, Sarah, Taylor, Hannah, Amanda, Megan, Rachel

Southwest Jessica, Ashley, Stephanie, Jennifer, Samantha, Sarah, Elizabeth, Emily, Amanda, Nicole

Noncontinental United States Jessica, Ashley, Taylor, Rachel, Kayla, Mary, Nicole, Maria, Courtney, Amanda

Boy Names

Northeast Michael, Matthew, Nicholas, Christopher, Joseph, Ryan, Tyler, Andrew, John, Daniel

Southeast Michael, Christopher, Joshua, Brandon, Matthew, Austin, William, James, Tyler, Jacob

Midwest Michael, Jacob, Tyler, Matthew, Nicholas, Zachary, Joshua, Austin, Brandon, Christopher

Northwest Jacob, Austin, Tyler, Michael, Joshua, Andrew, Matthew, Brandon, Christopher, Nicholas

Southwest Michael, Daniel, Jose, Christopher, David, Andrew, Joshua, Anthony, Matthew, Brandon

Noncontinental United States Joshua, Michael, Brandon, Matthew, Justin, Christopher, Tyler, Joseph, Ryan, John

Source: From The Baby Name Countdown, Fifth Edition, *by Janet Schwegel (Marlowe & Company, 2001).*

Top Five Baby Names by U.S. State for 2004*

Girl Names

Alabama	Emma, Madison, Emily, Hannah, Anna
Alaska	Emma, Madison, Hannah, Grace, Emily
Arizona	Emily, Isabella, Emma, Ashley, Madison
Arkansas	Madison, Emily, Emma, Hannah, Olivia
California	Emily, Ashley, Samantha, Isabella, Natalie
Colorado	Emma, Emily, Isabella, Madison, Ashley
Connecticut	Emily, Olivia, Emma, Isabella, Samantha
Delaware	Madison, Olivia, Emily, Elizabeth, Emma
District of Columbia	Sophia, Katherine, Kayla, Elizabeth, Caroline
Florida	Emily, Isabella, Madison, Emma, Ashley
Georgia	Emily, Madison, Emma, Hannah, Sarah
Hawaii	Emma, Isabella, Emily, Kayla, Chloe
Idaho	Emma, Emily, Alexis, Abigail, Hannah
Illinois	Emily, Emma, Olivia, Abigail, Madison
Indiana	Emma, Madison, Abigail, Emily, Olivia
Iowa	Emma, Madison, Grace, Olivia, Abigail
Kansas	Emma, Emily, Madison, Abigail, Grace
Kentucky	Madison, Emily, Hannah, Emma, Abigail
Louisiana	Madison, Emma, Emily, Hannah, Alexis
Maine	Emma, Emily, Madison, Hannah, Abigail
Maryland	Madison, Emily, Emma, Kayla, Hannah
Massachusetts	Emily, Emma, Olivia, Isabella, Abigail
Michigan	Emma, Madison, Emily, Olivia, Hannah
Minnesota	Emma, Grace, Olivia, Emily, Abigail
Mississippi	Madison, Emily, Hannah, Anna, Emma
Missouri	Emma, Madison, Emily, Abigail, Olivia
Montana	Madison, Emma, Grace, Hannah, Emily
Nebraska	Emma, Emily, Madison, Grace, Hannah
Nevada	Ashley, Madison, Emily, Emma, Isabella
New Hampshire	Emma, Emily, Abigail, Hannah, Madison
New Jersey	Emily, Olivia, Isabella, Samantha, Ashley
New Mexico	Alyssa, Isabella, Alexis, Emily, Madison
New York	Emily, Emma, Olivia, Isabella, Ashley

2004 is the latest year for which information was available at the time of printing.

North Carolina	Emma, Emily, Madison, Hannah, Abigail
North Dakota	Madison, Emma, Emily, Grace, Olivia
Ohio	Emma, Madison, Emily, Olivia, Hannah
Oklahoma	Madison, Emily, Emma, Alexis, Hannah
Oregon	Emily, Emma, Madison, Grace, Hannah
Pennsylvania	Emily, Emma, Madison, Olivia, Abigail
Rhode Island	Emily, Madison, Isabella, Emma, Olivia
South Carolina	Madison, Emily, Emma, Hannah, Abigail
South Dakota	Madison, Emma, Emily, Olivia, Hannah
Tennessee	Madison, Emma, Emily, Hannah, Abigail
Texas	Emily, Ashley, Madison, Emma, Alyssa
Utah	Emma, Madison, Emily, Olivia, Abigail
Vermont	Emma, Emily, Madison, Olivia, Abigail
Virginia	Emily, Madison, Emma, Hannah, Olivia
Washington	Emma, Emily, Olivia, Isabella, Madison
West Virginia	Madison, Emily, Hannah, Emma, Alexis
Wisconsin	Emma, Olivia, Emily, Abigail, Grace
Wyoming	Madison, Emma, Alexis, Elizabeth, Hannah

Boy Names

Alabama	William, Jacob, John, Joshua, James
Alaska	Ethan, Joseph, James, Samuel, Tyler
Arizona	Jose, Jacob, Anthony, Daniel, Angel
Arkansas	Jacob, William, Ethan, Joshua, Michael
California	Daniel, Anthony, Andrew, Jose, Jacob
Colorado	Jacob, Joshua, Ethan, Daniel, Alexander
Connecticut	Michael, Ryan, Matthew, Nicholas, Joseph
Delaware	Ryan, Michael, Joshua, Matthew, Nicholas
District of Columbia	William, John, Alexander, Joshua, Anthony
Florida	Michael, Joshua, Jacob, Anthony, Daniel
Georgia	William, Joshua, Jacob, Christopher, Michael
Hawaii	Joshua, Noah, Ethan, Jacob, Elijah
Idaho	Ethan, Tyler, Jacob, Logan, Michael
Illinois	Michael, Jacob, Daniel, Anthony, Joseph
Indiana	Jacob, Ethan, Andrew, Joshua, Michael
Iowa	Jacob, Ethan, Logan, Andrew, Samuel

Kansas	Jacob, Ethan, Michael, Alexander, Andrew
Kentucky	Jacob, Ethan, William, James, Logan
Louisiana	Ethan, Joshua, Jacob, Michael, Christopher
Maine	Jacob, Ethan, Samuel, Benjamin, Logan
Maryland	Michael, Jacob, Joshua, Ryan, Matthew
Massachusetts	Michael, Matthew, Ryan, Nicholas, Andrew
Michigan	Jacob, Ethan, Michael, Andrew, Joshua
Minnesota	Jacob, Ethan, Samuel, Andrew, Benjamin
Mississippi	William, James, John, Joshua, Michael
Missouri	Jacob, Ethan, Andrew, Tyler, Michael
Montana	Jacob, Ethan, William, Michael, Joseph
Nebraska	Jacob, Ethan, Samuel, Joshua, Alexander
Nevada	Anthony, Jacob, Joshua, Daniel, Michael
New Hampshire	Jacob, Ryan, Matthew, Ethan, Nicholas
New Jersey	Michael, Matthew, Nicholas, Ryan, Joseph
New Mexico	Jacob, Joshua, Matthew, Daniel, Isaiah
New York	Michael, Matthew, Joseph, Daniel, Ryan
North Carolina	William, Jacob, Joshua, Michael, Ethan
North Dakota	Ethan, Jacob, Andrew, Logan, Mason
Ohio	Jacob, Ethan, Andrew, Michael, Matthew
Oklahoma	Jacob, Ethan, Joshua, Michael, Tyler
Oregon	Ethan, Jacob, Daniel, Alexander, Andrew
Pennsylvania	Michael, Jacob, Ryan, Matthew, Nicholas
Rhode Island	Michael, Matthew, Jacob, Alexander, Nicholas
South Carolina	William, Jacob, James, Joshua, Christopher
South Dakota	Ethan, Jacob, Logan, Mason, Dylan
Tennessee	William, Jacob, Ethan, Joshua, James
Texas	Jose, Jacob, Joshua, Daniel, David
Utah	Ethan, Jacob, Joshua, Samuel, Andrew
Vermont	Jacob, Ryan, William, Ethan, Matthew
Virginia	Jacob, William, Joshua, Michael, Ethan
Washington	Jacob, Ethan, Andrew, Alexander, Joshua
West Virginia	Jacob, Ethan, Logan, Tyler, Hunter
Wisconsin	Ethan, Jacob, Alexander, Tyler, Samuel
Wyoming	Michael, Hunter, Jacob, Ethan, Joshua

Most Popular Names by Major U.S. City

Girl Names

Boston	Isabella, Emily, Sophia, Emma, Olivia, Grace, Katherine, Elizabeth, Abigail, Caroline
Denver	Ashley, Isabella, Jennifer, Elizabeth, Sophia, Emily, Samantha, Emma, Michelle, Jacqueline
Los Angeles	Ashley, Samantha, Emily, Jennifer, Natalie, Jessica, Kimberly, Brianna, Stephanie, Jasmine
New York	Emily, Ashley, Kayla, Sarah, Samantha, Brianna, Isabella, Nicole, Rachel, Jessica

Boy Names

Boston	Michael, John, Anthony, Christopher, Alexander, David, James, Joseph, Joshua, William
Denver	Jose, Angel, Daniel, David, Jonathan, Jesus, Andrew, Joshua, Juan, Luis
Los Angeles	Daniel, Anthony, Andrew, Angel, Jose, David, Joshua, Matthew, Christopher, Jonathan
New York	Michael, Justin, Daniel, Matthew, Christopher, Anthony, David, Joshua, Joseph, Kevin

Named for Cities

Girl Names

Acadia	Canada	Eden	North Carolina	Milan	Italy
Adeline	Illinois	Florence	Italy	Morgan	Louisiana
Adena	Ohio	Geneva	Switzerland	Olympia	Washington
Allison	Ohio	Hailey	Idaho	Paris	France
Aspen	Colorado	Helena	Montana	Portland	Oregon, Maine
Atlanta	Georgia	Jersey	New Jersey	Raleigh	North Carolina
Bethany (Beach)	Delaware	Jordan	Utah	Salem	Massachusetts
		Kelsey	England	Savannah	Georgia
Brooklyn	New York	Kennedy	Minnesota	Selma	Alabama
Cameron	Missouri	Kingston	Jamaica	Sharon	Massachusetts
Carmel	California	Lee	Massachusetts	Shelby	North Carolina
Catalina	California	Leslie	Michigan	Siena	Italy
Charlotte	North Carolina	London	England	Sierra	California
Chelsea	Massachusetts, Michigan	Lourdes	France	Sydney	Australia
		Madison	Wisconsin	Valencia	Spain
Cheyenne	Wyoming	Marion	Ohio	Venice	Italy
Devon	England	Melba	Idaho	Victoria	Canada

Boy Names

Abbott	Texas	Chase	Virginia	Harlem	New York
Acton	Massachusetts	Chester	Pennsylvania	Houston	Texas
Aiken	South Carolina	Cleveland	Ohio	Hudson	New York
Albany	New York	Clyde	Ohio	Hunter	North Dakota
Alden	Michigan	Cody	Wyoming	Jackson	Mississippi
Alton	Illinois	Cortez	Colorado	Kyle	Texas
Amory	Mississippi	Dallas	Texas	Kent	England
Austin	Texas	Dalton	Georgia	Logan	Utah
Baden	Germany	Davis	California	Melbourne	Australia
Baldwin	Kansas	Denver	Colorado	Ogden	Utah
Beaumont	Texas	Diego (San)	California	Owen	Canada
Blair	Nebraska	Douglas	Wyoming	Phoenix	Arizona
Boston	Massachusetts	Durand	Wisconsin	Quincy	Massachusetts
Brandon	Canada	Edmond	Oklahoma	Riley	Kansas
Brighton	Colorado	Eugene	Oregon	Stamford	Connecticut
Camden	Maine, New Jersey	Flint	Michigan	Trenton	New Jersey
		Garrett	Indiana	Troy	New York
Camillus	New York	Gary	Indiana	Tyler	Texas
Carson	Nevada	Gibson	Illinois	Wyatt	Indiana
Charleston	West Virginia	Hamilton	Bermuda		

Top 100 Most Popular Names for 2004

Note: These are listed in order of popularity.

Girl Names

Emily	Jasmine	Paige	Gabriella
Emma	Sydney	Lily	Avery
Madison	Victoria	Faith	Marissa
Olivia	Ella	Zoe	Ariana
Hannah	Mia	Stephanie	Audrey
Abigail	Morgan	Jenna	Jada
Isabella	Julia	Andrea	Autumn
Ashley	Kaitlyn	Riley	Evelyn
Samantha	Rachel	Katelyn	Jocelyn
Elizabeth	Katherine	Angelina	Maya
Alexis	Megan	Kimberly	Arianna
Sarah	Alexandra	Madeline	Isabel
Grace	Jennifer	Mary	Amber
Alyssa	Destiny	Leah	Melanie
Sophia	Allison	Lillian	Diana
Lauren	Savannah	Michelle	Danielle
Brianna	Haley	Amanda	Sierra
Kayla	Mackenzie	Sara	Leslie
Natalie	Brooke	Sofia	Aaliyah
Anna	Maria	Jordan	Erin
Jessica	Nicole	Alexa	Amelia
Taylor	Makayla	Rebecca	Molly
Chloe	Trinity	Gabrielle	Claire
Hailey	Kylie	Caroline	Bailey
Ava	Kaylee	Vanessa	Melissa

Boy Names

Jacob	Zachary	Gavin	Ashton
Michael	Logan	Mason	Steven
Joshua	Jose	Aaron	Jeremiah
Matthew	Noah	Juan	Timothy
Ethan	Justin	Kyle	Chase
Andrew	Elijah	Charles	Devin
Daniel	Gabriel	Luis	Seth
William	Caleb	Adam	Jaden
Joseph	Kevin	Brian	Colin
Christopher	Austin	Aiden	Cody
Anthony	Robert	Eric	Landon
Ryan	Thomas	Jayden	Carter
Nicholas	Connor	Alex	Hayden
David	Evan	Bryan	Xavier
Alexander	Aidan	Sean	Wyatt
Tyler	Jack	Owen	Dominic
James	Luke	Lucas	Richard
John	Jordan	Nathaniel	Antonio
Dylan	Angel	Ian	Jesse
Nathan	Isaiah	Jesus	Blake
Jonathan	Isaac	Carlos	Sebastian
Brandon	Jason	Adrian	Miguel
Samuel	Jackson	Diego	Jake
Christian	Hunter	Julian	Alejandro
Benjamin	Cameron	Cole	Patrick

Most Popular Names by Year

Girl Names

2004 Emily, Emma, Madison, Olivia, Hannah, Abigail, Isabella, Ashley, Samantha, Elizabeth

2003 Emily, Emma, Madison, Hannah, Olivia, Abigail, Alexis, Ashley, Elizabeth, Samantha

2002 Emily, Madison, Hannah, Emma, Alexis, Ashley, Abigail, Sarah, Samantha, Olivia

2001 Emily, Madison, Hannah, Ashley, Alexis, Sarah, Samantha, Abigail, Elizabeth, Olivia

2000 Emily, Hannah, Madison, Ashley, Sarah, Alexis, Samantha, Jessica, Taylor, Elizabeth

1999 Emily, Hannah, Alexis, Sarah, Samantha, Ashley, Madison, Taylor, Jessica, Elizabeth

1998 Emily, Hannah, Samantha, Ashley, Sarah, Alexis, Taylor, Jessica, Madison, Elizabeth

1997 Emily, Jessica, Ashley, Sarah, Hannah, Samantha, Taylor, Alexis, Elizabeth, Madison

1996 Emily, Jessica, Ashley, Sarah, Samantha, Taylor, Hannah, Alexis, Rachel, Elizabeth

1995 Jessica, Ashley, Emily, Samantha, Sarah, Taylor, Hannah, Brittany, Amanda, Elizabeth

1994 Jessica, Ashley, Emily, Samantha, Sarah, Taylor, Brittany, Amanda, Elizabeth, Megan

1993 Jessica, Ashley, Sarah, Samantha, Emily, Brittany, Taylor, Amanda, Elizabeth, Stephanie

1992 Ashley, Jessica, Amanda, Brittany, Sarah, Samantha, Emily, Stephanie, Elizabeth, Megan

1991 Ashley, Jessica, Brittany, Amanda, Samantha, Sarah, Stephanie, Jennifer, Elizabeth, Emily

1990 Jessica, Ashley, Brittany, Amanda, Samantha, Sarah, Stephanie, Jennifer, Elizabeth, Lauren

Boy Names

2004 Jacob, Michael, Joshua, Matthew, Ethan, Andrew, Daniel, William, Joseph, Christopher

2003 Jacob, Michael, Joshua, Matthew, Andrew, Ethan, Joseph, Daniel, Christopher, Anthony

2002 Jacob, Michael, Joshua, Matthew, Ethan, Andrew, Joseph, Christopher, Nicholas, Daniel

2001 Jacob, Michael, Matthew, Joshua, Christopher, Nicholas, Andrew, Joseph, Daniel, William

2000 Jacob, Michael, Matthew, Joshua, Christopher, Nicholas, Andrew, Joseph, Daniel, Tyler

1999 Jacob, Michael, Matthew, Joshua, Christopher, Nicholas, Andrew, Joseph, Tyler, Daniel

1998 Michael, Jacob, Matthew, Joshua, Christopher, Nicholas, Brandon, Tyler, Andrew, Austin

1997 Michael, Jacob, Matthew, Christopher, Joshua, Nicholas, Brandon, Andrew, Austin, Tyler

1996 Michael, Matthew, Jacob, Christopher, Joshua, Nicholas, Tyler, Brandon, Austin, Andrew

1995 Michael, Matthew, Christopher, Jacob, Joshua, Nicholas, Tyler, Brandon, Daniel, Austin

1994 Michael, Christopher, Matthew, Joshua, Tyler, Brandon, Jacob, Daniel, Nicholas, Andrew

1993 Michael, Christopher, Matthew, Joshua, Tyler, Brandon, Daniel, Nicholas, Jacob, Andrew

1992 Michael, Christopher, Matthew, Joshua, Andrew, Brandon, Daniel, Tyler, James, David

1991 Michael, Christopher, Matthew, Joshua, Andrew, Daniel, James, David, Joseph, John

1990 Michael, Christopher, Matthew, Joshua, Daniel, David, Andrew, James, Justin, Joseph

Most Popular Names by Decade

Girl Names

2000s	Emily, Madison, Hannah, Emma, Ashley, Alexis, Samantha, Sarah, Abigail, Olivia
1990s	Jessica, Ashley, Emily, Samantha, Sarah, Amanda, Brittany, Elizabeth, Taylor, Megan
1980s	Jessica, Jennifer, Amanda, Ashley, Sarah, Stephanie, Melissa, Nicole, Elizabeth, Heather
1970s	Jennifer, Amy, Melissa, Michelle, Kimberly, Lisa, Angela, Heather, Stephanie, Nicole
1960s	Lisa, Mary, Susan, Karen, Kimberly, Patricia, Linda, Donna, Michelle, Cynthia
1950s	Mary, Linda, Patricia, Susan, Deborah, Barbara, Debra, Karen, Nancy, Donna
1940s	Mary, Linda, Barbara, Patricia, Carol, Sandra, Nancy, Sharon, Judith, Susan
1930s	Mary, Betty, Barbara, Shirley, Patricia, Dorothy, Joan, Margaret, Nancy, Helen
1920s	Mary, Dorothy, Helen, Betty, Margaret, Ruth, Virginia, Doris, Mildred, Frances
1910s	Mary, Helen, Dorothy, Margaret, Ruth, Mildred, Anna, Elizabeth, Frances, Virginia
1900s	Mary, Helen, Margaret, Anna, Ruth, Elizabeth, Dorothy, Marie, Florence, Mildred
1890s	Mary, Anna, Margaret, Helen, Elizabeth, Ruth, Florence, Ethel, Emma, Marie
1880s	Mary, Anna, Emma, Elizabeth, Margaret, Minnie, Ida, Bertha, Clara, Alice

Boy Names

2000s	Jacob, Michael, Joshua, Matthew, Andrew, Christopher, Joseph, Nicholas, Daniel, William
1990s	Michael, Christopher, Matthew, Joshua, Jacob, Nicholas, Andrew, Daniel, Tyler, Joseph
1980s	Michael, Christopher, Matthew, Joshua, David, James, Daniel, Robert, John, Joseph
1970s	Michael, Christopher, Jason, David, James, John, Robert, Brian, William, Matthew
1960s	Michael, David, John, James, Robert, Mark, William, Richard, Thomas, Jeffrey
1950s	James, Michael, Robert, John, David, William, Richard, Thomas, Mark, Charles
1940s	James, Robert, John, William, Richard, David, Charles, Thomas, Michael, Ronald
1930s	Robert, James, John, William, Richard, Charles, Donald, George, Thomas, Joseph
1920s	Robert, John, James, William, Charles, George, Joseph, Richard, Edward, Donald
1910s	John, William, James, Robert, Joseph, George, Charles, Edward, Frank, Thomas
1900s	John, William, James, George, Charles, Robert, Joseph, Frank, Edward, Thomas
1890s	John, William, James, George, Charles, Joseph, Frank, Robert, Edward, Henry
1880s	John, William, James, George, Frank, Joseph, Henry, Robert, Thomas

Cultural Cache

Giving your baby a name that reflects your cultural heritage puts the child in touch with his or her roots and is a wonderful way to proclaim your identity and honor your family's tradition.

This chapter gives you an overview of names that cross cultural lines. Whether you're honoring your own heritage or looking to embrace another, the lists in this chapter will help you choose the name that best reflects your child's identity.

African/African American Names

Girl Names

Aba	Habika	Latanya	Quanda	Talisha
Abeni	Halima	Lateefah	Rashida	Tamika
Abiba	Isoke	Latisha	Raziya	Tamira
Afric	Jariah	Latoya	Safiya	Tamyra
Aissa	Jendayi	Limber	Saidah	Tandice
Anada	Kadija	Maizah	Salihah	Tanginika
Arziki	Kambo	Malika	Shandi	Taniel
Baako	Kanene	Mandisa	Shandra	Tanisha
Beyonce	Kapera	Marjani	Shantell	Tapanga
Caimile	Karimah	Mekell	Shaquana	Tariana
Catava	Kasinda	Moesha	Shasmecka	Temima
Chipo	Keisha	Monisha	Shateque	Timberly
Corentine	Kendis	Muncel	Sibongile	Tyrell
Dericia	Kesia	Nabelung	Sidone	Tyronica
Ebere	Lakeesha	Nakeisha	Sitembile	Yetty
Faizah	Lakin	Narkeasha	Sukutai	Zabia
Femi	Lanelle	Nichelle	Takiyah	Zalika
Fola	Laqueta	Niesha	Tale	Zarina
Gaynelle	Laquinta	Pemba	Talisa	Zina

Boy Names

Africa	Essien	Lakin	Sulaiman	Trory
Aitan	Faraji	Mablevi	Tabansi	Tyrell
Chata	Ibeamaka	Mykelti	Tabari	Uba
Chiamaka	Jabari	Nabulung	Tamarr	Ulan
Chike	Jamar	Naeem	Tameron	Vashon
Dakarai	Jayvyn	Obiajulu	Taurean	Yobachi
Deion	Jelani	Razi	Tavarius	Zabia
Denzel	Jevonte	Runako	Tavon	Zaid
Deshawn	Juma	Roshaun	Terrel	Zareb
Dewayne	Kendis	Salim	Tevin	Zeshawn
Duante	Khalon	Shaquille		

Chinese Names

Girl Names

Ah lam	Chyou	Hua	Lien	Mingmei
An	Da xia	Hui fang	Ling	Sun
Bo	Fang	Jin	Mee/Mei	Tao
Chu hua	Fang hua	Jing wei	Mei xing	Xiao
Chow	Genji	Jun	Mei zhen	Yin
Chun	Guanyin	Lian		

Boy Names

An	Deshi	Jing	Quon	Wen
Bo	Gan	Kong	Shen	Yu
Chan	Ho	Li	Shing	Yuan
Chen	Hsin	Liang	Sun	Zhong
Chung	Huang fu	Manchu	Tung	
Cong	Jin	Ming	Wang	

English/Scottish/Welsh Names

Girl Names

Addison	Dale	Jemma	Ona	Stockard
Afton	Dana	Jolene	Osma	Sybella
Aileen	Deisy	Karsen	Paisley	Taci
Alden	Delsie	Kendra	Paiton	Taite
Alvina	Dixie	Kimber	Patia	Tanner
Arden	Edie	Kirby	Piper	Tatum
Arleigh	Effie	Landon	Primrose	Taya
Artis	Ellen	Laury	Quinn	Tegan
Ashlin	Elspeth	Leeza	Ragine	Tinble
Berlynn	Eppie	Leslie	Rayna	Torri
Berti	Faren	Liana	Reggi	Twyla
Binney	Floris	Lolly	Remington	Tyne
Blair	Georgie	Lynell	Rennie	Udele
Blythe	Gilda	Mada	Romy	Vina
Bonnie	Guinevere	Maggie	Rowan	Waverly
Briton	Haiden	Maretta	Rue	Weslee
Bronwyn	Halsey	Maribel	Sable	Willie
Bryce	Haven	Marley	Sada	Winifred
Cady	Henna	Marlo	Sebrina	Yudelle
Charla	Hollyn	May	Sela	Zeta
Chenelle	Iolanthe	Meredith	Sheldon	
Christal	Jamey	Minta	Stacia	
Clare	Janeth	Nara	Starleen	
Corliss	Jannie	Odella	Starr	

Boy Names

Adney	Brigham	Ellison	Kelton	Radbert
Ahearn	Buckley	Emerson	Kenley	Raine
Alcott	Burleigh	Ewing	Kennan	Rance
Aldrich	Burris	Falkner	Kidd	Rayburn
Alford	Byrd	Farnell	Kirkland	Reed
Alistair	Calen	Farold	Kolton	Rhys
Angus	Calvert	Fielding	Kyler	Rigby
Arledge	Carl	Fife	Laird	Rochester
Arundel	Carlton	Fiske	Lathrop	Rockwell
Ashford	Case	Ford	Lave	Rollie
Atley	Chance	Frey	Lawford	Ross
Atwell	Chick	Fuller	Layton	Royce
Audric	Churchill	Garen	Lewin	Rudyard
Ayers	Clifton	Garth	Lindell	Saxon
Bancroft	Colby	Geary	Locke	Shaw
Barker	Colter	Germain	Manley	Sidwell
Barnes	Corwin	Gil	March	Snowden
Barric	Crandall	Grant	Massey	Spalding
Bartram	Dalbert	Gresham	Mayhew	Storm
Bayard	Dallan	Hagley	Mick	Stuart
Beacher	Darby	Halbert	Miller	Swain
Beck	Davis	Halsey	Mitchell	Tate
Bell	Dean	Hamish	Nevin	Thorley
Birkitt	Denham	Hammet	Niles	Tilford
Bishop	Derward	Hedley	Norwood	Troy
Blake	Diamond	Hubie	Ogden	Tucker
Booker	Draper	Hurst	Onslow	Vance
Boyd	Drummond	Hutton	Orrick	Wade
Braden	Dunley	Ives	Paden	Walker
Bardshaw	Dyson	Jagger	Palmer	Ward
Bowen	Ebner	Jarett	Pelton	Wesley
Bramwell	Edward	Jeremy	Penn	Will
Brayden	Egerton	Judson	Pierson	Zane

French Names

Girl Names

Alair	Charlotte	Françoise	Liana	Pippi
Amarante	Cherelle	Frederique	Lisette	Rayna
Amélie	Colette	Gaby	Lyla	Remi
Ami	Daryl	Geneva	Mallory	Rue
Ariane	Déja	Genevieve	Manon	Sarotte
Babette	Desi	Gigi	Mardi	Sharice
Bedelia	Dominique	Helene	Marguerite	Solange
Berneta	Elita	Isabeau	Merane	Sorrel
Blaise	Eloise	Ivette	Miette	Susette
Brie	Emmaline	Jae	Mignon	Sylvie
Brienne	Etoile	Jardena	Monique	Talia
Cami	Evonne	Jenay	Noelle	Tayce
Camille	Faye	Joelle	Oralia	Tempest
Caron	Felicity	Juliet	Orane	Valerie
Chantal	Fontanna	Lacy	Page	Virginie

Boy Names

Alain	Chante	Garrison	Maxime	Simeon
Alaire	Chase	Geraud	Montrell	Sully
Amando	Clark	Giles	Neville	Telford
Andre	Clement	Gregoire	Norris	Thayer
Antoine	Cornell	Hackett	Olivier	Thibault
Aramis	Coyne	Harbin	Pascal	Trent
Averill	Darcy	Herve	Pembroke	Troy
Beau	Dax	Holland	Phillippe	Vardon
Belden	Delano	Jacques	Pierre	Verrill
Benoit	Demont	Jules	Prewitt	Victoir
Bernard	Destin	Lamar	Raynard	Wyatt
Boden	Donatien	Lance	Renny	Yves
Boone	Edouard	Laurent	Ross	
Borden	Fabron	Luc	Saber	
Cassius	Ferrand	Marc	Sargent	
Chaney	Gage	Mason	Sennett	

German Names

Girl Names

Adalia	Callan	Faiga	Lorelei	Richelle
Adelina	Carleigh	Frederika	Lorraine	Roderica
Adolfina	Chay	Frieda	Louise	Senta
Agneta	Chloris	Gerda	Madison	Serilda
Alberta	Clay	Giselle	Mallory	Ula
Amara	Dagmar	Gretchen	Marlene	Ulrika
Antje	Dagna	Heidi	Mathilda	Ulva
Arabelle	Dame	Henrietta	Minna	Unna
Aubrey	Ebba	Idonia	Morgen	Uta
Ava	Edwina	Ilse	Nixie	Viveka
Berit	Emily	Jarvia	Norberta	Wanda
Bernadette	Emma	Jenell	Odelia	Zelda
Berta	Erika	Leyna	Orlantha	Zelinda
Bluma	Ernestine	Liese	Pepin	Zelma

Boy Names

Abelard	Brandeis	Fremont	Leopold	Ritter
Adelfried	Burke	Garin	Loring	Roderick
Adelino	Conrad	Gerard	Louis/Lewis	Rudolph
Adelmo	Derek	Gilbert	Luther	Stein
Adler	Dieter	Hackett	Madison	Strom
Adolph	Dutch	Hahn	Manfred	Tab
Alaric	Eberhard	Heller	Merrill	Ulbrecht
Albert	Eldwin	Herman	Nevin	Varick
Alger	Ellery	Imre	Norbert	Verner
Arnold	Emery	Johann	Odell	Vilhelm
Baldwin	Emil	Kellen	Otis	Warner
Barend	Ernest	Kiefer	Penrod	Yale
Bergen	Ferdinand	Lamar	Raynard	Yohann
Blaz	Frederick	Lance	Redmond	Zelig

Greek Names

Girl Names

Adara	Charis	Galen	Maris	Saba
Agnes	Cleo	Gemini	Medora	Sibley
Alessa	Colette	Hera	Melinda	Sofi
Alexandra	Corrina	Hermione	Nyssa	Stefania
Amari	Damaris	Hilary	Ola	Sula
Andrea	Daphne	Iona	Olympia	Tahlia
Astra	Daria	Irene	Ophelia	Tassos
Athena	Delfina	Jacey	Pallas	Thaddea
Basha	Demetria	Kairos	Pandora	Triana
Beryl	Dionne	Kalliope	Peri	Trina
Calla	Elana	Kyra	Petra	Ursula
Callista	Elisha	Leanore	Phillippa	Vanna
Carissa	Eudora	Lydia	Phoebe	Xena
Casandra	Fantasia	Magdalen	Rita	Yolie

Boy Names

Adonis	Cyril	Hermes	Nicholas	Talos
Ajax	Damen	Iakobos	Orion	Thanos
Alec	Darius	Icarus	Otis	Tibalt
Apollo	Deion	Isaak	Panos	Titus
Ares	Elias	Jason	Paris	Topher
Arion	Erastus	Julius	Pello	Ulysses
Aristo	Eros	Kit	Petar	Urian
Avram	Euclid	Kostas	Rastus	Vassos
Basil	Feodore	Kyros	Rouvin	Xenos
Carsten	Gale	Lazarus	Sandro	Yanni
Christos	Giles	Lex	Stavros	Yorick
Cohn	Gregorios	Makis	Stefanos	Zenon
Colson	Hamon	Maron	Strom	Zeus
Corydon	Hector	Myron	Tad	Zorba

Hawaiian Names

Girl Names

Akela	Haimi	Kamea	Lani	Noelani
Alana	Haleigha	Kane	Lanikai	Okelani
Aloha	Iolana	Keandra	Lokelani	Oliana
Alohi	Kai	Keilana	Makani	Peni
Anani	Kaili	Kekona	Malu	Roselani
Aloani	Kalama	Kiana	Mily	Ululani
Aulii	Kalea	Kiele	Nalani	Wanika
Edena	Kalia	Lana		

Boy Names

Akamu	Kaili	Keahi	Liko	Meka
Analu	Kalani	Keanu	Loe	Moke
Aulii	Kalei	Kelii	Maik	Nalani
Bane	Kale	Keon	Makaio	Oke
Havika	Kane	Kimo	Makan	Palani
Kahoku	Kanoa	Konala	Malo	Pekelo
Kai	Kapono	Leilani	Mauli	

Hispanic/Latino Names

Girl Names

Abril	Fe	Karmen	Osana	Ursulina
Adella	Flor	Kasandra	Paquita	Usoa
Aidia	Friera	Katia	Pepita	Valentina
Beatriz	Gitana	Lara	Pia	Veta
Benita	Gotzone	Leya	Querida	Vina
Brigida	Gustava	Linda	Quinta	Xalbadora
Camila	Hermosa	Lupe	Regina	Xaviera
Carisa	Honoria	Maitea	Ria	Xevera
Carola	Hortensia	Marietta	Rocio	Yadra
Daria	Ines/Inez	Mercedes	Sabana	Yoana
Devera	Irene	Neiva	Sancia	Yolanda
Dulce	Isabel	Nina	Seina	Zanetta
Elena	Jacinta	Noemi	Teodora	Zita
Emilie	Jimena	Olinda	Terciero	Zurine
Enriqua	Joaquina	Ora	Trella	

Boy Names

Abran	Eloy	Ivan	Oliverio	Tabor
Adan	Fanuco	Javier	Orlan	Timo
Adriano	Felix	Jerrold	Oro	Turi
Beltran	Fraco	Joaquin	Pablo	Ulises
Berto	Gaspar	Kemen	Pedro	Urbano
Carlos	Gervasio	Lazaro	Ponce	Veto
Casimiro	Guido	Leonel	Rafael	Vicente
Cesar	Hector	Lisandro	Ramon	Vidal
Dario	Hilario	Mario	Reyes	Xabat
Delmar	Hugo	Monte	Salvadore	Xalvador
Donatello	Iago	Neron	Senon	Yago
Edgardo	Ignado	Nicolas	Stefano	Zacarias
Efraim				

Irish Names

Girl Names

Adan	Doreen	Honour/Honoria	Maeve	Shae
Ailey	Duvessa	Ida	Moira	Shanessa
Aislinn	Eileen	Ilene	Muriel	Shannon
Akaisha	Ennis	Ina	Nelda	Sheena
Brea	Eveleen	Jana	Noreen	Sinead
Breen	Fallon	Kacey	Nuala	Tara/Tari/Taryn
Brenna	Farran	Kallie	Ohnicio	Teagan
Bridget	Fiona	Keara	Oma	Treasa/Treise
Cacey	Gale	Kelsey	Orla	Unity
Caitlynn	Gladys	Kerri	Padraigin	Uny
Cassidy	Glenna	Leena	Richael	Vevila
Ciannait	Hiolair	Leila	Rory	Vevina
Ciar	Hisolda	Liadan	Ryann	Zaira
Darnell				

Boy Names

Abban	Daire	Haley	Moriarty	Quinn
Adare	Daman	Hurley	Murphy	Rearden
Aeary	Darby	Inerney	Neilan	Rian
Aiden	Devlin	Inis/Innes	Nevan	Roark
Bain	Eman	Jarlath	Nolyn	Shamus
Beacan	Evin	Justin	Odell	Shane
Blaine	Ewan	Loaghaire	Odran	Shea
Braden	Fallon	Kagan	Ossian	Sheridon
Cahir	Farren	Kean	Padric	Teague
Carey	Finnegan	Laughlin	Peyton	Tiernan
Carrick	Galvin	Lorcan	Pierce	Torrence
Colm	Gannon	Liam	Quigley	Uistean
Conroy	Griffin	Maclean	Quinlan	Ward
Cormack	Hagan	Miles		

Italian Names

Girl Names

Alessandra	Caterina	Francesca	Maria	Serafina
Angela	Colomba	Gema	Marta	Silvia
Anna	Concetta	Ghita	Matilde	Simona
Artemia	Cornelia	Gioia	Maura	Tamara
Aryana	Dalia	Giovanna	Mia	Teresa
Benedetta	Delinda	Gisella	Mila	Valeria
Berenice	Diana	Ines	Miriam	Vedette
Bianca	Donatella	Jovanna	Nicola	Venecia
Candida	Elena	Justina	Oriana	Vera
Carmela	Emilia	Karah	Paola	Zola
Carmelina	Enza	Lia	Pia	
Carola	Ester	Lilla	Priscilla	
Capri	Eva	Lucia	Renata	
Caprice	Felicita	Luisa	Rita	
Carla	Franca	Marcella	Rosa	

Boy Names

Aldo	Dante	Genovese	Marco	Santo
Angelo	Dino	Geraldo	Milan	Sergio
Antonio	Domenico	Giancarlo	Napoleon	Siro
Armando	Donato	Gianni	Nicolo	Taddeo
Arturo	Edoardo	Gino	Nino	Tazio
Bartolomeo	Emanuele	Giorgio	Oscar	Tulio
Benito	Enrico	Guido	Otello	Uberto
Boris	Ermanno	Indro	Paco	Ugo
Bruno	Fabiano	Ivo	Paolo	Vito
Carlo	Federico	Jacopo	Pietro	Walter
Carmine	Flavio	Lanz	Raimondo	
Claudio	Francesco	Lazaro	Raul	
Cola	Franco	Leonardo	Renardo	
Corrado	Furio	Luca	Ruggerio	
Cristoforo	Gaspare	Luigi	Salvatore	

Japanese Names

Girl Names

Ai	Hoshi	Kumiko	Miyuki	Sakura	Tera
Aiko	Ima	Kuri	Morie	Sasa	Tetsu
Akako	Ishi	Kyoko	Mura	Sato	Toki
Aki	Iva	Leiko	Nami	Sawa	Tomi
Akina	Jin	Machi	Naomi	Sayo	Tora
Amaya	Kaede	Mai	Nara	Seki	Tori
Aneko	Kagami	Maiko	Nishi	Sen	Toshi
Asa	Kaiya	Mari	Nori	Shika	Uma
Ayame	Kameko	Mariko	Noriko	Shina	Umeko
Chika	Kami	Masago	Nozomi	Sorano	Usagi
Chiyo	Kei	Masako	Nyoko	Suki	Uta
Cho	Keiko	Matsuko	Rai	Sumi	Wakana
Dai	Kiaria	Michi	Raku	Suzu	Washi
Etsu	Kiku	Midori	Rei	Taka	Yasu
Gen	Kimi	Mieko	Ren	Takara	Yayoi
Gin	Kioko	Mika	Rini	Taki	Yei
Hachi	Kita	Miki	Rui	Tamaka	Yoko
Hama	Kiwa	Mina	Ruri	Tamiko	Yoi
Hana	Kohana	Mine	Ryo	Tanaka	Yumi
Hanako	Koko	Mio	Sachi	Tani	Yuri
Haya	Koto	Miwa	Sada	Taree	
Hisa	Kuma	Miya	Saki	Tazu	

Boy Names

Akemi	Hoshi	Kaori	Manzo	Naoko	Taro
Akira	Jiro	Kazuo	Mareo	Raidon	Tomi
Benjiro	Jo	Keitaro	Maro	Renjiro	Tomo
Botan	Joben	Ken	Masahiro	Ringo	Toyo
Danno	Joji	Kentaro	Masao	Ronin	Udo
Fujita	Jomei	Kin	Masato	Saburo	Yasashiku
Goro	Jun	Kioshi	Michio	Samuru	Yasuo
Haru	Kado	Kisho	Miki	Sen	Yogi
Hideaki	Kana	Kiyoshi	Minoru	Shiro	Yoshi
Hiromasa	Kanaye	Makoto	Montaro	Takeo	Yukio
Hiroshi	Kane	Mamoru	Morio	Tani	Zen
Hisoka					

Native American Names

Girl Names

Abey	Donoma	Kay	Nuttah	Talulah
Adoette	Dyani	Kwanita	Odina	Tiponi
Alameda	Elu	Leotie	Olathe	Tiva
Alawa	Enola	Lulu	Onida	Tuwa
Aleshanee	Eyota	Luyu	Opa	Una
Amitola	Fala	Magena	Pelipa	Unega
Aponi	Galilahi	Mai	Peta	Urika
Awendela	Genesee	Migisi	Poloma	Usdi
Ayita	Honovi	Muna	Quanah	Utina
Bena	Hurit	Nadie	Sihu	Wachiwi
Bly	Huyana	Nascha	Sokanon	Weayaya
Chapawee	Ituha	Nata	Suleta	Wyanet
Chenoa	Kachina	Nova	Tablita	Zonta
Doli	Kai	Nuna	Tadewi	

Boy Names

Adahy	Elsu	Kwahu	Nigan	Tawa
Ahanu	Etu	Lallo	Nikan	Tokala
Alo	Gad	Langundo	Nitis	Tyee
Ashkii	Gosheven	Lenno	Nodin	Viho
Atohi	Hania	Lusio	Ogima	Waban
Bemossed	Hassun	Mahkah	Paco	Wahkan
Bidziil	Helaku	Maska	Patwin	Wamblee
Chayton	Holata	Mikasi	Rowtag	Wapi
Chogan	Huritt	Misu	Sakima	Wicasa
Cochise	Illanipi	Mohe	Shilah	Wuliton
Dakotah	Kele	Mojag	Tadi	Wynono
Dichali	Keme	Nahele	Taima	Yahto
Dyami	Kitchi	Napayshni	Takoda	Yas
Elan	Koi	Nashoba	Tatonga	Yuma

Persian Names

Girl Names

Alea	Esther	Jessamine	Mehri	Peri
Armani	Fila	Khina	Melika	Roxana
Ayesha	Gatha	Kira	Melody	Sadira
Aylin	Gita	Ladan	Mila	Soraya
Azarin	Haleh	Laleh	Mina	Souzan
Bibiyana	Hawa	Leila	Mitra	Taraneh
Bita	Hester	Lila	Nadia	Yasmin
Cyra	Hestia	Mahubeh	Nahid	Zenda
Dana	Jaleh	Manoush	Narda	Zohreh
Donya	Jasmin	Marjan	Pari	

Boy Names

Aban	Bahram	Fazel	Kamal	Rasheed
Abbas	Behdad	Feroz	Karim	Reza
Adar	Bijan	Firouz	Kasper	Rohan
Ahmad	Borna	Ghadir	Kaveh	Said
Akbar	Cass	Habib	Kian	Sami
Amir	Cyrus	Hadi	Masoud	Shah
Aram	Dareh	Hafez	Mehdi	Sohrab
Arash	Davood	Hamid	Mohsen	Tabor
Arman	Ebi	Hassan	Nard	Taher
Asad	Eskander	Jafar	Nasim	Xerxes
Atash	Faraz	Jalal	Omid	Zakaria
Azad	Farhad	Javed	Rami	

Russian/Eastern European Names

Girl Names

Alka	Felicia	Lacey	Oksana	Valeska
Ana	Feodora	Lara	Olesia	Vania
Anastasia	Filipina	Larissa	Olga	Vanka
Anezka	Galina	Lida	Olien	Vanya
Aniela	Helina	Lilia	Raisa	Vera
Anstice	Ivanna	Luba	Rasien	Verushka
Avel	Jadwiga	Marian	Rayna/Reina	Viera
Basha	Jelena	Marina	Ryba	Yalena
Beta	Jolanta	Marinka	Sasha	Yeva
Bohdana	Julya	Marjeta	Sashenka	Yuri
Celestyn	Kamila	Mila	Savina	Zasha
Cyzarine	Karel/Karol	Nadezda	Sonia/Sonya	Zdenka
Danuta	Kate/Katerina	Natalya	Svetlana	Zelenka
Dusana	Kisa	Natasha	Talia	Zilya
Ekaterina	Kiska	Natasia	Tanya	Zofia
Eliska	Klementyna	Nika	Tesia	Zotia
Ewa	Kludia	Nikita	Tola	Zuzana

Boy Names

Akim	Erek	Kazimir	Nelek	Tanek
Anstice	Evzen	Kirill	Nikita	Tomas
Antoni	Filip	Kliment	Oldrich	Uri/Uriah/Urie
Aurek	Fyodor	Konrad	Oleg	Ustin
Avel	Gavrie	Konstantin	Osip	Vadim
Bazyli	Gavril	Kostya	Pavel	Vanya
Bedrich	Gerik	Lesta	Radek	Vasily
Boris	Ilya	Lev	Rurik	Viktor
Damek	Ivan	Maksim	Sacha	Vilem
Dana	Jakub	Marcin	Semyon	Walenty
Demyan	Jarek	Mikhail	Sevastian	Yakov
Dobry	Josef	Milos	Stefan	Yerik
Dusan	Karel	Naum	Strom	Yevgeni
Egor	Kaspar			

Scandinavian Names

Girl Names

Abbellonna	Dorothea	Ingrid	Mia	Susanna
Agata	Ebba	Irena	Monika	Thora
Agneta	Elke	Janna/Jesine	Nissa	Tilda
Amalia	Erika	Jette	Oda	Tova/Tove
Anke	Eva	Johanna/Jonna	Ola	Ulla
Anneliese	Freja	Karen/Karin	Petrine	Ulrika
Barbro	Freya	Karita	Petronilla	Ulrike
Beatrix	Gala	Katrine	Quenby	Unn
Birgit/Birgitta/ Birgitte	Gisela	Klara	Rae	Vanja
	Greet/Gret/Greta	Laila	Rakel	Vega
Brynhild	Guro	Lena/Lene	Rebekka	Vera
Carina	Hanna	Lisabet/Lisbet	Runa	Vilhemina/ Wilhelmina
Celia	Hedda/Hedvig	Louisa/Lovisa	Sanna	
Charlotta	Helena	Marcy	Sibella/Sibilla/ Sibylla	Viveka
Cornelia	Hildegard	Margareta/Margit		Ylwa
Dagmar	Idonea/Idony/ Idun	Matilda/Matilde	Sigrid	
Dania			Sonja/Sonje	

Boy Names

Aksel	Dyre	Ingmar	Niklaus	Tait
Amund	Edvard	Ivar	Odin	Thorwald
Anders	Egil	Jakob	Olaf/Olav/Olof	Torgeir
Anton	Emil	Jorgen	Ove	Ulf
Balder	Erik	Josef	Pal/Pavel	Ulrik
Benedikt	Filip	Karl	Peder/Pieter	Urban
Bjorn	Fiske	Konstantin	Per	Uwe
Borg	Fredrik	Kristoffer	Quinby	Valdermar
Canute	Frans	Larson	Ragnar	Verner
Carolus	Gamel	Ludvig	Rikard	Viktor
Claus	Garth	Maarten	Roth	Von
Cornelis	Georg	Matheu	Rurik	Waldemar
Dag	Greger/Gregor	Michiel	Sigmund	Werner
Davin	Haakon	Morten	Soren	Willem
Diederik/Dierk/ Dirk	Hendrik	Natanael	Stefan	
	Igor	Nels	Sven	

Hunting Through History

Names taken from ancient times—Persian, Norse, Egyptian, Sanskrit, or Romany/Gypsy—can carry a lot of weight and history. And who knows, maybe naming your baby after a mythological character or pioneer may up the ante for his or her greatness!

If your penchant is toward the more modern, we offer choices from the Old West for your modern-day cowboy or cowgirl.

Perhaps your child was born on a day that holds significance. Why not name him or her after that day, time, month, or week? We cover a lot of history in this chapter.

Ancient Names

Girl Names

Name	Origin	Name	Origin	Name	Origin
Abtin	Persian	Frigg	Old Norse	Nebta	Egyptian
Ahmose	Egyptian	Gerd	Old Norse	Neferu	Egyptian
Anis	Romany/Gypsy	Gita	Sanskrit	Peneli	Romany/Gypsy
Ardeshir	Persian	Grid	Old Norse	Priya	Sanskrit
Aria	Persian	Gudrun	Old Norse	Rennefer	Egyptian
Aruna	Sanskrit	Heidrun	Old Norse	Saga	Old Norse
Asha	Sanskrit	Hekenu	Egyptian	Senen	Egyptian
Bameket	Egyptian	Indira	Sanskrit	Sif	Old Norse
Deva	Sanskrit	Isis	Egyptian	Signy	Old Norse
Djab	Egyptian	Jaya	Sanskrit	Sigrun	Old Norse
Eir	Old Norse	Kasra	Persian	Siv	Old Norse
Emmanaia	Romany/Gypsy	Khety	Egyptian	Talaitha	Romany/Gypsy
Everilda	Romany/Gypsy	Leela	Sanskrit	Tetisheri	Egyptian
Freya	Old Norse	Meena	Sanskrit	Valkryie	Old Norse

Boy Names

Name	Origin	Name	Origin	Name	Origin
Abtin	Persian	Gunnar	Old Norse	Prakash	Sanskrit
Alvis	Old Norse	Hormoz	Persian	Rahotep	Egyptian
Ambrosius	Romany/Gypsy	Huni	Egyptian	Rama	Sanskrit
Ankhhaf	Egyptian	Imhotep	Egyptian	Ranjit	Sanskrit
Ardalan	Persian	Ing	Old Norse	Sanjay	Sanskrit
Balder	Old Norse	Jarl	Old Norse	Sigurd	Old Norse
Banefre	Egyptian	Krishna	Sanskrit	Sindri	Old Norse
Behrooz	Persian	Kourosh	Persian	Sohrab	Persian
Caspar	Romany/Gypsy	Kumar	Sanskrit	Tem	Romany/Gypsy
Cyrus	Persian	Lakshmi	Sanskrit	Thor	Old Norse
Darius	Persian	Loki	Old Norse	Tobar	Romany/Gypsy
Dipak	Sanskrit	Mahesh	Sanskrit	Tyr	Old Norse
Djau	Egyptian	Nataraj	Sanskrit	Unas	Egyptian
Emaus	Romany/Gypsy	Nedes	Egyptian	Vidar	Old Norse
Frey	Old Norse	Njord	Old Norse	Volund	Old Norse
Freyr	Old Norse	Odin	Old Norse	Xerxes	Persian
Gagino	Romany/Gypsy	Othi	Romany/Gypsy	Zindel	Romany/Gypsy
Gandale	Old Norse	Persepolis	Persian		

Names from Mythology/Legends

Girl Names

Acantha	Cassandra	Guinevere	Polyhymnia
Aegle	Ceridwen	Iblis	Rhiannon
Aella	Clarine	Isolde	Tanith
Agaue	Clio	Lachesis	Tara
Aglaia	Clotho	Lynelle	Terpsichore
Agrona	Cotovatre	Melpomene	Thalia
Atropos	Diana	Mnemosyne	Tryamon
Avalon	Dido	Nimaine/Nineve	Urania
Bedegrayne	Erato	Ourania	Venus
Branwen	Euphrosyne	Pandora	Viviane
Calliope	Euterpe	Phoebe	Ysolde

Boy Names

Ahura Mazda	Cavalon	Lancelot	Rion
Aleyn	Charon	Leander	Rivalen
Arthur (King)	Coeus	Marrock	Robin (Hood)
Atlas	Dagonet	Merlin	Ryons
Awarnach	Damon	Octha	Uther
Balduf	Dionysus	Odysseus	Valkyrie
Beowulf	Drystan	Parsifal	Vidar
Blaise	Enki	Pelleas	Vortigem
Breri	Frollo	Percival	Zephyr
Cabal	Hermes	Prometheus	

Calendar-Based Names

Girl Names

Aba	Aviva	Kesa	Sorley
Abmaba	Brook	Koleyn	Spring
Aki	Cerelia	Kudio	Summer
Akiyama	Chyou	Kwaku	Verda
Akosua	Easter	Kwashi	Vernice
Ajua	Ekua	Laverne	Wednesday
April	Epua	May	Welya
Arbor	February	June	Winter
Autumn	Jesen	Season	Zima

Boy Names

Abeeku	Dack	Koffi	Sarngin
Arley	Daren	Koleyn	Somerton
Arslan	Edan	Kwamin	Theron
August	Equinox	Kwaku	Ver
Averil	Estio	Kwau	Verano
Badar	Hiemo	Leo	Wen
Botan	Hurley	Noel	Yule
Cam	Jarek	Quillan	Zeeman
Cerella	Kell	Ramadan	Zenos
Chand	Kevat		

Historical Firsts

Girl Names

Historical Name	Year	Noteworthiness
Anne Bradstreet	1650	First female American writer to be published
Annie Moore	1892	First immigrant to pass through Ellis Island
Antonia Novello	1990	First female U.S. Surgeon General
Arabella Mansfield	1869	First woman lawyer
Barbara Walters	1976	First female newscaster on network TV
Diane Crump	1970	First female jockey to ride in the Kentucky Derby
Emily Warner	1973	First female commercial airline pilot
Geraldine Ferraro	1984	First female vice presidential nominee in a major party (Democrat)
Gertrude Ederle	1926	First woman to swim the English Channel
Henrietta Johnson	1707	First female professional American artist
Janet Guthrie	1986	First woman to race in the Indy 500
Jacqueline Means	1977	First woman to become an ordained Episcopal priest
Mary Kies	1809	First woman issued a U.S. patent
Nellie Tayloe Ross	1925	First female U.S. governor (Wyoming)
Sally Jean Priesand	1972	First female ordained rabbi in the United States
Sandra Day O'Connor	1981	First female Supreme Court Justice
Susanna Medora Salter	1887	First female elected mayor in the United States
Tenley Albright	1953	First American to win Women's World Figure Skating Championship
Victoria Woodhull	1872	First woman to run for U.S. president
Wallis Simpson	1936	First *Time* magazine "Woman of the Year"
Wilma Mankiller	1983	First woman to lead a major Native American tribe (Cherokee)

Boy Names

Historical Name	Year	Noteworthiness
Al Jolson	1927	Played lead role in first talking picture, *The Jazz Singer*
Alan Shepard Jr.	1961	First American in space
Benjamin Franklin	1753	First U.S. postmaster
Chadwick Haheo Rowan	1993	First non-Japanese sumo wrestler
Charles Lindbergh	1927	First man to fly solo across the Atlantic Ocean
Chuck Yaeger	1947	First person to break the sound barrier
Christiaan Barnard	1967	Performed first human heart transplant
David Farragut	1866	First admiral in the U.S. Navy
Edmund Hillary (Sir)	1953	First climber to reach top of Mt. Everest
Elias Haskett Derby	1805	America's first millionaire
John Jay	1789	First U.S. Supreme Court Justice
John McDermott	1897	First Boston Marathon winner
Neil Armstrong	1969	First man to walk on the moon
Maurice Garin	1903	First Tour de France winner
Roald Amundsen	1911	First man to reach the South Pole
Roger Bannister	1954	First person to break the four-minute mile
Samuel Hopkins	1790	Awarded U.S. patent #1
Steve Fossett	2002	First balloonist to fly solo around the world
Tim Hyer	1841	First boxing champion
Yuri Alekseyevich Gagarin	1961	First human in space

Heroes and Heroines

Girl Names

Amelia Earhart
Anne Hutchinson
Clara Barton
Deborah Sampson
Dolley Madison
Elizabeth Cady
  Stanton
Emma Lazarus
Florence Nightingale
Gloria Steinem
Harriet Beecher Stowe
Helen Keller
Jane Addams
Lucretia Mott
Lucy Stone
Margaret Corbin
Maria Weston
  Chapman
Marie Curie
Mary Wollstonecraft
Molly Pitcher
Penina Moise
Rebecca Gratz
Rosa Parks
Sojourner Truth
Susan B. Anthony
Zora Neale Hurston

Boy Names

Aaron Lopez
Adolphus Simeon
  Solomons
Charles Calistus
  Burleigh
Crispus Attucks
Edward Rosewater
Francis Salvador
Frederick Douglass
George Washington
  Carver
John Calhoun
Leon Dyer (Col.)
Leopold Karpeles
Levi Strauss
Louis Pasteur
Nathan Hale
Paul Revere
Robert E. Lee
Sam Houston
Solomon Bush
Theodore Parker
Thomas Jefferson
Ulysses S. Grant
Wendell Phillips
William Lloyd
  Garrison

Pioneers/Explorers

Girl Names

Christa McAuliffe
Elizabeth I (Queen)
Isabella Eberhardt
Louise Boyd
Mae Jemison
Martha Ballard
Mary Kingsley
Roberta Bondar
Sacajawea
Sally Ride
Sue Hendrickson
Sylvia Earle
Valentina Tereshova

Boy Names

Alexander Mackenzie
Amerigo Vespucci
Bartolomeu Dias
Christopher
  Columbus
Daniel Boone
David Thompson
Edmund Hillary
Eric the Red
Ferdinand Magellan
Francis Drake
Henry Hudson
Hernán Cortés
Jacques Cousteau
James Cook
Jedediah Smith
John Cabot
Juan de Cartegena
Kit Carson
Leif Eriksson
Marco Polo
Matthew Henson
Meriwether Lewis
Ponce de Leon
Samuel de Champlain
Sebastian Cabot
Walter Raleigh
William Clark
Zebulon Pike

Cowboys and Cowgirls

Girl Names

Annie Oakley

Belle Starr

Dale Evans

Diane Fletcher

Helen Hunt Jackson

Lucille Mulhall

Martha "Calamity Jane" Cannary

Patsy Montana

Pauline Cushman

Rose Maddox

Boy Names

Allen "Rocky" Lane

Bill Pickett

Bob Leavitt

Buffalo Bill

Buster Crabbe

Butch Cassidy

Cooper Smith

Eddie Dean

Gene Autry

George Glenn

Jay "Tonto" Silverheels

Jesse James

John Wayne

John Henry "Doc" Holliday

Monte Hale

Nat Love

Roy Rogers

Sunset Carson

Tagg Oakley

Tom Mix

Will Rogers

Wyatt Earp

Names from Religion

Some parents look to their religion for guidance when choosing a more spiritual name for their baby. In this chapter, you'll find a wide range of choices, from Greek and Roman gods of ancient history; to angel names; to names of virtues; to historical names, such as those of popes, saints, and religious leaders. You'll also find names with Christian, Jewish, Buddhist, Hindu, Muslim, and Wiccan backgrounds.

And even if you've chosen a name already, this chapter can fill you in on its history or religious significance.

Names of Greek and Roman Gods

Girl Names

Goddess	Reign
Amphitrite	Sea goddess
Aphrodite	Goddess of love and beauty
Artemis	Goddess of the moon; huntress
Athena	Goddess of wisdom
Bellona	Goddess of war
Demeter	Goddess of agriculture
Dione	Titan goddess
Eos	Goddess of the dawn
Eris	Goddess of discord
Flora	Goddess of flowers
Fortuna	Goddess of fortune
Gaea	Goddess of the earth
Hebe	Goddess of youth
Hecate	Goddess of sorcery and witchcraft
Hestia	Goddess of the hearth
Iris	Goddess of the rainbow
Istra	Goddess of psyche
Lucina	Goddess of childbirth
Mnemosyne	Goddess of memory
Nike	Goddess of victory
Nyx	Goddess of the night
Pales	Goddess of shepherds and herdsmen
Selene	Moon goddess
Terra	Earth goddess

Boy Names

God	Reign
Apollo	God of beauty
Atlas	Titan god
Cronus	God of harvests
Eros	God of love
Helios	God of the sun
Hephaestus	God of fire
Hercules	Hero (son of Zeus)
Hermes	God of physicians and thieves
Hyman	God of marriage
Hypnos	God of sleep
Janus	God of gates and doors
Momus	God of ridicule
Morpheus	God of dreams
Pluto	God of Hades
Plutus	God of wealth
Pontus	Sea god
Poseidon	Sea god
Proteus	Sea god
Quirinus	War god
Silvanus	God of the woods and fields
Terminus	God of boundaries and landmarks
Thanatos	God of death
Vertumnus	God of fruits and vegetables

Angels

Girl Names

Angel	Reign	Angel	Reign
Amriel	Angel of May	Muriel	Angel of June
Arael	Angel of birds	Nitika	Angel of precious stones
Cassiel	The earthly mother	Oriel	Angel of destiny
Dabria	One of five angels who transcribed books Ezra dictated	Pariel	Angel who wards off evil
		Sofiel	Angel of fruits and vegetables
Dara	Angel of rains and rivers	Talia	Angel who escorts the sun on its daily course
Dina	Guardian angel of wisdom		
Hariel	Angel of tame animals	Tariel	Angel of summer
Laila	Angel who guides spirits at their birth		

Boy Names

Angel	Reign	Angel	Reign
Aban	Angel of October	Kadi	Angel who presides over Friday
Arel	Angel of fire	Lucifer	Angel of the morning star
Asasiel	One of five angels who transcribed books Ezra dictated	Malchidiel	Angel of March
		Manuel	Angel who oversees the Cancer zodiac sign
Asmodel	Angel of April		
Azar	Angel of November	Michael	Angel who holds the keys to the kingdom of heaven
Barchiel	Angel of February		
Dai	Angel of December	Murdad	Angel of July
Elijah	Legendary prophet-turned-angel	Raphael	Angel of healing
Ethan	One of five angels who transcribed books Ezra dictated	Sauriel	One of five angels who transcribed books Ezra dictated
Farris	Angel who oversees second hour of the night	Seleucia	One of five angels who transcribed books Ezra dictated
Gabriel	Angel who sits at left hand of God	Uriel	Inspiration of writers and teachers
Geron	Angel called during magic-based prayer	Yale	Angel who attends throne of God
Hamal	Angel of water	Yahriel	Angel of the moon
Hamaliel	Angel of August	Zachriel	Angel of memory
Irin	An exalted angel; twin of Qaddis	Zaniel	Angel of Monday and the Libra zodiac sign
Javan	Guardian angel of Greece	Zamael	Angel of joy
Joel	Archangel who suggested Adam name things	Zazel	Angel summoned for love invocations

Biblical Names

Girl Names

Aaliyah	Dara	Ivah	Keturah	Rhoda
Abira	Dayla	Ivana	Keziah	Ruth
Abital	Delilah	Jale	Leah	Salome
Ada	Dinah	Jane	Lemuela	Samaria
Adalia	Eden	Janna	Lois	Sapphira
Ahava	Edna	Japhia	Lydia	Sela
Amissa	Eleora	Jedida	Mahalath	Seraphina
Apphia	Ellen	Jemima	Marsena	Shera
Ascah	Esther	Jensine	Martha	Shobi
Asenath	Eunice	Jerusha	Mehitabel	Susanna
Atarah	Eve	Joakima	Miriam	Tabitha
Athaliah	Galya	Joan	Moriah	Talitha
Aviva	Geva	Joelle	Myra	Tamar
Bathsheba	Gilana	Jonina	Naomi	Tirza
Bethany	Hadassah	Jora	Neriah	Tryphena
Beulah	Hali	Jordane	Peninnah	Vashti
Bracha	Hana	Josephine	Persis	Zillah
Candace	Helah	Judith	Phoebe	Zilpah
Carmel	Ideh	Justine	Rachel	Zipporah
Cassia	Ilana	Kadisha	Rebekah	Zoe
Chanah				

Boy Names

Aaron	Boaz	Gershon	Job	Pallu
Abel	Caesar	Gideon	Joel	Paul
Abijah	Cain	Goliath	Jonah	Peter
Abner	Carmi	Gomer	Jonathan	Phares
Abraham	Carpus	Haggai	Joram	Pontius
Absolom	Cephus	Haran	Joseph	Raphael
Achan	Cyrus	Heber	Joshua	Reuben
Adam	Daniel	Hillel	Josiah	Reuel
Adlai	Darius	Hiram	Judah	Rufus
Allon	David	Hosea	Julius	Samson
Alphaeus	Demetrius	Ira	Kenan	Samuel
Alvah	Ebenezer	Isaiah	Laban	Saul
Amal	Edom	Ishmael	Lamech	Seth
Ammiel	Ehud	Israel	Levi	Shadrach
Amon	Elam	Ithamar	Luke	Shiloh
Amos	Elazar	Jabez	Madai	Silas
Amram	Elihu	Jabin	Malachi	Simeon
Ananias	Elijah	Jachin	Mark	Simon
Anath	Elkanah	Jacob	Meshach	Solomon
Ara	Emanuel	Jadon	Micah	Timothy
Archelaus	Enoch	Jairus	Moses	Tiras
Asa	Eran	James	Nahum	Tobias
Asher	Esau	Japhet	Nathan	Uri
Azariah	Ethan	Jared	Nehemiah	Uriel
Barnabas	Ezekiel	Jason	Nicodemus	Uzi
Bartholomew	Ezra	Javan	Noah	Zachariah
Baruch	Felix	Jeremiah	Obadiah	Zalmon
Benaiah	Gabriel	Jericho	Omar	Zared
Bethuel	Garrison	Jesse	Oren	Zebulon

Names of Saints

Girl Names

Adela

Agape

Agatha

Agnes

Alice

Anastasia Patricia

Angela Merici

Antonia

Anysia

Audrey

Aurea

Barbara

Basilissa

Beatrice

Bertilla Boscardin

Brigid

Catherine of Siena

Cecilia

Chionia

Christina

Clare of Assisi

Colette

Dymphna

Eulalia of Merida

Eve

Felicity

Flora of Beaulieu

Gemma Galgani

Genevieve

Gertrude of Helfta

Hilda

Hyacintha Mariscotti

Irene

Ita

Joan Delanoue

Julia Billiart

Juliana Falconieri

Julitta of Caesarea

Kateri Tekakwitha

Lilian

Lucy of Syracuse

Madeleine Sophie Barat

Matilda

Maura of Troyes

Melania the Younger

Mercedes

Monica

Nonnita

Patricia

Raphaela Mary Porras

Rita of Cascia

Rose of Lima

Rufina

Sabina

Scholastica

Seraphina

Solangia

Sunniva

Ursula

Veronica Giuliana

Zita

Boy Names

Adalbert	Damian	Jerome	Otto
Aedan	Denis	Joachim	Owen
Albert the Great	Dewi	Jordan of Saxony	Patrick
Aloysius	Dominic of Silos	Jude	Paul Miki
Amator	Donatus	Julian the Hospitaller	Peter Canisius
Ambrose	Dunstan	Julius	Philip Neri
Anselm	Eadbert	Justus	Quentin
Apollo	Edmund the Martyr	Kenneth	Radbod
Arsenius the Great	Elmo	Landry	Raymund
Austin of Canterbury	Fabian	Laserian	Roderic
Bairre	Fergus	Laurence	Romanus
Barnabas	Francis of Assisi	Leger	Rupert of Salzburg
Benedict	Frederick of Utrecht	Leonard	Silvin
Benen	Gatian	Lucius	Stephen of Hungary
Blaan	George the Great	Luke	Tarasius
Boris	Gerard Majella	Macartan	Teilo
Brendan	Gerlac	Marcellus	Ternan
Bruno	Germanus	Marius	Theodore
Caedmon	Gildas the Wise	Mark	Timothy
Cajetan	Giles	Martin	Tobias
Canice	Gleb	Maximilian	Tutilo
Castor	Godfrey	Medard	Urban V
Chad	Guy of Cortona	Modan	Victor Maurus
Charles Borromeo	Harvey	Montanus	Vincent de Paul
Ciaran	Henry of Cocket	Nicholas	Walter of L'Esterp
Clement	Hervé	Nino	Wenceslaus
Colm	Hugh of Rouen	Norbert	Wolstan
Conrad	Ivo of Chartres	Odo of Cluny	Wulfstan
Cyprian	James	Oliver Plunket	Zachary

Names of Religious Leaders

Girl Names

Agnes

Aimee Semple Mcpherson

Barbara Harris

Elizabeth Fry

Harriet Martineau

Helen Prejean (Sister)

Jeanette Rankin

Joan of Arc

Marianne Williamson

Mary Daly

Mary Baker Eddy

Mother Cabrini

Mother Seton

Mother Teresa

Suzanne Langer

Sylvia Pankhurst

Tammy Faye Bakker

Boy Names

Al Sharpton (Reverend)

Augustine (Saint)

Bertrand Russell

Billy Graham

Brigham Young

Buddha

Charles Spurgeon

Chatam Sofer (Rabbi)

Confucius

Desmond Tutu (Bishop)

Dietrich Bonhoeffer

Edwin Chapin

Emanuel Swedenborg

Ernest Dimnet

Ezra Taft Benson

Francis of Assisi (Saint)

Frederick Buechner

Fulton Sheen

George Fox

Gordon B. Hinckley (president, Church of Latter Day Saints)

Harry Fosdick

Henry Ward Beecher

Ignatius Loyola (Saint)

Immanuel Kant

Isaac Watts

Prophet Isaiah

Jeremy Collier

Jerry Falwell

Jesse Jackson Sr. (Reverend)

Jesus Christ

Jim Bakker

Jimmy Swaggart

John the Baptist

John Wesley

Joseph Smith

Karol Wojtyla (Pope John Paul II)

Lao-Tzu

Li Hongzhi (Master)

Louis Farrakhan

Mahatma Gandhi

Martin Luther King Jr. (Dr.)

Martin Luther

Max Weber

Mohammed

Moses

Norman Vincent Peale

Pat Robertson (Reverend)

Paul (Saint)

Paul Tillich

Peter Marshall

Phillips Brooks

Reinhold Niebuhr

Robert Schuller

Ron L. Hubbard

Rowan Williams (Archbishop of Canterbury)

Ruhollah Khomeini (Ayatollah)

Siddha Nagarjuna

Tenzin Gyatso (Dalai Lama)

Thomas Aquinas

W. Deen Mohammed (Imam)

William Channing

Zoroaster

Names of Popes

Girl Names

Not applicable.

Boy Names

Adeodatus	Donus	Liberius	Simplicius
Adrian	Eleutherius	Linus	Siricius
Agapetus	Eugene	Lucius	Sisinnius
Agatho	Eusebius	Marcellinus	Sixtus
Alexander	Eutychian	Marcellus	Soter
Anacletus	Evaristus	Marcus	Stephen
Anastasius	Fabian	Marinus	Sylvester
Anicetus	Felix	Martin	Symmachus
Anterus	Formosus	Miltiades	Telesphorus
Benedict	Gelasius	Nicholas	Theodore
Boniface	Gregory	Paschal	Urban
Caius	Hilarius	Paul	Valentine
Callistus	Honorius	Pelagius	Victor
Celestine	Hormisdas	Peter	Vigilius
Clement	Hyginus	Pius	Vitalian
Conon	Innocent	Pontain	Zachary
Constantine	John	Romanus	Zephyrinus
Cornelius	John Paul	Sabinian	Zosimus
Damasus	Julius	Sergius	
Deusdedit	Lando	Severinus	
Dionysius	Leo	Silverius	

Buddhist Names

Girl Names

An	Da Shin	Hiten	Myoki
Anzan	Dainin	Ishu	Roshin
Bankei	Eido	Jakushitsu	Saiun
Chen-chio	Etsudo	Jimin	Shinjo
Chen-tao	Fuyo	Koge	Showa
Chinshu	Gyo Shin	Mu Ji Yo	Taido
Chorei	Hakue	Myo Ka	Tennen

Boy Names

Abhaya	Eryu	Kozan	Seiko
Ana	Fo-hai	Lung-t'an	Seiryu
Bankei	Fo-hsing	Ma-tzu	Seung Sahn
Banko	Fudoki	Mu-nan	Shisen
Banzan	Genjo	Mugen	Shoju Rojin
Bassui	Genko	Nan Shin	Suriak
Chan Khong	Hakaku	Nanruy	T'su Yu
Chimon	Hui K'o	Niao-ka	Tamon
Chotan	Hui-chao	Nyogen	Tan Gong
Daeshim	Itsu Ro	Quang Tu	Unkan
Daido	Jikai	Reiju	Wu-pen
Dai-In	Jiryu	Ryushin	Ya'o Xia'ng
Doryo	Kakumyo	Sariputra	Zanchu
Engu	Kando	Seido	Zendo
Enmei	Kogen	Seigan	Zuiki

Jewish/Hebrew Names

Girl Names

Aaliyah	Azalia	Hali	Maria
Abie	Bara	Hana	Marisha
Abira	Basha	Hanne	Netta
Abra	Bethesda	Hava	Nisi
Achazia	Bettina	Heba	Odelia
Ada	Bracha	Hedia	Raphaela
Adalia	Carmel	Hedva	Rena
Adamina	Chanah	Ideh	Sadie
Adelaide	Chaya	Ilana	Saloma
Adena	Daba	Iva	Samara
Aderes	Dalia	Ivana/Ivy	Shira
Adie	Damaris	Jael	Soshannah
Adina	Daniela	Jaen	Simona
Adine	Dara	Jamee	Tamara
Ahava	Davan	Jardena	Thadine
Ailsa	Davine	Jensine	Thomasina
Akiva	Daya	Jezebel	Tivona
Aliza	Dayla	Jobey	Tove
Alumit	Delilah	Joelle	Uma
Amissa	Edria	Jora	Varda
Anke	Efrosini	Jordane	Vidette
Araminta	Eilis	Kazia	Yachne
Arashel	Eleora	Kefira	Yadira
Arella	Else	Lailie	Ydel
Ariel/Ariella	Emanuela	Lexine	Yesmina
Asa	Endora	Lia	Yoninah
Asenka	Evelina	Lilith	Zahar
Asisa	Galya	Magda	Zehava
Astera	Gana	Magdalene	Zerlinda
Atara	Genesis	Malca	Zila
Aviva	Geva	Malina	Zisel
Ayala	Hadara	Mangena	Zita
Ayla	Hadassa	Mara	Zuriel

Boy Names

Aaron	Brighton	Israel	Nadav	Teman
Abbott	Britt	Itzak	Nathan	Thaddeus
Abdiel	Cain	Jacob	Nathaniel	Timur
Abel	Caleb	Jarlath	Nehemiah	Tivon
Abie	Chaika	Jaron	Nirel	Tobias
Abijah	Chaim	Jedidiah	Nisi	Tovi
Abner	Dagan	Jeremiah	Noadiah	Udeh
Abraham	Daniel	Jesus	Noah	Uriah
Abram	Doron	Jonah	Obadiah	Uzi
Abrahsa	Dov	Jonas	Omar	Vered
Acacio	Eban	Jorgen	Oran	Yadid
Adam	Ebenezer	Joseph	Oren	Yadon
Addai	Eden	Joshua	Osaze	Yakov
Adlai	Eisig	Josiah	Osborne	Yan
Adley	Eli	Jude	Palti	Yanis
Admon	Elias	Kabos	Ranen	Yarin
Adon	Elijah	Kaniel	Raphael	Yaron
Ahab	Ely	Laban	Ravid	Yehudi
Ahmik	Emanuel	Label	Reuben	Zabulon
Aitan	Ephraim	Lazarus	Reuel	Zaccheo
Amiel	Ethan	Lemuel	Rishon	Zachariah
Amos	Ethel	Leshem	Roni	Zakai
Ardon	Ezekiel	Levi	Sachiel	Zane
Ari	Ezio	Lot	Sagiv	Zared
Armon	Ezra	Malachi	Saloman	Zazu
Arnon	Gabai	Matai	Saul	Zebediah
Asher	Gabriel	Matthew	Seff	Zedekiah
Axel	Genesis	Mehetable	Seraphim	Zephan
Barnabas	Gersham	Mendel	Seth	Zev
Barnaby	Gideon	Michael	Shulamith	Ziff
Bartholomew	Hosea	Mihaly	Simon	Ziv
Baruch	Hyman	Mordecai	Sivan	
Benjamin	Ichabod	Moses	Solomon	
Benson	Isaac	Nachmanke	Talman	

Hindu Names

Girl Names

Akuti	Indu	Menaka	Pusti	Subhaga
Anjali	Jahnavi	Mohini	Radhika	Subhuja
Anuradha	Jamuna	Nalini	Rani	Sudevi
Anusha	Jaya	Nanda	Rati	Sunita
Aparna	Jayani	Narmada	Reena	Suravinda
Aruna	Juhi	Neelam	Rekha	Surotama
Asha	Jyoti	Neerja	Revati	Surya
Banu	Kala	Nidhi	Rima	Susila
Basanti	Kanchana	Nidra	Roshni	Suvrata
Bhama	Kanya	Nira	Rudrani	Tapi
Bharati	Kausalya	Nirmala	Rupali	Taruna
Bina	Kavita	Nirupa	Sabita	Tejal
Bindiya	Kirti	Nisha	Sachi	Tulasi
Charu	Komal	Nitya	Sangita	Tusti
Chhaya	Kriti	Padma	Sanjna	Uma
Chitra	Kshama	Padmini	Sapna	Urmila
Chitrangda	Lakshmi	Pallavi	Sarasvati	Urvasi
Darshana	Lalita	Parnika	Sarmistha	Uttara
Deepa	Lolaksi	Parvati	Saryu	Vanita
Devaki	Madhu	Pavani	Savarna	Varsha
Dipti	Madhur	Pivari	Savita	Varuni
Divya	Mala	Pooja	Seema	Vasanta
Dristi	Malati	Prachi	Shanti	Vasumati
Ekta	Mallika	Prisha	Shobha	Vidya
Gayatri	Malti	Pritha	Shreya	Vimala
Gita	Mamta	Priti	Shubha	Vinata
Gopi	Manushi	Priya	Smirti	Vineeta
Harhsa	Marisa	Punita	Somatra	Visala
Hema	Matangi	Purandhri	Sraddha	Yaksha
Hina	Medha	Purnima	Subhadra	Yauvani
Indira	Meena			

Boy Names

Abhay	Dhananjay	Madhav	Pranav	Siddharth
Abhijit	Dharuna	Mahabala	Prasata	Srinivas
Achyuta	Dhatri	Mahesh	Prasoon	Sudesha
Aditya	Dilip	Maitreya	Pravin	Sudeva
Ajatashatru	Dinesh	Mandhatri	Prem	Sukumar
Ajay	Duranjaya	Manik	Prithu	Sumit
Akaash	Durjaya	Mehul	Privrata	Suresh
Akshay	Eknath	Mohan	Purujit	Surya
Amal	Gajendra	Mohit	Pusan	Taksa
Amar	Ganesh	Mukul	Raj	Tarang
Amit	Girish	Nachik	Rajeev	Tushar
Anand	Gopal	Nagesh	Rakesh	Udai
Anay	Hari	Namdev	Ram	Upendra
Anoop	Harsh	Nandin	Ramanuja	Urjavaha
Arjun	Hitesh	Narayana	Randir	Vairaja
Aseem	Iravan	Naresh	Rantidev	Variya
Asija	Jaideep	Narsi	Ravi	Varun
Asuman	Jayant	Navin	Rohit	Vasava
Asvin	Jeevan	Neel	Sagar	Vasuman
Atharvan	Jimuta	Nimai	Sahadev	Veer
Atul	Jitendra	Nimish	Samrat	Vidvan
Badal	Kalidas	Niramitra	Samudra	Vijay
Balaji	Kamadev	Omprakash	Sandeep	Vikram
Balavan	Kapil	Pandya	Sanjay	Vimal
Bharat	Kartikeya	Paramartha	Sanjeev	Vinay
Bhudev	Kavi	Parnab	Sarat	Vinod
Bramha	Keshav	Prabhakar	Satrujit	Virat
Chandra	Kirit	Prabhu	Saunak	Visvajit
Cholan	Kusagra	Pradeep	Shalabh	Vivatma
Dattatreya	Kush	Pramath	Shashwat	Yashodhara
Devarsi	Lokesh	Pramsu	Shiv	Yogendra

Muslim Names

Girl Names

Abia	Ghada	Lateefah	Omaira	Sommer
Akilah	Habiba	Lila	Polla	Talitha
Alea	Hana	Lina	Qadira	Tara
Alima	Hayfa	Lucine	Rafa	Thana
Aliye	Jamila	Lydia	Rana	Ulima
Amina	Janan	Mahala	Rida	Vega
Anan	Jarita	Manar	Rukan	Waheeda
Anisa	Jenna	Maritza	Saba	Walad
Bibi	Kadejah	Maysa	Safiya	Yaminah
Callie	Kaela	Mouna	Sana	Yesenia
Emani	Karida	Nadira	Saree	Zahra
Faizah	Laela	Nekia	Shakera	Zia
Fatima	Lakia	Nima	Skye	Zulima

Boy Names

Abbud	Fahd	Jakeem	Mustafa	Sharif
Abdulaziz	Faisal	Jawhar	Nabil	Suhail
Aden	Fakih	Jumah	Nadim	Syed
Adham	Faris	Kadar	Nadir	Tahir
Ahmad	Fatin	Kadeem	Naji	Tamir
Akil	Ferran	Kale	Nasser	Tarik
Alam	Gamal	Kasib	Nuri	Wahid
Ali	Ghazi	Khalid	Omar	Waleed
Altair	Haddad	Lateef	Qamar	Wasim
Amar	Haidar	Mahdi	Rahul	Xavier
Asadel	Hakim	Mahmoud	Rasheed	Yasir
Azeem	Hamza	Malcolm	Reyhan	Yusuf
Basam	Hasan	Malek	Riyad	Zaid
Borak	Hilel	Marwan	Salam	Zahir
Boutros	Hussain	Mohammed	Samman	Zaki
Caleb	Imad	Muhammad	Seif	Zimraan
Coman	Isam	Munir	Shakir	Zuhayr
Dekel	Jabir			

Wiccan Names

Girl Names

Abiona	Aludra	Esme	Jana	Marinette	Rae Beth
Adalia	Anais	Evadne	Jocosa	Medea	Rhiannon
Ailis	Aruna	Fai	Kachina	Meroe	Ryanne
Alanna	Aurora	Farica	Kalinda	Morgan	Sheera
Alcina	Brietta	Feronia	Keelin	Milliani	Tala
Aldora	Candra	Fulvia	Kisa	Nimue	Talia
Alina	Chanda	Githa	Kisha	Pamphile	Talitha
Alivia	Cindeigh	Hekt	Llewellyn	Qiana	Vanita
Alleta	Ella	Idalis	Louhi	Radella	Xandria

Boy Names

Barrett	Charles	Mabon
Blaise	Colborn	Paul Beyerl

Names from Virtues

Girl Names

Adore	Chastity	Eternal	Honesty	Mercy	Purity
Affinity	Cherish	Ethereal	Honor	Merry	Sacrifice
Amiable	Compassion	Faith	Hope	Mirth	Serena
Amity	Concord	Felicity	Humbleness	Modesty	Sobriety
Amour	Constance	Fidelity	Humility	Muse	Solace
Beauty	Courage	Fortitude	Infinity	Noble	Spirituality
Bliss	Courtesy	Fortune	Integrity	Patience	Sympathy
Blythe	Delight	Freedom	Joy	Peacefulness	Temperance
Bonny	Desire	Gentle	Kindness	Pity	Tranquility
Chance	Destiny	Glory	Knowledge	Pleasance	Truth
Charisma	Divinity	Grace	Liberty	Providence	Winsome
Charity	Essence	Harmony	Love	Prudence	Wisdom

Boy Names

Chance	Justice	Merit	Valor	Wisdom
Chivalry	Loyal	Tenacious	Verity	Zeal
Gallant	Lucky	True		

Part 2

Giant Alphabetical List of Names, Origins, and Meanings

After you've gathered some possible names for your baby, you can jump ahead to Part 2, which lists the historical origins, meanings, and spelling variations of all the names in Part 1—plus thousands of others. Once you know what the names actually mean, you may find some that just "fit" better than others. Or if you're impatient, you can also jump ahead to this part, without having looked at Part 1, and start scanning the A-to-Z master list for possible name candidates.

Boy Names

A

Aaron (Hebrew) Shining light. (Arabic) Messenger. *Aaren, Aabron, Aaran, Aarin, Aaronn, Aarron, Aaryn, Aeron, Aharon, Ahron, Ahran, Ahren, Aranne, Arin, Arran, Arron, Aren, Aron, Aronne, Haroun, Harun*

Aban (Irish) Little king. *Abban*

Abbas (Hebrew, Arabic) Father. *Ab, Abba, Abbe, Abbey, Abbie, Abo*

Abbott (Arabic) Father. *Abad, Abbe, Abbot, Abba, Abbe, Abboid*

Naming Rights

Using a family name is a great way to begin the baby-naming process. But if the name isn't what you want to call your baby, consider using the family name as a middle name, or plan to call the baby by the middle name of your choice.

Abdiel (Hebrew) Servant of God.

Abdulaziz (Arabic) Slave of God.

Abel (Hebrew) Breath. *Able, Abell*

Abelard (German) Resolute. *Abelardo, Abalard, Abelhard, Abilard, Adalard, Adelard*

Abhay (Hindi) Fearless. *Abhaya*

Abhijit (Hindi) Victorious. *Abhijeet*

Abhorson (Scottish) Lives by the river. *Abhor*

Abijah (Hebrew) God is my Father.

Abner (Hebrew) Father of light.

Abraham (Hebrew) Father of a multitude. *Abram, Abramo, Avraham, Avram, Avrom, Aberham, Abhiram, Abrahaim, Abrahame, Abrahamo, Abrahan, Abrahon, Abraheem, Abrahem, Abrahim, Abrahm, Abe, Abie, Abra, Ibrahim, Braham, Bram*

Abrahsa (Hebrew) Father.

Absolom (Hebrew) My father is peace. *Absalon, Absolum, Abselon*

Abtin (Persian) Fereidoun's father.

Abuna (Arabic) Our father.

Acacio (Hebrew) The Lord holds.

Ace (Latin) Unity. *Acie, Acer, Acey*

Achachak (Native American) Spirit.

Achan (Biblical) He who troubleth.

Achilles (Greek) A mythical Trojan war hero. *Achille, Achilleo, Achill, Achillea, Akil, Akilles*

Achuta (Hindi) Untouchable.

Ackley (Old English) Meadow of oaks.

Acton (Old English) Town with many oaks.

Acura (American) Luxury automobile brand.

Adahy (Native American) Lives in the woods.

Adalai (Hebrew) Refuge of God. (Arabic) Just. *Adlai*

Adalbert (Old German) Noble.

Adalgiso (Old German) Noble hostage.

Adam (Hebrew) Earth. *Ad, Adamo, Adams, Adamson, Adan, Adao, Addam, Addams, Addem, Addie, Addis, Addison, Addy, Ade, Adem, Adhamh, Adie, Adnet, Adnon, Adnot, Adamec, Adamek, Adamik*

Adan (Irish) Warm. *Aden, Adin, Adian, Aidan, Aiden, Aedan*

Adar (Hebrew) Noble. *Addar*

Adare (Irish) From the ford of the oak tree.

Addai (Hebrew) Man of God.

Addison (Old English) Adam's son. *Adison, Addisen, Addisun, Addyson, Adisson, Adyson*

Adelbert (Old German) Famous for nobility. *Albert, Delbert*

Adelfried (Old German) He who protects the descendants.

Adelino (Old German) Noble.

Adelmio (Old German) Of noble birth.

Adelmo (Old German) Noble protector.

Ademaro (Old German) Glorious in battle.

Adeodatus (Latin) Given by God.

Adger (Old English) Happy spear. (Scottish) Oak tree ford. *Adar, Agar, Ager, Adair*

Adham (Arabic) Black.

Adie (German) Noble, kind; often used as a nickname. *Addie, Addy, Adolph*

Adin (Hebrew) Delicate.

Aditya (Hindi) Lord of the sun.

Adler (German) Eagle. *Addler, Adlar*

Adley (Hebrew) Just.

Admon (Hebrew) Red peony.

Adney (English) Dweller on the island. *Adny*

Adolph (German) Noble wolf. *Adolf, Adolfo, Adolphe, Adolphus, Adolfus*

Adon (Hebrew) Lord.

Adonis (Greek) Handsome mythological figure. *Andonis*

Adred (Science fiction) Character from *Star Trek: Deep Space Nine*.

Adrian (Greek) Rich. (Latin) Dark one. *Adrien, Adrianus, Adriano, Adarian, Adorjan, Adrain, Adreian, Adreyan, Adriann, Adriane, Adrianne, Adriean, Adrion, Adrionn, Adrionne, Adron, Adryan, Adryn, Adryon, Hadrian, Hadrianus*

Naming Rights

Remember, your baby must live with the name you choose for the rest of his or her life, so although a unique name and spelling might be favorable, consider that the child may always have his or her name mispronounced or misspelled, which can be very frustrating.

Aeary (Irish) Scholar.

Aegeon (Shakespeareanan) From *The Comedy of Errors*.

Aemilius (Latin) Eager. *Aimil, Aymil, Emelen, Emelio, Emil, Emile, Emilan, Emiliano, Emilianus, Emilio, Emilion, Emilyan, Emlen, Emlin, Emlyn, Emlynn*

Afram (African) A river in Ghana.

Africa (Latin) From Africa. *Afrate, Afro*

Afton (Celtic) From the Afton River. *Affton*

Agamemnon (Greek) King of Mycenae who led the Greeks in the Trojan War.

Agapetus (Spanish) Beloved.

Agatho (Italian) A Catholic saint and pope from Sicily.

Agrippa (Hebrew) One who causes great pain at birth.

Ahab (Hebrew) Uncle.

Ahanu (Native American) He laughs.

Ahearn (Celtic) Lord of the horses. *Ahearne, Aherin, Ahern, Aherne*

Ahmad (Arabic) To praise. *Achmad, Achmed, Ahmed, Ahamad, Ahamed, Ahmaad, Ahmaud, Amad, Amahd, Amed*

Ahmik (Hebrew) Strength of God's flock.

Ahren (Old German) Eagle.

Ahura (Hindi) Lord.

Aiken (Old English) Made of oak. *Aicken, Aikin, Ayken*

Aimon (Spanish) Homebody. *Aimond, Aymon, Haimon, Heman, Eamon, Edmund*

Aitan (Hebrew) Strong.

Ajatashatru (Hindi) Without enemies.

Ajax (Greek) Eagle.

Ajay (Hindi) Conqueror. *Aj, Aja, Ajae, Ajai, Ajaye, Ajee, Ajit*

Akaash (Hindi) Sky. *Aakash, Akasha*

Akamu (Hawaiian) Red earth. *Adamu, Akanah*

Akbar (Arabic) Powerful.

Akecheta (Native American) Fighter.

Akemi (Japenese) Beautiful dawn.

Akim (Hebrew) The Lord will judge.

Akira (Scottish) Anchor. (Japanese) Distinct. *Akio, Akiyo*

Aksel (Old German) Father of peace. *Aksell, Ax, Axe, Axel*

Akshay (Hindi) Indestructible. *Akshaj, Akshaya*

Alam (Hindi) The whole world. *Aalam*

Alan (Gaelic) Handsome. *Allen, Allan, Alain, Alun, Allon*

Alarbus (Shakespeareanan) From *Titus Andronicus*.

Alaric (German) Noble ruler. *Alarick, Alarico, Alarik, Aleric, Allaric, Allarick, Alric, Alrick, Alrik*

Al-Ashab (Arabic) Gray.

Alastair (Scottish) Defender of mankind; version of Alexander. *Alistair, Alistaire, Alastaire, Alister, Alaster, Alasdair, Alaisdair, Alaistair, Alaister, Alasteir, Alastor, Aleister, Allaistar, Allastair, Allaster, Allastir, Allysdair, Alystair*

Alban (Latin) White. *Alben, Albin, Albion, Albany, Albain, Albean, Albein, Alby*

Albert (German) Noble, bright; famous. *Alberto, Albertine, Albertus, Albrecht, Adelbert, Aubert, Elbert, Bertel, Berty, Bertie, Al, Alby, Albie, Ailbert, Albyrt, Albyrte, Alvertos*

Albrecht (German) Noble, intelligent. *Albert, Adelbert, Alberto*

Alcander (Greek) Manly, strong. *Alcindor, Alcandor*

Alcibiades (Shakespeareanan) From *Timon of Athens*. (Greek) Violent force; Athenian general and politian during the Poloponessian War. *Alkibiades*

Alcott (Old English) Old cottage. *Alcot, Walcott, Walcot*

Alden (Middle English) Antique. *Aldan, Aldwin, Aldean, Aldin, Elden*

Alder (Middle English) Type of birch tree. (Old English) Revered one. *Elder, Aldus, Aldair*

Aldo (English) Old and wise. *Aldous, Alds, Aldus*

Aldrich (Old English) Old king. *Aldrych, Aldred, Aldren, Aldridge, Aldric, Aldrick, Aldrige, Aldritch, Alldric, Alldrich, Alldrick, Alldridge*

Aleron (French) Knight. (Latin) Winged.

Alexander (Greek) Protector of mankind. *Alakesander, Alec, Aleck, Alejandro, Alek, Alkeos, Aleks, Aleksey, Alesandro, Alessandro, Alejo, Alex, Alexas, Alexei, Alexio, Alysander, Alexandre, Aleksander, Alick, Alik, Alyc, Alyck, Alyk, Iksander, Ixsander, Sandro, Sander, Sanders, Sandor, Sandy, Sandie, Sacha, Sasha, Xander*

Aleyn (English) A fisher king in Arthurian legend.

Alfonso (Old German) Noble and ready. *Alfons, Alonso, Alonzo, Alphonse, Alphonsus, Affonso, Alfonse, Alfonsus, Alfonza, Alfonzo*

Alford (English) From the old ford.

Alfred (Old English) Wise counsel. *Alf, Alfredo, Ailfrid, Alfeo, Alfric, Alfie, Alfrid, Allie, Elfred, Fred, Freddie*

Alger (German) Noble warrior. *Algar, Allgar, Elgar, Elger*

Algernon (French) Mustachioed. *Algie, Algenon, Algin, Algon*

Ali (Arabic) Greatest; exhalted. (Muslim) Protected by God. *Aly*

Alice (Old German) Of good cheer.

Allard (Old English) Noble and brave. *Alard, Ellard*

Allston (Old English) Al's town. *Alston, Alton*

Almas (Muslim) A diamond.

Alo (Native American) Spiritual guide.

Aloysius (Old German) Famous warrior. *Ahlois, Aloess, Alois, Alosius, Aloisio, Aloys, Lewis, Louis, Ludwick, Ludwig, Lutwick*

Alphaeus (Hebrew) Changing.

Alphus (Hebrew) He who follows after. *Alfaeus, Alfeos, Alfeus, Alpheaus, Alphoeus*

Altair (Arabic) Bird. (Greek) Star.

Alton (Old English) From the old town.

Alva (Hebrew) His highness. *Alvah*

Alvertos (Old English) Shepherd. *Adalverto, Alvert, Alvertis, Alvertos*

Alvin (Old English) Elf wine; cartoon character. *Alwyn*

Alvis (Old Norse) All wise. *Alviss, Elvis*

Alzen (Science fiction) Character from *Star Trek Voyager*.

Amadeus (Latin) Love of God. *Amado, Amadeo, Amadis*

Amal (Hebrew) Labor. (Arabic) Hope. *Amahl*

Amando (Latin) Loves God. *Amandus, Amand, Amandio, Amaniel*

Amanin (Science fiction) Character from *Star Wars*. *Amanaman*

Amar (Greek) Immortal. *Amare, Amaree, Amari, Amario, Amarjit, Amaro, Amarande*

Amaros (Arabic) Moon. *Amard, Amare, Amard, Amari, Amaro, Amaru, Amaral, Amaran, Amarco, Amardo, Amaree, Amareh, Amaren, Amares, Amargi, Amaria, Amaril, Amarin, Amario, Amariy, Amarja, Amarok, Amaron, Amaroo, Amaroq, Amarri, Amarsa, Amarth, Amarti, Amarya, Amaraja, Amaraji, Amarand, Amarant, Amarapa, Amarbir, Amarcus, Amardad, Amardev, Amardip, Amardit, Amareet, Amaresh, Amaresa, Amarfis, Amariah, Amarian, Amariea*

Amator (Latin) Lover.

Ambrose (Greek) Immortal. *Ambie, Ambrosi, Ambrosio, Ambroise, Ambros, Ambrosius, Emrys*

Amedeo (Italian) Painter (1884–1920) known for the use of graceful, elongated lines.

Amerigo (Italian) Industrious. *Americo, Americus*

Ames (Latin) Loves. (French) Friend.

Amherst (English) Place name: Amherst, Massachusetts.

Amiel (Hebrew) The Lord of my people. *Ammiel*

Amiens (Shakespeareanan) From *As You Like It.* (French) Place name: a city in northern France on the Somme River.

Amir (Arabic) Princely. *Aamir, Aamer, Amire, Amiri, Ameer, Amyr*

Amit (Hindi) Boundless, endless. *Amitan, Amreet*

Amon (Hebrew) Trustworthy, faithful. *Amun, Eamon, Eammon*

Amory (Latin) Loving; for girl or boy. *Amery, Amor, Emory, Emery*

Amos (Hebrew) Troubled. *Amose*

Amram (Hebrew) Father of Aaron and Moses. *Amrem, Amrym*

Amund (Scandinavian) Divine protection.

An (Chinese) Peace. *Ana*

Anacletus (Greek) Calling forth. *Anakletos, Cletus*

Analu (Hawaiian) Manly.

Anand (Hindi) Bliss. *Ananda, Anant, Ananth*

Ananias (Hindi) God will hear. (Biblical) The cloud of the Lord.

Anastasius (Greek) Reborn. *Anas, Anastacio, Anastacios, Anastagio, Anastas, Anastase, Anastasi, Anastasio, Anastasios, Anastice, Anastisis, Athanasius*

Anath (Hebrew) Answer.

Anatole (Greek) East. *Anatoly, Anatol, Anatoley, Anatoli, Anatolio, Anatoliy, Anitoly*

Anay (Hindi) Radha's husband.

Ancel (German) Deity. *Ansel, Ancell, Ancelot, Anselm*

Anderson (Swedish) Son of Andrew. *Andersen, Anders, Andy*

Andrew (Greek) Valiant, courageous. *Anders, Andor, Andre, Andreas, Andrae, Andrei, Andres, Andros, Andy, Aindrea, Andery, Andonis, Andru, Andrue, Audrew, Andie, Andrews, Andrzej, Drew*

Andromeda (Greek) A constellation in the Northern Hemisphere.

Angel (English) Messenger. *Ange, Angel, Angelico, Angell, Angelo, Angil, Angyl*

Angus (Gaelic) Superb or unique. *Aeneas*

Anicetus (Old French) Unconquerable. *Aniceta, Anicetta, Anniceta, Annicetta*

Anker (Greek) Manly. *Ankur*

Ankhhaf (Arabic) The oldest son of Pharaoh Seneferu; high-ranking religious and political adviser of Khafre. *Ankh haf*

Annan (Celtic) From the stream.

Annas (Hebrew) High priest. *Ananias, Anish, Anis*

Anoop (Hindi) Incomparable, the best. *Anup*

Anselm (Old German) Deity. *Ansel, Ancell, Ancelot*

Anson (English) Son of a nobleman. *Ansen, Ansun, Ansonia, Hansen, Hanson*

Naming Rights

Choose a name based on its meaning. Sometimes, learning the meaning of a name can either steer you away from it or draw you closer to it. Names with positive meanings are the best choice.

Anstice (Greek) Resurrected.

Antenor (Greek) An elder of Troy.

Anterus (Roman) A saint.

Anthony (Latin) Priceless. (Greek) Flourishing. *Anthonee, Anthoney, Anthonie, Anthonio, Antonius, Antoine, Anton, Antoni, Antony, Antonio, Antanee, Antanie, Antenee, Anthan, Anthey, Anthney, Anathony, Anothony, Antavas, Anfernee, Anthany, Anthey, Anthone, Anthonie, Anthonou, Antione, Anthoy, Antjuan, Antajuan, Anthjuan, Antuan, Tony, Tonio*

Antigonus (Greek) Like the ancestor. (Shakespearean) From *The Winter's Tale.*

Antiochus (Shakespearean) From *Pericles.*

Antipholus (Shakespearean) From *The Comedy of Errors.*

Apemantus (Shakespearan) From *The Life of Timon of Athens.*

Apenimon (Native American) Worthy of trust.

Apollo (Greek) Manly. *Apollos, Apolo, Apolonio, Appollo*

Apostolos (Greek) Disciple.

Aquarius (Latin) A constellation, the Water Bearer; the eleventh sign of the Zodiac.

Aquila (Latin) Strong as an eagle. *Acquilla, Aquil, Aquilas, Aquiles, Aquilino, Aquilla, Aquille, Aquillino*

Ara (Arabic) Opinions.

Aragorn (Fiction) Character from *The Lord of the Rings* by J.R.R. Tolkien.

Arali (African) Basement of the earth.

Aram (Assyrian) High place. *Aramia, Arra, Arram*

Aramis (French) Fictional swordsman. *Airamis, Aramys*

Arandis (Science fiction) Character from *Star Trek: Deep Space Nine.*

Arash (Arabic) Hero.

Arcadicus (Latin) Of or pertaining to Arcadia; pastoral. *Arcadia, Arcadien, Arcadian*

Archangelo (Latin) Principal angel. *Arcangello, Arcangelo*

Archelaus (Greek) Ruler of the people.

Archibald (English) Bold prince. *Arch, Arche, Archie, Archy, Archaimbaud, Archambault, Archibaldo, Archibold, Arkady, Arky*

Archidamus (Shakespearean) From *The Winter's Tale.*

Archimedes (Greek) To think about first.

Ardalan (Persian) Hurried.

Arden (Latin) Passionate; for boy or girl. *Ardelia, Ardis, Ardon, Ardan, Ardene, Ardian, Ardie, Ardn, Ardin*

Arel (Hebrew) Lion of God.

Ares (Greek) God of war.

Aretino (Italian) Attacker.

Argus (Greek) Bright.

Aries (English) A constellation. *Ares, Arie, Ariez*

Arion (Greek) Enchanted; a poet who was rescued by dolphins after being thrown into the sea. (Hebrew) Melodious. *Arian, Arien, Ario, Arione, Aryon*

Aristide (Greek) Descended from the best. *Aristedes, Aristo, Aristeed, Aristidis*

Aristotle (Hebrew) Lion. *Arelk, Arey, Aristito, Aristokles, Aristotelis*

Arjun (Sanskrit) The white one. *Arjuna, Arjin, Arjune, Arjen*

Arland (German) Famous throughout the land. *Arles, Arleigh, Arlo, Arly, Arlie, Arlen, Arliss, Arlyss*

Arledge (Old English) Lives at the hare's lake. *Arlidge, Arlledge*

Arley (Old English) From the hare. *Arlie, Arleigh, Harleigh, Harley, Harly, Hartley*

Arlo (Old English) From the protected town. *Harlow*

Armand (German) Warrior; variation of Herman. *Arman, Armon, Armond, Armondo, Armad, Armanda, Armando, Armands, Armanno, Armaude, Armenta, Herman, Hermann*

Armani (African) Faith.

Armstrong (Old English) Strong-armed warrior.

Arnold (German) Eagle and powerful. *Arnaud, Arnault, Arnie, Arnald, Arno, Arne, Arnell, Arnel, Arness, Arnot, Arnaldo, Arnoll, Arndt, Arnulfo*

Arnon (Hebrew) Rushing stream. *Arnan*

Arrigo (Italian) Estate ruler. *Enrico*

Arsenio (Greek) Masculine. *Arsenius, Arsenyo, Arsinio, Arsinyo*

Arslan (Arabic) Lion hero.

Arthur (Welsh) Bear hero. *Artur, Art, Artair, Artek, Arth, Arta, Arthor, Aurthar, Aurther, Aurthur, Artie, Arty, Arturo, Arturis, Arte, D'Artagnan*

Aruiragus (Latin) Melodies. (Shakespearean) From *Cymbeline.*

Arundel (Old English) He who dwells with eagles.

Arvid (Scandinavian) The eagle's tree.

Arwen (English) Noble, royal; muse. Character from *The Lord of the Rings* by J.R.R. Tolkien.

Asa (Hebrew) Healer. *Assa, Asaa, Ase*

Asad (Arabic) Most prosperous one. *Asadel, Asael, Asadour*

Aseem (Hindi) Limitless. *Asim*

Asher (Hebrew) Fortunate. *Asser, Ashe, Ashbel, Ashar, Ashor, Ashur, Anschel*

Ashkii (Native American) Sacred child.

Ashley (Old English) Ash tree; for boy or girl. *Ashleigh, Ashford, Ash, Ashe, Ashby, Ashlie, Ashling, Asheley, Ashelie, Ashlan, Ashlen, Ashlin, Ashlone, Ashlinn, Ashly, Aslan, Ashten, Ashton*

Asija (Hindi) A great sage.

Asmodel (Greek) Angel of patience; guardian of April ruling the Zodiac sign of Taurus.

Asphar (Hebrew) Pool in the desert.

Aster (Greek) Star.

Astin (English) A variation of August. *Asten, Aston*

Asuman (Hindi) Lord of vital breaths.

Asvin (Hindi) God of medicine.

Atash (Persian) Fire.

Athan (Greek) Immortal.

Athanasios (Greek) Noble.

Atharvan (Hindi) Knower of the Arthara vedas.

Athelstan (Old English) Noble stone.

Athol (Scottish) Place name: New Ireland; coming from Ireland.

Athos (Greek) Zeus.

Atilla (Hungarian) Beloved father. *Attila, Atila, Attal, Attilio, Atalik*

Atlas (Greek) Mythical Titan who supported the earth on his back.

Atley (English) From the meadow. *Atlea, Atlee, Atleigh, Atli, Attley*

Atohi (Native American) Woods.

Atticus (Latin) From Athens.

Attilio (Italian) Little father. *Attila, Atilio, Atilla, Attilah*

Atul (Hindi) Matchless.

Atwell (English) Lives by the spring.

Auburn (Latin) Fair. *Alban, Aubin*

Audie (English) Old friend. *Auden, Audi, Audley, Audy, Audiel*

Audio (American) Sound.

Audric (French) Wise ruler. *Audrick, Audrik*

August (Latin) Exalted. *Agosto, Auguste, Augustine, Augustina, Augie, Augustus, Augusta, Gus, Gussy, Gussie, Gusta*

Augwynne (Science fiction) Character from *Star Wars*.

Aulii (Hawaiian) Delicious.

Aurelius (Latin) Golden one. *Aurel, Aurele, Aurek, Aurelian, Aurelio, Aurelian, Areliano, Aurey, Auryn*

Auriga (Latin) Wagoner.

Austin (Latin) Useful. *Austen, Austan, Austun*

Autolocus (Greek) He who is wolf; self-luminous. (Shakespearean) From *A Winter's Tale. Autolycus, Autolykos*

Avel (Greek) Breath.

Averill (Old English) Boar warrior. *Averil, Averell, Averel, Averiel, Averyl, Averyll, Avrel, Avrell, Avryll, Everill, Everil, Haverl, Haverhill*

Avery (English) Counselor. *Averey, Averi, Averie, Avrey, Avry, Avary*

Avicus (German) Honorable.

Avis (Latin) A bird. *Avice*

Avon (Welsh) A river in England.

Avonmore (Irish) From the great river.

Awarnach (Old English) From Arthurian legend; a giant.

Axel (Swedish) Divine source of life. *Axtel, Axl, Aksel, Axell, Axil, Axill, Axyle*

Ayers (English) Heir to a fortune.

Azad (Arabic) Independent.

Azar (Persian) Fire.

Azariah (Hebrew) Servant of Nego. *Abednego*

Azeem (Arabic) Defender. *Azim, Aseem, Asim*

Azen (Science fiction) Character from *Star Trek Voyager*.

B

Babyface (American) One with a baby face. Singer whose real name is Kenneth Edmonds.

Badal (Hindi) Cloud.

Baden (Welsh) From Baddon. *Baddan, Badden, Badan, Baddon, Bade, Badin, Badon, Badyn, Baedan, Baede, Baeden, Baedin, Baedon*

Badr (Arabic) Full moon. *Badar*

Bahram (Persian) Name of a Persian King. *Bairam*

Bain (Irish) Lives near the pale bridge, bridge over white water. *Bainbridge, Bainbrydge, Banbrigge, Baine, Bayn, Bayne, Baynn*

Bairre (Irish) White, fair.

Baker (English) Occupational surname. *Backstere, Baecere, Bax, Baxter, Baxley, Bakir, Bakker, Bakory, Bakr*

Bala (Hindi) Young strength.

Balaji (Hindi) Lord Venkatesh; name of Vishnu.

Balavan (Hindi) Powerful.

Balder (English) Bold, courageous army. (Norse) Mythological son of Odin. (Swedish) God of light. *Baldr, Baldur, Baldhere, Baldier*

Baldev (Hindi) Full of strength. *Balbir, Balduf*

Baldwin (German) Bold friend. *Baldwyn, Maldwyn, Win, Wyn*

Balin (Hindi) Mighty warrior. *Bali, Baline, Balyn, Blyne, Baylen, Baylin, Baylon, Valin*

Ballard (Old English) Dancing song. *Ballad, Balard, Balerd, Ballerd*

Ballentine (English) Strength, valor.

Ballinamore (Irish) From the great river.

Baltasar (German, Spanish) Protect the king. One of the three wise men. *Baltazar, Baltsaros, Baldassare, Baldasare, Balthazar, Balthazzar, Balshazar, Belshazzar*

Banagher (Irish) Pointed hill.

Bancroft (Old English) Bean field. *Bankroft, Bancrofft*

Bane (Hawaiian) Long-awaited child. *Baen, Baene, Ban*

Banefre Origin and meaning unknown.

Banji (African) Second born of twins.

Banjo (American) Musical instrument.

Banke (Hindi) Lord Krishna.

Banko (Japanese) Everlasting. (Shakespearean) From *MacBeth. Banquo*

Banzan (Japanese) Indestructible mountain.

Baptiste (Greek) Baptizer; named for John the Baptist. *Baptista, Baptysta, Battista*

Barbaras (Hebrew) Meaning unknown. *Barabba*

Barber (Latin) Beard. *Barbour*

Barclay (Old English) Birch meadow. *Barklay, Barkley,*

Barksdale, Berkeley, Berkley, Barchiel, Barcley, Barclae, Barkleigh, Barkli

Bardalph (English) Ax-wielding wolf, ferocious. *Bardolf, Bardolph, Bardulf, Barwolf, Bardow, Bardowl, Bardulph, Bardawulf, Bardolfe*

Bardshaw Origin and meaning unknown.

Barker (English) Tanner of leather. *Bercher, Berbicarius, Berbicis, Barger, Berger, Barkker*

Barnabas (Hebrew) Son of prophecy. *Barnaby, Barney, Barnie, Barn, Bama, Barnabie, Barnabe, Barnabus, Barnebas, Barnes*

Barnett (Old English) Noble man. (German) Mighty as a bear. *Barret, Barrett, Barr, Barnet, Barnete, Barnette, Baronette*

Baron (German) Nobleman; derived title. *Barron, Baaron, Barin, Baronie, Baryn, Beron*

Barric (English) From the barley or the grain farm. *Barrick, Beric, Barrik, Baryc, Baryck, Baryk, Berric, Berrick, Beryc, Beryk*

Barry (Irish) Spear thrower. (Welsh) Son of Harry. *Barrie, Barris, Barie, Barrymore, Berry, Bari*

Bartholomew (Hebrew) Furrow. *Barth, Bart, Barthol, Bartel, Bartlett, Bartley, Barton, Bertol, Bartold, Bat, Tholy, Tolly, Bartolomeo, Bartolomeu, Bartholemew*

Bartram (Danish) Glorious raven. *Barthram*

Baruch (Hebrew) Blessed. *Boruch*

Basil (Greek) Royal. (Arabic) Brave. *Basile, Basilo, Basilia, Basia, Vasilis, Vasily, Bazyli*

Basim (Arabic) Smiling. *Bassam, Bassem, Basaam, Baseem, Basam, Basant, Bassim*

Baso (Sephardic) Glass. (Basque) Woods.

Bassanio (Shakespearean) From *The Merchant of Venice.*

Bassett (Old French) Short, low. *Basse, Basset*

Bassianus (Shakespearean) From *Titus Andronicus.*

Bassui (Japanese) High above average.

Batai (Science fiction) Character from *Star Trek: Next Generation.*

Bates (Greek) One who walks or haunts. (Hebrew) Son of Talmai.

Bayard (Old French) Bay horse. (English) Reddish-brown hair. *Baylor, Bayless, Baird, Baeyard, Baiardo, Baiyard, Bayardo, Bayerd, Bayrd*

Beacan (Irish) Small. *Beacen, Becan, Becen, Becin, Becon, Becyn*

Beacher (Old English) Dweller by the beech tree. *Beecher, Beach, Beachy, Beech, Beechy*

Beardsley (Old English) Beard, wood.

Beau (French) Beautiful. *Beaumont, Beauregard, Bo, Beaux*

Beck (Swedish) Brook. *Bek, Beckett*

Bede (Old English) Prayer.

Bedrich (Czechoslovakian) Peaceful ruler. *Fredrick*

Behdad (Persian) Given honor.

Behruz (Persian) A good day. *Behrooz*

Bela (Hebrew) Destruction. *Béla, Belah, Belay*

Belar (Science fiction) Character from *Star Trek: Deep Space Nine*.

Belarius (Shakespearean) From *Cymbaline*.

Beldon (Old English) Beautiful pasture. *Belden, Belidon, Beldin, Belldin, Belldon, Belldyn, Bellden, Balidyn*

Bellamy (Old French) Handsome friend. *Bell, Belami, Belamie, Belamy, Bellamey, Bellamie*

Beltran (Spanish) Bright raven.

Bemossed (Native American) Walker.

Bemus (Greek) Platform. *Bemis*

Benaiah (Hebrew) Yahweh has created.

Benedict (Latin) Blessed. *Benedick, Benedikt, Benecio, Benito*

What's in a Name

The Benedictine Order is the longest-lasting Catholic monastic order, which traces its history to **Saint Benedict,** who founded the monastery of Monte Cassino in 529. His model was that of a family, with the abbot as father and the monks as brothers. He also developed a plan of life for the monastery that stressed balance and moderation. Monks refrained from eating certain types of foods and kept regular hours for prayer, work, sacred reading, and sleep. Benedict's "rules" influence even modern-day monasticism.

Benen (Irish) Blessed.

Benjamin (Hebrew) Son of my right hand. *Benji, Benjie, Bennie, Benny, Ben, Benjy, Benyamin*

Benjiro (Japanese) Enjoys peace.

Bennett (Latin) Anglicized version of Benedict. *Benett, Benner, Benoit, Benn, Bentley, Benet, Benette, Benit, Benitt, Bennet, Bennette, Benyt, Benytt*

Benson (Hebrew) Ben's son. *Bensen, Bennsan, Bennsen, Bennsin, Bennsyn, Bensin, Benssen, Bensson, Bensyn*

Bentfield Origin and meaning unknown.

Bentley (Old English) From the moor. *Bentlee, Bentleah, Bentlie, Bentleigh*

Benvenuto (Italian) Welcome.

Benvolio (Latin) Happy face. (Shakespearean) From *The Tragedy of Romeo and Juliet*.

Beowulf (Anglo) Intelligent wolf.

Bergen (German) Mountain dweller. *Bergan, Bergin*

Berk (Turkish) Solid, firm. *Berc, Berck, Berke*

Bernard (German) Bold as a bear. *Barnard, Barney, Barnie, Barny, Bernd, Berndt, Bern, Berne, Bernardo, Bernhard, Bernhardt, Bernie, Bjorn, Barend, Barnum, Barn, Barnardine, Berend*

Bernstein (German) Amber, the bear's stone. *Berstein*

Berto (Spanish) Bright flame. *Robert, Burto*

Bertram (German) Bright. *Bertrem, Bertolt, Bertold, Bertil, Bertol, Berton, Bert, Bertrand*

Bethuel (Hebrew) House of God. *Bethel*

Bevin (Irish) One with a sweet song; son of Evan. *Bevan, Bevis*

Bharat (Hindi) India; universal monarch.

Bhudev (Hindi) Lord of the earth.

Bidziil (Native American) He is strong.

Bijan (Persian) Hero.

Bing (Chinese) Soldier, ice.

Bingham (German) Kettle-shaped hollow. *Bing, Binghamton, Binghampton, Binge, Binga*

Biondello (Italian) Shield. (Shakespearean) From *The Taming of the Shrew*.

Birch (Old English) White, birch tree. *Birche, Birket, Birk, Birkee, Birkey, Birky, Birkhead, Birkhed, Birkit, Birkett, Berch, Berche, Burch, Byrch, Byrche*

Birchard Origin and meaning unknown.

Bishop (English) A bishop. (Greek) Overseer. *Bish, Bishup*

Bjorn (Scandinavian) Bear. *Beorn, Bjomolf, Bjami, Bjame, Bjarne, Bjorne*

Blaan (Gaelic) Yellow; a Scottish saint. (Irish) Thin, lean. (English) River. *Bla, Blaney, Blane, Blayne, Blayn, Blayney*

Blackburn (English) Black brook. *Blackbern, Blackberne, Blackburne*

Blade (English) Knife, sword; glory. *Bladen, Bladon, Bladyn, Blae, Blaed, Blaid, Blaide, Blayd, Blayde*

Blaine (English) Source of a river. (Irish) Thin, lean. *Blayne, Blain, Blane*

Blair (Irish) Plain. *Blaire, Blare, Blayr, Blayre*

Blaise (French) Stammerer. *Blais, Blasius, Blazej, Blaisot, Blasi, Blasien*

Blake (Old English) Fair-haired. *Blanchard, Blanco, Blakely, Blayk*

Blaz (Old German) Unwavering protector.

Blaze (American) Flame. (English) Trail mark made on a tree. (Latin) Stutter. *Blayze, Blayse, Blayz, Blayzz, Blazen, Blazer*

Boaz (Hebrew) Swift, strong. *Boas, Booz, Bos, Boz*

Boden (Old French) Herald. *Bodain, Bodein, Bodene, Bodin, Bodine, Bodyn, Bodyne*

Bogart (German) Strong as a bow. *Bogar, Bogey, Bogie, Bogy*

Bonar (French) Gentle. *Bona, Bonar, Bonnar*

Boniface (French) Good fate. *Bonifacio, Bonifaz, Bonifacius, Bonifaco, Bonifacey, Bonifacy*

Bono (American) All good.

Booker (Old English) Beech tree.

Boone (Latin) Good. *Bon, Bone, Bonne, Boon, Boonie, Boony*

Booth (Old English) Hut. *Boothe, Boote, Boot, Bothe*

Borachio (Italian) Lightning. (Shakespearean) From *Much Ado About Nothing.*

Borak (Arabic) Lightning. Al Borak was the legendary horse that bore Muhammad from Earth to the seventh heaven. *Borac, Borack*

Borden (Old English) Near the boar's den. (Old French) Cottage. *Bordan, Bordin, Bordon, Bordyn*

Borg (Old Norse) From the castle. *Borc, Borge*

Boris (Russian) Fight. *Bors, Borys, Boriss, Borja, Borris, Borya, Boryenka, Borys*

Borna (Persian) Youthful one.

Boston (American) Place name: Boston, Massachusetts.

Boswell (Old French) Forested town. *Bosworth, Bos, Boswel, Bozwell*

Botan (Japanese) Peony. *Boten, Botin, Boton, Botyn*

Boult (Shakespearean) From *Pericles.*

Boutros (Arabic) Small rock; form of Peter. *Botros, Butrus, Badrosian, Bedros, Butras, Boutro*

Bowen (Welsh) Son of Owen. *Bowie, Bowan, Bowin, Bowon, Bowyn, Bowynn*

Boyce (French) Woodland. *Boice, Boise, Boycey, Boycie, Boyse*

Boyd (Irish) Blond. *Boid, Boydan, Boyde, Boyden, Boydin, Boydon, Boydyn*

Boyet (Shakespearean) From *Love's Labours Lost.*

Brabantio (Shakespearean) From *Othello.*

Braden (Irish) Brave. *Bradin, Brayden, Braedon, Braedan, Braeden, Bradden, Bradine, Bradun, Breden*

Bradley (Old English) Broad meadow. *Brad, Bradford, Brady, Braid, Braddlea, Braddlee, Braddleigh, Braddli, Braddlie, Braddly, Bradleigh, Bradlie, Braddley, Bradlay*

Bram (Irish) Raven. *Brame, Bramm, Bramdon*

Bramha (Hindi) Third major deity.

Bramwell (English) Bramble well. *Branwell, Bramwel, Bramwele, Bramwyll*

Branch (Latin) Extension.

Brandeis (German) Dweller on a burned clearing.

Brandon (Old English) Fiery hill. *Branden, Brand, Bran, Brenden, Brendan, Brant, Brent, Brennen, Brennan, Branford*

Brant (English) Marked by fire. *Brand, Brannt, Brante, Branton*

Braulio (Italian) Meadow on the hillside. *Braili, Brauliuo, Brauli*

Brawley (English) Meadow on the hillside. *Brawlea, Brawlee, Brawleigh, Brawli, Brawlie, Brawly*

Brent (Old English) Steep hill. *Brendt, Brente, Brentson, Brentt*

Breri (English) A messenger.

Brett (Irish) Native of Brittany. *Bret, Bretton, Brit, Britt, Brette, Bretlin, Bhrett, Brente, Bhrett*

Brewster (Old English) Brewer. *Brew, Brewer, Brewstar*

Brian (Irish) Strong. *Bryan, Bryon, Bryant, Brien, Briant, Briand, Briann, Brianne, Briano, Brainao, Briaun*

Briar (English) Shrub or small tree. (French) Heather. *Brier, Brierly*

Brigham (Old English) One who lives near a bridge. (Old French) Soldier. *Bringham, Brigg, Briggs*

Brighton (English) From the bright town. *Breighton, Bright, Brightin, Bryton*

Brinley (Old English) Tawny. *Brin, Brinlea, Brinlee, Brinlei, Brinleigh, Brinli, Brinlie, Brinly, Brynlea, Brynlei, Brynleigh*

Brock (Old English) Badger. *Braxton, Brocton, Broc, Brockley, Brockleah, Brocleigh, Brockly, Brocke, Brockett, Brok, Broque*

Broderick (English) Broad ridge. *Rick, Brod, Roderick, Brod, Broddy, Broderic, Brodrik, Brodrig, Brodderrick, Broderyk, Brodrick*

Bromley (Old English) Brush-covered meadow. *Bromwell, Bromwood, Bromlee, Bromleigh, Bromli, Bromlie, Bromly*

Bronco (Spanish) Rough, unbroken horse.

Bronson (German) Brown's son. (English) Color name; son of the dark man. *Brown, Broun, Bruno, Bruin, Bruins, Berowne, Bronsen, Bronnson, Bronsin, Bronsonn*

Naming Rights

Before committing yourself and your baby to a name, say the entire name out loud several times. Does it sound right? Does it "flow"? Does it rhyme? If so, does the rhyme sound good?

Bronwen (Welsh) Dark and pure. *Bronwyn*

Bronze (Italian) A metal; yellowish to copper brown.

Brook (Old English) Stream; brook. *Brooke, Brooks, Brookes, Brooc, Brooker, Brookin*

Brooklyn (Modern English) Beautiful brook.

Bruce (French) Thicket. *Brooce, Broose, Brucey, Brucy, Brue, Bruis, Bruse*

Bryce (English) Son of a nobleman. *Brice, Bryson, Brycen, Bryceton, Bryse, Bryston*

Buckley (Old English) Meadow of deer. *Buckminster, Buck, Bucky, Buckner, Bucklee, Buckleigh, Buckly, Buclie, Buklee, Buclea, Buckli, Bucklie*

Bud (Old English) Herald. (German) To puff up. *Buddy, Buddie, Budd*

Buddha (Buddhist) Wise one.

Bukka (Hindi) Heart, loving, sincere.

Burdette (English) Small bird. *Berdet, Berdett, Berdette, Burdet, Burdette*

Burgess (Old English) Free citizen; shopkeeper. *Burg, Bergess, Bergen, Birgess, Burges, Burgiss, Byrgess*

Burke (German) Castle. *Bourke, Burk, Birk, Birke, Byrk, Byrke*

Burle (English) Knotted wood. (German) Boundary line. *Burl, Burleigh, Burley, Berl, Byrl, Byrle*

Burne (Old English) Brook. *Burns, Byrne, Burney, Beirne*

Burr (Swedish) Youth. *Bur*

Burt (Old English) Fortress, bright flame. *Burton, Bert, Berton*

Buster (Old English) One who breaks things. *Bustar*

Butch (American) Manly. *Butcher*

Buzz (Irish) Village in the woods. *Busby, Buzzy*

Byrd (English) Like a bird. *Bird, Birdie, Byrdie*

Byron (French) Cottage. (English) At the cowshed. *Byran, Byren, Byrom, Beyron, Birin, Biron, Buiron*

C

Cabal (French) Joined by a secret. (English) Arthur's dog in legend of King Arthur. *Cafall*

Cable (Old French) Rope. *Cabel, Cab, Cabe, Cabell*

Cade (Old English) Round. (Welsh) Pure. (French) Cask. Short form of Cadence. *Caide, Caden, Caiden, Cayden, Kade, Kaden, Kayde, Codey, Codi, Codie, Cody, Coty*

Caedmon (Irish) Wise warrior. *Cadman*

Caelan (Irish) Victorious people. *Cailean, Cailin, Caelen, Calan, Caley*

Caelum (Latin) Celestial. *Caelus, Chaelus, Caellum*

Caesar (Greek) Long-haired; hairy. (Latin) A fine head of hair. Famous emperor. (Shakespearean) From *Julius Caesar. Cesar, Czar, Kaiser, Caesarae, Caesare, Caesario, Casarius, Caeser, Casa, Caseare*

Cage (English) Enclosed space.

Cahir (English) Warrior.

Cain (Hebrew) Craftsman; spear. *Caine, Kane, Kain, Kaine, Chaim, Connie*

Caithness (Scottish) River valleys by fertile farm and croft land. (Shakespearean) From *Macbeth.*

Caius (Latin) Rejoice; variation of Gaius. *Cai, Caio, Kay, Kaye, Keye, Keyes, Keys, Cais*

Cajetan (Italian) From Gaeta; variation of Gaetan. *Cajetano, Kajetan, Kajetano*

Calbraith Origin and meaning unknown.

Calder (Old English) River of stones. (Irish) Lives near stony river. *Caulder, Caldre*

Caldwell (Old English) Cold spring. *Cadwell, Cadmus*

Caleb (Hebrew) Faithful; dog; bold. *Cale, Cal, Cleve, Cliff, Colby*

Calen (Scottish) Victorius people. *Calin, Caelan, Clean*

Calhoun (Old English) Warrior. (Irish) The narrow woods. *Callhoun, Colhoun, Colquhoun, Calhaun*

Caliban (Shakespearean) From *The Tempest.*

Callistus (Latin) Chalice. (Greek) Most lovely. *Calisto, Calixto, Callis, Callice, Callys, Callyx, Calliste, Calix, Calixte, Callixtus, Calleas, Callinicus,*

Calvert (Old English) Shepherd. *Calvex, Calbert*

Calvin (Latin) Bald. *Calvyn, Calvine, Calvino, Kalvin, Vinnie*

Camden (Scottish, Irish) Winding valley. *Camdin, Camdon, Camdyn*

Cameron (Old English) Bent nose. *Camm, Camaeron, Camedon, Camren, Camryn, Camry, Camyron, Kameron, Kamrey, Camren, Camron*

Camillo (Latin) Free-born child; noble; masculine of Camille. *Camillus, Camilus, Camilo, Kamillo, Kamilo*

Campbell (French) Beautiful field. (Irish) Crooked mouth. *Campbel, Camp*

Canaan (French) Church official; large gun. *Cannen, Cannin, Canning, Cannyn*

Cancer (Greek) Sign of the zodiac; the crab.

Candidius (Latin) Pure, sincere. (Shakespearean) From *Antony and Cleopatra.*

Canice (Irish) Handsome.

Canon (French) Official of the church. *Cannon, Cannan, Canning, Kanon*

Canute (Scandinavian) Knot. *Cnut, Knut, Knute*

Caphis (Shakespearean) From *Timon of Athens.*

Capricornus (Latin) Horned goat; constellation of the Zodiac. *Cap*

Capucius (Latin) Ambassador. (Shakespearean) From *Henry VIII.*

Capulet (Shakespearean) From *Romeo and Juliet.*

Carden (Irish) From the black fortress. (Old English) Wool carder. *Card, Cardin, Cardon, Cardew*

Carew (Latin) Chariot; run. *Carewe, Crew, Crewe, Rew*

Carey (Irish) Dark ones; near the castle. *Cary, Carrey*

Carl (Old German) Free man; a variation of Charles. *Karl, Karel, Caroll, Carroll, Carlisle, Carlyle, Caryl, Carel, Carlos, Carlito, Carrlos*

Carleton (Old English) Carl's town. *Carlton, Carlson, Carston*

Carlow (Irish) Quadruple lake. *Carlowe, Carlo*

Carlyle (Old English) Carl's island. *Carlisle, Carl, Lyle, Lisle, Carley, Carlile*

Carmelo (Hebrew) From the garden. (Italian) Fruitful orchard. *Carmel, Carmeli, Carmello, Karmel, Karmelo, Karmello*

Carmine (Italian) Song. *Carmi, Carman, Carmen, Carmin, Carmino, Karman, Karmen*

Carnelian (Latin) A red gemstone.

Carolus (French) Strong. (Scandinavian) Freeman. (Old German) Man. *Carroll, Carrol, Caroll, Cary, Caryl, Caryll*

Carpus (Hebrew) Fruit, fruitful.

Carrick (Irish) Rocky cliff or cape.

Carson (Scandinavian) Son of marsh-dwellers. *Carsen, Carsyn, Carvell*

Carsten (Greek) Anointed. (German) Follower of Christ. *Cristian, Cristiano, Karsten, Kristen, Kristian*

Carter (Old English) Cart driver. *Cartier, Cartrell*

Carvell (Old English) Wood carver. (French) Swampy dwelling. *Carvel, Carvil, Carville*

Cashmere (Kashmir) Peacemaker; luxurious fabric from Kashmir.

Casimir (Slavic) Peacemaker. *Casimeer, Casmire, Casimiro, Casmir, Caz, Kasimir, Kasimiro, Kazimierz, Kazimir, Cace, Cacey, Casey, Cayce, Caycey, Kasey, Casimer*

Caspar (Persian) Keeper of the treasure. *Casper, Cass, Gaspar, Gaspard, Gasparo, Gasper, Jasper, Kaspar, Kasper*

Cassius (Latin) Vain. *Cassian, Casius, Cash, Cass, Cassio*

Castor (Greek) Beaver. *Caster, Castorio, Kastor, Kaster*

Catcher (Old English) One who catches, as in a ball.

Cato (Latin) All-knowing. *Caton, Cayto, Kaeto, Kato*

Cavalon (English) Name of a king; *The Legend of King Arthur*.

Cedar (English) Cedar tree.

Cedric (Welsh) Gift of splendor. (Old English) War leader. *Caddaric, Ced, Cedrick, Cedrik, Cedro, Cedrych, Cerdric, Sedrick, Sedrik, Kedrick, Chadrick*

Celesto (Latin) Heavenly. (Italian) High; lofty. *Célestine, Celestino, Celindo, Selestine, Selestino, Silestino, Celso, Celsius, Celsus*

Centaurus (Greek) Mythical beast.

Naming Rights

A baby deserves a name that conveys a positive, desirable value to you and to him or her throughout life. Don't choose a name you associate with stupidity, dullness, or awkwardness. Avoid names that remind you of people you dislike, and name your child after someone you truly admire.

Cepheus (Latin) Small rock. *Cephus, Cephas*

Cerek (Polish) Lordly.

Cerimon (Shakespearean) From *Pericles*.

Cerny (Czechoslovakian) Black.

Cetus (Latin) A constellation; the whale.

Chad (Old English) Warlike. *Chadwick, Chaddie, Chadric, Chadrick, Chadwyck*

Chaim (Hebrew) Life; masculine form of Eve. *Hyman, Hymen, Hymie, Cahyim, Cahyyam, Chayim, Chayyim, Haim, Hayvim, Hayyim, Hy, Haym, Cahya, Manny, Chaika, Cain, Chai, Chaimek, Chaym, Chayme*

Chainey (French) Oak tree. *Chaney, Chalney, Chany, Cheney*

Chancellor (Old French) Secretary. *Chauncey, Chancey, Chancelor, Chansellor, Chanseler, Chaunce, Chanse, Chantz, Chanze, Choncey*

Chandler (French) Candle maker. *Chan, Chand, Chandlor*

Chandra (Hindi) Bright, radiant.

Channing (Old English) Knowing. (Old French) Cannon. *Cannon, Canal, Canon, Chann, Channe, Channon*

Chante (Jamaican) Song.

Charles (Old English) Manly. *Charlie, Charley, Chuck, Chas, Chars, Chaz, Chip, Chico, Chick, Charlemagne, Carel, Carlo, Charlot, Charls, Karol, Karolek, Karolik, Karoly*

Charon (Greek) Fierceness.

Chase (Old French) Hunter. *Chace, Chasen, Chayce, Chayse*

Chata (African) Ending.

Chatam (Native American) Hawk.

Chatan (Hebrew) Groom.

Chayton (Sioux) Falcon.

Chatillon (English, Shakespearean) From *As You Like It*.

Chen (Chinese) Great.

Chesmu (Native American) Gritty.

Chester (Latin) Camp. *Ches, Chess, Cheston*

Cheveyo (Native American) Spirit warrior.

Chevy (French) Knight. (Old English) Hunt. *Chevie, Chevalier, Chevrolet, Cheval, Chevall*

Cheyenne (Native American) Red people. *Chayan, Chayann, Shayan, Shayanne*

Chiamaka (African) God is splendid.

Chike (African) Power of God.

Chilton (Old English) Farm by the spring. *Chill, Chil, Chilly*

Chimon (Japanese) Wisdom gate.

Chiron (Greek) Wise teacher. *Kiron*

Chivalry (Old French) Knightliness; gallantry.

Chogan (Native American) Blackbird.

Chotan (Japanese) Deep pool.

Christian (Greek) Anointed. *Christiaan, Chrestian, Karstan, Kristo, Cristian, Kristian, Krystian, Krystiano, Cristobel, Christiano, Christianos*

Christopher (Greek) Christbearer. *Cristo, Christo, Christos, Christ, Christion, Christop, Christoper, Christophe, Christpher, Cristobal, Cristopher, Kristofer, Christof, Christoph, Kristof, Kristo, Cristy, Christophe, Kester, Cristoforo*

What's in a Name

The name **Christopher** is derived from the Greek word *Christos*, for "Christ," and *phero*, meaning "to bear." Christopher was the saint who carried Jesus across a river, earning the status of patron saint of travelers.

Chung (Chinese) Intelligent, wise one. (Vietnamese) Common.

Churchill (English) Lives near the church hill. *Churchil*

Ciaran (Irish) Small and dark-skinned. *Kiernan, Kieron, Key, Kerwin, Kirwin, Kerry, Kern, Kerr, Ceirnin, Carra*

Cicero (Latin) Historian. *Ciro, Cecero, Ciceron*

Ciel (French) From heaven.

Cipriano (Spanish, Greek) From Cyprus. *Ciprien, Ciprian, Cyprian, Cyprien, Siprian, Siprien, Sipryan*

Ciqala (Native American) Little one.

Circinus (French) Constellation designated by eighteenth-century astronomer Nicolas-Louis de Lacaille.

Cirrillo (Italian) Lordly. *Cirilo, Cirilio, Cyrilo, Cyryllo, Cyrylo*

Cisco (Spanish) Free; form of Francis and Francisco. *Francesco, Frisco, Paco, Pancho*

Clachas (English, Shakespearean) From *Troilus and Cressida.*

Claiborne (Old English) Born of the earth. *Clayborne, Claybourne, Claibourne, Clayton, Claiborn, Claibourn, Clayborn*

Clancy (Irish) Offspring of a redheaded soldier. *Clancey, Claney, Clan*

Clarence (Latin) Clear. *Claron, Clarendon, Claran, Clarance, Clarens, Claron, Clarons, Claronz, Clarrance, Clarrence, Klarance, Klarenz*

Clark (Old English) Cleric. *Clarke, Clarkson, Clerc, Clerk*

Claude (Latin) Lame. *Claud, Claudie, Claudio, Cloyd, Clyde, Colt, Claudius, Claudell, Claudio, Claudius, Claudan, Claidianus, Claudido, Claudien, Claudino, Claudon, Clodito, Clodo, Clodomiro, Klaudio*

Claus (Greek) People of victory; diminutive of Nicholas. *Claes, Clause, Klaus*

Clay (German) Adhere. *Clayland, Clayton, Klay, Klayton*

Cleavant (English) A steep bank; cliff. *Cleavon, Cleevant, Cleeve, Cleevont*

Clement (Latin) Merciful. *Clements, Clemens, Clemmons, Clemon, Clem, Clemendo, Clemente, Clementino, Clementius, Clemmie, Clemmy, Klemens, Klement, Klementos, Kliment*

Cleomenes (English, Shakespearean) From *Hamlet; Julius Caesar.*

Cleon (Greek) Famous one. *Clem, Colin, Collin, Cullen*

Cleveland (Old English) Land near the hill. *Cleve, Clive, Cleavon, Cleaveland, Cleavland, Cleon, Clevon*

Clifford (Old English) Hill. *Clifton, Clyff, Clyfford, Clyford, Clinton, Clint, Clive*

Cloten (English, Shakespearean) From *Julius Caesar.*

Clovis (German) Famous warrior; variation on Louis. *Clodoveo, Clovisto, Clovio, Clovito, Clothilde, Clotilde*

Clyde (Welsh) Heard from afar. *Clydell, Cloyd*

Cochise (Native American) Wood.

Coeus (Greek) Mythical name; father of Leto.

Cohn (Greek) Victory of the people. *Cailean*

Cola (American) Soft drink.

Colar (French) Victorious people.

Colbert (German) A seaman. (Old English) Renowned mariner. *Colvert, Culbert*

Colborn (Old English) Cold brook. *Colbourn, Colbourne, Colburn, Collbourn, Collburn, Collborn*

Colin (Irish) Youth. (Greek) Victor. Short form of Nicholas. *Collins, Colan, Colyn, Coilin*

Colm (Irish) Of Saint Columba (Latin) Dove. Short for Columba or Columban. *Callum, Collumbano, Colombain, Colum, Columbano, Columbanus, Columkille*

Colson (English) Triumphant people.

Colter (Old English) Colt herder. *Coltrane, Coulter*

Colton (English) Coal town. *Kolton, Coleton, Colton, Colston, Colsten, Colten, Coltin, Kolt*

Colville (Native American) Tribe located in eastern part of the state of Washington. (French) Derived from Colville-Sur-Mer in Normandy, France. (Science fiction) Character from *Dr. Who. Colvile, Colvill*

Coman (Arabic) Noble.

Cominius (Shakespearean) From *A Midsummer Night's Dream.*

Conall (Irish) Friendship. *Connall, Connell, Conal*

Conan (Gaelic) Wise. *Con, Condon, Conin, Conant, Conn, Conon*

Confucius (Chinese) Philosopher.

Cong (Chinese) Intelligent.

Conner (Irish) Desire. *Conners, Connor, O'Conner, O'Connor, Conor, Konnor*

Conrad (Old German) Brave counsel. *Rad, Konrad, Conroy, Cort, Con, Conrado, Curt, Kurt*

Constantine (Latin) Constant; steadfast. *Constans, Constanz, Constant, Constantin, Constantino, Constantius, Costa, Konstantin, Konstantio, Konstanz, Constantinos*

Constanzo (Italian) Constant, firm.

Conway (Welsh) River. *Conwy*

Coolio (American) American rapper.

Cooper (Latin) Cask. (Old English) Barrel maker. *Coop, Kuper*

Copper (Old English) Mineral; reddish-brown.

Corbin (Old French) Raven. *Corbett, Corbet, Corben, Corbie, Corbit, Corbitt, Corbyn, Corvin, Korbin, Korbyn, Corwin, Corwan, Corwyn*

Cordell (Latin) Rope. *Cord, Cordas, Kordell, Cordale, Corday, Cordelle, Kordelle*

Corin (Latin) Spear. *Coren, Corrin, Cyran, Koren, Korin, Korrin*

Cormack (Irish) Chariot driver. *Cormac, Cormick, Cormic*

Cornelius (Latin) Horn; hornblower. *Cornel, Corneille, Cornelio, Cornelious, Cornelus, Corney, Cornilius, Kornelious, Kornelis, Kornelius, Neal, Neel, Neil, Neely, Carnell, Cornell*

Corrado (Italian) Bold; sage counselor. *Corradeo*

Cortez (Spanish) Courteous; variation of Curtis. *Coretes, Kortes, Kortez, Curtiss, Curtice, Curtis*

Corvette (American) Model name of Chevrolet car.

Corvus (Latin) Raven.

Corydon (Greek) Battle-ready; lark. *Coridon, Coryden, Coryell*

Cosimo (Greek) Perfect universe. *Cozmo, Cosmé, Kosmo*

Costante (Latin) Firm; constant. *Constant*

Costard (Shakespearean) From *Love's Labor's Lost.*

Courtland (Old English) The king's land. *Cortland, Court*

Courvoisier (French) Brand of liqueur developed by Emmanuel Courvoisier and his associate Louis Gallo in the Parisian suburb of Bercy; the colgnac of Napolean.

Coyne (French) Modest. *Coyan, Coye, Coy*

Craig (Irish) Crag. *Craigh, Cruz, Cyrus, Craigie, Craik, Kraig*

Crandall (English) Valley of cranes. *Crandal, Crandell*

Cranmer (Shakespearean) From *Henry V.*

Crawford (Old English) Ford of the crows. *Crawfurd*

Creighton (Old English) Town near a creek. *Creigh, Cree, Crichton*

Crispin (Latin) Curly. *Crispen, Crispus, Crispo, Krispen, Crisp, Crespen, Crespin, Crepin, Crispian, Crispino, Crisspin*

Crockett (Middle English) Crook. *Crock, Crocket, Croquet, Croquett, Krock*

Cromwell (Shakespearean) From *Henry VIII.* (Old English) Winding stream.

Cronus (Greek) A titan; mythical father of Zeus. *Cronan*

Cruz (Spanish) Cross bearer. *Cruzito*

Cuba (Spanish) The country.

Cullen (Irish) Handsome. *Culley, Cullan, Cullinan*

Cupid (English) Cherub. (Latin) Desire, passion; god of love. (Shakespearean) From *Henry VIII.*

Curan (Irish) Hero. (Shakespearean) From *Timon of Athens. Curran, Curon, Curren, Currin, Curron*

Curio (English) Gentleman attending the duke. (Shakespearean) From *King Lear.*

Currier (Old English) Churn. *Curran, Currie, Curry, Currey, Curren, Currer*

What's in a Name

Charlotte Brontë wrote several novels under the androgynous pen name Currer (**Currier**) Bell, including *Jane Eyre* in 1847. At the time, the publishing industry looked down on female writers.

Curtis (Latin) Court. (Old French) Courteous. *Curtys, Kurt, Kurtis, Kurtiss*

Cuyler (Irish) Chapel.

Cyd (Greek) Public hill; variation on Sydney. *Cydney*

Cygnus (Latin) A northern constellation; the swan.

Cymbeline (Shakespearean) From *Taming of the Shrew.*

Cyril (Greek) Lordly. *Cyrilla, Cyra, Cy, Ciril, Cirilio, Cyrill, Cyrille, Cirillo, Cirilo, Cyrillus, Kiril, Kyril*

Cyrus (Persian) The sun. *Cy, Ciro*

D

Dabney (French) From Aubigny, France. *Dabnee, Dabnie, Dabny*

Dacian (English) Of the Nobility. (Irish) Southener. (Latin) From Dacia, near Rome.

Dack (English) From the French town Dax.

Daelen (English) Small valley. Alternate form of Dale. *Daelan, Daelin, Daelon, Daelyn, Daelyne*

Daeshim (Korean) Great mind.

Dag (Scandinavian) Day. *Dagmar, Dagney, Dagny, Dagget, Dailey, Daily, Daley, Day, Dayton, Daymond, Daeg, Deegan*

Dagan (Hebrew) Grain. *Daegan, Daegon, Dagen, Dagon, Dageon, Dagin, Dagyn*

Dagobert (German) Bright day. *Dagbert, Dogoberto*

Dagonet (English) *The Legend of King Arthur*; Arthur's fool.

Dai (Japanese) Big.

Dai-In (Japanese) Hidden greatness.

Daido (Japanese) Great way.

Dailan (English) Pride's people. (Irish) From the Dale. Unseeing. *Daelan, Daelen, Daelin, Dailen, Dalan, Dalain, Dallen, Dallin, Dalyn*

Daire (Irish) Wealthy.

Dakarai (African) Happy. *Dakairi, Dakar, Dakari, Dakarri, Dakara, Dakaraia*

Dakin (English) One who comes from Denmark; a variant form of "Danish." *Dane, Daine*

Dakota (Native American) Friend. *Dakodah, Dakodas, Dokcota, Dakkota, Dakoata, Dkotha, Dokotta, Dekot, Dokata, Dakottah*

Dalbert (German) From a bright place. *Dalbiret, Dalburt, Dalbyrt*

Dale (Old English) Valley. (German) Valley dweller. *Dal, Dallan, Dallen, Dallin, Dallon, Dalton, Daley, Dalibor, Daly, Dayle, Dawley*

Dalit (Hebrew) To draw water.

Dallas (Irish) Skilled. *Dalieass, Dall, Dalles, Dallus, Dallys, Dalys, Dellis*

Dallin (English) Pride's people. (Irish) From the dale. *Dallon, Dallen, Dallen*

Dalton (English) From the valley. *Dalaton, Dalltan, Dallten, Dalltin, Dallton, Dalltyn, Dalt, Daltan, Dalten, Daltin, Daltyn, Delton*

Damasus (Greek) From Damascus. *Damaskenos, Damaskinos*

Damek (Czechoslovakian) Earth. *Damick, Damicke, Damik, Damyk*

Damien (Greek) Tamer. *Damian, Damon, Daimen, Daman, Damen, Demyan, Damaiaon, Damaien, Damaun, Damayon, Dame, Damean, Damián, Damiane, Damiann, Damiano, Damianos, Damiyan, Damján, Damyen, Damyin, Damyyn, Daymian, Dema, Daemien, Damie, Damienne,*

Damieon, Damiion, Damine, Damionne, Damiyon, Dammion, Damyon

Dana (Norse) From Denmark. *Daen, Dain, Dane, Dayn, Dene, Daina, Danah, Dayna*

Daniel (Hebrew) God is my judge. *Dan, Danny, Danni, Danno, Daniels, Danilo, Danil, Dana, Danna, Danniell, Danyl, Danal, Danieal, Daniyal, Dannal, Dannial, Danick, Danik, Dannick, Danek, Danieko, Danika, Danyck, Dacso, Dainel, Dan'l, Danel, Dániel, Daniël, Danielius, Daniell, Daniels, Danielson, Danukas, Dasco, Deniel, Doneal, Eoniel, Donois, Nelo, Danile, Danniele, Danielo, Danil, Danila, Danilka, Danylo*

Dante (Latin) Enduring one. *Darte, Danton, Duran, Durant, Dantae, Danté, Danatay, Danaté, Dant, Dantay, Dantee, Dauntay, Dauntaye, Daunté, Dauntrae*

Darby (Irish) Free man. *Derby, Dar, Darbey, Derbe, Derbee, Debey, Derbi, Derbie*

Darcy (Irish) Dark. *D'Arcy, Darcie, Darcey, Darci, Darsy, Darsey, Daray, Daray, Darce, Darcel, Darcio*

Dard (Greek) Son of Zeus.

Dareh (Persian) Wealthy. *Dare*

Dario (Spanish) Well-off. *Daryo*

Darius (Persian) King. (Greek) Wealthy. *Daria, Darien, Darian, Darreus, Darrias, Darriuss, Darryus, Derrious, Derrius, Darrus, Derris, Dairus, Darieus, Darioush, Dariuse, Dariush, Dariuss, Dariusz, Darrios, Darus, Daryos, Daryus*

Darod (Science fiction) Character from *Star Trek Voyager*.

Darrell (Old French) Beloved. *Darryl, Darryll, Daryl, Daryll, Darlin, Darlen, Darleen, Darlynn, Dare, Deryl, Darrel, Darrilo, Derrell, Darral, Darrall, Darril, Darrill, Darrol, Dahrll, Daril, Darl, Darly, Daroyl, Darryle, Daryell, Darylle, Derryl*

Darren (Old English) Rocky hill. *Darrin, Darin, Darra, Darryn, Darrion, Daren, Darran, Darrience, Darun, Dearron*

Dartmouth (English) Port's name; Ivy League college.

Darwin (Old English) Beloved friend. *Darwyn, Darwynn, Derwin, Derwynn, Darwen*

Dashiell (French) Page boy.

Dathan (English) Beloved gift of God. *Dathen*

Dattatreya (Hindi) Son of the god Atria.

David (Hebrew) Beloved. *Davida, Davidde, Davide, Davina, Davita, Dave, Davey, Davy, Davie, Davi, Davyd, Davis, Davidson, Dawes, Dawson, Dewi, Dewey, Devlin, Devi, Devid, Dabi, Daevid, Daevyd, Dafydd, Daived, Daivid, Daivyd, Dauid, Dav, Daved, Daveed, Davidd, Davidek, Davido, Davood, Davoud, Davydas, Davydd, Davyde, Dayvid, Deved, Devid, Devidd, Devidde, Devyd, Devydd, Devydde, Devod, Davison, Davyson, Dawed, Dawud, Dawyt, Dawit, Dawid*

Davin (Scandinavian) Bright Finn. *Davon, Davyn, Dawan, Dawin, Dayvon, Daevin, Davan, Deavan, Deaven*

Davood (Persian) Beloved.

Dawson (English) Son of David. *Dawsan, Dawsen, Dawsin, Dawsyn, Dayson*

Dax (French) A town in southwestern France that dates to before Roman occupation. (English) Water. (Science fiction) Character from *Star Trek: Deep Space Nine*.

Dayton (Old English) Bright town. *Daiton, Daeton, Daythan, Daython, Daytonn, Deyton*

Deacon (Greek) Messenger. *Declan, Deakin, Deicon, Deke, Deycon*

Dean (Old English) Valley. *Deane, Dino, Deen, Deene, Dene, Deyn, Deyne, Dyn, Dyne*

Deandre (American) Strong. (English) Courageous, valiant man. *Dandrae, Dandre, Dandray, Dandras, Dondrea, Deandrae, Deandres, Deandrey, Deeandre, Deiandre, Deyandre, Dondre*

Decretas (Latin) Lord, an earthly man. (Shakespearean) From *Antony and Cleopatra*.

Deepak (Hindi) Small lamp; kindle. *Dipak*

Deion (African American) God of wine and revelry. (Greek) Short form of Dennis. *Dion, Deione, Deionte, Deionta*

Deiondre (African American) Valley. *Deiondray, Deiondré*

Deiphobus (Shakespearean) From *Troilus and Cressia*.

Dekel (Hebrew) Palm tree. *Dekal, Dekil, Dekyl*

Delano (French) From the elder tree grove. (Irish) Dark. *Delaney, Delane, Del, Delanio, Delayno, Dellano*

Dele (African American) Meaning unknown.

Delmore (Latin) Sea. *Delmar, Delmer*

Delmonte (American) Corporate brand name.

Demarco (Italian) Warring. (English) Male. *Damarco, Demarcco, Demarcio, Demarkco, Demarko, D'Marco*

Dembe (African) Peace.

Demetrius (Greek) Lover of the earth. *Demitiri, Demetrios, Dimitri, Dimitry, Dimity, Demeter, Demetre, Demetri, Demetris, Demmy, Dmitri*

Demont (French) Mountain. *Demontre, Demonte, Demontae, Demonta*

Dempsey (Irish) Proud. *Dempsie, Dempsy*

Denholm (Scandinavian) Home of the Danes. *Denholme, Denham, Denby, Denim*

Dennis (Greek) Fine wine lover. *Denis, Dennys, Dennison, Denniston, Denzel, Denzil, Denzell, Denit, Dennet, Dennett, Dennit, Dion, Denny, Tennis, Tennyson*

Denton (English) Happy home. *Dent, Denten, Dentin, Dentown*

Denver (English) Green valley. *Denvor*

Denzel (African American) Wild one. (English) Place name near Cornwall. (Welsh) High stronghold. *Denzil, Danzel, Danzell, Dennzel, Denzal, Denzall, Denzell*

Deo (Greek) Godlike.

Derek (German) Ruler. *Derik, Dirk, Derick, Derrick, Derrik, Derrike, Derych, Derry, Derex*

Dermot (Irish) Free of envy. *Kermit*

Derward (English) Deer keeper. *Derwood, Dirward, Durward, Dyrward*

Deshawn (Irish) God is gracious. *Dashaun, Dashawn, Deshon, D'Shawn, Dushawn*

Deshi (Chinese) Virtuous. *Déshì*

Desiderio (Spanish) Desire. *Desi, Desideryo*

Desmond (Latin) Society. *Desi, Des, Desmund, Dess*

Destin (French) Fate. *Destan, Desten, Destine, Deston, Destyn*

Deusdedit (Italian) Papal name.

Devarsi (Hindi) Sage of the Devas.

Deverell (Welsh) From the riverbank.

Devlin (Irish) Brave one. *Devlen, Devlyn, Devland*

Devon (Irish) Poet. *Devin, Deven, Deivon, Devohn, Devone, Devonn, Devonne, Divon, Devan*

Dewayne (Irish) Dark. (African American) From the wagon maker. *Dewain, Dewaine, Dewane, Dewon, Dewaun, Dewaune*

Dewei (Chinese) Of great principle.

Dewey (Welsh) Treasured one. *Dewi, Dewie, Dew, Dewy*

Dewitt (German) Blond. *DeWitt, Dewit, Dewyt, Dewytt, Wit*

Dexter (Latin) Right-handed. *Daxter, Decca, Deck, Decka, Dekka, Dex, Dextar, Dextor, Dextron, Dextur*

Dezso (Hungarian) Desired.

Dhananjay (Hindi) Arjuna.

Dharuna (Hindi) A rishi.

Dhatri (Hindi) Son of Vishnu.

Diallo (African) Bold.

Diamond (English) Brilliant. *Diaman, Diamante, Diamend, Diamont, Diamund, Dimond, Dimonte*

Dian (German) From the god of wine.

Dichali (Native American) Speaks a lot.

Dickinson (English) Powerful, rich ruler. *Dick, Dicken, Dickens, Dickenson, Dixon, Dix, Dickerson, Dikerson, Diksan*

Didier (French) Desire.

Diederik (Danish) Ruler of the people. *Dierk, Dirk, Dirck, Dierks*

Diego (Spanish) Supplanter. *Diaz, Jago*

Dieter (German) Army of the people. *Deiter, Deyter*

Dietrich (German) Ever-powerful ruler. *Deitrich, Deitrick, Deke, Didric, Didrick, Diedrich, Diedrick, Diedrik, Dieter, Dieterick, Dietric, Dietrick*

Digby (Old English) Settlement near a ditch. *Digbe, Digbee, Digbey, Digbie*

Dikembe (African American) Sports figure.

Dilip (Hindi) A king; ancestor of Rama.

Dillard (English) Faithful.

Dillon (Irish) Faithful. *Dil, Dill, Dillie, Dilly, Dillyn, Dilon, Dilyn, Dilynn*

Dimos (Spanish) Giving.

Dinesh (Hindi) Sun god.

Diokles (Mythology) Priest of Demeter; also Diocles.

Diomedes (Greek) An evil king.

Dionysus (Greek) Celebration. (Mythology) God of wine. *Dionysius, Dion, Dionicio, Dionisios, Dionesios, Dionisio, Dionustos,*

Dionysios, Dionysius, Dyonisius, Dyonisus

Dior (French) Present.

Disney (American) Corporate brand name.

Djau (Australian) Aboriginal tribe of Australia; mouth.

Doak Origin and meaning unknown.

Doane (English) Hill dweller. *Doan*

Dobry (Russian) Good. (Polish) Good. *Dobri, Dobrie*

Doc (English) Short for doctor; seventh son of the seventh son.

Dolabella (Shakespearean) From *Antony and Cleopatra.*

Dolf (German) Noble wolf. *Dolph, Dolfe, Dolff, Dolffe, Dolfi, Dolphe, Dolphus, Dulph, Dulphe*

Dominick (Latin) The Lord's. *Dominica, Dominique, Dominic, Domenico, Dominik, Domenick, Domingo, Dominy, Dom*

Domitus (Latin) Tamed. *Domitius*

Donalbain (Scottish) Great chief. (Shakespearean) From *Macbeth.*

Donald (Old English) Ruler of the world. *Don, Donn, Donnie, Donny, Donaldson, Donne, Donghal, Donal, Donley, Donnally, Donnell*

What's in a Name

The name **Donald** is derived from the Gaelic name *Domhnall,* which means "ruler of the world." Domhnall is the combination of *dumno* for "world," and *val* for "rule." Two kings of Scotland were named Donald.

Donatien (French) Gift. *Donathan, Donathon, Donatyen*

Donato (Latin) Given. (Italian) Gift. *Donatello, Donati, Donatus*

Dong (Vietnamese) Winter.

Donnelly (Irish) Dark warrior. *Donahue, Donnell, Donnel, Donner, Donovan, Donovon*

Donus (Italian) Papal name.

Dooley (Greek) Dark hero. *Dooly, Doolea, Doolee, Dooleigh, Dooli, Doolie, Dooly*

Doran (Greek, Hebrew) Gift. (Irish) Stranger. *Doron, Dorren, Dorran, Dore, Dorin, Dorryn, Doryn*

Dorian (Greek) Gift. *Dorien, Dorie, Dorrien, Dorrian*

Dorjan (Hungarian) Dark man.

Dornin (Romanian) Stranger.

Dorset (Old English) Tribe near the sea. *Dorsey*

Doryo (Japanese) Generosity.

Doud Origin and meaning unknown.

Douglas (Old English) Dark water. *Douglass, Doug, Dougie, Dug, Dugan, Dougal, Dugald, Dougles, Dugaid, Duglass*

Dov (Hebrew) Bear. *Dove, Dovi, Dovidas, Dowid, Dovid*

Dover (Old English) Water.

Doyle (Old English) Dark stranger. *Doyl, Doial, Doiale, Doiall, Doil, Doile, Doyal, Doyel, Doyele, Doyell, Doyelle*

Drake (Latin) Dragon. (German) Male swan. *Drago, Draco*

Draper (English) Fabric maker. *Dray, Draeper, Draiper, Drayper, Draypr*

Draylan (American) Science fiction. *Draylen, Draylin*

Drew (Welsh) Wise. *Drewe*

Droe (American) Science fiction.

Dromio (Shakespearean) From *The Comedy of Errors*.

Druce (Irish) Wise man.

Drummond (Scottish) Druid's mountain. *Drummund, Drumond, Drumund*

Drystan (Irish) Riot; sad.

Duane (Irish) Wagon maker. *Dwayne, Dwane, Dwain, Dwaine, Duwayne, Deune, Duain, Duaine, Duana*

Duante (African American) Wagon maker.

Dudley (Old English) People's meadow. *Dudly, Dudlea, Dudlee, Dudleigh, Dudli, Dudlie, Dud, Duddy*

Duer (Irish) Heroic.

Duffy (Scottish) Dark. *Duff, Duffey, Duffie*

Dugan (English) Worthy. *Doogan, Doogen, Dougan, Dougen, Douggan, Douggen, Dugen, Duggan*

Duke (Latin) Leader. *Duk, Dukey, Dukie, Duky*

Dumaine (Shakespearean) From *Love's Labour's Lost*.

Dume (African) The bull.

Duncan (Old English) Dark warrior. *Dunc, Dun, Doncan, Dunkan*

Dunley (English) Hilly meadow. *Dunleigh, Dunlee, Dunlea, Dunli, Dunlie, Dunly*

Dunn (English) Brown. *Dunne, Dun, Dune*

Dunstan (English) From the fortress. *Dunstin, Dunsten, Dunston, Dunstyn*

Durand (Latin) Enduring. *Durandt, Durante, Durant, Duran*

Durango (American) Model name of a Dodge truck.

Duranjaya (Hindi) Heroic son.

Duras (American) Science fiction.

Durdanius (Shakespearean) From *Julius Ceasar*.

Durjaya (Hindi) Difficult to conquer.

Durward (Old English) Gatekeeper. *Durwood, Durwald, Durwin, Derwood, Derward, Ward*

Dusan (Russian) God is my judge. *Dusen, Dusin, Dusyn*

Duscha (Slavic) Divine spirit.

Dustin (Old English) Dark stone. *Dusty, Dustan, Dunston, Dustain, Dustion, Dustynn*

Dutch (German) From the Netherlands.

Duvie Origin and meaning unknown.

Duy (Vietnamese) Save.

Dwalin (American) Science fiction.

Dweezil (Origin unknown) Nickname.

Dwight (Old English) Fair. *DeWitt, Dwhite, Dwite, Dwyte*

Dwyer (English) Fabric dyer.

Dyami (Native American) Eagle.

Dylan (Welsh) Sea. *Dillon, Dillan, Dyllan, Dyllon, Dylon*

Dyre (Scandinavian) Dear heart. *Dire*

Dyson (English) Short form of Dennison. *Dysen, Dysonn*

E

Eachan (Irish) Horseman. *Eachann*

Eadbert (Anglo-Saxon) Name of a king.

Eamon (Irish) Variation of Edmund. *Eamen, Amon*

Earc (Irish) Red.

Earl (Old English) Nobleman. *Earle, Earland, Early, Erie, Errol, Erroll, Airle, Earld, Earlie, Eorl, Erl*

Eben (Hebrew) Stone. *Eb, Ebenezer, Eban, Ebin, Ebon*

Eberhard (German) Strong wild boar. *Eber, Ebere, Eberardo, Eberhardt, Evard, Everard, Everardo, Everhardt, Everhart*

Ebi (African) Good thought.

Ebner (Hebrew) Father of light. *Ab, Abbey, Abbie, Abby, Abna, Abnar, Abner, Abnor, Avner, Eb, Ebbie, Ebby, Ebner*

Ebony (English) A hard wood. *Ebonie, Ebonee*

Eden (Hebrew) Delight. *Edan, Eaden, Eadin, Edin, Edyn, Eiden*

Edgar (Old English) Properous warrior. *Edgerton, Edger, Edgarton, Edgardo, Edgard*

Edison (English) Son of Edward. *Eddison, Edisen, Edyson, Edson*

Edme (Scottish) Protector; variation of Esme and Edmund.

Edmund (Old English) Rich warrior. *Edmond, Edmon, Edmonde, Edmondo, Edmand, Edmaund, Edmun, Ed, Ned, Ted, Teddy*

Edom (Hebrew) Of blood.

Edred (English) Name of a king.

Edsel (Old English) Rich. (American) Clunky car. *Edsell*

Edward (Old English) Rich guardian. *Eduard, Eduardo, Edoardo, Edouard, Edwards, Edwardson, Eddie, Eddy, Teddie, Neddie, Edvard, Edwardo*

What's in a Name

Edward means "rich guard," from the Old English *ead* for "rich" and *weard* for "guard." But the name is one of the very few still in use following the Norman Conquest. Saint Edward the Confessor, who was king of England right before the Conquest, was so popular that his name continued to be used throughout Europe while most other Old English names were replaced by Norman ones.

Edwin (Old English) Rich friend. *Edwyn, Eadwinn, Edwan, Edwen, Edwon*

Edwy (English) Name of a king.

Egan (Irish) Little fire. *Egon, Egil, Egen, Egann*

Egbert (English, German) Intelligent, formidably brilliant.

Egerton (Old English) Edge. *Egmont, Edgarton, Edgerton, Egeton*

Egil (Scandinavian) Awe-inspiring. *Eigil*

Eglamour (Shakespearean) From *Two Gentlemen of Verona*.

Egmont (German) Weapon, defender.

Egor (Russian) Farmer; variation of George.

Ehud (Hebrew) He who praises.

Eisig (Hebrew) He who laughs.

Eitan (Hebrew) Strong, firm. *Eithan, Eiton, Eita*

Eknath (Hindi) Poet, saint.

Elam (Hebrew) Highlands.

Elan (Hebrew) Tree. (Native American) Friendly.

Elazar (Hebrew) God has helped.

Elbert (German) Bright, famous. *Elberto*

Elder (Old English) Old. *Alder, Eldred*

Eldon (Old English) Ella's mound. *Elden*

Eldridge (Old English) Old counsel. *Elbridge, Eldredge, Eldrege, Eldrid, Eldrige*

Eldwin (English, German) Old, wise ruler; old friend. *Eldwinn, Eldwyn, Eldwynn*

Eleutherius (Latin) Free. *Eleuthere*

Elgin (English) Noble. (Irish) White. *Elgan, Elgen*

Elias (Hebrew) The Lord is God. *Elihu, Elyas, Ellis, Ellison, Ellsworth, Ellys, Ellias, Ellice, Elyas*

Elie (Greek) Light, variation of Eleanor. *Eli*

Elijah (Hebrew) God the Lord, the strong Lord. *Elija, Elijha, Elijiah, Elijuah, Elijuo, Eliya, Eliyah*

Eliot (Hebrew) High. *Eli, Ely, Elliot, Elliott, Eliott, Eliut, Eliud, Elliotte, Elyot*

Elisaku Origin and meaning unknown.

Elkanah (Hebrew) The zeal of God. *Elkan, Elkana, Elkin*

Ellery (Latin) Cheerful. *Elery, Ellory, Ellerey, Elory, Ellary*

Ellis (English, Greek, Hebrew) My God is Jehovah, variation of Elias from Elijah. *Ellison, Elis*

Elmer (Old English) Famous nobleman. *Elmo, Elman, Elmore, Ellmer*

Elrond (Fiction) Character from *The Lord of the Rings* by J.R.R. Tolkien.

Elsu (Native American) Flying falcon.

Elton (Old English) Ella's town. *Elten, Alton, Eldon, Ellton, Elthon*

Elvis (Scandinavian) Wise, sage. *Elvin, Elva, Elviz, Elvys*

Elwood (English) From the old forest. *Woody*

Eman (Irish) Earnest, sincere. *Emani*

Emanuel (Hebrew) God is with us. *Emanuele, Emmanuel, Immanuel, Imanuel, Manuel, Manny*

Emaus Origin and meaning unknown.

Emeril (Portuguese) Meaning unknown.

Emerson (Old English) Emery's son. *Emersen, Emmerson, Emmyrson, Emyrson*

Emery (German) Powerful home. *Emory, Emmery, Emmory*

Emile (Latin) Eager to please. *Aimil, Aymil, Emelen, Emelio, Emile, Emilian, Emiliano, Emilianus, Emilio, Emilion, Emilyan, Emlen, Emlin, Emlyn, Emlynn, Emil*

Eminem (American) Stage name for rapper Marshall Mathers.

Emmett (English) Hard worker, truth. *Emmitt, Emmot, Emmott, Emet, Emett, Emitt, Emmet*

Emrick (Welsh) Variation on the Greek for "immortal." *Emryk, Emrys, Emris, Emeric, Emerick, Emric*

Enapay (Native American) Brave.

Eneas (Greek) Praised. *Enneas, Ennes, Ennis*

Engelbert (Old German) Angel bright. *Bert, Berty, Ingelbert, Inglebert*

Engu (Japanese) Whole or complete fool.

Enki (Japanese) Postponement; the god who ruled over the Abzu.

Enkil Origin and meaning unknown.

Enmei (Japanese) Bright circle.

Enoch (Hebrew) Trained and vowed, dedicated; profound. *Enock, Enoc, Enok*

Enrique (Basque) Ruler of an estate. *Enrico, Quique, Enrico*

Eowyn (Hawaiian) God's gracious gift. *Keowynn, Keona*

Ephraim (Hebrew) Fruitful. *Ephrem, Efrem, Efraim, Ephrain, Ephram*

Equinox (Latin) Equal night.

Eran (Hebrew) Watchful, vigilant.

Erastus (Greek) Beloved. *Eraste, Rastus*

Eriberto (Italian) Glorious soldier. Form of Herbert. *Erberto*

Eric (Scandinavian) Ruler of all. *Aric, Ehrich, Ericc, Erick, Erico, Eryc, Erik, Erek, Eryk, Erikson*

Eridanus (Latin) Large southern constellation.

Eris (Greek) Goddess of strife.

Ermanno (Italian) A man of the army, warrior. *Ermano, Ermon, Erman, Armand, Harman*

Ernest (Old German) Vigorous. *Ernst, Earnest, Ernie, Ernestino, Ernesto, Ernestus*

Eros (Greek) God of love.

Errol (English) A nobleman; variation of Earl. *Earle, Earland, Early, Erie, Errol, Erroll, Earleen, Erleen, Erlene, Erle, Erryl*

Erskine (Old English) Green heights. *Erskin, Ersin*

Ervin (Hungarian) Variation of Irving. *Irvin, Irving, Ervan, Erwin, Erven, Erwan, Erwyn*

Eryu (Japanese) Dragon wisdom.

Esau (Hebrew) Hairy. *Esaw*

Escalus (English) An ancient lord. (Shakespearean) From *Measure for Measure*.

Escanes (Shakespearean) From *Pericles*.

Eskander (Persian) Defends mankind; a variation of Alexander. *Alexandre, Alejandro, Aleksandr, Aleksander, Ales, Aleksy, Oles, Lyaksandro, Aleksanteri, Aleksi, Elek, Sandor, Eskander,*

Iskender, Alekanekelo, Alexandrukas

Esmond (Old English) Protective grace. *Esmund, Desmond, Desmund*

ESPN (American) The TV sports network. *Espen*

Essien (African) Sixth-born son.

Estes (Latin) Estuary. *Eston*

Estio (Portuguese) Summer.

Etchemin (Native American) Canoe man.

Ethan (Latin) Constant. *Ethen, Etan*

Ethelbert (English) Splendid.

Ethelred (English) Name of a king. (German) Noble counselor.

Ethelwolf (English) A name of a king. *Ethelwulf*

Etienne (French) Crowned. *Estienne*

Ettore (Italian) Loyal.

Etu (Native American) Sun.

Eubie Origin and meaning unknown.

Euclid (Greek) Intelligent.

Eugene (Greek) Well-born. *Gene, Eugen, Eugeni, Eugenio, Evgeny, Ezven*

Eusebius (Latin) Pious.

Eustace (Greek) Fruitful. *Stace, Stacie*

Eutychian Origin and meaning unknown.

Evagelos (Greek) The evangelist. *Evangelos, Evangelo*

Evan (Irish) Young warrior. *Evans, Evann, Evaine, Even, Evin, Evon, Evyn, Evanston*

Evangelista (Greek) Good news giver; messenger of God.

Evangeleana, Evangeleanah, Evangeleane, Evangeleena, Evangeleene, Evangelia, Evangelica, Evangeline, Evangelique, Evangelique, Evangelista, Evangelyn, Evangelyna, Evangelynah, Evangelyne

Evaristus (Latin) Pleasing.

Everest (English) Name of Earth's tallest mountain.

Everett (German) Strong boar. *Everet, Everrett, Evert, Evrett, Everard*

Evzen (Slavic) Of noble birth.

Ewing (English) Friend of the law. *Ewan, Ewen, Ewart*

Ezekiel (Hebrew) The strength of God. *Ezakeil, Ezeeckel, Ezeck, Ezeckiel, Ezekeyial, Ezekial, Ezekielle, Ezequiel, Eziakah, Eziechiele*

Ezio (Latin) Like an eagle.

Ezra (Hebrew) Salvation. *Ezer, Esra, Ezera, Ezrah, Ezri, Ezzret*

Ezral (Science fiction) Character from *Star Trek Enterprise*.

F

Fabian (Latin) Bean. *Fabius, Fab, Fabyan, Fabia, Fabya, Fabiana, Fabiano, Fabain, Fabayan, Fabean, Fabien, Fabion*

Fabrizio (Latin) One with skilled hands. *Fabrizius*

Fabron (French) Blacksmith. *Fabra, Fabre, Fabriano, Fabroni, Fabryn*

Fagan (Gaelic) Ardent. *Fagen, Faegen, Faegin, Faegon, Faegyn, Faigen, Faigin, Faigon, Faigyn, Faygan, Faygen, Faygin, Faygon, Faygyn*

Fahd (Arabic) Panther. *Fahaad, Fahad*

Fairfax (Old English) Blond-haired. *Fairfield, Fair, Fayrfax, Fax*

Faisal (Arabic) Decisive, criterion. *Faysal, Faisel, Faisil, Faisl, Faiyaz, Faiz, Faizal, Faizel, Fasel, Fasil, Fayzal, Fayzel*

Fakih (Arabic) Smart, intelligent.

Falito (Italian) God has healed.

Falk (German) Surname relating to falconry. *Falxo, Falcko, Falckon, Falcon, Falconn, Falk, Falke, Falken, Faulco*

Falkner (English) Falconer, one who trains falcons. *Falconer, Falconner, Falconnor, Faulconer, Faulconner, Faulconnor, Faulkner*

Fallon (Celtic) Of a ruling family.

Falstaff (English) Kingly, noble. (Shakespearean) From *The Merry Wives of Windsor*.

Fanuco (Spanish) Free.

Faraji (African) Consolation. *Farajy*

Faraz (Arabic) Elevation. *Farhaz, Fariez*

Farley (Old English) Distant meadow. *Fairley, Fairleigh, Farland, Fairlea, Fairlee, Fairlei, Far, Farlay, Farly, Farlea, Farli, Farlie, Farlee, Farrleigh, Farrley*

Farnell (English) From the fern slope. *Farnal, Farnall, Farnalle, Farnel*

Farold (English) Mighty traveler. *Farr*

Farran (English) Wanderer. *Ferren, Farrun, Farron, Farryn, Firrin*

Farrar (Latin) Blacksmith. *Farra, Farar, Farron, Faron, Farrier, Farer, Farrer*

Farrell (Old English) Man of valor. *Farrel, Farrow, Faral, Farel, Farol, Faril, Farrill, Farryl, Farryll, Faryl, Ferol, Ferrel, Ferreell, Ferryl*

Fatin (Arabic) Captivating, seducer, alluring. *Faten, Fatine, Fatyn, Fatyne*

Fazel (Persian) Learned.

Federico (Spanish) Peaceful ruler. *Federick, Federic, Federigo, Federoquito*

Felix (Latin) Happiness. *Felice, Feliks, Felic, Felike, Fliks, Felo, Felizio, Filix, Filyx, Fylyx*

Fenton (English) From the settlement of the town on the moor. *Fen, Fennie, Fenny, Fentan, Fenten, Fentin, Fentun, Fentyn, Fintan, Finton*

Feodore (Russian) Variation of Theodore. *Feodor, Feador, Feadodor, Feaodore, Fedar, Fedinka, Fedor, Fedore, Fedya, Feedor*

Ferdinand (German) Courageous traveler. *Ferdie, Ferdy, Ferde, Ferd, Fernando, Fernandas, Ferdinan, Ferdinandus, Ferrando, Nando*

Fergus (Irish) Strong man. *Ferguson, Fergie, Fergis, Fergy, Fergun, Feargas, Ferguson, Fergusson, Furguson, Fyrgus*

Feroz (Hindi) Winner.

Ferran (Arabic) Baker. *Ferren, Feren, Farran, Feran, Feron, Ferrin, Ferron, Ferryn, Ferryl*

Ferrand (French) Gray-haired. *Gerand, Farran, Farrando, Farrant, Ferand, Ferrant*

Ferris (Latin) Iron. *Ferrys, Ferrell, Ferrel, Faris, Farris, Feris, Ferrice, Ferrise, Ferryce, Ferriss*

Feste (Latin) Festive, joyful. (Shakespearean) From *Twelfth Night*.

Festus (Biblical) Festive, joyful. *Festys*

Fielding (Old English) Field. *Field, Fielder, Fields*

50 Cent (American) Rapper name of Curtis James Jackson III.

Filip (Scandinavian) Variation of Philip. *Filippo, Filipe, Filipek, Filips, Fill, Fillip*

Finch (English) Small bird.

Finley (Celtic) Fair-haired one. *Finlay, Findlay, Finlea, Finlee, Finleigh, Finnlea, Finnleigh, Fynlay, Fynlea, Fynley, Fynnley*

Finnegan (Irish) Fair. *Finegan, Fineghan, Finneghan, Fynegan, Fyneghan, Fynnegan, Fynneghan*

Finnian (Irish) Fair-haired. *Finn, Finnie, Finny, Finian, Finley, Fyn, Fynn*

Fiorello (Italian) Little flower. *Fiore, Fiorelleigh, Fiorelley, Fiorelli, Fiorellie, Fiorelly, Fyorellee, Fyorello, Fyorellie, Fyorelly*

Firouz (Persian) Victorious.

Fiske (Swedish) Fisherman. *Fisk, Fysk, Fyske*

Fitz (English) Son; Fitz names were commonly given to the illegitimate sons of royalty. *Fitzgerald, Fitzroy, Fitzhugh, Fitzpatrick, Filz, Fits, Fyts, Fytz*

Flannery (Old French) Sheet of metal. (Irish) Red haired. *Flan, Flann, Flainn, Flanan, Flanin, Flannon, Flanyn, Flanon*

Flavian (Greek) Yellow, blond. *Flavel, Flavelle, Flavien, Flavyan, Flawian, Flawiusz, Flawyan*

Flavio (Italian) Gold or blond. *Flabio, Flavias, Flavious, Flavius, Flavyo*

Flavius (Latin) Blond, yellow-haired. *Flavian*

Fleance (Italian) Son of Banquo.

Fleming (English) A native of Flanders. *Flemming, Flemmyng, Flemyng*

Fletcher (Old French) Seller of arrows. *Flecher, Fletch*

Flint (English) Hard, quartz rock. *Flinte, Flynt, Flynte*

Florian (Latin) Flowering, blooming. *Florien, Florentino, Florinio, Florentin, Florentyn, Florus, Florion, Florrian, Flory, Floryant, Floryante*

Floritzel (Italian) Flower. *Flor*

Floyd (Welsh) The hollow. *Floid, Floyde*

Fluellen (Welsh) Like a lion.

Flynn (Irish) Son of the red-haired man. *Flinn, Flin, Flyn*

Fo-hai (Chinese) Buddha-ocean.

Fo-hsing (Chinese) Buddha-mind.

Fonty Origin and meaning unknown.

Ford (Old English) River crossing. *Forde*

Formosus (Latin) Finely formed.

Forrest (Old French) Out of the woods. *Forest, Forestt, Forrestt, Forrester, Forster, Foryst*

Fortinbras (Scandinavian) Norwegian king. (Shakespearean) From *Hamlet*.

Fortino (Italian) Fortunate, lucky. *Fortin, Fortine, Fortyn, Fortyne*

Foster (Old French) Forest keeper. *Forster*

G

Fox (English) Fox. *Foxx*

Fraco (Spanish) Weak.

Franchot (French) Nickname for Francis.

Francis (Old French) Free; an androgynous name, though Frances is generally used for girls and Francis for boys. *Franco, France, Franciskus, Francys, Frannie, Franny, Franscis, Fransis, Franus, Frencis*

Francisco (Spanish) Free land. *Francesco, Fransysco, Frasco*

Francois (French) Free. *François, Francoise*

Franklin (Old French) Free man. *Frank, Frankie, Franklyn, Francklen, Francklin, Franklynn, Francklyn, Francelen*

Franz (German) Free. *Frans, Frants, Fransz, Franzen, Franzie, Franzin, Franzl, Franzy*

Frasier (French) Strawberry. *Frazer, Fraser, Frazier, Fraizer, Fraze, Frazyer*

Frederick (German) Peaceful ruler. *Frederic, Frederico, Fred, Freddie, Fredrik, Freddy, Fritz, Fredderick, Fredek, Fréderick, Frédérik, Fredricks, Fredrik*

Freedom (English) Liberty.

Fremont (German) Guardian of freedom. *Fremonte*

Frey (Scandinavian) God of weather. *Frai, Fray, Frei*

Freyr (English) He who is foremost lord. (Norse) God of peace and prosperity.

Frisco (Spanish) Variation of Francis.

Fritz (German) Peaceful ruler. *Fritts, Fritson, Frizchen, Fritzl*

Frollo (English) *The Legend of King Arthur*; killed by Arthur.

Fudoki (Japanese) Immovable; unmoving wisdom.

Fujita (Japanese) Field.

Fuller (Old English) One who works with cloth. *Fuler*

Fulton (Old English) Town near the field. *Faulton, Folton*

Furio (Latin) Furious.

Fyodor (Russian) The gift of God. *Fydor, Fydore, Fyodore*

G

Gabai (Hebrew) Delight, adornment.

Gabriel (Hebrew) God is my strength. *Gabryel, Gabriello, Gavrila, Gab, Gabe, Gable, Gaberial, Gabrail, Gabriael, Gabrieal*

Gad (Native American) Juniper tree.

Gage (French) Pledge. *Gaige, Gaig, Gager, Gayg, Gayge*

Gaines (English) Increase in wealth. *Gaynes, Gainsborough, Gainor, Gaynor, Gains, Gayne*

Gaino Origin and meaning unknown.

Gajendra (Hindi) Elephant king.

Gale (English) Lively. *Gail, Gaile, Gayl, Gayle*

Galen (Greek) Tranquil. *Gaelan, Gaelen, Gaelin, Gaelyn, Gailen, Galan, Galin, Galon, Galyn*

Galileo (Italian) From Galilee.

Gallagher (Irish) Eager aide. *Gallagher, Gahan*

Gallant (English) Courageous.

Galloway (Latin) From Gaul. *Galway, Gallway, Gallowai, Gallwai, Galwai*

Gallus (Shakespearean) From *Anthony and Cleopatra*.

Galvin (Irish) Sparrows. *Gal, Gallven, Gallvin, Galvan, Galven, Galvon, Galvyn, Gall*

Gamal (Arabic) Camel. *Jamal, Jammal, Gamali, Jemaal, Gemal, Gemali, Gamall*

Gamel (English) The old one.

Gan (Hebrew) Garden. (Chinese) Daring. (Vietnamese) Near.

Gandale Origin and meaning unknown.

Ganesh (Hindi) A Hindi god.

Gannon (Irish) Fair complexion. *Ganan, Ganen, Ganin, Gannan, Gannen, Gannyn, Ganon, Ganyn*

Gao (Chinese) Tall, high.

Gardiner (Danish) Garden keeper. *Gardener, Gardenor, Gardner, Gardnard, Garden, Gard, Gardell, Gardenner, Gardie, Gardiner, Gardnar*

Garen (French) Guardian. *Garin, Garan, Garion, Garrion, Garyon*

Gareth (Norse) Enclosure. (French) Watchful. *Garth, Garret, Garreth, Gareth, Garit, Gary, Garry, Gar, Garette*

Garfield (English) Promontory. *Garfyeld*

Garland (French) Wreath. *Garlan, Garlon, Garlyn, Garlande, Garllan, Garlund*

Garner (Latin) Granary. (French) Sentry. *Garnar, Garnier, Garnit, Garnor, Garnyr*

Garrett (English) Strong. *Garett, Garrard, Garret, Garretson, Garrith, Garrot, Garyth, Garritt, Gerrity, Jared, Jarod, Jarret, Jarrett, Jarrot, Jarrott*

Garrison (French) Fort. *Garson, Garison, Garisson, Garris, Garryson, Garyson*

Gary (German) Spear carrier. *Garry, Garrie, Garvey, Garvie, Garvin, Gervis, Gervais, Gervase, Garrick, Garri, Gare, Gari, Garie*

Gaspar (Persian) Treasure bearer. *Gasper, Gaspare, Jasper, Caspar, Casper, Gaspard, Gasparo, Jaspar, Kaspar, Kasper, Gasparas, Gaspari, Gasparo, Gazsi*

Gaston (French) From Gascony. *Gascon, Gastone, Gastan, Gastaun, Gasten, Gastin, Gastyn*

Gatian (Hebrew) Family.

Gavin (Welsh) Hawk. *Gavan, Gav, Gavinn, Gavn, Gavohn, Gavon, Gavun, Gavynn, Gavino, Gaven*

Gavrie (Russian) Man of God.

Gavril (Slavic) Believer in God. *Gavriel, Gavi, Gavrel, Gavryel, Gavryele, Gavryell, Gavryelle, Gavy, Ganya, Gavrilla, Gavrilo, Gavryl, Gavryle, Gavryll, Gavrylle, Gavy*

Gawain (Welsh) Courteous. *Gawaine, Gawen, Gauvain, Gawayn, Gawwayne, Gawen, Gwayne, Gwayn*

Gawonii (Native American) He is speaking.

Gaylord (French) Brave. *Gaylard, Gayelord, Gaelor, Gaelord, Gailard, Gaillard, Gailor, Gailord, Gallard, Gayler, Gaylor*

Geary (English) Changeable. *Gearey, Gery, Gearee, Geari*

Gedeon (Hungarian) Warrior; a form of Gideon.

Geert (Germanic) Brave; strength.

Gelasius (Greek) Laughter.

Gemini (Latin) The twins.

Gene (English) Well-born. *Eugene, Genio, Jeno, Genek, Gena, Genya, Gine, Yevgeni, Yevgenij, Yevgeniy, Yengeny*

Genesis (Hebrew) Origin. *Gennesis, Ginesis, Jenesis, Jennesis*

Genjo (Chinese) Gold.

Genko (Japanese) Original silence.

Gennaro (Latin) Consecrated to God.

What's in a Name

Gennaro is the Italian form of the Roman name Januarius, for January—the name of month given in honor of the Roman god Janus. Saint Gennaro is the patron saint of Naples.

Genovese (Italian) From Genoa, Italy. *Geno, Genovis*

Geode (Greek) Earthlike.

Geoffrey (German) Peace. *Geoff, Gef, Geff, Geoffery, Giotta, Godfrey, Gottfried, Jeff, Geoffre, Geoffri, Geoffroy, Geoffry, Geofri*

Geordi (Greek) Hill near meadows.

George (Greek) Farmer. *Georg, Georges, Georgio, Giorgio, Giorgis, Georgius, Georgie, Georgi, Georgy, Geordie, Goran, Jorge, Jorges, Jorgen, Jerzy, Jiri, Juro, Jurik, Jur, Jeorg, Juergen, Jurgen, Jurek, Jorrin, Jurgi, Yegor, Yura, Yurchik, Yurik, Yusha, Yurko, Yoyi, Yuri, Egor, Zhorka, Seiorse*

Gerald (French) Spear warrior. *Gerard, Geraud, Gerardo, Gerhard, Gerhardt, Gerhart, Geraldo, Garold, Gerek, Gerrit, Garrod, Garrard, Gerbert, Girard, Girauld, Girault, Giraut, Gerry, Jerry, Jerard, Jarett, Jarrett*

Gerik (Polish) Prosperous spearman. *Geric, Gerick, Gérrick*

Gerlac (German) Spear thrower. *Gerlach, Gerlache, Gerlaich*

Germain (French) Bud. *Germane, Germayn, Germayne, Germin, Germon, Germyn, Jarman, Jermyn, Jermain, Jermaine*

Germanus (Latin) Brotherly. *German, Germaine, Germano, Jermayn, Jermayne*

Geron (French) Guard.

Gersham (Hebrew) Exile. *Gershom, Gersho, Geurson, Gursham, Gurshun*

Gershon (Yiddish) Stranger in exile. *Gershoom*

Gerson (Hungarian) Stranger banished. *Gerzon, Gersan, Gershawn*

Gervasio (Spanish) Warrior. *Gervase, Gervais, Gervaise, Gervasius, Gervaso, Gervayse, Gerwazy, Jarvey, Jarvis, Jervis, Garvas, Gervasy*

Ghadir (Arabic) Sword.

Ghazi (Arabic) Invader.

Giacomo (Hebrew) Replaces. *Gaimo, Giacamo, Giaco, Giacobbe, Giacobo, Giacopo, Gyacomo*

Gian (Hebrew) The Lord is gracious. *Ghian, Ghyan, Gianetto, Giannis, Giannos, Gyan*

Giancarlo (Italian) Gracious; powerful. *Giancarlos, Gianncarlo, Gyancarlo*

Giannes (Hebrew) Gift from God. *Gian, Gianne*

Gianni (Italian) God is gracious. *Giani, Gionni, Gianney, Gianni, Gianny*

Gideon (Hebrew) Mighty warrior. *Giddy, Gid, Gedeon, Gideone, Gydeon, Hedeon*

Gifford (English) A worthy gift. *Giff, Giffard, Gifferd, Giffie, Giffy, Gyfford, Gyford*

Gig (Spanish) Spear.

Gilbert (German) Bright desire. *Gilberto, Guilbert, Giggon, Gil, Gilly, Gip, Gipper, Gib, Gibby, Gibbs, Gibbes, Gibson, Gillett, Gillette, Wilbert, Wilbur, Bert*

Gildas (English) Guilded.

Giles (Greek) Shield of hides. (French) Youth. *Gyles, Gilles, Gillis, Gilean, Gileon, Gil, Gillette, Gillian, Egedio, Egide, Egidius, Gide, Jetes, Jyles*

Gilford (Old English) Ford near the wooded ravine. *Guilford, Gilmore, Gilroy*

Gino (Italian) Noble born. *Ghino, Gyno*

Gioacchino (Italian) Founded by God. *Gioaccino, Gio*

Giovanni (Italian) Gift from God. *Giannino, Giovann, Giovannie, Giovanno, Giovon, Giovanathon, Giovonni, Giovonnia, Giovonnie, Givonni*

Girish (Hindi) God of mountain.

Giuseppe (Hebrew) The Lord increases. *Giuseppi, Giuseppino, Giusseppe, Guiseppe, Guiseppi, Guiseppie, Guisseppe*

Glanville (French) Settlement of oak trees. *Glannville, Glanvil, Glanvill, Glanvyl, Glanvyll, Glanvylle*

Gleb (Russian) God of life.

Glen (Irish) Secluded wooded valley. *Glenn, Glenard, Glenon, Glendon, Glean, Gleann, Glennie, Glennis, Glennon, Glenny*

Godfrey (German) God's peace. *Goddard, Gottfried, Gotfrid, Goffredo, Giotto, Godofredo, Govert, Godrick, Godwin, Godin, Goddenn, Godding, Godard, Godhart, Gotthardt*

Goldman (Old English) To shine. *Gold, Goldwin, Goldwyn*

Goliath (Hebrew) Exile. *Golliath, Golyath*

Gomer (English) Good fight.

Gonzalo (Spanish) Wolf. *Consalvo, Goncalve, Gonsalve, Gonzales, Gonzoalos, Gonzalous, Gonzelee, Gonzolo*

Gopal (Hindi) Lord Krishna.

Goran (Greek) Farmer. *Gorin, Gorren, Gorrin*

Gordon (Old English) Fertilized pasture. *Gordan, Gordie, Gordy, Gordo, Gorton, Gore, Gorham, Gorrell, Gord, Gordain, Gorden, Gordin, Gordonn, Gordun, Gordyn*

Gorman (Irish) Small blue-eyed one. *Gormen*

Goro (Japanese) Fifth.

Gosheven (Native American) Leaper.

Gower (Old English) Crooked coastline. (French) Harness maker. *Gowell, Gowar*

Grady (Latin) Rank. *Gradea Gradee, Gradey, Gradi, Gradie, Graidee, Graidey, Graidi, Graidie, Graidy, Graydee, Graydee*

Graham (Latin) Grain. (English) Gray home. *Gram, Graeme, Grahame, Graeham, Graehame, Grahem, Grahim, Grahime, Grahm, Graihame, Grayham, Greyham, Greyhame*

Grand (English) Grand; superior.

Granger (French) Farm steward. *Grainger, Grange, Graynger*

Grant (French) To give. *Grandt, Grantham, Granthem*

Granville (French) Big town. *Gran, Granvel, Granvil, Granvile, Granvill, Granvyl, Granvyll, Granvylle, Grenville, Greville*

Gratiano (Italian) Grace. (Shakespearean) From *The Merchant of Venice*.

Gray (Old English) To shine. *Grey, Grayson, Graydon, Griswold, Greeley, Graye, Grai, Greye*

Green (English) The color green. (Shakespearean) From *King Richard II*. *Greener*

Greer (Greek) Watchful. *Grier, Grear*

Gregory (Greek) Watchman. *Gregorius, Gregorios, Gregori, Gregoire, Gregor, Greger, Gregorio, Gregoor, Griogair, Grioghar, Gregus, Gragos, Greis, Grischa, Grigor, Grigori, Gries, Gero, Greg, Graig, Greig, Gregg, Gregson, Grig, Grigg, Grigson, McGregor*

Gremio (English) Enrages. (Shakespearean) From *The Taming of the Shrew*.

Gresham (English) From the grazeland. *Grisham*

Griffin (English) A mythological beast—half lion, half eagle—charged with watching over golden treasures. (Latin) Hooked nose. (Welsh) Red, ruddy. *Gryphon, Griffon, Griffith, Griff, Griffie, Griffyn, Griffynn, Gryffin, Gryffyn*

Griffith (Welsh) Fierce chief. *Griffeth, Gryffith, Griffy, Griffie*

Grover (English) One who tends the groves. *Grove*

Grumio (English) Enrages. (Shakespearean) From *The Taming of the Shrew*.

Guadalupe (Arabic) Wolf valley. *Guadalope*

Guard (English) Sentry, watchman.

Guiderius (Latin) Guide. (Shakespearean) From *Cymbeline*.

Guido (Spanish) Guide.

Guildenstern (English) Courtier. (Shakespearean) From *Hamlet*.

Guillermo (Spanish) Resolute, protector. *Guillaume, Guilherme, Gillermo, Gughilmo, Gwillyn, Gwilym, William*

Guinness (English) Brand of beer.

Guion Origin and meaning unknown.

Gunnar (Old Norse) War. *Gunn, Gunther, Gunter, Guntar, Guner, Guenter, Guntero, Gun, Guenther*

Gustave (Swedish) Goth. *Gustavo, Gustavus, Gustav, Gustaf, Gus, Gustaaf, Gustaof, Gustava, Gustaves, Gustavius, Gustavs, Gustik, Gustus, Gusztav*

Guthrie (Irish) War hero. *Guthree, Guthrey, Guthry, Guthre, Guthri*

Guy (French) Guide. *Guie, Guyon*

H

Haakon (Scandinavian) Highborn. *Haaken, Hakon, Hacon, Hagan, Hakan, Hako*

Habib (Arabic) Loved one; beloved. *Habeeb, Habyb*

Hackett (French) Little hewer of wood. *Hacket, Hackit, Hackitt, Hackyt, Hackytt*

Haddad (Arabic) Blacksmith. *Hadad*

Hadden (Old English) Heath. *Haddon, Haddan, Haddyn*

Hadi (Arabic) Rightly guide. *Haddi, Hadee, Hady*

Hadley (Old English) Heather meadow. *Had, Hadlea, Hadlee, Hadleigh, Hadly, Leigh*

Hadrian (Greek) Wealthy; form of Adrian. *Hadrien, Hadrion, Hadryan, Hadryen, Hadryin, Hadryon, Hadryn*

Hafez (Arabic) Keeper.

Hagan (Irish) Little Hugh. (German) Strong. *Haggan*

Haggai (Hebrew) Feast.

Hagley (Old English) Enclosed meadow. *Haglea, Haglee, Hagleigh, Hagly, Hagli, Haglie, Hagly*

Hahn (German) Rooster.

Haidar (Arabic) Lion. *Haider, Haydar, Hyder*

Haing (Cambodian) Cambodian American physician and actor best known for Academy Award for *The Killing Field*.

Hakaku (Japanese) White crane.

Hakeem (Arabic) Wise. *Hakim, Hakam, Hakem, Hakiem, Hakym*

Halbert (Old English) Shining hero. *Bert, Halbirt, Halburt, Halbyrt*

Haldor (Norse) Rock of Thor; Norse god of thunder.

Haley (Old English) Hay meadow. *Hailey, Haily, Haleigh, Halley, Hallie, Hayleigh, Hayley, Hayli*

Hall (Old English) Meeting room.

Hallam (Old English) The valley. *Halam, Hallem*

Halsey (Old English) From Hal's island. *Hallsey, Hallsy, Halsy, Hallsea, Halsea*

Hamal (Arabic) Lamb. *Amahl, Amal, Hamahl, Hamel, Hamol*

Hamaliel (American) Angel of logic, August. *Humatiel*

Hamid (Arabic) Thankful to God. *Haamid, Hamaad, Hamadi, Hamd, Hamdrem, Hammad, Hammyd, Hammydd, Humayd, Mohammed*

Hamilton (Old English) Flat-topped hill. *Hamel, Hamelton, Hamil, Hamill, Hamell, Hammill, Hamiltyn, Hamylton*

Hamish (Scottish) He who supplants; form of James. *Hamysh*

Hamlet (Old German) Home. (Shakespearean) From *Hamlet*. *Hamlit, Hamlin, Hammond, Hampton, Ham, Hamlot*

Hammet (German) Village; home. *Hammett, Hamnet, Hamnett*

Hamon (Greek) The faithful one.

Hamza (Arabic) Lion. *Hamze, Hamzah, Hamzeh, Hamzia*

Hania (Native American) Spirit warrior.

Hannes (Scandinavian) The Lord is gracious. (Hindi) Swan. *Hans, Hanns, Hansel, Hanss, Hanzel, Hanes, Hanus*

Hannibal (Old English) Steep incline. *Han, Hanley, Hannybal, Hanybal, Anibal*

Haran (Hebrew) Mountaineer.

Harbin (German) Little warrior. *Harban, Haren, Harbon, Harbyn*

Hardicanute (Norse) Hard nose.

Hardy (Old English) Good health. *Hardin, Harden, Harding, Hardley, Hardee, Hard, Hardey, Hardi, Hardie*

Hari (Hindi) Sun; Vishnu. *Harin*

Harkin (Irish) Dark red. *Harkan, Harken, Harkon, Harkyn*

Harlan (German) Flax. (Old English) Rabbit archer. *Harlin, Harley, Harlow, Harford, Harland, Harlen, Harlenn, Harlyn, Harlynn*

Harlem (American) Place name: Harlem, New York.

Harmon (Greek) Harmony. (Old English) Soldier. (Latin) Noble. *Harman, Harm, Harmann, Hermen, Harmin, Harmond, Harms, Harmyn*

Harold (Old German) Commander. *Hereld, Harry, Hal, Hiraldo, Harild, Haryld, Herald, Herold, Heronim, Heryld, Harolda, Harrel, Harrell, Heroldo, Herlad, Herrold, Herrick, Herryck*

Harper (Old Norse) Whaler. *Harpo, Harp*

Harry (Old English) Army ruler. (German) Ruler of the household. *Harris, Harrison, Harray, Harrey, Harri, Harrie, Hary*

Harsh (Arabic) Joy. *Harshad, Harshal, Harshi, Harshini, Harshit, Harshita*

Harshul (Hindi) Deer.

Hart (English) Stag. *Harte, Hartley, Hartman, Hartwell, Hartwig, Heart*

Haru (Japanese) Born in spring.

Harun (Arabic) Superior.

Harvey (Old German) Battle. *Harve, Herve, Harv, Harvard, Harvee, Harvy, Herv, Harvie*

Hasan (Arabic) Good-looking. *Hassan, Hassun, Hasain, Hasaun, Hashaan, Hason*

Haskel (English) Ash tree; form of Ezekiel. *Haskell*

Hastings (Old English) Son of the austere man. *Hastey, Hastie, Hasting, Hasty*

Havika (Hawaiian) Beloved.

Hawk (Old English) Falcon. *Hawke, Hawkin, Hawkins*

Hawthorne (Old English) Where hawthorn trees grow. *Hawthorn*

Hayden (Old English) Hay field. *Haydn, Haydan, Haydenn, Haydin, Haydun, Haydyn, Heydan, Heyden, Heydin, Heydn, Heydon, Heydun, Heydyn*

Hayes (Old English) Hedged area. *Hays, Hais, Haiz, Haize, Hayse, Hayz*

Haywood (Old English) Hedged forest. *Heywood, Heiwood, Woody*

Heathcliff (English) Cliff near a heath. *Heath, Heafclif, Heafcliff, Heaffclif, Heaffcliff, Heaffcliffe, Heaffclyffe, Heathclif, Heathcliffe, Heathclyffe*

Heaton (English) High ground. *Heatan, Heaten, Heatin, Heatyn*

Heber (Hebrew) Partner. *Hebor, Hebar*

Hector (Greek) Anchor. *Hektor, Heckter, Hecktir, Hecktore, Hecktur, Hectar, Hektar, Heckter, Hektir, Hektore, Hektur*

Hedley (Old English) Heathered meadow. *Headleigh, Headley, Headly, Hedly, Heddlea, Heddlee, Heddleigh, Heddley, Heddli, Heddlie*

Heinrich (German) Ruler of the household. *Heine, Heini, Heinie, Heiner, Heinreich, Heinric, Heinriche, Heinrick, Heinrik, Heynric, Heynrich, Heynrick, Heynrik, Hinric, Hinrich, Hinrick, Hynric, Hynrich, Hynrick, Hynrik*

Heinz (Hebrew) God is gracious. *Hines*

Helaku (Native American) Full of sun.

Helicanus (Shakespearean) From *Pericles.*

Helios (Greek) God of the sun.

Heller (German) The sun.

Hello (French) Greeting; surprise. *Halo*

Helmut (English) Helmet. *Hellmut, Helmuth, Helmaer, Hellmuth*

Hendrick (Old English) Lord's manor. *Hendric, Hedric, Hedrick, Hendrik, Henric, Henrik, Heindric, Heindrick, Hendricks, Hendrickson, Hendrikus, Hendrix, Hendryc, Hendryck, Hendrycks, Hendryx*

Henley (Old English) High meadows. *Henlee, Henlie, Henlea, Henleigh, Henli, Henly*

Hennessy (Irish) Surname.

Henry (German) House ruler. *Henri, Harry, Hal, Hawkin, Hawkins, Harrison, Harris, Henriot, Heinrich, Heinz, Henke, Henryk, Hank, Henny, Henderson, Hawke, Enrique, Enrico, Enzio, Parry, Petty*

Hephaestus (Greek) God of the crafts.

Herbert (Old English) Exalted ruler. (German) Shining army. *Herbie, Herb, Bert, Bertie, Erberto, Harbert, Heribert, Heriberto*

Hercules (Greek) Hera's glory. *Ercole, Ercolo, Ercule, Herakles, Hercule, Herculie, Herc*

Herman (German) Soldier. *Hermann, Hermie, Hermy, Herm, Herrick, Armand, Armando, Ermanno*

Hermes (Greek) Messenger. *Ermes, Hermilio, Hermite, Hermus*

Hernan (Spanish) Adventurous. (German) Peacemaker.

Herring (English) Small fish.

Hershel (German) Deer. *Herschel, Hersh, Hersch, Hirsh, Hirsch, Hertz, Heshel, Hershey, Hersey, Herschell, Herzel, Herzl, Heschel, Hirschel, Hirschl*

Herve (English) Bitter. *Herv, Hervee, Hervey, Hervi, Hervie, Hervy*

Hezekiah (Hebrew) God is my strength. *Hezekia, Hezekial, Hezeki, Hez, Hazikiah, Hezekyah, Hezikyah*

Hiamovi (Native American) High chief. *Hyamovi*

Hickory (English) Hickory tree.

Hideaki (Japanese) Clever. *Hideo, Hydeaki*

Hiemo (Latin) Winter.

Hieronymus (Greek) Holy name. *Hieronymous*

Hilario (Spanish) Happy. (Latin) Cheerful. *Hilarius*

Hildebrand (German) Battle sword. *Hildabrand, Hildreth, Hill, Hildo, Hildebrando*

Hilel (Hebrew) Greatly praised. *Hillel, Hylel, Hyllel*

Hilton (Old English) Hill settlement. *Hylton, Hillton*

Hinto (Native American) Blue. *Hynto*

Hipparchus (Greek) Greek astronomer who flourished in the late second century B.C. *Hipparcos*

Hippias (Greek) Tyrant of Athens in fifth century B.C.; sophist; teacher of philosophy; quibbler.

Hippocrates (Greek) A horse.

Hiram (Hebrew) Noble one. *Hyram, Hi, Hy, Hyrum, Hirom, Huram*

Hiromasa (Japanese) Fair; just.

Hiroshi (Japanese) Generous. *Hyroshi*

Hisoka (Japanese) Secretive. *Hysoka*

Hitesh (Hindi) Good person.

Ho (Chinese) Good.

Hobart (Danish) Bart's Hill. (German) Bright mind; bright spirit. *Hobert, Hobie, Bart, Hobard, Hobarte, Hoebard, Hoebart*

Hodding (Dutch) Bricklayer.

Hogan (Irish) Youth. *Hogen, Hoin, Hogun, Hogyn*

Hogarth (Norse) Hilltop garden. *Hogie, Hoagy*

Holata (Native American) Alligator.

Holden (Old English) Valley. *Holdin, Holbrook, Holdan, Holdin, Holdon, Holdun, Holdyn*

Holgernes (Shakespearean) From *Love's Labour's Lost*.

Holland (French) Place name: province of the Netherlands. (Shakespearean) From *Henry VI*. *Holand, Hollan*

Hollis (Old English) Holy day; grove of holly trees. *Holliss, Hollister, Hollie, Holly, Hollys, Hollyss*

Holm (Norse) Island. *Holms, Holmes*

Homer (Greek) Promise. *Homar, Homere, Homero, Homeros, Homerus, Omero*

Honore (French) Honored one. *Honoratus, Honoray, Honorio, Honorato*

Honorius (Latin) Man of honor. (Italian) Honor.

Honovi (Native American) Strong.

Hopper (American) Celebrity baby name.

Horace (Greek) Behold. (Latin) Keeper of the hours. *Horacio, Horatio, Horatius, Horazio, Orazio*

Hormisdas (Italian) Saint Hormisdas was a widower and a Roman deacon at the time of his ascension to the papal throne.

Hormoz (Arabic) A character in Shahnameh, eleventh-century "Epic of Kings" by the Persian poet Firdowski.

Horst (German) Thicket.

Hortensio (Italian) Garden. (Latin) The garden lover. (Shakespearean) From *The Taming of the Shrew. Hortensius*

Horton (Latin) Garden. (Old English) Gray settlement. *Horton, Orton, Hortan, Hort, Hortun, Hortyn*

Hosea (Hebrew) Salvation. *Hoshea, Hoseia, Hosheia, Hosheah*

Hoshi (Japanese) Star.

Houston (English) Town house. *Hewson, Huston, Hutcheson, Hutchinson, Houstyn, Houstun, Houstan*

Hovie (American) Legendary southern gospel singer Hovie Lister.

Howard (English) Protector of the home. *Howie, Ward, Howerd*

Howe (English) Hill. *Hough, Houghton, Howell, Howel, Howells, Howden*

Hoyt (English) Small boat. *Hoyle, Hoit, Hoyts, Hoyce*

Hsin (Chinese) After ancient dynasty. (Norse) Spirit.

Huang fu (Chinese) Rich future.

Hubert (German) Shining spirit. *Hubbard, Hubbell, Hub, Huberto, Hubie, Uberto, Hubirt, Hubyrt, Hugibert, Huibert*

Hudson (Old English) Son of Hud. *Hud, Hudsan, Hudsin, Hudsyn*

Hugh (German) Bright soul. *Hew, Huey, Hughie, Hughes, Huet, Hugi, Hugo, Ugo*

Hui K'o (Chinese) Able wisdom.

Hui-chao (Chinese) Wise illumination.

Hulk (Old English) Heavyweight. (American) Comic character.

Humbert (German) Famous giant. *Umberto, Humberto, Humbirt, Humbyrt*

Hume (Norse) Lakeside hill; careful. *Holm, Holmes*

Humphrey (Old English) Peaceful force. *Humphry, Humfrey, Humpty, Humph, Humpy, Humfrid, Humfried, Humpherey, Humphree, Humphrys, Hunfredo*

Naming Rights

Throughout history, famous people have boosted the popularity of the names they bear. If you would like to name a child after a famous person you admire, there's nothing wrong with that as long as you avoid names that may conspicuously draw attention to the original, such as Elvis, Madonna, Bart Simpson, or Willy Wonka.

Huni (German) Peace.

Hunt (Old English) Search. *Hunter, Huntington, Huntley, Hunta*

Huritt (Native American) Handsome.

Hurley (Irish) Sea tide. *Hurlee, Hurleigh, Hurly, Hurlea, Hurli, Hurlie*

Hurst (English) Thicket of trees. *Hearst, Hirst, Hyrst*

Hussain (Arabic) Good, small handsome one. *Husain, Husayn, Huscin, Hossain,*

Husani, Husian, Hussan, Hussin, Hussayn

Hutch (German) Hutch dweller. *Hutchinson*

Hutton (Old English) Settlement on the bluff. *Hut, Hutan, Huten, Hutin, Huton, Hutt, Huttan, Hutten, Huttin, Huttun, Huttyn, Hutun, Hutyn*

Huxley (English) Ash-tree field. *Huxly, Huxford, Huxleigh, Huxlea, Huxlee, Huxlie*

Hyatt (Old English) Lofty gate. *Hayatt, Hiatt, Hiatte, Hyat, Hyatte*

Hydrus (Greek) Lesser snake.

Hyginus (Greek) Healthy.

Hyman (Hebrew) Life; god of marriage. *Hyland, Hy, Hayim, Hayvim, Hayyim*

Hypnos (Greek) God of sleep.

I

Iachima (Japanese) Lotus.

Iago (Latin, Spanish) Supplanter. (Shakespearean) From *Othello. Jago*

Iakobos (Greek) Supplanter. *Iakov, Iakovos, Iakovs*

Naming Rights

When your baby is born, you realize the name choice is more a matter of feeling than logic. Remember, your feelings and your partner's matter more than the opinions your friends and family offer. Remain firm in your resolve to stick with the name you genuinely love.

Ian (Scottish) God is gracious. *Ianna, Ianthe, Iantha, Iain, Iane, Iin, Ion, Eian*

Ib (Danish) Oath of Baol.

Ibeamaka (African) The agnates are splendid.

Ibrahim (Arabic) Form of Abraham. *Ibraham, Ibraheem, Ibraheim, Ibrahiem, Ibrahiim, Ibrahaim*

Icarus (Greek) A legendary figure. *Icharus*

Ichabod (Hebrew) Departed glory. *Icobod*

Idris (Welsh) Eager lord. *Idrees, Idres, Idress, Idriece, Idriss, Idrissa, Idriys, Idrease, Idreus, Idriys, Idys, Idryss*

Ignado (Spanish) Fire. *Ignacio, Ignazio, Ignaas, Ignac, Ignaz*

Ignatius (Latin) Fiery. *Iggy, Ignaze, Ignace, Ignatz, Ignacey, Ignacius, Ignatas, Ignatios, Ignatus, Ignatys*

Igor (Scandinavian) Hero; form of George. *Igoryok*

Ike (Hebrew) He will laugh. *Ikee, Ikey, Ikke*

Ilan (Hebrew) Tree. *Eilon, Elam, Elan, Ilon*

Ilia (Hebrew) God is Lord. *Ilya, Ilija, Illia, Illya, Ilyah*

Ilias (Greek) The Lord is my God. (Hebrew) Jehovah is God. (Arabic) A prophet's name. *Illyas, Ilyas, Ilyes*

Ilie (Slavic) The Lord is God.

Illanipi (Native American) Amazing.

Imad (Arabic) Support, pillar.

Imhotep (Egyptian) He comes in peace.

Immanuel (Hebrew) God with us. *Imanol, Imanuel, Immanual, Immanuele, Emanuel, Emanuele, Emmanouil, Emmanuel, Emmanuelle, Manny, Manoel, Manuel, Imanual, Imanuele, Immuneal*

Imre (Hebrew) Well-spoken. *Imray, Imrie, Imri*

Inder (Hindi) Godlike. *Inderjit, Inderpal, Inderjeet, Inderpreet, Inderveer, Indervir, Indra, Inderbir, Indrajit*

Indiana (English) The land of the Indians. *Indy*

Indigo (Greek) Dark blue.

Indro (Italian) Man of the forest, woodsman.

Inerney (Irish) Steward of church lands.

Ing (German) Mythical fertility god. *Inge*

Ingmar (Scandinavian) Famous son. *Ingamar, Ingemar, Ingamur*

Ingvar (Scandinavian) He who is foremost. *Ingvarr, Yngvar, Ingevar*

Ingram (German) Raven. *Ingraham, Ingham, Ingrem, Ingrim, Gram, Graham*

Innis (Irish) Island. *Iniss, Inis, Inniss, Innys, Innyss*

Innocent (Latin) Harmless. (English) Innocence. *Innocenty, Inocencio, Innocentz, Innocenz, Innocenzyo, Inocenci, Inocente, Inocenzio*

Inyri (Science fiction) A character from *Star Wars*.

Ioan (Greek) God is gracious. (Hebrew) Gift from God. *Ioann, Ioannes, Ioane, Ioannis, Ione, Ioannikios, Ionel*

Ira (Hebrew) Watchful. *Irah*

Iravan (Hindi) Son of Arjuna/Uloopi.

Irin (Hebrew) Those who watch; peace.

Irving (Old English) Sea friend. *Irvin, Irvine, Irwin, Irwyn, Irven, Irvinn, Irvon, Irvyn, Irvyne*

Isaac (Hebrew) Laughter. *Ike, Zach, Isaak, Yitzchak, Isak, Itzak, Isac, Ishaq, Isiac, Issac, Izak, Issaic, Issiac, Isaack, Isaakios, Isacco*

Isaiah (Hebrew) Salvation of the Lord. *Isa, Isiah, Isaih, Issiah, Izaiah, Izaya, Izayah, Izeyah, Isaia, Isaid, Isish, Isaya, Isayah, Issia, Izaiha, Izayaih, Izayiah*

Isam (Arabic) Safeguard.

Ishan (Hindi) Direction. *Ishaan, Ishaun*

Ishmael (Hebrew) God will hear. *Ismael, Isamael, Ishma, Ishmail, Ishmale, Ishmeal, Ishmeil, Ishmel, Ismail, Isamail, Ishmil*

Isidro (Spanish) Gifted with many ideas. *Chidro, Isidoro*

Naming Rights

Keep your baby's name a secret until after he or she has been born. That way you can avoid any arguments and the pressure to name the baby after Aunt Millie, and people won't be able to comment on the name and try to put you off or influence you to change your mind.

Israel (Hebrew) Wrestled with God. *Isreal, Israhel, Isrell, Isrrael, Izrael, Isrieal, Iser, Israele, Isser, Izrael*

Ithamar (Hebrew) Island of the palm tree. *Itamar, Ittamar*

Itsu (Japanese) One. *Ichi*

Ivan (Russian) God is gracious. *Evan, Ivanchik, Ivann, Ivano, Iven, Ivon, Ivyn, Iván, Ivas, Ivin, Ivun*

Ives (Old English) Little archer. *Yvo, Ives, Yvan, Yves, Ive*

Ivo (German) Cut wood. *Ivor, Yvonne, Ivonnie, Yvo*

J

Jabari (Swahili) Fearless. *Jabahri, Jabarae, Jabare, Jabaree, Jabarei, Jabarie, Jabarri, Jabarrie, Jabary, Jabbaree, Jabbari, Jabiari, Jabier, Jabori, Jaborie*

Jabez (Hebrew) Born in pain. *Jabe, Jabar, Jaber*

Jabin (Hebrew) God has created. *Jabain, Jabien, Jabon, Jabyn*

Jabir (Arabic) Comforter. *Jabiri, Jabori, Jabyr*

Jace (American) Moon. (Greek) Healer. *J. C., Jacee, Jaci, Jacie, Jaece, Jaecee, Jaecey*

Jacek (Polish) Lily; male. *Jaeci, Jaice, Jaicee, Jaicey, Jaici, Jaice, Jaicy*

Jachin (Hebrew) He who strengthens. *Jacin*

Jackal (Sanskrit) Wild dog. *Jackel, Jackell, Jackyl, Jackyll*

Jacob (Hebrew) The supplanter. *Jakob, Jacobo, Jacopo, Jacoba, Jacobson, Jacobi, Jacobine, Jacobina, Jayme, Jacques, Jacinto, Jascha, Jake, Jackob, Jakub, Jack,* Jackson, Jeb, Cob, Cobb, Giacobo, Giacomo, Iago, Iacovo, Yago, Yaacov, Yacov, Yakov, Jaccob, Jachob, Jaco, Jacobb, Jacub, Jaecob, Jaicob, Jalu, Jecis, Jeks, Jeska, Jocek, Jock, Jocob, Jocobb, Jokubus

Jacques (French) Supplanter; substitute. *Jaques, Jacquel, Jacque, Jacquan, Jackques, Jackquise, Jacot, Jacquees, Jacquese, Jacquess, Jacquet, Jacquett, Jacquis, Jacquise, Jarques, Jarquis, Jacquez, Jaquez, Jaquese, Jaqueus, Jaqueze, Jaquis, Jaquise, Jaquze*

Jacy (Native American) Moon.

Jaden (Hebrew) God heard. *Jadon, Jayden, Jadee, Jadeen, Jadenn, Jadeon, Jadyne, Jadan, Jadin, Jaiden*

Jafar (Sanskrit) Little stream. *Ja'far, Jafari, Jaffar, Jaffer, Jafur*

Jagger (English) Carter. *Gagger, Jagar, Jaggar*

Jaguar (Spanish) Jaguar. *Jagguar*

Jaideep (Hindi) Light of the universe.

Jair (Spanish) God enlightens. *Jairo, Jairay, Jaire, Jayrus*

Jairus (Hebrew) My light; who diffuses light.

Jakeem (Arabic) Uplifted. *Jakeam, Jakim, Jakym*

Jalal (Hindi) Revered. *Jalaal, Jalil*

Jaleel (Arabic) Loftiness, glory. *Jaleell, Jaleil, Jalel, Jalal*

Jamar (African American) Handsome. *Jamaar, Jamaari, Jamaarie, Jamahrae, Jamair, Jamara, Jamaras, Jamaraus, Jamarr, Jamarre, Jamarrea, Jamarree, Jamarri, Jamarvis, Jamaur, Jammar, Jarmar, Jarmarr, Jaumar, Jemaar, Jemar, Jimar, Jamal, Jamalle*

James (Hebrew) Supplanter, substitute; the patron saint of Spain. *Jaymes, Jaime, Jaymie, Jamy, Jaimie, Jamesy, Jameson Jamey, Jan, Jay, Jim, Jimmy, Jimmie, Jimbo, Diego, Giacomo, Seamus, Sheamus, Shamus, Hamish, Santiago, Jaemes, Jaimes, Jaemie, Jaemy, Jaimie, Jame, Jameyel, Jaml, Jamiu, Jamiah, Jamian, Jamiee, Jamme, Jammey, Jammie, Jammy, Jamye, Jameze, Jamze, Jamieson, Jamison, Jamiesen*

Jan (Slavic) God is gracious. *Jahn, Jana, Janae, Jann, Jano, Jenda, Jhan, Yan*

Janus (Latin) Passageway. *Jannese, Jannus, Januario, Janusz*

Japhet (Hebrew) Handsome. *Japheth, Japeth, Yaphet*

Jared (Hebrew) Descending. *Jarrod, Jarett, Jarrett, Ja'red, Jaraed, Jahred, Jaired, Jaredd, Jareid, Jerred*

Jarek (Polish) Born in January. *Januarius, Januisz, Jarec, Jareck, Jaric, Jarick, Jarik, Jarrek, Jarric, Jarrick, Jaryc, Jaryck, Jaryk*

Jarl (Scandinavian) Earl; nobleman. *Jarlee, Jarleigh, Jarley, Jarli, Jarlie, Jarly*

Jarlath (Latin) In control. *Jarlaf, Jarlen*

Jaron (Hebrew) He will sing. *J'ron, Jaaron, Jaeron, Jairon, Jarone, Jayron, Jayrone, Jayronn, Je Ronn*

Jarrell (English) Mighty spearman. *Jarrel, Jerall, Jerrell, Jaerel, Jaerell, Jaerill, Jaeryl, Jaeryll, Jairel, Jairell, Jarael, Jareil, Jarelle, Jariel, Jarryl, Jarryll, Jayryl, Jayryll, Jharell*

Jarvis (Old German) True spear. *Jervis, Jaravis, Jarv, Jarvaris, Jarvas, Jarvaska, Jarvey, Jarvez, Jarvise, Jarvius, Jarvorice, Jarvoris, Jarvous, Jarvus, Jarvyc, Jarvyce, Jarvys, Jarvyse, Jervey*

Jason (Greek) Healer. *Jayson, Jase, Jaasan, Jaasen, Jaasin, Jaason, Jaasun, Jaasyn, Jaesan, Jaesen, Jaeson, Jaesun, Jaesyn, Jahsan, Jahsen, Jahson, Jasan, Jasaun, Jasin, Jasten, Jasun, Jasyn*

Jasper (French) Red, brown, or yellow stone. *Jaspar, Jazper, Jespar*

Javan (Hebrew) Deceiver, one who makes sadness. (Latin) Angel of Greece. *Jaavan, Jaewan, Javyn, Jayvin, Jayvine, Javen, Javin, Jaevin, Javine, Javian, Javion, Javionne, Javien, Javone, Javoney, Javonne, Javonta, Javona, Javontey, Javaughn, Jahvaughan, JaVaughn, Javon, Jaavon, Jaevon, Jaewon, Jahvon, Javaon, Javohn, Javoni, Javonn, Javonni, Javonnie, Javoun, Javontae, Javontay, Javonte, Javonté, Javonnte, Javontai, Javontaye, Javontee*

Javier (French) Enlightened. (Spanish) New house. *Javy, Xavier, Xever*

Jawhar (Arabic) Jewel; essence.

Jax (English) God has been gracious. *Jaxon, Jaxen, Jaxsen, Jaxsun, Jaxun*

Jaxon (English) God has been gracious, has shown favor. (American) Son of Jack. *Jacson, Jacksen, Jacsin, Jacson, Jakson*

Jay (Old French) Jay bird. (English) Supplanter; substitute. *Jai, Jaybird, Jave, Jeays, Jeyes*

Naming Rights

Check out the rhythm when choosing names. Baby's first name should complement his or her last (and middle). Vary the number of syllables from the first to the last name.

Jay-Z (American) Celebrity nickname. *Jaze*

Jayant (Hindi) Victorious.

Jayvyn (African) Light spirit.

Jean (French) Form of John. *Jéan, Jeannah, Jeannot, Jeano, Jeanot, Jeanty, Jene*

Jebediah (Hebrew) Beloved by God. *Jedidiah, Jedediah, Jed, Yedidiyah, Jebadia, Jebadiah, Jebadieh, Jebidia, Jebidiah, Jebidya, Jebydia, Jebydiah, Jebydya, Jebydyah, Jedadiah, Jeddediah, Jededia, Jedidia, Jedidiyah, Yedidya*

Jeevan (Hindi) Life.

Jeeves (American) Common English term for butler.

Jeffrey (Old French) Peaceful. *Jeffrie, Jeffry, Jefferey, Geoffrey, Geoff, Godfrey, Jeff, Jefferson, Jeffers, Joffrey, Jeffries, Jeffery, Jeffaree, Jefarey, Jeffari, Jefarie, Jefary, Jeferee, Jeferey, Jeferi, Jeferie, Jefery, Jeffaree, Jeffarey, Jeffari, Jeffarie, Jeffary, Jeffeory, Jefferay, Jefferee, Jeffereoy, Jefferi, Jefferie, Jefferies, Jeffory*

Jelani (Swahili) Mighty. *Jel, Jelan, Jelanee, Jelaney, Jelanie, Jelany, Jelaun*

Jemond (French) Worldly. *Jemon, Jémond, Jemonde, Jemone, Jemun, Jemund*

Jeremiah (Hebrew) Exalted of God. *Jeremia, Yirmeyah, Jerry, Jerrie, Jerri, Jeri, Jere, Jerimiha, Jerimya, Jerimiah, Geremiah, Jaramia, Jemeriah, Jemiah, Jeramiha, Jereias, Jeremaya, Jeremia, Jeremial, Jeremija, Jeremya, Jeremyah*

Jeremy (Hebrew) Chosen by God. *Jeremias, Geremia, Jerry, Dermot, Jaremay, Jaremy, Jereamy, Jeremry, Jérémy, Jeremye, Jereomy, Jeriemy, Jerime, Jerimy, Jerremy*

Jericho (Arabic) City of the moon. *Jericko, Jeriko, Jerricko, Jerricoh, Jerriko, Jerrycko, Jerryko, Jeric, Jerick, Jerric, Jerico, Jerrico, Jerryco*

Jermyn (Latin) German. *German, Germain, Germaine, Jermaine, Jer-Mon, Jeremaine, Jeremane, Jerimane, Jerman, Jermane, Jermanie, Jermanne, Jermany, Jermayn, Jermayne, Jermiane, Jermine, Jermoney, Jhirmaine*

Jerome (Latin) Sacred name. *Jerrome, Gerome, Jerry, Jeroen, Jerom, Jérome, Jérôme, Jeromo, Jerrome, Jeromy, Jeromee, Jeromey, Jeromie, Jerromy*

What's in a Name

In the legend of Saint **Jerome,** a lion entered his schoolroom and frightened away everyone but Jerome. When he noticed that the lion had a thorn in its paw, he removed it. The lion never left his side after that.

Jerrold (Spanish) Rules by the spear. *Jeraldo, Jerold, Jerrald*

Jerry (German) Mighty spear-man. *Jehri, Jeree, Jeri, Jerie, Jeris, Jerison, Jerree, Jerri, Jerrie, Jery*

Jesper (French) Jasperstone.

Jesse (Hebrew) Wealth. *Jescey, Jesie, Jessyie, Jesy, Jezzey, Jezzi, Jessie, Jezzy, Jesree, Jese, Jesee, Jesi, Jezze, Jezzee*

Jesus (Hebrew) God will help. *Yesus, Jecho, Jessus, Jesu, Jezus, Josu, Jesús*

Jet (English) Hard, black min-eral. *Jetson, Jetter*

Jethro (Hebrew) Preeminence. *Jethroe, Jeth, Jethroe, Jetro, Jetrow, Jettro*

Jevonte (African American) Son of Jeptheh. *Jevonta, Jevontae, Jevontaye, Jevonté*

Jiang (Chinese) Fire.

Jikai (Japanese) Ocean of com-passion.

Jin (Chinese) Gold.

Jing (Chinese) Essence.

Jintao (Korean) Meaning unknown.

Jiro (Japanese) Second son.

Jiryu (Japanese) Compassionate dragon.

Jitendra (Hindi) Conqueror.

Joachim (Hebrew) God will judge. *Joaquin, Akim, Jocheim, Jokim, Joakim, Jov*

Job (Hebrew) Afflicted. *Jobe, Jobert*

Joben (Japanese) Enjoys clean-liness. *Joban, Jobin, Jobon, Jobyn*

Jody (Hebrew) God will increase. For a boy or girl. *Jodie, Jodey, Jodiha, Joedee, Joedey, Joedi, Joedy*

Joel (Hebrew) The Lord is God. *Yohel, Jolson, Joël, Jôel, Joell, Joelle, Joely, Jole, Yoel*

John (Hebrew) God's grace. *Johnny, Johnnie, Jack, Jock, Jocko, Johann, Johan, Jenner, Janos, Jovan, Juan, Johannes, Johnson, Johnavon, Jansen, Janson, Jones, Jackson, Jenkins, Hanson, Hansen, Jonnel, Hans, Ivan, Ian, Iaian, Eoin, Sean, Shawn, Shane, Seain, Zane, Jaenda, Janco, Jantje, Jian, Joen, Johne, Jone, Jontavius, Johahn, Johanan, Johane, Johannan, Johaun, Johon, Jehan, Jehann, Jenkin, Jenkins, Jenkyn, Jenkyns, Jennings, Jens, Jense, Jentz, Jones, Joenes, Joennes, Joenns, Johnsie, Joness, Jonesy, Juhana, Juha, Juhanah, Juhanna, Juhannah, Juho*

Joji (Japanese) A form of George.

Jomei (Japanese) Spreads light. *Jomey*

Jonas (Hebrew) Dove. *Jonah, Yonas, Yonah, Jonahs, Jonass, Jonaus, Jonelis, Jonukas, Jonus, Jonutis, Jonys, Joonas*

Jonathan (Hebrew) God's gift. *Jonathon, Jon, Nathan, Nate, Nat, Jonatha, Jonathin, Jonathun, Jonathyn, Jonethen, Jonnatha, Jonnathun, Jonathen, Jonaton, Jonnathon, Jonthon, Jounathon, Yanaton, Jonatane, Jonate, Jonattan, Jonnattan, Johnthan*

Joram (Hebrew) Jehovah is exalted. *Joran, Jorim*

Jordan (Hebrew) Descender. *Giordano, Jordy, Jordie, Jory, Jordaan, Jordae, Jordain, Jordaine, Jordane, Jordani, Jordanio, Jordann, Jordanny, Jordano, Jordany, Jordáo, Jordayne, Jordun, Jorrdan, Jorden, Jordin, Jordon, Jordyn, Jeordon, Johordun, Jordenn*

Joseph (Hebrew) He shall add. *Josef, Jozef, Yoseph, Yosayf, José, Joe, Jo, Joey, Josie, Josiah, Josias, Jessup, Giuseppe, Isoep, Iosef, Seosaidh, Osip, Pepe, Pepito, Jazeps, Jooseppi, Joseba, Josep, Josephat, Josephe, Josephie, Josephus, Josheph, Josip, Joska, Joza, Joze, Jozeph, Jozhe, Jozio, Jozka, Jozsi, Jozzepi, Jupp, Jusepe, Juziu, Beppe, Bepe, Beppy, Cheche, Iokepa, Keo, Pepa, Peppe, Pino, Sepp, Yeska, Yosef, Yousef, Youssel, Yusef, Yusif, Zeusef*

Joshua (Hebrew) God of salva-tion. *Yehosha, Josh, Josiah, Joshawa, Johsua, Johusa, Joshau, Joshaua, Joshauh, Joshawah, Joshia, Joshuaa, Joshuea, Joshuia, Joshula, Joshus, Joshusa, Joshuwa, Joshwa, Jousha, Jozshua, Jozsua, Jozua, Joshua, Joshuah, Joshue*

Juan (Spanish) God is gracious, the grace. (Hebrew) Gift from God. *Juanch, Juanchito, Juane, Juann, Juanun*

Judd (Hebrew) Praised. *Jud, Juda, Judah, Judas, Jude, Juddson, Yehudah, Yehuda, Yehudi, Judda, Juddah, Juddas, Judge*

Judson (English) Son of Judd.

Juhani (Finnish) God is gracious.

Julian (Latin) Youthful. (English) Love's child. *Julien, Julyan, Julius, Jules, Jule, Julio, Giulo, Julian, Joles, Julas, Julean, Juliaan, Julianne, Julion, Julyan, Julyin, Julyon, Juliano, Julen, Juliene, Julienn, Julienne, Jullien, Jullin, Julyen, Julio, Juleo, Juliyo, Julyo, Julias, Julious, Juliusz, Jullius, Juluis*

Juma (Arabic) Born on a Friday. *Jumah, Jimoh*

Jun (Chinese) Truthful. *Joon, Junnie*

Junichiro (Japanese) Meaning unknown.

Junius (Latin) Young. *June, Junius, Junio, Junot*

Jussi (Finnish) Gift from God.

Justin (Old French) Justice. *Justice, Justis, Justino, Justus, Justinian, Juste, Justyn, Jastin, Jobst, Jost, Jusa, Just, Justain, Justek, Justian, Justinas, Justinius, Justinn, Justins, Justn, Justo, Justton, Justukas, Justun, Ustin, Iestyn, Iustin, Yustyn*

K

Kabir (Hindi) Spiritual leader.

Kabonero (African) Symbol.

Kabonesa (African) Born in hard times.

Kabos (Hebrew) Swindler.

Kabr (Hindi) Grass.

Kacy (American) Happy. *K. C., Kace, Kacee, Kase, Kasee, Kasy, Kaycee*

Kada (Hungarian) Meaning unknown.

Kadar (Arabic) Powerful. *Kade, Kedar*

Kade (Gaelic) Swamp.

Kadeem (African American) Newly created.

Kaden (American) Exciting. *Cade, Caden, Caiden, Caidin, Caidon, Caydan, Cayden, Caydin, Caydon, Kadan, Kadon, Kadyn, Kaiden*

Kadi (Irish) Pure. (American) Angel who presides over Friday.

Kadin (Arabic) Friend, companion. *Kadeen, Kaden*

Kadir (Arabic) Green. *Kadeer*

Kadmiel (Hebrew) God is first.

Kado (Japanese) Entrance.

Kaelan (Irish) Strong. *Kael, Kaelen, Kaelin, Kaelyn*

Kateo (American) Good judgment. *Cato, Cayto, Caytoe, Kato*

Kaga (Native American) A writer.

Kagan (German) A thinker.

Kahale (Hawaiian) Homebody.

Kahanu (Hawaiian) He breathes.

Kahil (Arabic) Friend, lover. *Cahil, Kahlil, Kaleel, Khaleel, Khalil*

Kahoku (Hawaiian) Star.

Kaholo (Hawaiian) Boy who runs.

Kai (Hawaiian) Ocean. (Greek) Earth. (Native American) Sea, willow tree. (Scottish) Fire. (Welsh) Keeper of the keys.

Kaid (English) Round; happy. *Caiden, Cayde, Caydin, Kaden, Kadin, Kayd*

Kaikara (Ugandan) Traditional name of God.

Kaikeapona (Hawaiian) Smooth skin.

Kailin (Irish) Sporty. *Kailyn, Kale, Kalen, Kaley, Kalin, Kailen, Kaylen*

Kainon (Science fiction) Character from *Star Trek: Deep Space Nine.*

Kaipo (Hawaiian) Embraces.

Kaisha (Japanese) To rewrite.

Kaj (Scandinavian) Earthy.

Kakumyo (Japanese) Clear awakening.

Kala (Hindi) Black.

Kalama (Hawaiian) Source of light. *Kalan*

Kalani (Polynesian) Gallon.

Kalb (Arabic) Dog. *Kaleb*

Kale (Hawaiian) Strong and manly. *Kail, Kayle, Kaylee, Kayley, Kaylie, Kalolo, Karolo*

Kaleb (African) Old Testament Cain. *Caleb*

Kalei (Hawaiian) Joy. *Kalea*

Kaleo (Hawaiian) Pure.

Kalepa (Hawaiian) Faithful. *Kaleba*

Kalidas (Hindi) The poet, musician; slave of goddess Kali.

Kalil (Arabic) Beautiful, good friend. *Kahill, Kailil, Khalil*

Kalin (Greek) Handsome. *Kallan, Kallin, Kallon, Kallun, Kalon, Kaltin, Kalyn*

Kalkin (Hindi) Tenth incarnation of God. *Vishnu*

Kallen (Greek) Handsome. *Kallan, Kallin, Kallon, Kallun, Kalon, Kalun, Kalyn*

Kalman (Hungarian) Strong and manly.

Kalpanath (Hindi) Meaning unknown.

Kalvin (Latin) Blessing; form of Calvin. *Kal*

Kamadev (Hindi) God of love.

Kameron (Scottish) Crooked nose. *Kameren, Kammeron, Kammi, Kammie, Kammy, Kamran, Kamrin, Kamron*

Kamil (Arabic) Perfection. *Camillo, Kamillo*

Kamlesh (Hindi) God of lotus.

Kamon (American) Alligator. *Cayman, Caymun, Kame, Kammy, Kayman, Kayman*

Kana (Hawaiian) God is my judge. *Kaniela*

Kanak (Hindi) Gold.

Kanan (Hindi) Forest.

Kanaye (Japanese) Zealous one.

Kance (American) Attractive; combo of Kane and Chance. *Cance, Cans, Kaince, Kans, Kanse, Kaynce*

Kando (Japanese) Penetrating insight.

Kane (Hawaiian) Man, the eastern sky. (Irish) Honor, tribute. (Japanese) Doubly accomplished, golden, man. (Scottish) Warlike. *Cathan, Kaine, Kain, Kayne, Keyne, Cane, Cain, Caine, Kainen*

Kanoa (Hawaiian) Free.

Kaniel (Hebrew) Stalk, reed. *Kan, Kani, Kanny*

Kant (German) Philosopher. *Cant*

Kaori (Japanese) Strong.

Kaper (American) Capricious. *Cape, Caper, Kahper, Kape*

Kapil (Hindi) Name of a rishi.

Kaplony (Hungarian) Tiger.

Kapolcs (Hungarian) Meaning unknown.

Kapono (Hawaiian) Righteous.

Karcher (German) Beautiful blond boy.

Kardal (Arabic) Mustard seed.

Kardos (Hungarian) Swordsman.

Kareem (Arabic) Charitable. *Kareem, Karim*

Karel (Czechoslovakian) Man; Carl's town. *Karlicek, Karlik, Karlousek, Karol, Karoly*

Karey (Greek) Pure. (Welsh) Castle; rocky island. *Karee, Kari, Karrey, Karry*

Karif (Arabic) Fall born. *Kareef*

Karl (German) Man; Carl's town. *Karlen, Karlens, Karlin*

Karmel (Hebrew) Red-haired. *Carmel, Carmelo, Karmeli, Karmelli, Karmelo, Karmello, Karmi*

Karney (Irish) Wins. *Carney*

Karr (Scandinavian) Curly hair. *Carr*

Karsa (Hungarian) Falcon.

Karsten (Greek) Blessed, anointed one.

Kartal (Hungarian) Eagle.

Kartik (Hindi) Name of a month.

Kartikeya (Hindi) God of war; son of Shiva and Parvati.

Kasch (German) Like a blackbird.

Kaseem (Arabic) Divides. *Kasceem, Kaseym, Kasim, Kazeem*

Kasen (Latin) Protected with a helmet.

Kasey (Irish) Form of Casey. *Kasi, Kasie*

Kasi (African) Leaving. *Kasee, Kasey, Kasie*

Kasib (Arabic) Fertile. *Kaseeb*

Kasimir (Old Slavic) Demands peace. *Casmir, Casimir, Kazimir*

Kaspar (Persian) A treasured secret. *Caspar, Casper, Kasp, Kasper*

Kass (German) Standout among men. *Cass, Kasse*

Kassidy (Irish) Clever; curly haired. *Kass, Kassidi, Kassidie, Kassie*

Kateb (Arabic) Writer.

Katzir (Hebrew) Reaping. *Katzeer*

Kaufman (Last name as first name) Serious. *Kauffmann, Kaufmann*

Kaul (Arabic) Trustworthy. *Kahlil, Kalee, Khalil, Khaleel*

Kaushal (Hindi) Perfect.

Kaushik (Hindi) Sage Vishramitra.

Kaveh (Persian) Hero.

Kavan (Irish) Good-looking. *Cavan, Kaven, Kavin*

Kavi (Hindi) Poet.

Kay (Welsh, German) Rejoicer; fort; joyful. *Kai, Kay, Kaye, Kaysie, Keh, MacKay*

Kayin (Yoruban) Celebrated child.

Kaylen (Irish) Laughing. *Kaylan, Kaylin, Kaylon, Kaylyn*

Kayven (Irish) Handsome. *Cavan, Kavan, Kave*

Kazuo (Japanese) First son.

Keahi (Hawaiian) Fire.

Keandre (American) Grateful. *Keondre*

Keane (English) Sharp; bold. *Kean, Keen, Keene*

Keanu (Hawaiian) Cool breeze over the mountians. *Keahnu*

Kearn (German) Dark. *Kearny, Kearn, Kerne, Kerney*

Kearney (Celtic) Warrior. *Karney, Karny, Kearns, Kerney, Kirney*

Keary (Celtic) Father's dark child. *Kear, Care*

Keaton (English) Hawk's nest. *Keeton, Keiton, Keyton*

Kedar (Arabic) Strong; powerful. (Hebrew) Blackness, sorrow. (Hindi) Raga.

Keefe (Gaelic) Lovable and handsome; noble. *Keefer, Keever*

Keegan (Gaelic) Little fierce one. *Keagan, Kagen, Keegen, Kegan*

Keeland (Gaelic) Little and slender. *Keelan, Kealon, Kealian, Keilan, Keillan, Kelan*

Keeley (Irish) Handsome. *Kealey, Kealy, Keelee, Keelie, Keely, Keilie*

Keemo (Vietnamese) Friendly.

Keenan (Gaelic) Little ancient one. *Keenen, Kienen, Kienan, Kenan*

Kegan (Celtic) Fiery.

Keir (Celtic) Dark-skinned. *Kieron, Kerr, Keiron, Kieran*

Keitaro (Japanese) Blessed.

Keith (Irish) Warrior descending. (Scottish) From the battle-ground. (Welsh) Forest. *Keath, Keeth, Keith*

Kekoa (Hawaiian) Warrior.

Kelan (Irish) Tiny, slender. *Caolan, Kelin, Kelen, Keelan*

Kelby (Norse) From the farm by the springs. *Kellby, Kelbie, Kelbey*

Kele (Native American) Sparrow. *Kelle*

Keled (Hungarian) A royal clan of the Scythians.

Keleman (Hungarian) Gentle, kind. *Kelemen*

Kelii (Hawaiian) Wealthy.

Kell (English) From the spring.

Kellen (German) Swamp. (Irish) Powerful. *Kel, Kelen, Kelin, Kell, Keilan, Kellin, Kelly, Kelyn, Keler, Kelher, Kylher*

Kelly (Irish) Warrior. *Kellie, Kelley*

Kelsey (Scandinavian) Island of ships. (English) Island. *Kelsy, Kelsie, Kelse, Kelsi, Kelso*

Kelton (Irish) Energetic. *Keldon, Kelltin, Kellton, Kelten, Keltin, Keltonn*

Kelvin (English) River man. (Irish) From the narrow river. (Scottish) Friend of ships. *Kelvan, Kelven, Kelvyn, Kel, Keloun*

Kem (Irish) Warrior chief. (Teutonic) To cover, veil, or hide. *Kam*

Kemenes (Hungarian) Furnace maker.

Kemp (Middle English) Champion. *Kempy, Kem, Kemper, Kemplen, Kempson*

Kenan (Hebrew) Possession. *Cainan*

Kendall (Celtic) Ruler of the valley. *Kendal, Kendell, Kendel, Kendalia, Kendaline, Kenna, Kendra, Ken, Kenny, Kenni, Kindall, Kindell*

Kende (Hungarian) Name of honor.

Kendis (African American) Pure.

Kendrick (Irish) Son of Henry. (Scottish) Royal chieftain. *Kendric, Kendryck, Kendrik*

Kenelm (Old English) Brave; helmet.

Kenley (Old English) Dweller at the king's meadow. *Kenly, Kenlie, Kenleigh, Kenlea, Kenlee*

Kenn (Welsh) Clear water.

Kennard (English) Strong. *Kennair, Kennerd*

Kennedy (Gaelic) Helmeted chief. *Kennady, Kenny, Ken, Canady*

Kenneth (English) Royal obligation. (Irish) Handsome. (Scottish) Good-looking, fair. *Ken, Kevin, Kennet, Kenny, Kenney, Kenn*

Kenrich (Welsh) Chief hero, royal ruler. *Kenrick, Kenway, Kenley, Kennard*

Kent (Old English) Border; coast; bright white. *Kennt, Kentt*

Kentaro (Japanese) Large baby boy.

Kentay (African American) Outrageous. *Keon, Keontae, Keontee*

Kentlee (English) Dignified. *Ken, Kenny, Kent, Kentlea, Kentleigh, Kently*

Kenton (Old English) From the king's estate. *Kentan, Kentin, Kenton*

Kenyon (Gaelic) Blond-haired. *Ken, Kenjon, Kenny, Kenyawn, Kenyun*

Keon (Irish) Well-born. *Keion, Keonne, Keyon, Kion, Kionn*

Keona (Hawaiian) God's gracious gift. *Keowynn*

Kepano (Hawaiian) Crown. *Kekepana, Tepano*

Kepler (German) Loves astrology; starry-eyed. *Kappler, Keppel, Keppeler, Keppler*

Ker (English) House. (Norse) Marshland. *Kerr, Keir, Kirby, Kir*

Kerecsen (Hungarian) Falcon.

Kermit (Gaelic) Freeman. *Kerm, Kermee, Kermet, Kermey, Kermi, Kermie*

Kern (Gaelic) Dark. *Curran, Kearn, Kearne, Kearns*

Kerr (Scandinavian) Serious. *Karr, Kerre, Kurr*

Kerry (Gaelic) Dark eyes. *Keri, Kerrie, Kerwin, Kerri, Kerrin*

Kers (Indian) Name of a plant.

Kersen (Indonesian) Cherry.

Kerwin (Irish) Dark. *Kerwen, Kirwin, Kerwyn, Kerwen*

Keshav (Hindi) Krishna's name.

Keshawn (African American) Friendly. *Kesh, Keshaun, Keyshawn, Shawn*

Kesley (Irish) From the gray fortress. (Scottish) An ancient surname. *Keslee, Kesli, Kezley*

Kester (English) From the Roman camp. (Scottish) Bearing Christ.

Kestrel (English) Soars.

Ketan (Hindi) Home, banner

Ketchum (American) Place name: Ketchum, Idaho. *Catch, Ketch, Ketcham, Ketchim*

Kettil (Scandinavian) Self-sacrificing. *Keld, Kjeld, Ketil, Ketti*

Kevat (Finnish) Spring.

Keve (Hungarian) Pebble.

Kevin (Gaelic) Gentle; lovable. *Kevan, Keven, Kev, Kevon*

Keyon (Old English) Guiding; leading. *Kieon, Key*

Khadim (Hindi) Forever. *Kadeem, Kadeen, Kahdeem, Khadeem*

Khairi (Swahili) Kingly. (Arabic) Charitable, beneficent.

Khalid (Arabic) Immortal. *Khaled*

Khalon (African American) Little king.

Khambis Origin and meaning unknown.

Khambrel (American) Articulate. *Kambrel, Kham, Khambrell, Khambrelle, Khambryll, Khamme, Khammie, Khammy*

Khorshed (Persian) Sun.

Khortdad (Persian) Perfection.

Khoury (Arabic) Priest.

Khyber (Hindi) Place name: passage of Khyer Pass, land that links Pakistan and Afghanistan. *Kibe, Kiber, Kyber*

Kian (Irish) Archaic.

Kiefer (German) Barrel maker. *Keefer, Keifer*

Kieran (Gaelic) Small and dark-skinned. *Kiernan, Kieron, Key, Kerwin, Kirwin, Kerry, Kern, Kerr, Ceirnin, Carra, Ciaran*

Kiki (Spanish) Ruler of the household.

Killian (Irish) Strife, battle, small, fierce. (Scottish) The little warlike one. *Kilian, Kelian, Kilean, Kiliane, Kilien, Killiean, Killien, Killienn, Killion, Kyllian, Kyllien*

Kim (Old English) Chief. *Kym, Kimmi, Kimmey, Kimmy, Kimball, Kimble, Kimbell, Kemble*

Kimberley (Old English) Land belonging to Cyneburg; royal fortress meadow. *Kimberly, Kymberly, Kimby, Kim, Kimmi, Kimmie, Kimmy*

Kin (Japanese) Golden.

Kincaid (Scottish) Vigorous. *Kincaide, Kinkaid*

King (Old English) Ruler. *Kingsley, Kingston, Kingswell*

Kinga (Hungarian) Brave warrior.

Kingsley (English) Royal nature. *King, Kings, Kingslea, Kingslee, Kingsleigh, Kingsly, Kins*

Kinnel (Gaelic) Dweller at the head of the cliff.

Kinsey (Old English) Victorious prince; child. *Kensey, Kinsie*

Kintan (Hindi) Wearing a crown.

Kipling (Middle English) One who cures salmon or herring.

Kipp (Old English) Wearing a crown; sharply pointed hill. *Kinnard, Kinnell, Kippy, Kipper, Kipp*

Kirby (English) Village of the church. *Kerbey, Kerbi, Kerbie, Kirbey, Kirbie*

Kirill (Greek) The lord. *Kiril, Kirillos, Kyril*

Kirit (Hindi) Crown, tiara.

Kirk (Old Norse) From the church. *Kirkley, Kirkwood, Kirby, Kurk, Kirkus, Kirkland*

Kishi (Japanese) Knight.

Kisho (Japanese) One who knows his own mind.

Kishore (Hindi) Young.

Kit (Greek) Michievious. *Kitt*

Kix (American) Dry cereal.

Kiyiyah (Native American) Wailing wolf.

Kiyoshi (Japanese) Quiet.

Klaus (German) Victorious people. *Claus, Claas, Klause*

Klay (English) Reliable; immortal; clay pit. *Klaie, Klaye*

Klein (German) Small. *Kleiner, Kleinert, Kline*

Klemens (Latin) Gentle. *Klemenis, Klement, Kliment, Klemet, Klimiek*

Kliment (Czechoslovakian) Gentle.

Knightley (English) Protects. *Knight, Knightlea, Knightlee, Knightlie, Knightly, Knights*

Knoton (Native American) The wind.

Knowles (English) Outdoorsman. *Knowlie, Knowls, Nowles*

Knox (Old English) From the hills. *Knoll*

Knute (Scandinavian) Knot. *Canute, Cnut, Knut*

Kobe (Hebrew) Cunning. *Kobee, Kobi, Koby, Kobey*

Kody (English) Brash. *Kodee, Kodey, Kodi, Kodie, Kodye*

Kofi (African American) Friday born.

Kogen (Japanese) Wild, untamed source.

Kohana (Native American) Fast.

Koi (Native American) Panther.

Koichi (Japanese) One light.

Kolby (English) Dark-haired. (Scandinavian) From the dark country. *Kelby, Kole, Kollby, Colby, Koelby, Kohlby, Koleby, Kollby*

Koleyn (Aboriginal) Winter.

Kolos (Hungarian) Scholar.

Kolton (English) Coal town.

Konala (Hawaiian) World ruler.

Kong (Chinese) Void.

Konnor (Irish) Brilliant; another spelling of Connor. *Konnar, Konner*

Konrad (German) Bold adviser. *Conrad, Khonred, Kort, Kord*

Konstantin (Russian) Forceful. *Konstantine, Tino, Tinos, Konstantyne*

Konstantinos (Greek) Steadfast. *Constance, Konstance, Konstant, Tino, Tinos*

Kont (Hungarian) Meaning unknown.

Kontar (Ghanese) Only child.

Korey (Irish) Lovable. *Kori, Korrey, Korrie*

Korvin (Latin) Crow. *Corvin*

Koshy (American) Jolly. *Koshee, Koshey, Koshi*

Kosmo (Greek) Likes order. *Kosmy, Cosmos*

Kostas (Russian) Loyal.

Koster (American) Spiritual. *Kost, Kostar, Koste, Koster*

Kostya (Russian) Steadfast. (Slavic) Faithful.

Kourosh (Old Persian) Sunlike. (Modern Persian) Great.

Kovan (Bohemian) Smithwork.

Kozan (Japanese) Ancient mountain.

Kozma (Greek) Decoration.

Kripa (Hindi) Has a twin sister. *Kripi*

Krischnan (Greek) Christian. *Krister*

Krishna (Sanskrit) Pleasing. *Krisha, Krishnah*

Kristoffer (Greek) Bearing of Christ. *Kristofer, Krist*

Krunal (Hindi) Meaning unknown.

Kuldeep (Hindi) Light of family.

Kulvir (Hindi) Brave soul of the community.

> **Naming Rights**
>
> Often, first and last names with the same first letter do not sound right together, so shake it up a bit by steering away from letter redundancy. Also, if the last name ends with a vowel, the first name usually should not. The first name should not end with a syllable that rhymes with the first syllable of the last name.

Kumar (Sanskrit) A son.

Kunal (Hindi) Son of emperor Ashok.

Kund (Hungarian) A name of honor.

Kurt (German) Bold counselor.

Kusagra (Hindi) A king.

Kush (Hindi) Son of Rama.

Kushan (Hindi) Meaning unknown.

Kwahu (Hopi) Eagle.

Kwamin (African American) Born on Saturday. *Kwame, Kwamee, Kwami*

Kwau (African) Born on Thursday.

Kyan (African American) Little king. *Kyann*

Kyle (Irish) The narrows; a place where cattle graze; a wood; a church. (Scottish) From a narrow strait; the name of a Scottish region. *Kylie, Kyleigh, Leigh, Lei, Kyli*

Kyler (English) Peaceful. (Dutch) Archer. (Irish) The narrows; a wood; a church. *Cuyler, Kieler, Kiler, Kye, Kylor*

Kyrone (African American) Brash. *Keirohn, Keiron, Keirone, Keirown, Kirone, Kyron*

Kyros (Greek) Master.

Kyzer (American) Wild spirit. *Kaizer, Kizer, Kyze*

L

La Vonn (African American) The small one. *La Vaun, La Voun*

Laakea (Hawaiian) Holy light.

Laban (Hebrew) White. *Lavan*

Labaron (French) The baron. *LaBaron, LaBaronne*

Label (Hebrew) Lion.

Labhras (Irish) Introspective. (Latin) Crowned with laurel. *Lubhras*

Laborc (Hungarian) Brave panther.

Lachlan (Scottish) Feisty. *Lachlann, Lacklan, Lackland, Lock, Locklan, Laughlin*

Ladd (Middle English) Young man. *Laddie, Laddy*

Ladislav (Czechoslovakian) Famous ruler. *Ladislao, Ladislaw, Ladislaus*

Lado (African American) Second-born son.

Ladomér (Hungarian) Trapper.

Lael (Hebrew) Belonging to Jehovah. *Lale*

Laertes (Greek) Action-oriented.

Lafe (American) Punctual. *Laafe, Laife, Laiffe*

Laionela (Hawaiian) Lion.

Laird (Scottish) Lord; landed gentry. *Layrd, Layrde*

Lake (English) Tranquil water.

Laken (African American) Treasure. *Lakin*

Lakista (African American) Meaning unknown.

Lakota (Native American) Friend.

Lakshman (Hindi) Brother of Rama.

Lakshmi (Hindi) A lucky omen; the Hindi goddess of beauty and wealth.

Lakshya (Hindi) Target.

Lalit (Hindi) Of great beauty, beautiful.

Lallo (Native American) Little boy.

Lam (Vietnamese) Full understanding, knowledge. *Lammie, Lammy*

Laman (Vietnamese) Happy, content.

Lamar (Latin) The sea. *Lamarr, Lemar, Lemarr, Lamair, Lamaris, Lamarre, Larmar*

Lamberto (Latin) Wealthy in land; brilliant. *Lambert, Lammert*

Lamech (African American) Powerful.

Lamont (Norse) Lawyer. *Lamond, La Monte, Lammont*

Lance (French) Lancer. (German) Spear. *Lancelot, Launcelot, Ancel*

Lander (Middle English) Occupational name meaning "landowner"; also place name: Lander, Wyoming. *Landor, Landry, Landis, Landers, Landman*

Landis (Anglo-Saxon) Rough land. *Land, Landes, Landice, Landise, Landly, Landus*

Lando (German) Famous throughout the land. (American) Masculine. *Land, Landow*

Landon (Old English) Long hill. *Landan, Landen, Landyn, Landun*

Landry (French) Entrepreneur. *Landree, Landre, Landri, Landrie, Landrue*

Lane (Middle English) Narrow road. *Laine, Layne, Layna*

Lang (Old English) Long. (German) A tall man. *Langdon, Langford, Langley, Langston, Langhorne, Langtry*

Langden (English) Long hill. *Lang, Langdon, Langdun*

Langston (English) Long-suffering. *Lang, Langstan, Langsten*

Lansa (Native American) Lance.

Lantos (Hungarian) Lute player.

Lanty (Irish) Lively. *Laughun, Leachlainn, Lochlainn, Lochlann*

Lantz (Yiddish) Lancer.

Lao-Tzu (Chinese) Old master; old child. Chinese philosopher who is traditionally regarded as the founder of Taoism.

Laramie (French) Pensive. *Laramee, Laramey, Larami, Laramy, Laremy*

Larenzo (Spanish) Bold and spirited. *Lorenso, Lorenzo, Lorenz*

Lariat (American) Word as a name; roper. *Lare, Lari*

Larkin (Irish) Cruel. *Lark, Larkan, Larken, Larkie, Larky*

Larnell (American) Generous. *Larn, Larndelle, Larndey, Larne*

Laron (French) Thief. *Laran, Laraun, Laren, Larin, Laronn, Laryn*

Larrimore (French) One who provides arms. *Larimore, Larmer, Larmor*

Lars (Scandinavian) Crowned with laurel. *Larse, Larson, Larris, Laris, Larse, Larz*

Laserian (Irish) Flame. *Lasairian, Lasirian*

Lassen (Place name). A mountain peak in California. *Lase, Lasen, Lassan, Lassun*

Lassiter (American) Witty. *Lassater, Lasseter, Lassie, Lassy*

László (Hungarian) Might; fame. *Laslo*

Lateef (Arabic) Gentle man.

Lathrop (English) Home-loving. *Lathe, Lathrap, Latrope, Laythrep, Laye*

Latimer (Middle English) Interpreter. *Lattimore, Latymer*

Lauaki (Polynesian) Best.

Laughlin (Irish) Servant.

Launcelot (French) Romantic. *Lance, Lancelott, Launce*

Laurence (Latin) Glorified. *Larence, Laurance, Laurans, Laure, Lorence*

What's in a Name

The name **Laurence** comes from the Roman name *Laurentius*, which means "of Laurentum," a city in ancient Italy. Saint Laurence was a third-century deacon and martyr who, when commanded to turn over the Church's treasures, presented the sick and the poor.

Laurent (French) Martyred. *Laurynt*

Lavan (Hebrew) White.

Lavaughn (African American) Perky. *Lavan, Lavon, Lavonn, Levan, Levaughn*

Lavesh (Hindi) Crumb.

Lawler (Gaelic) Soft-spoken. *Lawford, Loller, Lollar*

Lawrence (Latin) Laurel crown. *Laurence, Lawrance, Lorenz, Loren, Laurens, Lorin, Lorcan, Lon, Lonnie, Loring, Lawford, Lawley, Lawton, Lawler, Laughton, Lawry, Larry, Laurent, Lorenzo, Lauritz, Lorne, Lawson, Lars, Larson, Larkin, Labhras*

Lawson (Old English) Son of Lawrence.

Layton (Old English) One from the meadow farm. *Leighton, Lay, Leigh, Layland*

Lazarus (Hebrew) God's helper. *Lazre, Lazar, Lazaro, Laszlo, El'azar, Lázár*

Leander (Greek) Lion man. *Liander, Leandre, Leandro*

Lear (German) Of the meadow. *Leare, Leere*

Leavery (American) Giving. *Leautree, Leautri, Leautry, Levry, Lo, Lotree, Lotrey, Lotri, Lotry*

LeBron (African American) King.

Lech (Polish) Glory of the Poles. *Lecholsaw, Leslaw, Leszek*

Lee (Old English) Glade. (Gaelic) Poet. (Chinese) Plum. *Leigh*

Leggett (French) Messenger. *Legate, Leggitt, Liggett*

Legolas (Old English) Highest angel.

Lehel (Hungarian) Breathes.

Lei (Chinese) Thunder.

Leif (Old Norse) Beloved. *Leaf, Lief*

Leighton (English) Meadow, farm. *Laytan, Layton, Leighten, Leightun, Laeton, Laiton, Laeeton, Leiton, Leyton*

Leith (Scottish) Wide river. *Leathan*

Lél (Hungarian) Bugler.

Leland (Old English) From the meadowland. *Leeland, Leighlon, Leiland, Lelan, Lelond*

Lemuel (Hebrew) Devoted to God; belonging to God. *Lemmie, Lemmy, Lemy*

Len (Native American) Flute. (German) Courage. (American) Like a lion. *Lenny*

Lenno (Native American) Man.

Lennon (Gaelic) Cloak; little cape. *Lenin, Lenn, Lennen*

Lennor (Gypsy) Summer.

Lennox (Scottish) Amid the elms; from the field of elm trees. *Lenox, Lenix, Lennie, Lenny, Len*

Lensar (English) With his parents. *Lendar*

Leon (Greek) Lion. *Leo, Leone, Leonidas, Leosko, Leonato*

Leonard (German) Lion-hearted. *Lennard, Lenard, Lennart, Leonardo, Leonhard, Leon, Leo, Lennie, Lenny, Len, Lénárd, Leonárd, Leó*

Leonidas (Greek) One who is bold as a lion. *Leonidis, Leonid*

Leopold (Old German) Bold leader. *Luitpold, Leupold, Leopoldo*

Leor (Hebrew) I have light.

Leron (Arabic) The song is mine. *Lyron, Lirone, Lerone, Liron*

Leroy (Old French) The king. *Leroi, Lee, Roy*

Leshem (Hebrew) Precious stone.

Leslie (Scottish) Low meadow. *Les, Leslea, Lesley, Lesly, Lezly*

Lesta (Russian) From town of Leicester. *Leisti*

Lester (Latin) Legion camp. *Les, Leicester*

Levar (American) Soft-spoken. *Levarr*

Levente (Latin) Rising. (Hungarian) Being. *Levent, Lavant, Lavante*

Leverett (French) Baby rabbit. *Lev, Leveret, Leverit, Leveritt*

Levi (Hebrew) United. *Lev, Levey, Levin, Levon, Levy*

Lex (English) Defender of mankind. *Lexi, Lexie, Lexin*

Li (Chinese) Strength.

Li-Liang (Chinese) Powerful.

Liam (Irish) Unwavering protector. *Lliam, Lyam*

Liang (Chinese) Excellent; good. *Lyang*

Libero (Portuguese) Freedom. *Liberio*

Libor (Czechoslovakian) Freedom. *Libeck, Liborek, Libek*

Liko (Chinese) Buddhist nun.

Lincoln (Old English) Home by the pond. *Linc, Link*

Lind (Old English) Linden tree. *Lin, Linden, Lyndon, Lindell, Lindberg, Lindley, Lindon, Lindt, Linford, Linely, Linton*

Lindberg (German) Mountain of linden trees. *Lin, Lind, Lindburg, Lindie, Lindy, Lyndberg, Lydburgh*

Lindell (English) Valley of linden trees. *Lindall, Lyndell, Lyndall, Lindel*

Lindsay (English) Island of linden trees. *Lyndsey, Lindsee, Lindsy, Lyndsay, Lindsee, Lindsey*

Linus (Greek) Flax. *Linas, Line, Lines*

Lionel (French) Fierce. (Latin) Little lion. *Li, Lion, Lionell, Lye, Lyon, Lyonel, Lyonell, Leonel, Lonell, Lonnell*

Lipót (Hungarian) Brave.

Lisandro (Spanish) Liberator.

Lisiate (Polynesian) Brave king.

Lisimba (African American) Harmed by a lion.

Litton (Old English) Hillside town. *Lyten, Lyton, Lytton*

Livingston (English) Leif's settlement. *Livingstone*

Llewellyn (Old English) Ruling. *Llewelleyn, Llewelin, Lewellin, Lewellen*

Lloyd (Old Welsh) Gray-haired. *Floyd, Loyd*

Loaghaire (Irish) Calf herder; shepard. *Laoghaire*

Locke (English) Fort. *Lock, Lockwood*

Loe (Hawaiian) King.

Logan (Scottish) Little hollow.

Loikanos (Greek) Man from Lucania, an area in southern Italy. *Lukianos*

Lokesh (Hindi) Lord Brahma.

Lokni (Native American) Raining through the roof.

Lombardi (Italian) Winner. *Bardi, Bardy, Lom, Lombard, Lombardy*

Lon (Gaelic) Fierce. *Lonny*

Lonato (Native American) Flint.

London (English) Fierce ruler of the world.

Long (Vietnamese) Dragon.

Lono (Hawaiian) God of farming.

Loránd (Hungarian) Brave warrior. *Lóránt*

Lorcan (Irish) Little fierce one. *Lorcen, Lorcin, Lorcon*

Lord (English) Lord; noble title.

Loredo (Spanish) Smart; cowboy. *Lorado, Loredoh, Lorre, Lorrey*

Naming Rights

Talk about it—or not. Other than the inevitable, "Is it a boy or a girl?" question, the next in line will be, "What name have you chosen?" Talking with your spouse, family, and friends makes it a team effort, and it's fun for everyone involved, too. You might even have a baby-naming party. Check out your family tree or call relatives, especially those you haven't talked to in a while. Don't expect a unanimous decision, but everyone will feel like they helped play a role in an important family decision. On the flip side, however, too many name choices and people involved in the naming ritual could be overwhelming.

Loren (Latin) Hopeful; winning. *Lorin, Lorrin*

Lorenzo (Spanish, Italian) Bold; spirited. *Larenzo, Loranzo, Lore, Lorence, Lorenso, Lorentz, Lorenz, Lorrie, Lorry*

Lőrinc (Hungarian) Laurentian.

Loring (German) Famous in war.

Lorne (Latin) Grounded. *Lorn*

Lot (Hebrew) Furtive; hidden; covered. *Lott*

Loudon (American) Enthusiastic. *Louden, Lowden, Lowdon, Lewdan, Lewdin, Lewdon, Lowdan, Lowdin, Lowdon, Lowdyn*

Louis (German) Famed warrior. *Lewis, Lewes, Luis, Louie, Lewie, Lou, Lew, Lu, Ludwig, Ludvig, Luigi, Lodovico, Luthias, Llewellyn, Clovis, Chlodwig, Lajos*

Lowell (English) Young wolf. *Lowel*

Loys (American) Loyal. *Loyce, Loyse*

Luc (French) Light; laidback. *Lucca, Luke*

Lucan (Irish) Light.

Lucas (Latin) Bringer of light. (Greek) Patron saint of doctors, artists, and creatives. *Lucca, Luces, Luka, Lukas, Luke, Lukes, Lukus*

Lucian (Latin) Soothing. *Lew, Luyciyan, Lushun*

Lucius (Latin) Light. *Luca, Lucan, Lucca, Luce, Lucian, Luciano, Lucien, Lucio, Lucias*

Lucky (American) Lucky. *Luckee, Luckey, Luckie*

Ludacris (African American) Rapper, musician.

Ludlow (English) Hill of the leader. *Ludlowe*

Ludomir (Czechoslovakian) Famous people. *Ludek*

Ludoslaw (Polish) Glorious people.

Ludovic (Slavic) Smart; spiritual. *Luddovik, Lude, Ludovik, Ludvic, Vick*

Ludvig (Scandinavian) Famous warrior.

Ludwig (German) Famous fighter. *Lugweg, Lugwige, Ludwik*

Lugono (African) Sleep.

Luister (African) One who listens.

Luke (English) Bringer of light. *Luc, Lucas, Luckas, Luchas, Luca, Luka, Lukas, Lucais, Lucan, Lucian, Lucien, Lucius, Luciano, Lukyan, Lukian, Lukács*

Lukman (North African) Forecaster.

Lulani (Hawaiian) Pinnacle of heaven.

Lundy (Scottish) Child born on Monday.

Lunn (Irish) Strong; warlike. *Lon, Lonn, Lun*

Lunt (Scandinavian) From the grove.

Lusk (English) Hearty. *Lus, Luske, Luskee, Luskey, Luski, Lusky*

Luther (German) Warrior. *Luthar, Lutera, Lothaire, Lotario*

Lykaios (Greek) Wolfish, of a wolf, wolflike.

Lyle (Old French) Island. *Lisle, Lyell, Lysle*

Lyman (Middle English) From the meadow. *Leyman, Leaman*

Lynch (Irish) Mariner.

Lyndal (English) Valley with lime trees. *Lindal, Lyndell*

Lyndall (English) Nature lover; valley of lime trees. *Lyndell, Lynd, Lyndal*

Lyndon (Old English) Linden tree. *Lindon, Linden*

Lynn (English) Verbose; waterfall. *Lyn, Lin, Linn, Lynne*

Lynton (English) Town of nature lovers; town with lime trees. *Linton*

Lyon (Latin) Shining one. Place name: second-largest metropolitan area in France.

Lyre (Old English) A harp, lyre.

Lysander (Greek) Liberator; emancipation. *Lisander*

Lyulf (German) Combative. *Lyulfe, Lyulff*

M

Maarten (Dutch) Fondness of war.

Mablevi (African American) Do not deceive.

Mabon (Welsh) Son, or a knight, in Aurthurian legend.

Macario (Spanish) Happy. *Macareo, Makario*

Macartan (Irish) Son of Artan.

Macbeth (Scottish) Son of Beth. (Shakespearean) From *Macbeth*.

Macduff (Scottish) Son of the Blackman. (Shakespearean) From *Macbeth*.

Mace (Latin) Aromatic spice. (Old English) A medieval weapon used by a knight.

Mackenzie (Gaelic) Son of the wise leader. *Mackie, Kenzie, Max, Mackinzie, Mackenzy*

Mackinley (Irish) Educated. (Scottish) Son of Kinley.

Maclean (Irish) Son of Leander. (Scottish) Son of the servant of John. *Maclain, McLain, McLaine, Macleane*

Macmorris (Irish) Son of Morris.

Macon (Middle English) To make. *Makon, Macomb*

Macy (Old French) Matthew's estate. *Macey, Mace, Maceo, Maci, Macie*

Madai (Hebrew) A measure; judging; a garment.

Madan (Hindi) Cupid. *Madden, Maddin, Maddyn, Maden, Madin, Madyn*

Maddock (Old Welsh) Champion; good fortune. *Madock, Madoc, Madog, Maddox, Madox, Maidoc, Maddy*

Maddox (English) Giving. *Maddocks, Maddy, Madox*

Madhav (Hindi) Krishna.

Madison (Old English) Son of a mighty warrior; son of Maud. *Maddison, Maddy*

Madock (American) Giving. *Maddock, Maddy, Madac*

Maemi (Japenese) Honest child.

Magar (Russian) Groom's attendant. *Magarious*

Magee (Irish) Practical; lively; son of Hugh. *Mackie, Maggy, McGee, MacGee, MacGhee*

Magic (Latin) Supernatural. *Magik, Magique, Magikos*

Magnar (Polish) Strength; warrior.

Magne (Norse) Fierce warrior.

Magnus (Latin) The great one. *Manus, Magnuson, Magnum, Maghnus, Magnes, Magnuss, Manius*

Maguire (Irish) Subtle. *McGuire*

Mahabala (Hindi) Strength.

Mahan (American) Cowboy. *Mahahn, Mahand, Mahen, Mayhan*

Mahatma (Sanskrit) Great soul.

Mahavira (Hindi) Son of Priyavrata.

Mahdi (African) The expected one. (Arabic) Guided to the right path. *Mahde, Mahdee, Mahdy*

Mahesh (Hindi) A great ruler; Lord Shiva.

Mahkah (Native American) Earth.

Mahpee (Native American) Sky.

Maik (Hawaiian) Now.

Main (Welsh) Slender. *Mainess, Mane, Maness*

Maitland (Old English) Dweller in the meadow.

Maitreya (Hindi) The name of a sage.

Major (Latin) Greater; military rank. *Majeur, Majors, Majorie*

Makaio (Hawaiian) Gift of god. *Makayo*

Makalo (African) Wandering.

Makan (Hawaiian) Wind. *Makani, Makanie, Makany*

Makayla (Hebrew) Who is like God.

Makepeace (Old English) Peacemaker.

Makis (Hebrew) Gift from God. *Makys*

Makoto (Japanese) Sincere, honest.

Maksim (Russian) The greatest. *Maxim*

Malachi (Hebrew) Messenger of God. *Malachy, Malachai, Malaki, Maleki*

Malchidiel (Latin) Fullness of God. Angel of March.

Malcom (Scottish) Disciple of Saint Columbia. (Arabic) Dove. *Mal, Colm, Malcolm, Malkalm, Malkelm, Malkolm*

Malik (Arabic) Master. *Malek*

Mallin (English) Strong, little warrior, rowdy. *Malen, Malin, Mallan, Mallen, Mallie, Mally*

Mallory (French) Wild spirit. (German) Army counselor. *Mal, Mallie, Malloree, Mallrie, Malory*

Mallow (Irish) By the river Allo.

Malo (Hawaiian) Winner.

Maloney (Irish) Religious; serves Saint John. *Mal, Malone, Malonie, Malony*

Malvolio (Spanish) Steward.

Mamillius (Latin) Young prince.

Mamoru (Japanese) Earth. *Mamo*

Manavendra (Hindi) A king; king among men.

Manchu (Chinese) Pure.

Manco (Peruvian) King.

Mandar (Hindi) Tree of heaven; flower.

Mandek (Polish) Army man.

Mandel (German) Almond. *Mandee, Mandell, Mandela, Mandie*

Mander (English) From me.

Mandhatri (Hindi) Prince.

Manfred (German) Man of peace. *Manferd, Manford, Mannfred, Mannye, Manny*

Manik (Hindi) Ruby; gem.

Manish (Hindi) Intellect; god of mind

Manley (Old English) Man of the meadow. *Manly, Manning, Mansfield*

Manmohan (Hindi) Pleasing.

Manning (Old English) Son of the hero. *Mann, Man*

Mannix (Celtic) Monk. *Manix, Mann, Mannicks*

Manoj (Hindi) Born of mind.

Mansfield (English) From a field by a small river. *Manesfeld, Mans, Mansfeld, Mansfielde*

Mansour (Arabic) One who triumphs.

Mansukh (Hindi) Pleasing.

Mansur (Arabic) Divinely aided. *Mansoor, Mansour*

Manu (African) Second-born son. (Hawaiian) Bird. (Hindi) Lawmaker.

Manuel (Spanish) God is with us. *Mano, Manolo, Manny, Mani, Mannuel, Manual, Manuale, Manuell, Manuelo*

Manus (American) Strong-willed. *Manes, Mann, Mannas, Mannes, Mannis, Mannus*

Manzo (Japanese) 10,000-fold-strong; third son.

Mar (Latin) The sea.

Marcade (Latin) Warlike.

Marcel (French) Little hammer. *Marcello, Marcellus, Marcellino, Marcellinus*

Marcellus (Latin) Martial, warlike. *Marcel, Marcelis, Marsellus, Marsey*

March (Latin) Walk forth.

Marcin (Polish) Warlike.

Marco (Italian, Spanish) Warring. *Marc, Mark, Marko*

Marcus (Latin) Warlike.

Marden (Old English) From the valley with the pool.

Mardian (French) Tuesday.

Marek (Polish, Slavic) Warlike.

Mareo (Japanese) Rare, uncommon.

Margarelon (Latin) Son of a king.

Mariano (Italian) Bitter; sea of bitterness. *Maryano*

Marin (French) Ocean-loving. *Maren, Marino, Maryn*

Marinos (Greek) Of the sea; sailor. *Marinka, Marina, Mariono, Marynos, Marynus*

Marinus (Latin) Of the sea. *Marino*

Mario (Hebrew) Bitter; king-ruler. *Marion, Mariana*

Marius (Latin) Sailor.

Marjun (Spanish) Contentious. *Marhwon, Marwon, Marwond*

Mark (Latin) Warlike; hammer; defender. *Marek, Marc, Marcus, Markus, Marcel, Marceau, Marque, Marco, Marek, Marko, Marus, Markos, Marks, Marx, March, Marius, Marquette, Marquis, Marky, Markie, Marilo, Márk, Markó, Márkus, Markis*

Markandeya (Hindi) A sage.

Markham (English) Homebody. *Marcum, Markhum, Markum*

Marland (English) From the march. *Merle*

Marley (English) Secretive. *Marlee, Marleigh, Marly*

Marlin (Hebrew) Bitter; fish. *Marllin*

Marlon (Old French) Little hawk. *Marlan, Marlin, Marlyn, Marly, Marlo, Marlis, Marlys*

Marlow (Old English) From the hillside lake. *Marlowe, Marlo*

Marmaduke (Celtic) Leader of the seas. *Duke, Marmadook, Marmahduke*

Maro (Japanese) Myself.

Marót (Slavic) Moravian.

Marques (African American) Noble. (Portuguese) Warlike. *Marqes, Marqis, Marquez, Marquis*

Marrock (English) A knight thought to be a werewolf. *Marrok*

Mars (Latin) Bold warrior; Roman god of war.

Marsden (Old English) Field near water. *Marsdon, Marston, Marland, Marley, Marden, Marwood, Mardyth*

Marsh (English) Handsome. *Marr, Mars, Marsch, Marsey*

Marshall (French) Keeper of the horses; military title. *Marshal, Marschall, Marsh, Marshe, Marshell*

Marston (English) From the farm by the pool; town near the marsh. *Marstan, Marsten, Marsdon*

Martin (English) Warrior of Mars, warlike, warring. *Mart, Marten, Martie, Marton, Marty, Maartan, Maartin, Martain, Martine, Marton, Mertin*

Martino (Italian) Warlike. *Martiniano*

Martius (Latin) Warring.

Marvel (French) To wonder; admire. *Marvell, Marvil, Marvill, Marvyl, Marvyll*

Marvin (English) Beautiful sea; good friend; lover of the sea. *Mervin, Mervyn, Merwin, Merwyn, Myrwyn, Murvyn, Myrvyn, Marv*

What's in a Name

The name **Martin** is derived from the Roman god Mars. Saint Martin of Tours, the patron saint of France, was a fourth-century bishop who, according to legend, came across a beggar in the middle of winter and ripped his cloak in two, giving half to the beggar so he wouldn't freeze. Martin Luther King is a more modern-day namesake.

Masahiro (Japanese) Wise.

Masakazu (Japanese) First son of Masa.

Masao (Japanese) Vibrant.

Masato (Japanese) Justice.

Masatoshi (Japanese) Meaning unknown.

Mashawn (African American) Vivacious. *Masean, Mashaun, Mayshawn*

Maska (Native American) Strong.

Maslin (Old French) Little twin; little Thomas. *Maslen*

Mason (French) Stoneworker. *Masen, Mase, Masin, Masoon, Masun, Masyn*

Masoud (Arabic) Happy; lucky. *Masood*

Massey (English) Doubly excellent. *Maccey, Masey, Massi*

Massimo (Italian) Greatest. *Masimo, Massey, Massimmo, Massimiliano*

Matai (Hebrew) Gift of God. *Matteo, Matthäus, Mateus, Mateo, Matthew, Matthias, Matias, Matia, Mattias, Matze,*

Mathew, Mathias, Matthias, Mattieu, Matheu, Matyus, Matthuas, Mathern, Mayhew, Mattheson, Matthieson, Matthews, Mattheus, Mathe, Mattison, Massey, Matt, Matty, Mats, Máté, Mátyás

Matanga (Hindi) Sage; adviser to Devi

Mateo (Greek) Devoted to God. *Matteo*

Mather (Old English) Strong army.

Matheson (English) Son of God's gift. *Mathesen, Mathisen, Mathison, Mathysen, Mathyson*

Mathias (German) Gift of God. *Mathies, Mathyes, Matt, Matthias*

Matlal (Aztec) Dark green, net.

Matlock (American) Rancher. *Lock, Mattlock*

Mats (Scandinavian) Gift from God. *Matthew, Matthias, Matias, Matts, Matz*

Matthew (Hebrew) God's gift. *Matt, Matteo, Matthias, Mattias*

Mattison (Hebrew) Son of Matt; worldly. *Matisen, Matison, Matisen, Mattysen, Mattyson, Matysen, Matyson*

Mauli (Hawaiian) Black.

Maurice (Latin) Dark-skinned; like a Moor. *Morris, Morse, Maury, Morry, Morey, Morrie, Moritz, Moriz, Morets, Meuriz, Moss, Morrell, Mauricio, Maurizio, Murray, Maryse, Morrison*

Maurizio (Italian) Dark. *Marits, Maritza, Moritz, Moritza, Moritzio*

Maury (Italian) Dark-skinned; a Moor. *Maure, Amaury, Mauro*

Maverick (American) Wildly independent. (English) Nonconforming. *Maveric, Maverik, Maveryck, Mavric, Mavrick, Mavrik*

Max (Latin) The greatest. *Maximilien, Maximiliano, Maximus, Maxim, Maximo, Maxfield, Maximino, Maximilian, Maxey, Maxie, Mac, Maxa, Mack, Maks, Maksim, Massimiliano*

Maxwell (English) Capable. (Latin) Great. (Scottish) Mack's well. *Maxwel, Maxwill*

Mayer (English) Headman, mayor. (Hebrew) One who brightens. (Latin) Great. *Meyer, Meir, Meier, Mayr, Myer, Mayor, Myerson*

Maynard (Anglo-Saxon) Remarkable strength; powerful; brave. *Mainard, Maynhard*

Mayo (Irish) Nature-loving; yew tree. *Maio, Maioh, Moy, Mayes, Mayoh, Mays*

Mayon (Hindi) The black God. *Mayan, Mayun, Maion*

Mcaffie (Scottish) Charming. *Mac, Mack, Mackey, MacAfee, McAffee, McAffie*

Mcauliffe (Irish) Bookish. *Macaulif, Macauliff*

Mccauley (Scottish) Son of righteousness. *Mccaulay, Macauley*

McCoy (Irish) Son of Hugh.

McKinley (Scottish) Son of Kinley. *MacKinley*

Mead (Old English) Meadow. *Meade, Meed, Meid*

Meallan (Irish) Sweet. *Maylan, Meall*

Mecaenus (Shakespearean) From *Antony and Cleopatra*.

Medárd (Hungarian) Great, strong.

Megyer (Hungarian) Pearl. *Magyar*

Mehdi (Hindi) A flower.

Mehetabel (Hebrew) Favored by God; God is doing good. *Mehitabel, Mehitabelle, Metabel, Hetty, Hitty*

Mehul (Hindi) Rain. *Mukul*

Meka (Hawaiian) Eyes.

Melancton (Greek) Black flower. *Melanchthon*

Melborn (English) From the mill stream. *Melbourne*

Melbourne (English) Mill stream. *Mel, Melborn, Melbourn, Melburn, Melburne*

Melburn (English) From the mill stream. *Melburne, Milvourn, Milburn*

Meldon (English) From the hillside mill. *Melden, Meldin, Meldyn*

Melik (Slavic) His kingdom; his counselor.

Melor (English) Old English hillside; town by the mill. *Mel*

Melun (Greek) Dark-skinned.

Melvin (Celtic) Chief. *Malvin, Melvyn, Mel, Mal*

Menas (Shakespearean) From *Antony and Cleopatra.*

Mendel (Middle English) Repairman. *Mel, Mendelssohn, Menachem, Menahem, Mendal, Mendell, Mendie, Mendy, Mendyl*

Menecrates (Shakespearean) From *Antony and Cleopatra.*

Menelaus (Shakespearean) From *Troilus and Cressida.*

Menteith (Shakespearean) From *Macbeth.*

Menyhért (Hungarian) Royal; light.

Mercer (Middle English) Storekeeper. *Merce*

Mercury (Italian) God of invention. (Latin) God of trade.

Mercutio (Shakespearean) From *Romeo and Juliet.*

Meredith (Old Welsh) Protector of the *sea. Meridith, Merry, Meri, Merideth, Merydeth, Merydith, Merydyth*

Merit (Latin) Deserving of good fortune. *Merritt*

Meriweather (Latin) Fair weather.

Merlin (Celtic, Anglo-Saxon, Welsh) Sea; falcon; sea hill. *Merlyn, Marlin, Marlen, Marwin, Mervin, Merv, Merle*

Merrick (English) Ruler of the sea. *Mere, Meric, Merik, Merrack, Merrick*

Merrill (Irish) Bright sea. (French) Famous. *Merral, Meril, Merrel, Meryl, Myrl, Myril, Merle, Merrick, Merton*

Merton (English) From the farm by the sea. *Mert, Mertan, Merten, Mertin, Murton*

Meshach (Hebrew) That draws with force.

Messala (Italian) Supporter of Brutus.

Mete (Slavic) Gentle. (Greek) Pearl. *Mette*

Meyer (German) A farmer. *Mayeer, Mayer, Meier, Myer*

Mica (Hebrew) Prophet. (Latin) A mineral. *Micah, Michah, Micajah*

Michael (Hebrew) Who is like God. *Michail, Mikhail, Mikas, Mikel, Michel, Miguel, Michel-angelo, Micah, Michiel, Micha,* *Mischa, Mitchell, Mitch, Michau, Mikkel, Michel, Michele, Mihon, Mikhos, Mihal, Mick, Mickey, Micky, Mike, Mikey, Mickie, Midge, Mihály, Mikó*

Michelangelo (Italian) God's angel; messenger; artist. *Michel, Michelanjelo, Mikalangelo, Mikel, Mikelangelo*

Michio (Japanese) Man with the strength of 3,000.

Mickey (Irish) Who is like God. *Mickee, Micki, Myckee, Mycki, Myckie, Mycky, Mykee, Mykie, Myky*

Miguel (Portuguese) Like the Lord.

Mihaly (Hebrew) He who is like God. *Mihai, Mihail, Mihaly*

Mihir (Hindi) The sun.

Mikasi (Native American) Coyote.

Mikhail (Russian) Godlike; graceful. *Mika, Mikey, Mikkail, Mykhey*

Miko (Finnish) One who is like God.

Miksa (Hungarian) Similar to God.

Milán (Hungarian) Kind.

Miles (English) Merciful. (German) A soldier. (Irish) Servant. *Myles, Milan, Milah, Miles, Mila*

Milind (Hindi) A honeybee.

Naming Rights

Choose a name because of the historical meaning that springs forth from a language used by your ancestors.

Millard (Old English) Caretaker of the mill. *Milard, Millerd, Millurd*

Miller (Old English) One who mills. *Mills, Millson*

Milo (German) Soft-hearted. *Milos, Mye, Mylo*

Miloslav (Russian) Peace celebration.

Milton (Old English) From the mill town. *Milten, Milty, Milt, Melton*

Miner (Latin) Youth.

Minesh (Hindi) Meaning unknown.

Ming (Chinese) After a dynasty.

Minoru (Japanese) Fruitful.

Miroslav (Slavic) Famous. *Miroslaw*

Misu (Native American) Rippling brook. *Mysu*

Mitali (Hindi) Friend.

Mitchell (American, English, Hebrew) He who is like God. *Mitch, Mitchel, Mitchelle, Mitchill, Mitshell, Mytchil*

Mitesh (Hindi) One with few desires.

Mladen (Slavic) Forever in youth.

Moby (Fiction) The great white whale; *Moby Dick* by Herman Melville.

Mog (Indian) High lord.

Mohamed (Arabic) Praiseworthy; glorified. *Mohammad, Mohammed, Mohamid, Mohamud, Muhammod*

Mohan (Hindi) Charming; fascinating.

Mohanan (Irish) Believer. *Mon, Monaghan, Monehan, Monnahan*

Mohe (Native American) Elk.

Mohin (Hindi) Attractive.

Mohit (Hindi) Ensnarled by beauty.

Mohsen (Arabic) Son, child.

Mojag (Native American) Never silent.

Moke (Hawaiian) Drawn from the water.

Momus (Greek) God of mockery and fault-finding.

Monroe (Irish) Mouth of the Roe River; wheelwright. *Munroe, Munro, Monro*

Montague (French) Steep mountain; residence name. *Mont, Montagew, Montagu, Montegue*

Montana (Spanish) Mountain. *Montano, Montaine*

Montano (Latin) Mountain. *Montana, Montaine, Montanus*

Montaro (Japanese) Big boy.

Monte (English) Wealthy man's mountain. *Monti, Monty*

Montego (Spanish) Mountainous.

Montel (Spanish) Mountain.

Montenegro (Spanish) Black mountain.

Montgomery (French) Mountain hunter. (English) Rich man's mountain. *Mongomerey, Monte, Montgomry, Montgomerie, Mountgomery*

Montraie (African American) Fussy. *Montray, Montraye*

Montrell (French) Royal mountain. Place name: Montreal, Quebec. *Montrel, Montrelle*

Montrose (French) High and mighty. *Montroce, Montros*

Mór (Hungarian) Moorish. *Móric, Moore*

Mordecai (Hebrew) Warrior. *Mordechai, Mort, Mordy, Morty*

Mordock (Science fiction) Character from *Star Trek the Next Generation.*

Moreland (English) From the moors; marshlands. *Mooreland, Moorland, Moorlande, Morland, Morlande*

Morgan (Irish) Lives by the sea.

Moriarty (Irish) Sea warrior; expert seaman.

Morio (Japanese) Forest.

Morley (English) English moor; meadow. Outdoors loving. *More, Morlee, Morly, Morrs, Morlee, Morleigh, Morry, Morrie, Lee*

Moroni (Arabic) Place name: capital of Comoros, located on the western coast of Grand Comore island. *Maroney, Maroni, Marony, Moroney, Morony*

Morpheus (Greek) God of dreams.

Morris (Latin) Dark-skinned. *Maurice, Morrie, Morry, Morse, Moss, Morrison*

Morrison (English) Son of Morris. (Scottish) Son of the servant Mary. *Morrisen, Morrysen, Morryson*

Mortimer (French) Still water. *Morty, Mort, Mortemer, Mortymer*

Morton (Anglo-Saxon) City on the moor. *Morten, Mortyn, Morty, Mort*

Morven (Old English) Child of the sea.

Moses (Hebrew) Drawn out of the water. *Mose, Moe, Mosya, Moey, Moss, Moshe, Moishe, Mosheh, Moyes, Moyse, Mosie*

Motega (Native American) New arrow.

Mowgli (Fiction) Character from *The Jungle Book* by Rudyard Kipling.

Mu-nan (Japanese) The man who never turned back.

Mugen (Japanese) Infinity.

Muhammad (Arabic) Praised one. *Muhammed, Mohamad, Mohammed, Mohamed, Moham-mad, Mohamet, Mahmoud, Mehemet, Mehmet, Ahmad, Ahmet, Amad, Amed, Hamid, Hamad, Hammed*

Mukasa (Ugandan) God's chief administrator.

Mukki (Native American) Child.

Mukta (Hindi) A pearl.

Mukul (Hindi) Bud.

Mukunda (Hindi) Variation of Lord Krishna; freedom giver.

Mulder (American) Of the dark. *Muldyr*

Mull (Middle English) Grinder. *Muller, Müller*

Mumtaz (Arabic) Excellent; conspicuous.

Munir (Arabic) Sparkling; brilliant; shining. *Munira, Munirah*

Murdad (Persian) Immortality. Angel of July.

Murdock (Scottish) Victorious at sea. *Merdock, Merdok, Murdoch, Murdock, Murdok, Murtagh*

Murfain (American) Bold spirit. *Merfaine, Murf, Murfee, Murfy, Murphy*

Murphy (Irish) Sea warrior. *Merfee, Murphee, Murphree, Murphey, Murphi, Murphie*

Murray (Celtic) Sailor. *Muray, Murrey, Murry, Moray*

Mustafa (Arabic) The chosen one. *Mostafa, Mostafah, Mostaffa, Mustafe, Mustaffa, Mustafo, Mustofo*

Mustanen (Finnish) Black.

Mutius (Shakespearean) From *Titus Andronicus*.

Muzaffer (Turkish) Meaning unknown.

Mykelti (African American) He who is like God.

Myles (English) Merciful. (Irish) Servant. (Latin) Soldier. (Greek) Inventor of the corn mill.

Myrle (American) Able. *Merl, Merle, Myrie, Myryee*

Myron (Greek) Sweet oil.

N

Nabendu (Hindi) New moon.

Nabil (Arabic) Noble.

Nabulung (African American) Do not receive.

Nachiketa (Hindi) An ancient Rishi, fire. *Nachik*

Nachman (Hebrew) Comforter. *Menachem, Menahem, Nacham, Nachmann, Nahum*

Nachmanke (Hebrew) Compassionate one; one who comforts.

Nachum (Hebrew) Comfort. *Nabum, Nachman, Nechum, Nehum*

Nadav (Hebrew) Noble; a generous one.

Nadim (Hindi) Friend. *Nadeem*

Nadir (Hebrew) Pledge.

Naeem (African American) Benevolent.

Naftali (African) Runs in woods. *Naphtali, Neftali, Nefthali, Nephtali, Nephthali*

Nagel (English) Smooth. *Naegel, Nageler, Nagelle, Nagle, Nagler*

Nagesh (Hindi) Lord Shiva.

Nahele (Hawaiian) Forest.

Nahir (Hebrew) Light. *Naheer, Nahar*

Nahum (Hebrew) The comforter. *Naum*

Naimish (Hindi) Meaning unknown.

Nairne (Scottish) From the narrow river glade.

Naji (Arabic) To save. *Nagi, Naj*

Najib (Arabic) Noble. *Nageeb, Nagib, Najeeb*

Nakul (Hindi) Name of one of the Pandavas.

Nalan (Hindi) Lotus.

Nalani (Hawaiian) Heaven's calm.

Namdev (Hindi) Poet; saint; variation of Lord Vishnu.

Nan Shin (Japanese) Gentle mind, natural mind.

Nanda (Sanskrit) Joy.

Nandin (Hindi) The delightful; follower of Shiva.

Nándor (Hungarian) Short for Ferdinand.

Nantan (Apache Indian) Spokesman.

Naoko (Japanese) Direct.

Napoleon (Italian) Fierce one from Naples. (African American) Lion in a new city. *Nappie, Nappy, Nap, Leon, Leo*

Narayana (Hindi) Vishnu, refuge of man.

Narciso (Latin) A lily; daffodil.

Narcissus (Greek) Self-love. *Narcisus*

Nard (Persian) Chess game.

Naresh (Hindi) Ruler of men.

Narik (Science fiction) Character from *Star Trek the Next Generation*.

Narsi (Hindi) Poet; saint.

Nartana (Hindi) Makes others dance.

Nasario (Spanish) Dedicated to God. *Nasar, Nasareo, Nassario, Nazareo, Nazarlo, Nazaro, Nazor*

Nash (Old English) Cliff. *Nashe*

Nashoba (Native American) Wolf. *Neshoba*

Nasim (Arabic) Fresh.

Nasser (Arabic) Winning. *Naser, Nasir, Nasr, Nassar, Nasse, Nassee, Nassor*

Nassir (Arabic) Protector. *Nas, Nasir*

Nataraj (Sanskrit) King of dance.

Nathaniel (Hebrew) Gift of God. *Nathanael, Nathan, Nataniel, Natan, Nate, Nat, Natty, Nataniele, Nathon, Natt*

Nato (American) Gentle. *Nate, Natoe, Natoh*

Naum (Hebrew) The comforter.

Naveen (Hindi) New, modern. *Navin*

Nayan (Hindi) Eye.

Nazaire (French) From Nazareth. *Nasareo, Nasarrio, Nazario, Nazarius, Nazaro, Nazar*

Neal (Gaelic) Champion. *Neil, Neill, Nial, Niall, Neale, Neel, Niels, Niel, Niles, Nels, Nils, O'Neill, Neely*

Nebraska (Native American) Flat water. Place name: thirty-seventh state of the United States of America. *Neb*

Nectarios (Greek) Sweet nectar; immortal man. *Nectaire, Nectarius, Nektario, Nektarios, Nektarius*

Ned (English) Prosperous guardian.

Nedes (Old English) Necessity.

Nedim (Turkish) Meaning unknown.

Nedrun (American) Difficult. *Ned, Nedd, Neddy, Nedran, Nedro*

Neel (Hind) Blue. *Neelendra, Neelmani*

Neeraj (Hind) Born in water.

Nehemiah (Hebrew) God's compassion. *Nechemia, Nechemiah, Nechemya, Nechemyah, Nemiah, Nemo*

Nehru (East Indian) Canal.

Neil (Irish) Champion. *Neal, Neale, Neall, Nealle, Nealon, Neile, Neill, Neils, Nels, Nial, Niall, Nialle, Niel, Niels, Nigel, Niles, Nilo*

Naming Rights

Sometimes, the mother's maiden name is used as a first or middle name. Also, if needed to keep family members happy, a child can be given two middle names.

Neilan (Irish) Champion.

Nek (Italian) Meaning unknown. *Neko*

Nektarios (Greek) Nectar. *Nectarios*

Nelek (Polish) Like a horn.

Nellie (English) Short for Nelson; singing. *Nell, Nellee, Nelli, Nells, Nelly*

Nels (Scandinavian) Champion; form of Neil.

Nelson (Old English) Son of a champion; son of Neil. *Nealson, Neilson, Nilson, Nelly, Nellie*

Nemesio (Spanish) Justice. *Nemo*

Nemo (Latin) No name; nobody.

Neo (Greek) New.

Neper (Spanish) New city.

Neptune (Latin) Roman god of the sea. *Neptunne*

Nereus (Greek) Of the sea. *Nereo*

Nero (Latin) Strong. *Neron, Nerone*

Neron (Spanish) Strong, stern.

Nesbit (English) Curve in the road. *Nasbit, Naisbitt, Nesbitt, Nisbet, Nisbett*

Nesim (Turkish) Meaning unknown.

Nesip (Turkish) Meaning unknown.

Nestor (Greek) Traveler; wisdom. *Nesta, Nest*

Nevan (Irish) Little saint; holy. *Neven,*

Neville (French) From the new farmland. *Nevil, Nevile, Newland, Nev, Nevelson*

Nevin (German) Nephew. (Irish) The servant of the saints. *Nevins, Neffe, Nefin, Nevyns, Nivyn, Nyvin*

Newbury (English) Use of surname as a first name; renewal. *Newbery, Newberry, Newburry, Newborough, Newburgh*

Newell (Old English, French) From the manor; kernel. *Newall, Newlin, Newland, Newbold, Newgate, Newton*

Newlyn (Old Welsh) Pool. *Newlin, Newl, Newlynn, Nule*

Newman (Old English) Newcomer. *Neuman, Neumann, Numen, Newmie*

Newt (English) New.

Niao-ka (Chinese) Bird's nest.

Nicandro (Spanish) A man who excels. *Nicandreo, Nicandrios, Nicandros, Nikander, Nikandreo, Nikandrios*

Nicholas (Greek) Victorious people. *Nicolas, Nikolas, Nikolie, Niko, Nikolaus, Nicklaus, Nicola, Nick, Nicky, Nikki, Nikita, Nickita, Nikos, Nikolai, Nikola, Nicholai, Nicanor, Nikos, Nicos, Nichol, Nichols, Nicolson, Nicol, Nicolo, Nikolos, Nicko, Nicodemus, Nils, Niles, Nixon, Cole, Colin, Colet, Claus, Klaus, Klas, Klaas, Miklós*

What's in a Name

Nicholas comes from the Greek name *Nikolaos*, meaning "victory of the people." Saint Nicholas was a fourth-century bishop from Asia Minor who reportedly saved the daughters of a poor man from lives as prostitutes. But he is also more commonly known for his annual habit of bestowing gifts on children around the world on Christmas Eve, as Santa Claus.

Nicodemus (Greek) Victory of the people. *Nicodemo, Nikodema*

Niels (Scandinavian) Victorious. *Neels*

Nigan (Native American) In the lead.

Nigel (Latin) Dark one. *Nigal, Nigiel, Nigil*

Nihar (Hindi) Mist; fog; dew.

Nikan (Native American) My friend.

Nike (Greek) Victory. *Nykee, Nykie, Nyke*

Nikhil (Russian) Victor.

Nikos (Greek) Victor. *Nicos, Niko, Nikolos*

Nilay (Hindi) Home, heaven.

Nile (English) Smooth. *Ni, Niles, Niley, Nyles, Nyley*

Nils (Danish) Champion.

Nimai (Hindi) Name of Lord Krishna. *Nimay*

Nimbus (Latin) Rain cloud; halo.

Nimesh (Hindi) Meaning unknown. *Nimish*

Nimrod (Hebrew) Renegade. *Nimrodd, Nymrod*

Nino (Italian) God is gracious. *Ninoshka*

Ninyun (American) Spirited. *Ninian, Ninion, Ninyan, Nynyun*

Niraj (Hindi) Lotus flower.

Niramitra (Hindi) Son of pandava Sahadeva.

Niranjan (Hindi) Name of a river; goddess Durga; the night of the full moon.

Nirav (Hindi) Quiet, without sound.

Nirel (Hebrew) God's field. *Niriel, Niria, Nira, Nir, Nyree*

Nishad (Hindi) Seventh note on the Indian musical scale. *Ni*

Nishan (Armenian) Sign.

Nisi (Hebrew) Emblem.

Nitesh (Hindi) Heartbeat of the earth.

Nitis (Native American) Good friend. *Netis*

Nitya-Sundara (Hindi) Good-looking.

Njord (Old Norse) Man of the north.

Noadiah (Hebrew) God assembles.

Noah (Hebrew) Comfort; wanderer. *Noa, Noe, Noach, Noel, Noam*

Noble (Latin) Honorable one; well-born. *Nobel, Nobile*

Nocona (Native American) Wanderer. *Nokoni*

Nodin (American) Wind. (Native American) Windy day.

Noe (Spanish) Peace, rest. *Noeh, Noey*

Noel (French) Christmas. *Noël, Nowell, Natale, Natal*

Noi (Laos) Small. *Sanoi*

Nolan (Irish) Renowned, noble. (Scottish) Famous, a champion. *Nolen, Nolin, Nolyn, Nowlan*

Nona (Latin) Ninth.

Noor (Hindi) Light.

Norb (Scandinavian) Innovative. *Norberto, Norbie, Norbs, Norby*

Norbert (German) Blond hero.

Nordin (Nordic) Handsome. *Nord, Nordan, Norde, Nordee, Nordeen, Nordun*

Norman (English) Man from the north. *Normie, Normal, Norm, Norris, Norville, Normand*

Norris (English) Northerner. *Noris, Norreys, Norrie, Norriss, Norry*

North (Old English) From the north. *Northcliff, Northrup, Norton, Norvin, Norwin, Norwyn, Norward, Norwell, Norwood, Nowles*

Northcliff (English) Northern cliff. *Northcliffe, Northclyff, Northclyffe*

Northrop (English) Northern farm. *Northrup*

Norton (English) Northern town. *Nort, Nortan, Norten*

Norval (Scottish) Northern village. *Norvel*

Norvell (English) North well. *Norve, Norville, Norval, Norvill, Norvyl*

Norvin (English) Northern friend. *Norvyn, Norwin, Norwyn*

Norwin (English) Friendly. *Norvin, Norwen, Norwind, Norwinn*

Noy (Hebrew) Beauty; decoration.

Numa (Arabic) Kindness. *Numah*

Nuncio (Italian) Messenger. *Nunzio*

Nuri (Arabic) Fire. *Noori, Nur, Nuriel, Nuris*

Nuriel (Hebrew) Light of God. *Nooriel, Nuriya, Nuriyah, Nurya*

Nuru (African) Light; born in daylight.

Nuys (English) Place name: Van Nuys, California. *Nies, Nyes, Nys*

Nwa (African) Son.

Nye (Middle English) Island dweller.

Nyék (Hungarian) Borderlands.

Nyle (Old English) Island. *Nyl, Nyles*

O

Oakley (Old English) From the oak meadow. *Oakes, Oakie, Oaklee, Oakleigh, Oakly, Oklie*

Obadiah (Hebrew) Servant of God. *Obed, Obie, Obe*

Obedience (American) To obey.

Obelia (Greek) Pillar of strength; needle.

Obelix (Greek) Pillar of strength. *Obelius*

Oberon (German) Bear heart. *Auberon, Auberron, Obaron, Oberahn, Oberone, Oburahn*

Obert (German) Wealthy.

Obiajulu (African American) The heart is consoled.

Obsidian (English) Glassy black volcanic rock.

Ocean (Greek) Sea. *Oceane, Oceanus*

Oceana (Greek) From the sea.

Ochen (Ugandan) One of the twins.

Octavius (Latin) Eighth child. (Shakespearean) From *Antony and Cleopatra; Julius Caesar*. *Octavus, Octavio, Octavian, Tavie, Tavy, Oktávián, Octavia*

Octha (English) *The Legend of King Arthur*.

Oda (Norse) Small pointed spear.

Odakota (Native American) Friend.

Oddvar (Norse) The spear's point.

Odea (Greek) Walker by the road.

Oded (Hebrew) Strong. *Odeda*

Odele (Greek) Wealthy; melody.

Odell (English) Otter. (Irish) Used as a surname. (Scandinavian) Little wealthy one. *Ode, Odie, Odyll, Odall, Odele*

Odessa (Greek) Odyssey, journey, voyage.

Odette (English) Wealthy one. (German) Elfin spear. (Greek) Melody.

Odhran (Irish) Pale green.

Odil (French) Rich.

Odilon (French) Wealthy.

Odin (Norse) Head god in Norse mythology. *Odan, Oden*

Odina (Latin) Mountain.

Odion (Nigerian) First of twins.

Odis (German) Wealthy. *Otis*

Odo (French) Name of a bishop. (Scandinavian) Rich. (Science fiction) Character from *Star Trek: Deep Space Nine*. *Audo, Oddo, Odoh*

Odon (Hungarian) Wealthy protector; keeper of the fief.

Odran (Irish) Pale green. *Odren, Odrin, Odron, Odryn*

Odysseus (Greek) Full of wrath.

Offa (English) Name of a king.

Ogden (Old English) From the oak valley. *Oggie, Denny, Den*

Ogilvy (Scottish) From the high peak. *Ogilvie, Gil, Gilie, Gilly*

Ogima (Native American) Chief.

Oguz (Hungarian) Arrow.

Ohanna (Armenian) God's gracious gift.

Ohanzee (Native American) Shadow. *Ohanze*

Ohio (Native American) Large river.

Oihane (Spanish) From the forest.

Oisin (Irish) Little deer.

Oistin (Latin) Venerable. (Irish) Majestic. *Oistan, Oisten*

Oja (African) He came of a hard birth.

Ojal (Hindi) Vision.

Okal (African) To cross.

Okalani (Hawaiian) Heaven.

Okan (Turkish) Meaning unknown.

Okapi (African) Animal with a long neck.

Oke (Hawaiian) Divine strength. *Oscar*

Okelani (Hawaiian) From heaven.

Oki (Japanese) Ocean-centered.

Okoth (African) Born when it was raining.

Oksana (Russian) Glory be to God.

Olaf (Old Norse) Talisman; ancestor. *Olav, Olof, Olin, Olen, Olie*

Olajuwon (Yoruba) Wealth and honor are God's gift. *Olajuwan, Olujuwon, Olajowuan, Olajuwa, Oljuwoun*

Olan (Scandinavian) Royal ancestor. *Olin, Illee*

Olathe (Native American) Beautiful.

Olayinka (Yoruban) Honors surround me.

Olcay (Turkish) Meaning unknown.

Oldrich (Czechoslovakian) One with riches and power. *Olda, Oldra, Oldrisek, Olecek, Olik, Olouvsek*

Oleg (Slavic) One who is holy.

Olag, Olig

Oleos (Spanish) Holy oil used in church. *Leo*

Olesia (Polish) Helper and defender of mankind.

Olga (Russian) Holy.

Oliana (Hawaiian) Oleander.

Olier (French) Meaning unknown.

Olin (Old English) Holly. *Olney, Olinda*

Olindo (Spanish) Protector. *Olinda*

Oliver (Old Norse) Kind one. (Latin) Olive tree. (French) Peace. *Olivier, Olivero, Olley, Olly, Ollie, Noll, Nolly*

Naming Rights

People with less-than-common first names are usually greeted with pleasure, interest, and intrigue—as long as the name isn't *too* unique.

Olwen (Welsh) White footprint.

Olympe (French) Olympian.

Olympia (Greek) Of Mount Olympus; heavenly.

Oma (Arabic) Commander. (Hebrew) Cedar tree. (Irish) Olive color.

Omaha (Native American) Above all others upon a stream. Place name: Omaha, Nebraska.

Omana (Hindi) A woman.

Omar (Arabic) Long-lived; highest; follower of the prophet. (Hebrew) He who speaks; bitter. *Omer, Omir*

Omarjeet (Hindi) Meaning unknown.

Omega (Greek) Great.

Omprakash (Indian) Light of God.

Omri (Hebrew) Sheaf of corn.

On (Chinese) Peace.

Ona (Lithuanian) Graceful one.

Onaedo (African) Gold.

Onan (Turkish) Wealthy.

Onaona (Hawaiian) Sweet smell. *Onaonah*

Onawa (Native American) Awake.

Ond (Hungarian) Tenth child.

Ondrea (Slavic) Strong, courageous.

Oneida (Native American) Eagerly awaited.

Onelia (Hungarian) Torch light.

Onenn (Breton) Meaning unknown.

Oni (Native American) Born on holy ground.

Onida (Native American) The expected one.

Onofre (Spanish) Defender of peace.

Onslow (Arabic) Hill of the passionate one. (English) From the zealous one's hill.

Ontibile (African) God is watching over me.

Oona (Irish) Unity; one.

Opa (Native American) Owl.

Ora (Spanish) Gold.

Oral (Latin) Speaker; word.

Oralee (Hebrew) Lord is my light.

Oran (Irish) Green. (Scottish) Pale-skinned. *Orin, Orren, Oren, Orran, Orrin, Oram, Orrie*

Orane (French) Rising. (Irish) Green.

Orbán (Hungarian) City dweller; educated man. *Orbó, Oros*

Orde (Latin) Beginning. *Ordell*

Orea (Greek) Mountains.

Orelious (Latin) Gold. *Orelius*

Oren (Hebrew, Gaelic) Ash tree; pale; pine tree.

Orenda (Iroquois Indian) Magic power.

Orestes (Greek) Leader. *Oresta, Oreste*

Oria (Latin) From the Orient.

Oriel (Old French) Golden; angel of destiny.

Orien (Latin) The Orient; east. *Oreon, Ori*

Orinda (Teutonic) Fire serpent.

Oringo (African) He who likes the hunt.

Oriole (Latin) Fair-haired.

Orion (Greek) Son of fire. (Mythology) Orion the hunter was placed in the sky as a constellation. *Orien, Oris*

Örkény (Hungarian) Frightening man.

Orlan (English) From the pointed hill. (German) Renowned in the land.

Orlando (Latin) Bright sun. *Orly, Lando, Orlanda*

Orlantha (Old German) From the land.

Orleans (French) Golden.

Orli (Hebrew) The light is mine.

Orly (Hebrew) Light.

Orma (African) Free men.

Orman (Old English) Spearman.

Ormand (German) Serpent.

Ormanda (German) Of the sea.

Ormond (English) Kind-hearted. *Ormand, Ormande, Orme, Ormon, Ormund, Ormunde*

Ormos (Hungarian) Like a cliff.

Ornice (Hebrew) Cedar tree.

Oro (Spanish) Gold.

Orrick (English) From the ancient oak tree. *Oric, Orick, Orreck, Orrik*

Orrin (Greek) Mountain. *Orestes, Orest*

Naming Rights

How many names should baby have? Because of today's complex society, most parents think their children should have at least a first and a middle name. But it's not uncommon in other parts of the world for a child to have up to 10 names! China is one country where this is a common practice.

Örs (Hungarian) Hero.

Orson (English) Ormond's son. (French) Little bear. *Orsen, Orsin, Orsini, Sonny*

Orville (French) From the golden village. *Orvalle, Orval*

Osama (Arabic) Lionlike.

Osanna (Greek) Praise.

Osaze (Hebrew) Favored by God. *Osaz*

Osbert (Old English) Inspired; divine. *Osborn, Osborne, Osmar, Osmond, Osmund, Osted, Ostric, Osmen, Osman, Ossie*

Osborn (English) Divine warrior. (German) Divine bear. *Osbourne, Orburn, Osburne*

Oscar (Old Norse) Divine spear. *Osgood, Oskur, Oszkár*

Osgood (English) Goth of the Heavens. *Osgude, Ozgood*

Osias (Greek) Salvation.

Osip (Hebrew) God will multiply; God shall add.

Osma (Latin) God's servant.

Osman (Arabic) Tender youth. *Osmen, Osmin*

Osmond (Old English) God; protector.

Osric (English) Divine ruler.

Ossian (Irish) Fawn.

Ossie (English) God's divine power.

Osten (German) East. *Ostin, Ostyn*

Oswald (Old English) Divinely powerful. *Oswell, Ossie, Ozzie, Oswald, Oswall, Oswell, Oswaldo*

Oswin (Old English) God; friend. *Osvin, Oswinn, Oswyn, Owwynn*

Oszlár (Hungarian) Meaning unknown.

Othello (Italian) Prosperous. (Shakespearean) From *The Tragedy of Othello*.

Othi (Romany/Gypsy) Meaning unknown.

Otieno (African) Born at night.

Otis (German) Wealthy. (Greek) One who hears well. *Otho, Otello, Otilio*

Otto (German) Wealthy.

Ouida (French) Warrior.

Ove (Norse) Awe; the spear's point.

Overton (English) The upper town.

Ovid (Latin) Lamb.

Ovidio (Spanish) Shepherd. *Ovido*

Owen (Irish) Born to nobility; warrior. *Owyn, Ewan, Ewen, Owens, Owaine, Owan, Owayne, Owin, Owine*

Oxford (Old English) From where the oxen ford. *Oxton, Oxon*

Oya (Native American) Strength.

Oz (Hebrew) Strength. *Ozzy, Ozzie*

Ozan (Turkish) Meaning unknown. *Özcan*

Ozaner (Turkish) Meaning unknown.

Ozor (Hungarian) Name of an ethnic group.

Özséb (Hungarian) Pious.

Ozsvát (Hungarian) Deity; might.

P

Pablo (Spanish) Borrowed.

Pacey (English) Born on Easter or Passover. *Pace, Paice, Payce*

Packard (Old English) One who packs.

Paco (Native American) Bald eagle. (Spanish) Free. (Italian) Pack. *Packo, Pako, Paquito*

Paddy (Irish) Nobleman. *Paddee, Paddey, Paddi, Pady*

Paden (Scottish) Royal.

Padraig (Irish) Nobleman. *Padraic*

Page (French) Young attendant. *Paige, Payge, Padgett*

Paki (Egyptian) A witness.

Pal (Scandinavian) Small.

Palani (Hawaiian) Free man. *Palanee, Palaney, Palany*

Pallaton (Native American) Fighter.

Pallav (Hindi) Young shoots and leaves.

Pallu (Hebrew) Admirable; hidden.

Palmer (Old English) Palm-bearing pilgrim.

Palti (Hebrew) My escape.

Pancho (Spanish) Tuft, plume.

Pancrazio (Italian) Supreme ruler; all powerful.

Pandarus (Latin) Gifted.

Pandita (Hindi) Scholar.

Pandya (Hindi) Meaning unknown.

Pankaj (Hindi) Lotus flower.

Panos (Greek) A rock.

Panthea (Greek) Of all the gods.

Paolo (Italian) Small.

Parag (Hindi) Pollen.

Paramartha (Hindi) Great entity.

Paras (Hindi) Touchstone.

Paris (French) Place name: Paris, France. (Italian) Lover. (Greek) A character in mythology. *Paras, Pares, Parys*

Parker (Old English) Cultivated land. *Parke, Park, Parkley, Parks*

Parlan (Gaelic) Ploughman, farmer.

Parnab Origin and meaning unknown.

Parr (Old English) From the stable.

Parry (Welsh) Son of Harry.

Parsifal (English) Valley piercer.

Parth (Hindi) A name given to Arjun by Lord Krishna. *Partha*

Pascal (French) Born at Easter. *Paschal, Pasqual, Pasquale, Pascali, Pascha, Pace*

Patamon (Native American) Raging.

Patch (American) Small rock.

Patern (Breton) Meaning unknown. *Padern, Padarn*

Patrick (Latin) Noble one. *Patrice, Padraic, Padraig, Padruig, Pat, Paddy, Patterson, Paterson, Pattison, Rick, Ricky*

What's in a Name

Patrick, the patron saint of Ireland, adopted his name, which comes from the Roman name Patricius, meaning "nobleman," from his given name of Sucat. He was captured as a youth by Irish raiders and enslaved for 6 years before he escaped and made his way back to his home in Britain. Later he turned to the church, became a bishop, and returned to Ireland to preach Christianity. He is credited with converting the entire country at that time.

Patroclus (Greek) Character in Iliad by *Homer*. (Shakespearean) From *Troilus and Cressida*.

Patwin (Native American) Man.

Pau (Hebrew) Howling; sighing.

Paul (Latin) Little one. *Pol, Pawl, Pablo, Paolo, Pauly, Pauley, Pawley, Pavel, Paulin, Pavlo, Paulo, Paulus, Powell, Pál*

Paulo (African) Place of rest.

Paulos (German) Small.

Pavel (Slavic) Little.

Pavlos (Slavic) Little.

Pavo (Slavic) Little.

Paxton (Teutonic, Old English) Trader; town of peace.

Paytah (Native American) Fire.

Payton (Old English) Warrior's estate.

Pázmán (Hungarian) Right; man.

Peabo (African) Peaceful.

Peace (Latin) Peace; tranquility.

Peder (Greek) Stone.

Pedro (Spanish) A rock.

Peers (English) A rock.

Peja (Slavic) He that opens, that is liberty.

Pekelo (Hawaiian) Stone.

Pelagius (Latin) Sea.

Pell (Old English) Scarf. *Pelton, Pelham*

Pelleas (English) A fisher king.

Pellegrin (Hungarian) Pilgrim.

Pello (Greek) Stone.

Pelton (English) From the farm by a pool. *Peltan, Pelten, Peltin*

Pembroke (Welsh) From the headland; rocky hill. *Pembrok, Pembrook*

Penda (English) Name of a king. (African) Beloved.

Penley (Old English) Enclosed meadow. *Penn*

Penn (Old English) Enclosure.

Penrod (German) Esteemed commander. *Penn*

Pentele (Hungarian) Merciful; lion.

Per (Swedish) A small rock.

Percival (Old French) Pierce the veil. *Perceval, Percheval, Parsifal, Parsefal, Perce, Percy, Perci*

Percy (French) Piercing the valley.

Peregrin (Latin) Falcon. *Peregrine, Peregryn*

Pericles (Greek) Famous Greek orator.

Peril (Latin) A trial or test.

Pernell (French) Little rock.

Perry (Middle English) Small rock. *Pierrey, Parry, Perianne, Perian, Perrin, Perin*

Persepolis (Persian) Place name: Persepolis, southern Iran.

Perseus (Greek) Son of Danae and Zeus.

Perth (Celtic) Thorny bush.

Peter (Latin) Rock, stone. *Pete, Petey, Pietor, Pytor, Petr, Pieter, Piotr, Pietro, Pedro, Pierre, Piers, Pierce, Peer, Pero, Piero, Peder, Per, Pelle, Peadair, Petrus, Peterson, Perrin, Perkin, Perkins, Parnell, Parle, Parkin, Parkinson, Petrie, Petri, Petronio, Pierson, Péter, Petò, Petúr, Pyotr*

Petrucio (Shakespearean) From *The Taming of the Shrew*.

Peyton (Irish) Warrior's town.

Phares (Biblical) Of a great house; bursting through.

Phelan (Gaelic) Little wolf.

Philander (Greek) Lover of mankind.

Philario (Italian) Friend.

Philemon (Greek) Kiss.

Philip (Greek) Horse lover. *Phillip, Phillipa, Philipe, Philippos, Philo, Phillips, Phelps, Phipps, Philipson, Phillips, Philby, Phil, Philly, Felipe, Filippo, Filip, Filbert*

Philo (Greek) Loving. (Latin) Lover of horses.

Philostrate (Greek) Master.

Philotus (Greek) Servant to Tinon.

Phinneaus (Hebrew) Oracle. *Phineas, Pinchas*

Phoenix (Greek) Mystical bird; purple.

Phornello (African) Succeed.

Phuoc (Vietnamese) Good luck. *Phuc*

Phuong (Vietnamese) Destiny.

Pierce (English) Rock. *Pearce, Piercy, Pears, Piers*

Pierre (French) Rock.

Piers (English) Stone, rock.

Pierson (Old English) Son of Peter. (Irish) Stone. *Pearson*

Pilan (Native American) Supreme essence. *Pillan, Pyllan*

Pindarus (Shakespearean) From *Julius Caesar*.

Pino (Italian) A lover of horses.

Pisano (Italian) Sculptor.

Piusz (Hungarian) Pious. *Pious, Pius*

Piyush (Hindi) Nectar.

Placido (Latin) Tranquility.

Platinum (Latin) Silver-white precious metal.

Plato (Greek) Strong shoulders.

Platon (Greek) Broad-shouldered.

Platt (French) Ground without slope.

Pluto (Greek) God of the dead; God of the underworld. Ninth planet from the sun.

Plutus (Greek) God of wealth.

Polixenes (Slavic) People.

Polk (Scottish) From the pool or pit; eleventh president of the United States. (Slavic) People.

Polo (African) Alligator.

Polonius (Shakespearean) From *Hamlet*.

Ponce (Spanish) Fifth.

Pongor (Hungarian) All might. *Pongrác*

Pontain Place name.

Pontius (Latin) Marine; belonging to the sea; the fifth.

Pontus (Hebrew) Sea god.

Porfio (Spanish) Purple.

Porter (French) Gatekeeper; carrier. *Porteur*

Poseidon (Greek) God of the sea.

Powa (Native American) Wealthy.

Powell (English) Alert. (Old Welsh) Son of Howell. *Powers, Power, Powal, Powall, Powel, Powil*

Prabhakar (Hindi) Cause of luster.

Prabhu (Hindi) Great.

Prabodh (Indian) Consolation.

Pradeep (Hindi) Light.

Praful (Indian) Blooming.

Prakash (Hindi) Light.

Pramsu (Hindi) A scholar.

Pranav (Hindi) Om or Aum; the sacred syllable for Om.

Pranay (Hindi) Love, romance.

Prasata (Hindi) Father of Draupad.

Prassana (Hindi) Cheerful.

Pratap (Hindi) Glory; dignity; majesty.

Pratik (Hindi) Symbol.

Pratyush (Hindi) Meaning unknown.

Pravat (Thai) History.

Praveen (Hindi) Proficient.

Pravin (Hindi) Capable.

Prem (Hindi) Love.

Prentice (Middle English) Apprentice. *Prentiss*

Preston (Old English) Dweller at the church; priest's settlement. *Prescott, Presley, Priestley, Priestly, Priest, Prestan, Presten, Prestin*

Naming Rights

Get Dad involved in the naming process. Split the responsibilities between who chooses the first or middle names, or work together on a compromise for all names.

Prewitt (Old French) Valiant one. *Pruitt, Pruit, Prue, Prewet, Prewit, Prewitt*

Priam (Greek) King of Troy.

Price (Old Welsh) Urgent one. *Pryce*

Primel (Breton) Meaning unknown. *Primael, Privel*

Primo (Italian) First one. *Prime*

Prince (Latin) Royal son.

Prithu (Hindi) First Ksatriya; son of Vena.

Privrata (Hindi) Son of Satarupa.

Proculeius (Italian) Friend of Caesar.

Prometheus (Greek) Forethought.

Prosper (Latin) Fortune. *Prospero*

Proteus (Greek) Sea god.

Pryor (Latin) Head of the priory. *Prior*

Ptolemy (Greek) Star cluster. *Ptolemäus*

Pundarik (Hindi) White in color.

Purujit (Hindi) Conqueror of many.

Pusan (Hindi) A sage.

Putnam (Old English) From the sire's estate. *Putney*

Q

Qabil (Arabic) Able.

Qadim (Arabic) Ancient.

Qadir (Arabic) Talented. *Qadar*

Qamar (Arabic) Moon.

Qasim (Arabic) Provider.

Qimat (Hindi) Valued.

Qing-Nan (Chinese) The younger generation.

Quaashie (African American) Ambitious.

Quaddus (African American) Bright.

Quade (Latin) Fourth. *Quaid, Quaide*

Quadrees (African American) Four. *Kwadrees, Quadrhys*

Quan (Vietnamese) Dignified.

Quan Van (Vietnamese) Authorized.

Quanah (Native American) Good-smelling.

Quang Tu (Vietnamese) Clear.

Quannell (African American) Strong-willed. *Kwan, Kwanell, Kwanelle, Quan, Quanelle, Quannel*

Quant (Latin) Knowing his worth. *Quanta, Quantae, Quantal, Quantay, Quantea, Quantey, Quantez*

Quarren (African American) Tenacious. *Quarron, Quaronne, Kwarohn, Kwaronne*

Quashawn (African American) Tenacious. *Kwashan, Kwashaun, Kwashawn, Quasha, Quashie, Quashy, Quasean, Quashaan, Quashan, Quashaun*

Quasim (Arabic) He who divides goods among his people.

Qudamah (Arabic) Courage. *Qudam, Qudama*

Qued (Native American) Decorated robe.

Quelatikan (Native American) Blue horn.

Quennel (Old French) Dweller by the oak tree. *Quenal, Quenall, Quenel, Quennal, Quennall, Quennel*

 **Naming Rights**

Will your baby be a Junior? Some studies show that boys who are named after their fathers scored lower on average on psychological measures, including those with a capacity for status, well-being, responsibility, and respect. Remember, though, that these are averages. If you name your child after Dad, give him a unique middle name.

Quentin (Latin) Fifth-born child. *Quinton, Quenten, Quenton, Quintin, Quent, Quint, Quinto, Quintilian, Quintus*

Quick (American) Fast, remarkable.

Quico (Spanish) Short for many Spanish names; high rank. *Paco*

Quigley (Irish) Maternal side. *Quiglee, Quigly, Quiggly, Quiggy*

Quillan (Irish) Cub. *Quill, Quillen, Quillon*

Quimby (Norse) A woman's house. *Quenby, Quin, Quinby*

Quinby (Scandinavian) From the queen's estate.

Quincy (French) Estate belonging to the fifth son. *Quince, Quincey, Quin*

Quinlan (Irish) Well-shaped, athletic. *Quindlen, Quinley, Quinlin, Quinly*

Quinn (Irish) Fifth son's estate. *Quin*

Quintavius (African American) Fifth child. *Quint*

Quinto (Spanish) Home ruler. *Quiqui*

Quiqui (Spanish) Friend, short for Enrique. *Kaka, Keke Quinto, Quiquin*

Quirin (English) Magic spell.

Quirinus (Latin) Roman god of war.

Quito (Spanish) Lively. *Kito*

Qunnoune (Native American) Tall.

Quoitrel (African American) Equalizer. *Kwotrel, Quitrelle*

Quon (Chinese) Bright.

Qusay (Arabic) Distant. *Quassay*

R

Raashid (Arabic) Wise man.

Rab (Scottish) Bright; fame. *Rabbie*

Rabbit (Old English) Long-eared; hare; clover flower.

Rad (Scandinavian) Helpful; confident. *Radd*

Radbert (English) Intelligent. *Rad*

Radcliff (Old English) Red cliff. *Radcliffe, Radclyffe, Radclyf, Radford, Radley, Radnor, Rad*

Radek (Czechoslovakian) Famous ruler. *Radacek, Radan, Radik, Radko, Radouvsek, Radovs*

Radford (English) Helpful. *Rad, Radferd*

Radley (English) Red meadow. *Radlea, Radlee, Radleigh, Radly*

Radman (Slavic) Joy.

Radnor (English) Red stone.

Radomér (Hungarian) Happy; peace.

Radoslav (Czechoslovakian) Happy and glorious.

Radwan (Arabic) Delight. *Radwen, Radwin, Radwon*

Rae (Old English) Doe. *Ray, Rai*

Raeburn (Teutonic) Dweller by the stream.

Raeshon (American) Form of Raeshawn; brainy. *Rayshawn, Rashone, Reshawn*

Rafa (Hebrew) Cure. *Rapha*

Rafael (Hebrew) God has healed. *Raphael, Rafel, Rafello, Raffaello*

Rafferty (Irish) Prosperous. *Rafe, Rafer, Raferty, Raff, Raffer, Raffi, Raffy*

Raghnall (Irish) Powerful judgment. *Rognvaldr*

Ragin (Hindi) Advice.

Ragnar (Norse) A wise leader. *Rainer, Rayner, Raynor*

Rahn (American) King's adviser. *Rahnney, Rahnny*

Rahotep (Egyptian) Ruler.

Rahul (Arabic) Wolf counselor. (Hindi) Son of Lord Buddha.

Raidon (Japanese) Thunder god.

Raimy (African American) Compassionate. *Raimee*

Rainart (German) Great judgment. *Rainhard, Rainhardt, Reinart, Reinhard, Reinhardt, Reinhart*

Raine (English) Wise ruler. *Rain, Rainey, Raini, Rains, Raney, Rayne*

Rainier (Latin) Ruler. *Rainer, Raner*

Raivata (Hindi) A Manu.

Raj (Hindi) A king. *Rajan, Rajani*

Rajab (Muslim) Seventh month of the Muslim lunar calendar. *Ragab*

Rajanikant (Hindi) Sun; lord of the night.

Rajeev (Arabic) Spring.

Rajendra (Hindi) God.

Rajesh (Hindi) King.

Rajiv (Sanskrit) Striped. (Hindi) Lotus flower. *Rajeev*

Rakesh (Hindi) Lord of the night; sun.

Raleigh (Old English) Dweller by the deer meadow. *Rawley, Rawly, Rawls, Leigh, Lee*

Ralph (Old English) Wolf; wise counsel. *Ralf, Raff, Raffi, Rolf, Rolph, Raoul, Raul, Ralston*

Ram (Hindi) Lord Rama. *Ramm*

Ramadan (Arabic) Ninth month at the end of the Muslim year.

Raman (Hindi) Cupid.

Ramanuja (Hindi) A saint.

Rambures (Shakespearean) From *Henry V.*

Ramesh (Hindi) Ruler of Rama.

Rami (Arabic) Loving.

Ramiro (Basque) Great judge. *Ramero, Ramirez*

Ramon (Geman) Mighty protector. *Raymon*

Ramsey (Old English) Ram's land. *Ramsay, Ransden*

Rance (French) A kind of Belgian marble. *Rancel, Rancell, Ransel, Ransell*

Randal (English) Secretive. *Randahl, Randel, Randey, Randull, Randall*

Randolph (Anglo-Saxon) Shield; wolf. *Randolf, Randall, Randal, Randell, Randl, Randle, Randy, Rankin, Rand, Ran, Randie, Ranulf, Dolf, Dolph*

Ranen (Hebrew) Joyous. *Ranon*

Ranger (French) Dweller in the field. *Rainger*

Ranjan (Hindi) Entertaining.

Ranjeet (Hindi) Victor in war.

Ranjit (Hindi) The delighted one.

Ransford (Old English) Raven's ford.

Ransley (Old English) Raven's meadow. *Ransleigh, Ransly*

Ransom (Old English) Son of the shield. (Latin) Redeemer. *Ransome, Ranson, Rankin, Rance*

Rantidev (Hindi) Devotee of Narayana.

Raphael (Hebrew) Healed by God. *Rafael, Rafaelle, Rafaello, Rafe, Rafer, Rafi, Raff, Raph, Rafferty, Rafal*

Rashaan (Arabic) Young gift of god.

Rashid (Swahili) Wise adviser. *Rasheed, Rasheid, Rasheyd*

Rashne (Persian) Judge.

Rashon (African American) Newly created. *Rachan, Rashaan, Rasham, Rashan, Rashawn, Reshaun, Reshawn*

Rastus (Greek) The loving one.

Ratri (Hindi) Night.

Raul (French) Wolf counselor.

Raven (Old English) A raven. *Ravey, Ravyen*

Ravi (Hindi) Benevolent; sun god. *Rav, Ravee*

Ravid (Hebrew) Wander.

Ravindra (Hindi) Protector of ravens.

Ravinger (Old English) Ravine. *Ravi, Ravinia*

Rawdan (English) Hilly, adventurous. *Rawden, Rawdin, Rawdon*

Rawleigh (American) Form of Raleigh. *Rawlee, Rawli*

Rawlins (Old English) Son of a little wise wolf. *Rawlings, Rawson*

Ray (French) Kingly. *Rayce, Raydell, Rayder, Raydon, Rayford, Raylen, Raynell*

Rayburn (Old English) From the deer stream. *Rayborn, Raybourne, Rayburne*

Rayce (American) Counselor. (English) Race. *Racee*

Raymond (Old English) Worthy protector. *Raymund, Ramon, Raimundo, Raimund, Reamonn, Rayner, Wray*

Raynard (French) Wise; bold; courageous. *Raynard, Renard, Reinhard, Raynor, Reinhart, Rinehart, Renaud, Reynaud, Reynart, Reyner, Rey*

Razi (African American) Secret. *Raz, Raziel*

Read (Old English) Red-haired; reed. *Reed, Reid, Reading, Reade*

Reagan (Irish) Kingly. *Ragan, Raghan, Reagen, Reegen, Regan*

Redford (Old English) From the red ford. *Redfield, Redgrave, Redman, Redwald, Redd, Redding, Red*

Redmond (German) Adviser. *Radmond, Radmund, Redmond, Redmund*

Reece (Old Welsh) Enthusiastic. *Riece, Reace, Rase, Rice, Rhys, Rhett, Rett*

Reed (English) Red-haired. *Read, Reede, Reid*

Reese (Welsh) Ardent one. *Rhys, Ries*

Reeve (Middle English) Bailiff. *Reave, Reeves*

Regan (Gaelic) Little king. *Reagan, Rayghun, Reagen, Regen, Regino, Regent*

Reginald (Old English) Powerful one. *Reggie, Reggy, Reg, Reynolds, Reynold, Reinwald, Regnauld, Reinald, Renault, Rene, Rinaldo, Renato, Reinhold, Raghnall*

Regis (Latin) Kingly, regal. *Reggis*

Regō (Hungarian) Meaning unknown.

Rehan (Arabic) Flower.

Rehor (Czechoslovakian) To awaken. *Harek, Horik, Rehak, Rehorek, Rehurek*

Rei (Japanese) Law.

Reinhart (German) Brave-hearted. *Reinhard, Reinhardt, Rhinehard, Rhinehart*

Reinhold (German) Wise, powerful ruler.

Rembrandt (Dutch) Sword adviser.

Remi (French) Fun-loving. *Remee, Remey, Remmy, Remy*

Remington (Old English) From the raven's home. *Remmy, Remy, Remmie, Remme*

Remus (Latin) Swift oarsman.

Renard (Teutonic) Counsel hard.

Rendor (Hungarian) Policeman.

Renee (Latin) Reborn. *Rene, Rennie, Renny, Renato, René*

Renfrew (Old Welsh) From the still waters. *Renfred, Renshaw, Renton, Rinfro*

Renny (Gaelic) Small but mighty.

Reuben (Hebrew) Behold, a son. *Rube, Ruben, Reubin, Rubin, Reuven, Reuby, Ben, Benny*

Reuel (Hebrew) Friend of God.

Rex (Latin) King. *Rei, Roi, Rexford, Rexer*

Reyes (Spanish) King. *Rey*

Reynaldo (Spanish) Counselor; ruler.

Reynold (English) Knowledge-able tutor. *Ranald, Ranold, Reinhold, Renald, Renale, Rey, Reye, Reynolds*

Reza (Slavic) Reaper.

Rezsõ (Hungarian) Meaning unknown.

Rhett (English, Welsh) A stream. *Rhette*

Rhodes (Greek) Field of roses. (English) Lives near the crucifix. *Rhodas, Rodas, Rhoades*

Rian (Irish) Little king. *Rion*

Richard (English) Rich and powerful ruler. *Ricard, Ricardo, Richerd, Richman, Ricker, Richmond, Richardson, Rickward, Rickert, Rikkert, Rickard, Richart, Riocard, Ritchie, Rich, Rick, Rickie, Ricky, Rocco, Dick, Dickie, Dicky*

Rico (Spanish) Noble ruler. *Reco, Reko, Ricko, Rikko, Riko*

Rider (Old English) Horseman. *Ryder*

Ridge (English) From the ridge. *Rigg*

Ridgley (English) By the meadow's edge. *Ridgeleigh, Ridgeley, Ridglea, Ridglee, Ridgleigh*

Ridley (Old English) Reed clearing; cleared wood. *Riddley, Ridlea, Ridleigh, Ridly*

Rigby (Old English) Valley of the ruler. *Rigbie, Rigbye, Rygby*

Rigel (Arabic) Foot; star in the constellation Orion.

Rikard (German) Powerful ruler.

Rikin (Hindi) Meaning unknown.

Riley (Gaelic) Valiant. *Ryley, Reilly*

Rimon (Arabic) Pomegranite.

Ring (German) A ring. *Ringling, Ringo*

Ringo (Japanese) Apple; peace be with you.

Rio (Spanish) A river. *Reo*

Riordan (Gaelic) Poet. *Rearden, Reardon*

Ripley (Old English) Dweller in the noisy meadow. *Ripleigh, Rypley, Rip*

Ris (English) Outdoorsman. *Rislea, Rislee, Risleigh, Riz*

Rishab (Hindi) The musical note Re.

Rishi (Hindi) Sage.

Rishley (Old English) From the wild meadow. *Riston*

Rishon (Hebrew) First.

Ritch (American) Leader. *Rich, Richey, Ritchal, Ritchi*

Ritchell (Vietnamese) Nasty; gross. *Ritchel, Ratchell*

Ritter (German) Knight. *Ritt*

Rivalen (English) Tristan's father.

Rivan (Science fiction) Character from *Star Wars*.

Rivers (English) River; by the riverbank. *River, Rio*

Riyad (Arabic) Gardens. *Riyadh*

Rizal (Hindi) Bringer of good news. *Rizzy*

Roald (Teutonic) Fame, power.

Roam (American) Wanderer. *Roamey, Roma, Rome*

Roan (English) From the rowan tree. (Irish) Little red-haired one.

Roarke (Irish) Famous ruler. *Ruark, Rourke, Rorke*

Robert (Old English) Bright; famous. *Robbi, Robbie, Robbee, Robby, Róbert, Roberto, Rupert, Rubert, Robertson, Robin, Robinson, Robbins, Robben, Riobard, Robby, Robbie, Robey, Rober, Rab, Rob, Bobby, Bob, Bert, Berty, Tito, Dob, Dobbs*

Naming Rights

If you name your child a popular name, they will rarely be in a group without 4 or 5 other people who have the same name. They'll have to have their last initial attached before people can distinguish them.

Robi (Hungarian) Shining with fame.

Robin (English) Famous brilliance.

Robson (English) Sterling character. *Robb, Robbon, Robsen*

Rocco (Italian) Rest. *Roc, Rock, Rok, Rokka, Roko*

Rochester (Old English) Rock fortress. *Rocky, Rock, Rocho, Roche, Rockley, Rockwell, Rockne, Rocker*

Rockleigh (English) Dependable; outdoorsy. *Rocklee, Rockley, Roklee*

Rockwell (English) From the rocky spring. *Rockwelle*

Roden (English) Red valley.

Roderick (German) Famous one. *Rodrick, Broderick, Rodrigo, Roderich, Rodrigue, Rodney, Rod, Rodd, Roddy, Rodman, Rodmond, Rory, Rick, Ricky*

Rodman (Old English) Famous.

Rodney (Old English) Famous one's island. *Roddy, Rod*

Rodolf (Dutch) Famous wolf.

Roe (English) Small deer. *Roebuck*

Rogan (Gaelic) Red-haired. *Roan*

Rogelio (Spanish) Beautiful one.

Roger (German) Famous spearman; quiet. *Rodger, Rodgers, Rogers, Rogerio, Rog, Ruggiero, Rudiger, Rodiger, Rutger, Rüdiger*

Rohan (Hindi) Sandlewood. (Irish) Red-haired one.

Rohit (Hindi) Red color.

Roka (Japanese) Wave.

Rókus (Hungarian) Meaning unknown.

Roland (German) From the famous land. *Rolland, Rowland, Rollan, Rollin, Rollins, Rolando, Rodhlann, Rowe, Rollo, Rolly, Orlando, Rolt, Roland*

Roldan (English) Powerful, mighty.

Rolf (German) Kind adviser. *Rolfee, Rolfie, Rolph*

Rollins (German) Dignified. *Rolin, Rolins, Rollin, Rolyn*

Romain (French) A roman.

Roman (Hebrew) Strong, powerful. (Latin) Place name: Rome, Italy; from Rome. *Romano, Romanos, Romula, Romulos, Romulus*

Romeo (Italian) Pilgrim to Rome; romantic lover. (Shakespearean) From *Romeo and Juliet*. *Rome, Roman, Romain*

Ronak (Hindi) Embellishment.

Ronald (Old Norse) Mighty. *Ronnie, Ronny, Ron, Renaldo, Ronan, Naldo*

Ronan (Celtic) A pledge.

Rondell (Welsh) Grand. *Ronde, Rondel*

Roni (Hebrew) Shout for joy; my song of joy.

Ronin (Japanese) Samurai without a master.

Rooney (Gaelic) Red-haired. *Roon, Roone, Rune*

Roosevelt (Dutch) Field of roses. *Rooseveldt, Rosevelt*

Rooster (American) Animal as name; loud.

Rory (Gaelic) Red king. *Rurik, Roric, Ruaidhri*

Roscoe (Old Norse) From the deer forest. *Rosco, Roskie, Rosko*

Rosencrantz (English) A Shakespearean character.

Roshan (Hindi) One who emanates light.

Roshaun (African American) Shining light. *RoShawn, Rashon*

Rosling (Scottish) Redhead; explosive. *Roslin, Rozling*

Ross (Scottish) From the peninsula. (French) Red-haired. (English) Wood. (German) Rose-colored. *Rossano, Rosse, Roswald*

Roswald (German) Mighty horse. *Roswalt*

Roswell (English) Rose spring. *Roswel, Roswelle, Rozwell*

Roth (German) Red-haired. *Rothe, Rauth*

Rouvin (Hebrew) Behold, a son.

Rowan (Old English) Tree with red berries. *Rowen, Rowe, Rowell, Rowley, Rowson*

Rowley (English) Unevenly cleared meadow. *Rowlea, Rowlee, Rawleigh, Rowlie, Rowly*

Rowtag (Native American) Fire.

Roy (Old French) Regal one. *Royal, Royale, Royall, Roi, Roye*

Royal (French) Of the king, regal.

Royce (English) Son of the king. *Roice, Royse*

Ruben (Hebrew) Behold, a son.

Ruchir (Hindi) Beautiful.

Rudd (English) Ruddy. *Reed*

Rudeger (German) Friendly. *Rudger, Rudgyr, Rudigar, Rudiger, Rudy*

Rudolph (German) Wolf. *Rudolf, Rodolf, Rodolphe, Rodolfo, Raoul, Rudy, Rudie, Rudi, Rolf, Rolph, Rollo, Rollin, Dolph*

Rudyard (Old English) From the red gate. *Ruddy, Rudy*

Rufus (Latin) Red-haired one. *Ruphus, Rufe, Ruff, Rufford*

Rugby (English) From the raven's estate.

Ruggerio (Italian) Famous warrior. *Rugerio, Rugger, Ruge*

Ruhollah (Persian) The Spirit of Allah.

Runako (African American) Handsome.

Rune (English) Rune. (German) A secret. (Scandinavian) Secret lore.

Rupert (French) Famous; bright.

Rupesh (Hindi) Lord of beauty.

Rush (French) Red-haired. *Rousse, Rusk, Ruskin, Rust*

Russel (French) Red-haired; foxlike. *Russell, Russ, Rusty, Rusti*

Rutherford (Old English) From the cattle ford. *Ruthren, Rutherfurd, Rutherfyrd*

Ryan (Gaelic) Little king. *Rhine, Rhyan, Rhyne, Ry, Ryane, Ryen, Rian, Ryanne, Ryun*

Ryder (English) A horseman. *Rydar*

Rylan (Old English) Dweller in the rye field. *Ryland, Ryle, Rycroft, Ryman, Ryton*

Ryo (Spanish) A river; the Rio Grande. *Rio*

Ryogi (Japanese) Defender of nobility. *Ryoji*

Ryoichi (Japanese) First son of Ryo.

Ryons (Irish) Kingly. *Ryon*

Ryozo (Japanese) Third son of Ryo.

Ryuichi (Japanese) First son of Ryu.

Ryzard (Polish) Brave ruler; variant of Richard.

S

Saad (Hebrew) Assistance. *Saadia, Saadiah, Daadya, Saadyah*

Saahdia (Aramic) Helped by the Lord. *Saadya, Seadya*

Saarik (Hindi) Bird. *Saariq, Sareek, Sareeq, Sariq*

Sabene (Latin) Optimist. *Sabe, Sabeen, Sabin, Sabyn, Sabyne*

Saber (French) Sword. *Sabar, Sabe, Sabre*

Sabinian (Latin) Name of an ancient Roman clan. *Sabin, Sabine, Sabino*

Saburo (Japanese) Third son.

Sacha (Russian) Helper and defender of mankind. *Sasha, Sascha*

Sachchit (Hindi) Truth; consciousness.

Sachiel (Hebrew) Angel of water.

Sachin (Hindi) Lord Indra.

Saddam (Arabic) Powerful ruler.

Sadi (Turkish) Meaning unknown. *Sadie, Sady*

Sadler (English) Practical. *Sadd, Sadlar, Sadlur*

Safak (Turkish) Second month of Islamic calendar. *Safer, Safyr*

Sagar (Hindi) King. *Samrat, Satyavrat*

Sagaz (Spanish) Clever. *Saga, Sago*

Sage (English) Wise; herb. *Saje*

Sagittarius (Latin) A constellation of the southern hemisphere; the archer; a sign of the Zodiac.

Sagiv (Hebrew) Mighty, with strength.

Sahadev (Hindi) Prince.

Sahale (Native American) Above.

Sahen (Hindi) Falcon.

Sahib (Hindi) Sir.

Said (Arabic) Happy. *Saeed, Daied, Saiyid, Sayeed, Sayid, Syed*

Sakima (Native American) King.

Salim (African American) Peace. *Saleem, Salem, Salima, Selim*

Salisbury (English) Born in the willows. *Salisbery, Salisberry, Saulsberry, Saulsbery, Saulsbury, Saulisbury*

Saloman (Hebrew) Peaceful. *Salomi, Solomon, Schlomo, Shlomo, Soloman, Salomon, Salmon, Sholem, Shalom, Solom, Salamon*

Salter (English) A salt seller. *Salt*

Salvador (Spanish) Savior. *Salvatore, Sauveur, Sal*

Sam (Hebrew) To hear. *Sammie, Sammy, Samuel, Samouel, Samuele, Samuello*

Samien (Arabic) To be heard.

Samir (Hindi) Wind.

Sammon (Arabic) Grocer.

Sampath (Hindi) Meaning unknown.

Samson (Hebrew) Like the sun; His ministry. *Sampson, Sanson, Sansone, Sam, Sammy*

Samudra (Hindi) Lord of the ocean.

Samuel (Hebrew) Heard God; asked God. *Samuele, Samuelson, Samelle, Sam, Sammy, Sammie, Shemuel, Schmuel, Shem*

Sanat (Hindi) Lord Brahma.

Sanborn (English) One with nature. *Sanborne, Sanbourn, Sandy*

Sandeep (Hindi) Rishi (Sega of Gods); named after Sandipani.

Sanders (Middle English) Alexander's son. *Sander, Sandy, Sands, Sanderson, Saunders, Saunderson*

Sandhurst (English) From the sandy thicket; undaunted. *Sandhirst*

Sandon (Old English) From the sandy hill.

Sandor (Hungarian) Helper and defender of mankind.

Sanford (Old English) Dweller at the sandy ford. *Sanborn, Sandy, Sandford*

Sanjay (Hindi) Protector.

Sanjeev (Hindi) Love; life. *Sanjiv*

Sanjog (Hindi) Coincidence.

Sankara (Hindi) Auspicious.

Santiago (Spanish) Supplanter. *Santi, Chago, Diego*

Santo (Italian) A saint. *Santos*

Santosh (Hindi) Contentment.

Sapan (Hindi) Dream.

Sarasvan (Hindi) Meaning unknown.

Sarat (Hindi) A sage; autumn.

Sargent (French) Military man. *Sargant, Sargeant, Sergent*

Sarkis (Russian) Royalty Sak; lord.

Sarngin (Hindi) Name of God.

Sarojin (Hindi) Lotuslike.

Sarosh (Persian) Prayer.

Saswata (Hindi) Meaning unknown.

Satayu (Hindi) Brother of Amavasu and Vivasu.

Satch (French) Small bag. *Satchel*

Satrujit (Hindi) A son of Vatsa.

Saturn (Latin) Mythology: god of agriculture. Sixth planet from the sun.

Saturnin (Spanish) From planet Saturn; melancholy. *Saturnino*

Satyen (Hindi) Lord of truth.

Saudeep (Hindi) Meaning unknown.

Saul (Hebrew) Asked for. *Sol, Sauly, Solly*

Saunak (Hindi) Sage.

Saurabh (Hindi) Fragrance.

Sauron (Fiction) Character from *The Lord of the Rings* by J.R.R. Tolkien.

Saverio (Italian) Owner of the new house.

Sawyer (Middle English) Woodsman. *Saw, Sayer, Sayers, Sayre, Sayres*

Saxon (English) Germanic tribe. *Saxe, Saxen*

Sayer (Welsh) Carpenter. *Sayers, Sayre, Sayres*

Scanlon (Irish) Devious. *Scan, Scanlin, Scanlun, Scanne*

Scarus (English) Friend to Marc Antony.

Schae (American) Safe, careful. *Schay*

Schaffer (German) Watchful. *Schaffur, Shaffer*

Schmidt (German) Hard-working blacksmith. *Schmit*

Schneider (German) Stylish. *Sneider, Snider*

Schuyler (Dutch) Shield; scholar. *Skyler, Skylar, Sky, Skye, Ciel*

Scott (Old English) From Scotland. *Scot, Scotty, Scottie, Escott*

Scout (American) First explorer.

Scully (Scottish) Town crier; herald. *Scullee, Sculley, Scullie*

Seabert (Old English) Sea-glorious. *Seabright, Sebert, Seberg, Seabrook, Seabury, Sea*

Seal (American) Water; natural; singer.

Seamus (Gaelic) Replacement; bonus. *Seemus, Semus*

Sean (Celtic) God's grace. *Shawn, Shaun, Sian*

Searles (English) Fortified. *Searl, Searle, Serles, Serls*

Seaton (English) From the farm by the sea. *Seaton, Seeten, Seetin, Seeton, Seton*

Sebastian (Latin) Revered one. *Sebastien, Bastien, Bastian, Sebestyén*

Sebes (Hungarian) Fast.

Sedgley (American) Classy. *Sedg, Sedge, Segdeley, Sedgely*

Sedgwick (English) From the place of swords; defensive. *Sedgewick, Sedgewyck, Sedgwyck*

Seferino (Spanish) Flying in the wind. *Cerfirino, Sebarino, Sephirio, Zefarin, Zefirino, Zephir, Zephyr*

Seff (Hebrew) A wolf.

Seger (English) Sea spear; sea warrior; singer. *Seager, Seeger, Sega, Segur, Segar, Seegar, Sigar*

Seif (Arabic) Sword of religion.

Seiichi (Japanese) First son of Sei.

Seiko (Japanese) Force; truth.

Selby (English) From a village of mansions. *Selbey, Shelbey, Shelbie, Shelby*

Seldon (English) From the willow valley. *Selden, Sellden, Shelden*

Selestino (Spanish) Heavenly. *Celeste, Celestino, Celey, Sele, Selestyna*

Seleucus (Latin) Shaken; beaten by the waves.

Selim (Turkish) Peace.

Selvon (American) Gregarious. *Sel, Selman, Selv, Selvaughn, Selvawn*

Selwyn (English) Friend from the mansion. *Selwin, Selwinn, Selwyn, Selwynne*

Semih (Turkish) Meaning unknown.

Sempronius (Latin) Kinsman to Titus.

Semyon (Russian) The listener.

Senach (Gaelic) Meaning unknown.

Senajit (Hindi) Victory over army.

Sencer (Turkish) Meaning unknown.

Senichi (Japanese) First son of Sen.

Senior (French) Older. *Sennyur, Senyur, Sinior*

Sennett (French) Wise. *Senet*

Senon (Spanish) Given life by Zeus. *Sennon*

Septimus (Latin) Seventh-born son.

Seraphim (Hebrew) Burning ones; angels; ardent. *Sarafin, Saraphim, Serafim, Serafin, Serafino, Seraphimus*

Serge (Latin) Attendant. *Sergius, Sergei, Sergio*

Sergeant (French) Officer, leader. *Sarge, Sargent*

Sergei (Russian) Good-looking. *Serge, Sergeeo, Sergeoh, Sergyo*

Servan (Breton) Meaning unknown.

Sesame (Greek) A plant bearing small, flat seeds. (American) A children's television show: *Sesame Street*. *Sesamey, Sessame, Sessamee*

Seth (Hebrew) Apppointed one. *Sethia*

Seton (English) From the sea town.

Seung (Korean) Successor; winning.

Seven (American) A number. *Sevene, Sevin*

Severin (English) River in England. (French) Severe. *Saverino, Sverinus, Severyn*

Severinus (Latin) Severe. *Severen*

Sevilin (Turkish) Beloved.

Seward (Old English) From the sea. *Sewell, Severn, Sward*

Sewell (English) Seaward. *Seawell, Seawel, Sewel*

Sextus (Latin) Born sixth.

Seymour (French) Marshy land near the sea; prayer. *Seamor, Seamore, Seamour, Si, Sy*

Seyton (Shakespearean) From *Macbeth*.

Sezni (French) Old, wise. *Senan, Sane*

Shade (English) Secretive. *Shadee, Shadey, Shady, Shayd*

Shadow (English) Mystique. *Shade, Shadoe*

Shadrach (Arabic) Survived. *Shad, Shadd, Shadrack, Shadreck, Shadryack*

Shafir (Hebrew) Handsome. *Shafeer, Shafer, Shefer*

Shah (Arabic) The king.

Shailen (Hebrew) Gift.

Shailesh (Hindi) God of mountain, Himalaya.

Shakar (Arabic) Grateful.

Shakil (Arabic) Attractive. *Shakeel, Shakill, Shakille, Shaqueel, Shaquil, Shaquille*

Shakir (Arabic) Grateful.

Shalabh (Hindi) Easy.

Shalin (Hindi) Cotton plant; modest.

Shaman (Native American) Holy man. *Schamane, Shamain, Shamon, Shayman*

Shamus (Irish) Supplanter. *Schaemus, Shamus, Shamuss*

Shane (Irish) God is gracious. *Shain, Shay, Shayne*

Shankar (Hindi) He who gives happiness.

Shannon (Irish) Old. *Shana, Shanan, Shane, Shanen, Shann, Shannan, Shannen, Shanon*

Shantanu (Hindi) A king.

Shante (American) Poised. *Shantae, Shantay*

Shaquille (African American) Handsome. *Shaq, Shakeel, Shaquil, Shaquill*

Sharad (Hindi) Autumn.

Sharif (Arabic) Honest; honorable; noble. *Seif, Shareef*

Shashi (Hindi) The moon; moonbeam.

Shashwat (Hindi) Everlasting.

Shaun (Irish) God's gift.

Shaw (Old English) A grove.

Shea (Irish) Hawklike; stately. *Shae, Shai, Shay, Shaye*

Sheehan (Gaelic) Little peaceful one. *Sheen*

Shelby (English) Village on the ledge; ledge estate. *Shel, Shelbee, Shelbey, Shelbie, Shelbe, Shelbi*

Sheldon (English) Protected hill. *Sheldin, Shelton*

Shelley (Old English) Clearing on a bank; ledge estate. *Shelly, Shelli, Shell*

Shen (Chinese) Spiritual, deep-thinking.

Shepherd (Old English) One who herds sheep. *Shepard, Sheppard, Shepley, Shep*

Shepley (English) From the sheep meadow. *Sheplea, Shepleigh, Shepply, Shipley*

Sherborn (English) From the bright, shiny stream. *Sherborne, Sherbourn, Sherburn, Sherburne*

Sheridon (Irish) Wild one. *Sharidan, Sheridan, Sheridon, Sherr, Shuridun*

Sherlock (Old English) White-haired. *Sherlocke, Shurlock*

Sherman (Old English) Wool cutter. *Sherwin, Sherborne, Sherm, Shurman*

Sherrick (Irish) Surname; already gone. *Sherric, Sherrik, Sherryc, Sherryck, Sherwynne*

Sherwood (Old English) Bright forest.

Shevon (African American) Zany. *Shavonne, Shevaughan, Shevaughn*

Shilah (Native American) Brother.

Shiloh (Hebrew) Peaceful. *Shile, Shilo, Shy, Shye*

Shimon (Hebrew) Providing well.

Shing (Chinese) Victory.

Shinichi (Japanese) First son of Shin.

Shipley (Old English) From the deep meadow. *Shipton*

Shiro (Japanese) Fourth-born son.

Shiv (Hindi) Lord Shiva.

Shivendu (Hindi) Pure moon.

Shoichi (Japanese) First son of Sho.

Shontae (African American) Hopeful. *Shauntae, Shauntay, Shawntae, Shontay, Shontee, Shonti, Shontie, Shonty*

Shishir (Hindi) Winter.

Shuichi (Japanese) First son of Shu.

Shulamith (Hebrew) Peaceful. *Shulamit*

Shunichi (Japanese) First son of Shun.

Shunnar (Arabic) Pleasant.

Shyam (Hindi) Variation of Lord Krishna.

Shylock (Hebrew) Banker.

Siamak (Persian) Bringer of joy; great emperor Sia.

Sid (French) From Saint-Denis, France. *Cyd, Sidd, Siddie, Siddy, Syd, Sydd*

Siddel (Old English) From the wide valley. *Sydell, Sidwell*

Sidwell (English) From the broad well.

Sierra (Spanish) Dangerous. *See-see, Serra, Siera, Seirrah*

Sigebryht (Anglo-Saxon) Victory; bright.

Sigfried (Teutonic) Victory peace. *Siegfred, Sig, Sigfred, Sigfrid*

Sigmund (Teutonic) Victory shield; victory protector. *Siegmund, Sigismond, Sigismundo, Siffre, Sigvard, Siggy, Ziggy*

Sigurd (Old Norse) A victorious guardian.

Silas (Latin) Wood.

Siler (English) Meaning unknown. *Syler*

Silvester (Latin) Woodman. *Sylvester, Sly, Sylvestro, Silvestre, Silvanus, Silas, Syl, Sil, Szilveszter*

Silvano (Italian) Forest. *Silvan, Silvani, Silvia, Sylvan*

Silvio (Latin) Belonging to the forest; silver. *Silvan, Silvin*

Silvius (Latin) Forest dweller.

Simba (African) Lion.

Simeon (English) Hear, listen.

Similien (French) Surname used as a first name.

Simon (Hebrew) He who hears. *Simeon, Siomonn, Sim, Shimon, Semjén*

Simonides (Greek) King of Pentapolis.

Simpson (Hebrew) Simplistic. *Simpsen, Simpsun, Simson*

Sinan (Turkish) Spearhead.

Sinbad (German) A sparkling prince. *Sindbad*

Sinclair (French) Saint Clair.

Sindri (Old Norse) Glittering.

Singh (Hindi) Lion.

Sinjon (French) Saint John.

Sisyphus (Greek) From mythology; a cruel king.

Sivan (Hebrew) The ninth month on the ecclesiastical calendar and third month of the civil year on the Hebrew calendar.

Sivney (Irish) Satisfied. *Sivneigh, Sivnie*

Siward (English) A general. (Irish) Surname used as a first name.

Skeet (Middle English) Speedy. *Skeets, Skeat, Skeeter*

Skipp (Old Norse) Ship owner. *Skipper, Skippy, Skip*

Skjøld (Scandinavian) Meaning unknown.

Sklaer (Dutch) Protective. *Skilar, Skye, Skyeler*

Skye (English) Sky; sheltering. *Sky, Skyy*

Slade (Old English) Child of the valley. *Slaid, Slaide, Slayd, Slayde*

Slate (English) A fine-grained rock.

Slevin (Gaelic) Mountaineer.

Sloan (Gaelic) Warrior. *Sloane, Slone, Sloane*

Smith (English) Blacksmith. *Smyth, Smythe, Smitty, Smits*

Snehal (Hindi) Friendly.

Snorre (Scandinavian) Variation of Snorri; meaning unknown. Snorri Sturluson was a celebrated twelfth-century Icelandic historian and politician.

Snowden (Old English) From the snow-covered hill. *Snowdun, Snow*

So (Vietnamese) First-born; smart.

Socrates (Greek) Philosophical; brilliant. *Socratez, Socratis, Sokrates*

Sofronio (Greek) Self-controlled. *Sophronio*

Soham (Hindi) Presence of divinity in the soul.

Sol (Latin) The sun. *Solly*

Solan (Latin) Soul seeker.

Solanio (Italian) A friend to Antonio.

Solinus (Greek) Duke of Ephisus.

Solomon (Hebrew) Peaceful; perfect. *Salamon, Sol, Soloman*

Solt (Hungarian) Name of an honor.

Sølve (Scandinavian) Meaning unknown.

Sólyom (Hungarian) Falcon.

Som (Indian) Sun.

Soma (Hungarian) A kind of berry.

Somerby (English) From the summer village. *Somerbie, Somersby, Sommersby*

Somerly (Irish) Summer sailor. *Somerled. Sorley, Sommerleigh*

Somerton (English) The summer estate.

Sommar (English) Summer. *Somer, Somers, Somm, Sommars, Sommer*

Sonnagh (Welsh) Mound; rampart.

Soren (Danish) Thunder; war. *Soryn*

Sorrel (French) Bitter; from the tree. *Sorre, Sorrell, Sorrey*

Soteria (Greek) Salvation.

Soterios (Greek) Saviour.

Spalding (English) Divided field. *Spaulding*

Sparky (Latin) Ball of fire; joyful. *Spark, Sparkee, Sparkey, Spurki, Spurkie*

Spaulding (English) Divided field. *Spalding, Spaldying, Spauldyng*

Speck (Old English) A small mark; surname used as a first name.

Speers (English) Good with spears; swift-moving. *Speares, Spears, Spiers*

Spencer (Old English) Dispenser, keeper. *Spence, Spenser*

Spider (American) Scary. *Spyder*

Spike (Old English) Long, heavy nail. *Spyke*

Spiridon (Greek) Like a breath of fresh air. *Speero, Spero, Spiridon, Spiro, Spiros, Spyridon, Spyros*

Srijan (Hindi) Creation.

Srikant (Hindi) Lover of wealth.

Srinath (Hindi) Meaning unknown.

Srinivas (Hindi) Abode of wealth.

Sriram (Hindi) Lord Rama.

Stacey (Latin) Stable. *Stace, Stacee, Stacie, Stacy, Staci, Stasia, Stasya, Tasia*

Staffan (Swedish) A garland.

Stafford (English) Dignified. *Staff, Staffard, Stafferd, Staffi, Staffie, Staffor*

Stamford (English) From the stony ford. *Stemford*

Stamos (Greek) Reasonable. *Stammos, Stamohs*

Stanbury (English) Fortified. *Stanberry, Stanbery, Stanburghe, Stansberry, Stansburghe, Stansbury*

Stancliff (English) From the stone cliff; prepared. *Stancliffe, Stanclyffe, Stanscliff, Stanscliffe*

Stanislaw (Latin) Camp of glory; stone clearing. *Stanislao, Stanislau, Stanislav, Stanislaus, Stanislav, Sztaniszláv, Stanislas, Stanislavsky, Stan, Aineislis, Stasio*

Stanley (Old English) From the rocky meadow. *Stanly, Stanleigh, Stanbury, Stanberry, Standish, Stanfield, Stanford, Stanhope, Stanmore, Stanton, Stanway, Stanwick, Stanwyck*

Stanwick (English) Born in village of stone. *Stanwicke, Stanwyck*

Stark (German) High energy. *Starke, Starkey*

Starr (English) Bright. *Star, Starri, Starrie*

Stavros (Greek) Crowned with wreath.

Steadman (English) Landowner; wealthy. *Steadmann, Sted, Stedmann*

Stefan (German) Crown; wreath. *Stef, Stefano, Stefanos, Stefos, Stephano, Stephanos*

Stein (German) Stone. *Steyn, Stine, Styne, Steiner, Steen, Steinway, Steinbeck, Steinberg, Steinmetz*

Steinar (Scandinavian) Muse; rock. *Steinard, Steinart, Steinhardt*

Stephen (Greek) Crown. *Steven, Stefan, Stephan, Stepan, Steve, Stevie, Steven, Stefano, Stephens, Stevens, Stevenson, Stephenson, Etienne, Esteban, Estevan, Steffan*

Sterling (English) Genuine, valued. *Stirling*

Sterne (Middle English) Serious-minded. *Stern, Stearn, Stearne*

> ### What's in a Name
>
> **Stephen** is a name with a history of leadership. The name itself comes from the Greek name *Stephanos*, meaning "crown." Saint Stephen was an early Christian martyr; another Saint Stephen is the patron saint of Hungary and the first Christian king of the country in the tenth century. Stephen has also been the name of 10 popes as well as the moniker of kings from England, Poland, and Serbia.

Stetson (English) Cowboy hat.

Stewart (Teutonic) Keeper of the estate. *Stuart, Steward, Stew, Stu*

Stieran (Scandinavian) Wandering. *Steeran, Steeren, Steeryn, Stieren, Stieryn*

Stiles (English) Practical. *Stile, Styles*

Sting (English) Singer.

Stoke (English) Village.

Stokley (Old English) From the tree-stump meadow. *Stockley, Stockton, Stockwell, Stockman, Stokeley*

Stone (American) Stone, rock. *Stonee, Stoney*

Storm (English) Storm, tempest. *Storme*

Stoyan (Bulgarian) To stay.

Strato (Shakespearean) From *Julius Caesar*.

Stratton (Scottish) Home-loving. *Straton, Strattawn*

Strom (German) Stream. (Czechoslovakian) Tree. (Greek) Bed.

Stroud (Old English) From the thicket. *Stroude, Stod*

Stuart (English) Careful; watchful. *Stewart, Stu*

Studs (Old English) A house.

Sudarshan (Hindi) Handsome. *Sudarsana*

Sudesha (Hindi) A son of Krishna; good country.

Sudeva (Hindi) Good. *Deva*

Sudhansu (Hindi) Moon.

Sudhir (Hindi) Great scholar; calm; resolute; brave.

Sukarman (Hindi) Reciter of 1,000 Samhitas.

Sukumar (Hindi) Tender; handsome.

Sulaiman (African American) Peaceful. *Suleiman, Suleyuman*

Sulio (Breton) Meaning unknown. *Suliau, Suliag*

Sullivan (Gaelic) Black eyes. *Sullyvan*

Sully (Gaelic) To stain.

Sumadhur (Hindi) Very sweet.

Sumantu (Hindi) Meaning unknown.

Sumati (Hindi) Wisdom.

Sumit (Hindi) A good friend.

Sumner (French) Summoner. *Sumenor, Sumnor*

Sun (Chinese) Bending; decreasing; goodness; sun.

Sundara (Hindi) Beautiful. *Sundar, Sundarama, Sunder*

Sunil (Hindi) Blue, sapphire.

Sunny (English) Bright disposition, cheerful. *Sunnie, Sunnee, Sonny, Sunday*

Surány (Hungarian) Name of an honor.

Suresh (Hindi) The ruler of the gods.

Surya (Hindi) The sun.

Sutherland (Norse) From the southern land. *Sutton, Sutcliff, Suffield, Sundy*

Suvrata (Hindi) A child of Daksa.

Svein (Anglo-Saxon) Youth.

Sven (Scandinavian) Youth. *Swen, Svend, Svenson, Svensen, Swensen, Swenson*

Swain (Middle English) Knight's attendant. *Swaine, Swayne, Swayze*

Swapnil (Hindi) Dreamlike.

Sweeny (Gaelic) Little hero. *Sweeney*

Sydney (English) From Sidon. *Sy, Syd*

Sylvester (English, Latin) From the forest. *Silvester, Silvestre, Silvestro, Sly*

Szabolcs (Hungarian) Meaning unknown.

Szalók (Hungarian) Meaning unknown.

Szemere (Hungarian) Small man; demolisher.

Szervác (Hungarian) Freed.

Szescõ (Hungarian) Meaning unknown.

Szevér (Hungarian) Serious; strict. *Szörény*

T

Tab (German, Middle English) Brilliant; drummer. *Tabb, Taber, Tabor, Tabbert, Taburer, Tabby*

Tabansi (African American) One who endures.

Tabari (African American) After famous Muslim historian.

Tabor (Hungarian) Camp. *Taber, Taibor, Tayber, Taybor, Tavor*

Tadc (Celtic) Poet, philosopher.

Taddeo (Italian) Courageous; one who praises.

Tadi (Omaha Indian) Wind.

Taft (English) Flowing. *Tafte, Taftie*

Tahir (Arabic) Chaste, pure.

Tai (Vietnamese, American) Talent; from Thailand.

Taimah (Native American) Thunder. *Taima, Taiomah, Tama, Tamah*

Tajo (Spanish) Day.

Takeshi (Japanese) Bamboo.

Taksa (Hindi) Son of Bharata.

Taksony (Hungarian) Well-fed; content; merciless; wild.

Taku (Japanese) Small; young.

Talbot (French) Reward. *Tally, Tallie*

Talman (Hebrew) To injure; to oppress.

Talon (English) Sharp claw. *Talan, Tawlon*

Talor (Hindi) Morning dew.

Talos (Greek) Giant protector of Minos Island.

Tamarius (African American) Stubborn. *Tam, Tamerius, T'Marius*

Tamir (Arabic) Pure, tall, stately.

Tancredo (Italian) Of thoughtful counsel. *Tancrede*

Tanek (Polish) Immortal.

Taner (Turkish) Seed. *Tane*

Tanner (Old English) Leather worker. *Tan, Tanier, Tann, Tanney, Tannie, Tanny*

Tansy (Greek) Immortal. (Native American) Name of a flower.

Tapan (Hindi) The sun.

Tarasios (Greek) Of Tarentum. *Taras*

Tardos (Hungarian) Bald.

Tariq (Arabic) Star; path. *Tarik, Taric, Tareeq, Tareek, Tareec*

Tarján (Hungarian) Name of an honor.

Tarkan (Turkish) Meaning unknown.

Taro (Japanese) First-born male.

Tarun (Hindi) Young.

Tas (Hungarian) Well-fed; stone.

Tate (Old English) Cheerful. (Native American) Long-winded talker.

Tathal (Welsh) Meaning unknown.

Tathan (Welsh) Meaning unknown.

Taurin (Latin) Born under the sign of Taurus. *Taurinus*

Tavarius (African American) Misfortune; fun-loving. *Tav, Taverius, Tavurius, Tavvy*

Tavis (Scottish) Twin. *Tevis, Tav, Tavish, Tamsin*

Tavon (African American) Nature.

Taylor (Middle English) Tailor. *Tailor, Tay, Tie*

Teague (Irish) Poet; handsome. (Scottish) Philosopher. *Tadhg, Tege*

Tearlach (Scottish) Manly.

Tecer (Turkish) Meaning unknown.

Tee (Gaelic) House.

Tegan (Celtic) Doe.

Tej (Hindi) Splendor.

Telford (French) Works in iron. *Telfer, Telfor, Telfour*

Telo (Old French) Surname used as a first name. *Teliau, Thélo, Théliau*

Tem (English) Country.

Temani (Hebrew) Of Teman.

Temo (Hebrew) Right hand; south.

Templeton (English) Town near the temple. *Temple, Templeten*

Tenenan (French) Meaning unknown. *Tinidor, Tenedor*

Tennessee (Native American) The state.

Tennyson (Middle English) Son of Dennis. *Tennison, Tennessee, Tenny*

Terach (Hebrew) Wild goat; contentious. *Tera, Terah*

Tercan (Turkish) Meaning unknown.

Terence (Latin) Polished, tender. *Terrence, Terance, Terencio, Terentius, Terry, Teri, Terris, Torrance*

Terje (Norse) Of Thor's spear.

Terrel (Old English) Thunderer. *Terel, Terele, Terell, Terille, Terral, Terrelle, Tirrill, Tyril, Terrill, Tirell, Terris, Tyrell, Rell*

Tétény (Hungarian) Chieftain Töhötöm.

Teulyddog (Welsh) Meaning unknown.

Tevaughn (African American) Tiger. *Tev, Tevan, Tevaughan, Tivan, Tivaughan*

Tevin (African American) Son of Kevin.

Tewdwr (Welsh) Meaning unknown.

Tezer (Turkish) Meaning unknown.

Thabit (Arabic) Firm.

Thaddeus (Latin) Courageous; praiser. *Thaddeus, Thaddaus, Thaddea, Thada, Taddeo, Tadeo, Tadeusz, Tadgh, Thad, Taddy, Tadda, Tad, Ted, Thadea*

Thai (Vietnamese) Many, multiple.

Thaman (Hindi) Name of a god.

Than (Burmese) Million. *Tan*

Thane (Old English) Attendant warrior.

Thanos (Greek) Noble. *Thonasis*

Thaonawyuthe (Native American) One who interrupts. *Thaowayuthe*

Thatcher (Old English) Roof fixer. *Thacher, Thatch, Thaxter*

Theobold (German) The boldest. *Teoboldo, Tibalt, Tybalt, Thebault, Thibaud, Thibaut, Theo*

Theodore (Greek) Gift of God. *Theodor, Teodore, Teodoro, Teddy, Ted, Feodor, Fedor, Fyodor, Telly, Teodor*

Theodoric (Teutonic) Ruler of the people. *Thierry*

Theophilus (Greek) Beloved of God. *Teofil, Theophile*

Theron (Greek) Hunter. *Therron, Theryon*

Thiassi (Scandinavian) Ancient mythological figure. *Thiazi, Thjazi*

Thibaud (French) Rule of the people.

Thierry (Teutonic) People's ruler.

Thomas (Greek) Twin. *Tomas, Tomaso, Tom, Thom, Thos, Tommy, Thompson, Thomson, Massey, Tamas*

What's in a Name

Although **Thomas**, which means "twin" in Aramaic, was the one of the 12 apostles in the Bible who doubted Jesus' resurrection, many modern-day Thomases have proven less cynical. Philosopher Thomas Hobbes, inventor Thomas Edison, President Thomas Jefferson, and even Thomas the Tank Engine have proven Thomas is a solid, respectable name.

Thompson (English) Prepared. *Thom, Thompsen, Thompsun, Thomson*

Thong (Vietnamese) Smart.

Thor (Old Norse) Thunder. *Thorbert, Thordis, Tor, Soren, Sören, Søren*

Thoralf (Scandinavian) Thunder. *Thord, Thorfinn, Thorgeirr, Thorgils, Thorgrim, Thorkell*

Thorin (Scandinavian) Form of Thor, god of thunder. *Thorrin, Thors*

Thorley (English) Thor's meadow. *Thorlea, Thorlee, Thorleigh, Thorly, Torley*

Thorne (Old English) Thorn tree. *Thorn, Thorndyke, Thornton, Thornley*

Thorndike (English) Thorny riverbank. *Thorndyck, Thorndyke*

Thorpe (Old English) From the village. *Thorp*

Thorstein (Scandinavian) Son of Thor.

Thurborn (Teutonic) Dweller by Thor's stream.

Thurlow (Old English) Thor's hill. *Thorald, Thorbert, Thorburn, Thorley, Thurmon, Thurman, Thurmond, Thurber, Thormond, Torold, Terrell*

Thurston (Norse) Thor's stone. *Thorstan, Thorstein, Thorsteinn, Thorsten, Thurstain, Thurstin, Thorston, Torstein, Torsten, Torston, Turstan*

Tibalt (Greek) People's prince.

Tiernan (Celtic, Gaelic) Lord. *Tierney, Tyrnan*

Tihamér (Hungarian) Likes silence.

Tilak (Hindi) Auspicious.

Timeus (Greek) Perfect.

Timoleon (Greek) I honor what I say.

Timon (Greek) Worthy. (Shakespearean) From *The Life of Timon of Athens*. *Timan, Timen, Timin*

Timothy (Greek) Honoring God. *Timotheus, Timoteo, Timmy, Timmie, Tim, Timon, Timo*

What's in a Name

The name **Timothy** is the product of combining the Greek name *Timao*, meaning "to honor," with *Theos*, which means "God." Saint Timothy accompanied the apostle Paul on some of his missionary journeys.

Timur (Hebrew) Date; palm tree. (Russian) Conqueror. *Tomor, Tömör*

Tinh (Vietnamese) Mindful, aware.

Titus (Greek) Of the giants. *Tito, Titan*

Titusz (Hungarian) Dove; honored.

Tivadar (Hungarian) Gift of God.

Tivon (Hebrew) Lover of nature.

Tobias (Hebrew) God is good. *Tobia, Tobiah, Toby, Tobit, Tobin, Tova, Tobey, Tóbiás*

Todd (Middle English) Fox. *Tod*

Tolbert (English) Bright prospects. *Talbart, Talbert, Tolbart, Tolburt, Tollee, Tolley*

Tomaj (Hungarian) Name of a clan.

Tomer (Hebrew) Tall.

Tomkin (Old English) Little. *Tom, Tompkin, Tomlin, Torsten*

Tomo (Japanese) A twin.

Tong (Vietnamese) Fragrant.

Tony (Latin) Praiseworthy. (Greek) Flourishing. Nickname for Anthony. *Tonee, Toney, Tonie*

Torin (Celtic) Chief.

Tormod (Scottish) Thunder spirit.

Torrance (Irish) From the low hills. *Torey, Torrey, Torry, Tori, Torr*

Toste (Scandinavian) Warrior.

Tostig (Old English) Name of an earl.

Tov (Hebrew) Good. *Tovi, Toviel, Toviya, Tuvia, Tuviah, Tuviya*

Townsend (Old English) From the end of town. *Towne, Townley, Townes*

Toyo (Japanese) Plentiful.

Tracy (Greek) Harvester. (Latin) Courageous. (Irish) Battler. *Trace, Tracey, Treacy*

Trahaearn (Welsh) Strong as iron. *Trahern, Tray*

Tranter (Old English) Wagoneer.

Travis (French) Crossing. *Tavers, Traver, Travers, Traves, Travess, Travey, Travus, Travuss, Travys, Trever, Trevor*

Tremayne (Scottish) House by the stones; farm with a stone monolith. *Tramaine, Treemayne, Trem, Tremain, Tremaine, Tremane, Tremen*

Tremeur (French) Meaning unknown. *Treveur*

Trent (Latin) Torrent; rapid stream. (Old English) Dweller by the Trent. *Trenton*

Trenus (Latin) Meaning unknown.

Trevor (Irish) Cautious. *Trefor*

Trey (Middle English) Third-born, three. *Trae, Tre, Treye, Tray*

Trigve (Norwegian) Meaning unknown.

Tripp (Old English) Traveler.

Trisanu (Hindi) Meaning unknown.

Tristan (Old Welsh, Latin) Noisy one; laborer. *Trestan, Trestyn, Trist, Tristram, Tristen, Tristyn*

Troilus (Shakespearean) From *Troilus and Cressida*.

Trory (African American) The red one.

Truman (Old English) Disciple. *Truesdale, True, Trueman*

Tryggvi (Scandinavian) True. *Trygg, Tryggve*

Tuathal (Celtic) Meaning unknown.

Tucker (Middle English) Tailor. *Tuckman, Tuck*

Tudfwlch (Welsh) Meaning unknown.

Tudur (Welsh) Divine gift.

Tugdual (French) Meaning unknown. *Tual, Tugal*

Tujan (French) Meaning unknown. *Tugen, Tujen*

Tuncer (Turkish) Meaning unknown.

Tung (Chinese) Universal.

Turiau (French) Meaning unknown. *Turio*

Turner (Middle English) Carpenter.

Turpin (Old Norse) Thunder. *Finn*

Tushar (Hindi) Snow.

Tuvya (Hebrew) Goodness of God.

Twain (Middle English) Two pieces.

Tye (Old English) Enclosed. *Tie, Tigh, Tighe, Tiegh, Tynan, Tai*

Tyee (Native American) Chief.

Tyler (Middle English) Tiler; roofer. *Tylor*

Tymon (Greek) Honoring God.

Tyne (Old English) River. *Tain, Tine*

Tyrek (Hebrew) Rock; sharp. *Ty*

Tyrell (African American) Thunder ruler.

Tyrone (Greek) King. *Tyron*

Tyson (English) Son of Ty; fiery. (French) Explosive. (German) Son of the German. *Tison, Tiszon, Tycen, Tyeson, Tysin*

Tzuriel (Hebrew) God is my rock.

U

Ualtar (Irish) Ruler of the army. *Uaitcir, Ualteir*

Uang (Chinese) Great.

Uata (Ploynesian) Army leader. *Uate*

Uba (African American) Wealthy.

Ubadah (Arabic) He who serves God.

Ubanwa (African) Wealth in children.

Uben (German) Practice. *Ubaldo, Ube*

Uberto (German) Bright mind.

Ubrig (German) Big. *Ubrigg, Ubryg, Ubrygg*

Ubrigens (German) Bothered. *Ubrigins, Ubrigyns*

Ubul (Hungarian) Meaning unknown.

Uchtred (English) Cries. *Uchtrid, Uchtryd, Uctred, Uctrid, Uctryd, Uktred, Uktrid*

Udai (Hindi) To arrive. *Uday, Uhayan*

Udall (English) Certain, valley of trees. *Eudall, Udahl, Udawl, Yudall*

Udeh (Hebrew) Praise.

Udel (English) Yew grove. *Dell, Eudel, Uddal, Udell*

Udenwa (African) Thriving.

Udit (Hindi) Risen.

Udo (Teutonic) One with great fortune, prosperous.

Udolf (English) Wealthy wolf. *Udolfo, Udoplh*

Uehudah (Hebrew) Meaning unknown.

Ufuk (Turkish) Meaning unknown.

Ugo (Italian) Bright in mind and spirit.

Ugod (Hungarian) Name of a clan.

Ugor (Hungarian) Meaning unknown. *Ugron*

Ugur (Turkish) Meaning unknown.

Uhila (Polynesian) Lightning.

Uhr (German) Disturbed.

Uhubitu (Native American) Dirty water.

Uilleach (Irish) Ready. *Uilleack, Uilleak, Uilliac, Uilliack, Uilliak, Uillyac, Uillyack, Uillyak*

Uilleam (Irish) Determined guardian. *Uilliam*

Uilleog (Irish) Small protector. *Uilleac, Uilioc, Uilliog, Uillyog*

Uiseann (Irish) One who conquers. *Uinsionn*

Uistean (Irish) Intelligent.

Ujala (Hindi) Shining. *Ujaala*

Ukel (American) Player. *Ukal, Uke, Ukil*

Ulan (African American) First-born twin. (Russian) Place name: Ulan, Russia. *Ulane, Ulen, Ulin, Ulon*

Uland (Teutonic) Noble country. (African) First-born twin. *Ulande, Ulandus*

Ulani (Polynesian) Cheerful.

Ulas (German) Noble.

Naming Rights

Pick names that just sound good and say them, along with middle and last names, for a month to see how they sound. At the end of the month, one of them will probably become your favorite.

Ulbrecht (German) Noble; bright.

Ulbrich (German) Aristocratic.

Uleki (Hawaiian) Wrathful. *Ulekee, Ulekie, Uleky, Ulesi*

Ulexite (German) A mineral; silky white crystalline; discovered by G. L. Ulex.

Ulf (Teutonic) Wolf.

Ulffr (Scandinavian) Wolflike; courageous. *Ulff, Ulv*

Ulfred (Norse) Noble.

Ulgar (German) High born.

Ulices (Latin) Wrathful; wanderer. *Uly*

Ulick (Scandinavian) Bright; rewarding mind. *Ulic, Ulyc, Ulyck*

Ulises (Latin) Wrathful

Ull (Scandinavian) Glory.

Ulland (English) Noble lord. *Uland, Ullund*

Ullock (Irish) Nobleman.

Ulman (German) The wolf's infamy. *Ulmann, Ullman, Ullmann*

Ulmer (English) Famous wolf. *Ullmar, Ulmar*

Ulriah (German) Powerful wolf. *Ulria, Ulrya, Ulryah*

Ulrich (German) Wolf ruler. *Ulric, Ulrick, Udolf, Ulger, Ull, Ulu*

Ulrik (Scandinavian) Noble ruler.

Ulster (Scandinavian) Wolf.

Ultan (Celtic) From an old name. *Ultann*

Ultar (Scandinavian) Wolf. *Ultarr*

Ulucan (Turkish) Meaning unknown.

Ulysses (Latin) The hateful one, wounded in the thigh. *Ule, Ulesses, Ulises, Uilioc*

Umar (Arabic) Longevity.

Umber (French) Brown, plain.

Umberto (Italian) Famous German.

Umed (Hindi) Desire.

Umher (Arabic) Controlling.

Umi (African) Life. *Umie, Umy*

Unaduti (Native American) Wooly head.

Ungus (Irish) One victor.

Unitas (American) United.

Unkan (Japanese) Cloud valley.

Unkas (Native American) Fox. *Uncas, Wonkas*

Unni (Norse) Modest.

Unser (German) Surname as a first name. (American) Racing family.

Unten (English) Not a friend. *Untenn*

Unus (Latin) One. *Unuss*

Unwin (English) Enemy. *Unwinn, Unwyn*

Updike (Scottish) Surname used as a first name.

Upendra (Hindi) An element.

Upjohn (English) Creative. *Upjon*

Naming Rights

Think about what your baby's name will sound like if you have to yell it through the neighborhood at dinnertime. Practice it. Ask the neighbors what they think!

Upton (English) From the upper town. *Uppton, Uptawn, Upten, Uptown, Upshaw*

Upwood (English) Forest on a hill.

Uranus (Greek) Heaven.

Urban (Latin) From the city. *Urb, Urbain, Urbaine, Urbane, Urben, Urbin, Urbano, Urbanus, Urbaine, Urbane, Urvan*

Uri (Hebrew) Light; God of light. *Urie, Uriah, Uria, Uriel, Uriell, Urian*

Urian (Greek) Heaven. *Urion*

Urias (Hebrew) Lord as my light, old-fashioned. *Uraeus, Uri, Uria, Urius*

Urien (Greek) Heaven. *Turien, Turio*

Urjasz (Polish) God is light.

Urjavaha (Hindi) Of the Nimi dynasty.

Uros (Hungarian) Little lord.

Ursan (Latin) Bear. *Urs, Urson*

Urvano (Spanish) City boy. *Urbano*

Urvil (Hindi) The sea.

Urvine (Place name) Form of Irvine, California. *Urveen, Urvene, Urvi*

Ury (Hebrew) Shining.

Usaid (Arabic) Laughs.

Usaku (Japanese) Moonlit.

Usamah (Arabic) Lion. *Usama*

Useni (African) Tell me.

Usher (English) Bringer.

Usi (African) Smoke.

Ustin (Russian) Variation of Justin.

Utah (Place name) U.S. state.

Utatci (Native American) Bear scratching.

Uther (English) Arthur's father.

Uthman (Arabic) Bird. *Othman, Usman*

Utt (Arabic) Wise and kind.

Uttam (Hindi) Third Manu; founding father of human beings. (Sanskrit) Best.

Utz (American) Befriends all.

Uwe (German) Universal ruler.

Uzi (Hebrew) My strength.

Uziah (Hebrew) God is my strength. *Uzia, Uziya, Uzziah*

Uziel (Hebrew) Powerful. *Uzziel*

Uzoma (African American) Born on a trip.

Uzondu (African) Attracts others.

Uzor (Hungarian) Name of an ethnic group. *Ozor*

V

Vachel (French) Cow tender; small cow. *Vachell*

Vaclav (Slavic) Great glory.

Vadim (Russian) Powerful ruler. *Vadik, Wadim, Wadik*

Vadin (Hindi) Educated orator.

Vaduz (German) Place name: Vaduz, Germany.

Vaesna (Cambodian) Lucky.

Vahe (Armenian) Victor.

Vaibhav (Hindi) Riches.

Vail (English, French, Latin) From the valley. *Bail, Bale, Vaile, Vaill, Vale, Valle*

Vaino (Finnish) Wagon builder.

Vairaja (Hindi) Son of Virat.

Val (Latin) Strong; powerful; healthy. *Vall*

Vala (Polynesian) Loincloth.

Valdermar (German) Famous ruler. *Valdemarr, Waldemar*

Valen (English) Strong.

Valentin (Latin) Good health. *Valentino, Valente*

Valentine (Latin) Strong. *Val, Valentin, Valentino, Valentyn*

Valerian (Latin) Healthy. *Valerie, Valerien, Valerio, Valery, Valeryan*

Valeray (French) Strong.

Valeri (Russian) Athletic, mighty. *Val, Valerian, Valerio, Valry*

Valerian (Russian) Strong leader. *Valerien, Valerio, Valerious, Valery, Valeryan*

Vali (Scandinavian) Brave man.

Valin (Hindi) Mighty soldier. *Valen, Valyn*

Valmihi (Hindi) Ant hill.

Valor (Latin) Boldness; bravery.

Valu (Polynesian) Eight.

Van (Dutch) Dyke. *Vann, Von, Vonn*

Vance (Middle English) Dweller at the windmill. *Van, Vancelo, Vann*

Vanda (Lithuanian) Ruling people. *Vandele*

Vandan (Hindi) Saved.

Vander (Greek) Short for Evander. *Vand*

Vandiver (American) Quiet. *Van, Vand, Vandaver, Vandever*

Vandwon (African American) Covert. *Vandawon, Vandjuan*

Vandyke (Dutch) From the dyke. *VanDyck*

Vane (Middle English) Wind; banner.

Vaninadh (Hindi) Husband of Saraswati, the goddess of knowledge.

Vannevar (Scandinavian) Good.

Vanslow (Scandinavian) Sophisticated. *Vansalo, Vanselow, Vanslaw*

Vanya (Russian) God is gracious. *Vanek, Vanka*

Naming Rights

Vanya, which is a nickname of Ivan, is the Russian/Czechoslovakian form of John.

Varden (French) From the green hill. *Vartan, Vardon*

Vardhamma (Hindi) Growth. *Vardhaman*

Varen (Hindi) Superior.

Varesh (Hindi) God is superior.

Varick (German) Protecting ruler. *Varric, Warick, Warrick*

Varil (French) Faithful.

Variya (Hindi) Excellent one.

Varkey (American) Boisterous.

Várkony (Hungarian) Name of an Avar, ethnic group. *Varsany*

Varlan (American) Tough. *Varland, Varlen, Varlin*

Varma (Hindi) Faithful.

Varner (German) Surname used as a first name; formidable. *Varn*

Varocher (French) Meaning unknown.

Varrius (Latin) Gentleman, servant to the duke.

Vartan (Armenian) Rose. *Varoun*

Varun (Hindi) Lord of the waters. *Varin, Varoon*

Vas (Slavic) Protective. *Vaston, Vastun, Vasya*

Vasant (Hindi) Spring season.

Vasava (Hindi) Indra.

Vashon (African American) God is gracious, merciful. *Vashaun, Vashonne*

Vasil (Czechoslovakian) Kingly. *Basil, Vasile, Vasilek, Vasili, Vasilios, Vasilis, Vasilos, Vasily, Vassily*

Vasilios (Greek) With royal blood, regal. *Vasily, Wasily, Vassily, Vasilis*

Vasin (Hindi) Rules all.

Vassil (Bulgarian) King. *Vass*

Vasu (Sanskrit) Rich boy.

Vasudev (Hindi) Variation of Lord Krishna. *Vasu*

Vasuman (Hindi) Born of fire.

Vaughan (Celtic) Little, small. *Vaughn*

Vavrin (Czechoslovakian) Laurel.

Vavrinec (Czechoslovakian) Crowned with laurels. *Lawrence*

Vayk (Hungarian) Rich.

Vea (Polynesian) Chief. *Veamalohi, Veatama*

Veda (Sanskrit) Eternal knowledge. *Vedis*

Vedanga (Hindi) Knowledge. *Vedas*

Veejay (American) Talkative. *V. J. Vee-Jay, Vejay*

Veer (Hindi) Brave.

Vega (Arabic) Falling star.

Vegas (Spanish) Meadows. (American) Place name: Las Vegas, Nevada. *Vega*

Veleslav (Czechoslovakian) Great glory. *Vela, Velek, Velousek*

Velle (American) Tough. *Vell, Velley, Velly, Veltree*

Veltry (African American) Hopeful.

Venacio (Spanish) Glorious.

Vencel (Slavic) Wreath; glory. *Wenzel, Wazlaw, Vaclav, Venceslas, Vyacheslav*

Venec (Czechoslovakian) Wreath. *Veniec*

Venedict (Russian) Blessed. *Venedikt, Venka, Venya*

Venezio (Italian) Glorious. *Venetziano, Veneziano*

Ventidius (Shakespearean) From *Antony and Cleopatra*.

Venturo (Italian) Lucky. *Venturio*

Verdun (French) Fort on a hill. Place name: Verdun, France, and Verdun, Quebec. *Verden, Ferdon*

Vere (French) True. *Veir, Ver, Vir*

Vered (Hebrew) Rose.

Vergel (Latin) Rod bearer. *Vergele*

Verges (English) A head borough.

Verile (German) Macho. *Verill, Verille, Verol, Verrill*

Verity (French) Truth.

Verlin (Latin) Blooming. (American) Spring. *Verle, Verlon*

Verlyn (African American) Growing. *Verle, Velin, Verllin, Verlon, Virlie, Vyrle*

Vermont (French) Green mountain. Place name: fourteenth state.

Vern (Latin) Springlike. *Verne, Vernie*

Verner (German) Defending army. *Verner, Virnir*

Vernon (French) Alder tree. (Latin) Spring. *Vern, Verda, Verne, Verney*

Verrier (French) Faithful.

Verrill (French) Faithful. *Verill, Verrall, Verrell, Verrol, Veryl*

Versey (English) Full of song.

Vertumnus (Latin) Changing. Roman mythology: god of the seasons, plant growth and gardens.

Vester (Latin) He who guards the fire.

Vesuvio (Italian) Smoke; volcano in southern Italy.

Viau (Breton) Lively. *Vial, Vital*

Vicente (Spanish) Winner. *Vic, Vincentay, Visente*

Victor (Latin) Victor; conqueror. *Viktor, Vitorio, Vittorio, Vick, Vic, Vince*

Vid (German) Sylvan man. *Vida, Vidos*

Vida (Latin) Life. (Hebrew) Dearly loved.

Vidal (Spanish) Full of vitality. *Bidal, Videl, Videlio*

Vidar (Scandinavian) Soldier.

Vidkun (Scandinavian) Vast experience.

Vidor (Hungarian) Happy.

Vidvan (Hindi) Scholar.

Viet (Vietnamese) Destroy.

Viggo (Scandinavian) Exhuberant. *Viggoa, Vigo*

Vigilius (Latin) Alert, vigilant.

Vihs (Hindi) Increase.

Vijay (Hindi) Victorious. *Bijay, Vijun*

Vijayendra (Hindi) Victorious god of the sky. *Vijendra*

Vikas (Hindi) Progress.

Vikesh (Hindi) The moon.

Vikram (Hindi) Glorious king.

Vikrant (Hindi) Brave.

Vila (Czechoslovakian) Clever; resolute; mischievous. *Vilek, Vilem, Vilhelm, Vili, Viliam, Vilko, Ville, Vilmos*

Vilem (German) Determined guardian. *Vilhelm*

Viljalmr (Scandinavian) Resolute protector.

Viljo (Scandinavian) Guardian.

Villard (French) Village man.

Villiers (French) Kindhearted.

Vilmos (German) Steady soldier. *Villmos*

Vimal (Hindi) Pure. *Vima*

Vinay (Hindi) Good behavior.

Vincent (Latin) Conquering. *Vinko, Vincente, Viken, Vikenti, Vikesha, Vin, Vince, Vicenzio, Vincenzo, Vinci, Vinco, Vinn, Vinnie, Vinny*

Vine (English) One who works in a vineyard.

Vineet (Hindi) Unassuming.

Vinod (Hindi) Pleasing.

Vinson (English) Son of Vincent. (Latin) Conquering. *Venson, Vince, Vins*

Vinton (English) Town of wine.

Vipin (Hind) Forest.

Vipul (Hindi) Plenty.

Viraj (Hindi) Splendor.

Virat (Hindi) Supreme being.

Vireo (Latin) Brave.

Virgil (Latin) Staff bearer. *Verge, Vergil, Vergilio, Virge, Virgie, Virgilio*

Vishal (Hindi) Immense.

Visvajit (Hindi) One who conquers the universe.

Visvakarman (Hindi) Architect; son of Yogasiddha.

Visvayu (Hindi) Brother of Amavasuand Satayu.

Viswanath (Hindi) The lord.

Vitalian (Italian) Life.

Vitaly (Greek) Life.

Vitas (Greek) Alive, vital. *Vidas, Vite, Vitalis*

Vitéz (Hungarian) Brave warrior.

Vito (Latin) Conquerer.

Vittorio (Italian) Victory.

Vitus (Latin) Winning.

Vivar (Greek) Alive. *Viv*

Vivatma (Hindi) Universal soul.

Vivek (Hindi) Discerning with wisdom.

Vlade (Slavic) Prince.

Vladilen (Russian) Prince.

Vladimir (Slavic) To rule with peace; regal. *Wolodymyr, Vlad, Vladislav*

Vladislav (Czechoslovakian) Glorious ruler. *Ladislav*

Vlas (Russian) One who stammers.

Vojtech (Czechoslovakian) Comforting soldier. *Vojta, Vojtek, Vojtresek*

Volf (Hebrew) Wolf.

Volker (German) People's guard. *Volker*

Volney (Greek) Hidden.

Voltimand (English) Courtier.

Volund (Norse) A wonderful smith.

Volya (Slavic) Hopes.

Von (Scandinavian) Hope. *Vaughn, Vonn, Vonne*

Naming Rights

When looking for names of your new little one, both parents should sit down with this book, browse through the chapter topics or the names and definition lists, and come up with your top three choices. You can then work together to begin narrowing the final selection down from there.

Voshon (African American) God's grace.

Vortigem (English) *The Legend of King Arthur;* name of a king.

Vougay (Breton) Meaning unknown. *Vouga, Nonna*

Vui (Vietnamese) Cheerful.

Vul (African) Saves.

W

Waage (Scandinavian) Wagon.

Waban (Native American) East wind.

Waclaw (Polish) Glorified.

Waco (American) Place name: Waco, Texas.

Wade (Middle English) A ford. *Wadley, Wadsworth, Waide, Wayde*

Wadell (English) Southerner. *Waddell, Wade*

Waden (American) God has heard. *Waden, Wedan*

Wadley (English) Ford meadow. *Wadleigh, Wadly*

Wadsworth (English) Homebody. *Waddsworth, Wadswurth*

Waggoner (German) Wagon maker.

Wagner (Dutch) Wagon driver. (German) Wagon maker. *Wagg, Waggner, Waggoner, Wagnar, Wargnur*

Wahid (Native American) Sacred. *Wahida*

Wahkan (Arabic) Unique, singular, unequalled.

Wain (English) Industrious.

Waite (English) Protector.

Wakefield (Old English) Wet field. *Wake, Wakeley, Wakeman*

Walbert (German) Protective, stodgy

Walchelim (Anglo-Norman) Meaning unknown.

Walcott (English) Lives in the Welshman's cottage. *Wallcot, Wallcott, Wolcott*

Waldemar (German) Mighty, famous. *Valdemar, Waldermar, Waldo*

Walden (Teutonic) Mighty. *Wald, Waldan, Waldi, Waldin, Waldo, Waldon, Waldy, Welti*

Waldo (Teutonic) Rule. *Waldemarr, Waldemar, Waldorf, Walfred, Walden*

Waldron (German) Mighty raven.

Waleed (Arabic) Newborn. *Waled, Walid*

Walenty (Polish) Strong.

Waleran (Anglo-Norman) Meaning unknown.

Wales (English) Place name: United Kingdom. *Wael, Wail, Wails, Wale, Waley, Wali, Waly*

Walker (Middle English) Cloth worker.

Wallace (Old English) Welshman. *Wallis, Wallas, Wally, Wallie, Walsh, Welsh, Welch, Wallach*

Waller (English) Man from Wales, smooth.

Walmir (English) The pond of the Welsh.

Walmond (German) Mighty protector.

Walsh (English) Inquisitive. *Walls, Welce, Welch, Wells, Welsh*

Walten (German) Ruler.

Walford (English) Wealthy.

Walfred (English) Loyal.

Walker (English) Distinctive. *Walk, Wally*

Walter (German) Powerful warrior, army ruler. *Walt, Wally, Walther, Watson, Watkins, Gautier, Gauthier, Ualtar*

Walton (Old English) Dweller by the wall. *Walt, Walten, Waltin*

Waltraut (German) Rule, strength. *Waltraud*

Walworth (English) Introvert.

Walwyn (English) Welsh friend. *Walwin, Walwinn, Walwynn, Walwynne, Welwyn*

Waman (Hindi) Falcon.

Wamblee (Native American) Eagle.

Wang (Chinese) Kingly.

Waqar (Arabic) Talkative.

Wapi (Native American) Lucky.

Warburton (English) Fortified town.

Ward (English) To guard, watchman. *Wardell, Warden, Wardley, Warfield, Warford, Warley, Warmond, Warton, Warwick*

Warden (English) Watchful. *Warde, Wardie, Wardin, Wardon*

Wardley (English) Careful. *Wardlea, Wardleigh*

Wardford (English) Watchman's river.

Ware (English) Aware, cautious. *Wardlea, Wardleigh*

Waring (English) Dashing. *Warend, Warin, Warring*

Wark (American) Watchful.

Warley (English) Meadow near the river.

Warner (German) Defending army. *Werner*

Warren (German) Watchman; gamekeeper; enclosure. *Ware, Waren, Waring, Warrenson, Warrin, Warriner, Warron, Warry, Worrin*

Warrick (English) Strong leader.

Warton (English) Defended town.

Warwen (American) Defensive. *Warn, Warwun*

Warwick (English) Settlement near the weir. *War, Warick, Warrick, Warweck, Warwyc, Warwyck, Wick*

Wasaki (African) The enemy.

Waseem (Arabic) Graceful; good-looking. *Wasseem*

Washburn (English) Bountiful; river. *Washbern, Washbie, Washby*

Washi (Japanese) Eagle.

Washington (Old English) Town near water. *Wash, Washe, Washing*

Wasim (Arabic) Good-looking.

Wassily (Russian) Royal; kingly.

Wat (English) Jolly.

Watford (English) Dam made of twigs and sticks.

Watson (Old English) Son of Walter. *Watkins, Watt*

Waverly (Old English) From the tree-lined meadow.

Wayde (English) River crossing. *Waydee*

Wayland (Old English) From the path land. *Waylon, Way*

Waylon (English) Land by the road.

Wayne (Old English) Wagon maker. *Waggoner*

Webb (English) Weaver.

Webster (Old English) Weaver. *Weber, Webley, Webb*

Welcome (English) Welcome guest.

Weldon (English) Hill with a well.

Wells (Old English) From the springs. *Welles, Weller, Welborne, Welby, Weldon, Welford, Welton*

Wen (Chinese) Cultured, ornamental.

Wenceslaus (Slavic) Great glory.

Wendell (Teutonic) A wend. *Wendel, Wedel*

Werner (Teutonic) Warrior. *Warin*

Wes (German) The west meadow.

Wesley (Old English) West meadow. *Wes, Wessely, Wess*

West (Old English) Westerly direction. *Weston, Westbrook, Westby, Westcott, Weston, Westleigh*

Westbrook (English) Brook on the west side.

Wetherby (Old English) Ram's meadow.

Wheaton (Old English) Wheat town.

Wheeler (Old English) A driver.

Whistler (English) He who whistles.

Whit (Old English) White. *White, Whitey, Whitcomb, Whitby, Whitelaw, Whitfield, Whitford, Whitley, Whitlock, Whitman, Whitmore, Whittaker*

Whitby (English) Farm with white walls.

Whitcomb (English) Light in the valley.

Whitfield (Old English) From a small field. *Whitley*

Whittaker (English) White field.

Wicasa (Native American) Sage.

Wid (English) Wide. *Wyd*

Wieslav (Slavic) One with great glory.

Wihtred (Anglo-Saxon) Meaning unknown.

Wilbert (German) Willful, bright; resolute.

Wilbur (Teutonic) Bright resolve.

Wiley (English) Of the willows.

Wilford (English) Ford by the willows.

Wilfred (Old English) Much peace. *Wilfrid, Wilfried*

Willard (Teutonic) Bold resolve.

William (Teutonic) Valiant protector. *Wil, Will, Willem, Wilhelm, Wilmos, Wilmot, Wilson, Williams, Williamson, Wills, Willie, Willy, Wiley, Wyley, Wilkie, Willkie, Wilkes, Wylkes, Willis, Wilton, Wilmer, Wilmar, Winton, Willard, Wilford, Guillaume, Guillermo, Vilhelm, Vilem, Viliam, Vasili, Vasily, Uilleam, Uilliam*

What's in a Name

William—the name borne by rulers of England and Germany (as well as a current English prince), heroes such as William Tell, and literary geniuses such as William Shakespeare—is from the German name Wilhelm, which was composed of the word *wil* for will, as in "want," and *helm*, meaning "protection."

Willis (German) Son of William.

Willow (English) Willow.

Wilmer (German) Determined and famous.

Wilson (German) Son of William

Wilton (English) Farm by the Spring. *Wilt.*

Winfield (German) Friend of the field.

Wingy (English) Winged like a bird.

Winifred (Old English) Friend of peace. *Winnie, Winny, Winni, Win, Winn, Wyn, Fred, Freddie, Freddy*

Winog (Breton) Meaning unknown.

Winslow (Old English) From the friend's hill. *Winchell, Windsor, Winfield, Winfred, Wingate, Winthrop, Winton, Wynton, Winward, Winfrey*

Winston (Old English) Joy stone, victory town.

Winter (Old English) Winter. *Wynter, Winters*

Winthrop (Old English) Friendly.

Wirt (English) Worthy.

Wisdom (English) Wisdom; common sense.

Wise (Irish) Ardent or wise.

Wissian (English) Guide.

Wite (Scottish) Knowledge; punishment.

Witton (English) From the wise man's estate.

Wlod (Polish) Ruler.

Wohehiv (Native American) Dull knife.

Wojtek (Polish) Happy soldier.

Wokaihwokomas (North American) White antelope.

Wolcott (English) Wolf's home.

Wolf (English) Wolf. *Wolfe*

Wolfe (English) The wolf.

Wolfgang (Teutonic) Wolf strife. *Wolf, Wolfe, Wolfie, Wolcott, Woolsey*

Wolfram (Teutonic) Wolf, raven. *Walram*

Wolstan Origin and meaning unknown.

Woo (Chinese) Martial art; military.

Wood (American) From the name Woody.

Woodis (English) Wood; forest.

Woodrow (Old English) Forester; row of houses by a wood. *Woodruff, Woodward, Woodie, Woody*

Woodson (English) Son of Wood.

Woorak (Australian) From the plain.

Wray (Scandinavian) From the corner.

Wren (Welsh) Chief.

Wright (Old English) Craftsman, carpenter.

Wu-pen (Chinese) Original consciousness.

Wulfhere (Anglo-Saxon) Name of a King.

Wulfnoth (Anglo-Saxon) Wolf.

Wulfsige (English) Victorious wolf.

Wulfstan Origin and meaning unknown.

Wuyi (Native American) Soaring turkey vulture.

W

Wyalan Origin and meaning unknown.

Wyatt (Old English, French) Little warrior, water. *Wyeth, Wyatte*

Wyclef (English) From the white cliff.

Wylie (Old English) Enchanting. *Wiley*

Wyndam (Old English) The field with the winding path. *Windham, Wyn*

Wynono (Native American) First born.

Wynton (English) Friend. *Winton*

Wynward (English) From the wine's forest. *Wynyard, Winward*

Wyome (Native American) Plain.

Wyson (English) Meaning unknown.

Wystan (Anglo-Saxon) Battle stone. *Winston*

Wythe (English) From the willow tree.

X

Xabat (Spanish) Savior.

Xalvador (Spanish) Savior.

Xanthus (Greek) Yellow, blond. *Xantha, Xanthe, Xanthos*

Xat (American) Saved. *Xatt*

Xaver (Spanish) New home.

Xaverius (Spanish) Owner of new house. *Xaverious, Xaveryus*

Xavier (Arabic) Bright; splendid. (Spanish) New home. *Saverio, Xaver, Xever, Javier, Giaffar, Jaffar, Zavey, Zavier*

Xavion (Spanish) Home.

Xaxon (American) Happy. *Zaxon*

Xayvion (African American) The new house. *Savion, Sayvion, Sayveon, Xaivon, Xayveon, Zayvion*

Xebec (French) From Quebec; cold. *Xebeck, Xebek*

Xenik (Russian) Sly. *Xenic, Xenick, Xenyc, Xenyck, Xenyk*

Xeno (Greek) Strange, foreign. *Xenoes, Zene, Zenno, Zenny, Zeno, Zenos*

Xenophon (Greek) Soldier, mercenary, and Athenian student of Socrates; strange voice.

Xerarch (Greek) Forest dweller. *Xerarche*

Xeres (Spanish) Older. *Xeries*

Xerxes (Persian) Prince, ruler, leader. *Xerk, Xerky, Zerk, Zerkes, Zerkez*

Xhosas (African) South African tribe. *Xhoses, Xhosys*

Xi-Wang (Chinese) Desire, hope.

Xiaoping (Chinese) Small bottle.

Ximen (Spanish) Obedient. *Ximenes, Ximon, Ximun*

What's in a Name

Saint Francis **Xavier**, patron saint of the Orient and missionaries, has been credited with popularizing the name Xavier, which means "the new house." Saint Francis Xavier likely lived in many houses through the years, as he was a missionary to China, Japan, and India.

Xin (Chinese) New. *Xian, Xoan*

Xing-fu (Chinese) Happiness.

Xuthus (Greek) Son of Helen.

Xyle (American) Helpful. *Zye, Zyle*

Xylo (Greek) Wood.

Xylon (Greek) Forester. One who lives in the forest.

Xyshaun (African American) Zany. *Xye, Zye, Zyshaun, Zyshawn*

Xyst (Greek) A portico; systematic. *Xist*

Xystum (Greek) Promenade. *Xistoum, Xistum, Xysoum*

Xystus (Greek) Promenade. *Xistus*

Y

Yaakov (Hebrew) Supplanter or heel. *Yanknv*

Yaar (Hebrew) Forest.

Yadid (Hewbrew) Beloved.

Yadon (Hebrew) He will judge. *Yadin*

Yago (Hebrew, Spanish) Supplanter.

Yahir (Hebrew) Haughty.

Yahto (Native American) Blue.

Yahya (Arabic) God is good. *Yihya*

Yair (Hebrew) God will teach. *Jair*

Yakim (Hebrew) God develops. *Jakim*

Yakov (Hebrew) The supplanter; held by the heel.

Yale (German, Old English) One who pays or produces; corner of land. *Yael*

What's in a Name

Another Y-name with Jewish roots is **Yakov**, from the Hebrew name *Ya'agov*, for "holder of the heel," or "supplanter," because the biblical Jacob was born holding the heel of his twin brother, Esau. He was the son of Isaac and Rebecca and the father of the 12 founders of the 12 tribes of Israel.

Yamal (Hindi) One of a twin.

Yamin (Hebrew) Right hand. *Jamin*

Yan (Hebrew) God's grace. *Jannai, Yann, Yannic, Yanni*

Yancy (Native American) Yankee. *Yance, Yancey, Yantsey, Yank*

Yanis (Hebrew) Gift from God.

Yannick (French) Gift from God.

Yannis (Greek) God is good. *John, Yannakis, Yanni, Yiannis*

Yanoach (Hebrew) Rest.

Yao (Chinese) Born on a Thursday.

Yaphet (Hebrew) Attractive. *Japhete, Japheth, Yapheth*

Yarb (Gypsy) Herb.

Yardley (English) Of the yard. *Yardlea, Yardlee, Yardleigh, Yardly*

Yarin (Hebrew) To understand. *Yaron*

Yas (Native American) Snow.

Yasahiro (Japanese) Peaceful.

Yasar (Arabic) Wealth, comfort, ease. *Yaser, Yasir, Yasser, Yassir*

Yasashiku (Japanese) Gentle, polite.

Yash (Hindi) Victorious glory.

Yashodhara (Hindi) One who has achieved fame.

Yashovarman (Hindi) Meaning unknown.

Yashpal (Hindi) Protector of fame.

Yasin (Arabic) Prophet.

Yasir (Arabic) To be rich, to be easy. *Yasser*

Yasuo (Japanese) Peaceful one. *Yaso*

Yates (Middle English) Gate-keeper. *Yeats*

Yauvani (Hindi) Full of youth.

Yazid (Arabic) Increasing, enhance.

Ye (Chinese) Universe.

Yechezkel (Hebrew) God strengthens. *Chaskel, Chatzkel, Kesel*

Yehudi (Hebrew) Praise God; a man from Judah; a Jew. *Yehuda*

Yemon (Japanese) Guardian.

Yen (Vietnamese) Calm.

Yeoman (English) Servant.

Yered (Hebrew) To come down. *Jered*

Yerik (Russian) Appointed by God; variation of Jeremiah.

Yervant (Armenian) An Armenian king.

Yeshaya (Hebrew) God lends.

Yevgeni (Russian) Noble; well-born. *Yevgeny*

Yigit (Turkish) Shall be redeemed.

Yitro (Hebrew) Plenty. *Yitran*

Yitzchak (Hebrew) Laughter. *Itzhak, Yitzhak*

Yo (Chinese) Bright.

Yobachi (African American) Pray to God.

Yogendra (Hindi) God of yoga.

Yogesh (Hindi) God of yoga.

Yogi (Japanese) One who practices yoga. (Sanskrit) Unity.

Yohann (German) Form of Johan.

Yonas (Hebrew) Dove.

Yonatan (Hebrew) Gift from God.

Yong (Chinese) Brave.

Yong-Sun (Korean) Courageous.

Yongvar (Norse) Of Ing's army. *Ingvarr*

Yorath (English) Worthy God. *Ialo, Iorwerth*

York (Old English, Celtic) Yew tree, from the farm of yew trees. *Yorick*

Yosef (Hebrew) God increases. *Yoseff, Yosif, Yousef, Yusef, Yusif, Yusuf, Yuzef*

What's in a Name

The name Joseph has many variations, including **Yosef**, which is from the Hebrew name *Yoseph*, meaning "he will add." In the Bible, Joseph was the eleventh son of Jacob—and his favorite. Feeling jealous, Joseph's brothers sent him to Egypt and told their father he had died. In Egypt, Joseph became an adviser to the pharaoh and years later reconciled with his brothers.

Yoshi (Japanese) Better, best.

Yoshifumi (Japanese) Respectful, good. *Yoshimitusu, Yoshiyuki*

Yotimo (Native American) Bee flying to its hive.

Yottoko (Native American) Mud from the river.

Youkioma (Native American) Flawless. *Youkeoma, Yukeoma, Yukioma*

Young-Ja (Korean) Forever stable.

Young-Jae (Korean) Forever prosperous.

Ysgarran (Welsh) Meaning unknown.

Yu (Chinese) Universe.

Yuan (Chinese) New.

Yucel (Turkish) Noble.

Yudhajit (Hindi) Victor in war.

Yukio (Japanese) Gets what he wants; God will nourish.

Yul (Mongolian) From the far horizon. *Yule*

Yule (English) Christmas.

Yuma (Native American) Son of the chief.

Yunis (Arabic) Dove. *Yunus*

Yurchik (Russian) Farmer; variation of George. *Yura, Yuri, Yurik, Yurko, Yurli, Yury*

Yuri (Russian) Variation of George. (Greek) Farmer.

Yusef (Arabic) To increase. *Yusuf*

Yutaka (Japanese) Fisherman.

Yutu (Native American) Coyote hunting.

Yuval (Hebrew) Brook. *Jubal*

Yves (Teutonic) Yew; archer. *Yvo, Ives, Yvan*

Z

Zabulon (Hebrew) To exhalt; honor.

Zaccheo (Hebrew) The one God remembers. *Zaccheus*

Zachary (Hebrew) God remembers; renowned by God. *Zacharias, Zakary, Zacarius, Zaccaria, Zachariah, Zechariah, Zackry, Zach, Zack, Zak, Zacharie, Zaccaria, Zacharyah*

What's in a Name

Zachary comes from the Hebrew name *Zekeryah*, which means "God remembers." Spelled *Zechariah*, Zachary was the author of the Book of Zechariah in the Bible's Old Testament.

Zachriel (Latin) Angel who rules over memory.

Zádor (Hungarian) Violent.

Zafer (Turkish) Victorious. *Zafar*

Zahavi (Hebrew) Gold.

Zahin (Islam) Intelligent.

Zahur (Egyptian) Name of a flower. *Zahir*

Zaid (African American) Increase; growth.

Zaide (Yiddish) Elder.

Zajzon (Hungarian) Meaning unknown.

Zakai (Hebrew) Innocent; one who is pure. *Zaki, Zakkai*

Zaki (Arabic) Smart.

Zakur (Hebrew) Masculine.

Zalán (Hungarian) Thrower, hitter.

Zale (Greek) Strength from the sea. *Zayle*

Zalman (Yiddish) Peaceful and quiet. *Zalmon*

Zamael (German) Angel of joy. *Samuel*

Zamir (Hebrew) Songbird.

Zámor (Hungarian) Plough land.

Zan (Hebrew) Well-fed.

Zander (Greek) Defender of man.

Zane (Arabic) Beloved. (Hebrew) God is gracious. *Zain, Zayne*

Zanebono (Italian) The good one.

Zani (English, Hebrew) Gift from the house.

Zaniel (Latin) Angel of Monday; the zodiac sign for Libra.

Zanipolo (Italian) Little gift of God.

Zann (Hebrew) Lily.

Zanobi (Latin) Scarcely alive.

Zaránd (Hungarian) Gold.

Zareb (African American) Protector.

Zared (Hebrew) Trap.

Zarek (Polish) May God protect the king.

Zashawn (African American) God is gracious; merciful. *Zeshawn*

Zavad (Hebrew) Present. *Zabad*

Zayd (Arabic) To increase. *Zaid, Zayed, Ziyad*

Zayden (Hebrew) Lucky. *Zaydin*

Zayn (Arabic) Beauty.

Zazel (Latin) Angel summoned for love invocations.

Zazu (Hebrew) Movement.

Zdenek (Czechoslovakian) One from Sidon; a winding sheet.

Zebedeo (Aramaic) Servant of God Zeb.

Zebediah (Hebrew) Portion of the lord.

Zebulon (Hebrew) Home.

Zedekiah (Hebrew) Justice of the lord. *Zed*

Zeeman (Dutch) Seaman.

Zefirino (Greek) Wind of spring. *Zefferino, Zefiro*

Zeke (Arabic) The memory of the lord.

Zeki (Turkish) Smart.

Zekö (Hungarian) Meaning unknown.

Zelig (German) The blessed one.

Zelipe (Spanish) Meaning unknown.

Zen (Japanese) Religious.

Zendo (Greek) One who devotes his life to God.

Zeno (Greek) Of Zeus.

Zenoa (Hebrew) Sign.

Zenobio (Greek) Strength of Jupiter.

Zenon (Spanish) Living.

Zenos (Greek) Gift of Zeus. *Zen*

Zephan (Hebrew) Treasured by God.

Zephyr (Greek) Wind. *Zephirin*

Zeren (Turkish) Meaning unknown.

Zerind (Hungarian) Serb.

Zero (Greek) Seeds.

Zétény (Hungarian) Meaning unknown.

Zeth (Greek) Investigator, researcher. *Zeticus, Zetico*

Zeus (Greek) Powerful one.

Zev (Hebrew) Deer, wolf. *Zvi, Zevie, Zivia, Ziva, Zeva*

Zhong (Chinese) Second brother.

Zhu (Chinese) Wish.

Zhuang (Chinese) Strong.

Ziff (Hebrew) Wolf.

Zig (American) Justice of the lord. *Ziggy*

Zimraan (Arabic) Praise; celebrated.

Zindel (Yiddish) Protector of mankind. *Zindil*

Zion (Hebrew) A sign; guarded land.

Ziph (Hebrew) Mouthful; falsehood.

Zircon (Arabic) A mineral name.

Zitkaduta (Native American) Redbird.

Zitomer (Czechoslovakian) To live in fame. *Zitek, Zitousek*

Ziv (Hebrew) Very bright. *Zivan, Zivi*

Ziven (Slavic) Vigorous and alive. *Zivon*

Zobor (Hungarian) Gathering.

Zoello (Greek) Son of Zoe. *Zoellus*

Zoltán (Hungarian) Chieftain. *Zolton*

Zombor (Hungarian) Buffalo. *Zsombor*

Zomier (Hebrew) One who prunes trees. *Zomer*

Zorba (Greek) Live each day.

Zorro (Slavic) Golden dawn.

Zorya (Slavic) Star.

Zosimo (Greek) Lively. *Zosimos, Zosimus, Zotico, Zoilo, Zoticus*

Zowie (Greek) Life.

Zsigmond (Hungarian) Victorious defender.

Zsolt (Hungarian) Name of an honor.

Zuhayr (Arabic) Sweet, having flowers. *Zuhair*

Zuriel (Hebrew) The Lord is my rock.

Zurl (Hebrew) Rock, strength of God.

Zvi (Scandinavian) Deer. *Zwi*

Zydrunas (Slavic) Morning sky.

Zygmunt (Polish) Victorious protector.

Girl Names

A

Aaliyah (Hebrew) Exalted. *Alea, Aleah, Alea, Aleaseya, Aliya, Alia, Aleeya, Aliyah, Allyiah*

Aamoir Origin and meaning unknown.

Aari (Hebrew) Like a beautiful melody. *Aarie, Aariel, Aaries, Aree, Arey, Aria, Ariana, Arie, Ariel, Ariealla, Ary*

Aase (Hebrew) Flower of the Lord. *Asaella*

Aba (African) Born on Thursday.

Abbellonna (Hebrew) Exhalation of breath; variation of Abel.

Abby (Latin) Head of a monastery; nickname for Abigail. *Abey, Abbey, Abbe, Abbie*

Abeni (African) Prayed for.

Abeque (Native American) Stays at home. *Abequa*

Abey (Native American) Leaf.

Abeytu (Native American) Green leaf.

Abia (Arabic) Great. *Abbia, Abiah, Abbiah*

Abiba (African) Child born after grandmother died.

Abie (Hebrew) Mother of many.

Abigail (Hebrew) A father's joy. *Abagail, Abbagail, Abbagale, Abbagayle, Abbegail, Abbegale, Abbegayle, Abbygail, Abbeygale, Abbygale, Abbygayle, Abigayle, Abigale, Abegail, Abegale, Abegayle, Abbiegail, Abbiegayle, Abbigael, Abbigail, Abby, Abbie, Gail*

Abiona (Yoruban) Born on a journey.

Abira (Hebrew) My strength. *Abbira, Abeera, Abeerah, Abeir, Aberah, Abiir, Abir*

Abital (Hebrew) My father is night dew.

Abmaba (African) Born on Thursday.

Abra (Hebrew) Mother of many nations; feminine form of Abraham. *Abree, Abri, Abria*

Abriana (Italian) Mother of nations. *Abrien, Abrienna, Abrienne, Abrion, Abbrienna, Abbryana, Abreana, Abreanna, Abreanne, Abreeana, Abreona, Abreonia, Abriann, Abrianna, Abryanna*

Abril (French) Secure, protected. *Abrille, Abrial, Abreal, Abriale, Abrielle*

Abtin (Persian) A character in *Shahnameh*; Fereidoun's father.

Acadia (Canadian) Place name in Canada. *Cadie, Caddie*

Acantha (Greek) Thorny.

Achazia (Hebrew) The Lord holds.

Ada (Hebrew) Adorned. (Latin) Of noble birth. *Adah, Adda, Addah, Addi, Addiah, Addie, Addy, Ade, Auda, Adailia, Adalee, Adara, Adah, Eda, Etta*

Adalgisa (German) Noble hostage.

Adalia (Spanish) Noble. *Adal, Adala, Adalea, Adaleah, Adali, Adalie, Adaly*

Adamina (Hebrew) Daughter of the earth.

Adan (Irish) Warm.

Adara (Greek) Beauty. *Adair, Adar, Adarah, Adare, Adarra, Adaire*

Addison (English) Daughter of Adam. *Adison, Addisen, Addisson, Addyson, Adyson, Adisen, Adysen*

Adelaide (German) Noble kind. *Adalia, Addie, Adela, Adelae, Adele, Adeleana, Adelena, Adelia, Adeline, Adelina, Adella, Adelle, Adelynn, Adelynne, Adie, Adilenna, Adiline, Adlin, Adlynn, Aline, Della*

Adelpha (Greek) Dear sister. *Adelphie*

Adena (Hebrew) Delicate. *Adina, Adinna, Adine, Adenna, Adeena, Aden*

Aderes (Latin) One who protects.

Adia (Swahili) Gift. *Addia, Adea, Adiah*

Adoette (Native American) Large tree. *Adooeette*

Adolfina (German) Noble wolf.

Adora (Latin) Beloved. *Adore, Adoree, Adoria, Dora*

Adrienne (Greek) Rich. (Latin) Dark. Feminine form of Adrian. *Adria, Adriane, Adrea, Adreah, Adrean, Adreana, Adreanah, Adreane, Adreann, Adreanna, Adreannah, Adreanne, Adreena, Adreenah, Adreene, Adria, Adriah, Adrian, Adrianah, Adrianne, Adrien, Adriena, Adrienah, Adriene, Adrienn, Adrienna, Adriennah, Adrina, Adrinah, Adrine, Adryan, Adryana, Adryanah, Adryane, Adryann, Adryannah*

Adsila (Native American) Blossom.

Aegle (Greek) Illuminated.

Aella (Irish) From Ireland. *Aellyn*

Aemilia (Latin) Rival. (German) Hard-working. Feminine form of Aemilius.

Affera (Hebrew) Young deer. *Affery, Aphra*

Affinity (Latin) Relationship by marriage.

Afra (Hebrew) Female deer. (Arabic) Color of the earth. *Affra, Affrey*

Afric (Irish) Pleasant. *Africa*

Afrodite (Greek) Goddess of love and beauty.

Afton (Old English) From the Afton River.

Agape (Greek) Love of the next.

Agata (Greek) Good. *Agatha, Agace, Agacia, Agafa, Agase, Agath, Agathi, Agathia, Agathie, Agatka, Agaue, Agethe, Aggie, Aggy, Agota, Agotha, Agueda, Akta, Agacia, Agafia*

Aglaia (Greek) Wisdom.

Agnes (Greek) Pure. *Adneda, Agenta, Aggie, Aggy, Agna, Agnella, Agnelle, Agnesa, Agnesca, Agnese, Agnessa, Agnesse, Agnessija, Agneta, Agnete, Agnetha, Agnetis, Agnette, Agnies, Agnieszka, Agnizika, Agnizica, Agnizka, Agnola, Aigneis, Agytha, Ameyce, Anis, Annais, Annes, Anneys, Anneyse, Annice, Annot, Annys, Ina, Ines, Inesila, Inessa, Inez, Nancy, Nesa, Nesta, Neza, Neziko, Ynes, Ynez*

Agrona (Old English) Goddess of strife and slaughter.

Ah lam (Chinese) Like an orchid. (Arabic) Witty, one who has pleasant dreams.

Naming Rights

Agnes is a Latin variation of the Greek word for "chaste." When Saint Agnes was martyred under Emperor Diocletian, the name became associated with the Latin word for "lamb"—*agnus*. That's why Saint Agnes is often depicted with a lamb by her side.

Ahava (Hebrew) Cherished one. *Ahave, Ahivia*

Ahmose (Hebrew) Mother of Hatshepsut.

Ai (Japanese) Love.

Aida (Old English) Joyful. *Aidah, Aidee, Aide*

Aidia (Spanish) Help.

Aiko (Japanese) Little loved one.

Aileen (Greek) Light; form of Helen. *Aila, Ailean, Aileana, Aileanah, Aileane, Ailee, Ailena, Ailenah, Ailene, Ailey, Alean, Aleana, Aleanah, Aleane, Aleen, Aleena, Aleenah, Aleene, Alena, Alene, Alina, Aline, Eilean, Eileana, Eileane, Eileen, Eileena, Eileene, Eilleen, Eleana, Eleanah, Eleane, Elena, Elenah, Elene, Ileana, Ileane, Ilina, Ilinah, Iline, Illean, Illeana, Illeanah, Illeane, Illian, Illiana, Illianah, Illiane, Illianna, Illiannah, Illianne, Leana, Leanah, Leane, Lena, Liana, Lianah, Lyan, Lyana, Lynah, Lyann, Lyanna, Lyannah, Lyanne*

Ailis (Irish) Honest.

Ailsa (Scottish) Island dweller; island of Alfsigr. *Ailis, Ailsha, Aylsah, Elsa, Elsha, Elshe*

Aimee (Latin) Beloved. *Ami, Amia, Amie, Amity*

Ainsley (Scottish) My meadow. *Aynsley, Ainsly, Ainslee, Ainsworth, Ainsleigh, Ainslie*

Aisha (Arabic) Life. *Aieshah, Aishah, Aisia, Ayeesha, Ayisha, Ayeisha*

Aislinn (Old English) Dream; form of Ashlyn. *Aislin, Aislyn, Aislynn, Aissah, Ayslin, Ayslinn, Ayslyn, Ayslynn, Ayssa, Ayssah*

Aissa (African) Grateful.

Aiyana (Native American) Eternal blossom.

Ajua (African) Born on Monday.

Akaisha (Irish) The akaisha flower.

Akako (Japanese) Red.

Akanah (Japanese) Red. *Akae, Akaho, Akane, Akari*

Akelah (Russian) She of fair skin.

Aki (Japanese) Autumn.

Akilah (Arabic) Intelligent. *Akeela, Akeelah, Akeila, Akeilah*

Akina (Japanese) Spring flower.

Akiva (Hebrew) Protect.

Akiyama (Japanese) Autumn mountain.

Akosua (African) Born on Sunday.

Akuti (Hindi) Princess.

Alair (French) Cheerful; version of Hillary. *Allaire*

Alameda (Native American) Grove of cottonwood.

Alana (Irish) Attractive, peaceful. (Hawaiian) Offering. Feminine form of Alan. *Alaina, Alanna, Allanah, Allannah, Alani, Alania, Alanis, Alyn, Allyn*

Alaqua (Native American) Sweet gum tree.

Alawa (Native American) Pea.

Alba (Latin) A thick or mass vegetation; feminine form of Albin. *Albany, Albine, Albani, Elba*

Alberta (German) Noble. (French) Bright. Feminine form of Albert. *Albertina, Albertyna*

Alcina (Greek) Strong-minded; name of a Greek enchantress. *Alceena, Alcine, Alsinia, Alzina*

Alcott (Old English) Old cottage. *Alcot, Walcott, Walcot*

Alden (Old English) Wise protector. *Aldan, Alldyn*

Aldora (Greek) Winged gift.

Aleshanee (Native American) She plays all the time.

Alethea (Greek) Truthful one. *Aletta, Alettah, Alithea, Alitheah, Alethia, Alithiah, Allathea, Allatheah, Allathia, Allathiah, Allethea, Alletheah, Allethia, Allethiah, Allythea, Allytheah, Allythia, Allythiah, Allythya, Allythyah, Alythea, Alytheah, Alythia, Alythiah, Alythya, Alythyah, Allethya, Allethyah*

Alexandra (Greek) Defender of mankind; feminine form of Alexander. *Alandra, Aleka, Alex, Alexa, Alexia, Alexis, Alexandria, Alexandrina, Alesandra, Alessa, Alessandra, Allesandra, Aleksey, Alexine, Alya, Aliki, Alejanda, Lexy, Lexie, Sandra, Zandra, Sanie, Sandy*

Alexandrite (Russian) Gemstone with special optical effects; named after Czar Alexander II.

Algoma (Native American) Valley of flowers.

Alice (German) Noble. (Greek) Truth. *Addala, Adelice, Adelicia, Ailis, Aleece, Aleese, Aletta, Alexis, Alicia, Aliceie, Aliciedik, Alicija, Alicija, Aliedik, Alika, Aliki, Ali, Alina, Aline, Aletta, Alisa, Alisan,*

Alise, Alisen, Alisin, Alison, Alisun, Alisyn, Alissa, Alisyn, Allie, Allisan, Allisen, Allisin, Allison, Allisun, Allisyn, Allyce, Ally, Allyse, Alyssa, Aliza, Alodia, Alse, Alyce, Alys, Alyse, Elice, Elise, Elisan, Elisen, Elisin, Elison, Elisun, Elisyn, Elsje, Ilyssa

Alida (Greek) Beautifully dressed. *Aleda, Aletta, Alette, Allida, Allidia, Alidia, Lida*

Alima (Arabic) Dancer. *Aleema, Aleemah, Alimah, Alyma, Alymah*

Alisha (Greek) Truthful. (German) Noble. *Aliscia, Alisea, Alishah, Alishay, Alishaye, Alishya, Alisyia, Alitsha, Allisia*

Alison (Irish) Of noble birth. *Aleason, Aleeson, Aleison, Aleighson, Alisan, Alisana, Alisanah, Alisen, Alisena, Alisenah, Alisin, Alisina, Alisinah, Alissa, Alissah, Alisson, Alissun, Alissyn, Alisun, Alisyn, Alisyna, Alisynah, Alisyne, Allisa, Allisah, Allisan, Allisanah, Allisen, Allisena, Allisenah, Allisin, Allisina, Allisinah, Allisine, Allison, Allisona, Allisonah, Allisone, Alliss, Allissa, Allisah, Allisun, Allisuna, Allisyn, Allysna, Allysyne, Alson, Alsona, Alsonah, Alsone, Alysan, Alysen, Alysena, Alysenah, Alysene, Alysin, Alysina, Alysinah, Alysine, Alyson, Alysonah, Alysone, Alysyn, Alysyna, Alysynah, Alysyne, Alyssa, Alyssah, Alysse, Alysun, Alysyn, Alyzan, Alyzana, Alyzane, Alyzen, Alyzena, Alyzene, Alyzin, Alyzina, Alyzine, Alyzyn, Alyzyn, Alyzyna, Alyzyne*

Alivia (English) Peace; form of Olivia. *Alivah*

Alixia (Greek) Defender of mankind; form of Alex. *Alixe, Allix, Alix, Alyx*

Aliye (Arabic) Noble. *Aliyeh*

Aliza (Hebrew) Joyous. *Aliz, Alizah, Alizee, Aliezah*

Alize (French) Gentle trade wind; name of a cognac.

Alka (Hindi) Girl with lovely hair. *Alaka*

Allaya (English) Highly exalted.

Allegra (Latin) Brisk and cheerful; a musical marking for a fast tempo.

Alleta (Scandinavian) Heroine; form of Halle.

Allirea (Aboriginal) Quartz.

Alma (Latin) Soul or nourishing. *Almah*

Aloani (Hindi) Cloud from heaven. (Hawaiian) Bright sky. Variation of *Aolani, Alohilani*

Aloha (Hawaiian) Love; Hawaiian form of "hello" and "good-bye."

Alohi (Hawaiian) Brilliant.

Alona (Hawaiian) Beautiful. *Alonnah, Alonya*

Aloysia (Old German) Famous in war.

Alsoomse (Native American) Independent.

Althea (Greek) Healer. *Allie, Alethea, Alithea, Altheah, Altheda, Althedah, Althia, Althiah, Althya, Althyah, Thea*

Altrina (Science fiction) Character from *Star Trek: Deep Space Nine*.

Aludra (Greek) Virgin.

Alumit (Hebrew) Secret.

Alva (Spanish) Fair complexion. *Alvah*

Alvina (Old English) Wise companion; feminine version of Alvin. *Alveen, Alveena, Alveenia, Alvenea, Alvinae, Alvine, Alvinea, Alvinia, Alvinna, Alvyna, Alwin, Alwyn*

Alyssa (Arabic) Moon goddess. *Alaysieh, Alaysia, Ahlyssa, Alissa, Allissa, Allyssa, Alyesa, Alyissa, Lasine*

Amadahy (Native American) Forest water.

Amanda (Latin) Love. *Amandah, Amandi, Amandy, Amanada, Mandy, Mandie*

Amara (Greek) Eternal beauty. *Amar, Amarah, Amari, Amaira, Amariah*

Amarante (Japanese) Flower that never fades.

Amari (Hindi) Immortal. *Amarta*

Amarie (English) Gracious under adversity.

Amaris (English) Child of the moon. *Amarys, Maris*

Amaya (Japanese) Night rain.

Amber (Arabic) Jewel. *Ambar, Ambarlea, Ambarlee, Ambarlei, Ambarleigh, Ambarley, Ambarli, Ambarlina, Ambarline, Ambarlie, Ambarly, Amberlea, Amberlee, Amberlei, Amberleigh, Amberley, Amberli, Amberlia, Amberliah, Amberlie, Amberlina, Amberline, Amberly, Amberlyah, Ambur, Amburlea, Amburlee, Amberlei, Amburleigh, Amburley, Amburli, Amburlia, Amburliah, Amburlie, Amburlina, Amburline, Amburly, Amburlya*

Ambrosia (Greek) Immortal; food of the gods. *Ambrosa, Ambrosiah*

Amelia (German) Industrious. *Amala, Amalah, Amalburga, Amalea, Amaleah, Amalee, Amaleigh, Amaleta, Amalia, Amali, Amalie, Amalita, Amalitah, Amela, Amelie, Amelija, Amelina, Amelinda, Amelindah, Ameline, Amelita, Amelitah, Amelynda, Amelyndah, Amilia, Amiliah, Amilina, Amiline, Amilinda, Amiline, Amilita, Amilitah, Ammilina, Ammileine, Amylia, Amyliah, Amylaya, Amylyah, Emelin, Emelia, Emelina, Emeline, Emelita, Emelitah, Emmelina,*

Emmeline, Emmilyn, Emmilyna, Emmilyne

Amerie (German) Industrious leader.

Amethyst (Greek) Wine, purple-violet gemstone believed to prevent drunkenness.

Ami (Hindi) Nectar. *Aami, Amii*

Amiable (Middle English) Good natured, likable.

Amina (Arabic) Trustworthy. *Aamena, Aamina, Aaminah, Ameena, Ameenah, Aminah, Aminda*

Aminta (Greek) The protector.

Amissa (Hebrew) Friend.

Amitola (Native American) Rainbow.

Amity (Latin) Friendly. *Amitee, Amitey, Amiti, Amitie, Amity, Amytee, Amytey, Amyti, Amytie, Amyty*

Amory (Latin) Loving; for girl or boy. *Emory, Emery*

Amour (French) Love.

Amphitrite (Greek) A sea goddess.

Amriel (Latin) Angel of the month of May.

Amy (Latin) Beloved. *Aime, Aimee, Aimey, Aimi, Aimia, Aimiah, Aimie, Aimy, Aimya, Aimyah, Amata, Amatah, Ame, Amee, Amei, Amey, Ami, Amia, Amiah, Amie, Amice, Amie, Amity, Amorett, Amoretta, Amorette, Amorita, Amoritta, Amorittah, Amoritta, Amoritte, Amoryt, Amoryta, Amorytah, Amoryte, Amorytt, Amorytta, Amoryttah, Amorytte*

An (Chinese) Peaceful.

Anaba (Native American) She turns from battle.

Anais (pronounced *AH-na-ees*) (Hebrew) Gracious. *Anaise*

Anan (Arabic) Clouds.

Anani (Hawaiian) Orange blossoms. *Nani*

Anara (Arabic) Pomegranate flower. *Anargu*

Anastasia (Greek) Resurrection. *Anastacia, Anastace, Anastice, Anastise, Anastiaciah, Anastacya, Anastacyah, Anastas, Anastase, Anastasee, Anastasie, Anastatia, Anestasia, Anastassia, Anastazia, Anastziah, Anastazya, Annestas, Annestasia, Annestassia, Anstace, Ansteece, Ansteese, Anstes, Anstey, Anstice, Anstice, Anstis, Natasha, Tasia, Tasha*

Andrea (Greek) Strong and brave; feminine form of Andrew. *Aindrea, Anderea, Andra, Andrah, Andreana, Andreanah, Andreane, Andreann, Andreanna, Andreannah, Andreanne, Andree, Andreean, Andreeana, Andree-anah, Andreeane, Andrel, Andrela, Andrelah, Andrell, Andrella, Andrellah, Andrelle, Andretta, Andrette, Andria, Andriah, Andrian, Andriann, Andrianna, Andriannah, Andrianne, Andrina, Adrinah, Andrya, Andryah, Andryan, Andryana, Andryanah, Andryanem Abdryann, Andryanna, Andryannah, Andryanne, Andryane, Andrena*

Andromache (Greek) Mythology. Andromache, wife of Hector, became Queen of Epirius. (Shakespearean) *Troilus and Cressida.*

Andromeda (Greek) Beautiful maiden rescued by Perseus.

Aneesa (Arabic) Of good company.

Aneko (Japanese) Older sister.

Anezka (Slavic) Pure.

Angela (Greek) Heavenly messenger. *Agnola, Aindrea, Ancela, Ange, Angel, Angele, Angell, Angella, Angellah, Angelica, Angelika, Angelin, Angelina,*

Angelinah, Angeline, Angeliqua, Angeliquah, Angelique, Angelle, Angelita, Angiola, Angelo, Aniela, Anja, Anjah, Anjal, Anjala, Anjalah, Anjel, Anjela, Anjelah, Anjella, Anjelle, Engel, Engela, Engelah, Enjele, Engelchen, Engelica, Engelika, Engell, Engella, Engellah, Engelle, Engelyca, Engelycka, Engelyka, Engeliqua, Engeliquah, Engelique, Enjel, Enjela, Enjelah, Enjele, Enjell, Enjella, Enjellah, Enjelle, Enjelliqua, Enjelliquah, Enjellique, Enjellyca, Enjellycah, Enjellycka, Enjellyka, Enjellyqua, Enjellyquah, Enjellyque

Angeni (Native American) Spirit.

Anisa (Arabic) Friendly.

Anita (Hebrew) Graceful. *Anitta, Anittah, Anitte, Annita, Annitah, Annite, Annitt, Annitta, Annittah, Annitte, Annyta, Annytah, Annytta, Annyttah, Annytte*

Anjali (Hindi) Offering with both hands.

Ann (Hebrew) Gift of God's favor. *Anabel, Anca, Anke, Ani, Ann, Anna, Anne, Anneka, Anica, Anicah, Anika, Anikah, Aniqua, Aniquah, Anita, Annchen, Annette, Annabel, Annabella, Annabelle, Annia, Annice, Annie, Annis, Annuska, Annys, Anya, Anyca, Anycah, Anyka, Anykah, Anyqua, Anyquah, Bella, Hannah*

Annabeth (English) Favor. A devout woman who saw infant Jesus presented at the temple in Jerusalem. Combination of Anna and Beth. *Anabeth*

Annalynn (English) Beautiful daughter. Combination of Anna and Lynn. *Annalynne, Analyn, Analynne*

Anneliese (German) Graceful satisfaction. *Analisa, Analise, Anetta, Analiese, Annalisa, Annalise, Annalyce, Annalyca, Annalys, Annalysa, Annalyse, Anneliese,*

Anneliesel, Annelys, Annelysa, Annelyse

Anstice (Greek) One who will rise again.

Antje (German) Grace.

Antlia (Latin) Air pump, a constellation.

Antonia (Greek) Flourishing. (Latin) Praiseworthy. Feminine form of Anthony. *Antonett, Antonetta, Antonette, Antoni, Antoniah, Antonias, Antonica, Antonicah, Antonie, Antoinette, Antonietta, Antoninas, Antonnia, Antonniah, Antonya, Antonyah, Toinetta, Toynetta, Toni, Tonia, Tonya, Toinette, Toynette, Tuanetta, Tueanette*

Anuradha (Hindi) Name of a star.

Anusha (Hindi) Beautiful morning.

Anya (Russian) Form of Anna. *Aaniyah, Aniya, Aniyah, Anja*

Anysia (Greek) Complete.

Anzan (Japanese) Quiet mountain.

Anzu (Japanese) Apricot.

Aoi (Japanese) Hollyhock.

Aparna (Hindi) Goddess Parvati.

Aphrodite (Greek) Goddess of love. *Afrodita, Afrodite, Aphrodita, Aphrodyta, Aphrodytah, Aphrodyte*

Aponi (Native American) Butterfly.

Apphia (Hebrew) Fruitful.

Apple (American) Popular fruit.

April (Latin) Blooming. *Aprel, Aprela, Aprelah, Aprella, Aprelle, Aprila, Aprilah, Aprilett, Apriletta, Aprilette, Aprill, Aprilla, Aprillah, Aprille, Apryl, Apryla, Aprylah, Apryll, Aprylla, Aprylle, Ava, Avril, Avrilett, Avriletta, Avrilette, Avryl, Avryla, Avrylah, Avryle, Avryll, Avrylla, Avryllah, Avrylle, Avryleett, Avryletta, Avryllettah, Avryllette*

Apus (Greek) Footless; a constellation.

Aqualina (Latin) Tender waters.

Aquamarine (Latin) A gemstone and color.

Aquene (Native American) Peace.

Ara (Arabic) Embellishing. *Aara, Aira, Arae, Arah, Araya*

Arabelle (German) Beautiful eagle. *Arabel, Arabele, Arabella, Arabela*

Arali (Greek) A name for the netherworld.

Araminta (English) Combined form of Arabella and Aminta; Character in *The Man Who Laughs* by eighteenth-century playwright Victor Hugo. (Hebrew) Lofty.

Arantxa (Old English) Thornbush.

Arashel (Hebrew) Strong and protected.

Arbor (Latin) Herb garden.

Arden (Latin) Passionate; for girl or boy. *Ardelia, Ardis, Ardon*

Ardeshir (Persian) A character in *Shanameh*, eleventh-century "Epic of Kings" by Firdowski.

Ardys (English) Warm.

Arella (Hebrew) Angel messenger.

Aretha (Greek) Virtuous. *Areata, Areatah, Areatha, Areathah, Areathia, Areathiah, Areeta, Areetah, Areetha, Areethah, Areethia, Areethiah, Areta, Aretah, Arethia, Arethiah, Aretta, Arettah, Arette, Aritha, Arithah, Arytha, Arythah, Arythia, Arythiah, Arythya, Arythyah, Retha, Rethah*

Aria (German) Melody. *Ari, Ariah, Ariann, Arianna, Ariannah, Arianne, Arya, Aryah, Aryan, Aryana, Aryanah, Aryane, Aryann, Aryanna, Aryannah, Aryanne*

Ariadne (Greek) The mythological daughter of King Minos of Crete. *Arianne, Arianna, Aria*

Ariana (Old English) Silver. (Greek) Holy. *Ariadne, Ariane, Arianna, Arianne, Arionna, Arriana, Ariane*

Ariel (Hebrew) Lion of God. *Arael, Arial, Aryel, Ario, Ari, Ariella, Ariela*

Aril (Latin) Bright seed cover.

Arissa (Greek) Best. *Arista*

Arleigh (Old English) Meadow of the hare.

Arlene (Irish) Pledge. *Arleen, Arline, Arlette, Arlynn, Arlyn, Arleine*

What's in a Name

In Greek mythology, **Ariadne** was the daughter of King Minos of Crete. She fell in love with Theseus and offered to give him a way out of the labyrinth if he promised to marry her. She provided a map and a thread for him to find his way out, but Theseus didn't live up to his end of the bargain and ditched her once they left Crete. Ariadne's still a pretty name, no matter what her track record.

Arlington (Place name) Arlington, Virginia.

Armani (African) Faith.

Arnon (Hebrew) Rushing stream; also a boy's name.

Arrietty (German) Home ruler; version of Harriet. *Arietta*

Artemia (Greek) Gift from Artemis. *Artemesia*

Artemis (Greek) Moon goddess.

Artis (Scottish) Bear. *Arthea, Arthelia, Arthette, Artice, Artina*

Aruna (Hindi) Dawn. *Aruni*

Arva (Latin) From the seashore.

Arziki (African) Prosperity.

Asa (Japanese) Born in the morning.

Ascah (Hebrew) Anklet.

Asenath (Hebrew) She belongs to her father.

Asenka (Hebrew) Graceful.

Asha (African) Life.

Ashanti (African) Thank you. *Asante, Achante, Achanti, Ashantae, Ashante, Ashantee, Ashantie, Ashauntae, Ashaunta, Ashaunti, Ashonti, Ashuntae, Ashunti*

Ashland (English) Place name.

Ashley (Old English) Ash tree; for girl or boy. *Ash, Ashe, Ashby, Ashford, Ashia, Ashiah, Ashla, Ashlana, Ashlanah, Ashlane, Ashlaney, Ashlea, Ashleah, Ashlee, Ashlei, Ashleigh, Ashlen, Ashlena, Ashlenah, Ashlene, Ashli, Ashlia, Ashliah, Ashlie, Ashlin, Ashlina, Ashlinah, Ashline, Ashling, Ashly, Ashlya, Ashlyah*

Asisa (Hebrew) Ripe.

Aspen (Old English) Tree. *Aspin, Aspyn*

Astrid (Greek) Star. (Old Norse) Super strength. *Asta, Astra, Astera, Astrah, Astrea, Astreah, Astred, Astree, Astrey, Astriah, Astrya, Astryah, Astyr*

Atara (Hebrew) A crown. *Atarah, Ataree*

Athaliah (Biblical) The time of the Lord.

Athena (Greek) Goddess of war. *Atheana, Atheanah, Athenah, Athene, Athenais, Atherlea, Atherleah, Atherlee, Atherlei,*

Atherleigh, Atherley, Atherli, Atherlia, Atherliah, Atherlie, Atherly, Atherlya, Atherlyah

Atlanta (American) Immoveable; place name. *Atalanta*

Atropos (Greek) One of the three Moirae, the Fates, the female deities who supervised fate rather than determined it. Atropos was the Fate who cut the thread or web of life.

Aubrey (German) Elf rule. *Aubree, Aubrie, Auberi, Aubary, Aubre, Aubrei, Aubreigh, Aubri, Aubry, Aubury, Aubray, Aubrea, Aubree, Aubery, Aubria*

Auburn (Latin) Fair. *Alban, Aubin*

Audrey (Old English) Noble strength. *Audey, Audie, Audra, Audrah, Audre, Audree, Audri, Audria, Audriah, Audrie, Audry, Audrye, Audrea, Audree, Audrya, Audryah, Etheldreda*

Augusta (Latin) Exalted. *Augustine, Augustina, Augie, Augustus, Augusta, Gus, Gussy, Gussie, Gusta*

Aulii (Hawaiian) Exquisite.

Aung Sun (Burmese) For father.

Aurelia (Latin) Gold. *Aurora, Aurea, Aurore, Aurelie*

Aureliano (Spanish) Golden.

Aurora (Greek) Goddess of the dawn. *Aurorah, Aurore, Aurure, Ora, Orah*

Autumn (Latin) Of woods. *Autum*

Ava (Latin) Birdlike. *Avalee, Avelina, Aveline, Avelyn, Avis, Avlynn, Avada, Avae, Aveen*

Avalon (Latin) Island. *Avalona, Avalonah, Avaloni, Avalonia, Avaloniah, Avalonie, Avalony, Avalonya, Avalonyah*

Avel (Greek) Breath.

Avery (English) Counselor.

Aviva (Hebrew) Springtime. *Avital, Avi, Avia, Avivah*

Avon (Old English) The river.

Avril (French) Month of April. *Averel, Averell, Averil, Averyl*

Awendela (Native American) Morning.

Ayala (Hebrew) Gazelle.

Ayame (Japanese) Iris.

Ayana (African) Beautiful flower. (Hindi) Innocent. *Ayanna, Ahyana, Ayan, Ayania, Ayna*

Ayasha (Arabic) Mohammed's wife. (Native American) Little one. *Ayesha*

Ayita (Native American) Worker.

Ayla (Hebrew) Oak tree. *Aylah, Aylana, Aylanah, Aylanna, Aylannah, Aylea, Aylee, Ayleena, Aylena, Aylene*

Aylin (Turkish) Moon halo.

Ayn (Hebrew) Prayer.

Azalea (Arabic) Democracy.

Azarin (Persian) Chamomile flower.

Azura (Persian) Sky blue. *Azure*

Azure (Biblical) He who assists; also a boy's name.

B

Baako (African) First-born.

Babette (French) Stranger. *Babbette, Babbie, Babeta, Babetta, Babs, Babita, Babidjana, Babet, Babetah, Babett, Babettah, Babittah*

Badriya (Muslim) Resembling the full moon.

Bailey (French) Bailiff. (Old English) Fortification. *Baily, Bayley, Bailee, Baylee, Bailea, Baileah, Bailel, Bailli*

Bambi (Italian) Child; little doll. *Bambino, Bambea, Bambee, Bambia, Bambiah, Bambie, Bamby, Bambya*

Bameket Origin and meaning unknown.

Bankei (Japanese) Ten thousand blessings.

Banu (Turkish) Woman. *Bano*

Bao (Chinese) Treasure; precious.

Bara (Hebrew) To choose. *Barra, Barah, Bára, Barra, Barrah*

Barbara (Latin) Foreign, strange. *Barbra, Barbro, Bararella, Barbie, Barby, Barbs, Barb, Babette, Babs, Bobbie*

Barika (Swahili) Bloom. *Barikah, Baryka, Barykah*

Basalt (Greek) Hard, dark, igneous rock.

Basanti (Hindi) Spring.

Basha (Hebrew) Daughter of God. *Basia, Batyah, Bashiah, Bashya, Bashyah, Basiah, Basya, Basyah, Bathia, Batia, Batya*

Bashira (Arabic) Joyful, happy. *Bashiga, Basheera, Bashirah*

Basilissa (Greek) Regal; feminine form of Basil. *Basile, Basilla*

Basimah (Arabic) Smile. *Basmah*

Bathsheba (Hebrew) Daughter of the oath. *Batsheva, Bathshua, Batya, Sheba, Batshevah, Bersaba, Bethsabee, Bethsheba*

Beata (Latin) Blessed. *Beatah, Beatta, Beeta, Beetah, Beita, Beitah, Beyta, Beytah*

Beatrice (Latin) Happy. *Beatrix, Beatriz, Bea, Beah, Beattie, Beatirsa, Trixie, Beezus, Beate, Beatty*

Becky (Hebrew) To tie, bind; enchantingly beautiful. *Rebecca, Becka, Becki, Beckie, Bekki, Ree,*

Riba, Rivalee, Rivi, Rivkah, Rivy, Becca, Reba, Rebeca, Rebeka, Rebekah, Reeba, Riva

Bedegrayne (English) From *The Legend of King Arthur*; infamous castle and forest where Arthur fought his battle against 11 kings. *Bedgraine*

Bedelia (French) Strength; mighty. (Irish) High goddess. *Bedeelia, Bedeliah, Bedelya, Bedelyah, Biddy, Bidelia*

Bela (Czechoslovakian) White. (Hungarian) Bright. *Belah, Belau, Belia, Beliah, Biela*

Belinda (Spanish) Beautiful. *Belynda, Belle, Linda, Bella, Belva, Beauty, Bellini, Belita, Bell, Belladonna, Belva, Belvia, Balina, Balinah, Balinda, Ballinda, Ballindah*

Bellona (Latin) The Roman goddess of war.

Bena (Hebrew) One of wisdom. *Benay, Benah, Benea, Benna, Bennah*

Benazir (Muslim) Incomparable.

Benedetta (Latin) Blessed. *Benita, Bente, Benetta, Benita*

Berit (German) Glorious, splendid, strength.

Berlynn (German) Bear. *Berlin, Berlinn, Berlyn, Berla, Berlinda, Berline, Berling, Berlync, Berlynne*

Bernadette (French) Brave as a bear. (English) Intelligent. Feminine version of Bernard. *Bern, Bernie, Bernadete, Berna, Bernadina, Berneta, Bernetta, Berni, Bernadine, Burnice, Burney, Burnette*

Bernice (Greek) Bringer of victory. *Berenice, Berry, Bunny, Berta, Berti, Bernica, Bernise, Bernyc, Bernyce, Bernyse, Bernicia*

Bertha (Saxon, Germanic) Glorious, beautiful. *Berti, Bertina, Bertie, Birtha, Birthe, Byrth, Byrtha, Byrthah*

Beryl (Hebrew) Jewel. *Berel, Beril, Berila, Berile, Berill, Berille, Berylla, Berylle*

Bess (Hebrew) God's oath; dedicated. *Bette, Betty, Elizabeth, Bestey, Belita, Besse, Bessie, Bessy, Betta, Betti, Bettine, Ealasidde, Elizabet, Elsabet, Elisabeth, Elisabetta, Elise, Elissa, Eilise, Elisa, Eliza, Elsa, Elsbeth, Babette, Belle, Beth, Bettina, Bet, Beta*

Bethany (Hebrew) House of mercy. *Betheny, Bethesda, Bethel*

Bettina (Hebrew) House of God. (Spanish) Majestic. Combination of Beth and Tina. *Betina, Betine, Bettyne, Betyne*

Beulah (Hebrew) Married. *Beula, Beulla, Beullah*

Beverly (Old English) Meadow of beavers. *Beverley, Beverlee, Beverely, Bev, Beverle, Beverlea, Beverleah, Beverleigh*

Beyonce (African American) Beyond others.

Bharati (Hindi) Goddess of knowledge and arts.

Bhuma (Hindi) Earth. *Bhoomi*

Bianca (Italian) White; fair. *Biancha, Blanche, Blancha, Blanca, Branca, Blanch, Blake, Biancca, Biancia, Bianco*

Bibi (Arabic) Lady. *Bibiyana, Bibiana, BeBe, Beebee, Byby*

Billie (English) Resolution; wise. *Billy, Bille, Billye, Billea, Billeah, Bilee, Bilei, Bileigh, Biley, Byli, Bylli, Bylly, Byly*

Bina (Hindi) A musical instrument. (Hebrew) Intelligence, understanding. *Sabina, Binah, Binney, Binta, Bintah, Byna, Bynah*

Bindiya (Hindi) Drop or point.

Binney (German) From the name Bingham: kettle-shaped hollow. *Bin, Bing, Binnie, Binnee, Binni, Binny*

Birdee (English) Birdlike. *Birdie, Bird, Birde, Birdea, Birdella, Birdena, Birdey, Birdi, Birdy*

Birgit (Irish) Defender. *Birgitte, Birgita, Birkita, Birget, Bergeta, Birgitt, Birgitta*

Bisa (African) Greatly loved.

Blaine (Gaelic) Lean. (Old English) Source of a river. *Blain, Blane*

Blair (Gaelic) Plain. *Blaire, Blare, Blayr, Blayre*

Blase (Latin) One who stammers. *Blaise, Blaze, Blais, Blaisia, Blaiz, Blaize, Blasha, Blasia, Blayse, Blayze, Blaza, Blazena, Blazia*

Bliss (English) Perfect joy. *Blis, Blisa, Blisasa, Blisse, Blys, Blysa, Blyss, Blyssa, Blysse*

Bloodstone (Greek) Green with red spots; the martyr's stone.

Blossom (Old English) Lovely.

Blue Angel (American) A sad angel.

Bluma (German) Flower. *Blooma*

Bly (Native American) Tall child.

Blythe (Old English) Joyous. *Blithe, Bligh, Bliss*

Bo (Norse) To live or dwell. (Hebrew) Strong and fast. (Scandinavian) Commanding. *Beau, Bow*

Bohdana (Russian) From God.

Bonnie (Scottish) Good. *Bonny, Boni, Boniface, Bonita, Bonnibel, Bonifacy, Bonea, Bonee, Boney, Bonne, Bonnell, Bonney, Bonni, Bonniah, Bonnin*

Bracha (Hebrew) A blessing.

Brandie (Dutch) A fiery spirit distilled from wine. (American) Sweet nectar. *Brandy, Brandee, Brandi, Branwen, Bronwen, Bronwyn, Brandea, Branddeece, Brandei, Brandyse*

Brea (Old English) Thin broth. *Bree, Bri, Breah, Breeah*

Breck (Irish) Freckled. *Breckin, Brecklyn, Brecklynn*

Breena (Irish) Fairy land. *Breenah, Breene, Breenea, Breenia, Breeniah, Breina, Breinah*

Brena (Irish) Raven; maiden with dark hair. *Brenna, Brenah, Brenie, Brenin, Brenn, Brennah, Brennaugh, Brenne*

Brenda (Old English) Sword. (Irish) Little raven. Feminine of Brandon; fiery hill. *Branda, Brynna, Bren, Brendie, Breonna, Brendah, Brendyl, Brennda, Brenndah, Brinda, Brindah, Brynnda, Brynndah*

Brice (Irish) Swift. (English) Son of a nobleman. *Bryce, Brick, Bristol, Brixey, Brixie*

Bridget (Irish) Resolute, strong. *Brigetta, Brigette, Brigitte, Brighid, Brigid, Britta, Brita, Britte, Brit, Biddy, Brie, Bree, Birgit, Birgitta, Brigada, Brigida, Brigita, Birgit, Brietta, Breanna, Brianna, Briana, Brianne, Brienne, Bryanne, Brid*

C

What's in a Name

Traditionally male or female names often become popular for the other gender after a well-known character or celebrity adopts it. **Brett**, for example, was historically a boy's name (and we list it in the "Boy Names" section), but became acceptable for girls after Ernest Hemingway named his female character Brett in *The Sun Also Rises*.

Brittany (English) Anglicized version of Bretagne, a section of France; from Britain. *Brita, Britta, Brittney, Brittny, Britny, Britannia, Britain, Britany, Britaney, Britt, Brittania, Britnee*

Brook (Old English) Stream. *Brooke, Brooks, Brookes, Brookie, Burne, Bhrooke, Brookee, Brookelle, Brookia*

Bruna (German) Brunette. (Yiddish) Brown. *Brona*

Bryn (Welsh) Hill. *Brynne, Brynhil, Brunhild, Brunhilde*

Bryony (English) Vine with small blossoms. *Brionie, Bryoni, Bryonee, Bryoney, Bryoni, Bryonia*

Buffy (Old English) Consecrated to God. *Bufee, Bufey, Buffee, Buffey, Buffi, Buffie, Buffye, Bufi, Bufie, Bufy*

Bunita (Australian) Meaning unknown.

Burnet (Modern English) Burnette.

Cacey (Irish) Vigilant. (African) Favorite. Variation of Casey. *Cace, Cacee, Cacia, Cacie, Cacy, Casee, Kacey, Kaci, Kacie, Kacy, Kasey, Kasie, Kassie, Kaycee, Kecia, Keesha, Keisha, Kesha, Keshia, Kesia, Kisha, Kizzy*

Cady (American) Simple happiness. (Old English) Rhythmic flow of sounds. Possibly a combination of Katy and Cody. *Cade, Cadee, Cadey, Cadi, Cadie, Cadye, Caidie, Kade, Kadee, Kadi, Kadie, Kady, Kayde*

Caitlin (Irish) Pure beauty; variation of Catherine. *Caitlyn, Kaitlin, Kaitlyn, Katelyn, Kaytlin, Catalina, Catelyn, Caitlan, Caitlynn*

Cala (Arabic) Castle.

Calandra (Greek) Lark; Calinda and Calynda are contemporary variants or blends with Linda. *Cal, Calandre, Calandia, Calandria, Calendre, Calinda, Callee, Calley, Cally, Calynda, Kalandra, Cayla, Ceil, Celia, Chloe, Cielo, Cleo*

Calantha (Greek) Beautiful blossoms. *Calanthe, Kalantha*

Calcite (Latin) Burnt lime; gray, colorless.

Calendula (Latin) Flower that blooms every month of the year.

Calista (Greek) Most beautiful. *Cala, Calesta, Calissa, Calisto, Calla, Callia, Callesta, Callista, Calliste, Callysta, Calyssa, Calysta, Kala, Kalesta, Kalista, Kalla, Kallesta, Kalli, Kallie, Kallista, Kally, Kallysta, Celeste, Celestine*

Callan (German) Chatter. (Irish) Powerful in battle. *Callen, Calynn, Kallan*

Calliope (Greek) Beautiful voice. *Callia, Callyope, Kalliope*

Callis (Latin) Cup. *Callys*

Calpurnia (Shakespearean) From *The Tragedy of Julius Caesar*.

Cambria (Latin) From Wales. *Cambaria, Cambree, Cambrie, Kambria*

Cameo (English, Italian, Latin) An engraved gem. *Cammeo, Kamea*

Camera (American) Photographic device.

Cameron (Old English) Bent nose. *Camm, Cam, Cami, Cammie, Camyron, Camryn*

Camille (Latin) Attendant at a religious ceremony. *Caimile, Camilla, Camila, Camelia, Camillia, Cammilla, Cammie, Cammy, Kamilla, Kamille, Mila*

Camira (Aboriginal) Of the wind.

Campbell (Latin) Beautiful field. (Scottish) Crooked mouth. *Cambel, Cambell, Kampbell*

Camry (Brand name) Model of a Toyota car.

Candace (Ethopian) Brilliantly white. (Greek) White-hot. *Candaice, Candase, Candayce, Candee, Candi, Candice, Candie, Candis, Candiss, Candys, Candyce, Dace, Dacee, Dacey, Dacie, Dacy, Kandace, Kandice, Kandiss, Kandy*

Candida (Latin) Bright; glowing white. *Candi, Candide, Candie, Candy*

Candra (Latin) Luminescent. (Greek) Pure and chaste. Variation of Candace.

Capri (Anglo-Saxon) Unpredictable, whimsical; variation on Caprice. *Capree, Caprey, Caprie, Capry*

Caprial Origin and meaning unknown.

Caprice (Italian) Fanciful.

Capreece, Capri, Capriana, Capricia, Caprise, Capryce

Cara (Latin) Dear. (Irish) Friend. (Italian) Beloved one. (Vietnamese) Diamond. *Carah, Caralie, Careen, Canna, Carine, Carita, Kara, Carra, Karra, Caragh, Caera*

Carey (Latin) Dear. (Irish) Pure. (Spanish) Dear. (Welsh) Near the castle. *Cari, Carie, Cary, Carry, Carrey, Carrie, Kerry, Kerrie*

Carin (Irish) Friend. (Italian) Beloved one. *Caryn, Caren, Karena, Karin, Karina, Karine, Karyn*

Carina (Greek) Pure. (Latin) Little darling. Variation of Catherine. *Careena, Careenna, Caaren, Cariana, Carinna, Caryna, Carynna, Kareena*

Carisa (Latin) Most beloved one. (Greek) Grace. *Caresa, Carrisa, Carissa, Caressa, Carisse, Carita, Charissa, Karisa, Karissa, Kharissa*

Carla (Latin) Strong one. (Old German) Freeholder. Feminine form of Carl. *Carlah, Carlana, Carlee, Carleen, Carleigh, Carlena, Carlene, Carletta, Carlette, Carley, Carlia, Carleigh, Carlina, Carlisa, Carlita, Carlla, Carlyn, Karlla, Karla, Karlie, Karly, Karleen, Carilla, Carlin*

Carlotta (Italian) Valiant, strong, free. (Spanish) Little and womanly. Variation of Charlotte or Caroline. *Carlota, Charlotta, Karlotte, Charlie, Charley, Lotta, Lottie, Lotty, Tottie, Totty*

Carmel (Hebrew) Garden or field of fruit. *Carmela, Carmelina, Canneline, Carmelita, Cannella, Carmen, Carma, Carmia, Carmelina, Carmeline, Carmelita, Carmella, Carmelle, Carmia, Carmiel, Carmina,*

Carmine, Carmita, Karmel, Karmela, Karmelita, Karmelle, Kamelit, Karmen, Lina, Lita, Melina, Mell, Melli, Mellie, Melly

Carnelian (Latin) Red gem.

What's in a Name

Ever wonder why Carmen Miranda's signature style included a hat full of tropical fruits? The name **Carmen** is most popular in Spanish-speaking countries, although the word is Hebrew for "garden" or "field of fruit." The crazy fruit-filled hat makes sense now, doesn't it?

Cornelian

Carol (English) Song. (Old German) Freeholder. English feminine form of Carolus. Originally a short form of Caroline; feminine form of Charles. *Carel, Carline, Caro, Carola, Carole, Caroll, Caroly, Carri, Carrola, Carroll, Caryl, Caryll, Karel, Kari, Karla, Karleen, Karli, Karlie, Karlina, Karlinka, Karlote, Karlotta, Karol, Karole, Karola, Karyl, Karyll, Karryl, Karryll, Kerril, Kerryl, Keryl*

Caroline (French) Little and strong; feminine form of Charles. *Caraleen, Caraleena, Caraline, Caralyn, Caralyne, Caralynn, Carilyn, Carilynne, Carolan, Carolann, Carolanne, Caroliana, Carolin, Carolina, Carolyn, Carolyne, Carolynn, Carolynne, Carollyn, Karaleen, Karaleena, Karalina, Karaline, Karalyn, Karalynna, Karalynne, Karoline, Karolinka, Karolyn, Karolyna, Karolyne, Karolynn, Karolynne, Leena, Lina, Sharla,*

Sharkeen, Sharlena, Sharlene, Sharline, Sharlyne

Caron (Welsh) Loving, kind. (French) Pure. Variation of Karen. *Caryn, Caren, Carin, Carren, Carron*

Carys (Welsh) To love.

Casey (Irish) Vigilant, watchful. *Cacey, Cacia, Cacie, Caisee, Caisey, Caisi, Caisie, Casee, Casi, Casie, Caycee, Caycey, Cayci, Caycie, Caysee, Caysey, Caysi, Caycie, Kaysey, Kaysi, Kaysie, Kaysy, Kaysyee*

Casmir (Slavic) Peacemaker.

Cassandra (Greek) The original prophet of doom in classical mythology. *Cassandre, Casandra, Cassaundra, Casandera, Cassandrea, Cassandry, Cassondra, Cassy, Cassia, Kasandera, Kassandra, Kassi, Kassie, Kassy, Kassia, Kass, Sande, Sandee, Sandera, Sandra, Sandy, Sandi, Sandie, Saundra, Sohndra, Sondra, Zandra*

Cassidy (Irish) Curly headed; clever. *Cassady, Cassidey, Kassadey, Kassidy, Kassodey*

Cassiel (Latin) Angel of Saturday; earthy mother.

Cassietta (African American) Cassietta George, "Queen of Good Gospel Music," Grammy Award–winning gospel singer in 1960s and 1970s.

Cassiopeia (Greek) Mother of Andromeda; clever. *Cassiopia, Kassioleia, Kassiopia*

Catava (African) Sleep.

Catera (Modern English) Blessed, pure. (Brand name) Model of a Cadillac car. *Katera, Katara, Katerra*

Cathay (Khitay) Name of semi-nomadic people who dominated northern China in tenth through twelfth centuries.

Catherine (Greek) Pure. *Cait, Caitey, Caitie, Caitlin, Caitlinn, Caitrin, Caitrine, Caitrinn, Caitriona, Caitrionagh, Caity, Cat, Cataleen, Catarina, Catarine, Cate, Cateline, Caterina, Catey, Catha, Cathaleen, Cathaline, Catharin, Cathatina, Catharine, Cathatyna, Catharyne, Cathe, Cathee, Cathelin, Cathelina, Cathelle, Catherin, Catherina, Catherinn, Catheryn, Cathi, Cathie, Cathirin, Cathiryn, Cathleen, Cathlene, Cathline, Cathlyne, Cathrine, Cathrinn, Cathryn, Cathrynn, Cathy, Cathye, Cathyleen, Catlina, Catlaina, Catriona, Catrionagh, Catryna, Cay, Caye, Cazzy, Ekaterina, Kait, Kaitey, Kaitie, Kaitlin, Kaitlinne, Kaitrin, Kaitrine, Kaitrinna, Kaitriona, Kaitrionaugh, Kasienka, Kasja, Kaska, Katarina, Katchen, Kate, Katee, Katell, Katelle, Katenka, Katerina, Katerinka, Katey, Katinka, Katha, Katharine, Katharyn, Katharyne, Kathee, Kathelina, Katheline, Katherin, Katherina, Katherine, Katheryn, Katherynn, Kathi, Kathie, Kathileen, Kathiryn, Kathleen, Kathlene, Kathleyn, Kathline, Kathyleen, Kathrine, Kathrinna, Kathryn, Kathryne, Kathy, Kathyrine, Katica, Katie, Katina, Katka, Katla, Katlaina, Katleen, Katoushka, Katrena, Katrine, Katrina, Katriona, Katrionaugh, Katryna, Katushka, Katy, Katya, Kittee, Kittie, Kitty, Trina, Trine, Trinette, Yekaterin, Yekaterina*

Catori (Hopi Indian) Spirit.

Cavanaugh (Middle English) Chubby. *Cavanagh, Kavanagh, Kavanaugh*

Ceara (Irish) Ruddy; dark; spear. *Caera, Ciara, Sierra, Chiara, Ciaran, Ciarra, Cieara, Ciera, Cierra, Kiara, Searra, Siara, Ciar*

Cecania (German) Freedom.

Cecilia (Latin) Blind one; the sixth; feminine form of Cecil. *Cacelie, C'Ceal, Cecelia, Ceceley, Cecely, Cecile, Cecilie, Ceciliane, Cecilyann, Cecyle, Cecylia, Ceil, Cecilija, Cecilla, Cecille, Cecily, Cile, Cilka, Cecilee, Cecilya, Celia, Celie, Cicely, Cilia, Cilla, Cilly, Cissie, Sela, Selia, Sheila, Sile, Sileas, Silke, Kikelia, Kikylia, Sacilia, Sasilia, Sasilie, Seelia, Seelie, Seely, Sesilia, Sessaley, Sesseelya, Sessile, Sessilly, Sessily, Cele, Cissie, Sissey, Sissie, Sissy*

Celandia (Greek) Swallow.

Celeste (Latin) Heavenly. *Cela, Celesse, Celesta, Celestena, Celestene, Celestia, Celestiel, Celestijna, Celestina, Celestine, Celesteen, Celesteene, Celestyn, Celestyna, Celestyne, Celeena, Celia, Celie, Celine, Celina, Celinda, Celisse, Celinka, Celka, Celleste, Celyna, Cesia, Cesya, Celinna, Celena, Salena, Salina, Selena, Selene, Seleena, Seline, Selinda, Selyna, Selyne, Saleste, Salestia, Seleste, Selestia, Selestina, Selestine, Selestyna, Selestyne, Silesta, Silestena, Silestia, Silestijna, Silestina, Silestyna, Silestyne, Tinka, Zelena*

Celica (Brand name) Model of a Toyota car.

Cerelia (Greek) Goddess of the harvest. (Latin) Relating to spring. *Cerella, Sarelia, Sarillia, Ceres*

Ceridwen (Welsh) Poetic goddess. *Kerridwyn*

Cerise (French) Cherry; cherry red. *Cerisa, Cerisse, Charisse, Cherise, Sarese, Sherise*

Cettina (Italian) Blessed, happy, bringer of joy.

Chablis (French) A dry white wine. *Chabley*

Chaka (Arabic) Chakra; energy center. (Hebrew) Life. *Chayka*

Chalan (Peruvian) Horse trainer.

Chalcedony (Greek) Quartz; a mystical stone.

Chalee (English) Meadow on the ledge. Variation for *Shelee*.

Chanah (Hebrew) Grace; variation of Hannah. *Chana, Chaanach, Chaanah, Chanach, Channa, Chanaiana, Cheyanne, Cheyenne, China, Chyna, Chynna, Connie*

Chance (Old French) A church official or chancellor.

Chandra (Sanskrit) Of the moon. (Hindi) Goddess Devi, foe of evil. *Chanda, Chandara, Chandria, Chandrama, Chandani, Chandy, Chaundra, Candi, Candy, Chante, Cinda, Cindi, Cindy, Cinthia, Cyndi, Cynthia*

Chanel (French) Canal; channel; perfume. *Chanell, Chanelle, Channelle, Chenelle, Shanel, Shanell, Shanelle, Shannel, Shannelle, Shenelle, Shynelle*

Chantal (Old French) Stone or singer. *Chantale, Chantalle, Chantel, Chantele, Chantell, Chantelle, Chantrell, Chauntel, Shantal, Shantalle, Shantel, Shantell, Shantelle, Shontel, Shontelle, Chandler*

Chapa (Native American) Superior.

Chapawee (Sioux Indian) Industrious.

Charisma (Greek) Grace; beauty; kindness. *Charis, Carisma, Chareesse, Charisa, Charise, Carisa, Carissa, Charissa, Charisse, Charysse, Cherish, Carrie, Carry, Cruz, Karas, Karis, Karisma, Karisse, Sherisa*

Charity (Latin) Loving and benevolent. *Carissa, Carita, Chareese, Charis, Charissa, Charisse, Charita, Charitee, Charitey, Charitye, Chariza, Charty, Cherri, Cherry, Sharitee,*

Sharitey, Sharity, Sharitye, Caridad, Carita, Caritas, Karita, Cordia, Cordie

Charlotte (French) Little and womanly; feminine of Charles. *Carlotta, Charlotta, Charlet, Charlette, Charlot*

Charu (Hindi) Charming.

Chastity (Latin) Purity, innocence. *Chasaty, Chasida, Chasity, Chassity, Chasta, Chastina, Chastine, Chastitee, Chastitey, Chiquita*

Chay (Old German) Man. (Irish) Fairy dwelling.

Chaya (Hebrew) Life.

Chelsea (Old English) River landing place. *Chelde, Chelsa, Chelsee, Chelseigh, Chelsi, Chalsie, Chelsie, Chellsie, Chelsy, Chelsey, Kelsie, Kelsey, Kelsy*

Chen (Chinese) Dawn.

Chen-chio (Chinese) Meaning unknown.

Chen-tao (Chinese) Meaning unknown.

Chenoa (Native American) White dove.

Chepi (Algonquin) Fairy.

Cheridah (Latin) Charity, kindness.

Cheriss (French) Precious.

Cheryl (French) Beloved. *Cherelle, Sherryl, Sherryll, Sherrill, Sheryl, Cheryle, Sheryle, Sher, Sherelle, Sherey, Sheri, Sherice, Sherie, Sherry, Cher, Chere, Cherée, Cheri, Cherie, Cherri, Cora, Corey, Cori, Corrie, Cory, Charalin, Charalyn, Charalynne, Charelin, Charelyn, Charelynn, Charilyn, Charilynn, Cheralin, Cheralyn, Cherilin, Cherilynn, Cherilynne, Cherralyn, Cherrilin, Cherrilyn, Cherrylene, Cherrylin, Cherryline, Cherrylyn, Cherylin, Cheryline, Cheryllyn, Cherylyn, Sharelyn, Sharelynne, Sharilynn, Sheralin, Sheralynne,*

Sherilin, Sherralin, Sherrilyn, Sherrylene, Sherryline, Sherrylyn, Sherylin, Sherylyn

Cheyenne (Native American) Courage. *Chana, Chayan, Chayanne, Cheyanna, Cheyanne, Chiana, Chianna, Chyanne, Shayan, Shayanne, Shyann, Shyanne*

Chhaya (Hindi) Shadow.

Chika (Japanese) Near.

Chimalis (Native American) Bluebird.

Chinara (Nigerian) God receives.

Chinshu (Japanese) Calm place.

Chione (Egyptian) Daughter of the Nile.

Chipo (African) A gift.

Chitrangda (Hindi) Portrait. *Chitra*

Chiyo (Japanese) Thousand years; eternal.

Cho (Japanese) Butterfly. (Korean) Beautiful.

Chon (Korean) Heaven.

Chorei (Japanese) Transparent spirituality.

Chosposi (Hopi Indian) Bluebird eye.

Chow (Chinese) Summer.

Christina (Greek) Anointed; feminine of Christian. *Christine, Cristina, Kristen, Kristin, Kristine, Kirsten, Kristina, Chrissa, Chrisstan, Christen, Christa, Christan, Christeen, Christeena, Christel, Christena, Christene, Christian, Christiana, Christiane, Christianna, Christie, Christin, Christine, Christini, Christinn, Christmar, Christyna, Chrystal, Chrystalle, Chrystee, Chrystel, Chrystelle, Chrystina, Chrystle, Crissey, Crissie, Crissy, Crista, Cristal, Cristel, Cristelle, Cristen, Cristena, Cristie, Cristin, Cristina,*

Cristine, Cristiona, Crysta, Crystal, Crystena, Crystene, Crystie, Crystina, Crystine, Crystyna, Khristeen, Khristena, Khristina, Khristine, Khristya, Kirstin, Krista, Kristeen, Kristel, Kristijna, Krysta, Krystal, Krystka, Krystle, Stina, Teena, Teyna, Tiny

Christy (English) Of Christ; variation of Christine. *Christi, Chrissti, Chrisstie, Chrissty, Cristy, Cristi, Kristi, Kristy*

Chu hua (Chinese) Chrysanthemum.

Chun (Chinese) Spring.

Chyou (Chinese) Autumn.

Ciannait (Irish) Ancient. *Ciana, Ciandra, Cianna*

Cinnabar (Greek) Red; also the name of a mineral.

Citrine (Middle English) Reddish yellow. (Latin) Citrus.

Claire (Latin) Bright. *Clare, Clara, Claral, Clarice, Clarissa, Clarisa, Clarisse, Clarrie, Clair, Claireen, Clairene, Claireta, Clairette, Clairey, Clairice, Clairinda, Clairissa, Clairita, Clairy, Clarabel, Clarabelle, Clarene, Claresta, Clareta, Claretta, Clarey, Clari, Claribel, Claribella, Claribelle, Clarice, Clarie, Clarinda, Clarine, Clarita, Claritza, Clarrie, Clarry, Clary, Claryce, Clayre, Clayrette, Clayrice, Clayrinda, Clayrissa, Clerissa, Cliara, Clorinda, Klaire, Klara, Klaretta, Klarissa, Klaryce, Klayre, Kliara, Klyara*

Claudette (French) Lame; feminine variation of Claude. *Claudia, Claudie, Cleta, Clyde, Claudella, Claudelle, Claudetta, Claudey, Claudina, Claudine, Claudy, Clodia, Klaudia, Klodia*

Clay (German) Adhere; mortal.

Clementine (Latin) Mild; clemency; giving mercy; feminine variation of Clemens. *Clem,*

Clemence, Clemency, Clementia, Clementina, Clementya, Clementyna, Clementyn, Clemmie, Clemmy, Klementijna, Klementina

Cleotha (African American) Cleotha Staples was a popular American gospel singer and member of The Staple Singers.

Clinique (Brand name) Cosmetics sold through Estée Lauder.

Clio (Greek) Praise. *Clea, Cleon, Cleopatra, Cleone, Cleonie, Cleta*

Clodagh (Irish) The river Clody named for a local female deity. *Cloda*

Cloris (Greek) Blooming; flower goddess. *Chloris*

Clotho (Greek) Weaver.

Coco (Spanish) Diminutive form of Soccoro; French pet name; Chanel cosmetics brand. *Cocoa*

Naming Rights

Take popularity into consideration. Names that are popular today may not be 20 years from now when your child is 20. Consider the trendiness of the name today.

Colette (Greek) Victory of the people. (French) Victorious. Diminutive of Nicole. *Coleta, Cosette*

Colleen (Irish) Girl; feminine form of Cole. *Colene, Coleen, Collena, Collene, Collie, Colline, Colly, Kolleen, Kolline, Celena, Celina, Celine, Clemmie*

Colomba (Latin) Dove. *Colum, Collie, Colly, Colombe, Columbia, Columbine*

Comfort (Latin) Strengthen.

Compassion (Latin) Sympathy.

Concepción (Latin) Conception; pure. *Cetta, Chiquin, Chita, Concetta, Concha, Concheta, Conchissa, Conchata, Conchita*

Concordia (Latin) Peace; harmony. *Concord, Concorde*

Constance (Latin) Faithful. *Connie, Constantia, Constanze, Constanza, Constantine, Constant*

Contessa (Italian) Royalty; feminine form of Count.

Cora (Greek) Heart, maiden. *Coretta, Corita, Corin, Corina, Coralee, Coralie, Corabel, Corabella, Corabelle, Corabellita, Coralia, Coralie, Coralyn, Corazon, Coree, Corella, Corena, Corene, Corentine, Corey, Cori, Corie, Corilla, Corine, Corinne, Corisa, Corissa, Corita, Corlene, Correen, Corrella, Correlle, Correna, Correnda, Correne, Correy, Corri, Corrie, Corrina, Corrine, Corrissa, Corry, Corynna, Corynne, Coryssa, Kora, Korabell, Kore, Koreen, Koretta, Korey, Korilla, Korina, Korinne, Korry, Koryne, Korynna, Koryssa, Corentine*

Coral (Latin) Rock. *Coralee, Coralena, Coralia, Coralie, Coraline, Corallina, Coralline, Coraly, Coralyn, Coralyne, Creola, Koral, Korall, Koralie, Koralline*

Cordelia (Latin) Rope maker. (Irish) Daughter of the sea. Feminine of Cordell. *Delia, Cordy, Kordelia, Cordelie, Cordella, Cordelle, Cordey, Cordi, Cordie, Cordy, Delie, Della, Kordelia, Kordella, Kordelle*

Corky (Latin) Lively, buoyant. (English) Hill, hallow.

Corliss (Old English) Cheerful and generous; feminine form of Carl or Carlisle. *Corlee, Corless, Corley, Corlie, Corly*

Cornelia (Latin) Horn; feminine form of Cornelius. *Cornell, Cornel, Cornalia, Corneelija, Cornela, Cornelija, Cornelya, Corelie, Cornella, Cornelle, Cornie, Korneelia, Korneelya, Kornelia, Kornelija, Kornelya, Neel, Neely, Nela, Nelia, Nell, Nella, Nellie, Nelly, Neal*

Corrina (Latin) Spear; variation of Corinne; feminine of Corin. *Coreen, Coreene, Coren, Korin, Carinna, Carinne, Corrianne, Corrienne, Corrinda, Corryn, Coryn, Corynn, Corynne, Karinne, Karynna*

Cotovatre (English) From *The Legend of King Arthur*; name of a lake.

Courage (English) Heart, confidence, valor.

Courtney (Old English) Courtly; courteous. *Courteney, Courtenay, Cortney, Cortie, Cordney, Cordni, Cortenay, Corteney, Cortland, Cortnee, Cortneigh, Courteneigh, Courtland, Courtlyn, Courtnay, Courtnee, Courtnie, Courtny, Kordney, Kortney, Kortni, Kourtenay, Kourtneigh, Kourtney, Kourtnee, Kourtnie*

Courtesy (French) Polite, gracious respect.

Cressida (Greek) Gold.

Cricket (American) Loud insect of the night.

Crisiant (Welsh) Like a crystal.

Cybill (Greek) Fortune-teller, soothsayer. *Sibyl, Cybil, Cybille*

Cyd (Greek) A public hill.

Cydney (French) From Saint-Denis. *Sydney, Cidney, Cydnee, Cydne, Cydnei, Cydnie*

Cynthia (Greek) Moon. *Cindie, Cyndi, Cindy, Cinda, Cinta, Cintia, Cindee, Cindi, Cinnie, Cinny, Cinthia, Cintia, Cinzia,*

Cyn, Cynda, Cyndee, Cyndia, Cyndie, Cyndra, Cyndy, Cynnie, Cynthea, Cynthie, Cynthya, Cyntia, Cytia, Kynthia, Kynthija, Sindee, Sindi, Sindy, Sindya, Sinnie, Sinny, Synda, Syndee, Syndi, Syndy, Syntha, Synthee, Syntheea, Synthia, Synthie, Synthya Cindeigh, Cinzia, Sintia

Cyra (Persian) Throne; sun; feminine form of Cyrus. *Cyrah, Cira, Cyrena, Cyrene, Cyrina, Kyra, Cytherea, Cytheria*

Cyzarine (Russian) Royalty. *Cyzars*

D

Da-Shin (Chinese) Peaceful heart.

Da-xia (Chinese) Hero.

Daba (Hebrew) Kind words.

Dabria (Latin) Name of an angel.

Daelen (English) Alternate form of Dale. *Daelan, Daelin, Daelon, Daelyn, Daelyne, Dalena, Daleena, Dalehna, Dalenna, Dalennah*

Dagen (Hebrew) Corn, grain. *Dagan, Daegon, Daegan, Dagon*

Dagmar (Danish) Joy of the land. (German) Glorious. *Dagmara, Dagmarah, Dagmaria, Dagmariah, Dagmarya, Dagmaryah*

Dagna (Scandinavian) Day. *Dagny, Dagne, Dagney, Dagnie, Dagnah, Dagnana, Dagnanna, Dagnee, Dagnia, Dagniah*

Dahlia (Scandinavian) Valley. (Botany) A flower. *Dahliah, Dahlya*

What's in a Name

The name **Dahlia** comes from a type of flower that was named for Swedish botanist Anders Dahl.

Dai (Japanese) Great. *Day, Daye, Dae*

Dainin (Buddhist) Graciously shining.

Daisy (Latin) Day's eye. *Daisey, Daisee, Daisie, Deisy, Deisi, Deissy, Daisi, Dasee, Dasey, Dasi, Dasie, Dasy*

Dakota (Native American) Friend. *Dakotah, Dakoda*

Dale (German) Valley dweller. *Dael, Daile, Dalena, Dallon, Dayle, Daela, Dahl, Dail, Daila, Dalene, Dalina, Daline, Dayl*

Dalia (Hebrew) Branch. *Dahlia, Daliah, Daelia, Dailia, Daleah, Daleia, Dalialah, Daliyah*

Damaris (Greek) Gentle. *Damara, Damar, Damarius, Damary, Damarylis, Damarys, Damarysa, Damaryss, Dameressa, Dameris, Damiris, Dammaris, Dammeris, Damris, Damriss, Damrissa, Demara, Demaras, Demaris, Demariss, Demarys, Demaryse, Demaryss, Demarysse*

Dame (German) Lady.

Damia (Greek) Goddess of the forces of nature. *Damiah, Damya, Damyah*

Damita (Spanish) Baby princess. *Dameeta, Dameetah, Dametia, Dametiah, Dametra, Dametrah, Damitah, Damyta, Damytah*

Dana (English) Bright as day. *Danna, Danae, Dayna, Daina, Danah, Danice, Danella, Daena, Daenah, Danaia, Dane, Danean, Daneana*

Danica (Latin) Morning star. *Danika, Danee, Daney, Danie, Danne, Dannee, Danney, Dannie, Dannii, Danny, Dannye, Dany*

Danielle (Hebrew) Judged by God. *Daniella, Daniele, Daniela, Dania, Dani, Danni, Danna, Danya, Danella, Danelle, Dannia, Danae, Daniah, Danja, Danyae, Daneil, Daneal, Daneala, Daneale, Daneel, Daneela, Daneila, Daneille, Danala, Danalle, Danal, Danele, Danell, Donella, Donnelle*

Dannon (American) God is my judge; form of Daniel. *Daenan, Daenen, Dainon, Danaan, Danon*

Danuta (Hebrew) God has judged. (Polish) Little deer; also used as boy's name.

Daphne (Greek) Laurel tree. *Daphnie, Daphney, Daphny, Daphnis, Daffi, Daffy, Daffye, Daphna, Dafnee, Dafney, Dafni, Dafnie, Dafny, Daphane, Daphaney, Daphanie, Daphany, Dapheney, Daphni, Daphnee*

What's in a Name

According to Greek legend, **Daphne** was the wood nymph who begged her father, the river god Peneus, to transform her into a laurel tree to escape the amorous attentions of Apollo. Still in love with her, Apollo declared that he would always wear a wreath of laurel leaves around his head.

Dara (Hebrew) Pearl of wisdom. *Darah, Darra, Daralice, Dahra, Dahrah, Daira, Dairah, Darja, Darra*

Darby (Irish) Free person. *Darbie, Darbra, Darbiana, Darbia, Darbiah, Darbi, Darb, Darbe, Darbea, Darbee, Darbye*

Darcie (Irish) Dark girl. (French) Of the fortress. *Darcey, Darcy, Darsy, Darsey, Darcee, Darci, Darcia, Darciah, Darcea, Darcee, Darsea, Darsee, Darsi, Darsie*

Darena (American) Famous and loved.

Daria (Greek) Wealthy. *Dari, Darya, Dariya, Darria, Darriah*

Darice (Persian) Queenly. *Dareece, Darees, Dareese, Daricia, Dariciah, Darisa, Darissa, Darycia, Darys, Darysa, Darysah, Daryse, Darysia*

Darlene (French) Little darling. *Darlie, Darleen, Darline, Darly, Daryl, Darryl, Darylle, Darelle, Darlita, Darlean, Darlee, Darleena, Darleenah, Darleene, Darlen, Darlena, Darlenah, Darlenne, Darlina, Darlinah, Darling, Darlyna, Darlynah, Darlyne, Darlynne, Darla, Darlah, Darlecia, Darli, Darlis*

Darnell (English) Hidden nook. *Darnel, Darnela, Darnelah, Darnele, Darnelle, Darnella, Darnellah, Darnyell, Darnyella, Darnyelle*

Darshana (Hindi) Sight; observation.

Darva (Slavic) Honey bee.

Daryn (Greek) Gifts. (Irish) Great. *Daron, Daryne, Darynn, Darynne, Darin, Darina, Darinah, Daryna, Darynah*

Dasha (Greek) Gift of God. *Dashae, Dashah, Dashenka*

Davan (Hebrew) Beloved one. *Dava, Daveigh, Davina*

Davine (Scottish) Friend; darling. *Devine, Davannah, Davean, Davee, Daveena, Davene, Daveon, Davey, Davi, Daviana, Davin, Davineen, Davinia, Davinna, Davria, Devean, Deveen, Devene*

Daw (Thai) Stars.

Dawn (English) Daybreak. *Dawne, Dawna, Dawana, Dawanna, Dawin, Dawina, Dawnee, Dawnetta, Dawnisha, Dawnlin, Dawnlynn, Dawanah, Dawandra, Dawandrea, Dawannah, Dawnah, Dawnn, Dawnna, Dawnnah, Dawnya*

Day (American) Light and hope. *Dey*

Daya (Hebrew) Bird. *Dayah*

Dayla (Hebrew) To draw water.

Dea (Greek) Goddess.

Debbani (Arabic) Gray.

Deborah (Hebrew) Bee. *Debra, Debrah, Debbie, Debby, Debbi, Debbye, Deb, Debi, Debo, Devera, Devora, Devorah, Devorit, Debbea, Debbee, Debbey, Debea, Debee, Debie, Deby, Debora, Debbora, Debbera, Debberah, Debborah, Debera, Deberah, Deboran, Debrha, Deborrah, Debroah, Dobra, Debbra, Debbrah, Debrea, Debria*

Deepa (Hindi) Light.

Deila (Old Norse) Quarrel, fight. (Place name) A part of land "La Delle" in Normandy.

Deiondre (African American) Valley. *Deandra*

Deja (French) Before. *Daja, Daeja, Daija, Dejae, Dejah, Dejon, Déja, Dejanae, Dajona, Dejana, Dejanah, Dejanai, Dejanay, Dejane, Dejanea, Dejanee, Dejanna, Dejannaye, Dejaena, Dejonae, Daijon, Dajan, Dajone, Dejonee, Dejonna*

Deka (African) Pleasing. *Dekah*

Delbin (Greek) Dolphin; name of a flower.

Delfina (Spanish) Dolphin. *Delfeena, Delfine, Delphina, Delpha, Delphe, Delphi, Delvina, Delfi, Delfie, Delfin, Delfinah, Delfyn, Delfyna, Dlfynah, Delfyne*

Delia (Place name) Delos, Greece; pet form of Bedelia. *Dehlia, Delea, Deleah, Deli, Deliah, Deliana, Delianne, Dellia, Delliah, Dellya, Delyah, Delya, Delyah*

Delight (Old French) Emotion.

Delilah (Hebrew) Delicate. *Dalila, Delila, Lila, Lilah, Dalialah, Daliliah, Delila, Delilia, Delilla, Delyla, Delylla*

Delinda (Latin) Anointed. *Gundelinda*

Della (Greek) Visible. (German) Noble. *Dell, Adella, Adela, Del, Dela, Delle, Delli, Dellie, Dells*

Delling (Scandinavian) Scintillating.

Delphine (Greek) Dolphin. (Place name) From Delphi, Greece. *Dolphine, Delphina, Delphinah, Delphinah, Delphinia, Delphiniah, Delphinie, Delphyna, Delphyne, Delvina, Delvinah, Delvine, Delvinia, Delviniah, Delvyna, Delvynah, Dolphina, Dolphinah, Dolphine, Dolphyn, Dolphyna, Dolphyne*

Delsie (English) God is my oath. *Delcea, Delcee, Desa, Delsea, Delsee, Delsey, Delsi, Delsia, Delsy, Delza*

Delta (Greek) The fourth. *Delte, Deltora, Deltra, Deltah, Deltar, Deltare, Deltaria, Deltarya, Deltaryah, Deltoria*

Delu (African) The only girl.

Demelza (Old English) Fort on a hill. *Demie, Demi*

Demetria (Greek) Goddess of the harvest. *Demeter, Demetra, Demetri, Demetrice, Demetris, Demmi, Demi, Demma, Deitra, Deetra, Detria, Demeetra, Demeetrah, Demeta, Demeteria, Demetrias, Demetrice, Demetriona, Demetrius, Dymeetra, Dymitrah, Dymetra, Dymitria, Dymitriah, Dymytria, Dymytrya, Dymytryah, Demee, Demey, Demia, Demiah, Demie, Demii, Demmee, Demmie, Demmy, Demy*

Denise (French) Mythology; a follower of Dionysus, the god of wine. *Deniece, Deniese, Denice, Denyse, Denyce, Deneise, Dennice, Denisse, Denesse, Danice, Danise, Denece, Denese, Deni, Denize, Denys, Deneece, Dineese, Dinice, Dynise, Dynice, Dynyce, Denicy, Denisha, Deneesha, Deniesha, Denishia*

Denita (English) God is my judge; form of Danielle. *Denitta, Danita, Danett, Danis, Daniss, Danitra, Danitrea, Danitria, Danitza, Daniz*

Denna (Hebrew) Valley. *Dena, Denaé, Deana, Dane, Deeyn, Denah, Dene, Denea, Deney, Denai, Denay, Denee, Deneé*

Denver (Place name) Green valley. Denver, Colorado. *Denvor*

Dericia (African American) Athletic.

Derora (Hebrew) Running streams. *Derorit, Derorice, Drora, Drorah, Drorit, Drorlya*

Derry (Irish) Redhead. *Deree, Derey, Deri, Derie, Derree, Derrey, Derri, Derrie, Dery*

Desdemona (Greek) Misery. *Desdemonda, Desmona*

Desiree (Latin) Crave. (French) Hoped for. *Desi, Desiderio, Desire, Desideria, Desea, Desee, Desey, Desie, Désir, Desira, Desy, Dezi, Dezia, Dezzia, Dezzie, Desira, Desirah, Desirai, Desireah, Désirée, Desirey, Desray, Desree, Dessie, Dessirae, Dessire, Dessiree, Desyrae, Desyrai, Desyray*

Desma (Greek) Pledge. *Desmé*

Despina (Greek) Young lady. *Despoina*

Destiny (French) Fate. (Ethiopian) Happy. *Destinee, Destany, Destiney, Destenee, Desteny. Desta, Destah, Desti, Destie, Desty, Destania, Destaney, Destani, Destanie, Destannee, Destanney, Destanni, Destannia, Destannie, Destanny, Desteni, Destenia, Destenie, Destin, Destine, Destinée, Destini, Destinie, Destiana, Destinne, Destinni, Destinnia, Destinnie, Destnie, Destyn, Destynia, Destyniah, Destynie, Destyny, Destynya, Destynyah*

Deva (Hindi) Celestial spirit. *Deeva, Deava, Deavah, Deevah, Devah, Diva, Divah, Dyva, Dyvah*

Devaki (Hindi) Black.

Devon (English) From Devonshire. *Deaven, Devonne, Devion, Devione, Devionne, Devone, Devoni, Devonn, Devonne, Devin, Devinne, Devan, Devana, Devanna, Deven, Devenne, Devondra, Deveyn, Devvon, Devyn, Devynn*

Devona (English) Defender. *Devonnah, Devonda*

Dextra (Latin) Flexible. *Dex, Dekstra, Dextrah, Dextria*

Dharma (Hindi) Ultimate law of all things. *Dharmetta*

Diamond (English) Brilliant. *Diaman, Diamanta, Diamante, Diamend, Diamenn, Diamont, Diamonte, Diamonta, Dimond, Dimonte, Diamon, Diamantina, Diamantra, Diamonda, Diamondah, Diamonde, Diamonia, Diamontina, Dimonda, Dimondah, Dimonde, Diamonique, Damonica, Diamoniqua, Diamandi*

Diana (Latin) Divine. *Diane, Diann, Dianne, Dianna, Dyan, Dyana, Dyanne, Diahann, Di, Diandra, Diantha, Deanna, Deanne, Daiana, Daianna, Diaana, Diaanah, Dianah, Dianalyn, Dianarose, Dianatris, Dianca, Dianelis, Diania, Dianiah, Dianiella, Dianielle, Dianita, Dianya, Dianyah, Dianys, Didi, Dihana, Dihanah, Dihanna, Diandre, Diandrea, Deane, Deeane, Deeanne, Diaan, Diaane, Diahann, Dian, Diani, Dianie, Dihan, Dihane, Dihann, Dihanne, Diahanna, Diannah, Diandre, Dianthah, Dianthe, Dyanthah, Dyanthe, Dyanthia, Dyanthiah, Dyanthya, Dyanthyah, Deann, Deahanne, Déanne, Dee-Ann, Deeann*

Diara (African) Gift.

Didina (French) Beloved.

Dido (Latin) Mythical queen of Carthage.

Diella (Latin) Worshipper of God. *Dielle*

Dierdre (Irish) Sorrowful. *Deirdre, Deirdra, Dierdra, Deidre, Deidre, Derdre, Dede, Diedra, Didra, Diedre, Deerdra, Deerdrah, Deerdre, Deirdree, Didi, Diérdre, Dierdrie, Dyerdre, Deidra, Deidrah, Deidrea, Deidrie, Dydree, Dydri, Dydrie, Dydry, Deedra, Deeddra, Deedrah, Deedrea, Deedri, Deedrie*

Dillian (Latin) Worshiped one. *Dilli, Dilliana, Dilliannah, Dilliane, Dillianne, Dylian, Dyliana, Dylianah, Dyliane, Dyllian, Dylliana, Dylliane, Dylliann, Dyllianna, Dylliannah, Dyllianne, Dylyan, Dylyana, Dylyanah, Dylane, Dylyann, Dylyanna, Dylyannah, Dylyanne*

Dimaia (American) Daughter of Maia.

Dinah (Hebrew) Judgment. *Dina, Deena, Deanna, Dena, Dynah, Dinna, Dinnah, Dyna, Dynna, Dynnah*

Dionne (Greek) Daughter of heaven. *Dion, Dione, Diona, Dionna, Dyon, Dyonne, Deonia, Deonyia, Dionah, Dyona, Dyonah, Diondra, Diondrea, Deonne, Deonee, Dioney, Dioni, Dionie, Dionis, Dionte, Diony, Dyone, Dyonee, Dyoney, Dyoni, Dyonie, Dyony*

Dionyza (Shakespearean) From *Pericles.*

Dior (French) Golden. *Diora, Diore, Diorre, Diorah, Diorra, Diorrah, Dyor, Dyora, Dyorah, Dyorra, Dyorrah, Dyorre*

Diotama (Greek) Great math teacher in Ancient Greece.

Dipti (Hindi) Brightness.

Diva (Latin) A goddess. *Devine, Divinia, Diveena, Divina, Divinah, Diviniah, Diviniea, Dyveena, Dyvina, Dyvinah, Dyvinia, Dyvyniah, Dyvyna, Dyvynah, Dyvynia*

Divinity (English) Divine.

Divya (Hindi) Heavenly.

Dixie (American) Southern girl. *Dixon, Dixi, Dix, Dixee, Dixey, Dixy, Dyxee, Dyxey, Dyxi, Dyxie, Dyxy*

Diza (Hebrew) Joyous. *Ditza, Ditzah, Dizah, Dyza, Dyzah*

Djab (French-Creole) Devil.

Dobara (Science fiction) Character from *Star Trek: The Next Generation.*

Dodie (Hebrew) Beloved. *Dodi, Dody, Doda, Dode, Dodea, Dodee, Dodey, Dodia, Dodiah, Dodya, Dodyah*

Doe (Middle English) Female deer. Nickname for almost any "D." *Dee, Dee Dee, Didi*

Doli (Native American) Bluebird. (African) Doll. (American) Sorrowful. Variation of Dolores.

Dolores (Latin) Lady of sorrows. *Deloris, Delores, Dorrie, Dolora, Dolly, Dolley, Deloria, Dolorcitas, Dolorita, Doloritas*

Domani (Italian) Tomorrow.

Dominique (French) Belonging to God. *Dominiqua, Dominica, Dominga, Domina, Domeniga, Dom, Domineque, Dominiquah, Domino, Dominoque, Dominuque, Domique, Dominah, Domyna, Dominah, Domyno, Domeneque, Domeniqua, Domeniquah, Domeneka, Domenicah, Domenicka, Domenika, Domineca, Domineka, Domini, Dominia, Dominiah, Dominicah, Dominick, Dominicka, Dominikah, Dominixe, Dominyika, Domka, Domnica, Domnicah, Domnicka, Domnika, Domonica, Domonice, Domonika*

Donatella (Italian) Gift. *Donatha, Donathia, Donathiah, Donathya, Donathyah, Donato, Donatta, Donetta, Donette, Donita, Donnette, Donnita, Donte*

Donelle (Irish) World leader.

Donna (Latin) Lady. *Dona, Donella, Donia, Donni, Donya, Donnica, Donae, Donah, Donalda, Donaldina, Donelda, Donellia, Doni, Donail, Donalea, Donalisa, Donay, Dondi, Dondra, Dondrea, Dondria, Donnae, Donnah, Donnai, Donnalee, Donnalen, Donnay, Donnaya, Donne, Donnell, Donni, Donny, Dontia*

Donoma (Native American) Sight of the sun.

Dora (Greek) Gift. *Doral, Doralyn, Dori, Dorita, Dore,*

Dory, Dorah, Doralia, Doraliah, Doralie, Doralisa, Doraly, Doralynn, Doran, Dorana, Dorchen, Dorece, Doreece, Dorelia, Dorella, Dorelle, Doresha, Doressa, Doretta, Dorielle, Dorika, Doriley, Dorilis, Dorion, Doro, Doralin, Doralina, Doraline, Doralyna, Doralynah, Doralyne, Doralynne, Dorlin, Dorrey, Dorie, Dorree, Dorri, Dorrie, Dorry, Dorinda, Dorindah, Dorynda, Doryndah

Dorcas (Greek) Gazelle. *Dorcia*

Doreen (French) Golden girl. *Dorene, Dorena, Dorina, Dorine, Doreene, Doreana, Doreanah, Doreena, Doreenah, Dorenah, Dorin, Doryn, Doryna, Dorynah, Doryne*

Doria (Greek) From the sea. *Doriah, Dorria, Dorrya, Dorryah, Dorya, Doryah*

Dorian (Greek) Sea; from Doris. *Dorean, Doriana, Doriane, Doriann, Dorianne, Dorin, Doreane, Dorianna, Dorina, Dorinah, Dorriane*

Doris (Greek) Of the sea. *Dorris, Dorice, Dore, Dory, Dorys, Dori, Doreece, Doreese, Dorisa, Dorise, Dorreece, Dorreese, Dorrise, Dorrys, Dorryse*

Dorothy (Greek) Gift of God. *Dorothea, Dorotea, Dorothee, Dorthy, Dortha, Dottie, Dot, Dotson, Dolly, Dolley, Dasya, Doortje, Dorathee, Dorathey, Dorothi, Dorathie, Dorathy, Dordei, Dordi, Dorefee, Dorethie, Doretta, Dorifey, Dorolice, Dorothie, Dorika, Doritha, Dorka, Dorle, Dorlisa, Doro, Dorofey, Dorlice, Dorosia, Dorota, Dorothey, Dorottya, Dorte, Doryfey, Dosi, Dossie, Dosya, Do, Doa, Dotea, Dotee, Dotey, Doti, Dotie, Dott, Dottea, Dottee, Dottey, Dotti, Doty*

Dorrit (Greek) Dwelling. (Hebrew) Generation. *Dorit, Doritt, Dorita, Dorite, Doritte, Dorrite, Doryt, Doryte, Dorytt, Dorytte*

Dree (Scottish) Suffering.

Drew (Greek) Courageous. *Dru, Drewa, Drewee, Drewia, Drewie, Drewy*

Dristi (Hindi) Sight.

Drucilla (Greek) Innocent. *Drusilla, Drusie, Drusy, Drucie, Druci, Drucela, Drucella, Drucill, Drucillah, Drucyla, Drucylah, Drucyle, Drucylla, Drucyllah, Drucylle, Druscila, Drucey, Drucy, Drusey, Drewcela, Drewcella, Drewcila, Drewcilla, Drewcyla, Drewcylah, Drewcylla, Drewcyllah, Drewsila, Drewsilah, Drewsilla, Drewsillah, Drewsyla, Drewsylah, Drewsylla, Drewsyllah, Druscilla, Druscille, Drusila, Drusylah, Drusyle, Drusylla, Drusyllah, Drusylle*

Duaa (Arabic) Prayer to God.

Naming Rights

What if you've fallen in love with two names but are only having one baby? Why not combine the two, for example, Leigh and Anne combined become Leighanne.

Duenna (Spanish) Protector of friends. *Duena, Duenah, Duennah*

Duff (English) Baker.

Dulcie (Spanish, Latin) Sweet. *Dulcinea, Dulcine, Dulce, Dulsie, Delcina, Delcine, Douce, Douci,* *Doucie, Dulcea, Dulcee, Dulcey, Dulci, Dulcia, Dulciana, Dulciane, Dulciann, Dulcianna, Dulcianne, Dulcibel, Dulcebela, Dulcibell, Dulcibella, Dulcibelle, Dulcie, Dulcy, Dulse, Dulsea, Dulsee, Dulsey, Dulsi, Dulsy, Delsine, Dulcina, Dulsia, Dulsibell, Dulsiana, Dulsine*

Dumi (African) The inspirer.

Dusana (Russian) A spirit, soul.

Dustin (German) Valiant fighter. (English) Brown rock. *Dustine, Dustina, Dusteena, Dustyn, Dust, Dustain, Dustan, Dusten, Dustion, Duston, Dustynn, Dustean, Dusteana, Dusteanah, Dusteane, Dusteenah, Dusteene, Dustinah, Dustyna, Dustynah, Dustyne*

Dusty (English) Dusty place. *Dustie, Dusti, Dustea, Dustee, Dustey*

Duvessa (Irish) Dark beauty.

Duyen (Vietnamese) Charm and grace.

Dyani (Native American) Deer. *Dianee, Dianey, Diani, Dianie, Diany, Dyanee, Dyaney, Dyanie, Dyany*

Dylan (Welsh) Sea. *Dylane, Dylin, Dylana, Dylann, Dylen, Dylaan, Dylanee, Dylanie, Dyllan, Dylynn*

Dyllis (Welsh) Sincere. *Dylis, Dylissa, Dylissah, Dyllys, Dyllysa, Dyllyse, Dylys, Dylysa, Dylysah, Dylyse, Dylyss, Dylyssa, Dylyssah*

Dymphna (Irish) Patron saint of the mentally ill. *Dympna*

Dysis (Greek) Sunset.

E

Earlene (Irish) Pledge; feminine form of Earl. *Earla, Earlean, Earline, Earleen, Erleen, Erlene, Erlenne, Erline, Erlina, Erlinda, Erla*

Eartha (Old English) Earth.

Easter (American) From the holiday.

Ebba (German, Anglo-Saxon) Strength; return of the tide.

Ebere (African) Mercy.

Ebony (Greek) Hard wood. *Ebonie, Ebonee*

Ecaterina (Romanian) Innocent.

Edda (Old English) Rich. *Eda*

Eden (Hebrew) Delight. *Edie, Edan, Edena, Edene, Edin, Edyn*

Edena (Hawaiian) Delightful. (Babylonian) A plain. (Hebrew) Delight. *Edna, Eden, Edene, Edenia, Edin, Edon, Edona, Edyne*

Edith (Old English) Expensive gift. *Edithe, Eadith, Ede, Edetta, Edette, Editta, Edyta, Edyth, Edythe, Edita, Editha*

Edna (Hebrew) Pleasure, rejuvenation. *Adna, Ednah, Ednita*

Edria (Hebrew) Mighty. *Edreah, Edriah, Edra, Edrya*

Edwina (German) Prosperous friend; heir's axe. *Edwynna, Edwinna, Edwyna, Edweena, Edwena, Edwine*

Effie (Greek) Well-spoken; short form of Euphemia. *Efea, Effi, Effy, Efi, Ephie*

Efrosini (Hebrew) A fawn or a bird.

Eido (Japanese) Illuminating way.

Eileen (Greek) Light. *Ilene, Alene, Eileene, Eilena, Eilina, Eilyn, Eillen, Eleen, Elene, Eilene, Eiline*

Eilis (Gaelic) Noble, kind.

Eir (Scandinavian) Goddess of healing.

Ekta (Hindi) Unity.

Naming Rights

Consider what your baby's initials will spell. Imagine what a mono-grammed baby spoon would look like with the initials DOG inscribed on it because your beautiful daughter's name was Dorothy Olivia Granger. Be sure to choose a name that doesn't spell out an unexpected word.

Ekua (African) Born of Wednesday.

Elaine (French) Variation of Helen. *Elaina, Elayne, Elana, Elena, Alaine, Alana, Laine, Laney*

Elam (Hebrew) Highlands.

Elani (Greek) Light.

Eleanor (Greek) Mercy. *Eleanore, Eleanora, Elinor, Elinore, Ellie, Nell, Leonore, Leonora, Eliana, Elana, Elanor, Elanore, Elenor, Elenore, Eleonor, Elianore, Ellenor, Ellinor, Ellinore, Elynor, Elanie*

Electra (Greek) Bright; the shining one. *Elektra*

Eleora (Hebrew) The Lord is my light.

Elfriede (German) Peaceful ruler. *Elfreda, Elfrida, Elfredda, Elfreeda, Elfreyda, Elfreida*

Eliann (Hebrew) My God has answered.

Elise (French) Consecrated by God; variation of Elizabeth. *Lise, Elisa, Elisha, Elissa, Elyssa, Elyse, Elysse, Eilis, Eilise, Elisee, Elisie, Elisse, Ellice, Ellise, Ellyce, Ellyse, Ellyze, Elyci, Alise, Alyse, Alysse, Alyssa, Alysa*

Elita (French) Special one. *Ellita, Ellitia, Ellitie, Ilida, Lida*

Elizabeth (Hebrew) Consecrated to God. *Elisabeth, Lisbeth, Liz, Lizzie, Liza, Eliza, Ellie, Elsa, Else, Beth, Bess, Betty, Bette, Bettie, Betsy, Aliza, Libby, Elspeth, Elsbeth, Elsbet, Elspet, Isabel, Isabelle, Isabella*

Elke (Greek) A variation of Axelia; protector of mankind. *Elki, Ilki*

Ella (Old German) All. *Ellie*

Elladan (Science fiction) Character from *The Lord of the Rings* by J.R.R. Tolkien.

Elle (French) Woman, girl.

Ellen (English) Light. A variation of Helen. *Ellyn, Elen, Elyn, Ellin, Elin, Ellan, Ellene, Ellynn, Ellynne*

Elma (Greek) Amiable.

Elodie (Greek) Marshy, white blossom. *Elodee, Elody*

Eloise (French) Intelligent; smart. *Elouise, Elois, Eloisa, Ell, El*

Elu (Native American) Full of grace.

Elvira (Spanish) Variation of German for "close." *Elvyra, Elvera, Elvie, Elva, Elvina*

Emani (Arabic) Believer. *Imani, Amani, Emoni, Emonie, Amoni, Imoni*

Emanuelle (Hebrew) God is with us. *Emmanuella, Emanuela, Manuella, Emmanuelle, Emanuel*

Emeraude (French) Emerald.

Emiline (Old German) Labor. *Emmeline, Emaline, Emmaline, Emyln, Emelyn, Emylin, Emiline, Emmiline, Emmilyne*

Emily (Latin) Eager. *Emilie, Emilee, Emmilie, Emmily, Emil, Em, Emilia, Emile, Emeline, Emileigh, Emiliee, Emmilee,*

Emylee, Emalee, Emeli, Emelia, Emely, Emilly, Emmaly, Emmie, Emmilly, Emmylee, Emmy, Emmye

Emlyn (Welsh) Brave and noble warrior. *Emlin*

Emma (German) All-embracing. *Emmie, Emmett, Emmet, Emmot, Emmott*

Emmanaia (Science fiction) Name from *Gaming Fiction*.

Emmylou (German) Whole or complete.

Endora (Hebrew) Fountain.

Enid (Welsh) Soul.

Ennis (Irish) Sole or only choice.

Enola (Native American) Magnolia.

Enriqua (Spanish) Ruler.

Enya (Scottish) Jewel; blazing. *Enia, Eniah, Enyah*

Enza (Latin) Citizen or descendent of Laurento.

Eos (Greek) The dawn.

Eppie (Greek) Well spoken of. (English) A diminutive of Euphemia or Hephzibah, also used as an independent name.

Epua (Swahili) Clear away or remove.

Naming Rights

You've always loved the name Emily—until the day you realized it was the number-one choice for girl babies throughout the country. What to do? Go ahead and use a popular name? Choose a less well-known name? Choose an alternate spelling? All are viable options.

Erato (Armenian, Greek) Muse of erotic poetry.

Erica (Scandinavian) Ever-powerful; honorable ruler. *Erika, Ericca, Ericka, Errica*

Erin (Irish) Western island. *Eryn, Erinn, Erinna, Erynn, Earin, Earrin, Eran, Eren, Erian, Errin, Erynna*

Eris (Greek) Goddess of strife.

Ermine (Latin) Noble. (German) Soldier. Form of Hermina. *Ermin, Ermina, Erminda, Erma, Erminie*

Ernestine (Old German) Earnest, vigorous. *Earnestine, Ernesta, Ernie, Erna, Ernaline, Ernesia, Ernestina, Ernesztina*

Esme (Latin) Esteem. *Esmee, Esma, Esmie*

Esmerelda (Spanish) Emerald. *Esmeralda, Esmarelda, Esmaralda, Esmiralda, Esmirelda*

Esperanza (Spanish) Hope. *Esperance, Esparanza, Esperansa, Esperanta, Esperenza*

Essence (Latin) The embodiment; spirit of; that which is. *Essencee, Essences, Essenes, Essense, Essynce*

Estelle (Latin) Star. *Estel, Estella, Estela, Estele, Estell, Esthella, Stella, Estie, Estee, Estelina*

Esther (Persian) Star. *Ester, Esthur, Eszter, Esta, Essie, Ettie, Hester, Hesther, Hettie*

Etenia (Native American) Wealthy.

Eternal (Latin) Without beginning or end.

Eternity (American) Everlasting.

Ethel (Old English) Noble. *Ethelda, Adele, Ethelred, Ethelbert*

Ethereal (Greek) Lightness.

Etoile (French) Star.

Etsu (Japanese) Delight.

Etta (Old German) Little. *Ettie, Etty, Etka, Etke, Itta*

Eudana (Science fiction) Character from *Star Trek Voyager*.

Eudora (Greek) Good gift. *Eudor*

Eugenia (Greek) Well-born. *Eugenie, Eugina, Evgenia*

Eulalia (Greek) Fair of speech. *Eula, Eulalie, Eulalee, Eulia*

Eunice (Greek) Victorious. *Eunyce, Eunise, Euniss, Unice*

Euphemia (Greek) Spoken well of. *Effam, Eufemia, Euphan, Euphemie, Euphie*

Euphrosyne (Greek) Joy.

Eustacia (Latin) Tranquil. *Eustasia, Stace, Stacie*

Euterpe (Greek) Muse of the flute.

Evadne (Greek) A water nymph.

Evangeline (Greek) Messenger of good news. *Evangelyn, Evangaline, Evangalyne*

Eve (Hebrew) Life. *Eva, Evy, Evie, Evita, Evander, Ev, Ewa, Ava*

Evelyn (English) Hazelnut; variation of Eve. *Eveline, Eveleen, Evelina, Evalyn, Aveline, Avaline, Avelina, Avalina, Evalina, Evette*

What's in a Name

Evelyn is a prime example of a name that's switched genders in the last century. Though now generally a girl's name, in the past it was more common as a boy's. The author of *Brideshead Revisited*, Evelyn Waugh, married a woman named Evelyn Gardner. Friends called them he-Evelyn and she-Evelyn.

Everilda (English) The slayer of the boar. *Everlid*

Evian (Place name) From the town in France famous for Evian springwater. *Evan*

Evonne (French) Young archer. (Scandinavian) The wood of the Yew tree. *Evon, Evonna, Evanne, Evenie, Evenne, Eveny, Evone, Evoni, Evonnie, Eyvone, Evyn, Evony, Ivonne, Yvonne, Vonni, Vonnie, Vonny*

Ewa (Polish) Life.

Eyota (Native American) Greatest one.

F

Fabiana (Italian) Bean farmer. *Fabianah, Fabianna, Fabiannah, Fabienna, Fabiennah, Fabyana, Fabyanah, Fabyanna, Fabyannah*

Fai (Chinese) Brilliant light.

Faiga (Germanic) A bird.

Faith (Latin) Trust. *Faithful, Faythe, Fayth, Fidelity, Faeth, Faethe, Faithe*

Faizah (African) Victory. *Faiza, Fayza, Fayzah*

Fala (Native American) A crow.

Fallon (Celtic) Of a ruling family. *Falon, Fallan, Fallen, Fallenn, Fallenna, Fallona, Fallonah, Fallonya, Fallonyah*

Falynn (English) Beautiful fairy. *Faelyn, Faelynn, Failyn, Failynn, Faylinn, Faylynne, Felyn*

Fang (Chinese) Fragrant; sweet-smelling.

Fang hua (Chinese) Fragrant flower.

Fanny (English) Free; from France; nickname for Frances. *Fannie, Fanette, Fanci, Fancie, Fancia, Fania, Fannia*

Naming Rights

If you genuinely like the idea of naming your baby after a family member, then by all means go ahead. However, if you feel obligated to do so but secretly dislike the name because it sounds too old or reminds you of a relative you never liked, think of an alternative. Try using the family member's name as a middle name. Or use a variant or alternate spelling of the family name.

Fanta (Africa) Beautiful day.

Fantasia (Latin) Imagination. *Fantasy, Fantasya, Fantaysia, Fantazia, Fiantasi*

Faren (English) Wanderer. *Faran, Farana, Farane, Farin, Faron, Faryn, Feran, Fare, Farine, Faronah, Ferin, Feron*

Farica (German) Chief of peace. *Faricah, Faricka, Farika, Fariqua, Fariquah, Farique, Faryca, Farycah, Farycka, Faryque*

Farrah (Old English) Beautiful. *Farah, Farra, Farria, Farriah, Farrya, Farryah, Farya, Faryah, Fayre*

Farran (Irish) Adventurous. *Farrin, Farrand, Ferrin, Ferron, Ferran, Farren, Farrahn, Ferryn*

Fatima (Arabic) Daughter of the prophet. *Fatema, Fathma, Fatime, Fattim, Fatyma, Fatymah*

Fawn (Latin) Young deer. *Faun, Fauna, Fawne, Fawna, Faunah, Faunia, Fauniah, Fauny, Faunya, Faunyah, Fawnah, Fawnia, Fawniah, Fawnna, Fawny, Fawnya, Fawnyah*

Fay (Old French) Fairy. *Faye, Fey, Fae, Fai, Faie, Faya, Fayah, Fayana, Fayette, Fei, Feya, Feyah, Feye*

Fayla (Nigerian) Lucky. *Fayola, Faiola, Faiolah, Fayolah, Feyla*

Fe (Spanish) Trust.

February (American) The second month.

Feena (Irish) Small fawn. *Feana, Feanah, Feenah*

Felicia (Latin) Fortunate, happy; feminine of Felix. *Felice, Felicity, Felicita, Felisse, Feliciana, Felyce, Phylice, Philicia, Phylicia, Falica, Falisa, Felisca, Felissa, Feliza*

Femi (Egyptian) Love. *Feme, Femia, Femiah, Femie, Femmi, Femmie, Femy, Femyah*

Feodora (Russian) God's gift. *Fedora, Fedorah, Fedoria, Fedorra*

Fern (Old English) Leafy plant. *Ferne, Fearn, Fearne, Fernly, Ferna, Ferni, Firn, Firne, Furn, Furne, Fyrn, Fyrne*

Feronia (Latin) Goddess of springs and woods.

Fidelity (Latin) Faithful. *Fidel, Fidelia, Fidelio, Fidella, Fidea, Fideah, Fidela, Fidelah, Fidele, Fideliah*

Fifine (French) He shall add. *Fifi, Feefeem, Fefe, Fefi, Fefie, Fiffi, Fiffy, Fifina, Fifinah*

Fila (Persian) Lover. *Filiah, Filya, Fylia, Fyliah, Fylya, Fylyah*

Filipina (Polish) Lover of horses. *Filippina, Filpina, Filipa, Felippa, Felipe, Felipa, Philippa*

Filmena (Greek) Love song. *Filemon, Filomenah, Filomene, Filomina, Filominah, Filomyna, Filomyne, Fylomena, Fylomenah, Fylomina, Fylomine, Fylomyna, Fylomyne*

Fiolla (American) Science fiction. *Fiola*

Fiona (Old English) White. *Fione, Fionn, Feeona, Feeonah, Feonia, Feoniah, Fionna, Fionnah, Fionni, Fionniah, Fieonne, Fionnea, Feonnee, Fyona, Fyoniah, Fyoni*

Fiorella (Italian) Little flower. *Fiorelle*

Fiorenza (Italian) Flower.

Flannery (Celtic) Sheet of metal, flat land. *Flanneree, Flannerey, Flanneri, Flannerie*

Flavia (Latin) Blond, golden hair. *Flaviah, Flavianna, Flavianne, Flaviar, Flavien, Flavienne, Flaviere, Flavya, Flawia, Flawya*

Fleur (French) Flower. *Fleure, Fleuree, Fleuret, Fleurett, Fleuretta, Fleurettah, Floretta, Florettah, Florette, Flouretta, Flourette*

Florence (Latin) Blooming flower; flourishing. *Flora, Flor, Floria, Florida, Florie, Floris, Florrie, Fleur, Flower, Florenz, Florentia, Flory, Floryn, Flossie, Flo*

Fola (African) Honor. *Floah*

Fonda (Spanish) Earth; grounded; profound. *Fondah, Fondea, Fonta, Fontah*

Fontanna (French) Fountain. *Fountanne, Fountain, Fontaina, Fontainah, Fontaine, Fontana, Fontannah, Fontanne, Fontayn, Fontayna, Fontaynah, Fontayne*

Fortitude (Latin) Strength; courage.

Fortuna (Latin) Fortune. *Fortunah, Fortunata, Fortunate, Fortunia, Fortuniah, Fortunya, Fortunyah*

Fortune (French) Given to luck. *Fortunne, Fortunee, Fortoona*

Franca (Latin) Free. (Place name) From France; form of Frances. *Franc, Francka, Francki, Franka, Frankah, Franke, Frankee, Frankia, Frankyah*

Frances (Old French) Free; an androgynous name, though Frances is generally used for girls and Francis for boys. *Francesca, Francisca, Fran, Franny, Fanny, Francine, Francene, Francess, Francesta*

Frederica (German) Peaceful ruler. *Fredericka, Frederika, Frederique, Fritzie, Fritzi, Federica, Feriga, Fredalena, Fredaline, Frederina, Fredith, Fredora*

Naming Rights

Affirm your ethnicity, religion, or heritage by naming your baby in a manner that honors those ideals.

Freedom (English) Liberty.

Freya (Scandinavian) Goddess of love, fertility, and beauty. *Frey, Freyah*

Frida (Spanish) Peaceful ruler; nickname for Frederica. *Fridah, Frideborg, Fryda, Frydah, Frydda, Fryddah*

Frieda (German) Peace. *Friede, Freida, Fredie, Freda, Friedah, Winifred, Freide, Freydah, Freyda*

Friera (Spanish) Sister.

Frigg (Norse) Beloved.

Fulvia (Latin) Blond.

Fuyo (Japanese) Peony.

G

Gabriela (Hebrew) Feminine version of Gabriel. *Gabriella, Gabrielle, Gabriele, Gavrila, Gavra, Galia, Galya, Gabby, Gaby, Gabi*

Gaea (Greek) Earth. *Gaia, Gaiah, Gaiea, Gaya, Gayah*

Gaeriel (American) Science fiction; hero of God.

Gaetana (Italian) From Gaeta. *Gaetan, Gaetane, Gaetanah, Gaetanna, Gaetanne, Gaitana, Gaitane, Gaitanah, Gaitann, Gaytana, Gaytane, Gaytanne*

Gail (Irish) Stranger. (Old Norse) To sing. *Gayle, Gale, Galatea, Gael, Gaela, Gaell, Gaylia*

Gala (English) Joyful. *Galah, Galla, Gallah*

Galen (English) Festive. *Gaelen, Gaellen, Galane, Galean, Galleene, Gallen, Galyn, Galyne, Gaylaine, Gaylyn*

Galiana (German) Haughty. *Galayna, Galianah, Galiane, Galiena*

Galilahi (Native American) Attractive.

Galina (Greek) Full of light. *Galaina, Galainah, Galaine, Galinah, Galine, Galinka, Gallin, Gallina, Galyna, Galynah*

Galya (Hebrew) God shall redeem. *Galia, Gallia, Gallya*

Gana (Hebrew) Garden. *Ganah, Ganit, Gania, Ganiah, Ganice, Ganyah*

Gardenia (English) Flower. *Deenia, Gardeen, Gardeene, Gardeena, Gardin, Gardina, Gardinia, Gardyn, Gardyna, Gardynia*

Garland (French) Wreath. *Garlan, Garlon, Garlyn, Garlana, Garlanah, Garlinda, Garlinde, Garlynd, Galrlynde*

Garnet (Latin) Red seed. *Garnett, Garnette, Granata, Grenata, Grenatta, Garnetta, Garnettah, Garnete, Garnetah*

Gatha (Hindi) Song.

Gay (French) Merry. *Gaye, Gae, Gai, Gaea, Gaia*

Gayatri (Hindi) Mother of the Vedas; goddess.

Gaynelle (African American) Happy. *Gaynell*

Gayora (Hebrew) Valley of the sun.

Geena (American) Nobility. *Gena, Gen, Geana, Geeandra, Geina, Geneene, Genelle, Genette, Jena, Jeena*

Gelasia (Greek) Laughter.

Gelilah (Hebrew) Rolling hills.

Gelsey (Persian) A variety of jasmine (gelsemium). *Gelsi, Gelsy*

Gemini (Greek) Twin. *Gemelle, Gemina, Geminia, Geminine, Gemmina*

Gemma (Latin) Precious stone (pronounce it with a soft "g," as in "gemstone"). *Gema, Gem, Jemma, Jemmsa, Gemah, Gemee, Gemmah, Gemmey, Gemmia, Gemmy*

Genene (Scottish) God is gracious. *Geanine, Geannine, Genine, Gineen, Ginene, Jeanine*

Genesee (Native American) Beautiful valley.

Genesis (Latin) Birth. *Genesia, Genes, Genisis, Genysis, Genesys, Genisys, Genysys, Genicis, Jenesis, Yenesis*

Geneva (French) Juniper berry. *Genevia, Genny, Geneve, Genevie, Genneeva, Genneevah, Ginneva, Gyniva, Gynniva, Gynnivah*

Genevieve (Welsh) White wave. *Genavee, Genaveve, Genevie, Geniveve, Gineveve, Ginevieve, Ginevive, Guinevieve, Guinivive*

Genji (Chinese) Gold.

Gentle (American) Kind. *Gentil, Gentille, Gentlle*

Georgia (Greek) Farmer; feminine version of George. *Georgea, Georgina, Georgiana, Georgianna, Georgine, Georgette, Georgeen, Georgeena, Georgeanne, Georgienne, Giorgia, Georgie, Georgy, Gina, Gerda, Gruzia, Jirka, Jirca, Jirina, Jorgina*

Geraldine (German) Hard spear; feminine version of Gerald. *Geraldene, Gereldine, Geraldyne, Gerry, Geri, Gerri, Gerrie, Geralda, Geraldeen, Gerhardine*

Germain (English) Bud. *German, Germaine, Jarman, Jermyn, Jermain, Jermayne, Jermaine, Jermana, Germine, Germyn*

Gertrude (German) Adored warrior. *Gerta, Gerd, Gerda, Gerte, Gertie, Gerty, Gert, Jera, Jerica, Trude, Truta, Trudy, Trudie, Trudi, True*

Gervaise (French) Strong. *Gerva, Gervaisa, Gervayse, Gervis*

Geva (Hebrew) Hill. *Gevah*

Ghada (Arabic) Young woman. *Gada, Gadah, Ghadah*

Ghislaine (French) Sweet; pledge.

Gig (English) Horse-drawn carriage.

Gilana (Hebrew) Joy. *Gila, Gilah, Gilanah, Gilane, Gilania, Gilenia Gylana, Gylanah, Gylan, Gylane*

Gilda (Irish) Servant of God. (English) Gold-coated. *Gylda, Gildah, Gilde, Guilda, Guildah, Guylda, Guyldah, Gylda, Gyldah*

Gill (Latin) Youthful. *Gili, Gilli, Gillie, Gilly, Gyl, Gyll*

Gilla (Hebrew) My joy is in the Lord. *Giliah, Gilana, Gila, Gilah*

Gillian (Latin) Graceful, blessing; variation of Juliana. *Gillianne, Gilliana, Gilian, Gillianah, Gillien, Gillyan, Gillyana, Gillyanah, Giliane*

Gilora (Science fiction) Character from *Star Trek: Deep Space Nine.*

Ginger (Latin) Flower. *Gin, Ginja, Ginjah, Ginjar, Ginjer, Gynger, Gynya, Gynyah*

Gioia (Italian) Joy. *Gioya, Joya*

Giordana (Italian) Descending. *Giadana, Giadanah, Giadanna, Giodana, Giodanna, Giordanah, Giordanna, Giordannah, Gyodana, Gyodanna*

Giovanna (Italian) God is good. *Giovana, Giovanah, Giovannah, Giovanne, Giovannica, Giovona, Giovonah, Giovonnah, Gyovana, Gyovanna*

Giselle (English) Sword pledge. *Gisella, Gisela, Gizella, Gizelle, Gigi, Ghisele, Giseli, Gysell, Gyselle, Gizela*

Gita (Hebrew) Good. *Gitah, Gitel, Gittel, Ghita, Gitka, Gyta, Gytah, Geeta*

Gitana (Spanish) Gypsy. *Gitane, Gypsy, Gipsy, Gitanna, Jeetanna*

Githa (English) Gift. *Getta, Gittah*

Giuseppina (Hebrew) He shall add. *Guiseppina, Josephine*

Gladys (Welsh) Version of Claudia. *Gladiss, Gladyce, Gleda, Glad, Gladdys, Gleddis, Gleddys, Gladyss, Gladuse*

Glen (Irish) Secluded wooded valley. *Glenn, Glenna, Glena, Glenda, Glyn, Glynn, Glynnis, Glynis, Glenetta, Glenne*

Gloria (Latin) Glory. *Glora, Glorya, Glory, Gloriana, Glorianne, Glorea, Gloriah, Gloriela, Gloriella, Gloryah*

Godiva (Old English) Gift of God. *Godivah, Godyva, Godyvah*

Golda (Old English) To shine. *Goldie, Golden, Gaoldarina, Goldarine, Goldee, Goldi, Goldina, Goldy, Goldia, Goldyah*

Goneril (Shakespearean) From *King Lear.*

Gopi (Hindi) Cowherd girl.

Gotzone (Spanish) Angel.

What's in a Name

Although "Godiva" today is generally associated with fine chocolates, Lady **Godiva** is believed to have been an eleventh-century noblewoman and wife of Leofric, Earl of Mercia. A patron of the arts, she was frustrated at the town's lack of interest, so she pleaded with her husband to lower taxes so members of the community could afford time to enjoy the arts. He agreed, on one condition: that she ride through the marketplace on horseback with nothing on. Thinking she would never go through with it, he was astonished when she pranced through town *au naturel.* Taxes were subsequently abolished.

Grace (Latin) Graceful, blessing. *Gracey, Gracie, Graza, Grazia, Grazina, Greyse, Graice, Graise, Grase, Greice*

Gratia (Latin) Grateful. *Gratiana*

Graziella (Italian) Form of Grace. *Graziel, Graziela, Graziele, Graziell, Grazielle, Graziosa, Grazyna*

Greer (Greek) Watchful. *Gregoria, Gregorina, Grear, Grier, Gryer*

Greta (Greek) Precious jewel. *Greet, Gret, Grata, Gratah, Greata, Greatah, Gretah, Gretha, Grieta, Gryta*

> **What's in a Name**
>
> According to Roman mythology, the Graces—which the Greeks called the "Charities"—personified truth, beauty, and charm. Their individual names were *Thalia*, meaning "flowering"; *Aglaia*, "wisdom"; and *Euphrosyne*, "joy." Although the individual names are uncommon today, **Grace** is extremely popular.

Gretchen (German) Little pearl. *Gretchan, Gretchin, Gretchon, Gretchun, Gretchyn, Margaret*

Grid (Norse) A wife of Odin.

Griselda (German) Gray warrior. *Grizelda, Grishilda, Grishilde, Griseldis, Grisa, Gris, Chriselda, Selda, Zelda*

Gro (Norse) Gardener.

Guadalupe (Spanish) River of black stones. *Guadalup, Guadelupe, Guadlupe, Guadulupe, Gudalupe*

Guanyin (Chinese) Goddess of Mercy.

Gudrun (Scandinavian) Battler. *Gudren, Gudrin, Gudrina, Gudrine, Gudrinn, Gudrinna, Gudrinne, Gudruna*

Guinevere (Irish) White wave; French version is Genevieve. *Guenevere, Gwendoline, Gwendolyn, Gwendaline, Gwendolen, Gwen, Gwenn, Gwenne, Gwenith, Gwenyth, Gwyneth, Gwyn, Guenn, Gwynne, Gwyndolyn, Jennifer*

Gunda (Scandinavian) Warrior. *Gundah, Gundala, Gunta*

Guro (Norse) Divinely inspired; wisdom.

Gustava (Latin) Majestic. *Gus, Gussi, Gussie, Gussy, Gusta*

Gyo Shin (Japanese) Heart of dawn.

H

Habiba (Arabic) Loved one. *Habibah, Habibeh, Habibi, Haviva, Havivah, Hebiba*

Habika (African) Sweetheart.

Hachi (Native American) River.

Hadara (Hebrew) Beauty. *Hadarah, Hadarit, Haduraq, Hadariah, Hadaria, Hadarya, Hadaryah*

Hadassa (Hebrew) Myrtle. *Hadassah, Hadas, Haddasa, Haddasah*

Haiden (English) Hedged valley. *Haden, Hadyn, Haeden, Haidn, Haidyn*

Haimi (Hawaiian) The Seeker.

Haiwee (Native American) Dove.

Hakue (Japanese) Pure blessing.

Haley (Norse) Hero. (Irish) Wise one. *Hailey, Hayley, Haylee, Haile, Hally, Halley, Halli, Hallie, Hale, Hali, Haleigh, Haleigha, Haleh, Hollis*

Halima (Arabic) Gentle. *Halime, Haleema, Haleemah, Haleima, Halimah, Helima, Helyma, Helymah*

Hallam (German) From the hills.

Halle (Scandinavian) Heroine. *Halla*

Halona (Native American) Fortunate. *Hallona, Hallonah, Halonah, Haloona, Haona*

Halsey (Old English) From Hall's island. *Halsea, Halsie*

Halston (English) Stone town.

Hama (Japanese) Beach.

Hanako (Japanese) Flower child.

Hannah (Hebrew) God is merciful; graceful one. *Hanna, Hana, Hannia, Hannya, Hanniah, Hania, Hanne, Hanita, Hanka, Hannicka, Hannele, Channa*

> **What's in a Name**
>
> Palindromic names are names that are the same spelled backward and forward, such as Bob, Hannah, Eve, Ada, and Aviva.

Harhsa (Hindi) Joy.

Hariel (Hebrew) Ruler of animals.

Harmony (Greek) Harmony. (Old English) Soldier. *Harmonie, Harmene, Harmeni, Harmon, Harmone, Harmonee, Harmonei, Harmoney, Harmoni, Harmonia, Harmoniah, Harmonya, Harmonyah*

Naming Rights

Because you can inject creativity and originality in the process of choosing a name, you have more choices and variations than you might have originally thought. Don't immediately disqualify a name with a less-than-common spelling or pronunciation. Do, however, use common sense to spare your child future frustration.

Harper (Old Norse) Whaler. *Harp, Harpo*

Harriet (French) Ruler of the household; feminine variation of Harry. *Harriette, Hariot, Harriott, Hattie, Hatty, Hetty, Happy, Etta, Etty, Harrie, Harrietta, Hatsee, Hatsey, Hatsie, Hatsy*

Hava (Hebrew) Life. *Chaba, Chaya, Chayka, Eve, Kaija, Havah, Havvah*

Haven (Dutch) Harbor. *Hagen, Hagan, Hogan, Hazen, Havis*

Hawa (African) Desire.

Haya (Japanese) Quick; light. (Arabic) Humble. *Haia, Haiah, Hayah*

Hayfa (Arabic) Shapely. *Haifa, Haifah, Hayfah*

Hazel (Old English) Hazel tree. *Hazella, Hazela, Hazlit, Hazlet, Haslett, Haize, Haizelah, Haizell, Haizella, Haizellah, Haizelle, Hayzal, Hayzaline, Hazall*

Heather (English) A heath or shrub. *Heath, Hether, Heathar, Heatherlee, Heatherly, Hethar*

Heavenly (American) Spiritual. *Heaven, Heavyn, Heven, Hevenley, Heavynlie, Heavenleah, Heavenlee, Heavenlei, Heavenli, Heavenlie*

Heba (Hebrew) Gift from God. *Hebah*

Hebe (Greek) Youth. *Hebee, Hebey, Hebi, Hebia, Hebie, Heby*

Hecate (Greek) Mythical witchcraft goddess.

Hecuba (Greek) Mother of Paris and Hector.

Hedia (Hebrew) God's voice. *Hediah, Hedya, Hedley, Hedaya, Heddah, Hedu*

Hedva (Hebrew) Joy.

Hedwig (Old English) Hidden weapon. *Hedvig, Heddy, Hedy, Hedda, Havoise, Hedvick, Hedvicka, Hedvige, Hedvika, Hedwiga, Hedwyg, Hedwyga, Hendvig, Hendvyg, Jadviga*

HeeWon (Korean) Garden.

Heidi (German) Noble and serene; shortened version of Adelheid or Hedwig. *Heidy, Haidee, Heida, Heidea, Heidee, Heidey, Heydy, Hidea, Hidee, Hidey, Hede, Hedee, Hiede, Hiedi, Hydi*

Heidrun (Norse) The goat who supplies mead for the Gods.

Hekenu (Egyptian) Mythology; falcon-headed god.

Hekt (Egyptian) Goddess of birth, fertility.

Hela (Norse) Goddess of the underworld.

Helen (Greek) Torch. *Helene, Helena, Helina, Helaine, Elaine, Elayne, Eleanor, Elinor, Eileen, Elena, Elene, Galina, Lenora, Lena, Lenny, Nelly, Jelena, Jelika*

Heliotrope (Latin) Flower, faithfulness.

Hema (Hindi) Snow.

Henna (Hindi) A tree or shrub of the Middle East, having fragrant red or white flowers. (English) Rule. *Hena, Henaa, Henah, Heni, Henia, Henka, Hennah, Henny, Henya*

Henrietta (German) House ruler; feminine variation of Henry. *Henriette, Hendrike, Henrika, Henriot, Henriqueta, Hetty, Enrica, Enriqueta, Henriquetta, Henryetah, Henryette*

Hepziba (Hebrew) My love is with her. *Hepzibah, Hephziba, Hephzibah, Chepziba, Eppie, Hefzia, Hefziba, Hephziba, Hepsie, Hepsibah, Hepzi, Hepzia, Hetta, Yetta, Yettie*

Hera (Greek) Queen; jealous. *Herah, Heria, Heriah, Herya, Heryah*

Hermia (Greek) Messenger. *Hemita, Hermilda, Herminia*

Hermione (Greek) Earthy; feminine variation of Hermes, the messenger of the gods. *Hermine, Herma, Hermia, Hermina, Hemine, Herminna*

Hermosa (Spanish) Beautiful. *Hermosah*

Hero (Greek) Defender.

Hertha (Old English) Earth. *Eartha, Erda, Ertha, Herta, Heartha, Hearthea, Heartheah, Herthia, Hearthiah, Herthyah, Hertah, Herthah, Herthiah, Herthya, Herthyah, Hirtha*

Hester (Dutch) Star. (Latin) A variation of Esther. *Hesther, Hetty, Hetti, Hettie, Hetta, Hessie, Hessi, Hessye, Hestar, Hestarr*

Hestia (Greek) Goddess of the hearth. *Hestea, Hesti, Hestiah, Hestie, Hesty, Hestya, Hestyah*

Hila (Hebrew) Praise. *Hillah, Hilly, Hilla, Hillela, Hillel*

Hilary (Greek) Cheer. *Hillary, Hilaire, Hilaria, Hilliard, Hilar, Hill, Hilly, Ilario, Laris, Hillari, Hillery, Hillerie, Hilleree*

Hilda (German) Warrior. *Hilde, Hildy, Hildegard, Hildegarde, Hildegaurd, Hildegaurda, Hildegaurde, Hildred, Hyldaa-gaurde, Hyldaaguard, Hyldagard, Hyldagarde, Hyldegarde, Hyldeguard, Hyldeguarde, Hildie*

Hinda (Hebrew) Doe. *Hindah, Hindey, Hindie, Hindy, Hynda, Hyndah*

Hiolair (Irish) Happy.

What's in a Name

Hilary is both the masculine and feminine form of *Hilarius*, a Roman name derived from the Latin word *hilaris*, for "cheerful." The contemporary meaning of the word *hilarious* is "very funny" or "amusing."

Hippolyta (Greek) Freer of horses. *Hippolyte*

Hisa (Japanese) Long-lasting.

Hisolda (Irish) Fair.

Hiten (Hindi) Meaning unknown.

Hollace (Old English) Near the holly bush. *Holles, Holless, Holliss, Hollyss, Holice, Holisa, Holisah, Holissah, Hollice, Hollyce, Hollys, Hollyssa, Hollyse*

Holly (Old English) Holly bush. *Hollye, Holli, Hollie, Hollyn, Holea, Holeah, Holee, Hollei, Holleigh, Hollye, Holy*

Honesty (Latin) To be truthful. *Honestee, Honestey, Honestie, Honestah, Honesta, Honestia*

Honey (English) Sweet. (German) A familiar alternative to "darling" or "dear." *Honig, Honeah, Honalee, Honea, Honeah, Honee, Honi, Honia, Honiah, Honnea, Honnee, Honney, Honni, Hony*

Hong (Vietnamese) Pink; rosy.

Honor (Latin) Dignified. (French) Nobleman. *Honore, Honour, Honora, Honoria, Nora, Norah, Noria, Norry, Honner, Honorah, Honnor, Honorin, Honorine, Honourah*

Honovi (Native American) Strong deer.

Hope (Old English) Faith.

Hortense (Latin) Gardener. *Hortensia, Hartencia, Hartinsia, Hortenxia, Hortinzia, Ortensia, Hortensiah, Hortensya, Hortensyah*

Hosea (Hebrew) Salvation. *Hosia, Hosiah*

Hoshi (Japanese) Star. *Hoshee, Hoshey, Hoshie, Hoshiko, Hoshiyo, Hoshy*

Hua (Chinese) Blossom.

Hui fang (Chinese) Nice flower.

Humbleness (Latin) Virtue.

Humility (Latin) A virtuous trait. *Humiliah, Humillia, Humilliah, Humylia, Humyliah, Humylya, Humylyah*

Hurit (Native American) Beautiful.

Huyana (Native American) Rain falling.

Hyacinth (Greek) Blue crystal. *Hyacynth, Hyacintha, Hyacinthia, Cintha, Cinthia, Cinthie, Hyacintie, Jacinda, Jacinta, Jancintha, Jacinthe, Jacynth, Hyacinthie*

Hydra (Greek) Water snake.

I

Ianthe (Greek) Violet flower. *Iantha, Ianthia, Ianthina, Iolanthe, Iolanda, Iolande, Ianthya, Ianthyah, Ianthyna*

Iblis (English) From *The Legend of King Arthur*, wife of Lancelot.

Icess (Egyptian) Form of Isis. *Ices, Icesis, Icia, Icis, Icesse, Isis, Icey, Icy*

Ida (Old German) Youthful. *Idana, Idanna, Idena, Idah, Idaia, Idalia, Idalis, Idaly, Idamae, Idania, Idarine, Idaya, Ide, Idys, Idette, Idalee, Ita, Idah, Idarina, Idda, Idetta, Idella, Iida, Yda, Ydah, Idal*

Idalis (English) Happy, noble laborer. *Idalise, Idelis, Idalesse, Idaliz, Idallas, Idallis, Idelys*

Ideh (Hebrew) Praise.

Idelle (Welsh) Form of Ida. *Idell, Idella, Idil, Idele, Idela, Idelah*

Idina (Old English) Variant of Edina.

Idit (Hebrew) Choicest.

Idonea (Scandinavian) Eternal youth. *Idony, Idun, Idonia*

Iesha (American) Woman; form of Aisha. *Ieaisha, Ieasha, Ieashe, Ieesha, Ieeshia, Ieisha, Ieishia, Iescha, Ieshah, Ieshea, Iesheia*

Ikia (Hebrew) God is my salvation. *Ikea, Ikeia, Ikiia, Ikiea, Ikeyia, Ikaisha, Ikeesha, Ikeeshia, Ikeishia, Ikeshia, Ikiah, Ikya, Ikyah*

Ilana (Hebrew) Tree. *Illana, Ilanna, Ilani, Ilania, Ilainie, Illeana, Ileanne, Alana, Allana, Alanna, Ilaina, Ilainah, Ileinah, Ileinee, Ileyna, Ileynah, Ileyni, Ileynie, Ilanah, Ilaney, Illani, Illanie, Ilanit, Illanna, Illannah*

Ilaria (Italian) Form of Hilary.

Ilena (Greek) Form of Helena. *Ileena, Ileina, Ilina, Ilyna, Ilinee, Ileanne, Ileen, Ileenah, Ilini, Ilynah, Ilyni, Ilynie*

Ilene (Irish) Light. *Helen, Eileen, Ilean, Ileane, Ileanne, Ileen, Ileine, Ilyne*

Ilisa (Scottish) Consecrated to God; form of Elisa. *Ilissa, Illissa, Illisa, Illysa, Ilysa, Ilyssa, Ilyza, Ilicia, Ilisah, Ilissah*

Ilsa (German) Consecrated to God. (English) Noble; derived from Elizabeth. *Ilse, Ilise, Ilse, Ilisa*

Ima (Japanese) Now; the present. *Imah*

Imelda (German) Battle. *Ymelda, Imalda, Imeldah, Melda*

Imogene (Latin) Image; last born. *Imogen, Imojeen, Imojean, Imogenia, Innogen, Innogene, Emogen, Emogene, Imagene, Imagina, Imajean, Imogine, Imogyn, Imojeen*

Ina (Irish) Pure. *Ena, Inanne*

India (Hindi) From India. *Indeah, Indee, Indiah, Indi, Indie, Indya, Indiya, Indea, Indeya*

Indira (Hindi) God of heaven and thunderstorms; Goddess Lakshmi. *Indiara, Indra, Indre, Indyra, Indyrah*

Indu (Hindi) Moon.

Ines (Spanish) Gentle. *Inez, Inesa, Inessa*

Infiniti (Brand name) Luxury car brand. *Infinity*

Ingrid (Scandinavian) Hero's daughter; derived from Ing, the god of fertility. *Inga, Inge, Inger, Ingmar, Ingrede*

Innis (Irish) Island. *Innes*

Integrity (Latin) Completeness, purity.

Iolana (Hawaiian) To soar like an eagle, hawk.

Iolite (Greek) Violet; water sapphire; the path to enlightenment.

Iona (Greek) Flower name; purple jewel. *Ione, Ioney, Ioni, Ionia, Iyona*

Iras (Hebrew) Flower. *Iriss, Irisse, Irys, Iryssa, Irysse*

Irene (Greek) Peace. *Irena, Ireene, Irina, Erina, Irenea, Ireneah*

Iris (Greek) Goddess of the rainbow. *Irys, Irisa, Irisha, Irissa, Iryssa, Irita, Irysa*

Irma (German) Whole. *Irmin, Irmina, Irminia, Erman, Ermingarde, Irmingarde, Irmah*

Isabeau (French) Consecrated to God; variation of Elizabeth.

Isabel (Spanish) Consecrated to God; variation of Elizabeth. *Isabella, Isabelle, Isabal, Isabeli, Ishbel, Isobel, Izabel, Izabele, Izabella, Isbel, Iseaabal, Issabel, Issie*

What's in a Name

Isabel is either an ancient Spanish variation of Elizabeth or an Arabic/Hebrew/Aramaic word for "daughter of Ba'al." Ba'al means "lord" or "possessor" and was the common name for local deities associated with occurrences such as storms and fertility.

Isela (Hebrew) Devoted to God. (German) A pledge. *Gisela, Isel*

Ishara (Hindi) Rich.

Ishi (Japanese) Rock. *Ishiko, Ishiyo, Shiko*

Isidore (Greek) Gift of Isis, the Egyptian goddess associated with fertility. *Isidor, Isisdora, Isadora, Izzy, Dora, Dorie, Dory, Isadorya, Izadora, Izadorah, Izadore*

Isoke (African) Satisfying gift. *Isoka, Isokah*

Isolda (Old English) Fair. *Isolde, Yseult, Isault, Isolad, Izolde*

Istas (Native American) Snow.

Istra (Nordic Mythology) The Norse counterpart of Psyche, Cupid's wife.

Itala (Italian) From Italy. *Italo, Italus, Italea, Italeah, Italei, Italie, Italy, Italya, Italyah*

Ituha (Native American) Sturdy oak.

Itzel (Spanish) Protected. *Itesel, Itsel, Itssel, Itza, Itzell, Itchel, Itzallana*

Iva (Hebrew) God's great gift. (Japanese) Yew tree. *Ivah*

Ivana (Hebrew) God is gracious. *Ivanka, Ivanna, Ivania, Ivannia, Ivannah*

Ivette (French) Archer. *Ivete, Iveth, Ivetha, Ivett, Ivetta*

Ivory (Latin) White as elephant tusks. *Ivoory, Ivori, Ivorine, Ivree, Ivoree, Ivorey*

Ivria (Hebrew) From the other side of the river. *Ivriah, Ivrit*

Ivy (Old English) Vine. *Ive, Ives, Ivey, Ivie, Ivi, Ivye*

Iyana (Hebrew) Form of Ian. *Iyanah, Iyannah, Iyannia*

Iyanla Origin and meaning unknown.

J

Jacey (Greek) Familiar form of Jacinta. *Jacy, Jaci, Jaycie, Jacci, Jacia, Jaciah, Jaciel, Jaciela, Jaciele*

Jacinta (Greek) Attractive. *Jacinth, Jacant, Jacent, Jacenta, Jacentah, Jacente, Jacintah, Jacintia, Jacinte, Jacintha, Jacinthia, Jacinthy*

Jacqueline (French) Supplanter, substitute; feminine variation of Jacob or James. *Jacquelyn, Jackelyn, Jacklin, Jaklyn, Jaclyn, Jackie, Jackey, Jackee, Jacqui, Jacquetta, Jacquith*

Jade (Spanish) Stone of the loins. *Ijada, Jada, Jadae, Jadah, Jadda, Jaddah, Jadea, Jadeah, Jadeann, Jadee, Jadera, Jadienne, Jaed*

Jadwiga (Polish) Refuge in war.

Jae (Latin) Jaybird. *Jaey*

Jael (Hebrew) Goat. *Jaele, Jaelea, Jaeli, Jaelei, Jaely, Jahlia, Jahlie, Jailey, Jaili, Jaelee, Jaeleigh, Jaeley*

Jaen (Hebrew) Ostrich.

Jahnavi (Hindi) Ganga River in India.

Jaimie (French) I love. *Jamee, Jamey, Jamie, Jaemey, Jaemi, Jaemia, Jaemiah, Jahmey, Jahmi, Jahmie, Jaime, Jaimeah, Jaimea*

Jakki (American) Substitute; familiar form of Jacqueline. *Jacki, Jakea, Jakee, Jakkea, Jakia, Jakete, Jaketah, Jakevah, Jakevia, Jaki, Jakie, Jakke, Jakkee, Jakkie, Jakky, Jaky*

Jakushitsu (Japanese) Tranquil space.

Jale (Turkish) Hoarfrost.

Jaleh (Persian) Dew.

Jamila (Arabic) Beautiful. *Jahmeala, Jahmil, Jahmille, Jahmillah, Jaimila, Jameale, Jamelah, Jahmela, Jahmylla, Jaimille, Jaimyla, Jahmyla*

Jamuna (Hindi) Holy river Yamanu.

Jana (Hebrew) Gracious, merciful. *Janna, Jaana, Jaanah, Janah, Janalee, Janalisa, Janya, Janyah*

Janan (Arabic) Heart. *Jananee, Jananey, Janani, Janania, Jananiah, Jananie, Janann, Jananni, Janany*

Jane (Hebrew) God is gracious; a feminine version of John. *Jayne, Jain, Jan, Janie, Jannie, Janet, Janot, Janeth, Janina, Janice, Janyce, Janis, Janith, Janna, Jina, Joan, Joanna, Jo Ann, Johanna, Joann, Joanne, Jovanna, Joni, Janey, Gianina, Giovanna, Juana, Juanita, Sinead, Shena, Sheena, Sine, Seonaid*

Janel (French) God is gracious; form of Jane. *Janell, Jannell, Jannelle, Jaenel, Jaenela, Jaenell, Jainel, Janelis, Janella, Janellah, Janielle, Janille, Jannella, Jaynele, Jaynelle*

Janese (Hebrew) God is gracious; form of Jane. *Janesey, Janess, Janesse, Janis*

Janica (Hebrew) God is gracious; form of Jane. *Janycka*

Jardena (Spanish) Garden. *Jardan, Jardana, Jardanah, Jardane, Jardania, Jarden, Jardene, Jardenia, Jardin, Jardina, Jardine, Jardyn, Jardyna, Jardyne, Jardynia*

Jariah (Hebrew) Splendid.

Jarita (Arabic) Earthen water jug. *Jara, Jareata, Jareatah, Jareet, Jareeta, Jareetah, Jaretta, Jari, Jaria, Jariah, Jarida, Jarika, Jarina, Jaytta, Jaryte, Jarytte*

Jarvia (German) Skilled with a spear. *Jarviah, Jarvya, Jarvyah*

Jasmine (Persian) A form of flowering olive. *Jasmin, Yasmin, Yasmine, Jasmina, Jessamine, Jessamyn, Jesmin, Jasmain, Jasmaine, Jasmane, Jassmain, Jassmaine, Jasman, Jasmeet, Jasmit, Jassmit*

Jaya (Hindi) Victory. *Jaea, Jaia, Jaiah, Jayah*

Jayani (Hindi) A sakti (power, energy) of Ganesha.

Jazz (American) Musical style of early and mid-1900s. *Jaz, Jazee, Jazey, Jazi, Jazie, Jazy, Jazzee, Jazzey, Jazzi, Jazzie, Jazzy*

Jeanne (Scottish) God is gracious. *Jean, Jeanette, Jeanine, Janine, Jeanie, Jeannie, Jannette, Jennette, Jeane, Jeania, Jeaneva, Jeanice, Jeen, Jeene*

Jedida (Hebrew) Beloved.

Jelena (Russian) Light; form of Helen. *Jelaina, Jelainah, Jelaine, Jelana, Jelanah, Jelane, Jelayna, Jelean, Jeleane, Jeleen, Jeleene, Jelene, Jelin, Jelyna, Jelyne, Jelynah*

Jemima (Hebrew) Dove. *Yemimah, Jemma, Jemmie, Jem, Gemma, Mimi, Gemima, Gemimah, Jamin, Jamima, Jemimah, Jemyma, Jemymah, Jema*

Jenay (Hebrew) Small bird. *Jena, Jenai, Jenea, Jennae, Jennay, Jennaye, Janée, Janea, Janee*

Jendayi (African) Give thanks.

Jenell (German) Knowledge, understanding, kindness. *Genell, Jenall, Jenalle, Jenel, Jenela, Jenelah, Jenele, Jenella, Jenille, Jennel, Jennele, Jennell, Jennille, Jinelle*

Jennifer (Old Welsh) White wave. *Jenifer, Jenyfer, Jenny, Jennie, Jinny, Jenni, Jen, Jena, Jennett, Jenet, Jenna, Jennifar, Jenafar, Jennafar*

Jenova (Hebrew) God is Jehovah.

Jensine (Welsh) White wave, white phantom; a form of Jennifer. *Jeni*

Jeong (Korean) Sentiment; pure. *Jyo*

Jerolyn (German) Mighty with a spear; variation of Geraldine. *Jeralyn, Jerelyn, Jerylin, Jeryl, Jerri*

Jersey (English) From a section of England.

Jerusha (Hebrew) Inheritance. *Jerushah, Yerusha*

Jesen (Scandinavian) Autumn.

Jesse (Hebrew) Wealth. *Jessie, Jessy, Jess, Jescie, Jesea, Jesee, Jesey, Jesie, Jessé, Jessea, Jessee, Jessey, Jessia*

Jessica (Hebrew) Wealthy one. *Jessyca, Jessika, Jessye, Jessi, Jessa, Jessalyn, Jessaca, Jessca, Jessia, Jessicka*

Jette (English) Jet-black mineral. *Jeta, Jetah, Jetia, Jetiah, Jetje, Jett, Jettah, Jetti, Jettia, Jettie, Jetty*

Jewel (Old French) Priceless gem. *Jewell, Jewelle, Bijoux, Jewal, Jewele, Jewelei, Jeweleigh, Jeweli, Jewelie, Jewely, Juel, Juela, Juele*

Jezebel (Hebrew) Impure. *Jesabel, Jesabela, Jesabelah, Jesabele, Jesabell, Jesabella, Jesabellah, Jesabelle, Jessabel, Jessebelle, Jez, Jezebela, Jezebelle*

Jill (English) Short form of Jillian. *Jil, Jyl, Jyll*

Jillian (Latin) Youthful. *Jilly, Jilian, Jiliana, Jilianah, Jiliane, Jiliann, Jilianna, Jiliannah, Jilleen, Jilliana, Jilyann, Jilyanna, Jilyannah, Jyllian*

Jimena (Hebrew) Substitute. *Jimi*

Jimin (Japanese) Compassionate.

Jin (Japanese) Tender. *Jyn*

Jing Wei (Chinese) Small bud.

Jira (African) Related by blood.

Jo Beth (English) Combination. *Jobeth, Joebeth, Joebethe, Joebetha, Johbeth, Johbetha, Johbethe*

Jo Dee (American) Combination of Jo (Hebrew) God is gracious and Dee (Welsh) black, dark; familiar form of Judith. *Jode, Jodea, Jodele, Jodell, Jodevea, Jodey, Joedey, Joedee, Joedi, Joedie, Joedy, Johdea, Johdee, Jowdie*

Joakima (Hebrew) The Lord will judge.

Joan (Hebrew) God is gracious. *Joaneil, Joanmarie, Joannanette, Joayn, Joenah, Joen, Joenn, Jonni*

Joanna (English) God is gracious; form of Joan. *Joanne, Jhoana, Jo-Ana, Joahna, Jaonah, Joandra, Joanka, Joananna, Joayna, Joenna*

Joaquina (Hebrew) God will establish. *Joaquinah, Joaquine, Joaquyn, Joaquyna, Joaquynah, Joaquyne*

Jobey (Hebrew) Afflicted. *Jobea, Jobee, Jobi, Jobie, Jobina, Jobia, Jobitt, Jobitta, Jobrina, Jobya, Jobye*

Jocelyn (Old English) Just one. *Jocelyne, Joceline, Joscelyne, Joseceline, Joscelin, Joslyn, Joslin, Josalin, Jossie, Jocie, Justine, Justina, Justa*

Jocosa (Latin) Gleeful.

Jody (American) Praised; variation of Joseph, for a boy or girl. *Jodie, Jodi, Jodee, Johdea, Johdee, Johdey, Johdi, Johdie, Johdy, Jowdee, Jowdey, Jowdi, Jowdy*

Joelle (Hebrew) The Lord is God. *Joella, Joellen, Joela, Joelah, Joele, Joeli, Joelia, Joelie, Joell, Joellah, Joelly, Jowele, Jowell, Jowelle, Joyelle*

Joey (American) God is gracious; familiar form of Jo.

Johanna (German) God is gracious; form of Joan. *Jonna, Johan, Johanah, Johanka, Johann, Johonna, Joyhanna, Joyhannah*

JoJo (American) Nickname.

Jolanta (Greek) Violet flower. *Joland, Jolanda, Jolande, Jolander, Jolanka, Jolánta, Jolante, Jolantha, Jolanthe*

Jolie (French) Pretty. *Jolene, Joline, Joli, Jolli, Jollie, Jolly, Joly, Jolye*

JoMei (Japanese) Spreads light.

Joni (American) Familiar form of Joan. *Joncee, Joncey, Jonci, Joncie, Jone, Jonee, Joney, Jonie, Jony, Jonilee*

Jonina (Hebrew) Dove. *Jona, Joneen, Joneena, Joneene, Joninah, Jonine, Jonnina, Jonyna, Jonynah*

Joo Mi (Korean) Meaning unknown.

Jora (Hebrew) Autumn rain. *Jorah, Jorai, Joria, Joriah*

Jordan (Hebrew) Descender. *Jordana, Jordanna, Jourdan, Jourdain, Jordane, Jordea, Jordee, Jordi, Jordian, Jordie*

Josephine (Hebrew) He shall increase; a feminine version of Joseph. *Josefine, Josefina, Josepha, Josephe, Josefa, Joette, Josette, Josetta, Josie, Josey, Jo, Giuseppina, Fifi*

Josie (Hebrew) God will increase; familiar form of Josephine. *Josey, Josi, Jossie, Joesey, Josia, Josiah, Josy, Josye*

Joss (German) Joyous; form of Jocelyn. *Jocalin, Jocelina, Jocelinah, Jocalina, Jocalyn, Jocelinn, Jocelynne, Jocelle, Joci, Jocia, Jocilyn, Jocilynn, Jocinta, Joscelin, Josilin, Jossalin*

Jovanna (Latin) Majestic. *Joevana, Jouvan, Jovado, Joval, Jovan, Jovann, Jovannah, Jovanniah, Jovannia, Joviana, Jovina, Jovon, Jonvonah, Jovonda, Jovone, Jovonia, Jovonn, Jovonnah, Jowan, Jowana,*

Jowanna

Joy (Latin) Rejoice. *Joi, Joia, Joice, Joyous, Jovita, Joyeuse, Joye, Joyeeta, Joyella, Joyvina, Joyah, Joyia*

Joyce (Latin) Joyous. *Joice, Joise, Joycee, Joycey, Joycia, Joyciah, Joycie, Joyse, Joysel*

Judith (Hebrew) Praised. *Judyth, Judy, Judi, Judie, Jude, Judit, Siobhan, Siubhan, Yehudith, Giuditta, Judett, Judetta, Judette, Judine, Judita, Judite, Juditha, Judithe, Juditt, Juditta, Juditte, Judyta, Judytt, Judytte, Jutka*

Juhy (Hindi) A flower. *Juhi*

Juice (American) Nickname.

Julia (Latin) Youthful; a feminine version of Julius. *Julya, Julie, Julianne, Juliana, Julina, Julianna, Juline, Joliette, Joletta, Jules, Juli, Giulia, Giulietta, Jewelea, Jeweleah, Jewelia, Jeweliah, Juelea, Jeuleah, Juliah, Julica, Juliea, Julija, Julita, Juliya*

Juliet (French) Youthful; form of Julia. (Shakespearean) From *Romeo and Juliet. Jewelett, Jewel-etta, Jewelette, Jeweliet, Jeweliete, Jewelyet, Jewlyett, Jewelyette, Jolet, Jolete, Juelet, Juelett, Julliet, Julliete, Jullietta, Julyeta, Julyetah, Julyetta, Julyettah*

Julitta (Spanish) Youthful; form of Julia. *Julit, Julitt, Julitte, Julittah, Julyta, Juleet, Juleetah, Juleete, Julet, Juleta, Juletah*

Jun (Chinese) Truthful.

June (Latin) Young. *Juin, Junia, Juniata, Junette, Junine, Juney, Juno, Juine, Juna, Junel, Junell, Junella, Junelle, Junett, Junetta, Juniet, Juen, Junieta, Junilla, Junille, Junina, Junita, Junn, Junula*

Juniper (Latin) Juniper berry.

Juno (Latin) Queen.

Justice (Latin) Form of Justus. *Justys, Justyse*

Justina (Italian) Just, righteous; form of Justus. *Justine, Justena, Justeyna, Justeynah, Justinah, Justinna, Justean, Justeane, Justeen, Justeene, Justein, Justeine, Justeyn, Justeyne*

Jyoti (Hindi) Light; flame.

Jysella (Science fiction) Character from *Star Wars*.

K

Kaatje (Dutch) Pure.

Kabibe (African) Little lady.

Kabira (African) Powerful.

Kacela (African) Hunter.

Kacey (Irish) Brave. *Casey, Casie, K. C., K. Cee, Kace, Kacee, Kaci, Kacy, Kasey, Kasie, Kaycee, Kaycie, Kaysie*

Kachelle (English) Stove tile; variation of German *Kachel*.

Kachine (Native American) Sacred dancer. *Cachina, Kachena, Kachina*

Kaci (Irish) Brave.

Kacia (Greek) Thorny. *Kaycia, Kaysia*

Kacondra (African American) Bold. *Condra, Connie, Conny, Kacon, Kacond, Kaecondra, Kakondra, Kaycondra*

Kacy (American) From initials K. C.

Kade (English, Scottish) Barrel; from the wetlands.

Kadejah (Arabic) Trustworthy.

Kaden (American) Charismatic. *Caden, Kadenn*

Kadence (French) Rhythmic flow of sounds.

Kadenza (Latin) Cadence; dances. *Cadenza, Kadena, Kadence*

Kadie (American) Virtuous. *Kadee*

Kadija (African) The prophet's wife. *Kadee*

Kadin (Arabic) Companion.

Kadisha (Hebrew) Holy. *Kadischa, Kadiza*

Kady (English) Sassy. *Cady, K.D., Kadee, Kadie, Kaydie, Kaydy*

Kaede (Japanese) Maple leaf.

Kaela (English) Keeper of the keys; pure.

Kaelin (Irish) Rejoicer; waterfall; pool; pure; impetuous. *Kaelan, Kaelen, Kaelinn, Kaeylynn, Kaelynne, Kaylin*

Kaelyn (American) Combination of Kae (Greek) Rejoicer and Lynn (English) Waterfall. *Kaelin, Kailyn, Kay-Lynn*

Kaethe (Greek) Pure.

Kagami (Japanese) Mirror.

Kahlilia (Arabic) Beloved, sweetheart. From *Khalil.*

Kai (Hawaiian) Sea. (Native American) Willow tree.

Kaia (Greek) Earth.

Kaida (Japanese) Little dragon.

Kaie (Celtic) Combat.

Kaija (Finnish) Pure. (Greek) Earth.

Kaila (Hebrew) Laurel; crown. *Kailah, Kail, Kala, Kalae, Kalah*

Kailani (Hawaiian) Sky.

Kailas (Hindi) Home of the Lord.

Kailey (American) Spunky; laurel; crown. *Kalee, Kaili, Kailie, Kaylee, Kaylei*

Kaili (Hawaiian) A deity. (American) Crown.

Kailyn (American, English) Laurel tree; keeper of the keys.

Kaimi (Hawaiian) The seeker.

Kainda (African) Hunter's daughter.

Kairi (Greek) Opportunity.

Kairos (Greek) Goddess from Jupiter.

Kaitlyn (Celtic, Irish) Little darling; pure-hearted. *Caitlin, Caitlyn, Kaitlan, Kaitland, Kaitlin, Kaitlynn, Kailyn, Kait-lynne, Kait, Katie, Kaydee, Katlan*

Kaiya (Japanese) Forgiveness.

Kajal (Hindi) Eyeliner.

Kajol (Hindi) Eyeliner.

Kajsa (Swedish) Pure. *Kaisa*

Kakra (Ghanese) Younger of twins.

Kala (Hindi) Black; royal, time.

Kalama (Hawaiian) Flaming torch.

Kalani (Hawaiian) The heavens. *Kalauni, Kaloni, Kaylanie*

Kalanit (Hebrew) Flower name.

Kalare (Latin) Bright; clear.

Kalea (Arabic) Sweet; bright. *Kahlea, Kahleah, Kailea, Kaileah, Kallea, Kalleah, Kaylea, Kayleagh, Khalea, Khaleah*

Kalei (American) Sweetheart. *Kahlei, Kailei, Kallei, Kaylei, Khalei*

Kaleigh (Hebrew) Beloved. (Arabic) Sweetheart. *Kalea*

Kalena (Hawaiian) Chaste. *Kaleena*

Kalene (Czechoslovakian) Flower. (Gaelic) A thin piece of land. (Polish) A flowering plant.

Kalet (French) Beautiful energy. *Kalay, Kalaye*

Kaley (Hawaiian) Hesitating. (American) Crown. Form of Kelly; energetic. *Kalee, Kaleigh, Kalleigh*

Kali (Hindi) The black one; form of the Hindi goddess Devi. (Hawaiian) Hesitating. (Greek) Beauty. *Kala, Kalli*

Kalia (Hawaiian) Beauty.

Kalidas (Greek) Most beautiful. *Kaleedus, Kali*

Kalie (Dutch) Keeper of the keys; pure. *Kali*

Kalika (Greek) Rosebud. *Kalyca*

Kalila (Arabic) Beloved. *Cailey, Cailie, Caylie, Kailey, Kaililah, Kaleah, Kalela, Kalie, Kalilah, Kaly, Kay, Kaykay, Kaylee, Kayllie, Kyle, Kylila, Kylilah*

Kalin (Irish) Pure. Form of Caleb.

Kalina (Hawaiian) Unblemished. *Kalinna, Kaylynna*

Kalinda (Hindi) Sun. (Sanskrit) Mountains. *Kaleenda, Kalin, Kalindi, Kalynda, Kalyndi*

Kalisa (American) Pretty and loving; combination of Kay and Lisa. *Caylisa, Kaleesa, Kalisha, Kaylssa, Kaylisa, Kaykay*

Kaliska (Miwok Indian) Coyote that chases deer.

Kalista (Greek) Most beautiful one.

Kaliyah (Arabic) Darling, sweetheart. *Kahlilah*

Kallan (American) Loving. *Kall, Kallen, Kallun*

Kalle (Finnish) Strong.

Kalli (Greek) Castle, fortress. *Callie, Kalley, Kali, Kallie, Kalie, Kally*

Kallie (Cambodian) Best.

Kallima (American) Butterfly.

Kalliope (Greek) Beautiful voice. *Calli, Calliope, Kalli, Kallyope*

Kallista (Greek) Pretty; bright-eyed. *Cala, Calesta, Calista, Callie, Callista, Cally, Kala, Kalesta, Kalista, Kalli, Kallie, Kally, Kallysta, Kalysta*

Kalliyan (Cambodian) Best.

Kalona (German) Amish town.

Kaloni (Hawaiian) The sky.

Kalonice (Greek) Beauty's victory.

Kalpana (Sanskrit) Imagination.

Kalyca (Greek) Rosebud.

Kalyn (American) Loved. (Arabic) Keeper of the keys. (English) Laurel tree. *Calynn, Calynne, Kaelyn, Kaelynn, Kalen, Kalinn, Kallyn*

Kama (Sanskrit) Love.

Kamakshi (Hindi) Goddess Parvati.

Kamala (Hindi) Lotus. *Camala, Kam, Kamali, Kamilla, Kammy, Kamalah*

Kamali (Rhodesian) Spirit protector.

Kamana (Hindi) Desire.

Kamaria (Swahili) Like the moon. *Kamara, Kamaarie*

Kambo (African) Must work for everything.

Kambrea (Latin) From Wales.

Kambria (Latin) Girl from Wales. *Kambra, Kambrie, Kambriea, Kambry*

Kamea (Hawaiian) Precious one. *Kameo, Kamea, Kamaya, Kammie, Kam, Mea, Maya*

Kameko (Japanese) Tortoise-child; symbol for long life.

Kamella (Hungarian) Young ceremonial attendant.

Kameron (American) Variant of Cameron; crooked nose; kind. *Kamren, Kamrin, Kamron*

Kami (Shinto) Above; God. (Slavic) Young attendant. *Cami, Cammie, Cammy, Kammie, Kammy, Kamelia, Kamille*

Kamila (Arabic) Perfect. (Slavic) Noble.

Kamilah (Arabic) The perfect one. *Camilla, Kamilla*

Kamilia (Slavic) Fragrant evergreen tree with fragrant flowers. *Kam, Kamila, Kammy, Milla, Kameela, Kamela, Kamella, Kamilla, Kamillah, Kamyla*

Kamin (Japanese) Joyful.

Kamna (Hindi) Desire.

Kamryn (American) Crooked nose. *Cameron*

Kanara (Hebrew) Tiny bird; lithe. *Kanarit, Kanarra*

Kanchana (Greek) White; pure. *Candace*

Kandace (Greek) Charming; glowing. *Candace, Candie, Candy, Dacie, Kandi, Kandice, Kandiss*

Kande (African) First-born daughter.

Kandice (English, Greek) Brilliant; white; clarity; pure.

Kandra (American) Light. *Candra*

Kane (Japanese) Two right thumbs. *Cathan, Kaine, Kain*

Kaneesha (American) Dark-skinned. *Caneesha, Kaneesh, Kaneice, Kaneisha, Kanesha, Kaneshia, Kaney, Kanish, Nesha*

Kanene (African) A little thing in the eye is big.

Kanesha (African American) Spontaneous. *Kaneesha, Kaneeshia, Kaneisha, Kanisha, Kannesha*

Kanga (Australian) Short for kangaroo; jumpy.

Kanika (Egyptian) Black cloth.

Kanisha (American) Pretty. *Kaneesha, Kanicia, Kenisha, Kinicia, Koneesha*

Kaniya (Hindi) Virgin. (Thai) Young lady. (Native American) Variation of *Niya*, meaning "champion."

Kanoni (African) Little bud.

Kansas (Sioux Indian) Derived from *Kansa* meaning "people of the south wind." (Place name) U.S. state.

Kantha (Hindi) Kantha represents the Hindi God Lord Shiva; recreation; wife.

Kanti (Native American) Sings.

Kanushi (Hindi) Meaning unknown.

Kanya (Asian) A young lady.

Kaori (Japanese) Fragrant, beautiful girl.

Kaoru (Japanese) Fragrant.

Kapera (African) This child, too, will die.

Kaprece (American) Capricious. *Caprice, Kapp, Kappy, Kapreece, Kapri, Kaprise, Kapryce, Karpreese*

Kapuki (African) First girl in the family.

Kara (Greek) Pure. *Karan, Karen, Karyn, Kasia, Katja, Kasen, Kassia, Katoka, Katrien, Kaysa*

Karan (American) Sweet melody.

Karana (Greek) Pure.

Karasi (African) Life and wisdom.

Karayan (Slavic) Dark one.

Karbie (American) Energetic. *Karbi, Karby*

Karel (American) Variation of *Carol*. (German) Meaning "farmer" and (English) meaning "strong." *Karell, Karelle*

Karen (Greek) Pure. *Caren, Carin, Caron, Caronn, Carren, Carrin, Carron, Carryn, Caryn, Carynn, Carynne, Kare, Kareen, Karenna, Kari, Karin, Karina, Karan, Karon, Karron, Karryn, Karyn, Keren, Kerran, Kerrin, Kerron, Kerrynn, Keryn, Kerynne, Taran, Taren, Taryn*

Karena (Scandinavian) Pure one.

Kari (Turkish) Flows like water. *Cari, Carrie, Keri, Kery, Kary*

Karian (American) Daring. *Kerian*

Karida (Arabic) Untouched, virginal. *Kareeda, Karita*

Karima (Arabic) Giving. *Kareema, Kareemah, Kareima, Kareimah, Karimah*

Karimah (African) Generous.

Karin (Greek) Pure. *Karen, Karine, Karinne, Karyn*

Karis (Greek) Graceful. *Karise, Karisse, Karyce*

Karise (Latin) Dearest one.

Karishma (Hindi) Miracle.

Karissa (Greek) Love; grace. *Carissa, Krissy, Sissa*

Karka (Hindi) Crab.

Karla (German) Strong; womanly. *Carla, Karlah, Karlie, Karlia, Karrla*

Karlee (Latin) Womanly; strong. *Karley, Karlie, Karly*

Karleen (American) Witty; combination of Karla and Arleen. *Karlene, Karline, Karly*

Karli (Turkish) Covered with snow. *Karlie*

Karlotta (German) Pretty; from Charlotte. *Karlota, Karlotte, Lotta, Lottee*

Karly (Latin) Strong-voiced. *Carly, Karlee, Karlie, Karlye*

Karlyn (Greek) Little and womanly.

Karma (Sanskrit) Action. *Karmah*

Karmel (Hebrew) Garden. *Carmen, Karmin, Karmine*

Karmen (Latin) Song.

Karmina (Hebrew) Song; songstress.

Karmiti (Native American) Trees.

Karna (African) Horn of an animal.

Karolina (Polish) Little and strong; form of Carolina. *Karaline, Karalyn, Karalynna, Karalynne, Karla, Karleen, Karlen, Karlene, Karli, Karlie, Karlina, Karlinka, Karo, Karoline, Karolinka, Karolyn, Karolyne, Karolynn, Karolynne*

Karrie (English) Melody, song.

Karrington (Welsh) Rocky town. *Carrington*

Karsen (American) Anointed one. *Carson, Karson, Carsen*

Karya (Hindi) Effect, product.

Karyn (English) Pure; variation of Katherine. *Karen, Karan, Karon*

Karyan (Armenian) The dark one.

Kasa (Hopi Indian) Fur-robe dress.

Kasandra (Greek) Helper of men.

Kasey (Irish) Vigiliant; alert. *Kaci, Casey*

Kashmir (Sanskrit place name) Region between India and Pakistan. *Cashmere, Cashmir, Kash, Kashmere*

Kasi (Hindi) Illuminating. *Casey, Kaci, Kass, Kassi, Kassie*

Kasia (Polish) Pure. From Katherine.

Kasie (Irish) Brave.

Kasinda (African) Born to a family with twins.

Kasmira (Old Slavic) Demands peace. *Kasamira, Kazamira*

KasrA (Persian) A character in "Shahnameh" the eleventh-century *Epic of Kings* by Firdowski.

Kassandra (Greek) Capricious. *Cassandra, Kass, Kasandra, Kassandrah, Kassie*

Kassia (Polish) From Katherine.

Kassidy (Celtic, Gaelic) Clever. *Cassidy, Cassir, Kasadee, Kassydi*

Kassie (Irish) Prophet; unheeded prophetess.

Kat (American) Pure; from Catherine.

Kata (Japanese) Worthy.

Katalin (Hungarian) Pure.

Katarina (Greek) Pure. (Latin) Virginal. *Katareena, Katarena, Katarinna, Kataryna, Katerina, Katyrna*

Katarra (Science fiction) Character from *Star Wars*.

Katarzyna (Czechoslovakian) Pure.

Katchi (American) Sassy. *Catshy, Cotchy, Kat, Kata, Katchie, Kati, Katshi, Katshie, Katshy, Katty, Kotchee, Kotchi, Kotchie*

Kate (Greek) Pure, virginal. *Cait, Caitie, Cate, Catee, Catey, Catie, Kait, Kaite, Kaitlin, Katee, Katey, Kathe, Kati, Katie, Katy*

Katelin (Irish) Pure, virginal. *Caitlin, Kaitlin, Kaitlynne, Kat, Katelynn, Kate-Lynn, Katline*

Katelyn (Celic, Gaelic) Pure beauty.

Katen (Irish) Pure, virginal.

Kateri (German) Pure; variation of Katherine.

Katerina (Slavic) Pure.

Katherine (Greek) Pure. *Katarina, Katharine, Kate, Kathryn, Kathreen, Katheryn, Katrin, Kathy, Katie, Kate, Katina, Katrina, Karen, Karin, Karyn, Karan, Karon, Kari, Karrie, Karry, Kara, Karina, Caren, Carin, Caryn, Cari, Carrie, Carry, Cara*

Kathleen (Celtic) Little darling. *Cathaleen, Cathaline, Cathaline, Cathleen, Kathaleen, Kathaleya, Kathaleyna, Kathaline, Kathelina, Katheline, Kathlene, Kathlin, Kathline, Kathlynn, Kathlyn, Kathie*

What's in a Name

The name **Katherine** has a history of being associated with a saint, two Russian empresses, and three of King Henry VIII's wives. Not too shabby. But what it means is still up for debate. It could be derived from the Greek name *Hekaterine*, meaning "each of the two," or the name of the goddess Hecate. Or it could be from the Roman variation of the Greek word for "pure"—a good choice for a little princess.

Katia (Slavic) Pure. *Kateeya, Kati, Katya*

Katima (American) Powerful daughter.

Katina (Greek) Pure; unsullied.

Katiuscia (English, Irish) Pure.

Katlin (Irish) Pure. *Katlyn, Katlynn*

Katoka (Hungarian) Pure.

Katrice (American) Graceful. *Katreese, Katrese, Katrie, Katrisse, Katry*

Katriel (Hebrew) God is my crown.

Katrin (German) Pure.

Katrina (German) Pure.

Katyayani (Hindi) Goddess Durga.

Kaula (Polynesian) Prophet.

Kausalya (Hindi) Highly skilled.

Kaveri (Hindi) Sacred river of India.

Kavi (Hindi) Poet.

Kavindra (Hindi) Mighty poet.

Kavita (Hindi) Poem.

Kawena (Hawaiian) Rosy reflection in the sky.

Kay (Hebrew) Crown of laurels.

Kaya (Hopi Indian) Wise child. (Japanese) Resting place. *Kaea, Kaja, Kayah, Kayia*

Kaydence (American) Musical.

Kayla (Hebrew) Crown of laurels. *Kaila, Kaylynn, Kailyn, Kaylene, Kaylah, Kayln, Kay*

Kaylana (American) From Kay and Lana.

Kaylee (American) From Kay and Lee. *Chaeli, Kayleigh*

Kayleen (American) Pure lass.

Kayley (American) Bright; beautiful. (Irish, Scottish, English) Slender; keeper of the keys. (Arabic) Laurel. *Kay, Kaylee, Kaylie, Kayli*

Kaylin (American) Pure; keeper of the keys. *Kaylyn, Kaylynn*

Kazanna (Hindi) Treasure. *Kasanna, Kazy, Kazi, Kizzy*

Kazia (Hebrew) Plant with cinnamonlike bark.

Keahi (Hawaiian) Flames; fire.

Keaira (Gaelic) Little dark one.

Keala (Hawaiian) Path.

Keandra (Hawaiian) Water baby.

Keanna (Irish) Ancient; variation of *Kian*.

Keanu (Hawaiian) Cool mountain breeze.

Keara (Irish) From a saint's name.

Kedma (Arabic) Toward the east.

Keedera (Science fiction) Character from *Star Trek: Deep Space Nine*.

Keegan (Irish) Small and fiery; bright flame.

Keeley (Irish) Lively; aggressive; beautiful.

Keelia (Irish) From Keely.

Keelin (Irish) Slender, fair.

Keelty (Gaelic) From the woods.

Keely (Gaelic) Beautiful and graceful. *Keeley, Kealy, Keel, Keelan, Keeler*

Keen (Gaelic) Brave.

Keena (Celtic) Brave.

Keeya (African) Garden flower.

Kefira (Hebrew) Young lioness.

Kehinde (Yoruban) Second of twins.

Kei (Japanese) Rapture; reverence.

Keiki (Hawaiian) Child.

Keiko (Japanese) Adored one.

Keilah (Hebrew) Citadel.

Keilana (Hawaiian) Adored one.

Keilantra (African American) Princess of the night sky; magical. *Keil, Keilei*

Keir (Celtic) Black.

Keira (Celtic) Black haired.

Keisha (African) Favorite. *Keasha, Keesha, Keeshah, Keicia, Keishah, Keshia, Keysha, Kicia*

Naming Rights

Your baby's middle name offers a unique naming opportunity. Use it to honor a family member when the name's not desirable as a first name, or use the middle name as a way to settle a name debate between you and your partner.

Keishla (African) Her life.

Keita (Celtic) Forest.

Keitha (Gaelic) Female warrior.

Kekona (Hawaiian) Second-born.

Kelby (German) Place by the flowing water. *Kelbea, Kelbeigh, Kelbey, Kellbie*

Kelcie (Scottish) Brave; ship island. *Kelsey, Kelcy, Chelsea, Kelsee, Kellsey, Kelsy*

Kelda (Scandinavian) Clear mountain spring. *Kelley, Kelly, Kel, Kell*

Kelila (Hebrew) Regal woman. *Kayla, Kayle, Kaylee, Kalula, Kelulah, Keluila, Kelylah, Kyla, Kyle*

Kelis (American) Beautiful.

Kella (Irish) Warrior.

Kellan (Gaelic) Warrior princess.

Kellen (Irish) Powerful.

Kelly (Irish) Church; warrior; wood; holly; farm by the spring. *Kel, Kelli, Kellie*

Kellyn (Irish) Powerful.

Kelsey (Scandinavian) Ceol's island; beautiful island; from the ship's island; shipping harbor. *Kelsi, Kelsie, Kelsy, Kelcie, Kelson, Kelton, Kels*

Kelsi (Scottish) Brave; ship island. *Kelsey, Kelcy, Kollsoy, Kelsee, Kelsie, Chelsea, Kelsy*

Kember (American) Zany. *Kem, Kemmie, Kimber*

Kempley (English) From a meadowland; rascal. *Kemplea, Kempleigh, Kemplie, Kemply*

Kenadia (American) Chief.

Kenda (English) Child of clear, cool water. *Kendi, Kendie, Kendy, Kennda, Kenndi, Kenndie, Kenndy*

Kendall (Celtic) Ruler of the valley. *Kendal, Kendell, Kendel, Kendalia, Kendaline, Kenna, Kendra, Ken, Kenny, Kenni, Kindall, Kindell*

Kendis (African American) Pure.

Kendra (Anglo-Saxon) Understanding; knowledge. *Kendrah, Kenna, Kennie, Kindra, Kinna, Kyndra*

Kenia (Hebrew) Animal horn. *Keneah*

Kenisha (American) Gorgeous woman.

Kenna (Celtic, Gaelic) Handsome.

Kennedy (Irish, Scottish) Chief with helmet. *Kennedi*

Kennice (English) Beautiful. *Kanice, Kaneese, Kanese, Kennise*

Kennis (Gaelic) Beautiful.

Kennita (American) Chief with helmet.

Kensington (Place name) An area to the west of Central London in the Royal Borough of Kensington and Chelsea. *Kenzi, Kenzy, Kenzington, Kensi, Kensy*

Kenya (Place name) Country on the continent of Africa. *Kennya*

Kenyangi (Ugandan) White egret.

Kenyatta (African) East African name meaning musician.

Kenyon (English) Blond; white-haired.

Keola (Hawaiian) The life.

Kepa (Basque) Stone.

Kera (Celtic, Gaelic) Pure.

Keran (Armenian) Wooden post.

Kerani (Hindi) Sacred bells.

Kerensa (Cornish) Love.

Kern (Celtic, Gaelic) Dark-haired child.

Kerry (Gaelic) Ciara's people; dark eyes. *Keri, Kerrie, Kerwin, Kerri, Kerrin*

Kerryn (American) Dusky and pure.

Kerstin (German) A Christian. *Kersten, Kerston, Kerstyn*

Kerzi (Turkish) Meaning unknown.

Kesare (Spanish) Long-haired.

Kesha (American) Laughing. *Kecia, Kesa, Keshah*

Keshia (African) The favorite.

Keshon (African American) Happy. *Keshann, Keshaun, Keshonn, Keshun, Keshawn*

Kesi (Swahili) Born when father was in trouble. *Kesee, Kesey, Kesie*

Kesia (African) Favorite. *Kessia, Kessiah, Kessya*

Kessie (Ghanese) Fat at birth.

Kestra (Science fiction) Character from *Star Trek: The Next Generation*.

Ketaki (Indian) Monsoon flower.

Ketika (Hindi) Meaning unknown.

Keturah (Hebrew) Fragrance.

Ketzia (Hebrew) Surface; cinnamonlike bark.

Kevina (Gaelic) Lively; from Kevin. (Irish) Beautiful. *Kevine, Kevinne, Kevyn, Kevynn, Kevynne*

Kevlyn (American) Handsome child; variation of Kevin.

Keyah (African) In good health.

Keyanna (American) Living with grace.

Keyla (American) Living with grace. *Keylon*

Kezia (Hebrew) Cassia; cinnamon. *Keesha, Keziah, Ketzia, Kezzy, Keisha, Keishia, Keshia, Lakeisha*

Khadijah (Arabic) The prophet's first wife; trustworthy. *Khadaja, Khadajah, Khadije, Khadijia*

Khalidah (Arabic) Immortal. *Khalidda, Khalita*

Khanh (Vietnamese) Meaning unknown.

Khara (Latin) Dearest. *Cara*

Khety (Egyptian) Meaning unknown.

Khina (Greek) Goose, nesting. (Iranian) Sweet voice; variation of KhinA.

Kia (African) Hill.

Kiah (Australian Aboriginal) From the beautiful place.

Kiana (Hawaiian) Moon goddess. *Kianah, Kiane*

Kiandra (English) From Kendra.

Kianga (African) Sunshine.

Kianna (Irish) Ancient. *Kiana, Kiani*

Kiara (Celtic, Gaelic) Small; dark.

Kiaria (Japanese) Fortunate.

Kiarra (Irish) Small; dark.

Kichi (Japanese) Fortunate.

Kiden (African) Female born after three boys.

Kiele (Hawaiian) Gardenia; fragrant blossom.

Kiera (Irish, Scottish) Dusky; dark-headed; dark; black. *Kyra, Kieran, Kiearra*

Kiersten (Scandinavian) Anointed.

Kieu (Vietnamese) Meaning unknown.

Kiho (African) Fog.

Kijana (African) Youth.

Kiki (Spanish) Short for names beginning with K.

Kiku (Japanese) A chrysanthemum.

Kilana (Science fiction) Character from *Star Trek: Deep Space Nine*.

Kilenya (Native American) Coughing fish.

Kiley (Irish) Good-looking; from the straits. *Kielea, Kielee, Kielei, Kieley, Kieli, Kielia, Kielie*

Killian (Irish) Little warrior. (Gaelic) Fierce. *Kilean, Kilian, Kiliane, Kilien, Killiean, Killien, Killion, Kyllien*

Kim (Old English) Chief. *Kym, Kimmi, Kimmey, Kimmy, Kimball, Kimble, Kimbell, Kemble*

Kimama (Native American) Butterfly.

Kimatra (Hindi) Seduce. *Kim*

Kimber (English) Leader. *Kim, Kimball, Kimberly, Kimberley*

Kimberley (Old English) Land belonging to Cyneburg; royal fortress; meadow. *Kimberly, Kimberlee, Kymberly, Kimby, Kim, Kimmi, Kimmie, Kimmy*

Kimi (Japanese) She who is without equal.

Kimimela (Native American) Butterfly.

Kimn (English) Ruler.

Kimora (Chinese) Meaning unknown.

Kin (Japanese) Golden.

Kina (Hawaiian) China.

Kindness (Anglo-Saxon) Warm-hearted and considerate.

Kineks (North American) Rosebud.

Kineta (Greek) Active one.

Kinfe (African) Wing.

Kinipela (Hawaiian) Wave.

Kinsey (English) Offspring. *Kensey, Kinnsee, Kinnsey, Kinnsie, Kinsee, Kinsie, Kinzee*

Kioko (Japanese) Meets world with happiness.

Kiona (Native American) Brown hills.

Kione (African) Someone who comes from nowhere.

Kipling (English) Cured salmon. *Kiplin*

Kipp (English) High hill.

Kippi (Old Norse) Tied together.

Kira (Persian) Sun. (Latin) Light. (Japanese) Sunlight. (Science fiction) Character from *Star Trek: Deep Space Nine*. *Keera, Kera, Kiera, Kierra, Kiria, Kiriah, Kirya, Kirra*

Kirabo (African) Gift from God.

Kiral (Turkish) Supreme chief.

Kiran (Hindi) Ray of light. *Kiranpal*

Kirana (Hindi) Ray of light.

Kirby (Anglo-Saxon) From the church town. *Kirbee, Kirbey, Kirbie*

Kiri (Cambodian) Mountain.

Kirima (Eskimo) A hill.

Kirit (Hindi) Crown.

Kiros (African) The king.

Kirra (Celtic) Dark lady.

Kirsi (Hindi) Amaranth blossoms.

Kirsten (Greek) Christian; stone church. *Kristine, Kristi, Kirstin, Kirstie, Kirsty, Kirsti, Kiersten, Kier*

Kirtana (Hindi) Praise.

Kirti (Hindi) Fame.

Kisa (Russian) Kitty.

Kisha (Slavic) Rainfall. *Keshah*

Kishi (Native American) Night.

Kiska (Russian) Pure.

Kismet (English) Fate; destiny. *Kismat, Kismete, Kismett*

Kissa (Ugandan) Born after twins. *Kisser*

Kita (Japanese) North.

Kitra (Hebrew) Crowned.

Kitty (Latin) Little cat. *Kit, Kittee, Kittey, Kitti, Kittie*

Kitu (Hindi) Meaning unknown.

Kiwa (Japanese) Born on the border.

Kiya (Australian) Always returning; pretty girl; from the name Kylie. *Kya*

Kiyoshi (Japanese) Quiet child.

Kizzy (Hebrew) Cinnamon. *Kissee, Kissie, Kiz, Kizzie*

Klara (Hungarian) Bright and famous. *Klari, Klarice, Klarika, Klarissa, Klarisza, Klaryssa*

Klarika (Hungarian) Brilliant.

Klarissa (German) Bright-minded. *Clarissa, Klarisa, Klarise*

Klavdia (Slavic) A lame one.

Klementyna (Polish) Mild; merciful. *Klementina, Clemence, Clementine*

Kludia Origin and meaning unknown.

Knowledge (Middle English) To confess, to recognize.

Kochava (Hebrew) Star.

Koge (Japanese) Fragrant flower.

Kogen (Japanese) Wild, untamed source. *Kogyn*

Kohana (Japanese) Little flower.

Koko (Native American) Night.

Koleyn (Native American) Coughing fish.

Kolina (Greek) Pure.

Kolton (English) Coal town.

Komal (Hindi) Tender.

Komala (Hindi) Delicate.

Konane (Hawaiian) Lunar glow.

Konstance (Latin) Loyal. *Constance, Kon, Konstanze*

Kora (Greek) A companion; maiden. *Korah, Kore, Korra*

Kordell (Latin) Warm-hearted. (Welsh) Sea jewel. (French) Rope maker. (English) From Cordell.

Koren (Greek) Maiden. *Kori, Korry, Korrie, Korin*

Kori (Greek) Girl.

Korina (Greek) Strong-willed; small girl. *Corinna, Koreena, Korena, Korinna, Koryna*

Kortney (English) Courteous.

Kory (American) Hollow.

Kosma (Greek) Universe; harmony.

Kostya (Slavic) Faithful.

Koto (Japanese) Harp.

Kourtney (English) From the court; dignified. *Courtney, Kortnee, Kortni, Kourtny, Kourtnie*

Kozue (Japanese) Tree branches.

Kreeli (American) Sweet and charming.

Krisalyn (American) Beautiful bearer of Christ.

Krista (Czechoslovakian) Christ-bearer; short for Christina. *Khrista, Krysta*

Kristal (English) Clear; brilliant; glass.

Kristen (Greek) Bright-eyed; follower of Christ. *Christen, Cristen, Kristin*

Kristi (Greek) Anointed follower of Christ.

Kristina (Greek) Anointed; Christ-bearer. *Christina, Krista, Kristie, Krysteena*

Kristine (Greek) Christ-bearer.

Kristy (Greek) Christ-bearer.

Kristyn (Greek) Christian; anointed; variation of Kristen.

Kriti (Hindi) A work of art.

Krupa (Hindi) Meaning unknown.

Krupali (Hindi) Meaning unknown.

Krysta (Czechoslovakian) Christian; anointed.

Krystal (American) A clear, brilliant glass. *Cristalle, Cristel, Crysta, Crystal, Crystalle, Khristalle, Khristel, Khrystle, Khrystalle, Kristel, Krys, Krystalle, Krystalline, Krystelle, Krystie, Krystle, Krystylle*

Krysten (Greek) Anointed follower of Christ.

Krystina (Greek) Anointed.

Krystyn (Scandinavian) Christian; anointed.

Ksena (Polish) Praise to God.

Kshama (Hindi) Forgiveness; patience; a form of the Devi.

Kuhuk (Hindi) Meaning unknown.

Kuma (Japanese) Bear.

Kumani (African) Destiny.

Kumi (Japanese) Long; continued beauty.

Kumiko (Japanese) Braid. *Kumi*

Kumud (Hindi) Lotus.

Kuniko (Japanese) Child from the country.

Kunti (Hindi) The mother of Pendavas.

Kura (Japanese) Treasure house.

Kuron (African) Thanks.

Kusum (Indian) A flower.

Kwanita (Native American) God is gracious.

Kwashi (African) Born on Sunday.

Kya (African) Diamond in the sky.

Kyara (Irish) Little and dark.

Kyla (Irish) Lovely. (Old English) Narrow; narrow channel. (Yiddish) Crown. *Kylene, Kylee, Ky, Kylah*

Kylar (English) Chapel; shelter.

Kyle (Irish) Narrow land; handsome.

Kylee (Celtic) Crown; from Kyla.

Kyleigh (Irish) Narrow land.

Kylene (Irish) Little piece of land.

Kylia (American) Narrow land.

Kylie (Aborigine) Boomerang. *Kayleigh, Kay, Leigh, Kayle*

Kyna (Gaelic) Wise. *Kyne, Cyna, Cyne*

Kynan (Welsh) Chief.

Kynthia (Greek) Born under the sign of cancer. *Cinthia, Cynthia*

Kyoko (Japanese) Mirror.

Kyra (Greek) Noble. *Kyrea, Kyree, Kyrie, Kyry*

Kyrene (Greek) Lord; ruler.

Kyria (Greek) Ladylike. *Kyrea, Kyree, Kyrie, Kyry*

Kyrielle (French) French verse.

L

L'Oréal (French) Brand name.

Laah (Hebrew) Weary.

Laasya (Hindi) Dance.

Labana (Hebrew) The moon; whiteness; frankincense.

Labdhi (Native American) Heavenly power.

Lacey (Latin) Cheerful. *Laci, Lacie, Lacy, Laicee, Laicey, Layce*

Lachelle (African American) Sweetheart. *Lachel, Lachell, Laschell, Lashelle*

Lachesis (Latin) Fury.

Lachlan (Celtic/Gaelic) From the lake.

Lacienega (Spanish) The swamp, marshes.

Lacy (Greek) Happy. *Lace, Laycee, Lacie, Lase*

Lada (Slavic) Goddess of love and fertility.

Ladan (American) Bright as day.

Ladawn (English) Sunrise.

Ladonna (Spanish) The woman.

Ladye (English) Lady.

Lae (Laos) Dark.

Lael (Hebrew) Of God.

Laela (Hebrew) Dark beauty; night. (Arabic) Born at night. *Lael, Laele*

Laetitia (Latin) Joy. *Leticia, Lateaciah, Lateacya, Latycia, Letisia, Letzyiah*

Laguna (Place name) Laguna Beach, California; water-loving. *Lagunah*

Lahela (Hawaiian) Innocent lamb.

Lahoma (Native American) The people.

Laila (Arabic) Night. (Hebrew) Dark beauty. *Laili, Laleh, Layla, Laylah, Leila*

Lailie (Hebrew) Born during light.

Laima (Slavic) Luck.

Lainey (English) Sun ray. *Laine*

Laisa (Biblical place name) Variation of Elasa, located north of Jerusalem.

Laisha (Hebrew) A lion.

Lajerrica (English) Powerful ruler.

Lake (English) Body of water.

Lakeisha (Swahili) Favorite one. *Lawanna, Latasha, Latoya, Latonya, Lakeesha*

Laken (American) From the lake.

Lakeshia (American) Joyful. *Keishia, Lakaisha, Lakeesha, Lakeishah, Lakezia, Lakisha*

Lakia (Arabic) Treasure.

Lakin (African American) Found treasure.

Lakota (Native American) Friend.

Laksha (Hindi) White rose.

Lakshmi (Hindi) Lucky omen. *Laxmi*

Lakyle (Gaelic) Half wood.

Lala (Slavic) Tulip.

Lalaine (American) Helpful and hardworking.

Lalan (Hindi) Nurturing.

Lalasa (Hindi) Love.

Laleh (Arabic) From Leila.

Lali (Greek) Well-spoken.

Lalima (Hindi) Redness.

Lalisa (English) Noble; kind.

Lalita (Hindi) Variety; beauty. *Lai, Lala, Lali, Lalitah, Lalite, Lalitte*

Lalitamohana (Hindi) Attractive, beautiful.

Lalo (Latin) To sing a lullaby.

Lama (Arabic) Darkness of lips.

Lamees (Arabic) Soft to the touch.

Lamis (Arabic) Soft.

Lamya (Arabic) Dark.

Lan (Vietnamese) Flower.

Lana (Polynesian) To float. *Lan, Lanna, Lanny*

Lanai (Hawaiian) Terrace; veranda.

Landen (English) Rough land.

Landon (English) Grassy plain.

Landrada (Spanish) Counselor.

Landry (English) Rough road.

Lane (Middle English) Narrow road. *Laine, Layne, Layna*

Lanelle (African American) Narrow road.

Lanette (American) Beautiful. *Lanetta, La-Net, LaNett, LaNette*

Laney (English) Path, roadway.

Lang (Scandinavian) Tall one.

Langley (English) Long meadow. *Langlee, Langli, Langlie, Langly*

Lani (Hawaiian) Sky; heaven. *Lannie*

Lanikai (Hawaiian) Heavenly sea.

Lanna (English, Irish) Good-looking, beautiful.

Lanni (Irish) Attractive.

Lansing (Place name) Lansing, Michigan. *Lanseng*

Lanza (Italian) Noble and eager.

Lapis (Egyptian) Lapis lazuli; gemstone.

Laquanna (African American) Outspoken. *Kwanna, LaQuanna, LaQwana, Quanna*

Laqueta (African American) The quiet one.

Laquetta (English) Wildflower. *Quetta, Etta*

Laquiesha (American, English) Joyful, happy. *Laquisha*

Laquinta (African American) The fifth.

Laquita (African) The fifth.

Lara (Latin) Well-known; name of a nymph.

Laraine (Latin) Sea bird. *Lareine, Larene, Loraine*

Larby (American) Pretty; form of Darby. *Larbee, Larbey, Larbi, Larbie*

Lareina (Greek, Spanish) Seagull; flies over water; the queen. *Larayna, Larayne, Lareine, Larena, Larrayna, Larreina*

Lari (English) Crowned with laurel. *Larie*

Laria (Greek) The stars are mine.

Larina (Greek) Sea gull.

Larisa (Greek) Cheerful one.

Larissa (Greek) Sea gull. *Lareesa, Lareese, Larresa, Laris*

Lark (English) A bird. *Larke, Larkin, Lirkin*

Larsen (Scandinavian) Laurel crowned. *Larson, Larssen, Larsson*

Larue (French) The street. *LaRue*

Larya (Slavic) Crowned with laurel.

Lashawn (African American) God is gracious.

Lashonda (American) God is gracious. *Lashanda, Lala, Lasha, LaShanda, LaShounda*

Lassie (Irish) Young girl, maiden.

Lasthenia (Latin) Herb of Pacific coast of North and South America; golden fields. (Greek) Natural philosopher; one of Plato's female students.

Lata (Hindi) A creeper; vines.

Latanya (African American) The fairy queen.

Latasha (American) Beauty. *Latacha, LaTasha, Latayshah, Latisha*

Lateefah (North African) Gentle; pleasant. *Latifa, Latiffa, Lateefa*

Latifah (African) Elegant. *Lateefa, Latifa, Latiffe, Latifuh*

Latika (Hindi) Small creeper.

Latisha (Latin) Great joy.

Latona (Greek) Goddess name.

Latonia (Latin) Mother of Apollo and Diana. *Latone, Latonea*

Latonya (African American) Praised woman. *Latonia, LaToya, Tonya*

Latoya (African American, American, Spanish) Praised woman; victorious one. *LaToyah, Toyah*

Latreece (American) Go-getter. *Latreese, Letrice*

Latrice (American) Weary; bringer of joy. *Tricey, Trice*

Laura (Latin) Laurel leaves; honor; fame; spirit. *Laure, Lora, Lori, Lorna, Laurie, Lorry, Laurel, Lauren, Lauryn, Lorin, Laurin, Laurien, Loryn, Laureen, Lauranne, Laurena, Lauretta, Laurette, Lorina, Lorene, Lauriette, Loretta, Lorette, Lorita, Lorenza, Lor*

Laurel (English) Crowned with laurel. *Laurell, Lorel, Lorell, Laural, Laurella, Laurelle, Lorella, Lourelle*

Lauren (French) Crowned with laurel. *Lauryn, Loren, Laurene, Laryn, Loryn*

Laurinda (Latin) Crowned with laurel; praise.

Lavada (American) Friendly and creative.

Lavani (Hindi) Grace. *Laboni*

Lavanya (Hindi) Grace.

Lave (Italian) Burning rock.

Laveda (Latin) Innocent one. *Lavella, Lavetta, Lavette, Levita*

Lavender (English) Purple-flowering plant.

Laverne (French) From the alder grove; springlike. *La Verne, Verna, Verne, Lally*

Lavey (Hebrew) Joined, attracted; from Levi.

Lavi (Hebrew) Lion.

Lavina (Latin) Woman of Rome.

Lavinia (Latin) Purity. *Lavine, Lavin*

Lavonn (American) Wood. *Lavonne, Lavaughan, Lavaughn, Lavon, Lavone, Lavonna, Lavonnah*

Lawanda (American) Little wanderer. *LaWanda, Lawonda*

Lawrence (Latin) Crowned with laurel.

Laxmi (Hindi) Meaning unknown.

Layla (African) Dark beauty; born at night. *Laela, Laila, Lala, Laya, Laylah, Laylie, Leila*

Layna (Greek) Light; truth. *Laynie*

Le (Chinese) Joy.

Lea (Hebrew) Meadow.

Leah (Hebrew) Weary. *Lea, Lia, Liah, Lee, Leatrice*

Leala (French) Loyal one.

Leandra (Greek) Lion woman. *Leandrea, Leanndra, Leeandra*

Leane (English) Gracious plum.

LeAnn (English) Light; variation of Helen.

Leann (Latin) Youthful.

Leanna (English) Graceful willow.

Leanne (English) Graceful plum.

Leanore (English) Torch. *Leonora*

Leatrix (American) Weary; bringer of joy.

Leauna (Latin) Young deer.

Leba (Yiddish) Beloved.

Lecea (American) Of noble birth.

Leda (Greek) Mother Creator. *Ledah, Lida, Lita*

Ledah (Hebrew) Birth. *Leda*

Ledell (Greek) Spartan queen.

Lee (Old English) Glade. (Gaelic) Poet. (English) Sheltered from the storm. (Irish) Poetic. (Chinese) Plum. *Leigh, Lea, Leanne, Leeanne, Leigh Anne, Li, Ly*

Leeann (English) Light; beautiful; woman.

Leelea (Sanskrit) Meaning unknown.

Leena (Russian) Illumination. *Lina, Lena*

Leetefa (Arabic) Delicate flower, sensitive. *Latifah, Lateiffa, Latifa, Ketifa*

Leeza (Hebrew) Devoted to God. *Leesa*

Lehana (African) One who refuses.

Lei (Chinese) Flower bud.

Leia (Hebrew) Weary.

Leigh (Old English) Meadow.

Leighanna (English) Gracious; poetic.

Leighna (American) Illustrious.

Leiko (Japanese) Arrogant.

Leila (Arabic) Dark as the night. *Lila, Lillah, Lyla, Leilia, Lela, Laila, Layla*

Leilana (Hawaiian) Heavenly flowers.

Leisel (German) Place in the district of Birkenfield in Rhineland-Palatinate.

Lela (Spanish) Lofty.

Lella (Latin) Lily.

Lemuela (Hebrew) Devoted to God. *Lemuelah, Lemuella, Lemuellah*

Lena (Hebrew) Dwelling. *Lina, Lenore, Leonore, Leonora, Leonne*

Lenci (Hungarian) Light.

Lene (Norwegian) Illustrious.

Lenka (Slavic) Illumination.

Lenora (Spanish) Brave as a lioness; from Leona.

Lenore (Greek) Light. *Lenor, Lenora*

Lenya (Russian) Lion.

Leola (Latin) Lion. *Leonarda, Leontine, Leontyne, Leona*

Leoma (German) Brave woman.

Leona (German) Lioness.

Leonie (German) Lioness.

Leonora (Greek) Light.

Leontyne (French) Like a lion.

Leopolda (Old German) Bold leader. *Leopoldine*

Leora (Hebrew) Light. *Liora, Leorah*

Leosa (Science fiction) Character from *Star Trek Voyager*.

Leotie (Native American) Flower of the prairie.

Lequoia (Native American) From the Sequoia tree.

Lesa (American) Consecrated to God.

Lesh (French) To restrain.

Lesley (Scottish) Gray fortress. *Lesle, Lesli, Leslie, Lesly, Leslye, Lezlie*

Leslie (Scottish) Dweller in the gray castle. (Old English) Small meadow. *Lesley, Lesly, Les, Lee*

Leta (Latin) Joy. (Swahili) Bringer. (Greek) Small with wings. *Leeta, Lita*

Letha (Greek) Forgetful; oblivion. *Lethia, Leitha, Leithia, Leda, Leta*

Lethia (Greek) Forgetfulness.

Leticia (Latin) Joy; gladness. *Letecia, Letisha, Letitia, Lettice, Tiesha*

Letitia (Latin) Joy. *Leticia, Letice, Letizia, Letycia, Leetice, Leta, Letty, Ticia, Tish, Latasha, Laetitia, Laticia*

Levana (Latin) Rising sun. *Livana*

Levia (Hebrew) Combined forces.

Lewa (African) Beautiful.

Lexi (Greek) Protector of mankind. *Lexsis, Lexus, Lexuss, Lexxus*

Lexie (English) Defender of mankind. (Greek) Variation of Alexandra.

Lexine (Hebrew) Helper and defender of mankind.

Lexis (English) Protector of mankind.

Lexus (Brand name) Make of car. *Lexorus, Lexsis, Lexxus*

Leya (Spanish) Loyalty.

Leyna (Old German) Little angel. *Leyns, Lenya*

Leyza Origin and meaning unknown.

Li (Chinese) Pretty; powerful.

Li Hua (Chinese) Pear blossom.

Li Mei (Chinese) Pretty rose.

Li Ming (Chinese) Pretty and bright.

Lia (Hebrew) Dependence. *Li, Liah*

Liadan (Irish) Gray lady.

Lian (Chinese) The graceful willow. *Leane, Leanne, Liane*

Liana (Hebrew) Vine; to bind; youth. *Lianna, Lianne, Liane, Leana*

Liani (Spanish) Daughter of the sun; variation of Elaina.

Liannaka (Dutch) Bringer of peace; hope. *Lan, Lani, Lanna, Anna*

Libba (Hebrew) Consecrated to God; from Elizabeth. *Libby, Libbi*

Libby (Hebrew) Consecrated to God.

Liberty (English) Freedom. *Libby*

Libra (Latin) The scales; equality.

Licia (Latin) Happy.

Lida (Russian) Beloved by all. *Leedah, Lyda*

Lidia (Greek) From Lydia, an ancient Asian land. *Lydia*

Lidiva Origin and meaning unknown.

Lien (Chinese) Lotus.

Lieneke (Dutch) Goddess of joy.

Liese (German) Beloved by God. *Liesl, Lieselotte*

Liesel (German) Dedicated and gracious. *Leesel, Leezel*

Lieu (Vietnamese) Willow tree.

Lila (Arabic) Night.

Lilac (Sanskrit) The lilac blossom; blue-purple.

Lilah (Arabic) Night.

Lilia (Slavic) Lilac. *Lileah, Lyleah, Lylia*

Lilian (Latin) Form of Lily. *Lillian*

Liliana (Latin) Lily flower. (English) Flower; innocence, purity; beauty.

Lilianna (Latin) Gracious lily.

Liliha (Hawaiian) Angry; disregard.

Lilika (Greek) Lily flower.

Lilike (Hungarian) Lily flower.

Lilith (Arabic) Of the night; night demon. *Lilyth, Lily*

What's in a Name

Lilith comes from the Assyrian word *lilitu*, meaning "of the night." In the Jewish and Islamic religions, Lilith was Adam's first wife, who was cast out of Eden and replaced by Eve because she would not submit to him. Adam and Lilith's offspring were the evil spirits of the world.

Lilka (Polish) Warrior maiden.

Lillian (English) Blend of Lily and Ann.

Lilliana (Latin) Lily flower.

Lillias (Latin) Lily.

Lilo (Hawaiian) Generous one.

Lilovarti (African) Joyfulness.

Liluye (Native American) Singing hawk while soaring.

Lily (Latin) A flower. *Lilian, Lily Ann, Lilian, Lilianne, Liliana, Lilias, Lilly, Lili, Lillie, Lilia, Lil, Lis*

Limber (African) Joyfulness.

Lin (Chinese) Beautiful; jade. *Linn, Lynn*

Lina (Greek) Tender; light of spirit. *Lena, Linah*

Linaeve (American) Tree of song.

Linda (Spanish) Pretty. *Lynda, Lindy, Lindi, Lin, Linden, Belinda*

Lindley (English) Pasture.

Lindsay (Old English) Linden island. *Lindsey, Lyndsay, Lyndsey, Lyndsy, Lynsey, Linsey, Lindy, Lindzee*

Linette (Middle French) Linnet bird; flaxen. *Lanette, Linet, Linnet, Lynette*

Ling (Chinese) Tinkling pieces of jade.

Linh (Vietnamese) Gentle spirit.

Linne (English) Waterfall.

Linnea (Scandinavian) Lime tree. *Lin, Linayah, Linea, Linnay, Lynnea*

Linore (Greek) From Lenore.

Liona (Italian) Lioness.

Liora (Hebrew) Light. (English) The laurel tree.

Lirit (Hebrew) Musical grace.

Lis (Scandinavian) Consecrated to God.

Lisa (Hebrew) Consecrated to God. *Lisette, Lisetta, Liza*

Lisabet (English) God of plenty; form of Elizabeth.

Lisbet (Hebrew) From Elizabeth.

Lise (German) Consecrated to God.

Lisea (Hebrew) Consecrated to God. *Lesa*

Liseli (Native American) Meaning unknown.

Lisette (French) Devoted to God. *Lissette*

Lisimba (African) Lion.

Lisle (French) Of the island.

Lisolette (Scandinavian) Little and strong; form of Caroline; variation of Liselette.

Lita (Latin) Light.

Litonya (Native American) Hummingbird darting.

Litsa (Greek) One who brings good news.

Litzy (Scandinavian) Devoted to God.

Liv (Norwegian) Life. *Leev*

Livana (Greek) Goddess. *Livanna, Livania, Livanya*

Livi (Latin) Olive branch; peace.

Livia (Hebrew) From Olivia.

Livvy (Greek) From Oliver.

Lixue (Chinese) Pretty snow.

Liz (English) Consecrated to God; variation of Elizabeth. *Lis, Lizzy, Lizzi*

Liza (Hebrew) Consecrated to God. *Leeza, Lizah, Lyza*

Lizbeth (Hebrew) From Elizabeth.

Lizeth (Hebrew) Devoted to God.

Lizette (English) God of plenty; variation of Elizabeth.

Lizina (Slavic) Consecrated to God.

Llewellyn (Welsh) Like a lion.

Lluvia (Spanish) Rain.

Loan (Vietnamese) Meaning unknown.

Loba (African) To talk.

Locke (Old English) Stronghold.

Loe (Hawaiian) King.

Logan (Scottish) Little hollow. *Logun*

Lois (Hebrew) Better. (French) Renowned fighter (German) Warrior. *Loes*

Lokelani (Hawaiian) Small red rose.

Loki (Scandinavian) Trickster god.

Lola (Spanish) Strong woman. *Lolita*

Lolaksi (Hindi) A sakti of Ganesha.

Lolita (Spanish) Manly; variation of Carlos.

Lolovivi (African) Love is sweet.

Lomasi (Native American) Pretty flower.

Lona (English) Lioness; ready for battle. *Lonee, Lonna*

London (English) Fortress of the moon.

Loni (English) Lion.

Lonikie (Dutch) Pretty one.

Lonna (Slavic) Light.

Lora (Latin) Laurel-crowned.

Lorand (Hungarian) Crowned with laurel. *Lorant*

Lore (Basque) A flower.

Lorelei (German) From the Rhine River.

Lorelle (American) Variation of Laurel.

Lorena (English) Crowned with laurel. *Loren, Lorren, Lorron, Lorryn, Loryn*

Lorene (American) Small victories.

Loretta (English) Small, wise one. *Lauretta, Lorretta*

Lori (Latin) Crowned with laurel. *Laurie, Loree, Lorie, Lory*

Lorinda (Latin) Crowned with laurel. *Larinda, Lorenda*

Loring (French) Famous in war.

Lorna (Celtic) Of Lorne. *Lorenah*

Lorraine (Old German) Where Lothar dwells. *Lorry, Lorrie, Loretta, Lorette, Lorne, Lorna, Lori*

Losira (Science fiction) Character from *Star Trek.*

Lotta (Latin) Petite beauty.

Lotte (German) Little and strong; old-fashioned; from Charlotte. *Lottee, Lotti, Lotty*

Lottie (Latin) Petite beauty.

Lotus (Greek) Dreamlike; lotus flower.

Louanna (German) Gracious warrior.

Louhi (Finnish) Mythology; goddess of death; snake.

Louisa (German) Fights with honor.

Louise (Old German) Warrior maiden. *Luise, Louisa, Louisiana, Luisa, Loise, Lois, Loyce, Lisette, Luana, Luane, Luwana, Lou, Lu, Lulu, Lulie, Ouise, Ouisa, Eloise, Eloisa, Aloysia, Liusadh*

Lourdes (Place name) Section of France where Virgin Mary was seen. *Lordes, Lordez*

Louvain (Place name) City in Belgium.

Love (Old English) Loved one. *Lovie, Luv*

Lovette (English) Little loved one.

Lovey (American) Loved one. *Lovie*

Lowri (Welsh) Crowned with laurels.

Luana (German) Graceful battle maiden. (Hawaiian) Content; peaceful.

Luba (Russian) A lover. *Liba, Lubah, Lyuba*

Luca (Italian) Bringer of light.

Luce (Latin) Light.

Lucetta (French) Bringer of light; illumination.

Lucia (Italian) Light.

Luciana (Italian, Latin) Illumination; light.

Lucie (French) From Lucille.

Lucille (Latin) Light. *Loucil, Loucile, Loucille, Lucyl, Lucile*

Lucina (German) Goddess of childbirth. *Lucena, Lucinah, Lucyna*

Lucinda (Latin) Bringer of light. *Lucinda, Lucinde, Lukene*

Lucine (Armenian) Moon.

Lucky (American) Fortunate; light.

Lucrece (Latin) Bringer of light.

Lucretia (Latin) Riches. *Lucrezia, Lucrece, Lucy*

Lucy (Latin) Light. *Lucie, Lucia, Luce, Lou, Lu, Luza, Luz, Luciana, Lucianna, Lucianne, Lucienne, Lucida, Lucile, Lucille, Lucette*

Luella (Old English) Elfin. *Louella, Loella, Luelle*

Luisa (Spanish) Warrior; variation of Louis. *Louisa, Luisah, Luiza, Luysa*

Lujuana (Spanish) Renowned warrior. *Lu*

Luka (Latin) Light.

Lukina (Ukrainian) Graceful and bright.

Lula (Arabic) Pearl.

Lulu (African, Arabic) Pearl.

Lumina (Latin) Of the light; glowing.

Luna (Latin) Moon. *Lune, Lunetta*

Lundy (Scandinavian) By the island. *Lundrea, Lundee, Lundi*

Lunette (French) Little moon.

Lupe (Latin) Wolf.

Lupita (Spanish) From Guadalupe.

Lux (Spanish) Light.

Luyu (Native American) Wild dove.

Luz (Spanish) Light.

Ly (Vietnamese) Reason.

Lyanne (Greek) Melodious. *Liann, Lianne, Lyan, Lyana, Lyaneth, Lyann*

Lycorida (Greek) Twilight. Variation of Lycoris.

Lycoris (Greek) Twilight.

Lydia (Greek) Woman from Persia; beauty. *Lydie, Lidia*

Lydie (Greek) A maiden from Lydia, Greece.

Lykaios (Greek) Wolfish; of a wolf; wolflike.

Lyla (French) From the island. *Lila, Lilah*

Lyle (French) From the island. *Lile*

Lyn (American) Beautiful.

Lynda (American, English) Beautiful. *Linda, Lindi, Lynde, Lynn*

Lynde (English) From the hill of linden trees.

Lyndon (English) Flexible.

Lyndsay (English) From Linden Tree Island. *Lyndsey, Lindsay*

Lynelle (American) Pretty. *Linelle, Lynel*

Lyneth (Welsh) Beautiful one.

Lynette (English) Bird; little beauty. *Lynet, Lynnet, Linett*

Lynley (English) Meadow near the brook.

Lynn (Anglo-Saxon) A cascade.

Lynna (English) Waterfall.

Lynnea (Latin) Pretty.

Lynsey (American) From the linden tree.

Lynton (English) Town near the brook.

Lyra (Greek) Song; expression of emotion.

Lyric (Greek) Melodic word. *Lyrec*

Lyris (Greek) A harp; lyre. *Liris, Lirisa, Lirise, Lyre*

Lysa (German) From Lisa.

Lysandra (Greek) One who is freed.

Lysette (American) Pretty little one. *Lysett*

Lysia (Hebrew) Consecrated to God.

M

Mab (Gaelic) Joy, happiness; intoxicating one; a queen in legend. *Mave, Mavis, Mabley, Mabinna*

Mabel (Latin) Lovable. *Maybelle, Mabel, Maibelle, Mabella, Maybelline, Mabil, Mabry, Amabel*

Mabyn (Welsh) Ever young.

Macaria (Greek) Daughter of Hercules and Deianara; blessed.

Macayle (Hebrew) Who is like God; form of Michaela.

Macha (Native American) Aurora.

Machi (Japanese) Ten thousand.

Machiko (Japanese) Child of Machi; fortunate one.

Mackenzie (Irish) Child of the wise leader. *Mackensi, Mackenze, Mackenzey, Mackenzi, Mykenzie*

Macy (Polish) Sea of bitterness. *Mace, Macie, Macey*

Mada (English) High tower. *Madah, Maida*

Madalena (Greek) From Madeline; high tower; jaunty. *Madalyna, Madaleyna, Madelyna, Madelayna, Madelen, Madeleyna*

Maddox (English) Son of the Lord. *Maddax, Maddee, Maddux*

Madeira (Spanish, Portuguese) Sweet wine; an island off the African coast.

Madelia (Greek) High tower.

Madeline (Greek) High tower. (Hebrew) Woman from Magdala; variation of Magdalene. *Marlene, Magdalene, Magdalen, Magdalena, Maigarena, Mayalen, Madeleine, Madleen, Madalynn, Madelynne, Madelaine, Madalena, Madelon, Madelyn, Madlin, Madigan, Marleen, Marlena, Marline, Maighdlin, Maudlin, Malina, Magda, Mady, Maddy, Maddie, Matty, Mala, Mae, May, Lena, Lene, Magdaline, Maddalena*

Madge (Greek) Pearl. *Madgie*

Madhavi (Hindi) Creeper with beautiful flowers; springtime.

Madhu (Hindi) Honey.

Madhul (Hindi) Sweet.

Madhulika (Hindi) Nectar.

Madhur (Hindi) Sweet.

Madhuri (Hindi) Sweet girl; sweet; sweetness.

Madison (English) Good; child of Maud. *Maddison, Maddy, Madisyn*

Madja (Danish) Meaning unknown.

Madonna (Latin) My lady.

Madra (Spanish) Mother. *Madre, Madrona, Madonna, Madraye, Madreah*

Mae (English) Flower; month of May. (Latin) Great. *May*

Maegan (Irish) Pearl.

Maeko (Japanese) Truthful child.

Maemi (Japanese) Honest child.

Maeron (Irish) Bitter.

Maeryn (Gaelic) Bitter.

Maeve (Irish) Joyous. (Celtic) Queen. (Greek) Goddess of song. (Latin) Purple flower. *Maeva, Maive, Mave, Mayve*

Magan (Hindi) Absorbed. (Teutonic) Power. (Greek) Competent. *Magana, Magahn*

Magara (Rhodesian) Child who constantly cries.

 **Naming Rights**

Remember, your baby's name is ultimately your decision. No law says you have to choose a name you don't like just because it's been used before in your family. Perhaps it's time to introduce a new name.

Magda (Hebrew) High tower; one who is elevated.

Magdalen (Greek) High tower. (Hebrew) A woman from Magdala. *Magdala, Magdalena, Magdalene, Magdalina, Magdalone, Magdelena, Magdelina*

Magena (Hebrew) A covering; protection. (Native American) The coming moon.

Maggie (English) Pearl.

Magna (Latin) Strength. (Norse) Large. *Magnilda, Magnea*

Magnolia (Latin) A flower; flowering tree. *Magnole*

Maha (African) Beautiful eyes.

Mahal (Polynesian) Love.

Mahala (Hebrew) Woman; tenderness; marrow. (Hawaiian) Woman; tenderness. (Native American) Woman. (Arabic) Powerful. *Mahalah, Mahalar, Mahela, Mahalia, Mahelia, Mehala*

Mahalath (Arabic) Lyre.

Mahalia (Hebrew) Affection.

Mahari (African) Forgiver.

Mahdi (African) The expected one.

Mahdis (Persian) Moonlike.

Mahima (Hindi) Greatness.

Mahina (Hawaiian) Moon.

Mahita (Hindi) Honorable.

Mahogany (English) Dark wood. *Mahagonie, Mahogony*

Mahola (Hebrew) Dance.

Mahsa (Persian) Like the moon.

Mahubeh (Arabic) Good greeting; good fortune; variation of Mahubah.

Mai (Japanese) Brightness. (Native American) Coyote. (Vietnamese) Flower. *Maie*

Maia (Greek) Mother; nurse. (English) Maiden. *Maiah, Maea*

Maida (Old English) Maiden. *Maidie, Maidy, Mady, Maidel, Mayda*

Maik (Hawaiian) Now.

Maiko (Japanese) Child of Mai.

Maili (Polynesian) Gentle breeze.

Maille (Gaelic) Sea of bitterness; form of Molly.

Maimun (Arabic) Lucky.

Maina (Hindi) Bird.

Maine (French) Mainland. *Mayne*

Maire (Irish) Bitter. *Mair*

Mairead (Scottish) Pearl. *Maired, Mared*

Mairi (Gaelic) Sea of bitterness; a version of Mary.

Mairwen (Welsh) Fair; a version of Mary.

Maisha (African) Life.

Maisie (Gaelic, Scottish) Pearl. *Maesee, Maesey, Maesi, Maesie, Maesy, Maisee, Maisey, Maisi, Maisy, Maize, Maizie, Margaret,*

Marjorie, Maysie, Mazee, Mazey, Mysie

Maitane (English) Dearly loved. (Spanish) Darling; beloved.

Maitea (Spanish) Love. *Maite, Maitena*

Maitland (English) Meadow. *Maitlande, Mateland, Matelande, Maytland, Matylande*

Maitryi (Hindi) Friendship. *Maitri*

Maizah (African, Arabic) Discerning.

Maj (Swedish) Pearl.

Maja (Arabic) Splendid.

Majondra (Spanish) Meaning unknown. *Majie, Maj, Jondra*

Maka (Native American) Earth.

Makaila (American) Who is like God.

Makaio (Hawaiian) Gift of God.

Makala (Hawaiian) Shrub.

Makana (Hawaiian) Gift.

Makani (Hawaiian) The wind.

Makara (Hindi) Born under Capricorn.

Makayla (American) Who is like God.

Makeena (American) Child of the wise; from McKenna.

Makelina (Hawaiian) From Magdelene.

Makiko (Japanese) Child of Maki.

Makya (Native American) One who hunts eagles.

Mala (Greek) High tower; variation of Magdelene.

Malachite (English) Precious gem.

Malaika (African) Angel.

Malana (Hawaiian) Light.

Malati (Hindi) Small, fragrant flower; Jasmine flower. *Malti*

Malavika (Hindi) From Malva.

Malaya (Filipino) Free. *Malae*

Malca (Hebrew) Queen. *Malka, Malcah*

Maleah (Hawaiian) Bitter.

Malha (Hebrew) Queen.

Mali (Southeast Asian) Flower; smart; funny; lucky. *Mal, Malee, Maley, Malie, Malley, Mallie, Maly*

Malia (Hawaiian) Calm and peaceful. *Maylia*

Maliha (Hindi) Strong; beautiful. (Arabic) Pretty; good-looking. *Mali, Malha, Hala*

Malika (Arabic) Queen; princess. (Slavic) Industrious. (Sanskrit) Garland. *Malik, Malikah*

Malila (Miwok Indian) Salmon going fast upstream.

Malin (Scandinavian) Woman from Magdela.

Malina (Hebrew) Tower. (Native American) Soothing. *Malinah, Malinna, Malyna, Malini*

Malinza (Science fiction) Character from *Star Wars*.

Malise (Celtic) Black; dark.

Malissa (Greek) Honey bee.

Malka (Hebrew) Queen.

Malkia (African) Queen.

Mallika (Hindi) Jasmine. *Malika*

Malloren (American) Laurel of bad luck.

Mallory (French) Without good fortune. (German) Army counselor. *Mallorie, Mallorey, Malori, Malory, Mal, Mally, Malin*

Mallow (Irish) By the river Allo.

Malti (Hindi) Small, fragrant flower.

Malu (Hawaiian) Peacefulness.

Malvina (Scottish) Armored chief. *Melvina, Malva, Malvie, Melvine, Mevin, Mally, Melly, Mal, Mel, Mellen*

Mamie (English) Bitter. *Mamee, Mamey, Mami, Mamy*

Mamiko (Japanese) Child of Mami.

Mamta (Hindi) Mother's love for child; wife of sage Asija.

Manar (Arabic) Guiding light. *Manaar, Manara*

Manasa (Hindi) Mind.

Manasi (Hindi) Born of the mind. *Manasie*

Manavi (Hindi) Wife of Manu.

Manda (Spanish) Warrior. *Mandakini*

Mandana (Persian) Everlasting.

Mandara (Hindi) Mythical tree; calm.

Mandeep (Hindi) Light of heart.

Mandel (German) Almond. *Mandell*

Mandelina (American) Lovable.

Mandisa (African) Sweet.

Mangena (Hebrew) Melody.

Manhattan (Place name) Island bordering lower Hudson River. (English) Whiskey. *Manny, Manda, Maisie*

Manisha (Hindi) Sharp intellect, genius; sagacity.

Manjari (Hindi) The sacred basil; blossom.

Manju (Hindi) Sweet.

Manjula (Hindi) Sweet.

Manjusha (Hindi) Treasure chest. (Sanskrit) A box of jewels.

Manon (French) Bitter.

Manoush (Arabic) Sweet sun.

Mansi (Hopi Indian) Plucked flower.

Manuela (Spanish) God is with us. *Manuella*

Manushi (Hindi) Human.

Manyara (African) You have been humbled.

Mapiya (Native American) Sky; heavenly.

Mara (Greek) Eternally beautiful. (Hebrew) Melody.

Marayna (Science fiction) Character from *Star Trek Voyager*.

Marcella (Latin) God of war; little hammer. *Marcy, Marcie, Marcelle, Marceline, Marclyn, Marcelin, Marciana*

Marcia (Latin) Martial, warlike; brave. *Marzia, Marsha, Marshe, Marcille, Marchita, Marchette, Marquita, Martia, Marcelia, Marcy, Marci, Marcie, Marcey, Marsi, Marsy, Marsie*

Mardi (French) Tuesday.

Mareel (Science fiction) Character from *Star Trek: Deep Space Nine*.

Maren (Latin) Sea; of the sea; bitter. *Marin, Marren, Marrin*

Maretta (Hebrew) Bitter. *Mari, Mary, Marella, Mariette*

Margaret (Greek, Persian, Hebrew, Irish, Latin) Child of light; pearl; jewel. *Maggie, Maggy, Magee, Mag, Margery, Margareta, Margarita, Margita, Margory, Marjorie, Marjory, Marget, Margret, Margette, Margalo, Marguerite, Margarida, Margiad, Margherita, Margarethe, Maergrethe, Margaretha, Margalith, Mairghread, Margo, Marjoe, Marga, Margot, Margaux, Marge, Margie, Marta, Madge, Mamie, Maymie, Maisie, Meg, Meggie, Midge, Gretchen, Gretel, Gretle, Greta, Grete, Garet, Peg, Peggy, Reta, Rita*

Marge (American) Pearl. *Marg*

Margo (French) Pearl. *Margot, Margeaux*

Maria (Hebrew) Bitter; the star of the sea. *Mary, Marya, Mariah, Marie, Malia, Ri, Mar*

Mariabella (Italian) Beautiful. *Mary, Mariabelle, Maribel, Maribelle*

Mariah (Hebrew) Bitter; star of the sea; God is my teacher. *Mariaha, Mariahna*

Mariam (Hebrew) Wife of Herod; bitter; mother of Jesus; wished-for child. *Mariamne, Mariama*

Marianne (French) Little; bitter. *Mary, Manya, Marianna, Mara, Marian, Marisha, Marilyn, Maire, Marion, Marrion, Mariana, Mariann, Mary-Ann, Maryanne*

Mariasha (Egyptian) Perfect one. (Hebrew) Bitter with sorrow.

Maribel (French) Beautiful. *Maribella, Maribelle*

Maricel (Latin) Full of grace. *Mar, Maricelle, Marcella*

Maridel (English) Beautiful; bitter.

Marie (French) Bitter. *Maree, Mary*

Mariel (German) Bitter. *Marielle, Mariella, Marietta, Mariette, Marette, Maretta*

Marietta (Italian) Little bitter; the star of the sea. *Marieta, Maryeta, Maryetta*

Marigold (Greek) A flower; mother of Jesus. *Mari, Golda, Goldie*

Mariko (Japanese) Child of Mari; circle.

Marilee (Greek, Spanish) Bitterness; God is with us. *Mary Lee, Marilea*

Marilynne (Hebrew) Descendent of Mary. *Marilyn*

Marina (Latin, Russian) Sea maiden. *Marin*

Marinette Origin and meaning unknown.

Marinka (Russian) Of the sea. *Marina*

Mariola (Spanish) Wild field plant from Texas.

Marion (French) Bitter; star of the sea. *Mariano, Mariana*

Mariposa (Spanish) Butterfly. *Mariposah, Maryposa*

Maris (Latin) Of the sea. *Marice, Meris, Marys*

Marisa (Spanish) Of the sea; bitter. *Marce, Maressa, Marissa, Marisse, Mariza, Marsie, Marysa, Maryssa, Merisa*

Marissa (Latin) Of the sea. *Marisa, Maris, Mari, Marina, Maressa, Maritza, Merisa, Merrisa, Marissah, Rissa*

Maritza (German) Of the sea.

Marjani (African) Coral.

Marjeta (Czechoslovakian) Pearl.

Marjorie (Greek) Pearl. *Marjory, Marjorey, Marjary, Margery, Margey, Margie, Marge, Margo, Marje, Marjy, Marcail*

Marla (English) Star of the sea. *Marlene, Magdala*

Marlee (Australian) On elder tree. *Marleigh, Marley, Marli, Marlie, Marly*

Marlene (Greek) Child of light; from the high tower. *Marlena, Marleen, Marline, Marly, Marlie, Marla, Lene, Lena, Madeline*

Marley (English) Marshy meadow; woman from Magdala. *Marlene*

Marliss (English) Woman of Magdala. *Marla, Molly, Marlene*

Marmara (Greek) Radiant.

Marna (Hebrew) Rejoice. *Marnie, Marni, Marny, Marnette, Marne*

Marnina (Hebrew) Cause of joy. *Marneena, Marnyna*

Marny (Scandinavian) From the sea.

Marsala (Italian) A town; a sweet, fortified wine.

Marsena (Hebrew) Bitterness of a bramble.

Marta (Arabic, English, Greek, Hebrew, Italian, Scandinavian, Spanish) Lady; mistress; bitter; pearl.

Martha (Aramic) A lady; mistress; who becomes bitter; provoking. *Marth, Marta, Martina, Marella, Martita, Marti, Marty, Mattie, Matty, Marthe, Masia*

Martina (Latin) Warlike; who loves everyone; warring. *Marta, Martine, Marty, Tina, Martin*

Maruti (Hindi) Lord Hanuman.

Marvelle (French) Miracle. *Marvel, Marvell, Marva, Marvella*

Mary (Hebrew) Bitter; rebellion. *Mari, Merry, Marie, Maria, Miriam, Marian, Mame, Mamie, Maymie, Mayme, May, Mally, Molly, Polly, Mara, Maretta, Marel, Marella, Maren, Marlo, Mariette, Marieta, Meriel, Mimi, Minette, Minnie, Minny, Mitzi, Madonna, Marilla, Marla, Marya, Muriel, Manon, Manette, Marija, Marika, Maire, Mare, Marquita, Maure, Mairin, Mair, Maura, Maureen, Moira, Moire, Moya, Muire, Masha, Mairi, Mariya, Mashia, Mash, Mariath*

Masago (Japanese) Sand.

Masako (Japanese) Child of Masa; justice.

Matana (Hebrew) Gift. (Arabic) Blessing. *Matanah, Matania, Matannia*

Matangi (Hindi) Devi.

Mathea (Hebrew) Gift of God. *Matthea, Mathia, Mattea, Mathia*

Mathilda (German) Battle maiden; strength; strong in war. *Matilda, Matelda, Maitilde, Mathylda, Mathilde, Matty, Mattye, Mattie, Maddy, Maddie, Mala, Tila, Tilly, Tillie, Tilda*

Matrika (Hindi) Mother; name of goddess.

Matsuko (Japanese) Pine-tree child.

Mattea (Hebrew) God's gift. *Mattaya*

Maud (English) Strength in battle; mighty battle maiden. *Maude, Maudie, Maudy, Maudine*

Maura (Irish) Dark-skinned; bitter; dark.

Maureen (French) Dark; dark-haired. (Irish) Bitter. *May, Maura, Mora, Moira, Moreen, Moria, Moriah, Maurin, Maurine, Morena, Maurizia, Mo*

Mauve (French) Violet.

Mavis (French) A small bird; song-thrush; joy. *Maves, Maeves, Maeve, Mauve, Meave, Maive*

Maxine (Latin) The greatest. *Maxeen, Maxene*

May (English) Month of May. (Hebrew) Bitter. (Latin) Great. *Mae, Mai, Maia, Maya, Maye, Mayes, Mays, Maize*

Maya (Greek) Mother. (Hindi) God's divine creative power.

Mayako (Japanese) Child of Maya.

Maysa (Arabic) Graceful.

Mayuko (Japanese) Child of Mayu.

Mayuri (Hindi) Peahen.

Meara (Gaelic) Merry, filled with mirth. *Mira, Meera*

Meckenzie (Gaelic) Daughter of the Wise Leader.

Meda (Native American) Priestess.

Medea (Greek) Ruling; goddess. (Latin) Middle child. *Medora, Media, Madora*

Medha (Hindi) Intelligence; a form of the Devi; Goddess Saraswati.

Medilion Origin and meaning unknown.

Medora (Greek, Latin) Ruling; middle child. *Medea, Meia, Madora*

Mee (Chinese) Beautiful.

Meena (Hindi) Precious blue stone. *Mina*

Meenakshi (Hindi) A woman with beautiful eyes.

Meera (Hebrew) Light. *Mira*

Megan (Greek) Mighty; strong, able; pearl; soft and gentle. *Meggy, Meghan, Meagan, Megann, Meggy, Meggie, Meg, Megs, Megless, Margaret, Maeghan*

Megara (Greek) Wife of Hercules; pearl.

Megha (Hindi) Cloud.

Meghana (Hindi) Raincloud.

Mehitabel (Hebrew) God is our joy. *Mehitabelle, Mehitabelle*

Mehri (Arabic) Kind; lovable; sunny.

Mei (Chinese) Plum. (Hawaiian) May. (Latin) Great one.

Meira (Hebrew) Light.

Mekell (African American) Who is like God. *Mekelle*

Mekia (Hawaiian) Eyes; member of the Royal Hawaiian Band who brought the first ukulele to the U.S. mainland.

Mela (Hindi) Religious gathering.

Melanctha (Greek) Black flower. *Melantha*

Melanie (Greek) Dark-skinned. *Melany, Melane, Melani, Melania, Melloney, Melonie, Melony, Milena, Melanya, Mellie, Melly, Mel, Mela*

Melba (Greek) Slender. (Latin) Mallow flower. *Melva, Malva*

Melenna (Greek) Yellow as canary. *Melena, Melina*

Melia (Greek) Industrious. (Hawaiian) Nymph daughter of Oceanus.

Melika (Arabic) Owner of slaves.

Melina (Latin) Bright canary yellow. *Melyna*

Melinda (Greek) Gentle one; honey. *Malinda, Malina, Malinde, Malena, Melina, Minda, Mindy, Mallie, Mally, Linda, Lindy*

Melisenda (French) Honest; diligent; sweet.

Melissa (Greek) Bee; honey bee. *Melicent, Mellissa, Millicent, Melisent, Melita, Melisse, Meli, Mellie, Melly, Mel, Millie, Milly, Missy, Lisa, Lissa, Lis*

Melitta (Greek) Honey sweet; honey bee; garden. *Melita, Melissa, Carmelita*

Melody (Greek) Song. *Melodie, Melodi, Melly, Mellie*

Melosa (Spanish) Gentle; sweet. *Melosia*

Melpomene (Greek) Tragedy. *Melpomeni*

Mena (Hindi) Mother of Menaka; wife of the Himalayas. *Meebah, Menah*

Menaka (Hindi) Celestial damsel.

Merane (French) Sea of bitterness. *Meraine, Meirane*

Mercedes (Latin) Ransom; virgin; merciful. (Brand name) Make of car. *Mary, Mercia, Mercy, Mercedees, Mercedeze, Mercedies*

What's in a Name

Emil Jellinek owned the rights to sell Daimler cars in Austria, Hungary, France, and the United States in the late 1800s. He sold the cars under his daughter's name—**Mercedes.** Daimler liked the name so much that in 1902, the company officially registered the name Mercedes as their car trademark.

Mercy (Middle English) Merciful; compassion; pity. *Merci, Mercia*

Meredith (Old Welsh) Protector of the sea. *Meridith, Merry, Meri*

Meridian (American) Perfect posture. *Meridiane*

Merit (Latin) Deserving. *Merritt, Merriwell*

Merla (French, Latin) Blackbird.

Merle (French) Blackbird. *Merl, Myrle, Meryl, Merlina, Myrlene, Merola, Merrill, Merla*

Merleen (English) Falcon. *Merlene*

Merlyn (French) Blackbird. (Welsh) The fort by the sea; falcon. *Merlin*

Meroe (Ethiopian) Former capital of Ancient Ethiopia.

Merry (Middle English) Mirthful, joyful. *Merri, Merrie, Merrilee, Merrily, Merrita, Merrielle, Meredith*

Mersadize (English) Princess.
Sadize, Sadi, Sadie

Meryl (German) Famous.
(French) Blackbird. (Irish)
Shining. *Meryle*

Mesha (Hindi) Ram; born under
the sign of Aries; burden; salvation.

Messina (African) The spoiler.
(Latin) The one in the middle.
Messena

Meta (Latin) Ambitious.
(German) Pearl. *Margaret.*

Mia (Italian) Mine. (Hebrew)
Bitter. (Scandinavian) Star of the
sea. *Miah*

Miakoda (Native American)
Power of the moon.

Michaela (Hebrew) Like God.
*Michaelina, Michaeline, Michelina,
Micaela, Mikaela, Miguela,
Michelle, Nichelle, Shelly, Shell,
Michal, Micheline, Michelyn,
Mickey, Mikhaeli, Mikaeli*

Michelle (Italian) Like the Lord;
close to God. *Michella, Michell,
Michellene*

Michi (Japanese) Righteous way.

Michiko (Japanese) Child of
Michi; beauty; wisdom.

Midge (Persian, Latin) Child of
light.

Midori (Japanese) Green.

Mieko (Japanese) Already prosperous.

Miette (French) Small, sweet
thing.

Migina (Omaha Indian) Moon
returning.

Migisi (Native American) Eagle.

Mignon (French) Dainty; petite;
delicate; graceful. *Mignonne,
Migonette, Migonn, Migonne*

Mihoko (Japanese) Child of
Miho.

Mika (Japanese) New moon.
(Native American) Intelligent
raccoon. (Russian) Child of
God.

Miki (Japanese) Flower stem.

Mila (Italian) Miracle. (Russian)
Dear one. *Camilla*

Milan (Place name) Milan, Italy.

Mildred (English) Gentle
adviser. *Mildrid, Mildraed,
Mildryd, Milly, Milli, Milley,
Millie, Hildred, Hil, Mil*

Milena (Slavic) The favored one.
Mela, Milina

Milissa (English) Bee. *Melissa*

Millicent (English) Industrious;
strength. *Millisent, Melicent,
Milly, Millie, Mili, Melly,
Melisande, Melisenda*

Mily (Hawaiian) Beautiful.
(English) Hard-working. *Milly*

Min (Korean) Cleverness; love;
smooth; fine; small.

Mina (Arabic) A place near
Makkah. (German) Love.
(Persian) Sky blue. *Meena, Mena,
Min, Minah, Myna, Mynah*

Minako (Japanese) Child of
Mina.

Minda (Hindi) Knowledge.

Mindel (Yiddish) Sea of bitterness.

Mine (Japanese) A resolute protector.

Minelli (American) Last name
used as first name, as in Liza
Minelli.

Minerva (Latin) Goddess of wisdom; power; thinker. *Minette,
Minnie, Minny*

Mingmei (Chinese) Smart; beautiful. *Mingmey*

Mink (American) Weasel-like.

Minka (Teutonic) Strong, resolute.

Minna (Old German) Love.
(Hebrew) Bitter. *Mina, Minnah,
Minette, Minetta, Minda, Myna,
Mindy, Willaminna*

Minta (Greek) Of the mint plant.
Mintha, Araminta, Mint

Mio (Spanish) Mine.

Mira (Latin) Wonder. (Spanish)
Behold. (Hebrew) Bitter. *Myra,
Mirila, Mirella, Mirelle, Mirielle,
Myrilla*

Mirabelle (Latin) Wonderful;
beautiful to look upon. *Mirabel,
Mirabella, Mirable, Marabel*

Miranda (Latin) Extraordinary;
to be admired; beautiful.
*Myranda, Meranda, Mira, Randy,
Mandy*

Miremba (Ugandan) Peace.

Mireya (Hebrew) God has spoken; miracle. *Mirielle, Mireille*

Miriam (Hebrew) Bitter; rebellion. *Miryam, Myriam, Mimi,
Mitzi, Miri, Mims, Mimsie,
Meryem, Mirjam, Mirem*

Mirth (Old English) Happiness;
mirth.

Misako (Japanese) Child of Misa.

Misha (Russian) Who is like
God. *Mishan*

Missy (Old English) Young girl.
Missie, Missye, Sissy

Misty (Old English) Covered by
mist. *Mistee*

Mitena (Native American)
Coming moon, new moon.

Mitexi (Native American) Sacred
moon.

Mitra (Hindi) Friend; the sun.

Mitsuko (Japanese) Child of
Mitsu.

Miwa (Japanese) Beautiful harmony.

Miya (Japanese) Sacred house.

Miyoko (Japanese) Beautiful generations; child of Miyo.

Miyuki (Japanese) Silence of deep snow.

Mnemosyne (Greek) Goddess of Mercy.

Modestus (Latin) Modest one.

Modesty (Latin) Modest one. *Modesta, Modestia, Modestine, Modeste, Modestus, Desty*

Moesha (African American) Drawn out of the water.

Mohini (Hindi) Most beautiful; enchantress.

Moira (Irish) Bitter; great. *Maura, Moyra, Maire, Mary*

Mollie (Irish) Bitter. *Maili, Molly, Mary*

Momoko (Japanese) Child of Momo.

Mona (Arabic) Peaceful. (Irish) Noble. (Greek) Solitary. *Monica*

Monica (Latin) Adviser; counselor. *Monca, Mona, Monique*

Monique (French) Wise. *Mon, Mone, Monee, Moneeqe, Moneeque, Moni, Moniqe*

Monisha (Hindi) Solitary life; Lord Krishna.

Montana (Spanish) Mountain, mountainous.

Moon (Korean) From the moon; letters.

Moon Unit (American) Universal appeal.

Mopsa (English) Shepherdess.

Mora (Spanish) Sweet berry.

Morgan (Welsh) Enchantress half-sister of Arthur; white sea; bright; dweller by the sea. *Morgana, Morganne, Morganica*

Morgance (Celtic) Sea-dweller.

Morgandy (Celtic) Little one from the edge of the sea.

Morgen (German) Morning.

Moria (Hebrew) My teacher is God. *Moriah, Moriel, Morit, Moryah*

Moselle (Hebrew) Drawn from the water. (French) A white wine. *Mosela, Mosella, Mozelle, Mosheh, Moses*

Mouna (Arabic) Wish, desire.

Mridul (Hindi) Soft. *Mridula*

Mrinalini (Hindi) Lotus.

Mukul (Hindi) Soul; bud.

Muna (Arabic) The Lord is with you. (Irish) Noble.

Muncel (African American) Strong and willing.

Muriel (Arabic) Myrrh. (Irish) Sea-bright. (Latin) Angel of June. *Murial, Meriel, Muireall*

Murphy (Irish) Sea warrior.

Muse (Greek) Nine daughters of Mnemosyne and Zeus; a guiding spirit.

Musetta (Old French) A ballad. *Musette, Musa, Muse*

Mutsuko (Japanese) Child of Mutsu.

Mya (Burmese) Emerald.

Mychau (Vietnamese) Great. *Mah Chow*

Myda (Greek) Wet, damp; moldy.

Myfanwy (Welsh) Sweet woman; the beloved one.

Myiesha (Arabic) Life's blessing.

Mykala (English) Who is like God.

Myoki (Japanese) Wondrous joy.

Myra (Latin) An aromatic shrub. *Miranda, Myrah, Myrra*

Myrna (Gaelic) Beloved. *Muirne, Merna, Mirna, Moina, Morna, Moyna*

Myrtle (Greek) A flower; symbol of victory; a tree. *Myrta, Myrtia, Myrtis, Mirtle, Mertle, Mertice, Mert, Myrtice, Myrtilla*

N

Nadda (Arabic) Generous.

Navila (Arabic) Born to nobility.

Nadezda (Czechoslovakian) One with hope.

Nadia (French) Hopeful. *Nada, Nade, Nadeen, Nadene, Nadi, Nadie, Nadina, Nadine, Nady*

Nadie (Russian) From the name Nadia.

Nadine (Slavic) Hope. *Nada, Nadina, Nadeen, Nadia, Nata, Nadya, Nadie, Nadezhda*

Nadira (Arabic) Precious; rare; pinnacle. *Nadirah, Nadra*

Naeva (French) Evening. *Naeve, Nahvon*

Nafeeza (Arabic) Precious thing. *Nafiza, Naf, Naffy, Naffo*

Nafuna (African) Delivered feet first.

Nagihan (Turkish) Meaning unknown.

Nahid (Arabic) Venus, goddess of love and beauty; one with full, round breasts.

Nahimana (Native American) Mystic.

Nahoko (Japanese) Child of Naho.

Naia (Greek) Flowing.

Naida (Greek) Water nymph. *Naiad, Naia, Naiia, Nayad, Nyad*

Nailah (African) Succeeding. *Naila*

Naimah (Arabic) Living a soft, enjoyable life. *Naeemah, Maima*

Naina (Hindi) Eyes.

Nairne (Scottish) From the narrow river glade.

Naiyah (Greek) Water nymph.

Naja (African) Stoic and strong. *Najah*

Najwa (African American) Passionate.

Nakeisha (African American) Her life.

Nakia (Egyptian) Pure; faithful. *Nakea*

Nala (African) Successful. *Nalah, Nalo*

Nalani (Hawaiian) Calmness of the skies. *Nalanie, Nalany*

Nalini (Sanskrit) Lovely.

Nalanie (Hawaiian) Heaven's calm.

Nallely (Hawaiian) Heaven's calm.

Namazzi (Ugandan) Water.

Nami (Japanese) Wave. *Namiko*

Namrata (Hindi) Modesty.

Nan (English) Gracious.

Naming Rights

Keeping the baby-to-be's name a secret is a good thing because many parents actually change their minds about the name as soon as the baby is born. Quite often, the name that has been decided upon just doesn't suit any longer once you are actually holding the baby in your arms.

Nanako (Japanese) Child of Nana.

Nanami (Japanese) Seven beauties; seven seas.

Nancy (Hebrew) Full of grace. *Nancee, Nansey, Nansee, Nana, Nanny, Nan, Nanette, Nannette, Nanine, Nanice, Nance*

Nanda (Hindi) A sakti of Ganesha.

Nandini (Hindi) Bestower of joy; daughter.

Nandita (Hindi) Happy.

Nanette (French) Gracious.

Nanna (Hebrew) Graceful one.

Nantale (Ugandan) Clan totem is a lion.

Naoko (Japanese) Child of Nao.

Naomi (Hebrew, Japanese) Pleasant one; above all, beauty. *Naoma, Noami, Mimi, Mimsy, Mims, Nomi, Omie*

Napea (Latin) Of the valley.

Napua (Hawaiian) The flowers.

Nara (Old English) Near one. (Gaelic) Joyous. (Native American) Place name. *Narah, Nera*

Narcissa (Greek) Self-love. *Narcisse*

Narcisse (French) Daffodil. *Narci, Narcis, Narcissa, Narcissie, Narcissey, Narsee, Narsey, Narsis*

Narda (Latin) Fervently anointed.

Narella (Greek) Bright one. *Narelle, Relly, Relle, Rell*

Nariko (Japanese) Thunder.

Narkaesha (African) Pretty.

Narmada (Indian) River.

Nascha (Native American) Owl.

Nasha (African) Born during the rainy season.

Nashaly (African) Born during the rainy season.

Nashwa (Egyptian) Wonderful feeling. *Nashy*

Nasia (Latin) From the name Natalie.

Nasiche (Ugandan) Born during the locust season.

Nasnan (Native American) Surrounded by song.

Nasya (Hebrew) Miracle. *Nasyah*

Nata (Native American) Speaker.

Natala (Slavic) Born on Christmas. *Natalah*

Natalia (Italian) Born on Christmas.

Natalie (Latin) Birthday; child born at Christmas. *Nataly, Natalee, Nataleigh, Natalia, Natalya, Nataline, Nathalia, Nathalie, Noel, Noelle, Novella, Natasha, Natosha, Natashi, Tosha, Tosh, Natasa, Natashia, Natalja, Natassia, Nastassia, Natividad, Netty, Nettie, Natty, Tally, Tallie, Tasha, Talia*

Natane (Arapaho Indian) Daughter.

Natania (Hebrew) Gift of God.

Nataniella (Hebrew) Gift of God. *Natanielle, Nathania, Natania, Nathanielle*

Natara (Arabic) Sacrifice. *Natarah, Nataria, Natarya*

Natasha (Greek) Rebirth; from Anastacia. *Nahtasha, Natashah, Natasa, Nastia*

Natesa (Hindi) Dance lord.

Nathaly (French) Birthday, especially the birth of Christ.

Natira (Science fiction) Character from *Star Trek*.

Natsuko (Japanese) Child of Natsu.

Nautica (English) Meaning unknown.

Navdeep (Hindi) Meaning unknown.

Naveena (Indian) New.

Nawar (Arabic) Flower.

Nayana (Hindi) Eye.

Nayeli (Native American) He who wrestles.

Nayely (Arabic) Highness; grace.

Nayoko (Japanese) Child of Nayo.

Naysa (Hebrew) Miracle of God.

Nazirah (Arabic) Equal; like.

Natsuko (Japanese) Child of Natsu.

Neala (Gaelic) Champion. *Niela, Nela, Neela, Neila, Nealah, Neilla, Nila*

Nebta (Egyptian) Meaning unknown.

Neci (Latin) Intense, fiery.

Necia (Latin) Fiery, passionate. *Necee, Neciah, Necie*

Neda (Slavic) Born on Sunday; sanctuary. *Nedda, Neddy, Ned, Nerida, Nedjelko, Nedo*

Nediva (Hebrew) Noble and generous.

Nedra (Latin) Awareness.

Neeharika (Hindi) Dewdrops.

Neelam (Hindi) Sapphire.

Neelja (Hindi) Meaning unknown.

Neema (Hindi) Prosperous.

Neena (Hindi) Mighty.

Neerja (Hindi) Lotus flower.

Neeta (Hindi) Upright.

Neferu (Egyptian) Meaning unknown.

Neha (Hindi) Rain.

Neith (Egyptian) Divine mother.

Neiva (Spanish) Snow.

Nekia (Arabic) Pure. *Nakiya, Nakiea, Nekeya, Neya, Nakia, Nakeia*

Nelda (English) By the alder tree. (Irish) Champion. *Neldah, Nell, Nellda, Nellie*

Nelia (Gaelic) Champion.

Nell (Greek) Stone. *Nelle*

Nelleke (Dutch) A horn.

Nellie (Greek) The bright one. *Nelly, Nellis, Nela, Nelda, Nelia, Nella, Nelita, Nelina, Nellwyn*

Nellis (Greek) Light.

Nelly (Greek) Stone.

Nenet (Arabic) Goddess of the deep.

Neola (Greek) Youthful.

Neoma (Greek) New moon. *Neona*

Neorah (Hebrew) Light.

Nerhim (Turkish) Meaning unknown.

Neria (Hebrew) Lamp of God; angel. *Neriah*

Nerice (American) Powerful woman.

Nerin (Greek) One from the sea.

Nerina (Greek) Sea nymph.

Nerissa (Latin) Daughter of the sea. *Neressa, Narissa, Nerisa, Nerisse*

Nerita (Spanish) Sea snail.

Neroli (Italian) Orange blossom. *Nerolia, Nerolie, Neroly, Nerole*

Nerys (Welsh) Lady. *Neris, Neriss, Nerisse*

Nessa (Old Norse) Headland. *Nesa, Nissa, Nessie*

Netis (Native American) Trustworthy.

Netta (Hebrew) A plant or shrub.

Neva (Spanish) Covered with snow. *Nevia, Nevea, Nevita*

Nevada (Latin) Snowy. *Nevedah*

Nevaeh (American) Heaven.

Nevala (Science fiction) Character from *Star Trek*.

Neveah (Slavic) Butterfly.

Neviah (Hebrew) Forecaster.

Nevina (Irish) Saint worshipper.

Neysa (Greek) Pure.

Nguyet (Vietnamese) Little one.

Nhi (Vietnamese) Little one.

Nhu (Vietnamese) Everything according to one's wishes.

Nhung (Vietnamese) Velvet.

Nia (Swahili) Purpose.

Nichelle (African American) Victorious maiden. *Nichele, Nishele*

Nichole (Greek) Victorious.

Nicia (Greek) Victorious army. *Nicanor*

Nickan (Persian) Goodness of grandparents.

Nicki (Greek) From the name Nicole.

Nickita (Russian) Victorious people.

Nicole (Greek) Victorious people. *Nichole, Nicola, Nikki, Nika, Nickie, Nicky, Nichola, Nicci, Nichelle, Nikolia, Nicoline, Nicolette, Nikole, Colette, Collette, Cosette, Lacole, Nykole, Nyky, Nykky, Nykki, Nyki*

Nidha (Asian) Sleep; night.

Nidra (Hindi) A form of the Devi.

Niesha (African American) Pure.

Nieve (Spanish) Snowy.

Nigella (Latin) Dark night.

Nijole (Slavic) Form of Nicole.

Niju (Hindi) Pansophist. *Nij*

Nika (Russian) Born on Sunday.

Nike (Greek) Victory.

Niki (English) Victorious people. *Nicky, Nicole*

Nikita (Greek, Russian, Slavic) Unconquered, victorious people.

Nikki (American) From Nicole.

Nikole (English) Victorious people.

Nile (Egyptian) From the River Nile.

Nilgun (Turkish) Meaning unknown.

Nilima (Hindi) Blueness.

Nilini (Hindi) Perpetuator of the Kuru race.

Niloufer (Hindi) From the heavens.

Nimah (Arabic) Blessing; loan. *Nima*

Nimeesha (African) Princess.

Nimisha (Hindi) Meaning unknown.

Nimmi (Hindi) Meaning unknown.

Nimue (English) Full of life, vibrant; variation of Vivian.

Nina (Spanish, Hebrew) Girl; grace. *Ninya, Ninette, Ninon*

Nineve (English) Full of life, vibrant; variation of Vivian.

Ninon (French) Form of Annie.

Niobe (Greek) Fern.

Nira (Hawaiian) Of the loom. (Hebrew) Plow.

Niradhara (Hindi) Meaning unknown.

Niral (Hindi) Meaning unknown.

Nirguna (Hindi) Meaning unknown.

Nirmala (Hindi) Pure; immaculate.

Nirupa (Hindi) A decree; command.

Nirvana (Hindi) Deep silence; ultimate bliss. *Nirvahna, Nirvanah, Vana*

Nirvelli (Tudas Indian) Water child.

Nisha (Hindi) Night.

Nishi (Japanese) West.

Nishtha (Indian) Devotion.

Nisi (Hebrew) Emblem.

Nissa (Scandinavian) Elf, fairy. *Nisse, Nissi, Nissan, Nissim*

Nita (Native American) Bear.

Nitara (Hindi) Deeply rooted.

Niti (Hindi) Meaning unknown.

Nitika (Native American) Angel of precious stone.

Nitsa (Greek) Light.

Nitu (Hindi) Meaning unknown.

Nituna (Native American) My daughter.

Nitya (Hindi) Goddess.

Nitza (Hebrew) Bud from a flower.

Nitzana (Hebrew) Blossom. *Nizana, Nitza*

Nivedita (Indian) Surrendered.

Nivea (Latin) Snow; reflecting the snow-white color.

Niverta (Hindi) Meaning unknown.

Nixie (German) Water sprite.

Niyati (Hindi) Fate.

Nizana (Hebrew) Flower bud.

Noble (Latin) Honorable one.

Noelani (Hawaiian) Beautiful girl from heaven.

Noella (French) Christmas. *Noelle*

Noemi (Hebrew) Pleasantness.

Nohely (Latin) Christmas. *Noheli*

Noire (Greek) Verdent; blooming.

Nokomis (Native American) Grandmother.

Nola (Latin) Of noble birth.

Noletta (Latin) Unwilling.

Nona (Latin) The ninth.

Nonnita (Celtic) Named for Saint Nonn; mother of Saint David of Wales. (Latin) Ninth. *Non, Nonh, Nonee, Noni, Nonie, Nonna, Nonyah*

Nora (Greek) The bright one; honor; light. *Norah, Norine, Noreen, Norina*

Norberta (German) Blond hero.

Nordica (German) From the north. *Norna*

Nori (Japanese) Doctrine.

Noriko (Japanese) Doctrine child; child of Nori.

Norina (English) Light.

Norma (Latin) Model.

Normandy (Place name) Province in France.

Notburga (German) Meaning unknown.

Noura (Arabic) Inner light. *Nourah*

Nova (Latin) New. *Noova, Novah, Novella, Novia*

Novia (Spanish) New; girlfriend.

Novyanna (Spanish) Lovely. *Novy, Novie*

Noya (Arabic) Beautiful, ornamented.

Nozomi (Japanese) Hope.

Nu (Vietnamese) Girl.

Nuala (Celtic, Gaelic) White-haired.

Nubia (Egyptian) From Nubia.

Nuna (Native American) Land.

Nura (Arabic) Light. *Noora, Noura, Nuriah*

Nuray (Turkish) White moon.

What's in a Name

Years ago, it was fashionable, or at least a tradition, to name children according to their birth order. For example, if it was a girl, the ninth child was typically given the name **Nona**, which is derived from the Latin word *nonus*, for "ninth." Likewise, **Quintus** was given to the fifth child, if it was a boy.

Nurhan (Turkish) Meaning unknown.

Nuria (Hebrew) God's fire. *Noor, Noura, Nur, Nuriah, Nuriel*

Nusa (Hungarian) Grace.

Nuttah (Native American) My heart.

Nya (Irish) Champion. *Neil, Niall, Neale*

Nyah (Irish) Champion. *Neil, Niall, Neale*

Nyasia (Irish) Champion. *Neil, Niall, Neale*

Nydia (Latin) Refuge, nest. *Nidia, Nidiah, Ny, Nydiah, Nydie, Nydya*

Nyeki (African) Second wife.

Nyla (Greek) Winner. *Nila*

Nyoko (Japanese) A gem; treasure.

Nysa (Greek) A new beginning. *Nisa, Nissa, Nyssa*

Nyssa (Greek) The beginning.

Nyx (Greek) Night. *Nix*

O

Oba (Nigeria) An ancient river goddess.

Obelia (Greek) Pillar of strength.

Obsession (Old English) Product name; to be obsessed; compulsive.

Oceana (Greek) From the sea.

Octavia (Latin) Eighth child. *Octave, Octavie, Occtavia, Ottavia, Tave, Tavi, Tavia, Tavie*

Oda (Norse) Small, pointed spear.

Odea (Greek) Walker by the road. *Odee*

Odeda (Hebrew) Strong.

Odele (Hebrew) Wealthy; melody.

Odelia (German, Hebrew) Little wealthy one; praise God. *Odella, Odelinda, Odilia, Odelette*

Odella (German) Little wealthy one.

Odera (Hebrew) Plough.

Odessa (Greek) Odyssey, journey, voyage.

Odetta (French) Melody.

Odette (French) Happy home.

Odil (French) Rich.

Odina (Latin) Mountain.

Ofa (English) Name of a king.

Ofelia (Greek) A helper. *Ofilia, Ofeelia, Ofellia, Ophelia*

Ofira (Hebrew) Gold.

Ohanna (Armenian) God's gracious gift.

Ohio (Native American) Large river.

Ohnicio (Irish) Honor.

Oihane (Spanish) From the forest.

Oistin (Latin) Venerable.

Ojal (Hindi) Vision.

Okal (African) To cross.

Okapi (African) Animal with a long neck.

Okelani (Hawaiian) From heaven.

Oki (Japanese) Ocean-centered.

Oksana (Russian) Glory be to God. *Oksanochka*

Ola (Hawaiian) Well-being.

Olathe (Native American) Beautiful.

Olayinka (Yoruban) Honors surround me.

Olba (Aboriginal) Red ochre.

Olcay (Turkish) Meaning unknown.

Olesia (Polish) Helper and defender of mankind.

Olga (Russian) Holy.

Oliana (Hawaiian) Oleander.

Olien (Russian) The dear one.

Olina (Hawaiian) Joyous.

Olinda (German) Protector of property.

Olisa (Native American) God.

Olive (Old Norse) Kind one. (Latin) Olive tree. (Old French) Peace. *Olivia, Olivya, Olivette, Ollie, Olly, Olva, Livia, Livy, Liv, Livvy, Nollie, Nola*

Olympia (Greek) Of Mount Olympus; heavenly. *Olympe, Olimpie*

Olwen (Welsh) White footprint.

Oma (Hebrew) Reverent. (German) Mother. (Arabic) Commanding.

Omaira (Arabic) Red.

Omaka (Maori) The place where the stream flows.

Omega (Greek) Great.

Ona (Lithuanian) Graceful one.

Onaedo (African) Gold.

Onaona (Hawaiian) Sweet smell.

Onawa (Native American) Awake.

Ondine (Latin) Water sprite.

Ondrea (Slavic) Strong, courageous.

Oneida (Native American) Eagerly awaited.

Onella (Hungarian) Torch light.

Oni (Native American) Born on holy ground.

Onida (Native American) The expected one.

Onora (Irish) Version of honor.

Ontibile (African) God is watching over me.

Onur (Turkish) Honor.

Onyx (Greek) Dark black; precious stone.

Oola (Aboriginal) Red lizard. (Irish) Apples. *Ulla*

Oona (Gaelic, Latin) Unity. *Ona, Oonaugh, Oonagh*

Opa (Native American) Owl.

Opal (Sanskrit) Jewel.

Naming Rights

Feel free to consider names from other traditions. If you really like the uniqueness of such a name, don't hold yourself back. There's one exception: when first names and last names are from very different origins, the result may be a peculiar-sounding combination such as Francesco Xavier Jones or Kaitlynne Oblina Hedgekowsky.

Opaline (French) Jewel; precious stone.

Ophelia (Greek) Useful; wise. *Ofelia, Ofilia, Ophelie, Phelia*

Ophira (Greek) Gold. *Oprah*

Oprah (Hebrew) Light; runaway.

Ora (Spanish) Gold.

Orana (Aboriginal) The moon.

Oralee (Hebrew) Lord is my light.

Oralia (Latin, Hebrew) Golden; light. *Orel, Orelda, Oriole, Orlene, Orlena, Orpah, Oralee, Oralie, Oral, Ora, Orah, Oria, Orlie, Orly, Orabel*

Orane (French) Rising.

Orchid (Latin) A flower.

Orea (Greek) Mountains.

Orenda (Iroquois Indian) Magic power.

Oria (Latin) From the Orient. (Latin) Dawn, sunrise. (Irish) Golden.

Oriana (Latin) Dawn. (Greek) East. *Oralia, Orelle, Orlanna*

Orianna (Latin) Golden; dawning. *Orienne*

Oriel (French) Golden; angel of destiny. *Orielle*

Orinda (Teutonic) Fire serpent.

Oriole (Latin) Fair-haired.

Orla (Latin) Golden woman.

Orlanda (Latin) Bright sun. *Orlie*

Orlantha (German) From the land.

Ormanda (German) Of the sea.

Ornella (Italian) A flowering ash tree.

Orpah (Hebrew) The neck; skull.

Orsa (Latin) Bear.

Ortensia (Latin) Gardener, farmer. *Hortense*

Osana (Spanish) Health.

Osma (Latin) God's servant.

Otylia (German) Lucky; heroine.

Ouida (French) Warrior woman.

Ova (Latin) Egg.

Ove (Norse) The spear's point.

Owena (Welsh) Well-born.

Ozora (Hebrew) The strength of the Lord.

P

Paavana (Hindi) Pure.

Paavani (Hindi) The Ganges River.

Paca (Spanish) Frenchman.

Padgett (Greek) Wisdom. *Padget, Paget, Pagett, Pagette*

Page (French) Intern. *Paige, Payge*

Paka (African) Kitten.

Pala (Native American) Water.

Palakika (Hawaiian) Version of Frances. *Farakika*

Palila (Hawaiian) Bird.

Pallas (Greek) Another name for Athena, goddess of the arts, goddess of wisdom.

Palmer (English) Palm tree. *Palima, Pammimirah, Pallma, Pallmara, Pallmyra, Palma, Palmira, Palmyra*

Paloma (Spanish) Dove. *Palloma, Palometa, Palomita, Peloma*

Pamela (Greek) Honey. *Pam, Pamala, Pamalia, Pamella, Pamelia, Pamelina, Pamilia, Pamilla, Pammela, Pammi, Pammie, Pammy*

Pana (Native American) Partridge.

Pandora (Greek) All gifted. *Panda, Pandorra, Panndora*

Panphila (Greek) She loves all. *Panfila, Panfyla, Panphyla*

Pansy (English) Flower. *Pansey, Pansie*

Panya (African) Mouse.

Paris (English) The city. *Parisa, Parris, Parrish*

Parthenia (Greek) Virginal. *Parthania, Parthena, Parthenie, Parthina, Parthine, Pathania, Pathena, Pathenia, Pathina*

Parvani (Hindi) The goddess Devi.

Pascale (French) Child of Easter; feminine version of Pascal. *Pascalette, Pascaline, Pascalle, Paschale*

Paterekia (Hawaiian) Aristocrat.

Patience (English) Patience. *Paciencia, Patient*

Patricia (English) Noble. *Pat, Patreece, Patreice, Patria, Patric, Patrica, Patrice, Patricka, Patrizia, Patsy, Patti, Pattie, Patty, Tricia, Trish, Trisha*

Pasua (African) Born by cesarean section.

Paula (Latin) Small. *Paola, Paolina, Paule, Pauleen, Paulene, Pauletta, Paulette, Paulie, Paulina, Pauline, Paulita, Pauly, Paulyn, Pavla, Pavlina, Pavlinka, Pola, Polcia, Pollie, Polly*

Pausha (Hindi) Name of the lunar month of Capricorn.

Pavana (Hindi) Wind. *Pavani*

Pax (Latin) Peace.

Paz (Hebrew) Gold. *Paza, Pazia, Paziah, Pazice, Pazit, Paziya, Pazya*

Pearl (Latin) Pearl; jewel. *Pearla, Pearle, Pearleen, Pearlena, Pearlette, Pearley, Pearline, Pearly, Perl, Perla, Perle, Perlette, Perley, Perlie, Perly*

Pedzi (African) Last child.

Pela (Hawaiian) Pretty. *Bela*

Pelagia (Greek, Polish) The ocean; sea-dweller. *Pelage, Pelageia, Pelagie, Pelegia, Pelgia, Pellagia*

Pelenakino (Hawaiian) Strong as a bear. *Peresekila, Peresila, Perisila*

Peliah (Hebrew) God's miracle. *Pelia*

Pelika (Hawaiian) Peaceful; version of Freda. *Ferida*

Pelipa (Native American) Lover of horses.

Pelulio (Hawaiian) Emerald. *Berulo*

Pemba (African) Meteorological power.

Penda (African) Beloved.

Penelope (Greek) Bobbin-weaver. *Lopa, Pela, Pelcia, Pen, Penelopa, Penina, Penine, Penna, Pennelope, Penni, Penny, Pinelopi, Piptisa, Popi*

Peninah (Hebrew) Coral. *Peni, Penie, Penina, Penini, Peninit*

Peony (English) Flower. *Peoni, Peonie*

Perry (French) Pear tree. *Peri, Perrey, Perri, Perrie*

Persis (Latin) From Persia. *Perssis*

Petronella (Latin) Roman clan name. *Pernel, Pernelle, Peronel, Peronelle, Petrina, Petronelle, Petronia, Petronilla, Pier, Pierette*

Petula (Latin) Sassy. *Petulah*

Petunia (English) Flower. *Petune*

Phedra (Greek) Bright. *Faydra, Fedra, Phadra, Phaedra, Phedre*

Philadelphia (Greek) City; brotherly love. *Philli, Phillie*

Philippa (Greek) Lover of horses. *Philipa, Philippine, Phillipina, Pippa, Pippy*

Philomena (Greek) Beloved. *Filomena, Philomene, Philomina*

Phoebe (Greek) Brilliant. *Pheabe, Phebe, Pheby, Phobe*

Phyllis (Greek) Green tree branch. *Philis, Phillis, Philliss, Phillys, Phylis, Phyllida, Phylliss*

Pia (Latin) Pious. *Peah, Piah*

Pinquana (Native American) Fragrant.

Pirene (Greek) The daughter of the river god Achelous.

> **What's in a Name**
>
> The Greek moon goddess Artemis was described as "phoibe," meaning bright and pure, which then evolved into the name **Phoebe**.

Pita (African) Fourth daughter.

Pixie (English) Tiny.

Placida (Spanish) Calm. *Plasida*

Pleasance (English) Pleasure. *Pleasant, Pleasants, Pleasence*

Pocahontas (Native American) Capricious.

Polly (English) Variation of Molly. *Pauleigh, Pollee, Polley, Polli, Pollie, Pollyann, Pollyanna, Pollyanne*

Pollyam (Hindi) Goddess of the plague.

Poppy (Latin) Flower. *Poppi*

Portia (Latin) Roman clan name. *Porcha, Porscha, Porsche, Porschia, Porsha*

Pragyata (Hindi) Wisdom.

Prarthana (Hindi) Prayer.

Prashanti (Hindi) Peace.

Pratiksha (Hindi) Meaning unknown.

Pratima (Hindi) Image.

Precious (American, Latin) Dear.

Preeti (Hindi) Love.

Preita (Finnish) Most loving one.

Prema (Hindi) Love.

Premila (Hindi) Meaning unknown.

Prerana (Hindi) Encouragement.

Preyasi (Hindi) Beloved.

Pribislava (Czechoslovakian) To help glorify. *Pribena, Pribka, Pribuska*

Prima (Italian) First one. *Primalia, Primetta, Primina, Priminia, Primula*

Primavera (Italian) Spring.

Primrose (English, Latin) The first rose.

Princell (English) Royal title. *Prin, Princesa, Princessa*

Priscilla (Latin) From ancient times. *Priss, Prissy, Prisca, Silla, Cilla, Cyla*

Prisma (Greek) Cut glass. *Prusma*

Pritha (Hindi) Mother of Pandavas.

Priti (Hindi) Satisfaction; renowned wife of Pulastya/Sukha.

Pritika (Hindi) Beloved. *Priyal, Priyam*

Priya (Hindi) Loved one, darling. *Priyal, Priyam, Priyanka, Priyasha, Priyata, Priyati*

Priyanka (Hindi) Dear one.

Providence (English) Providence.

Prudence (Latin) Foresight. *Prudy, Prue, Pru*

Prunella (French) Color of a plum.

Psyche (Greek) The soul.

Ptolema (Greek) Meaning unknown.

Pua (Polynesian) Flowering tree.

Puakai (Hawaiian) Ocean flower.

Puanani (Hawaiian) Beautiful flower.

Pulkita (Hindi) Meaning unknown.

Puma (Spanish) Mountain lion.

Pundari (Hindi) Meaning unknown.

Punita (Hindi) Pure.

Purandhri (Hindi) Beautiful woman.

Purity (English) Unsullied, clean.

Purnima (Hindi) Night of the full moon.

Purva (Hindi) Elder.

Purvaja (Hindi) Elder sister.

Purvi (Hindi) East.

Purvis (French) Provide.

Pusti (Hindi) Nourishment, a form of the Devi; wife of Ganapati.

Pyrena (Greek) Fiery.

Pyhrrha (Greek) Red.

Pythia (Greek) Prophet.

Q

Qadira (Arabic) Wields power. *Kadira*

Qamra (Arabic) Moon. *Kamra*

Qatai (Arabic) Conclusive. (Science fiction) A character from *Star Trek Voyager.*

Qitarah (Arabic) Aromatic. *Qeturah, Quetura, Queturah*

Quan (Chinese) Goddess of compassion.

Quanah (Native American) White coral beads. (English) Queenly. *Kwanda, Kwandah, Quandah, Qwanda*

Quanella (African American) Sparkling. *Kwannie, Quanela*

Quanesha (African American) Singing. *Kwaeesha, Kwannie, Quaneisha, Quanisha*

Quanika (American) Combination of Quan and Nika; joyful. *Kwantina, Kwantynna, Quantinna, Quantyna, Quawanica*

Quantina (American) Brave queen. *Kwantynna, Quantinna, Quantyna*

Quartilla (Latin) Fourth.

Quartz (German) Jewel, gem; crystalline.

Qubilah (Arabic) Agreement.

Queena (English) Queen. *Queen, Queenation, Queeneste, Queenette, Queenie, Quenny*

Queisha (American) Contented child. *Queysha, Queshia*

Quella (English) Pacify.

Quenby (Scandinavian) Womanly. *Quenbee, Quenbey, Quenbi, Quenbie, Quinbee, Quinbie, Quinby*

Querida (Spanish) Beloved.

Questa (French) Hunter. *Kesta*

Naming Rights

Should you choose a "gender-free" name for your baby? The old notion was that a gender-free name caused psychological problems. Studies have shown that to be untrue.

Queta (Spanish) Home ruler. *Keta*

Quiana (American) Gracious; queen; variation of Hannah. *Qiana, Qianna, Quiyanna*

Quianna (American) Grace. *Quiana, Qianna, Quianna, Quiyanna*

Quinby (Scandinavian) Living like royalty. *Quenby, Quin, Quinbie, Quinnie*

Quinceanos (Spanish) Fifteenth child. *Quin, Quince, Quincy*

Quinci (English) Fifth son's estate. *Quincy*

Quincylia (American) Popular, fifth child. *Cylia, Quince, Quincy*

Quinella (Latin) A girl who is as pretty as two. *Quinn*

Quinn (Gaelic, Greek) Wise; queen; fifth born.

Quintessa (Latin) Essence. *Quintessenz, Quinn, Tess, Tessa*

Quintina (Latin) Fifth. *Quin, Quinella, Quinetta, Quinette, Quintana, Quintessa, Quintona, Quintonice, Quinta*

Quirina (Latin) Contentious.

Quirita (Latin) Citizen.

Quisha (African American) Beautiful mind. *Keisha, Kesha, Key*

Quita (Latin) Peaceful. *Keeta, Keetah*

Quiterie (French) Tranquil.

Quorra (Italian) Heart.

R

Raanana (Hebrew) Fresh. *Ranana*

Rabab (Arabic) Pale cloud.

Rabiah (Arabic) Breeze. *Rabi, Rabia*

Rachel (Hebrew) Little lamb, ewe; one with purity. *Rachael, Raychel, Rachele, Rah'zell, Rahel, Raquel, Ray, Shelley, Shelly, Shellie, Chelle, Chellic*

Radella (Old English) Elfin adviser.

Radha (Hindi) Favorite friend.

Radhika (Hindi) Form of the Devi; fifth Sakti; wife of Krishna.

Radinka (Slavic) Active.

Rae (Scottish) Grace. (English) Doe. (German) Wise protection. *Raeann, Raelene, Ray, Raye, Rayette*

Raeka (Spanish) Beautiful; unique. *Rae*

Raelin (Celtic) *Raelyn, Rae*

Rafa (Hindi) Happy. *Rafah*

Naming Rights

Choosing a popular name for your child offers familiarity and ease with which others will use a name they know and can recognize immediately. A child with a popular name may have a leg up on acceptance in the peer group and does not have to explain how to spell or pronounce his or her name. Your child also will always be able to find the right personalized pencil, key chain, or T-shirt in novelty stores.

Rafaela (Spanish) God heals; feminine version of Raphael. *Rafa, Rafaelia, Rafaella, Rafella, Rafelle, Raffaela, Raffaele, Raphaella, Raphaelle, Refaela, Rephaela*

Ragini (Hindi) Melody.

Ragnhild (Norse) One who is wise in battle. *Ragnhilda, Ragnhilde, Ragnilda, Ranilida, Renilda, Renilde*

Rahab (Hebrew) Proud; quarrelsome.

Rai (Japanese) Trust.

Raimy (African) Compassionate. *Raimee*

Rain (Latin) Ruler. *Raine, Rein, Reign, Rayne, Rana, Rane, Raina, Ray*

Rainbow (English) An array of bright colors. *Rainbeau, Rainbo*

Rainelle (English) Combination of "rain" and "elle." *Rainell*

Raissa (Old French) Thinker. (Russian) Rose. (Greek) Rose. *Raisa*

Raizel (Hebrew) Rose. *Rayzel, Razel*

Raja (Arabic) Anticipation. *Raga, Ragya, Rajya*

Rajni (Hindi) Dark of the night. *Rajani*

Rakel (Hebrew) Ewe.

Rakhil (Hindi) Lamb.

Raksha (Hindi) The moon; protection.

Raku (Japanese) Pleasure.

Raleigh (English) Field of birds. *Raileigh, Railey, Raley, Rawleigh, Rawley*

Ralphina (English) Wolf counselor; feminine variation of Ralph. *Ralphine*

Ramla (Egyptian) One who predicts the future.

Ramona (Spanish) Wise protector. *Ramonda, Mona, Ramonah, Ramonna, Raymona*

Ramya (Hindi) Elegant, beautiful.

Ran (Scandinavian) Goddess of the sea.

Rana (Spanish) Frog. *Raniyah, Ranna, Ranya*

Randi (English, American) Wolf shield; form of Randall.

Rane (Norwegian) Queen; pure. *Rain, Raine, Ranie*

Rani (Hindi) A queen.

Ranielle (African American) God is my judge; variation of Danielle.

Ranjana (Hindi) Delightful.

Ranjita (Hindi) Adorned.

Ranveig (Scandinavian) Housewife. *Rannaug*

Raphaella (Hebrew) Healed by God. *Rafaella*

Rashida (African) Righteous. *Rasheda, Rasheeda, Rasheddah, Rasheida, Rashidah*

Rasia (Greek) Rose. *Rasine, Rasya*

Rasika (Hindi) Connoisseur.

Rasine (Polish) A rose. *Roisine*

Rasna (Hindi) The tongue.

Rati (Hindi) A Devi.

Raven (English) Dark haired; wise; a bird. *Ravan, Rave, Ravin*

Rawnie (Gypsy) Lady.

Rayanne (American) Grace; combination of Ray and Anne. *Rayann*

Rayelle (English) Lamb.

Raylene (French) Counselor; variation of Raymond. *Raylina*

Rayma (German) Wise protection. *Ray*

Rayna (Hebrew) Pure, clean. *Raina, Rana, Rane, Rania, Renana, Renait, Renatia, Renatya, Renina, Rinatia, Rinatya*

Raziya (African) Agreeable.

Rea (English) Manly. *Raya, Rhia, Ria*

Reba (Hebrew) The fourth; square; stooped.

Rebecca (Hebrew) Bound, tied. *Rebekah, Rebeckah, Rebeccah, Rebeca, Rebeka, Rebeque, Rebekka, Rebakah, Rebequa, Becky, Bekki, Becca, Becha, Becka, Riba, Reba, Riva, Reeba, Ree, Rivka, Rifka, Rivca, Rivy*

Reena (Hindi) Peaceful. *Reen, Reene*

Reese (Welsh) Enthusiastic. *Ree, Reece, Rees, Rere*

Regan (Irish, Scottish) King's heir.

Regina (Latin) Queenly. *Reggie, Gina, Rina, Regan, Reyna, Reine, Rein, Reina, Rain, Rane, Reyna, Rani, Raina, Rexy*

Rei (Japanese) Gratitude.

Reidun (Norwegian) Nest-lovely.

Reiko (Japanese) Child of Rei; gratitude.

Reilley (Irish) Rye. *Riley, Rielly*

Rekha (Hindi) Straight line. *Reka*

Reman (Hindi) Meaning unknown.

Remington (English) Town of the raven.

Remy (French) From Rheims. *Remi*

Ren (Japanese) Waterlily.

Rena (Hebrew) Peace; joyous song. *Reena, Rinah, Rinne*

Renata (Latin) Reborn. *Renate, Renée, Renette*

Rene (Greek) Peaceful. *Renee, Reene, Renne*

Renee (French) Born again. *Renata, Renay, Rene, Renelle, Reney, Reni, Renia, Renie, Renni, Rennie, Renny*

Renita (Latin) To be firm. *Reneeta*

Rennefer (Egyptian) The weaver.

Renora (Japanese) Compassion. (Science fiction) Character from *Star Trek: Deep Space Nine*.

Renuka (Hindi) Mother of Parasurma.

Reshma (Hindi) Silky.

Revati (Hindi) Wife of Balarama.

Revelation (Latin) Lacy; insight.

Rhea (Greek) Stream. (Latin) Poppy. *Ria, Rea*

What's in a Name

In Greek mythology, **Rhea** was the mother of Zeus, Hades, Poseidon, Demeter, Hera, and Hestia, and wife of Cronos. Her name is a Latin variation of the Greek word *Hreia*, which seems to mean something related to "stream" or "flow." Whatever the origins of her name, she was one powerful woman!

Rhiamon (Welsh) Witch. *Rhianon*

Rhiannon (Welsh) A mythological nymph. *Rheanna, Rheanne, Rhiana, Rhiann, Rhianna, Rhiannan, Rhianon, Rhuan, Riana, Riane, Rianna, Rianne, Riannon, Rianon, Riona*

Rhoda (Greek) A rose. *Rhodia, Rhodie, Rodie, Roe*

Rhodanthe (Greek) A rose.

Rhonda (Celtic) Good spear. *Rhonnda, Ronda*

Rhonwen (Welsh) Slender; fair. *Ronwen, Roweena, Roweina, Rowena, Rowina*

Rhoswen (Gaelic) White rose.

Rhu (Hindi) Pure.

Rhysati (Science fiction) Character from *Star Wars*.

Ria (Spanish) Mouth of a river.

Riana (Irish) Honorable.

Riane (Gaelic) Little king.

Riannon (Welsh) Great queen, witch, or goddess. *Rianne*

Ricarda (Italian) Powerful ruler; feminine version of Richard. *Rica, Ricca, Richarda, Richel, Richela, Richele, Richella, Richelle, Richenda, Richenza, Ricki, Rickie, Ricky, Riki, Rikki, Rikky*

Richael (Hebrew) Innocence of a lamb. (Irish) Name of a saint.

Richelle (German) Powerful ruler. (English) Brave one. *Ricarda, Ricky, Rikki*

Rickena (Czechoslovakian) Meaning unknown.

Rida (Arabic) Favored by God.

Riddhi (Hindi) Will follow.

Rieko (Japanese) Child of Rie.

Rigoberta (Spanish) Ridge.

Rihana (Arabic) Sweet basil.

Rikako (Japanese) Child of Rika.

Riku (Japanese) Land. *Rikuya*

Riley (Gaelic) Valiant. *Ryley, Reilly*

Rima (Hindi) White antelope.

Rimona (Hebrew) Pomegranate.

Rina (Hindi) Queen. *Reena, Riena*

Rinako (Japanese) Child of Rina.

Rinda (Scandinavian) Ancient mythological figure. *Rind*

Rini (Japanese) Little bunny.

Ripley (English) From the shouter's meadow.

Risa (Latin) Laughing one. *Risë, Risé*

Risako (Japanese) Child of Risa.

Rishabh (Hindi) Octave note.

Rishona (Hebrew) First.

Rita (Greek) Pearl; precious. *Reeta, Reta, Rheta, Rhetta*

Ritu (Hindi) Season.

Riva (French) River. *Rivy, Reeva, Rive, Rivi, Ria, Reva*

Rizpah (Greek) Hope. *Ritzpa*

Roana (Spanish) Reddish-brown skin.

Roberta (English) Bright; famous. *Ruperta, Robin, Robyn, Robbin, Robinette, Robina, Bobbi, Bobbie, Bobby, Bert, Berta, Bertie, Berthe*

Robin (English) Queen of morning. *Robbin, Robyn, Robbyn*

Rochelle (French) From the little rock. *Rochella, Rochette*

Rocio (Italian) Dewdrops.

Roderica (German) Famous one. *Roderika*

Rogan (Gaelic) Red-haired. *Roan*

Rohana (Hindi) Sandalwood.

Rohini (Hindi) A star.

Rolanda (German) From the famous sea. *Rolande, Rollande, Rolonda, Rolande*

Romana (Italian) From Rome. *Romy, Roma*

Rona (Gaelic) Covenant; oath.

Ronalda (Old Norse) Mighty.

Ronnell (African American) Feminine version of Ron. *Ronell, Ronelle, Ranell*

Rory (German, Scottish, Irish) Variation of Roderick; famous ruler; red. *Rorie, Rorrie, Rorry*

Rosa (Irish) Noted protector; rose; pink.

Rosalind (Spanish) Pretty rose. *Rosalinda, Rosaline, Roseline, Rosalyn, Roselyn, Rosey, Rosilind, Rose-Lyn, Roslin*

Rosalynda (Spanish) Beautiful. *Rosalinda*

Rosamund (German) Garden of flowers. *Rosamond, Rosamonde, Rosamunda, Rosamunde*

Rosanne (Latin) Gracious rose. *Rosanna, Roseanna, Roseannah, Rosehannah, Rozanna, Rozanne*

Rose (Latin) A flower. *Rosa, Rosie, Rosey, Roz, Rozsi, Rosalie, Rosalee, Rosalia, Rosetta, Rosette, Rosina, Rosena, Rasia, Rois, Rosita, Rosebud, Rosabell, Rosly, Roslin, Rosamund, Rosmund, Rosemonde, Rozamund, Roanee, Roanna, Rosaleen, Rosellen, Roselle, Rosella, Rosemary, Rosemarie, Chara, Charo*

Roselani (Hawaiian) Heavenly rose.

Rosemary (English) Bitter rose; fragrant herb.

Roshin (Japanese) Dewdrop mind.

Roshni (Hindi) Light.

Roslin (French) Little red-haired one. *Rosselin, Roslyn, Rose-Lynn, Rosalyn, Rosalind, Rosalinde, Rosalinda*

Rowan (English) From the rowan tree; tree with red berries.

Rowena (Welsh) Red-haired; rugged. *Rowana*

Roxanne (Persian) Brilliant one. *Roxane, Roxann, Roxanna, Roxie, Roxy, Rox, Roxana*

Ruby (French) Red gem. *Rubie, Rubee, Rubia, Rubina*

Ruchi (Hindi) Luster; beauty.

Ruchika (Hindi) Meaning unknown.

Ruchira (Hindi) Beautiful.

Rudrani (Hindi) A wife of Shiva.

Rue (Latin, Greek) Herb name; regret.

Ruffina (Italian) Red-haired.

Rui (French) Regal.

Rukan (Arabic) Steadfast.

Rukmini (Hindi) Wife of Lord Krishna.

Rumer (English) Gypsy.

Rumiko (Japanese) Child of Rumi.

Runa (Scandinavian) Secret lore.

Rupa (Hindi) Silver.

Rupal (Hindi) Meaning unknown.

Rupali (Hindi) Beautiful.

Ruri (Japanese) Emerald.

Ruth (Hebrew) Compassionate friend. *Ruthie, Ruthanne*

Ryan (Gaelic) Little king. *Ryen, Rian, Ryanne*

Ryba (Czechoslovakian) Fish.

Ryesen (English) Rye.

Ryo (American) River.

Ryoko (Japanese) Child of Ryo.

S

Saamiya (Arabic) Elevated; exalted; lofty.

Saba (Greek) Woman of Sheba. *Sabah*

Sabana (Latin, Spanish) From the open plain.

Sabeans (Hebrew) Captivity; conversion; old age.

Sabiha (Arabic) Forenoon; beautiful.

Sabina (Latin) Sabine woman. *Sabine, Savina, Saidhbhin, Sabiny, Biene, Bini, Bienchen, Sabse*

Sabirah (Arabic) Patient.

Sabita (Hindi) The sun; sweet; variation of Savita.

Sable (English) Dark-brown color fur; black. *Sabelle*

Sabola (Egyptian) Prophetess.

Sabra (Arabic) To rest. (Hebrew) Thorny cactus. *Sabe, Sabera, Sabrah*

Sabrina (Latin) From the border land. *Sabreena, Sabrena, Sabrinna*

Sachi (Hindi) Wife of Indrid. (Japanese) Bliss. *Sachee, Sachey, Sachie, Sachy, Sashi, Sashie*

Sachiko (Japanese) Bliss; child of Sachi.

Sacrifice (Old English) To make sacred.

Sada (Japanese) Pure one.

Sadah (Arabic) Good fortune; from Zada.

Sadb (Gaelic) Meaning unknown.

Sade (Nigerian) Honor confers a crown.

Sadhana (Hindi) Patience.

Sadie (English) Princess. *Sade, Sadee, Sady, Sadye, Shaday*

Sadira (Arabic) Ostrich returning from water.

Saeko (Japanese) Child of Sae.

Saeran (Welsh) Irish saint.

Safa (Arabic) Innocent.

Safak (Turkish) Meaning unknown.

Safara (African) Her place.

Naming Rights

If a certain name has a meaning you like but you don't want to use that particular name, why not use an anagram of it? Switch around the letters to form a new, unique name for your baby.

Saffi (Danish) Wisdom.

Saffron (English) Yellow flower. *Saffrone, Safron*

Safiya (African) Pure.

Saga (English) Journey.

Sagara (Hindi) Ocean.

Sage (French, English, Latin) Wise one; from the sagebrush plant; prophet. *Saige*

Sagira (Egyptian) Little one.

Sagittarius (Latin) The archer.

Sahana (Indian) A raga.

Sahara (Arabic) The moon. *Shahar*

Saheli (Hindi) Friend. *Sakhi, Sakina*

Sahiba (Hindi) Lady.

Sahila (Hindi) Guide.

Sahirah (Egyptian) Clean, pristine.

Sahyko (Native American) Mink.

Saida (Arabic) Fortunate one.

Saidah (African) Happy, fortunate.

Saige (English) Wise one. *Sage.*

Sailia Origin and meaning unknown.

Sailor (American, English) Mariner. *Sailie, Sailer, Saylor*

Saima (Arabic) Fasting woman.

Saiun (Japanese) Colorful sky. *Saiun.*

Sajili (Hindi) Decorated.

Sajni (Hindi) Beloved.

Sakari (Native American) Sweet.

Sakhi (Asian) Woman friend.

Saki (Japanese) Cloak; rice wine.

Sakiko (Japanese) Child of Saki.

Sakima (Native American) King. (Can be unisex.)

Sakina (Hindi) Friend.

Sakinah (Arabic) God-inspired peace of mind; tranquility. *Sakina*

Sakti (Hindi) Energy; goodness.

Sakuko (Japanese) Child of Saku.

Sakura (Japanese) Cherry blossoms.

Sakurako (Japanese) Child of Sakura.

Salal (English) A plant.

Salali (Native American) Squirrel.

Salama (Egyptian) Peaceful.

Saleema (Arabic) Peaceful.

Salena (Indian, Latin) The moon; salt.

Salene (French) Dignified one.

Salia (English) Princess.

Salihah (African) Correct.

Salimah (Arabic) Safe, healthy.

Salina (Latin, French) By the salt water; solemn. *Salena, Saleena*

Sally (Spanish) Saviour. *Salaidh, Sallye, Salli, Sallie, Sal*

Salma (Spanish) Ambitious.

Saloma (Hebrew) Peace. *Salome.*

Salome (Hebrew) Welcome; peace.

Saloni (Hindi) Dear, beautiful.

Salwa (Arabic) Solace, comfort. *Salva*

Samantha (Aramaic) Listens well. *Sammy, Sammi*

Samara (Hebrew) Ruled by God. (Latin) Seedling. *Samora*

Samatha (Hebrew) Listener of God.

Samiah (Arabic) Exalted.

Samicah (Hebrew) Meaning unknown. *Samika*

Samiksha (Hindi) Overview; analysis.

Samira (Arabic) Entertaining.

Samirah (Arabic) Entertaining companion.

Samma (Arabic) Sky, skye. *Sa, Samm, Ma*

Sammy-Jo (Hebrew) God is good; God has heard.

Sampriti (Hindi) Attachment.

Samta (Hindi) Meaning unknown.

Samuela (Hebrew) Her name is God. *Samuella, Samella*

Samularia (Latin) Sweet one forever. *Sammy, Lari, Laria.*

Samye (Tibetan) Place of first Buddhist monastery built in Tibet. Forest; thinkers; unexpected.

Sanako (Japanese) Child of Sana.

Sanam (Persian) Lover.

Sancha (Spanish) Holy. *Sanchia*

Sanchali (Indian) Movement.

Sanchay (Hindi) Collection. *Sandhaya, Sandhya*

Sanchaya (Indian) Meaning unknown.

Sancho (Spanish) Holy. *Sancha*

Sancia (Latin) Holy.

Sandia (Spanish) Watermelon.

Sandora (English) Defender of mankind. *Alexandra, Sandy, Sandrine*

Sandra (Greek) Helper and defender of mankind. *Sandrah*

Sandrine (Greek) Helper and defender of mankind. *Sandreen, Sandrene, Sandrin*

Sandya (Hindi) Sunset time; name of a god.

Sangita (Hindi) Musical.

Saniya (Hindi) Moment in time.

Sanjana (Indian) Gentle.

Sanjna (Hindi) Wife of the sun.

Sanjula (Hindi) Beautiful. *Sanjushree, Sohni*

Sanna (Scandinavian) Truth. *Sana*

Sanne (American) Lily.

Sanrevelle (Portuguese) Meaning unknown. *San, Rev, Revelle, Revla*

Santana (Spanish) Saintly. *Santanne, Santina*

Santina (Spanish) Little saint.

Sanura (Egyptian) Kitten.

Sanyogita (Hindi) Meaning unknown.

Sanyukta (Hindi) Union. *Sanjukta*

Saoirse (Celtic, Gaelic) Freedom.

Sapna (Hindi) Dream.

Sapphira (Greek) Blue jewel. *Saphira, Sapphire*

Sappho (Greek) First known woman poet; poetry.

Sarah (Hebrew) Princess, lady. *Sara, Sari, Sarri, Sary, Sarrie, Sarene, Sarina, Sarine, Sarita, Sairne, Sarett, Sadie, Sadey, Zarah, Zara, Zaria*

What's in a Name

At the age of 90, **Sarah**, the biblical wife of Abraham, gave birth to a son, Isaac. Her name means "lady" in Hebrew. Interestingly, Sarah was originally named Sarai, but God is said to have changed it to Sarah.

Sarahi (Hebrew) Princess.

Sarai (Hebrew) Quarrelsome. *Sari*

Saraid (Celtic) Excellent.

Sarasvati (Hindi) A goddess.

Saravati (Hindi) A river.

Sarea (Hebrew) Name of an angel.

Saree (Arabic) Most noble. *Sarie, Sary*

Sari (Hebrew) Princess. *Saree, Sarey, Sarie, Sarree, Sarrey, Sarri*

Sariah (Hebrew) My princess.

Saricia (Science fiction) Character from *Star Wars*.

Sarika (Hindi) Thrush.

Sarina (Latin) Serene, calm. *Sareena, Sarena, Sarrie*

Sarisha (Hindi) Charming.

Sarita (Hindi) Stream; river.

Sarmistha (Hindi) A daughter of Vrsaparvan.

Sarotte (French) Princess.

Saryu (Hindi) The river Sharayu in Ramayana.

Sasa (Japanese) Assistant.

Sasha (Russsian) Defender of mankind; variation of Alexander. *Sacha, Sachie, Sascha, Sasheen, Sashy*

Sashenka (Russian) Defender and helper of mankind.

Sashi (Hindi) Moon. (Japanese) To cut, to stab.

Sasilvia (Hawaiian) From the name Silvia.

Saskia (Slavic) Protector of mankind.

Sasthi (Hindi) Meaning unknown.

Satin (French) Smooth fabric. *Saten*

Satinka (Native American) Magic dancer.

Sato (Japanese) Sugar.

Satoko (Japanese) Child of Sato.

Satyavati (Hindi) Mother of Vyasa.

Saumya (Hindi) Mild.

Saundarya (Hindi) Meaning unknown.

Savana (Spanish) Treeless plain.

Savanna (Spanish) From the open plain Savannah. *Sava, Savana, Savanah*

Savarna (Hindi) Daughter of the ocean.

Savea (Scandinavian) The Swedish nation.

Savina (Russian) A Sabine woman. *Saveena, Savyna*

Savita (Hindi) Sun.

Savitri (Hindi) A form of the Devi; fourth Sakti.

Sawa (Japanese) A swamp.

Saxon (Latin, English) Large stone; swordsman.

Sayana (Hindi) Fourteenth-century commentator on the Vedas; tropical.

Sayo (Japanese) Born at night.

Sayoko (Japanese) Child of Sayo.

Scarlet (Middle English) Deep red. *Scarlett*

Schmetterling (German) Butterfly.

Schuyler (Dutch) Shield; scholar. *Schuylar*

Scholastica (Latin) Scholar.

Scota (Latin) An Irish woman.

Scout (French) Scout; watchman.

Seanna (Celtic) God's grace. *Shawna, Shawny, Shawnie, Shawnna, Shaune, Shauna, Siana, Shay*

Searlait (French) Petite.

Season (Latin) Planting time.

Sebastianne (Latin) Revered one. *Sebastiana, Sebastiane*

Sebastiona (French, Italian, Latin) Venerable, revered; a form of Sebastian.

Sebille (English) A fairy.

Sebrina (English) Princess.

Seda (Armenian) Forest voices.

Seema (Greek) Sprout. (Hindi) Limit; border.

Sefika (Turkish) Meaning unknown.

Seina (Spanish) Innocent.

Sekai (African) Laughter.

Seki (Japanese) Wonderful.

Sela (Hebrew) A rock. *Cela, Celia, Selah, Selia*

Selby (English) Of the manor house farm. *Selden, Seldon, Selwin, Selwyn*

Selena (Greek) Moon. *Selina, Selene, Selinda, Selly, Sellie, Sela, Selia, Sena, Celena, Celina, Celene, Celie, Celia*

Selima (Arabic) Peace. *Selema, Selemmah*

Selma (Scandinavian) Divinely protected. *Selle, Sellma, Salmah, Zelma*

Selina (Greek) Moon.

Sema (Greek) Divine omen.

Semele (Latin) Once.

Semine (Danish) Goddess of sun, moon, and stars. *Semina, Mina, Mine*

Semira (African) Fulfilled.

Semra (Turkish) Meaning unknown.

Sen (Vietnamese) Lotus flower.

Senalda (Spanish) A sign, symbol.

Senja (Finnish) Meaning unknown.

Sennett (French) Wise one. *Senet, Senta*

Senona (Spanish) Lively.

Senta (German) Assistant.

September (Latin) Seventh moon.

Septima (Latin) Seventh born. *Septimma, Septyma*

Sequoia (Native American) Giant redwood tree.

Sera (Latin) Heavenly, winged angel.

Serafina (Latin) Heavenly, winged angel.

Seraphina (Hebrew) Afire; angel; seraph. *Serafina, Sarafina, Serafine, Seraphine, Seraphim, Sera*

Serena (Latin) Peaceful one; calm. *Sarina, Serenna, Serenah, Serina*

Serenity (English) Peaceful disposition. *Serenitee, Serenitie*

Serilda (German) Armed maiden of war.

Serina (Latin) Serene, calm. *Sereena, Serin, Serinah, Serreena, Serrin, Serrina*

Serwa (African) Jewel.

Sesen (African) To wish for more.

Sesha (Hindi) Serpent who symbolizes time.

Settimia (Australian) Meaning unknown.

Sevati (Hindi) White rose.

Seve (Breton) Meaning unknown. *Seva*

Sevita (Hindi) Beloved.

Sexburth (Anglo-Saxon) Meaning unknown.

Sezen (Turkish) Meaning unknown.

Sezja (Russian) Protector.

Shada (Native American) Pelican.

Shae (English, Irish) A gift; fairy palace. *Shea, Shay*

Shaila (Hindi) Stone, mountain.

Shailaja (Hindi) Meaning unknown.

Shaili (Hindi) Style.

Shaina (Hebrew) Beautiful. *Shayna, Shane, Shania, Shayne*

Shaine (Hebrew) Beautiful. *Shaina, Shaynah, Shanie, Shayna, Shay, Shanna, Shana*

Shakila (African) Pretty.

Shakina (African) Beautiful one.

Shakira (Arabic) Grateful. *Shakera, Shakeera, Shakeerah, Shakeira, Shakyra, Skakarah*

Shako (Native American) Mint.

Shalini (Hindi) Modesty.

Shalom (Hebrew) Peace.

Shamara (Arabic) Ready for battle.

Shamira (Hebrew) Protector.

Shamita (Hindi) Peacemaker.

Shammara (Arabic) He girded his loins.

Shana (Hebrew) God is gracious. *Shanae, Shanaia*

Shanae (Hebrew) From Shana.

Shanata (Hindi) Peaceful.

Shandra (African American) God is gracious.

Shandy (English) Rambunctious. *Shandi*

Shanequa (American) From Moniqua; the adviser.

Shanessa (Irish) God is gracious. *Nessa*

Shani (Swahili) Marvelous.

Shania (Native American) I'm on my way.

Shanice (English) God is gracious. *Shaniece*

Shanika (Hindi) Gracious, beautiful.

Shaniqua (American) Adviser; variation of Moniqua.

Shaniya (Native American) I'm on my way.

Shanley (Gaelic) Child of the old hero.

Shanna (Hebrew) God is gracious; variation of Shannon; lovely. *Shanah, Shanea, Shannah*

Shannelle (French) Channel. *Chanel, Shanel, Schannel, Channel, Shannel, Shanelly*

Shannon (Irish) Wise one; river name. *Shan, Shanon, Shanen*

Shantah (Hindi) Peace; a name of a God. *Shanta, Shanti*

Shanata (Hindi) Peaceful.

Shantay (French) Enchanted.

Shante (Hindi) Rest, peace.

Shantell (Africa American) Song. *Chantel, Shantal, Shantel*

Shantelle (American) Stormy place. *Shantel, Telle, Telly, Shanty*

Shanti (Hindi) Peaceful, tranquil.

Shantina (American) Warrior princess. *Tina*

Shanton (French) We sing.

Shaquana (African American) Truth in life.

Sharay (Hebrew) My song, my lord. *Ray, Shay*

Sharda (Hindi) Meaning unknown.

Shari (Hebrew) Beloved. *Shary, Sherry*

Sharice (French) Precious.

Sharis (Hebrew) Flat plain.

Sharman (English) A fair share.

Sharmila (Hindi) Protected one.

Sharmistha (Hindi) Wife of Yayat.

Sharon (Hebrew) Princess. *Shari, Sharee, Shara, Sharen, Sharyn, Sharron, Charon, Sharry, Sherry, Sherri*

Sharseia Origin and meaning unknown.

Sharvani (Hindi) Goddess.

Shasa (African) Precious water.

Shashi (Hindi) The moon, moonbeam.

Shasmecka (African) Princess. *Shas*

Shasta (Native American) Three.

Shateque (African American) Follower.

Shauna (Irish) God is gracious; feminine form of Shaun. *Shaunna, Shawna*

Shawmbria (American) Combination of Shawn (Irish), God is gracious, and Bria (Irish), strong, virtuous, and honorable.

Shawn (Hebrew) God is gracious. *Shaunna, Shaun*

Shawnee (Irish) God's gift. *Shawn, Shawna, Sean*

Shawnnessy (Irish) God is gracious. *Saughnessy, O'Shaughnessy, Seannesy*

Shay (Irish) Stately one. *Shaye*

Shayla (Irish) Fairy palace.

Shaylee (Irish) Fairy princess of the field. *Shaylie, Shaleigh, Shaylea, Shaylee, Shealee*

Shayna (Hebrew) Beautiful.

Shayndel (Yiddish) Beautiful.

Shea (Irish) Fairy palace. *Shae, Shay*

Sheba (Hebrew) From Sheba. *Chebah, Sheeba, Sheebah*

Sheena (Irish) God's gracious gift.

Sheera (Hebrew) A song.

Sheetal (Hindi) Cool.

Sheila (Latin) Blind. *Sheilah, Sheela, Sheelah, Selia, Sheilagh*

Shela (Celtic) Musical.

Shelagh (Gaelic) Blind.

Shelah (Hebrew) Request.

Shelbi (English) Sheltered town. *Shelby*

Sheldon (English) From the farm on the ledge. *Shelden*

Shelley (English) From the ledge meadow; a variation of Michelle. *Sheli, Shelli, Shellie, Shelly*

Shenara Origin and meaning unknown.

Shenna (Irish) Shining. *Shenae, Shenea, Shena*

Shepry (American) Friendly and honest mediator.

Shera (Hebrew) Light-hearted. *Sheera, Sheerah, Sherah*

Sheri (Hebrew) From Sharon. *Sherri, Sherrie*

Sheridan (English, Irish, Scottish) Untamed; the wild one.

Sherill (English) Bright. *Cheril, Cherrill, Sherelle, Sheril, Sheryl, Sherrill, Cheryl*

Sherine (Hebrew) From Sharon.

Sherise (Greek) From the name Charisse.

Sherlyn (American) His song, his plain.

Sherri (Hebrew) Beloved. *Sherry*

Sheryl (English) Charity. *Cheryl, Sherri, Sherry, Cherie*

Sheyla (English) Gift of God.

Shian (Cheyenne Indian) A tribal name. *Shianne*

Shika (Japanese) Deer.

Shikah (Japanese) Gentle deer.

Shikha (Bengali) Flame.

Shima (Native American) Mother.

Shin (Korean) Belief.

Shina (Japanese) Virtue; good.

Shinko (Japanese) Faith.

Shira (Hebrew) Song. *Shirah, Shiri*

Shirley (English) Country meadow. *Shirlee, Sherlie, Shurlie, Shirleigh, Shirleen, Sherey, Shirl, Shurl, Shir*

Shirlyn (English) Bright meadow.

Shivani (Indian) Goddess Parvati.

Shobha (Hindi) Attractive. (Sanskrit) Brilliance.

Shobhna (Hindi) Ornamental, shining.

Shobi (Hebrew) Glorious.

Shoko (Japanese) Child of Sho.

Shoshannah (Hebrew) Rose. *Shoshanna, Shoshana, Shoshanah, Shosha*

Shradhdha (Hindi) Faith, trust.

Shreya (Hindi) Auspicious.

Shri (Hindi) Luster.

Shridevi (Hindi) Goddess.

Shrijani (Hindi) Creative.

Shruti (Hindi) Hearing.

Shu Fang (Chinese) Kind, gentle.

Shubha (Hindi) Meaning unknown.

Shubhada (Indian) Giver of luck.

Shulamit (Hebrew) Tranquil.

Shyann (French) A variation of Cheyenne. *Chayanne, Sheyenne*

Shyla (Hindi) Goddess. *Shila, Shy, Shylah*

Shylah (Celtic) Loyal to God; strong. *Shy, Shyla*

Shysie (Native American) Silent little one.

Sian (Welsh) God's gracious gift.

Sibel (Turkish) Meaning unknown. *Siebel, Sibella, Sibilla, Sibylla*

Sibley (Greek) Prophetess. *Sibyl, Sibylle, Sybil, Sybyl, Sybille, Sibille, Sibeal, Sybilline, Sibby, Sibbi, Sib, Cybil, Cybill*

Sibongile (African) Thanks.

Sibyl (Latin, Greek) Wise; seer; prophetic.

Siddhi (Hindi) Achievement; daughter of the god Daksha.

Sidone (African American) It is heard.

Sidonia (Italian) From Sidonia. *Sydania, Syndonia*

Sidonie (French) Flower.

Sidra (Latin) Like a star.

Sieglinde (German) Victory.

Sienna (Italian) Reddish brown.

Sierra (Spanish) Saw-tooth mountain range. *Cierra, Searah, Searrah, Siera, Sierrah, Sierre*

Signa (Scandinavian) Signal, sign.

Signe (Swedish) A sign; victorious.

Signild (Scandinavian) Meaning unknown.

Sigourney (French) Daring king.

Sigrid (Old Norse) Winning adviser. *Sigrath, Sigwald, Sigurd*

Sigrun (Scandinavian) A secret victory.

Siham (Arabic) Arrows.

Sihu (Native American) Flower.

Sika (African) Money.

Sila (Turkish) Homesick.

Sile (Scottish) Youthful; the blind one; the sixth.

Sileas (Latin) Youth.

Silei (Samoan) Meaning unknown.

Silke (German) Blind.

Silvana (Latin) Forest.

Silver (English) White.

Silvia (Latin) Woodland maid. *Sylvia, Silva, Silvie, Sylvie, Sylva, Silvana, Sylvana, Sylwia, Zilvia*

Sima (African) Treasure, prize.

Simba (Swahili) Lion.

Simone (Hebrew) One who hears. *Simona*

Simoni (Hindi) Obedient.

Simran (Hindi) God's gift.

Sine (Gaelic) God's gracious gift.

Sinead (Irish) Gracious.

Siobhan (Gaelic) God is gracious.

Siran (Armenian) Alluring.

Sirena (Greek) Siren.

Sirisha (Hindi) Flower.

Siroun (Armenian) Lovely.

Sirvat (Armenian) Rose.

Sissy (American) From the name Cecilia; familiar name for "sister." *Cissee, Cissey, Cissy, Sis, Sissi, Sissie*

Sistine (Italian) Spiritual. *Sisteen, Sisteene*

Sitara (Sanskrit) Morning star.

Sitembile (African) Trust.

Siusan (Scottish) Lily.

Siv (Norwegian) Kinship; wife of Thor. *Seev*

Siyanda (African) We are growing.

Skyla (English) Sky; sheltering. *Sky, Skylah*

Skylar (English) Eternal life; strength; love and beauty. *Skye, Sky, Skyrah, Schuyler, Skieler, Skilar, Skiler, Skyla, Skylie, Skylor*

Smita (Hindi) Smiling. *Susmita*

Smridhi (Hindi) Meaning unknown.

Smriti (Hindi) Recollection. (Hindi) A form of the Devi.

Snana (Native American) Jingles like bells.

Sneh (Hindi) Love.

Sneha (Hindi) Affection.

Snigdha (Hindi) Soft.

Snøfrid (Scandinavian) Meaning unknown.

Snow (American) Frozen rain. *Sno*

Snowy (American) White; pure.

Sofi (Greek) Wisdom. *Sofie, Sophie, Sophia, Sofia*

Sofiel (Spanish) Wise; angel of fruits and vegetables.

Sojourner (Old French) To stay for a time; name of former slave-turned-equal-justice advocate, Sojourner Truth.

Sokanon (Native American) Rain.

Solace (Latin) Comfort.

Solada (Thai) Listener.

Solana (Spanish) Sunshine. *Solande, Solanna, Solena, Solinda*

Solange (French) Rare jewel. *Solangia*

Soledad (Spanish) Solitary; health.

Soleil (French) Sun.

Solita (Latin) Alone. *Soleata, Soleeta, Soleita, Solitah, Solite, Solyta*

Solosolo (Samoan) Dry.

Somatra (Hindi) Excelling the moon.

Sommer (German) Summer season. *Somer, Somara, Sommar*

Sona (Hindi) Gold.

Sonakshi (Hindi) Golden eye.

Sonal (Hindi) Golden. *Sonali*

Sondra (Greek) Helper; defender of mankind.

Sonia (Russian) Wisdom. *Sonja, Sonya*

Sonika (Hindi) Golden.

Sonja (Scandinavian) Wisdom. *Sonjae, Sonjia*

Sonnenschein (German) Sunshine.

Sonora (Spanish) Pleasant-sounding.

Sonya (Latin) Wisdom. *Sonnya*

Soo (Korean) Excellence; long life.

Sophie (Greek) Wisdom. *Sofi, Sophia, Sofia, Sofie, Sophy, Sophronia, Sadhbh, Zofka*

Sophronia (Greek) Foresighted.

Sora (Native American) Chirping songbird.

Sorano (Japanese) Of the sky. *Sora*

Soraya (Arabic) Princess.

Sorcha (Gaelic) Bright.

Sorilbran (English) Smart.

Sorley (Scandinavian) Viking.

Sorrel (French) Bitter; from the tree. *Sorel, Sorrell, Sorie*

Sosanna (Irish) Lily. *Sosannah, Sosanah, Sosanna*

Soshannah (Hebrew) Lily.

Sosie (French) Double; look alike.

Souzan (Arabic) Fire.

Soyala (Native American) Winter solstice.

Sparrow (English) A bird.

Speranza (Italian) Hope. *Speranca*

Spica (Latin) Name of a star.

Spirituality (Greek) Spiritual; significance of life.

Spodumene (Greek) Burnt to ashes; ash-gray.

Spring (English) Spring season.

Sraddha (Hindi) Faith; a wife of Shiva.

Srilata (Hindi) Creeper.

Sripada (Hindi) Noble footprint. *Sripata*

Srishti (Hindi) Creation; nature.

Sruti (Hindi) Ability to hear.

Stacia (Greek) One who shall rise again. *Stacy, Staci, Stasia, Stasya, Tasia*

Star (American, English, Latin) A star. *Starr*

Starleen (English) Star.

Stefania (Greek) Crown. *Stephanie, Stephannie, Stepania, Stephania, Stefanie, Stephana, Stephanya, Steffie, Steffi, Stef, Stepha, Stefa, Fannie, Fanny, Stefka*

Stella (Latin) Star. (French) Variation of Estella. *Stela, Stellar, Star, Starr, Starla, Starling*

Stephaney (Greek) Crowned.

Stesha (Greek) Crowned one.

Stockard (English) From the yard of tree stumps. *Stockerd, Stockyrd*

Storm (English) Stormy weather; tempest. *Storme, Stormy, Stormie*

Subhadra (Hindi) A wife of Arjuna, a hero of the epic *Mahabharata.*

Subhaga (Hindi) A fortunate person.

Subhangi (Hindi) A fortunate person.

Subhuja (Hindi) Auspicious. *Apsara*

Suchi (Hindi) Radiant glow.

Suchitra (Hindi) Beautiful.

Sudevi (Hindi) Wife of Krishna.

Sudha (Hindi) Nectar.

Sudie (English) Lily.

Sujata (Hindi) Of noble birth, well-bred.

Sukanya (Hindi) Comely.

Suki (Japanese) Beloved.

Sugar (American, English) Sugar; sweet.

Suksma (Hindi) Fine.

Sukutai (African) Hug.

Sula (Icelandic) Large sea bird; peace.

Sulwyn (Welsh) Bright as the sun.

Suma (Egyptian, Japanese) To ask.

Sumana (Hindi) Flower.

Sumanna (Hindi) Good natured.

Sumati (Hindi) Wisdom.

Sumayah (Arabic) Pride.

Sumehra (Arabic) Beautiful face.

Sumey (Asian) Flower. *Sumy*

Sumi (Japanese) Clear, refined.

Sumitra (Indian, Hindi) Good friend; mother of Lakshamana.

Summer (English, Arabic) Summer season. *Sumar, Somar, Samar*

Sun (Korean) Goodness.

Sundarai (Hindi) Beautiful.

Sundeep (Punjabi) Light; enlightened. *Sundip*

Sunee (Hindi) Good thing.

Sunila (Hindi) Blue.

Sunita (Hindi) A daughter of the god Dharma. *Sunrita*

Suniti (Hindi) Good principles.

Sunniva (English, Scandinavian) Gift of the sun.

Suparna (Hindi) Leafy.

Suprabha (Hindi) Radiant.

Supriti (Hindi) True love.

Supriya (Hindi) Beloved.

Surabhi (Hindi) Wish-yielding cow.

Suravinda (Hindi) Beautiful. *Yaksa*

Surotama (Hindi) Auspicious. *Apsara*

Suruchi (Hindi) Good taste.

Surupa (Hindi) Beautiful.

Surya (Hindi) The sun.

Susan (Hebrew) Lily. *Susannah, Susanne, Susanna, Susi, Suse, Suisan, Suzanne, Suzanna, Sosana, Susette, Suzette, Sue Anne, Sue Ellen, Susy, Susie, Soos, Suzy, Suzie, Soozie, Sue, Sukie, Sukey, Zsa Zsa*

Sushanti (Hindi) Peace.

Sushma (Hindi) Beautiful woman.

Sushmita (Hindi) Smiling. *Susmita*

Susie (French) From the name Susan. *Susey, Susi, Susy, Suze, Suzi, Suzie, Suzy*

Susila (Hindi) Wife of Lord Krishna; clever in amorous sciences.

Suvarna (Hindi) Golden.

Suvrata (Hindi) A child of god Daksa.

Suzana (English) Lily. *Suzenna, Suzzanna, Suzanna, Suzannah*

Suzette (French) Little lilly. *Susette*

Svea (Scandinavian) The Swedish nation. *Svay*

Sveta (Slavic) Bright light.

Svetlana (Russian) Star. *Svetochka.*

Swarupa (Hindi) Truth.

Swati (Indian) Name of a star.

Sweta (Hindi) Fair complexioned.

Sybella (Greek) Prophetess, oracle.

Sybil (Greek) Prophet. *Sibel, Sibyl, Syb, Sybill, Sybille, Sybyl*

Sydelle (Hebrew) Princess.

Sydney (French) From the city of Saint-Denis. *Sidney, Sydny, Sid, Sidne, Sidoney, Sidonia, Siddie, Syd, Sydell, Sidell, Sydel*

Sydni (French) Contradiction of Saint-Denis. *Sydnee, Sidney*

Syeira (Gypsy) Princess.

Sylvia (Latin) From the forest. *Syl, Sylvea*

Symona (American) It is heard.

Symone (French) God is heard. *Simone, Simona, Simon, Symona*

Symphony (English, Greek, Latin) Concordant in sound. *Symfoni, Symphanie, Symphany, Symphoni, Symphonie*

Syna (Greek) Two together.

Synnove (Scandinavian) Sun gift.

Syrida Origin and meaning unknown.

Syshe (Yiddish) Street.

Szitakota (Slavic) Dragonfly.

T

Taa (Native American) Seed.

Taahira (Arabic) Pure, chaste.

Taalah (Origin unknown) Young palm tree.

Taanach (Hebrew) Who humbles thee.

Taariq (Swahili) Morning star.

Taban (Irish) Genius.

 Naming Rights

Some parents believe they can imbue their newborn child with personality traits they admire by choosing a name that coincides with those traits.

Tabassum (Arabic) Smiling.

Tabea (German) Meaning unknown.

Tabitha (Greek, Hebrew, Native American) Gazelle; roebuck; tiara. *Tabatha, Tabbie, Tabbi, Tabby*

Taborri (Native American) Voices that carry. *Taborah, Tabby*

Tacey (English) Silent, calm. *Tace, Tacita*

Taci (American) Strong, healthy.

Tacincala (Native American) Deer. *Tawi*

Tacita (Latin) To be silent. *Taceta, Tacetah, Tasita, Taycita*

Tacy (Latin) Silence.

Tadako (Japanese) Child of Tada.

Tadewi (Native American) Wind.

Tadi (Omaha Indian) Wind.

Tadita (Native American) Runner.

Taffy (Welsh) Beloved. *Taffea, Taffee, Taffey, Taffi, Tafy*

Tahirah (Arabic) Chaste, pure.

Tahlia (Hebrew) Morning dew. (American) Combination of Tai (Vietnamese), weather, talented, and Lia (Hebrew), dependence.

Tahnee (English) Little one.

Tahzai Origin and meaning unknown. *Tahzay*

Tai (Vietnamese) Talent. *Tie, Tye*

Taifa (African) Nation, tribe.

Tailynn Combination of Tai (Vietnamese), weather, talented, and Lynn (English), waterfall. (American) From Tai and Lynn.

Taido (Japanese) Gentle way.

Taima (Native American) Crash of thunder.

Taina (Spanish) Gracious; from Anna.

Taini (Native American) Returning moon.

Tainn (Native American) New moon.

Taipa (Miwok Indian) To spread wings.

Taite (English) Pleasant and bright.

Taja (African) To mention.

Tajsa (Polish) Princess; born at Christmas.

Taka (Japanese) Tall, honorable.

Takako (Japanese) Child of Taka.

Takala (African) Corn tassel. *Takalah*

Takara (Japanese) Treasure, precious object.

Taki (Japanese) Waterfall.

Takia (Arabic) Worshipper. *Taki, Tikia, Tykia*

Takira (American) Sun.

Takiyah (North African) Pious, righteous.

Takoda (Native American) Friend to all.

Tala (Native American) Stalking wolf.

Talaitha (African American) Inventive. *Talitha, Taleetha, Taleta, Taletha, Talith, Tally*

Talasi (Hopi) Indian corn-tassel flower.

Tale (African) Green.

Taleen (Armenian) Meaning unknown. *Tal, Taline, Talyn*

Talia (Hebrew) Dew from heaven. (Greek) Blooming. *Tahlia, Tali, Talya, Talyah, Tally, Tai,*

Talieya (Greek) Blooming.

Taline (Armenian) Monestary.

Talisa (African American) Consecrated to God. *Talisha, Talesa*

Talisha (African American) Damsel arise.

Talitha (Aramic) Angel who escorts the sun on its daily course. *Taleetha, Taleta, Taletha, Talith*

Taliyah (Greek) Blooming. *Taliya*

Tallis (French) Forest.

Tallulah (Choctaw Indian) Leaping water. *Tally, Tallie, Tallula, Talula, Talulah*

Tallya (Greek) Blooming.

Tallys (French) Forest.

Talon (English) Claw. *Taelon, Taelyn, Talen, Tallon*

Talor (Hebrew) Morning dew.

Tam (Vietnamese) Heart.

Tama (Native American) Thunderbolt. *Tamah*

Tamaka (Japanese) Bracelet.

Tamali (Hindi) Tree with very dark bark.

Tamanna (Hindi) Desire.

Tamara (Hebrew) Palm tree, spice. *Tamarah, Tamar, Tamarind, Tamika, Tamary*

Tamasha (African) Pageant.

Tamatha (American) Dear Tammy.

Tamber (American) Music pitch.

Tambre (English) Great joy; music. *Amber, Tambur*

Tambrey (American) Immortal. *Tambree*

Tameka (Arabic) Twin.

Tamesis (Greek) Goddess of the river.

Tamia (English) Palm tree; variation of Tamara.

Tamika (African American) People.

Tamiko (Japanese) Child of Tami.

Tamira (African American) A spice or palm tree.

Tamitha (Hebrew) Twin.

Tamma (Hebrew) Perfect.

Tammy (Hebrew) Perfect one. *Tammie, Tammye*

Tamra (Hebrew) A spice or palm tree. *Tamora, Tamorah*

Tamsyn (Native American, English) Benevolent. *Tamsa, Tamsan, Tamsin, Tamsen*

Tamya (American) Palm tree; variation of Tamara.

Tamyra (African American) A spice or palm tree. *Tamirah*

Tan (Vietnamese) New.

Tana (Slavic) Fairy queen.

Tanaka (Japanese) Dweller.

Tanasha (African American) Strong willed, persistent. *Tenyasha*

Naming Rights

Go through the phone book and see if any names jump out at you.

Tanashia (Origin unknown) Born on Christmas.

Tanaya (Hindi) Child of mine.

Tandice (African American) Team.

Tanesha (African) Strong. *Tanish, Tanisha, Tannesha*

Taney (Japanese) Valley. *Tahnee, Tahney, Tahni, Tanie*

Taneya (Russian) Fairy queen.

Tangia (American) The angel.

Tanginika (African American) Lake goddess.

Tani (Japanese) Valley. (Melanesian) Sweetheart. (Tonkinese) Youth. (Andalusian) Bull that charges randomly. *Tangee*

Tania (Slavic) A fairy queen of Tatiana. *Tanya*

Taniel (African American) Feminine form of Daniel.

Tanika (Hindi) Rope.

Tanisha (African American) Born on Monday.

Tanith (Greek) Goddess of love.

Taniya (English) Fairy queen. *Tanya, Tania, Tonya, Taniyah*

Tanner (English) Leather worker. *Tanner*

Tansy (Greek, Hopi Indian) Immortality; flower name.

Tanu (Hindi) Body; slim.

Tanuja (Hindi) Daughter.

Tanushi (Hindi) Beauty.

Tanvi (Hindi) A delicate girl.

Tanya (Russian) Fairy princess. *Tania, Tan, Tani, Tatiana, Tatjana*

Tanzi (English) Immortal.

Tapanga (African, Hebrew) Sweet; unpredictable. *Tata, Pangi*

Tapi (Hindi) Meaning unknown.

Tapti (Hindi) A river.

Tara (Celtic, Gaelic, Hindi) Rocky hill; tower. *Taria, Taryn*

Tarala (Hindi) Honeybee.

Tarana (African) Born during the day.

Taraneh (Arabic) Melody, song.

Tarannum (Hindi) Melody.

Tarangini (Indian) River.

Taree (Japanese) Arching branch.

Tareva-Chine' (Native American) Beautiful eyes. *Tu-Sha*

Taria (English) Crown.

Tariana (African American) Holy hillside.

Tariel (Origin unknown) Angel of summer.

Tarika (Hindi) Star.

Tarisai (African) Look, behold.

Tarja (Arabic) The stave of a poem. (Finnish) Wealthy.

Tarjani (Indian) First finger.

Tarquinia (Place name) Tarquinia, Italy.

Tarra (Australian) A creek.

Tarsha (Native American) Tan.

Taruna (Sanskrit) Young girl.

Taryn (Greek) Queen. *Tarin*

Tasanee (Thai) Beautiful view.

Tasha (Greek, Russian) Born on Christmas; short for Natasha.

Tashi (Asian, English) Prosperity; born on Christmas.

Tasia (Greek) Resurrection.

Tasmine (American) Twin. *Tasmin*

Tassilyn (American) Mythological name.

Tasya (Slavic) Resurrection.

Tate (English, Native American) To be cheerful; windy; a great talker.

Tatiana (Russian, Slavic) Fairy queen. *Tanya, Tatania, Tatia, Tatianna, Tatiannia, Tatie, Tattianna, Tatyana, Taynanna*

Tatum (English) Cheerful, bringer of joy. *Tait, Taitum, Tat, Tayte, Taite*

Tatyana (Latin, Russian) Fairy queen; silver haired.

Tauret (Egyptian) Goddess of pregnant women.

Tavia (Latin, Old English) Great. *Tay, Taves*

Tavita (Latin) Eighth.

Tawana (Native American) Tan hide.

Tawanda (German) Slender, young.

Tawnie (English) Little one, yellowish-brown. *Tawny*

Taya (English) From the name Taylor.

Tayce (French) Silence.

Tayen (Native American) New moon.

Tayla (English) Tailor. *Taila, Taylah*

Taylar (French) To cut. *Tayla*

Taylor (English) Tailor. *Tailor, Tay, Tie*

Tayna (English) Tailor.

Tazanna (Native American) Princess.

Tazara (African) Railway line.

Tazu (Japanese) Stork; longevity. *Taz, Tazi, Tazoo*

Tea (Spanish) Princess; aunt.

Teagan (Irish, Welsh) Attractive, beautiful. *Tegan, Teagen*

Teal (American, English, Scandinavian) Greenish-blue color, a duck.

Tebeth (Hebrew) Good, goodness.

Teca (Slavic) Summer.

Teddi (English) God-given; variation of Theodora.

Tedra (Greek) Outgoing. *Teddra, Tedrah*

Teena (Latin) Little one.

Tehya (Native American) Precious.

Teigra (Greek) Tiger.

Teishymn Origin and meaning unknown.

Tejal (Hindi) Lustrous.

Tejana (Spanish) Texan female.

Teji (Hindi) Enlightment.

Tekla (Greek) Divine fame. *Thekla*

Tekli (Polish) Famous for God.

Teleri (Welsh) From the River Tyleri.

Telissa (American) Combination of Talia (Greek), blooming, and Aisha (Arabic), woman.

Telma (Greek) Ambitious.

Telyn (Welsh) Harp.

Tema (Hebrew) Righteous; a palm tree.

Temima (African American) Whole; honest.

Temina (Hebrew) Honest.

Temira (Hebrew) Tall. *Temora, Timora*

Temperance (Latin) Moderate.

Tempest (French) Storm. *Tempestt, Tempyst*

Tena (English) Anointed; follower of Christ.

Tenaya (Origin unknown) Meaning unknown.

Tendai (African) Be thankful to God.

Tender (American) Sensitive.

Tendra (Science fiction) Character from *Star Wars*.

Teness (American) Meaning unknown.

Tenley Origin and meaning unknown.

Tennen (Japanese) Natural.

Tera (English) High hill.

Terah (Latin) Earth, hillside.

Teranika (Celtic, Gaelic) Earth's victory.

Terceiro (Spanish) Born third.

Terehasa (African) Blessed.

Tereixa (Galician) Reaper. *Thereasa*

Terena (Latin) Earthly. *Terrena, Terenna, Terrenna*

Terentia (Greek) Guardian.

Teresa (Spanish) Harvester. *Theresa*

Terhi (Finnish) Acorn.

Teri (English, Greek) Harvester, variation of Teresa.

Terin (Latin) Yellow singing bird; ash-colored.

Terpsichore (Greek) Dancing.

Terra (Latin) Earth. *Terry, Tera*

Terri (Greek) Harvester. *Teri, Terre, Terrey, Tery*

Terrylyn (American) Combination of Teri (Greek), reaper, and Lyn (English), waterfall.

Tertia (Latin) The third. *Ters, Tersh, Tersha, Tersia*

Teryl (English) Bright and vivacious.

Tesia (Polish) Loved by God.

Tess (Greek) Fourth-born. *Tessie*

Tessa (Italian) Countess. *Tesa, Teza*

Tessica (American) Wealthy harvester. *Tesica, Tessika*

Tetisheri (Egyptian) Matriarch of Egyptian royal family of the late seventeenth and early eighteenth centuries.

Tetsu (Japanese) Iron.

Tevy (Cambodian) Angel.

Texcean (Spanish) From Texas. *Tex*

Thaddea (Greek) Appreciative. *Thada, Thadda, Thaddeah*

Thadine (Hebrew) The praised. *Thadyne, Thady*

Thaisa (Greek) The bond. *Thais*

Thalassa (Greek) From the sea.

Thalia (Greek) Blooming; plentiful. *Taylie, Taylee, Thalius*

Than (Greek, Vietnamese) Death; brilliant.

Thana (Arabic) Gratitude.

Thandiwe (African) The loving one.

Thao (Vietnamese) Respectful of parents.

Thara (Arabic) Wealth.

Thea (Greek, Laos) Goddess; sort. *Teah, Teeah, Theah, Theeah, Tiah*

Theala (Science fiction) Character from *Star Wars*.

Thelma (Greek) Nursing. *Telma*

Thema (African) Queen.

Themis (Greek) Goddess of justice.

Themista Origin and meaning unknown.

Theodora (Greek) Gift of God. *Theora, Theda, Teodora, Theodosia, Thedora, Tedra, Feodora, Fedora, Dora, Theone, Theophania, Theophilia*

Theodosia (Greek) God-given.

Theola (Greek) Divine.

What's in a Name

Sometimes the short, or pet form, of a name becomes more popular than the original. Take **Thea**, for example. It's the short form of *Theodora*, which means "gift of God," from the Greek name "theos," for God, and "doron," gift. And there are even variations of Thea, such as with movie star Téa Leoni's name.

Theone (Greek) Godly.

Theophilia (Greek) Loved divinely.

Thera (Greek) Wild.

Theresa (Greek) Reaper. *Teresa, Teressa, Therese, Toireasa, Teri, Terri, Terry, Tessa, Tess, Tessie, Tessy, Tracey, Tracie, Tracy, Tressa, Tessica*

Therese (French) From Theresia.

Thi (Asian) Poetry.

Thirza (Hebrew) Sweet-natured; cypress tree. *Thyrza, Tirza, Tyrza*

Thisbe (Greek) Where the doves live.

Thistle (English) Thistle.

Thomasa (Greek) Twin. *Thomasina, Thomasine, Tomasina, Tommie, Tommy, Tammy, Tamsen, Tamsin, Tamson, Thomassa*

Thora (Old Norse) Thunder. *Thordia, Tora*

Thorborg (Scandinavian) Thunder.

Thracia (Greek) Place name: Thracia, Greece.

Thu (Asian) Autumn.

Thuraya (Arabic) Stars and the planets.

Thurid (Scandinavian) Wife of Thorstein the Red; viking.

Thuy (Vietnamese) Pure.

Thy (Asian) Poetry.

Thyra (Greek, Scandinavian) Shield-bearer. *Thira*

Thyrrni (Scandinavian) Loud.

Tia (Spanish, Greek) Aunt; princess. *Tianna, Tiana*

Tiana (Greek) Princess. *Tianna, Tyana*

Tiara (Latin) Crowned. *Teara, Tiarra, Tyara*

Tiaret (African) Lioness.

Tiarra (Hebrew) Crowned.

Tiegan (Aztec) Little princess in the big valley. *Tiegs, Tiegy*

Tien (Vietnamese) Fairy.

Tienette (Greek) Crowned with laurel. *Tiena, Tien*

Tiera (Latin, Spanish) Land; earth.

Tierra (Spanish) Earth; land.

Tiesha (Latin) Joy, happy; variation of Leticia.

Tieve (Celtic, Gaelic) Hillside.

Tiffany (French) Appearance of God. *Tiff, Tiffani, Tiffanie, Tifany, Tiphany, Tifanee, Tiffy, Tiffie, Fanny*

What's in a Name

Most people assume the name **Tiffany** is given in honor of the famed Tiffany and Co. jeweler in New York City, but the name's origins actually go farther back than that. Tiffany is a Medieval form of Theophania, which was frequently given to girls born on the Christian celebration of Epiphany, January 6. That was the day the Magi were said to have visited the baby Jesus. The name itself means "God appearing."

Tigerlily (Asian) Tigerlily; flower. (American) Lily; tiger.

Tilda (French, German) Mighty in war; maid of battles.

Tillie (German) Might, power.

Timandra (Greek) Daughter of hero Tyndareus.

Timberly (African American) Tall ruler.

Timera (Hebrew) Palm tree. *Tamara, Tamyra*

Timotha (English) To honor God.

Timothea (Greek) Honoring God. *Timaula, Timi*

Tina (Spanish) Majestic.

Tinble (English) Bell sounds.

Tineka-Jawana (African) Meaning unknown.

Ting (Chinese) Slim; graceful.

Tinisha (American) Born on Christmas.

Tiombe (African) Shy.

Tionne (Science fiction) Character from *Star Wars*.

Tiponya (Miwok Indian) Owl poking the hatching egg. *Tiponi*

Tira (Scottish) Land.

Tirza (Hebrew) Kindness. *Thirza, Tirzah*

Tisha (Latin) Form of Patricia; joyful. *Tesha, Ticia, Tishah*

Titania (Greek) Giant.

Titian (Greek) Red-gold.

Tiva (Native American) Dance.

Tivona (Hebrew) Lover of nature.

Toakase (Tonga) Woman of the sea. *Toa*

Tobit (Hebrew) Good.

Tokiko (Japanese) Child of Toki.

Tola (Polish) Priceless.

Tolena (French) Meaning unknown. *Toley*

Tolia (Polish) Worthy of praise.

Tolinka (Native American) Coyote's ear.

Tomai (Greek) Honoring Thomas.

Tomi (Japanese) Rich.

Tomiko (Japanese) Child of Tomi.

Tona (Greek) Flourishing. (Latin) Praiseworthy.

Toni (French) Worthy of praise.

Tonya (Latin) Worthy of praise.

Topanga (Native American) Where the mountain meets the sea.

Topaz (Latin) Yellow gemstone. *Tophaz*

Tora (Japanese) Tiger. (Hebrew) Law.

Toral (Hindi) Folk heroine.

Tori (Japanese) Bird. *Torree, Torri, Torrie, Torry, Tory*

Torie (American) Victorious.

Toril (Scandinavian) Female warrior. *Torill, Torille*

Tosca (Latin) From Tuscany, Italy.

Tosha (English, Greek) Born on Christmas.

Toshi (Latin) Inestimable.

Tosia (Latin) Inestimable.

Totie (English) Gift of God.

Tourmaline (Asian) Name of a gemstone.

Tova (Hebrew) Good. *Tove, Tovah*

Toyah (Scandinavian) Toy.

Toyo (Japanese) Plentiful.

Traci (English) Brave; summer. *Traice, Traicy, Traicey, Traici, Traicie, Tracee*

Tracy (French) Path, road. *Tracey*

Naming Rights

In many cultures and throughout history, a child's name is thought to reflect his or her deepest or truest self. A name, therefore, is inseparably entwined with the body's soul.

Trang (Vietnamese) Page.

Tranquilia (Spanish) Calm, tranquil.

Tranquility (Latin) God-inspired peace of mind; devout.

Treasa (Celtic) Strong.

Trella (Spanish) Star; from Estrella.

Tresa (Greek, Welsh) Harvester; the third.

Tressa (Greek) Reaping life's rewards. *Tresa, Tresah, Trisa*

Treva (Celtic) Prudent. *Treve*

Triana (Greek) Pure. *Trianna*

Tricia (Latin) Noble woman.

Trifine (Greek) Delicate. *Trifin, Trifina, Trifena, Trifene, Triffena*

Trilby (Italian) One who sings; musical trills.

Trilochana (Indian) Lord Shiva.

Trina (Greek) Fire; full of spirit; perfect. *Treena, Trinah, Trin*

Trind (Swedish) Pure.

Trinh (Vietnamese) Pure.

Trini (Latin) The Trinity.

Trinity (Latin) The holy three. *Trin, Triny, Triniti*

Trish (American) From Patricia.

Trisha (Latin) Of noble descent.

Trishna (Hindi) Thirst; a form of the Devi.

Trista (Latin) Sorrowful.

Tristana (Latin) Sad.

Tristessa (Latin) Sad woman.

Triveni (Hindi) Three sacred rivers.

Trixie (American) Bringer of joy.

Troy (French) Place name.

Tru (English) From Truly. *True*

Truda (Polish) Warrior woman.

Trude (German) From Gertrude.

Trudie (English) Strong, spear.

Trudy (English) Beloved.

Trula (German) True.

Trupti (Hindi) Satiatedness.

Trusha (Hindi) Thirst.

Tryamon (English) Fairy princess.

Tryna (Greek) Third.

Tryne (Dutch) Pure.

Tryphena (Latin) Dainty.

Tuesday (English) Day of the week.

Tuhina (Hindi) Dewdrop.

Tulasi (Hindi) A sacred plant; basil.

Tulia (Spanish) Destined for glory.

Tully (Irish) At peace with God. *Tulee, Tulei, Tuley, Tuli, Tulie, Tulli, Tuly*

Turquoise (French) A precious stone.

Tusti (Hindi) Peace; happiness; a form of the Devi.

Tuwa (Native American) Earth.

Tuyen (Vietnamese) Angel.

Twila (English) Creative. *Twyla*

Twyla (English) Third.

Tyanne (American) From Tyrus and Anne. *Ty*

Tydfill (Welsh) Meaning unknown.

Tyesha (African American) Duplicitous. *Tesha, Tisha, Tyeisha, Tyiesha, Tyisha*

Tyne (English) A river.

Tynice (American) Meaning unknown.

Tyra (Scandinavian) God of battle.

Tyree (Irish, Scottish) Island off Scotland.

Tyrell (African American) Thunder; ruler.

Tyrina (African American) Meaning unknown.

Tyronica (African American) Goddess of battle.

Tzila (Hebrew) Protection.

Tziporah (Hebrew) Bird.

Tzippa (Hebrew) Bird.

Tzofit (Hebrew) Hummingbird.

Tzvia (Hebrew) Deer or gazelle.

U

Uberta (Italian) Bright.

Uchenna (African) God's will.

Udaya (Hindi) Dawn.

Udele (English) Wealthy. *Uda, Udela, Udell, Udella, Udelle*

Udiya (Hebrew) Fire of God. *Udia, Uriela, Uriella*

Uinise (Polynesian) Fair victory.

Ujila (Hindi) Bright light. *Ujala, Ujjala, Ujvala*

Ujwala (Hindi) Bright, lustrous.

Ula (Irish) Sea jewel. (Scandinavian) Inherited estate.

Ulima (Arabic) Wise.

Ulla (German) Willful. *Ulah, Ullah*

Ulrika (German) Wolf ruler. *Ulrica, Ulrike*

Ultima (Latin) Last, endmost. *Ultimah*

Ultreia (Gaelic) Meaning unknown.

Ulu (African) Second-born girl.

Ululani (Hawaiian) Heavenly inspiration.

Ulva (German) She-wolf; brave.

Uma (Hindi) Mother; name for the Hindu goddess Devi. *Umah*

Umali (Hindi) Generous.

Umeko (Japanese) Child of the plum blossom.

Umm (Arabic) Mother.

Una (Latin) One, unity, wholeness. *Oona, Unah*

What's in a Name

One of David Letterman's favorite names, **Uma** (as in movie star Uma Thurman) is a name of the goddess Parvati in Hindi mythology. The word also means "flax" in Sanskrit.

Unaiza (Arabic) Meaning unknown.

Undine (Latin) Of the wave. Mythology; water spirits. *Unda, Onde, Ondine*

Unega (Native American) White.

Unity (English) Oneness, together.

Unn (Scandinavian) She who is loved. *Un*

Unnati (Hindi) Progress.

Unni (Norse) Modest.

Uny (Latin) Unity, together.

Urania (Greek) Heavenly; muse of astronomy. *Uraina, Urainia, Uraniya, Uranya*

Urbana (Latin) From the city. *Urbani, Urbanna, Urbannia*

Urbi (African) Princess.

Uriah (Hebrew) God is light. *Uria*

Uriana (Greek) The unknown.

Urika (Native American) Useful. *Ureka, Urica, Urikah, Uriqua*

Urmila (Hindi) Wife of Lakshmana.

Ursula (Latin) Little bear. *Ursola, Ursule, Orsola, Ursa, Ursie, Orsa, Urzula*

Ursulina (Spanish) Little bear.

Urvasi (Hindi) Most beautiful of Apsaras.

Usagi (Japanese) Moon. *Usa*

Usdi (Native American) Baby.

Usha (Hindi) Dawn.

Ushi (Chinese) Ox.

Ushmil (Hindi) Warm. *Ushria*

Ut (Vietnamese) East.

Uta (German) Fortunate maid of battle. *Ute*

Utina (Native American) Woman of my country. *Utahna, Uteana, Uteena, Utinah, Utona, Utyna*

Uttara (Hindi) Mother of Pariksit.

Uwimana (African) Daughter of God.

V

Vachya (Hindi) To speak.

Vada (Hebrew) Rose. *Vaida, Vay*

Vail (English) From the valley. *Vayle, Vale, Valle, Val*

Vailea (Polynesian) Water that talks.

Naming Rights

One of the hottest trends today is to name a baby after a place—a state, town, or region—or even a college or high school alma mater.

Vaishali (Hindi) Ancient city of India.

Vala (English) Chosen.

Valborg (Swedish) A powerful mountain.

Valda (Old Norse) Spirited warrior.

Valencia (Latin) Bravery. Place name: Valencia, Spain. *Valecia, Valence, Valensha, Valentia, Valenzia, Valinicia*

Valentine (Latin) Good health. *Valentina, Valeda, Valina, Vally, Val, Valtina, Valentiane*

Valerie (Latin) Strong. *Valeria, Valery, Valerian, Vally, Vallie, Val, Valarie, Vallerre*

Valeska (Polish) Glorious ruler.

Valisa (Latin) Wild one. *Vall, Vallie*

Valkyrie (Scandinavian) Fantastic. *Valkie, Valkee, Valkry*

Valonia (Latin) Of the vale. *Vallon, Valona*

Valora (Latin) The valorous. *Valoria, Valorie, Valory, Valorya*

Van (Dutch) Form of Von.

Vandana (Hindi) Worship.

Vanecia (Latin) Goddess of beauty and love. *Vanetia, Vanicia, Venecia, Venetia, Venezia, Venice, Venise, Venize*

Vanessa (Greek) A butterfly. *Vannia, Vanna, Vannie, Vanora, Nessa, Nessie, Nessy, Venissa*

Vani (Hindi) Alternate name for goddess Saraswati; knowledge.

Vanika (Hindi) Small forest.

Vanita (Hindi) Woman.

Vanja (Scandinavian) Version of John; grace.

Vanjan (Hindi) Meaning unknown.

Vanka (Russian) Favored by God.

Vanna (Asian, Greek) Golden colored; God's gift. *Vannaugh*

Vanora (Scottish) White wave. *Vannora*

Vanya (Russian) Gracious gift of God. *Wanja, Vanja, Vania, Wania, Wanya*

Varana (Hindi) River.

Varda (Hebrew) Rose. *Vadit, Vardah, Vardia, Vardice, Vardina, Vardis, Vardit*

Varsha (Hindi) Rain. *Varisha*

Varuni (Hindi) A Hindi goddess of wine and alcohol.

Vasanta (Hindi) Spring.

Vasavi (Hindi) Mental daughter of the Pitrs.

Vashti (Persian) Beautiful.

Vasiliki (Greek) Basil.

Vasudha (Hindi) Earth.

Vasumati (Hindi) Apsara of unequalled splendor.

Veda (Hindi) Knowledge, wisdom. *Veed, Vedad, Vedah, Devis, Veeda, Vida, Vita*

Vedette (French) From the guard tower. (Italian) Scout. *Vedett, Vedetta*

Veena (Hindi) A musical instrument; Beena.

Vega (Arabic) Falling star.

Velika (Slavic) Great. *Velikah, Velyka*

Velinda (African American) Combination of prefix Ve and Linda (Spanish), pretty; variation of Melinda. *Valinda*

Velma (Greek) Protector. *Valma, Vellma, Vilma, Vylma*

Velvet (English) Fabric.

Venecia (Italian) Place name: Venice, Italy.

Venice (Latin) Place name: Venice, Italy.

Venetia (Italian) From Venice, Italy.

Venetta (English) Newly created. *Veneta, Venette*

Venus (Greek) Goddess of love. *Venis*

Vera (Latin) True. (Slavic) Faith. *Verena, Verin, Verina, Verine, Verenia, Vere, Verouska*

Verda (Latin) Young. *Virdinia, Viridis*

Verdad (Spanish) Truth.

Verena (Teutonic) Defender. (Latin) Truthful. *Vereena, Verene, Verina, Verine, Veruchka, Veruschka, Verushka, Veryna*

Vernice (Latin) Brings victory. *Vernese, Vernessa, Vernis, Vernise, Vyrnesse*

Verity (Latin) Truth. *Verita, Veritie*

Veronica (Latin) True image. *Veronique, Ronnie, Ron, Nica, Nicky, Ronica*

Verran (Welsh) The short one.

Verushka (Russian) Meaning unknown.

Vesper (Latin) Evening. *Vespera*

Vesta (Latin) Guardian of the sacred fire.

What's in a Name

Although they don't sound much alike, **Veronica** is the Latin form of the name *Berenice*, meaning "true image," which is a reference to Saint Berenice, who wiped Jesus' face with a towel and discovered it had his image imprinted on it.

Vestal (Latin) Chaste, pure.

Veta (Spanish) Intelligent. *Vetah*

Vevay (Welsh) White wave.

Vevila (Gaelic) Woman with a melodious voice.

Vevina (Latin) Sweet lady.

Vibhuti (Hindi) Great personality.

Victoria (Latin) Victory. *Vicki, Vicky, Viktoria, Vitoria, Victoire, Victory, Vickie, Vic, Toria, Torey, Torri, Tori, Victorienne*

Vida (Hebrew) Beloved. *Veda, Veeda, Veida, Vidette, Vieda, Vita, Vitia*

Vidette (Hebrew) Dearly loved. *Vidett*

Vidonia (Latin) Vine; branch.

Vidya (Hindi) Wisdom; knowledge.

Vienna (Latin) From wine country. (Place name) Vienna, Austria. *Venia, Vennia, Vienne*

Viera (Slavic) Truth; faith.

Vigdis (Scandinavian) Goddess of war.

Vilette (French) Small town. *Vietta, Vilet, Vilea, Vilett, Viletta, Vylette*

Vilhemina (Russian) Resolute protector. *Vilhlmin, Vilhelmine, Vylhelmina*

Vimala (Hindi) Pure; the sakti of the Gayatri Devi.

Vina (Spanish) From the vineyard.

Vinata (Hindi) Humble; the mother of Garuda.

Vinaya (Hindi) Good behavior; modesty.

Vincentia (Latin) To conquer. *Vincenta, Vincentena, Vincentina, Vincentine, Vincetta, Vinia, Vinnie*

Vineeta (Hindi) Unassuming; humble.

Viola (Scandinavian) Violet.

Violet (Latin) Violet. *Viola*

Virgilia (Latin) Strong. *Virgilla*

Virginia (Latin) Chaste; maiden. *Virginie, Virgie, Virgy, Gina, Ginia, Ginny, Ginni, Ginger, Jinny*

Virgo (Latin) The virgin.

Viridis (Latin) Youthful and blooming. *Virdis, Virida, Viridia, Viridiana*

Virsila (Czechoslovakian) Little she-bear.

Visala (Hindi) Celestial Apsara.

Vita (Latin) Life. *Vitas, Verta, Vitia*

Viveka (German) Little woman; of the strong fortress. *Vivica*

Vivian (Latin) Living, lively. *Vivien, Vivianne, Viviana, Vivienne, Vyvyan, Vivyen, Vivyan, Vivie, Viv, Vibiana, Viveca*

Viviefont (Latin) Lively.

Voleta (Greek) Veiled one. *Voletta, Volette, Volettie*

Volumnia (Shakespearean) From *Coriolanus*.

Vondra (Czechoslovakian) A woman's love. *Vondrah*

Vrinda (Hindi) Virtue and strength.

Vyoma (Hindi) Sky. *Vyomika*

W

Wachiwi (Native American) Dancing girl.

Wade (American) Campy.

Wafa (Arabic) Faithful. *Wafiyya, Wafiyyah*

Waheeda (Hindi) Beautiful. (Arabic) Single. *Wahidah*

Waja (Arabic) Noble. *Wagiha, Wagihah, Wahija, Wajihah*

Wakana (Japanese) New blooms.

Wakanda (Sioux) Inner magical power. *Wakenda*

Walada (Arabic) Giving birth.

Walanika (Hawaiian) True image; version of Veronica. *Walonika, Welonika*

Walburga (Anglo-Saxon) A mighty defender; a fortress. *Walburg*

Walda (German) Strong protection. *Wallda, Welda, Wellda*

Walentya (Polish) Healthy.

Walida (Arabic) Newborn. *Wallidah*

Walker (English) Last name. *Walliker*

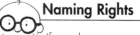 **Naming Rights**

If you have a passion for sports, consider choosing a name for your child that your favorite sports hero holds. Remember, though, that 10 or 20 years from now, baby's name could be a bit outdated.

Wallis (English) From Wales. *Wallie, Walliss, Wally, Wallys*

Waltraud (Teutonic) Rule strength.

Wanaao (Hawaiian) Sunrise.

Wanda (German) Wanderer. *Wenda, Wandis, Wendeline, Wendy, Vanda*

Waneta (English) Fair complexion. (Native American) Charger. *Wanetta, Wanette, Wanita*

Wangari (African) Leopard.

Wanika (Hawaiian) God's gracious gift.

Wanisha (American) Pure.

Wapeka (Native American) Skillful.

Wapin (Native American) Sunrise.

Waseme (African) Good-looking.

Washi (Japanese) Eagle.

Wasula (Native American) Bad hair.

Wateka (Native American) Meaning unknown.

Waverly (English) To wave, from the aspen trees. *Waverley*

Wawetseka (Native American) Pretty woman.

Weayaya (Native American) Setting sun.

Wednesday (American) Born on Wednesday.

Weetamoo (Native American) Lover. *Weetamoe, Weetamore, Weatamoo, Wetemoo*

Wendy (English) Fair. *Wenda, Wendee, Wenday, Wendi, Wendie, Wendye, Windy*

Weslee (English) Variation of Wesley.

Whitley (English) White field. *Whitelea, Whitlea, Whitlee, Whitly, Whittley, Witlee*

Whitney (English) From the white island. *Whitnee, Whitnie, Whitny, Whittney*

Whoopi (English) Excitable. *Yahoo, Yippee, Wahoo*

Widjan (Arabic) Ecstasy.

Wihtburth (Anglo-Saxon) Meaning unknown.

Wilda (English) Willow. *Willida, Wylda*

Wilfreda (English) Peaceful will; feminine version of Wilfred.

Wilhelmina (German) Feminine version of William; Will + helmet. *Wiletta, Wilette, Wilhelmine, Willa, Willamina, Willimina*

Willa (Teutonic) Fierce protector. *Wilma, Wilhelmina, Willamina, Wilhemine, Wihelma, Willette, Wilmette, Wyla, Willie, Willy, Will, Mina, Minnie, Minny, Billie, Billy, Helma, Vilma, Guillelmine, Guillemette, Vilhelmina*

Willow (English) Freedom; tree. *Willo*

Wilma (German) Protector. *Wilmette, Wilmina, Wylma*

Wilona (English) Desired. *Wilo, Wiloh, Wilonah, Wylona*

Winda (Swahili) Hunt.

Winema (Native American) Female chief.

Winifred (English) Friend of peace. *Winnie, Winny, Winni, Win, Winn, Wyn, Fred, Freddie, Freddy*

Winola (German) Enchanting friend.

Winona (Sioux) First-born daughter. *Winonah, Wenona*

Winsome (English) Pleasant and attractive.

Winter (English) Winter. *Wynter, Winters*

Wisdom (English) Wisdom; discerning.

Wislawa (Polish) Meaning unknown.

Wrenn (English) Small bird.

Wyanet (Native American) Beautiful.

Wyetta (African American) Feminine version of Wyatt.

Wynflæd (Anglo-Saxon) Meaning unknown.

Wynn (Welsh) Fair. *Wynne, Wyn, Wynnie, Winnie, Winny, Win, Winn, Weeny, Wyonna*

Wynonah (Native American) First-born. *Wenona, Wenonah, Winona, Winonah, Wynnona*

Wyome (Native American) Big field.

X

Xalbadora (Spanish) Savior.

Xanadu (Place name) An idyllic, exotic, fictional place. *Zanadu*

Xandria (Greek) Defender of man; version of Alexandra. *Xandra*

Xandy (Greek) Protector of man.

Xantha (Greek) Blond; yellow. *Xanthe, Xanth, Xanthie, Zanthie*

Xaviera (Arabic) Bright. (Basque) New house. *Xavière*

Xenia (Greek) Hospitable. *Xena*

Xenobia (Greek) Jewel of my father.

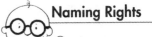

Naming Rights

Create a new name from a combination of names with meanings you're drawn to. For example, if you're drawn to names from nature, choose one that appeals to you and then select a virtue you admire. Then play around with the letter combinations to come up with a name that portrays the traits you find appealing.

Xevera (Spanish) Owns a new house.

Xiang (Chinese) Fragrant.

Xianthippe (Greek) Form of Xanthe, wife of Socrates.

Xiao (Spanish) Meaning unknown.

Xiao-Niao (Chinese) Small bird.

Xiao-Xing (Chinese) Morning star.

Ximena (Hebrew) Heroine; He heard.

Xin (Chinese) Elegant; beautiful.

Xiomara (Spanish) Ready for battle. *Xiomy*

Xiu Mei (Chinese) Beautiful plum.

Xuan (Vietnamese) Spring.

Xylia (Greek) Wood dweller. *Xyla, Xylina, Xylona*

Xylona (Greek) From the forest. *Xylina, Zylona, Zylina*

Xyza (Gothic) By the sea.

Y

Yaa (African) Born on Thursday.

Yaara (Hebrew) Honeycomb. *Yaari, Yaarit, Yara*

Yachi (Japanese) Good luck. *Yachiko, Yachiya*

Yachne (Hebrew) Gracious. *Yachna*

Yadira (Hebrew) Friend, companion.

Yadra (Spanish) Mother.

Yael (Hebrew) Mountain goat. *Jael, Yaala, Yaalat, Yaela, Yaella*

Yaffa (Hebrew) Beautiful.

Yaki (Japanese) Broiled; baked.

Yakira (Hebrew) Dear. *Yakara, Yekarah, Yakirah*

Yaksha (Hindi) A sister of Daksha.

Yale (English) Fertile moor. *Yaile, Yayle*

Yalika (Native American) Spring flowers.

Yama (Japanese) Mountain.

Yaminah (Arabic) Right and proper. *Yamina, Yamuna, Yemina*

Yamini (Hindi) Night. *Yamni*

Yamuna (Hindi) Sacred river; Juamana.

Yanaha (Native American) She confronts an enemy. *Yanaba*

Yanira (Hebrew) To understand.

Yardena (Hebrew) To descend. *Jardena*

Yardeniya (Hebrew) God's garden. *Jardenia, Yardenia*

Yardley (English) Open-minded. *Yardlee, Yardleigh, Yardli, Yardlie, Yardly*

Yarenna Origin and meaning unknown.

Yaravi (Inca) Song of love and death. *Yari, Yara*

Yarmilla (Slavic) Merchant.

Yashona (Hindi) Rich. *Yaseana, Yashauna, Yashawna, Yeseana, Yeshauna, Yeshawna, Yeshona*

Yasmine (Persian) Flowering olive. *Yasmeen, Yasmin*

Naming Rights

Naming your child for the time of his or her birth (Summer, Autumn, and so on) is a long-honored tradition, as is choosing a child's name to coincide with his or her astrological sign. Times of birth, days of the week, or months of the year are also popular choices.

Yasu (Japanese) Tranquil.

Yauvani (Hindi) Full of youth.

Yavonna (Hebrew) Beautiful.

Yayoi (Japanese) March.

Ydel (Hebrew) Praise. *Yidel*

Yeardley (English) Home enclosed in a meadow. *Yeardlee, Yeardleigh, Yeardli, Yeardlie, Yeardly*

Yedda (English) Singing. *Yetta*

Yei (Japanese) Flourishing.

Yejide (Yoruba) Image of her mother.

Yelena (Russian) Light. *Yalena*

Yenene (Miwok Indian) Wizard poisoning a sleeping person.

Yenta (Hebrew) Ruler at home. *Yentel, Yentele, Yentil*

Yesenia (Arabic) Flower.

Yesmina (Hebrew) Right hand; strength.

Yetty (African American) Ruler of the household.

Yeva (Russian) Live-giving.

Yin (Chinese) Silver.

Ylwa (Scandinavian) She-wolf. *Ylva*

Yoana (Hebrew) God's gift.

Yogini (Hindi) One who can control their senses; feminine form of yogi, one practiced in yoga.

Yogita (Hindi) One who can concentrate.

Yoi (Japanese) Born in the evening.

Yoki (Native American) Bluebird.

Yoko (Japanese) Positive.

Yolanda (Greek) Violet flower, modest. *Yolande, Yolantha, Iolanthe, Iolande, Eolande, Jolanda, Jolaunda, Jo, Yo, Landa*

Yolie (Greek) Violet flower.

Yomaris (Spanish) I am the sun. *Maris, Marisol*

Yon (Burmese) Rabbit.

Yona (Hebrew, Native American) Dove.

Yoninah (Hebrew) Dove. *Yonina*

Yori (Japanese) Honest.

Yoshiko (Japanese) Child of Yoshi.

Young (English) Newly begun; fresh.

Yovela (Hebrew) Rejoicing.

Ysolde (English) Lover of Tristan.

Yu (Chinese) Jade.

Yudelle (Hebrew) Praised, admired.

Yuka (Japanese) Snow; lucky.

Yukako (Japanese) Child of Yuka.

Yukiko (Japanese) Snow child.

Yula (Russian) Young; variation of Julia. *Yulenka, Yuliya, Yulya*

Yumi (Japanese) Beauty.

Yumiko (Japanese) Child of Yumi.

Yuri (Japanese) Lily.

Yuriko (Japanese) Child of Yuri.

Yusra (Arabic) Rich. *Yusrivva, Yusrvvah*

Yutsuko (Japanese) Child of Yutso.

Yvette (Teutonic) Yew; archer. *Yvonne, Yvo, Ivon, Ivona*

Yvonne (French, Greek) Archer. *Yvetta, Yvette, Yvone*

Z

Zaafirah (Arabic) Victorious; successful.

Zaanannim (Hebrew) Movings; a person asleep.

Zabana (Native American) Savannah; meadow.

Zabel (Slavic) Consecrated to God.

Zabia (African) First-born.

Zabrina (American) Fruitful desert flower. *Zabreena, Zabryna*

Zacharee (Hebrew) God is remembered.

Zaci (African) God of fatherhood.

Zada (Syrian) Lucky one. *Zaiada, Zayda*

Zadhiya (Japanese) Meaning unknown.

Zadie (English) Princess.

Zafaran (Arabic) Spice.

Zafina (Arabic) Victorious.

Zagir (Russian) Flower.

Zagros (Greek) Sweet, feminine.

Zahara (Arabic) Shining, luminous. *Zahar, Zahra*

Zahari (Hebrew) Blossom; flower the bright dawn.

Zahava (Hebrew) Golden. *Zahavah*

Zahidah (Arabic) Ascetic; abstentious.

Zahira (Arabic) Brilliant illumination.

Zahra (Arabic, Swahili) White; flowers. *Zara, Zarah*

Zahwa (African) Flower.

Zahwah (Arabic) Pretty.

Zaida (Arabic) Fortunate one. *Zada, Zai*

Zaide (Hebrew) Elder.

Zaila (African) Female.

Zaina (Arabic) Beautiful.

Zainab (Scandinavian) Beautiful.

Zair (Hebrew) Little; afflicted; in tribulation.

Zaira (Arabic) Rose. *Zahirah, Zaire, Zi, Zizi*

Zaire (African) From Zaire. *Zayaire*

Zakia (Hebrew) Bright, pure.

Zakiya (African) Smart, intelligent.

Zale (Greek) Sea strength. *Zaile, Zayle*

Zalia (Hebrew) Sea strength.

Zalika (African) Well-born.

Zaltana (Native American) High mountain.

Zama (Latin) Came from Zama.

Zambda (Hebrew) Meditation.

Zan (Hebrew) God is gracious. (Chinese) Support; praise.

Zana (Hebrew) Graceful lily. *Zanah*

Zanaide (Greek) Devoted to God.

Naming Rights

Both parents should write down their name choices separately. When comparing your lists, you might see you both came up with a same choice or two. Consider that a sign you're on the right track toward choosing your baby's name.

Zanda (English) Beautiful girl; independent.

Zandra (Greek) Defender of mankind. *Zandria, Andria, Andra*

Zane (Arabic) Beloved.

Zaneta (Spanish) God's gift. *Zanetta*

Zanette (French) God is gracious.

Zanita (Greek) Long teeth. *Zaneta, Zanetta, Zanette, Zanitt*

Zankhana (Hindi) Deep desire.

Zanna (Latin) Lily. *Zana, Zanah, Zannah*

Zanoah (Hebrew) Forgetfulness; desertion.

Zanta (African) Beautiful; a girl.

Zanthe (Greek) Light blond. *Zanth, Zanthi, Zanthie, Zanthy*

Zanubiya (Arabic) Name of a great Syrian queen.

Zaqaria (Indian) Meaning unknown.

Zara (Hebrew, Arabic) Dawn; princess. *Zarah, Zarry, Zari*

Zaray (Arabic) Beautiful flower.

Zarda Meaning and origin unknown.

Zareah (Hebrew) Leprosy; hornet.

Zareen (Hebrew) Golden.

Zarela (Spanish) Meaning unknown.

Zarephath (Hebrew) Ambush of the mouth.

Zaretan (Hebrew) Tribulation; perplexity.

Zaria (Arabic) Rose. *Zariah, Zari*

Zariel (American) Lion princess.

Zarifa (Arabic) Moves with grace.

Zarina (African) Golden.

Zarita (Spanish) Princess.

Zarna (Hindi) Meaning unknown.

Zarola (Arabic) Hunter.

Zasha (Russian) Pet form of Alexander. *Sasha*

Zasu (African) Meaning unknown.

Zati (Hebrew) Olive tree. *Zatthu*

Zavannah (English) Savannah; meadow.

Zavia (English) Bright; new house.

Zaviera (Spanish) Owner of the home.

Zavrina (American, English) Princess. *Sabrina*

Zawadi (African) Gift.

Zay (Arabic) Lucky.

Zayit (Hebrew) Olive.

Zaylin (American) Meaning unknown. *Zayla, Aylin*

Zayna (Arabic) Beauty.

Zayra (Hebrew) Princess.

Zaza (Hebrew) Golden.

Zdebka (Russian) Meaning unknown.

Zdenek (Czechoslovakian) One from Sidon; a winding sheet. *Zdenka*

Zeanes (Hebrew) Meaning unknown.

Zebina (Greek) One who is gifted.

Zea (Latin) Wheat.

Zee (Hebrew) Wolf. *Zeela, Zella, Zelmora, Zelnora*

Zeeba (Persian) Beautiful.

Zehava (Hebrew) Golden.

Zeitia (Galician) Meaning unknown.

Zelda (German) Woman warrior. *Selda*

Zelek (Hebrew) The shadow; noise of him who licks; laps.

Zelenka (Czechoslovakian) Little innocent one.

Zelia (Greek) Zeal.

Zelinda (German) Shield of victory. *Segelinde*

Zeljka (Slavic) Wish.

Zella (Hebrew) Wise and peaceful.

Zelotes (Hebrew) Zealous.

Zelma (German) Divinely protected.

Zelpha (Hebrew) Dignified. *Zilpha*

Zemaraim (Hebrew) Wool; pith.

Zemil (Hebrew) Joyous melody.

Zena (Greek) Alive.

Zenaide (Greek) One who has devoted his life to God.

Zenda (Arabic) Womanly.

Zenevieva (Irish) Pale.

Zenia (Greek) Hospitable.

Zenobia (Greek) Of Zeus. *Zenobie, Zena, Zenna, Zenina, Zinovia*

Zenon (Greek) Stranger. *Xenon.*

Zenzi (German) Growing.

Zeolia (English) Meaning unknown.

Zeph (Hebrew) Treasured by God.

Zephan (Irish) Saint.

Zephath (Hebrew) Beholds; covers.

Zequinha (Spanish) Meaning unknown.

Zera (Greek) Wolf.

Zerdali (Turkish) Wild apricot.

Zeredah (Hebrew) Ambush.

Zeresh (Hebrew) Misery; strange.

Zerlinda (Hebrew) Beautiful dawn.

Zeruah (Hebrew) Meaning unknown.

Zeta (Greek) Investigator; researcher.

Zethel (Hebrew) Meaning unknown.

Zeuti (Greek) Meaning unknown.

Zeva (Greek) Sword.

Zevida (Hebrew) Gift.

Zez (Hebrew) Meaning unknown.

Zhalore (Hebrew) Meaning unknown.

Zhengqiu (Chinese) Precious.

Zhenya (Russian) Of noble birth.

Zhi (Chinese) Wisdom.

Zhijuan (Chinese) Precious; beautiful.

Zi (Chinese) Graceful.

Zia (Hebrew, Latin) To tremble; a kind of grain. *Zea, Ziah*

Ziahon (Hebrew) Meaning unknown.

Ziarre (American) Goddess of the sky.

Ziazan (Armenian) Rainbow.

Zibiah (Hebrew) Doe.

Zigana (Hungarian) Gypsy girl.

Zila (Hebrew) Shadow. *Zilah, Zilla, Zillah, Zylia*

Zilli (African) My shadow. *Zili*

Zilya (Russian) Harvester.

Zima (Polish) Winter.

Zina (African) Name. *Zena, Zinah, Zine, Zinnie*

Zinaida (Greek) Of Zeus. *Zenais, Zina*

Zinnia (English) Name of a flower. (Latin) Colorful flowers. *Zinia, Zin, Zina, Zinnya, Zinya*

Ziona (Hebrew) A sign. *Zinoah, Zyona, Zyonah*

Zippora (Hebrew) Bird. *Zeporah, Zipporah*

Zisel (Hebrew) Sweet. *Zysel*

Zita (Hebrew, Persian) The seeker; virgin.

Zizi (Hungarian) Dedicated to God.

Zoe (Greek) Life. *Zoë, Zoey, Zoé*

Zofia (Polish) Wisdom.

Zohreh (Persian) Happy.

What's in a Name

The name **Zoe** has increased in popularity in recent years, perhaps because of its meaning: life. Hopeful, positive names are always good choices. Then again, it could be the popularity of top TV shows such as *The West Wing*, which has a character named Zoe, that have raised awareness of this cool name.

Zoila (African) Child.

Zoisite (Austrian) Type of mineral.

Zola (Italian) Ball of earth.

Zoleen (Hebrew) Meaning unknown.

Zona (Latin) Prostitute.

Zonda (Hebrew) Defender of mankind.

Zone Origin and meaning unknown.

Zonta (Native American) Honest, trustworthy.

Zora (Slavic) Golden dawn. *Zorah, Zoradah, Zohra, Zarya, Zoranna, Zorina, Zoriana, Zori, Zorie, Zorry*

Zosima (Greek) Lively.

Zotia (Polish) One with wisdom. *Zosia*

Zov Origin and meaning unknown.

Zsa Zsa (Hungarian) Rose; lily. *Zsusanna, Zsuzsanna*

Zula (Hebrew) Brilliant; ahead.

Zuleika (Arabic) Fair-haired. *Zuleyka*

Zulema (Arabic) Peace. *Zulima*

Zuriaa (Spanish) White; light-skinned.

Zuriel (Hebrew) God is my rock.

Zurine (Spanish) White.

Zuza (Czechoslovakian) Graceful lily.

Zuzana (Slavic) Rose.

Online Resources

americanbaby.com/ab/babynames/index.jhtml
Here you'll find favorite baby names, meanings, origins, personality traits, and even pictures of famous people associated with some of the names.

babycenter.com/babyname
This site offers lists of names sorted by sex, ethnic origin, and number of syllables.

babychatter.com
Lists of baby names, coupons, and free stuff can be found here.

babynameaddicts.com
More than 51,000 names and growing. This site offers names with meanings, origins, popularity graphs, surveys, and more. This site says it goes "above and beyond" in its offerings.

babynameguide.com
Lists of names by category, a personal favorites list, and top 100 boy and girl names.

babynamenetwork.com
An extensive database of names searchable by gender and origin. Also has lists showing popularity by decade and user rating.

babynames.com
Here you'll find baby names and their meanings, names listed by popularity, names from soap operas, and much more.

babynamesdirectory.com
This baby name directory offers the "easiest" way to choose the perfect name for your new addition. Baby names and their meanings, ethnic origin, and most popular baby names.

babynamesindia.com
This site includes pictures of the world's "cutest babies," pregnancy resources, nursery rhymes, and more.

babynamesofireland.com
List of 200 popular, unusual, and exotic Irish baby boy and girl names. Frank McCourt, Pulitzer prize–winning author of *Angela's Ashes*, helps with the pronunciation of each one and gives the meanings.

babynameworld.com

A database of baby names, searchable by origin, is what you'll find at this site. Find that perfect baby name along with the meaning.

babyzone.com/babynames

Finding the perfect name for your baby can be a daunting experience—until now. Babyzone offers tips and hints to help make the choice easier.

baby-names.adoption.com

Find the perfect baby name for your child by searching among 5,400 popular, unique, or unusual baby names and find their meanings, origins, and similar names.

baby-names-meanings.com

American, English surnames, meanings, historical meanings, name origins, how to choose names, fashion nicknames, traditional and religious names can be found here.

behindthename.com

This site offers a look into the history behind common first names.

ipl.org.ar/ref/QUE/FARQ/nameFARQ.html

The Internet Public Library offers names for babies. You can also type in questions if you're searching for the meaning of a name.

muslim-names.co.uk

An online database of Muslim baby names and their meanings for both boys and girls.

namenerds.com

This site is dedicated to all those who love names, those who are looking for names, or anyone who has a name.

popularbabynames.com

More than 10,000 baby names from around the world can be found here. The database includes names from major regions, religions, and languages. There are also baby formula, diaper and food coupons, samples, and freebies.

ssa.gov/OACT/babynames

This site features archived lists of given names in popularity ordered by gender and year of birth from the Social Security Administration.

yeahbaby.com

Here you'll find baby names and meanings.